THE COBURGS OF EUROPE

The Rise and Fall of Queen Victoria's European Family

By

Arturo E. Beéche

ISBN: 978-0-9854603-3-4

EUROHISTORY.COM

The Prince's Wing, Veste Coburg

Prologue

The House of Wettin, one of Europe's oldest ruling dynasties, dates back to the Middle Ages. The oldest member known with certainty is Dietrich I of Wettin, who died in 982. He was based in the county of Lisgau, an area located at the western edge of the Harz Mountains, now in modern-day Saxony. The family acquired Schloß Wettin around the year 1000 and soon after took the property's name as their dynastic name. Dedo I, son of Dietrich, received the title of "count" from Emperor Otto III. In the year 1030 Emperor Konrad II granted the Wettins the Eastern Marches as a fief. The family's prominence and allegiance to the empire, gained for Dedo II, Count of Wettin, the Margraviate of Meißen in 1089.

Nearly a decade later, Konrad of Meißen received the Margraviate of Lower Lusatia. Owing allegiance to the Emperor, Konrad joined the crusade in Palestine, where he spent considerable time battling the Arabs. By the time Konrad died in 1157, he had taken religious vows and entered the convent of Lautenberg, where he lived in daily meditation. His five surviving sons, starting a custom that was to weaken the Wettins for centuries, all shared in their father's considerable inheritance. Konrad's lands were partitioned and five new lines of Wettin rulers came into being: Otto became the Margrave of Meißen, Dietrich inherited the Margraviate of Lower Lusatia, Heinrich became Count of Wettin, Dedo became the Count of Groitzch, and Friedrich received the county of Bern. In time, these five brothers would create their own plethora of sub-branches, further diminishing the family's power.

The family's fortunes continued to rise through the medieval era and their allegiance to the empire brought them more lands, which of course they subdivided among the ruler's heirs. By 1425 they were already invested with the Landgraviate of Thüringen and the Duchy of Saxony. As ruler of Saxony, the Wettin duke became one of the prince-electors entrusted with the selection of the Holy Roman Emperor.

The various Thuringian properties ruled by the House of Wettin did not adopt the concept of primogeniture until the mid-Eighteenth Century. The custom of sharing the inheritance amongst all surviving sons led to each duke's properties being divided among his male offspring; when Duke Ernst I of Saxe-Gotha died in 1675, his realm was split between his six sons. Trade wars, political machinations, and personal enmity meant that borders were constantly redrawn. Complicating matters further, some dukes reigned as co-rulers: if a duke died without issue, his closest living male heir or heirs inherited his realm. As a result, the family's political power within the Holy Roman Empire was considerably weakened.

The Coburgs unfortunately shared the constant divisions and subdivisions that weakened their other Wettin cousins. In 1729 Duke Johann Ernst of Saxe-Coburg-Saalfeld died and his two surviving sons by different mothers, Christian Ernst and Franz Josias, succeeded their father. For sixteen years, they ruled jointly; after the 1745 death of the childless Christian Ernst, his brother reigned alone. Duke Franz Josias, said a contemporary, was *"very much looked up to. He was a tall, powerful man. He had lost an eye at tennis, formerly much played on the continent."* In 1747, to prevent further diminution of his lands, he adopted primogeniture, with the firstborn male son designated as successor to the Duke. If the firstborn died prior to inheriting, then his eldest surviving son or, in the absence of children, his next surviving brother, inherited. The succession was finally in order.

When Duke Ernst Friedrich succeeded his father in 1764, he faced a country in debt. Endless disputes over inheritance had led to chaos, though Ernst Friedrich's wife, the former Princess Sophia Antonia of Brunswick-Wolfenbüttel, played no small part in this financial fiasco. One of nineteen children born to Duke Ferdinand Albert II and his wife Antonia Amalia, formerly Princess of Brunswick-Blankenburg, Sophia Antonia felt entitled from birth. The Dukes of Brunswick-Wolfenbüttel were not only wealthy but also extremely well connected. One brother became Duke Karl I of Brunswick-Wolfenbüttel (1713-1780); another, Anton-Ulrik (1714-1774),

Duke Johann Ernst of Saxe-Coburg-Saalfeld.

married Duchess Elisabeth of Mecklenburg-Schwerin, and was the father of deposed, and imprisoned, Tsar Ivan VI of Russia. Elisabeth Christine (1715-1797), Sophia's sister, married King Friedrich the Great of Prussia; Louisa Amalia (1722-1780), another sister, married Friedrich the Great's brother Prince August Wilhelm of Prussia; and a third, Juliane Maria (1729-1796), wed King Frederik V of Denmark. Even Sophia Antonia's maternal aunts had made splendid dynastic marriages: Elisabeth Christine (1691-1750) to Holy Roman Emperor Charles VI (and thus was the mother of Empress Maria Theresa), and Charlotte (1694-1715) to Tsarevich Alexei Petrovich of Russia, Peter the Great's unfortunate son.

King Léopold I of the Belgians, Duke Ernst Friedrich's grandson, described him as "*a good-natured, easy, and well-meaning man.*" Ernst Friedrich's 1749 marriage to the prominent Sophia Antonia may have owed something to his father's adoption of primogeniture, thus ensuring the young man a larger inheritance and making him more attractive on the royal marriage market. Sophia Antonia knew that her marriage could not match the illustrious unions of her closest relations, but she was determined to live as she pleased, and according to the standards of her privileged youth. While her weak-willed husband tried to rule, Sophia Antonia spent his meager treasury into bankruptcy. Years later, her grandson King Léopold I of the Belgians best described her as "*too great a person for so small a duchy ... in a great monarchy [she] would most certainly have played a great part – perhaps not of the mildest, like her sister, the Queen of Denmark. She ruled everything in Coburg, and treated that little duchy as if it had been an empire. She was very generous, and in that respect did much harm, as she squandered the revenues in a dreadful manner. The duke stood very much in awe of his imperious wife.*" Furthermore, Leopold also wrote that, "*she brought into the family energy and superior qualities above the minute twaddle of these small establishments.*"

Duke Christian Ernst of Saxe-Coburg-Saalfeld.

Duke Ernst Friedrich found it impossible to recover financially and by the end of 1771 the duchy faced the complete collapse of its treasury. It was then that Ernst Friedrich's brother Prince Friedrich Josias interceded in Vienna. As a young man, Friedrich Josias had distinguished himself fighting for the Habsburgs. Although shot through the hand during the battle of Lobositz in 1759 during the Seven Years' War, his tenacity earned Empress Maria

Theresa's gratitude. Coburg ignored his injury and distinguished himself in further campaigns. In 1788 he was given general command of the Austrian Army during its invasion of Galicia and Bukovina; after defeating the much larger Turkish Army, he was given the rank of Austrian Imperial Field Marshal, and led his men when they liberated Bucharest, a city that had been under Ottoman rule for centuries. These accomplishments left Friedrich Josias a respected figure at the Habsburg Court, and when he asked the Hofburg to assist his impecunious brother, Emperor Joseph II promptly established a Debt Commission, whose sole purpose was to monitor government spending. Within two years, the duchy's finances improved and the Coburgs' worries seemed to fade. Thereafter, Habsburg rulers kept a close eye on the future of the Coburg family.

Coburg was peaceful, but the winds of war raged across Europe. In July 1789 the continent's myriad ruling dynasties received earth-shattering, and worrisome, news from Paris. On 14 July a crowd surrounded and ransacked the Bastille. Although the royal prison only housed two elderly convicts, it represented the French monarchy's eroding authority and its fall symbolized an end to the autocracy that Louis XIV had founded in the Seventeenth Century. Soon enough, Louis XVI and his family were forced to leave their golden isolation at Versailles and return to Paris, where the French Royal Family had not lived for generations. The French king no longer ruled.

Duke Franz Josias of Saxe-Coburg-Saalfeld.

The troublesome events that set Paris ablaze soon burned across the continent. The Habsburgs in Vienna worried that Parisian mobs would mistreat and insult their sister Marie Antoinette and her somnolent husband, Louis XVI. Even more worrisome for Emperors Joseph II and Leopold II were the menacing political threats carried on the pikes of French revolutionaries. The right of monarchs to rule over the destinies of their people was questioned and attacked, and the governance of Europe lay in the hands of a mob. The cancer emanating from France had to be stamped out at all costs, even if it plunged the continent into a major conflict.

The execution of King Louis XVI in January 1793, followed by that of Marie Antoinette later that same year, was the final straw for Vienna. Leopold II died in 1792; Franz II, his successor, believing that it was both his duty and his right to end the danger posed by the revolution that had toppled his uncle and aunt, earnestly launched into a war. That war would deeply affect the Ducal Family of Coburg. They suffered grave losses and experienced deep privations, yet would rise from the chaos stronger and determined to change relations between monarch and people.

Table of Contents

Prologue	ii
Chapter I – *The Beginning – "You, Handsome Coburg, Marry"*	4
Chapter II – *Enter Russia: A Fateful Journey*	11
Chapter III – *Enter Gotha: Power Expanded*	16
Chapter IV – *Enter Kohary: Untold Riches*	25
Chapter V – *Enter Great Britain: A Failed Attempt*	30
Chapter VI – *Princesses for Export & Alexandrina Victoria of Kent*	37
Chapter VII – *Enter Belgium: The Uncle of Europe*	44
Chapter VIII – *Enter Portugal: The Unlucky PromisingBrood*	53
Chapter IX – *Enter Great Britain Again: Prince Consort & Mater Familias*	62
Chapter X – *Return to Coburg & Gotha: A Duke from Great Britain & A Troubled Succession*	73
Chapter XI – *The Kohary Line: Wealth, Position & A New Throne*	88
Chapter XII – *Enter Bulgaria: Alas, A Crown at Last*	99
Chapter XIII – *Duke Carl Eduard: Fortune and Position Withered*	114
Chapter XIV – *The Coburgs of Windsor: A Dynasty's Name Changed*	143

Chapter XV – The Coburgs of Brussels: Despised & Beloved   170

Chapter XVI – The Coburgs of Vienna: Debacle & Ruin   193

Chapter XVII – The Coburgs of Lisbon: An Unsurprising End   224

Chapter XVIII – King Albert I's Descendants: Tragedy, War & Redemption   255

Chapter XIX – The Coburgs of Sofia: "Tantamount to an Invitation"   276

Chapter XX – The Women of Coburg: A Most Interesting Club   297

Chapter XXI – A Return to Coburg: "… and I Smiled"   332

Epilogue – A Roundabout Way to Coburg   347

Family Tree   356

Coburg Ancestries   358

Bibliography   361

Index   364

Acknowledgments   369

Copyright & Company Information   370

CHAPTER I
"You, Handsome Coburg, Marry"

When old Duke Ernst-Friedrich passed away in 1800, his son Duke Franz Friedrich Anton succeeded him. Born in 1750, Franz Friedrich Anton was an affable man with a soft look and rosy cheeks. His private, comprehensive education had left him with wide-ranging interests, including art and literature. He possessed, said his son Leopold, a deep knowledge of *"everything connected with fine arts."* Of the family, only Prince Albert – later the Prince Consort – came close, Leopold believed, to the old duke in his desire to acquire knowledge and appreciating fine arts. Franz Friedrich Anton nurtured the duchy's collection of 300,000 copperplate engravings, today on display at the walled, mountaintop castle of Veste Coburg, and he equipped his library with an extensive collection of books. In 1805, he even managed to repurchase Schloß Rosenau, a family summer residence that had temporarily passed from the family owing to his father's debts. Rosenau was to become a pleasure retreat for the Coburgs, the site of many important family gatherings.

An unfortunately short reign left the new Duke of Saxe-Coburg-Saalfeld with little political accomplishments, and he was at the mercy of the storms within his realm and raging in the much larger European theater. The few surviving portraits show him with a smooth look, though perhaps disinterested in acting the role he inherited. In one, he wears several orders, including the Russian Order of St. Andrew, bestowed by either Catherine the Great or her son Emperor Paul. Others convey a sense of the private man: the friend of the graphic arts, theater, music, and travel; the man who liked to wear fashionable clothes; and the culinary connoisseur who loved wine, champagne, and fresh oysters. One surviving image, though, contradicts the other carefree portraits and reflects more accurately the problems Franz Friedrich Anton faced: rather gloomy, it depicts a man overwhelmed by the heavy burden of his role, weighed down by responsibilities, deeply religious, and unsettled by the upheavals surrounding him.

Franz Friedrich Anton married twice. On 6 March 1776, he wed distant relation Princess Sophie of Saxe-Hildburghausen, but the couple's joy was short: Sophie died some seven months later. Another bride was quickly found so as not to risk the succession. A year later, Hereditary Prince Franz Friedrich Anton married Countess Augusta (1757-1831), eldest daughter of Count Heinrich XXIV of Reuß zu Ebersdorf and of his wife Carolina-Ernestine, née a Countess of Erbach-Schönberg. This marriage had profound consequences, catapulting the Coburgs into European prominence.

Augusta came from a much smaller dynasty than that of her imperious and financially irresponsible mother-in-law. She had been raised in Ebersdorf, a sleepy town not far from Coburg, and was not particularly dazzled by the trappings of royalty. Duchess Augusta of Saxe-Coburg-Saalfeld was one of many remarkable women in the House of Coburg. Though small of stature, she possessed a forcible character. Handsome rather than pretty, she had very well defined features, deep blue eyes, and a long nose – the latter a feature inherited by many of her descendants. Lively and intelligent, her mind was powerful and energetic; she seemed to be more interested in the ruling of her family's possessions than her husband, and they held her in the greatest regard. *"Protestant pietism, deep feeling for nature in 'Goethe's sense,' deep sensibility, and sense of romance, and their conception of art,"* were all united within her.

The new Duchess's principal mission was to be a good wife and mother, and to secure suitable futures for her own offspring – efforts at which she admirably succeeded. Under her 'rule,' the Coburgs finally began to achieve the political and dynastic prominence for which they later became renowned. Within a year of their marriage, Franz Friedrich Anton and Augusta welcomed their first child, Sophie (1778-1835). Nine other children followed: Antoinette (1779-1824); Juliane (1781-1860); a stillborn prince in 1782; Ernst I (1784-1844);

Above: Duke Franz Friedrich Anton of Saxe-Coburg-Saalfeld.

Left: Duchess Augusta of Saxe-Coburg-Saalfeld (née Reuß-Ebersdorf).

Top left: Princess Sophie (Countess of Mensdorff-Pouilly) – Top right: Princess Antoinette (Duchess of Württemberg).

Above: Princess Juliane (Grand Duchess Anna Feodorovna) – Right: Princess Victoria (Fürstin of Leiningen, Duchess of Kent).

Ferdinand (1785-1851); Victoria (1786-1861); Marianne (1788-1794); Leopold (1790-1865); and Maximilian (1792-1793). Conscientious and motherly, she insured the well being of her large family. Her son King Leopold remembered her as, *"in every respect distinguished; warm-hearted, possessing a most powerful understanding, she loved her grandchildren most tenderly."* Owing to the tenuous financial situation of the Duchy, Augusta improvised when it came to raising her children. Happy family life took precedence over luxury, and Augusta focused on personal responsibility and the fulfillment of one's duties. She believed that *"maternal care and a pronounced sense of family"* could not be separated from the *"idea of reason of state"* and of the political calculus. If they were to make a mark in the world, Augusta knew that two conditions were necessary: good looks (which the Coburg children thankfully possessed) and solid, enlightened educations. Augusta became the epicenter of the extensive Coburg family, in much the same way as her granddaughter Queen Victoria would later do, a benefactor with untold possibilities to help its fortunes. Augusta masterfully learned the art of secret diplomacy by acting as 'diplomatic agent' for her children and their ambitions and she was tireless in her quest.

Duke Franz Friedrich Anton was a flagrantly unfaithful man. His blacksmith once threatened him on learning that the Duke intended to seduce his nubile daughter. Yet Augusta was completely devoted to her husband as he faced the difficulties of rule. Coburg lay in the middle of military routes, and armies crisscrossed the small duchy as the early Napoleonic Wars played out. The country was ravaged and the treasury impoverished; Franz Friedrich Anton had to somehow fund an army and look after his people. At times the duchy seemed doomed, and constant worry soon overtook the Duke. *"My poor father,"* his son Leopold later said, *"suffering comparatively early in life from bad health, was the most amiable and human character – benevolence itself."*

Yet amiability and benevolence could not save Franz Friedrich Anton from premature illness. Throughout the autumn of 1806 his health worsened. *"Toward the end of November and the first days of December, our beloved benevolent father sank very fast, and died on the 9th of December,"* Leopold remembered. He summed the family's desolation by recalling that, *"the situation was a sad one."* His remains were buried in a small mausoleum in Coburg's Hofgarten.

The throne passed to Franz Friedrich Anton's eldest son Ernst, but real power and influence in Coburg remained with the widowed Duchess Augusta. Despite their marital difficulties, she had been genuinely devoted to her husband. On one of the anniversaries of his death she wrote, *"Only married couples can be tied in sorrow and joy, in deeds and responsibilities the way we were. Every year the knot of our married life became tighter. Enjoy a blissful rest dear and good husband. Thank you…for the many happy years we spent with no trace of a quarrel, not even an argument. Thank you for your goodness, attentiveness and kindness."*

Augusta's fascinating diary, one of the most reliable sources on the meteoric rise of the House of Coburg, reveals her everlasting sensibility and motherly love as well as her immovable faith in God. It also helps us better understand the privations suffered by the duchy during the Napoleonic occupation, as well as the utter despair felt by Germany's princes as the little Corsican humiliated their country. When her eldest son Duke Ernst I was kept from assuming his duties because of his support for Napoléon's enemies, Augusta took matters into her own hands and approached the French overlord. *"Ach! I can see now, for Ernst's sake, I must go in person to Napoléon and implore his protection and clemency, even though it will break my heart,"* she wrote. *"Yet the happiness of my children is well worth the sacrifice and I will do it quite willingly."* She was planning to meet the French Emperor at Warsaw but, as her youngest son Leopold related, *"Napoléon did not like such a visit, and she did not go further than Berlin."* Leopold later spoke about her life in Coburg: *"My good mother and all of us had no food and only could survive on what the French officials felt good to give us."* The battle of Leipzig was the turning point for the "holy" war against the French invaders. *"With tears in my eyes,"* Augusta wrote in her journal, *"I have thanked the Almighty…the battle of October 18, 1813, was the most sublime Toten feier* (death celebration) *for the fallen heroes of 1806. The humiliation of the German sons has been absolved."*

Augusta's thoughts were never far from her family. *"Filled with a thankfulness to God I close the day,"* she wrote in her diary. *"At 2pm Ernst has arrived, and my greatest wish to have my seven children around me has been fulfilled."* She defended and fought for her children's interests: anyone who upset their future plans was deemed an obstacle to her quest. Such was the sad fate that rained upon poor Pauline Panam, Ernst I's mistress, who

Above: Schloß Ehrenburg, Coburg, & Duke Johann Ernst of Saxe-Coburg. The Ehrenburg was the main residence of the ducal family in the center of Coburg. The palace was first built by Duke Johann Ernst in 1543 on a spot where a Franciscan monastery once stood. Like his father, Johann, Elector of Saxony, Johann Ernst, who died childless, was a protector of Lutheranism.

Right: an old print of the town of Coburg, with the Veste Coburg dominating the valley. In the middle of the image the tower of St. Moritz's Church is clearly visible as it dominates the town. From a distance, modern-day Coburg looks much the same.

recalled Augusta as a formidable lady *"whose presence caused a shiver."* Augusta blamed Panam for the collapse of Ernst's matrimonial prospects. In an interview with the old Duchess, Panam was the recipient of much motherly ire: *"The Duchess Mother began by pouring forth a volley of invectives. In vain did I fly to avoid her – in vain did I conceal myself in the corners of the apartments, whither she pursued me. I incessantly heard the clacking of her enormous slippers, which echoed over the flooring and announced her coming, or rather her fury-like approach."*

In later years Augusta established a voluminous correspondence with her children and grandchildren, keeping still a semi-tyrannical grip over her family. Her economy (some have called it avarice) became notorious, but the devotion and affection she showed to her entire family made her beloved by all. Even in old age, she traveled around Europe and also urged her children to make pilgrimages to the family 'nest' in Coburg. The Coburgs, in turn, greatly valued her openness and warmth, and her dedication to their interests.

When Augusta died in 1831, she left behind a family united toward achieving her goal of political greatness. Propitious marriages and fortuitous alliances became her legacy. *"Andere mogen Krieg fuhren, du gluckliches Österreich, heirate!"* ("While others fight war, you, handsome Austria, marry!") went the unofficial motto of Austria's Imperial Habsburgs. Soon a new saying swept across Europe: *"Du, gluckliches Coburg, heirate!"* ("You, handsome Coburg, marry!").

German Imperial Chancellor Prince Otto von Bismarck once derisively referred to the Coburgs as 'the stud farm of Europe.' Jealous he may have been, but quite correct he certainly was. Unlike her granddaughter Queen Victoria, no age bears Augusta's name, yet by the end of the Nineteenth Century Coburg descendants would sit on the thrones of Great Britain, Belgium, Portugal, and Bulgaria; occupy the ducal throne of Saxe-Coburg and Gotha; and become crown princesses and consorts to Prussia, Mexico, Austria, Saxony, Hohenzollern, Romania, Hesse and By Rhine, and Hohenlohe-Langenburg. In the Twentieth Century, their reach would extend to Sweden, Italy, and Luxembourg as well. With diligence, care, and cultivation, Augusta had sent her large brood of Coburgs from their small palace in quaint, old Coburg's Steingaße to courts and courtiers across the continent in a marriage offensive that overtook royal Europe.

That offensive had begun in 1795, with a fateful trip to Russia and a union that established an intricate web of alliances uniting the ruling houses of Europe, altered the fate of the Coburg dynasty, and forever changed the course of history.

From the top: Hereditary Prince Ernst, Prince Ferdinand and Prince Leopold of Saxe-Coburg-Saalfeld.

Empress Catherine the Great.

CHAPTER II
Enter Russia
A Fateful Journey

Emperor Peter the Great's death in 1725 had left the Russian succession in disarray. None of his sons survived him; Alexei, his heir, had been executed in 1718, leaving two young children from his marriage to Charlotte of Brunswick-Blankenburg: Natalia Alexeievna (1714-1728) and Peter Alexeievich (1715-1730). Although young Peter Alexeievich was the obvious heir, Peter the Great ignored tradition and nurtured the rise of his second wife Catherine to the throne. A humble peasant woman of obscure beginnings, the former Martha Skavronskaya had secretly married Peter the Great in 1710, taken the name Catherine, and borne him twelve children, including two surviving daughters, Anna Petrovna and Elisabeth I. Peter the Great crowned Catherine Empress in 1724; when he died the following year, he failed to name a successor, and the ambitious Catherine quickly took the throne with the help of her late husband's closest friends, including Prince Alexander Danilovich Menshikov, in whose employ she had been when she had first met her imperial lover. Catherine became the first of three women to rule Russia in the Eighteenth Century. She survived Peter by a mere two years, leaving a legacy of military expenditure reduction, public works, and the acquisition of Tsarskoye Selo, where the famed Catherine Palace still bears her name.

Catherine's step-grandson succeeded her as Emperor Peter II, largely through Menshikov's machinations with Austrian agents who forged the late Empress's will and manipulated the political environment to ensure his rise to power. Peter II, though, soon turned against the imperious Menshikov and had him arrested. Although betrothed to Princess Catherine Dolgorukova, Peter II died of smallpox on the day he was to be married and failed to name an heir.

The Privy Council chose Anna Ivanovna, daughter of Tsar Ivan V, as the new ruler of mighty Russia. Anna had lived in Courland, where her late husband had reigned as duke for two decades, before ascending the throne of her ancestors. Already in her late thirties, there was little chance that Anna would produce any legitimate heirs, and she turned to the descendants of her sister Catherine Ivanovna, who had died in 1733. From her marriage to Duke Karl Leopold of Mecklenburg-Schwerin, Catherine Ivanovna had one daughter, Anna Leopoldovna, who had married Duke Anton Ulrik of Brunswick-Wolfenbüttel. When, in 1740, they had a baby boy, Anna adopted him and named him as her heir. Within a few days the Empress was dead, and the Russian throne passed to the infant Ivan VI, with his mother Anna Leopoldovna selected as regent. However, machinations to dispose of the Brunswicks were already under way.

Elisabeth Petrovna, Peter the Great's last surviving child, had once been betrothed to a German prince, but the sickly youngster died before the wedding. Her father's ambition to marry her into the French Royal Family failed owing to her mother's obscure origins. When Anna came to the Russian Throne in 1730, no foreign court dared suggest any suitable husband to Elisabeth for fear of arousing the anger of her cousin the Empress. Frustrated in her enforced spinsterhood, Elisabeth Petrovna lost little time seeking out male company at her small court. She is said to have secretly married Alexei Razumovsky, a young Ukrainian peasant who remained her devoted companion for many years, and who supposedly fathered several of her illegitimate children.

It took Elisabeth Petrovna a little over a year to construct the conspiracy that would topple her cousins. In late November 1741, with the support of the Preobrazhensky Regiment, she went into action. The coup removed Ivan VI, Anna Leopoldovna, her husband, and a daughter: all were arrested and imprisoned. Anna

The parade grounds of the Catherine Palace, Tsarskoe Selo during the reign of Tsar Nicholas II.

Leopoldovna died after childbirth while still imprisoned in 1746, and Ivan VI was assassinated in 1764 after supporters tried to free him and restore him to the throne. In 1780, Anna Leopoldovna's surviving children, who had lived in isolation and with minimal social contact, were released to Dowager Queen Juliane Maria of Denmark and settled under house arrest in Horsens, Jutland. They all died unmarried.

Once on the throne, Empress Elisabeth quickly settled the succession. Russians would never have accepted the former peasant Razumovsky as an imperial consort, and Elisabeth was forced to choose as heir Duke Karl Peter Ulrik of Holstein-Gottorp, her sister Anna Petrovna's only son. Born in 1728, the young man was brought to Russia and given the name Peter to reinforce links to his late grandfather Peter the Great. In 1745, Peter married his cousin Princess Sophie of Anhalt-Zerbst, who took the name Catherine. It was a most unhappy marriage and the spouses felt deep revulsion for each other. Finally, in 1754, to the surprise of many members of the Russian Imperial Court, a child was produced (most likely fathered by Sergei Saltykov, Catherine's lover). The birth of Paul Petrovich secured the succession through yet another generation, giving his aunt Empress Elisabeth much peace of mind.

Peter III succeeded his aunt Elisabeth on her death in 1761 and immediately moved to isolate his wife Catherine. Catherine, though, had cultivated influence and power. Her husband's eccentricity and undisguised admiration for all things Prussian horrified the Imperial Court, and with the help of her current favorite, Gregory Orlov, Catherine staged a coup that deposed and arrested Peter III after a reign of just over six months. Eight days later, Gregory Orlov and his brothers assassinated the former Emperor at Ropsha, where he had been imprisoned.

Paul Petrovich, the young son and heir, never forgave his mother for her actions. Clinging to an idealized image of his late father, he blamed Catherine for Peter III's removal and death, and for usurping the throne for herself when he was rightful heir. Relations between mother and son were never easy, and might best be described as civil. In 1773, Catherine married Paul off to Princess Wilhelmina Louise of Hesse-Darmstadt. Known as Natalia Alexeievna in Russia, she died in childbirth in 1776. Later that same year, Catherine found her son a second wife, Sophia Dorothea of Württemberg, who took the name Maria Feodorovna in Russia.

Within a year, she produced the required heir, Alexander Pavlovich, and two years later she gave birth to a second son, the spare, Konstantin Pavlovich. This birth was to have momentous consequences for the Coburgs, as Konstantin's future bride was born in 1781 in the palace of Coburg's Hereditary Prince on the Steingaße.

Relations between Paul Petrovich and his mother did not improve after his second marriage. He felt ignored and resented the attention Catherine paid to her never-ending list of favorites. Paul and Maria Feodorovna produced ten children in all, six daughters and four sons. They lived in isolation from St. Petersburg as much as possible, focusing their lives on the imperial estates at Gatchina and at Pavlovsk, the latter perhaps the most exquisite royal residence in Europe. Catherine cared little about the girls and left them in their parents' care, but with the two eldest boys she repeated the pattern established by Elisabeth: as soon as Alexander and Konstantin were born, the babies were taken away from the parents. The pair became strangers to their parents as their doting grandmother showered them with attention and prepared

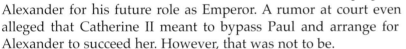
Grand Duchess Anna Feodorovna.

Alexander for his future role as Emperor. A rumor at court even alleged that Catherine II meant to bypass Paul and arrange for Alexander to succeed her. However, that was not to be.

Grand Duke Konstantin Pavlovich was born at Tsarskoye Selo on 27 April 1779. His grandmother named him after Constantine, founder of the Eastern Roman Empire. The political inference was clear: she meant to position Russia as a power capable of challenging the domination of the Ottoman Turks in the Balkans. Her dream encompassed not only expanded Russian borders and influence in the Balkans, but also the liberation of Constantinople from centuries of Ottoman rule. This geopolitical ambition was to consume Russia and bring the empire untold dangers, frustration and unnecessary loss.

Tsar Paul I.

Catherine saw to it that Paul and Maria Feodorovna had no role in Konstantin's upbringing or education. As in the case of her eldest grandson, Alexander Pavlovich, she regulated every detail of Konstantin's physical and mental education, leaving it to the men who were in her confidence to carry out her orders. Count Nicholas Saltykov, the principal tutor, soon transferred the burden to another courtier. Saltykov interfered personally only on exceptional occasions, and exercised no influence upon the passionate, restless, and headstrong boy's character. The only person who exerted a responsible influence was Frédéric-César La Harpe, who acted as tutor-in-chief from 1783 to May 1795 and educated both the Empress's grandsons. A Swiss citizen imbued with the ideals of the Enlightenment, La Harpe molded Alexander and Konstantin's minds with philosophies espoused by French revolutionaries in the hope that they would one-day

Empress Maria Feodorovna.

reform Russia. Despite his best efforts, La Harpe was to be sorely disappointed: both Alexander and Konstantin were first and foremost Romanovs.

In 1793, when still in his teens, Alexander Pavlovich married Princess Louise of Baden (1779-1826). Catherine II had selected the bride and dictated the union. Husband and wife were children plunged into an adult world for which they were ill suited. Unhappiness followed, compounded by the deaths of their two children at young ages.

Monarchy certainly needs an heir, but a spare is also necessary. That role fell to Grand Duke Konstantin Pavlovich, whose own marital career echoed that of his brother Alexander. Suffering from poor health, Catherine II made inquiries about a proper German spouse for her second grandson and, through various diplomatic channels, learned that the impoverished Hereditary Prince of Saxe-Coburg-Saalfeld had three healthy, blossoming daughters who promised to be beauties. "I was made aware," she wrote to Duke Ernst Friedrich, "of the kind qualities and distinguished talents possessed by the eldest princesses, granddaughters of your Serene Highness." Wanting to personally inspect the girls, she asked them to come to Russia. Preparations began in earnest and the Coburgs readied to visit St. Petersburg. Little did Duchess Augusta and her young daughter Juliane know what would come from this auspicious journey.

Born in Coburg in 1781, Princess Juliane was the most attractive of the Coburg sisters. Her sister-in-law, Louise of Saxe-Gotha, recalled that Juliane was, *"always pretty, lively and friendly."* These qualities endeared her to Catherine the Great when the Empress finally met her during her visit to Russia. *"The Duchess of Saxe-Coburg was beautiful and worthy of respect among women,"* the Empress wrote, *"and her daughters are pret-*

Grand Duke Konstantin Pavlovich.

ty. It's a pity that our groom must choose only one, would be good to keep all three. But it seems that our Paris gave the apple to the younger one, you'll see that he would prefer Julia among the sisters...she's really the best choice."

Konstantin Pavlovich was somewhat less enthusiastic. *"If I have to choose between one of these ugly creatures,"* he supposedly said, *"I shall marry the smallest and the youngest."* Marry her he did, in a ceremony held in St. Petersburg in February 1796. The alliance proved to be a masterstroke on Augusta's part. Her family now had true royal and imperial status, and invaluable ties to the epicenters of European power.

The new bride took the name Anna Feodorovna, but within a few years relations between the couple had deteriorated beyond repair. *"The eccentricities, fits of passion, the brutalities, and the savagery of Konstantin so terrified and alienated the poor girl that she refused to live with him not long after their ill-fated marriage,"* wrote one chronicler. *"Complaints of all kinds poured in upon Tsar Alexander concerning the unbearable brutality of his brother's conduct, forcing the Tsar to banish Konstantin from the Russian court under the guise of supervising affairs in the newly formed kingdom of Poland."* Leopold, Juliane's youngest brother once recalled, *"How strangely do things often come to pass…If the Grand Duke's choice had fallen on Antoinette, she would have suited that position wonderfully well."* He also expressed the opinion that the marriage collapsed in no small part due to difficulties and constant meddling created by Konstantin's mother.

In 1799 Anna Feodorovna was allowed to travel to Europe in search of medical treatment. While in Coburg, she told her family that she did not wish to return to Russia and instead wanted to divorce the brute she had married. Konstantin, if one believes memoirists of the time, was extremely jealous of his wife and treated her as his property, while being particularly brutish to the young girl. However, not wanting to cause a scandal that would damage their family's reputation, Juliane's parents convinced her to return to St. Petersburg and give it another try.

Once under her husband control again, Anna Feodorovna's life did not improve. In fact, a member of the court, Countess Golovina, recalled the married life of Anna Feodorovna was *"hard and impossible to maintain...in her modesty, she needed the friendship of [her sister-in-law] Elisabeth Alexeievna, who was able to smooth things out between the frequentlly quarreling spouses."* In 1801, taking advantage of the assassination of her father-in-law, Anna Feodorovna convinced Alexander I and Konstantin that she needed a cure in Germany. Duchess Augusta, who came to St. Petersburg to see her daughter, also fell victim to Anna's scheme. She took her back to Coburg and once safely ensconced in her hometown, Anna Feodorovna announced that she would not return to Russia. She asked Konstantin for a divorce, but he declined the request: *"You write to me that you were allowed to go into foreign lands,"* he informed her, *"because we are incompatible and because I cannot give you the love that you needed. But humbly I ask you to calm yourself in consideration to our lives together, besides all these facts confirm in writing, and that in addition to this other reason you don't have."*

Despite several attempts at reconciliation, Anna Feodorovna refused to ever set foot in Russia again. She eventually settled in Switzerland, where she purchased an estate, Elfenau, near Bern. Hidden away from the public eye, she gave birth to two illegitimate children, both fathered by courtiers. In 1808, she had a son who received the name Eduard Schmidt von Löwenfels, the last from the man who adopted him,

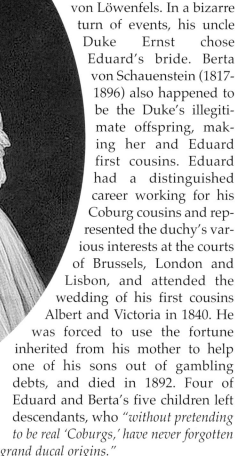

Grand Duchess Anna Feodorovna by Winterhalter.

Edgar Schmidt von Löwenfels, Coburg's Minister to Bern. Eduard's real father was a Frenchman by the name of Jules-Gabriel de Seigneux, who had served as an officer in the Prussian army. Four years later, Anna again gave birth, this time to a daughter, Louise-Hilda-Aglaé d'Aubert, fathered by Rodolphe Abraham de Schiferli, a Swiss professor who served both as tutor to Eduard and chamberlain to Anna. Interestingly, Eduard was later raised to the Saxon nobility with the last name Schmidt von Löwenfels. In a bizarre turn of events, his uncle Duke Ernst chose Eduard's bride. Berta von Schauenstein (1817-1896) also happened to be the Duke's illegitimate offspring, making her and Eduard first cousins. Eduard had a distinguished career working for his Coburg cousins and represented the duchy's various interests at the courts of Brussels, London and Lisbon, and attended the wedding of his first cousins Albert and Victoria in 1840. He was forced to use the fortune inherited from his mother to help one of his sons out of gambling debts, and died in 1892. Four of Eduard and Berta's five children left descendants, who *"without pretending to be real 'Coburgs,' have never forgotten their ducal and grand ducal origins."*

As for Anna, the family's repeated efforts at reconciliation with Konstantin only produced more acrimony and pain. The couple finally divorced in early 1820, an action that settled an irregular situation that had existed for nearly two decades. By the time of Anna Feodorovna's death in Switzerland in 1860, her family had largely forgotten her. A simple black slab marks her grave in Bern, inscribed with the words *"Mourir est mon gain et Christ est ma vie"* ("To die is my gain and Christ is my life") and serving as a reminder of her unfortunate existence.

CHAPTER III
Enter Gotha
Power Expanded

Ernst, the eldest son of Duke Franz Friedrich Anton and Duchess Augusta, succeeded his father as Duke of Coburg in 1806 at the young age of twenty-two. Born in 1784, he had been educated at court from 1791-1799 by a professor from the prestigious Gymnasyum Casimirianum, a Coburg school of some renown. Travel abroad was nearly impossible given the family's strained financial situation. However, in 1801 he went to St. Petersburg to see his sister Grand Duchess Anna Feodorovna; during the visit, he was made an officer of Imperial *Garde à Cheval*, one of the many honorary titles and positions Ernst collected during his lifetime.

Duke Ernst I, recalled the mother of his onetime mistress, Madame Panam, was *"a tall young man with the head rather stooping, covered with a profusion of curly black hair…His conduct was noble, his physiognomy handsome, his stature elegant."* He faced immediate difficulties on coming to the throne: the duchy's fortunes were at their lowest ebb and the continued Napoleonic wars had a disastrous effect on its economy. On hearing that Napoléon planned to annex Saxe-Coburg to his growing empire, Ernst lost little time departing for Paris to lobby on behalf of his realm, with his brother Leopold in tow.

Napoléon, though, refused to grant him an audience. As he waited, Ernst found himself captivated by the joyful and libertine atmosphere that reigned in Paris. He was seen at most of the fashionable salons and involved himself with the city's prettiest women. At the salon of Madame Panam, a well-known intriguer of dubious origins, he fell under the spell of her thirteen-year-old daughter Pauline. The young girl became his mistress overnight; when he returned to Coburg, Ernst tried to conceal Pauline's real role by appointing her a lady-in-waiting to his sister Grand Duchess Anna Feodorovna. Dowager Duchess Augusta, however, would not tolerate such shenanigans and banned her son's attempts. Unable to give up his paramour, Ernst hid Pauline in a gardener's cottage, dressing her as a boy to avoid any suspicions. The Duke's visits to Pauline's bedside continued and all would have continued rather easily had the poor girl not become pregnant. In a small town and court like Coburg, it was impossible to keep her pregnancy a secret and word of her unwelcome condition soon leaked to Dowager Duchess Augusta.

Negotiations had been underway between St. Petersburg and Coburg to arrange a marriage between Ernst and Grand Duchess Anna Pavlovna, Emperor Alexander I's sister; word of the pregnancy brought them to an end, much to Dowager Duchess Augusta's fury. Pauline Panam was called to an audience and ordered to renounce Duke Ernst. After the promise of a substantial monetary settlement, the poor girl left Coburg for Dresden, where she found protection under the wings of Grand Duke Konstantin, Ernst's brother-in-law. Konstantin eventually convinced Ernst to grant Pauline a pension for herself and for their baby son, who was given the name of Ernst-August Belmont. Years later, Pauline would take revenge on her ex-lover by writing a scurrilous book in which she accused Ernst of dastardly deeds, even insinuating that the Coburgs had tried to poison her. Fortunately for Ernst's reputation, Dowager Duchess Augusta's determination and self-control eventually saved her son's reputation and honor. Pauline Panam's statements were dismissed as nothing but the scornful tales of a frustrated lover.

Duke Ernst's close relations with the Romanovs saved him from Napoléon's wrath. Despite his dislike of the wily Coburger, Napoléon stopped short of deposing him, perhaps fearing that such a move against Alexander

I's brother-in-law would only further sour relations between France and Russia. Instead, he inflicted punitive measures on the duchy: Coburg was forced to provide troops and materiel to the war effort. Peace, in 1814, was received with great jubilation, if not by Duke Ernst, then certainly by his exhausted and war-weary subjects. The relief, though, was to be short: in 1815, after Napoléon escaped from Elba, Coburg was again forced to contribute troops, this time to defeat the Emperor. During this campaign, Ernst commanded the united Saxon Corps. His successful participation in the final defeat of Napoléon provided Ernst with considerable leverage when the Congress of Vienna met to decide the future of Europe.

The King of Saxony had remained loyal to his French ally. The Hohenzollerns, looking to devour the kingdom, demanded its annexation to Prussia and the total destruction of the Saxon monarchy. Much to their surprise, Duke Ernst led the opposition to such harsh measures that would obliterate a distant relation and a fellow sovereign. It was not that Ernst was fighting for the underdog: in his view, he was anticipating the eventual extinction of the Saxon Royal Family's Albertine line. If that happened, Coburg's lands might be greatly expanded, a possibility that Prussian annexation would preclude. Duke Ernst's approach was to become synonymous with the Coburgs: *"Venture nothing...keep everything."* This policy was to be the engine behind the dynasty's meteoric rise to European prominence.

In the aftermath of the Napoleonic Wars, Ernst's diplomatic endeavors led to considerable expansion of his lands. Claiming that Coburg had suffered grave losses during the wars, he demanded compensation. On 11 September 1816 his ambitious demands were met when Prussia ceded territories covering 464 square kilometers in Saarland. These lands, including St. Wendel, Kusel, and Tholey, are located near Neunkirchen, and were constituted into the principality of Lichtenberg. They provided yearly revenues amounting to £12,000, a considerable sum back then. Not surprisingly, Duke Ernst claimed that the new territories were his personal property, which he meant to govern without interference by politicians in Coburg, much less by those in St. Wendel. Disputes over revenue began a month after Duke Ernst took possession of the new lands. These quarrels marred Duke Ernst's tenure, and would not be solved until he sold his Saarland estates to Prussia in 1834. Money from this transaction allowed Duke Ernst the financial wherewithal to buy extensive properties in Austria and Lower Franconia. These were private transactions, and held as personal property by the duke and his descendants.

Emperor Napoléon I.

The Coburg succession, though, had not been settled and Duke Ernst remained unmarried. For a time it seemed as if he would wed Princess Hermine of Anhalt-Schaumburg (1797-1817), eldest daughter of Fürst Viktor II and of his wife Amalie, born a Princess of Nassau-Weilburg. In 1815, however, Hermine married Archduke Joseph of Austria, Palatine of Hungary, and the widower of Grand Duchess Alexandra Pavlovna, Juliane of Saxe-Coburg's sister-in-law. Poor Hermine's marital bliss did not last long as she died in childbirth in 1817 after delivering twins, Stephan and Hermine.

Never one to spend a night in solitude, Ernst had begun a relationship with a young lady named Sophie Fermepin during his Parisian stay in 1815. While his brothers were settling, Ferdinand with Princess Antonia of Kohary, and Leopold with Princess Charlotte of Wales, the insatiable Ernst was about to become the father of an illegitimate child, yet again. Ernst tried to cover up the liaison by marrying Sophie off to a captain in the Saxon army named Carl Schmidt, who in 1817 was ennobled in Coburg with the name von Schmidt-Schauenstein. However, and much to everyone's delight, amenable Carl died soon after the wedding. Sophie gave birth to her daughter, Berta von Schauenstein on 26 January 1817. Mother and daughter lived in Paris and at an estate Ernst bought for them. Her relationship with Ernst continued until his last days, in spite of his two marriages. The surreptitious lovebirds arranged yearly meetings, mainly in Wiesbaden, where they spent weeks in each other's embrace without being noticed by the outside world. Sophie lived the remaining years of her long life in Coburg, dying there in 1885.

The Panam and Fermepin affairs convinced Ernst's mother that it was time to find him a proper wife from an equal family, and Dowager Duchess Augusta would settle for nothing less than the best available for her wayward son. She did not have far to look, as the neighboring duchy of Saxe-Gotha-Altenburg offered her a pretty young bride, Princess Louise, who stood to inherit a sizable fortune. Duke August, her father, had no interest in hunting or riding, preferring to spend his leisure hours among his precious art collections while clad in silks and clothes with a distinctly feminine flair. He also wrote a poetic novel on the nature of love, including within its pages a homosexual couple. His first wife, the former Duchess Louise of Mecklenburg-Schwerin, had died in childbirth in early 1801, leaving August with a two week-old daughter, her namesake. One year later, he remarried, this time to Princess Karoline Amalie of Hesse-Kassel, a union that, perhaps not surprisingly, remained childless.

In Louise Ernst had not only a most attractive bride, but also one who could potentially add considerable territories to Coburg. The heir to Saxe-Gotha-Altenburg, Louise's uncle Friedrich, was not only childless but also mentally unstable, making it likely that she would one day inherit a considerable share of the family's estate. It was also hoped that the lively, sixteen-year-old Louise would manage to maintain thirty-three-year-old Ernst's amorous attentions long enough to begin a family. When the court at Gotha finally accepted Ernst, Dowager Duchess Augusta was overjoyed. The marriage, which took place in 1817 in the ducal capital of Gotha, witnessed lavish celebrations. Dowager Duchess Augusta wrote, *"The poor little bride was so trembling and overcome when she entered the room that she could not speak for crying. She is a sweet little thing, not beautiful, but very pretty through her charm and vivacity. Every feature of her face is expressive; her charming blue eyes under their long black eyelashes often look so sad, and then she is suddenly a gay, wild child. She has a pleasant voice, speaks well, and is at the same time so friendly and intelligent that one must like her. I hope she is still growing, as she is very small."* The people of Coburg greeted her joyously, and hopes for the future ran high.

Duchess Louise of Saxe-Coburg-Saalfeld.

Within a year of their wedding, Louise gave birth to an heir. Born in 1818 the baby boy was given the name of Ernst in honor of his very proud father. A second son arrived the following year: baptized with the name Albert, he was to become Louise's favorite son. However, these births did little to unite Ernst and Louise as a couple. After Albert's birth there were to be no more children and the marriage headed toward an abyss. Ernst and his duchess began to lead increasingly separate lives and were rarely seen together.

In truth, Ernst and Louise had very little in common. He was fond of hunting, a sport she abhorred; she loved dancing and parties, while he preferred entertaining within a small circle. Ernst found it impossible

Above: A map of Thuringia showing the various Saxon realms, as well as the lands ruled by the Princes of Reuß and Prussian controlled provinces in Saxony and Hannover. Coburg's acquisition of Gotha, and the territorial exchanges that followed, tripled Duke Ernst I's holdings.

Right: Schloß Ketschendorf, slightly outside Coburg, is a beautiful neo-Gothic structure that served as dower house to several widowed duchesses, among them Augusta, Marie and Alexandrine. Today, no longer owned by the Coburgs, it houses a youth hostel.

to find satisfaction in the arms of his inexperienced young wife, and did not remain faithful to her for long. Soon, he resumed his adventures with other ladies of the court. *"Ernst will go to Carlsbad,"* Louise confessed in despair, adding, *"How sad I already am you can well imagine, and mixed up with this is the tormenting feeling of jealousy. I am always afraid of the beauties there. Luckily he is to stay there only eight days."*

Once having fulfilled her main role to secure the succession and left alone, Louise sought companionship among her husband's courtiers. Sensitive and romantic, her young heart fluttered easily in its thirst for love and with the attentions she received from handsome young officers. Innocent flirtations soon turned serious when Alexander von Hanstein, a former Austrian cavalry officer attached to the Court Battalion, appeared. Described as a *"good looking young man, with black, curly hair, shining bright eyes, and resolute manner,"* von Hanstein *"sighed and languished like a turtle dove."* Louise even confessed that he *"did a thousand pretty, amorous things that amused me very much."* Soon, she threw caution to the wind and made her feelings for Hanstein known. Duke Ernst was not the man to tolerate public cuckolding, notwithstanding that his own treatment of Louise had been largely responsible for this state of affairs. Separation followed soon after and Ernst moved into his summer palace at Ketschendorff, while Louise retired to her beloved Rosenau, the birthplace of her young Albert.

The gentlefolk of Coburg reacted swiftly. Aware of the Duke's roving eye, most sided with young Louise. *"The Duchess,"* wrote Count Corneillan, *"has indeed committed mad pranks with her lovers, and has by no means concealed them. She is possessed of wild naiveté, and carries on with an artless, bold frankness that others conceal; at the same time she is lovable and seductive."* Louise relished this sympathetic popularity, writing to a friend that, *"the people love me to a degree of worship. They went in thousands to Rosenau. As I stepped into my carriage they burst through the hedges and railings cut the ropes and harnessed themselves to the carriage and pulled me from Rosenau, with unceasing shouts and hurrahs, through the town and stopped before the castle. The love was most touching and they were all armed. When I arrived at the castle I went on the balcony and thanked them for their love. After shouts and hurrahs, they solemnly sang Now Thank We All Our God!"*

Having convinced Louise to return to Coburg, the crowd headed to Ketschendorff, where the Duke, Dowager

Duchess Augusta, and the two young princes had retired. Ernst appeared on the balcony, agreeing to reunite his family in Coburg. That same evening, Ernst and Louise made their final public appearance together on the balcony of the Ehrenburg Palace. The peace was brief and the reconciliation failed. So upset were Coburgers by this state of affairs that they even made an attempt against the life of a court official charged with the inevitable divorce.

On 4 September, Louise departed Coburg for St. Wendel, never to return. *"At the stroke of midnight I left Coburg…and took the road to Brückenau; leaving my children was the most painful moment of all,"* she wrote. *"They have whooping cough, and said, 'Mamma cries because she got to go, when we are so ill.' The poor lambs, God be with them!"* Once the divorce was finalized, she quickly married von Hanstein, who just days earlier had been granted the title of Count Pölzig by the Duke of Saxe-Hildburghausen. Although her married life was happy, Louise she was haunted by all that had been abandoned. In March 1831, five years after her marriage, and while living in Paris, husband and wife went to see a famous dancer at the Opera. During the performance Louise collapsed from a serious hemorrhage and was carried unconscious from the theater. She died of uterine cancer on 30 August, four months before her thirty-first birthday. *"Don't damn me completely, but go on loving me,"* she had written to a friend. *"I have sacrificed everything, but don't also let me lose your friendly heart."* On hearing of her death, Leopold, her former brother-in-law, insisted that, *"Persian poetry corrupted Louise's mind."*

Duke Ernst I of Saxe-Coburg & Gotha.

The Coburg family did not wholly blame Louise for her actions, and she was freely mentioned in family circles with pity and sadness, not with reproach. Prince Albert himself *"never forgot her, and spoke with much tenderness and sorrow of his poor mother and was deeply affected by reading, after his marriage, the accounts of her sad and painful illness. One of the first gifts he made to the Queen was a little pin he received from his mother when a little child."* Princess Louise, Albert's daughter, was said to greatly resemble her grandmother.

Louise's last act had been bizarre: *"She settled a considerable annuity upon her second husband on condition that he should never part with her body! Should he pass even one night only in a house that did not at the same time harbor her mortal remains, he would loose his annuity. For years the luckless Count Pölzig dragged about with him the embalmed corpse of his spouse from place to place; but one morning, to his terror, he found that the precious coffin had vanished. When he found that his annuity continued to be paid, he soon became reconciled to his loss."*

The 1825 death of Duke Friedrich IV of Saxe-Gotha-Altenburg, Louise's childless uncle, brought a new redistribution of lands among the surviving branches of the Thuringian Wettins. When the four remaining Saxon duchies settled their negotiations in late 1826, Duke Ernst received the duchy of Saxe-Gotha; from the Duke of Saxe-Hildburghausen he received Königsberg (in Bavaria) and Sonnefeld, while from the Duke of Saxe-

Meiningen came the lands of Callenberg and Gauerstadt. In exchange, Duke Ernst gave the principality of Saalfeld, property in Themar and several localities on the left bank of the Steinach to the Duke of Saxe-Meiningen. From this time onward the family would be known as Saxe-Coburg and Gotha.

The new Duchy of Gotha was double the size of Coburg's territory, and Ernst I's fortunes improved considerably. Not only had his dynasty's territories been greatly expanded but also the substantial art collections gathered by generations of the duchy's extinct ducal family now landed in his hands. There were also several exquisite residences, including the Coburg inheritance. Most prominent among these was Schloß Friedenstein, *"the former ducal palace, built in 1643–1655. This imposing rectangular structure, with low square towers on the corners, is Germany's oldest early Baroque palace. The Palace Museum is home to valuable historic collections of art and cultural artifacts."* In lands formerly owned by a Benedictine abbey near Friedrichroda, Duke Ernst built a country retreat, Schloß Reinhardsbrunn, in English style and surrounded by a large pleasure park, where the Coburgs could hunt. His descendants owned this estate until the end of the Second World War, after which Communists expropriated Reinhardsbrunn. It now lays burnt out and nearly abandoned, its ruins an empty shell of what once was a magnificent residence.

A replenished treasury allowed Duke Ernst the luxury of engaging architects and artists to beautify, and modernize, Coburg. Schloß Ehrenburg, and the palace square in front, experienced considerable improvement, as did the town's ducal court theater, where the virtuoso Paganini performed in 1829. Later, in 1835, Ernst shifted his attention to improving the Veste Coburg, the massive fortress overlooking the town. Medieval moats were leveled and the ducal quarters modernized, while the castle's extensive art collections were expanded. By the time of Ernst's death, the ducal collection inside the Veste Coburg included more than 200 exquisite paintings.

Duchess Marie of Saxe-Coburg & Gotha.

Duke Ernst I married again in 1832, this time to his own niece Princess Marie of Württemberg. The union was somewhat happier than his previous marriage, but Ernst was never far away from the shadows of spite and infidelity. Marie certainly was a patient and submissive wife, remaining more a niece than a consort to her husband. Caroline Bauer remarked: *"She always looked remarkably serious. Never did a smile brighten her sulky face."* Marie was not unpleasant looking, with dark curls, good posture and regal manners, and she took an active part in the affairs of the duchy, showing herself weekly at the royal loggia of the newly built theater. Her personal tragedy was her inability to have children, and relations with her stepchildren were cool and with little affection. She once wrote about the two young princes: *"You think of me no more; you do not love me properly and you do not consider my advice being well-intentioned."* Yet she did not attend the confirmation of the princes or Queen Victoria's coronation, the latter with the excuse that the season was inclement to make the journey to London. Albert and Marie maintained correspondence throughout their lives, which has helped historians gain a better understanding of their relationship. Marie had a deep passion for literature, music, theatre, and art. The newly built Landestheater Coburg was opened on her 41st birthday. From 1842, Franz Liszt often came to Coburg to visit Marie. In 1836, she assumed the management of the *Gothaer Marien-Institut*, a private educational institution for girls. On in 1842, she donated funds for establishing an refuge

Schloß Greinburg, Austria. Perched over the banks of the mighty Danube River, Greinburg was purchased by Duke Ernst I with funds he obtained from the sale of the principality of Lichtenberg to Prussia. Greinburg continues under Coburg ownership and the Head of House visits frequently. It also houses a museum dedicated to the Coburgs.

for young children in Coburg, modeled on a similar institute in Gotha. The *"Marienschulstiftung"* (Marie School Foundation) opened its doors that same year and has run a Kindergarten since then. In 1869 it moved to a building where it continues housed until today. Duchess Marie died in Gotha in 1860.

Infidelity was second nature to Duke Ernst. Not only did he father at least four recognized children, but he is also alleged to have been the progenitor of countless others in both Coburg and Gotha. He ennobled Ernst-August, his son by Panam, as Knight of Hallenberg. The young man, however, had little contact with his father and siblings and died unmarried in 1832. Pauline Panam died in 1840 a deeply embittered woman, not without reason. Berta von Schauenstein fared better, as Ernst married her off to his nephew Eduard Schmidt von Löwenfels, himself the illegitimate child of Grand Duchess Anna Feodorovna. In 1838, he became the father of twin sons, Ernst and Robert, born to a notoriously ill-reputed adventuress by the name of Margaretha Braun. Baby Ernst died soon after birth, but his brother Robert lived long enough to be ennobled by Duke Ernst. In 1856, Robert was granted the title of Baron von Bruneck in the Austrian peerage, but he died that same year without leaving any descendants.

Duke Ernst was a difficult man and he ruled over a notoriously profligate court. His reign saw the family's holdings and possessions vastly increase. Aside from various estates in Bavaria, Lower Franconia, and Thuringia, Duke Ernst I acquired important properties in Austria from the Count of Dietrichstein, among them Greinburg, Kreuzen, Ruttenstein, Prandegg, Zellhof and Aich. Yet the treasury was in constant trouble and in arrears on its debts. Ernst had constant confrontations with authorities of the lands he ruled, and his efforts to bypass legalities and maneuver around constitutional restraints were both legendary and the source of countless political quarreling with elected officials. On many occasions he even tried to borrow funds from his son Albert.

In 1844 Duke Ernst I died at the age of fifty-nine, leaving a conflicting and troubled legacy of acquisitions and debts, marriages and mistresses. On hearing of his father's death, Prince Albert wrote, *"How I should like to be with you* [his brother Ernst] *and see the beloved face once more, though it is cold. We no longer have any home. This is a break that you cannot feel in the same way. Poor subjects, be a father to them!"*

Above: Prince Ferdinand of Saxe-Coburg & Gotha. An able administrator of his wife's huge fortune, Ferdinand also acquired large properties in Hungary, Austria and Slovakia.

To the right: Princess Antonia of Saxe-Coburg & Gotha. Born a Countess of Kohary, she was perhaps the richest bride of her time. Her father, who served in the inner circle of Emperor Franz I of Austria, owned vast properties within the empire. The absence of a male heir made the Count of Kohary designate his daughter as heir to the vast family fortune. Since Antonia, in spite of her riches, was a 'mere' countess, Franz I elevated her father, and consequently Antonia, to the princely rank. This was done retroactively to clear any doubt as to her eligibility to marry into the Coburg dynasty.

CHAPTER IV
Enter Kohary
Untold Riches

Prince Ferdinand, the second son of Duke Franz Friedrich Anton and Duchess Augusta, was renowned for his appearance. In a family graced with good looks, Ferdinand possessed finely chiseled features, good bone structure, a long aquiline nose, and jet-black hair that he had carefully curled with an iron. As a young man he served in the Austrian army; although markedly fond of the carefree atmosphere at the Viennese Court, he nonetheless enjoyed a good reputation.

It was while living in Austria that Prince Ferdinand made the acquaintance of a beautiful and exotic heiress, Countess Maria Antonia (Antoinette) Kohary de Csábrág et Szitnya, who had been born in Buda on July 2, 1797. Her father, Prince Franz Joseph von Kohary, served as Imperial Chancellor to Emperor Franz I, while her mother Maria Antonia was born a Countess von Waldstein-Wartenberg. As an only child (her three-year-old brother had died in 1792), Antonia stood to inherit what was then one of the premier fortunes in the Austrian Empire.

Count Franz Joseph von Kohary possessed a massive amount of property that spread over wide regions of present-day Hungary, Slovakia, and Lower Austria. These lands were partly imperial fiefdom, and partly Fideikommiss, an institutional foundation established in 1723 to hold estate property deemed inalienable from the Kohary inheritance, indivisible, and subject to certain succession rules on the Emperor's approval. The Fideikommiss was meant to provide the head of the aristocratic house with enough property and revenue to live in a style according to his position while preventing constant divisions caused by inheritance rights of other family members. Instead, lesser members received yearly pensions. Rules demanded that the lands be managed advantageously and profitably, and their hunting rights cultivated and protected. In exchange, estate income was paid to descendants and relatives of the Fidekommiss founder.

A serious relationship soon developed between Prince Ferdinand and Antonia, a good-looking woman whose Hungarian blood tempered her constitution. Her sister-in-law, Louise, described her as *"very tall, a beautiful figure, but a little thin. Wonderful dark eyes, long fair hair, a beautiful nose, and the prettiest mouth I know. She is very kind and friendly. We say 'thou' to each other, and have quickly become friends, as she is the same age as I, and sees things in the same way."* Ferdinand eventually asked for Antonia's hand. There were questions about the proposed union from the beginning. Antonia's parents were authoritarian, ambitious parvenus, and the marriage of their wealthy daughter to the mere cadet of a minor princely house from the Thuringian forests did not seem impressive enough, though the Coburg family's numerous royal connections eventually won their acquiescence. The Kohary family had been mere counts, and the issue of whether the marriage would be equal also kept tongues wagging. Though the marriage had little dynastic value, Ferdinand had to agree to raise all his children in the Roman Catholic faith; this provision excluded them from potential succession in Coburg, whose rules demanded a Protestant. For its part, the Coburg family, headed by the indomitable Duchess Augusta, welcomed the union and anticipated its many financial benefits. The wedding itself was a grand affair involving thousands of guests and incredible expense. Over three days, those invited to the festivities consumed 1,000 pigs, 1,600 sheep, and 10,000 chickens as some 800 musicians kept them entertained.

Dowager Duchess Augusta's delight with her new daughter-in-law almost certainly owed something to Antonia's immense dowry. *"I cannot be more satisfied in the darling Ferdinand has brought to our house,"* she wrote.

"The expression of her beautiful face reveals her generosity and goodness, her loving and friendly eyes seem to say: Are you happy with me? How can I make you happy? Pure, content, alien to any evil thought, she stands there charming and unassuming like the young maiden in a fairy tale."

The union between Ferdinand and Antonia was an exceedingly happy – and wealthy – one. On Antonia's father's death in 1826, the Kohary fiefdoms reverted to Emperor Franz I, who then awarded them to the highly decorated Prince Ferdinand for his services to Austria and Hungary. Old documents reveal this to have been roughly 53,500 hectares of land. Ferdinand took this opportunity to create his own Fideikommiss (The Prince Ferdinand von Coburg Fideikommiss), which further protected the family's vast landholdings from division among future descendants. This gave him control of some additional 107,000 hectares; combined with the Kohary inheritance, he now had nearly 420,000 acres of real estate measuring roughly 700 square miles – approximately ten times the size of the Principality of Liechtenstein. As a result, the Coburgs were the third largest landowners in Greater Hungary until the debacle following the Great War. The holder of the Fideikomiss was also tasked with advantageously and profitably managing the property. He also had to undertake the protection of wild game and hunting grounds. From the income raised by the Fideikommiss estates, the holder had to pay appanages and widows pensions to the descendants of the founder of the Kohary Fideikommiss.

Princess Antonia in later life.

By the terms of these arrangements, Ferdinand had to specify an heir in his Will. As his eldest son later renounced inheritance rights on marrying Queen Maria II of Portugal, Prince Ferdinand named his second son Prince August as his successor, while also specifying that the Prince Ferdinand von Coburg Fideikommiss and the Counts Kohary Fideikommiss were to be administered jointly. The conditions also stipulated that the holder of the Fideikommiss had to be Catholic. Antonia's parents had not insisted that Kohary become a part of the Coburg name; to differentiate the Catholic and Protestant branches of the Coburg family from this time on, however, it is easiest to refer to Ferdinand and Antonia's descendants as the Saxe-Coburg-Kohary line.

To provide an adequate residence for the head of the Fideikommiss, Prince Ferdinand had the old Kohary Palace and surrounding buildings – which were part of his wife's inheritance – pulled down between 1839-1843. In their place he had the present-day Coburg Palais built at Seilerstätte 3. Renowned architects and talented artisans worked tirelessly for five years, only distracted by the political repercussions of the February Revolution in 1848 and the overthrow of King Louis Philippe of France, eventual father-in-law of Ferdinand's son Prince August. Prince Ferdinand's vast wealth also allowed him the luxury of traveling in grand style. Several times he visited his sister Victoire in London, and made a strong impression on his little niece, the future Queen Victoria. Perhaps seeing in Ferdinand the father figure missing from her life, she described conversation with him as *"useful and extremely clever in seeing through things."*

Princess Antonia proved to be a loving wife and a dutiful mother. Unlike her husband, she rarely traveled, preferring to remain in the Austrian Empire in one of her many palaces and tending to her children. A son, Prince Ferdinand, was born in 1816, followed by Prince August in 1818; Princess Victoire, born in 1822; and Prince Leopold, born in 1824. True to family tradition, these Catholic Coburgs generally married well: Ferdinand became King Consort of Portugal; Prince August married Princess Clémentine of Orléans; and Princess Victoire married the Duke de Nemours, one of the sons of King Louis Philippe of France. Only Prince Leopold disappointed by marrying morganatically, the first in the family to do so.

Prince Ferdinand died in 1851 aged sixty-six years. His widow Antonia survived him by eleven years. She was a distant figure for the rest of the Coburgs, who remembered her but did not mention her in their correspondence. Antoinette, it seems, preferred to lead a quiet life spent in the background, a completely un-Coburg approach to one's existence, always present yet rarely making an impression. In later life, she was easily overshadowed by the far larger presence of her daughter-in-law Clémentine. Antonia died quietly in her vast Viennese palace on 25 September 1862. Her remains were transported to Coburg, where they rest for eternity in the Glockenberg Mausoleum with those of her beloved Ferdinand.

The Coburg-Kohary alliance, if not dynastically important, had at least been well received by all of Vienna, or so it was thought. Legend, though, holds that one of Antonia's close relations, expecting a considerable inheritance from her father, was furious upon learning that the fortune would go to Ferdinand and his children. In retaliation, this relative – according to rumor a man of the cloth – supposedly invoked a curse on the

Prince Leopold of Saxe-Coburg & Gotha, Ferdinand and Antonia's youngest son.

Above left: An early photograph circa 1855 of Princess Victoire, Duchess de Nemours, and her two sons: Gaston, Count d'Eu, and Ferdinand, Duke d'Alençon. Victoire was Prince Ferdinand and Princess Antonia's only daughter. She married Prince Louis, Duke de Nemours, second son of King Louis-Philippe of the French.

Above right: Prince Gaston, Count d'Eu, was the eldest son of Princess Victoire. In 1864 he traveled to Brazil and there on 1 October, married Princess Izabel, heir of Emperor Pedro II. Gaston's descendants form the present-day Imperial Family of Brazil.

Right: Prince Ferdinand, Duke d'Alençon, was Princess Victoire's second son. He married Sophie, Duchess in Bavaria, a sister of the mythical Empress Elisabeth of Austria.

The Duchess de Nemours was a great favorite at the court of King Louis Philippe, where her distinction, elegance and exquisite education gained her much favor. In England, Victoire was particularly close to her cousin, and namesake, Queen Victoria, who adored her Coburg cousin. Victoire died at Claremont House in 1857 from complications after delivering her fourth child.

Coburgs, something future history certainly seemed to support. A total of thirteen Coburg princes predeceased their fathers: the Duke of Clarence, eldest son of King Edward VII; Alfred Jr., only son of Duke Alfred of Saxe-Coburg & Gotha; Arthur Jr., only son of the Duke of Connaught; Hubertus, second son and heir of Duke Carl Eduard; Pedro V, eldest son of King Consort Ferdinand of Portugal; Leopold, only son of Prince Philipp; Pedro (Peter) August, eldest son of Prince Ludwig August, who went mad at an early age and was thus bypassed for inheritance matters as if he were dead; August Clemens, eldest son of Prince August Leopold; Johannes Albert, only son of Prince Johannes Heinrich; King Boris III, eldest son of King Ferdinand I of Bulgaria; Louis-Philippe, eldest son of King Léopold I of the Belgians; Leopold, Duke of Brabant, only son of King Léopold II; and Baudouin, eldest son of the Count of Flanders.

Perhaps the story was merely a myth, an attempt to make sense of the slew of tragedies that visited the House of Coburg after Prince Ferdinand received the Kohary inheritance. Yet there is no denying that, at times and in light of future tragedies, it must have seemed very real to many members of the family.

Chapter V
Enter Great Britain
A Failed Attempt

The greatest prize to be won in the aftermath of the Napoleonic Wars was the hand of Princess Charlotte of Wales, only legitimate grandchild of King George III. In and out of touch with reality for several decades George III had been supplanted in all but name by his son George, who ruled as Prince Regent. As the Prince's brothers had no legitimate heirs, it seemed certain that young Charlotte would inevitably become Queen. Finding her a proper husband was a grave matter of state, and as peace spread across Europe a stampede of eligible princes headed to London hoping to gain her hand.

Charlotte's life had not been easy. Her parents, the future George IV and his wife, Caroline of Brunswick, had both been incredibly unhappy in their disastrous marriage. George had found his wife – and her lack of hygiene – repellent, while Caroline was infuriated that her husband flaunted his mistresses. It was a small miracle that their union had even produced a daughter. Never properly education for her future role, Charlotte had been neglected and emerged as a young woman of conflicting impressions. She was, said one contemporary, blonde, with a *"handsome nose, a delicious mouth and fine teeth...She is full of spirit and positive in character. She seems to have an iron will in the smallest things."* Yet Grand Duchess Catherine Pavlovna recalled: *"Her manners are so extraordinary that they take one's breath away...She walks up to any man, young or old, especially the older men, takes them by the hand, and shakes it with all her strength...She looks like a boy, or rather a ragamuffin. I really am telling you nothing but the strictest of truth. She is ravishing, and it is a crime to have allowed her to acquire such habits."*

The Prince Regent initially proposed a marriage between his daughter and Prince Willem of Orange, future ruler of The Netherlands. The talks had been underway since 1807, when the King of The Netherlands suggested to Lord Malmesbury that the natural alliance between *"Holland and England should be strengthened by a marriage between his son and heir and the heir presumptive to the throne of England, Princess Charlotte."* There were potential benefits to such an alliance, including the possible combination of the Royal Navy and Dutch fleet, a proposition that would make *"Britannia's rule of the waves...unassailable."*

Willem of Orange was sent to Oxford to both get an education and become an Englishman, and his mother promptly reported his progress to the Prince Regent. In 1811, Orange was commissioned in the British Army and went on to serve under Wellington in Spain. Napoléon's defeat stripped portions of the Austrian Netherlands (present day Belgium) and incorporated them into a new constitutional monarchy in Holland. This all seemed promising, and yet even as the fathers schemed no one bothered to inform the young couple of the planned future union.

When Charlotte finally met Orange, she was not wholly disappointed. At least, the Dutchman was tall, slender and amenable, even though he had a plain face. *"I like his manner very well, as much as I have seen it,"* Charlotte told her father. Even though his daughter's reaction to Orange was lackluster at best, the Prince Regent was delighted and quickly convinced himself that the engagement was a fait-accompli. *"He is by no means as disagreeable as I expected,"* she told a friend. These were hardly the words of someone deeply impressed with her prospective husband; more to the point, having witnessed the disastrous union of her parents, Charlotte was determined to marry for love.

Prince Leopold of Saxe-Coburg-Saalfeld in Garter robes.

married he would not insist in her joining him when travel to Holland was necessary. While she appreciated Orange's honesty on the matter, Charlotte was most irritated at her father for having trapped her in a relationship without revealing what it required. It was the second crack in the plan: the first had come when Charlotte witnessed her father and Orange's own father drink themselves under the table at a dinner to celebrate her grandmother's birthday.

When the intended groom returned to his country, Charlotte had time and space to think things through. What she wanted out of marriage was independence and a household all her own, a path to freedom. *"Holland is a very Odd place I believe,"* she wrote. *"Even now I doubt being much amused there…We must see what we can do to make it more Londonish & dandyish."*

Grand Duchess Catherine Pavlovna, sister of Emperor Alexander I of Russia, happened to visit London that spring. Heartily disliking the Prince Regent and dismissing his brother the Duke of Clarence as 'vulgar,' she nonetheless befriended Charlotte. As she slowly gained the young girl's trust, the Grand Duchess felt that Charlotte was a prisoner of circumstance, manipulated by all of those around her, including her father. At a dinner party given by Lord and Lady Liverpool, Catherine cornered the Prince Regent and lobbied on Charlotte's behalf. *"When she is married,"* Catherine said, *"I hope she will know how to make up for her present imprisonment."*

"When she is married, Madame," George replied in annoyance, *"she will do her husband's will, just as at present she is doing mine."*

"Ah, yes," the Grand Duchess shot back. *"Your Royal Highness is right. Between husband and wife there can only be one will."*

"This is intolerable!" the Prince Regent told Princess Lieven, who sat at his side. Soon, Catherine would take up Charlotte's cause, and the Prince Regent would discover the power of a Romanov Grand Duchess.

At top: An artist's rendering of the first meeting of Prince Leopold and Princess Charlotte at the Pulteney Hotel, London. Grand Duchess Catherine Pavlovna sits between them. Above: A print of Princess Charlotte of Wales from around the time of her wedding.

The first difficulties arose when Orange insisted that, after the marriage, Charlotte spend several months a year in Holland with him. She was mortified by the thought of being away from England for that long, and hesitated. Orange, fearing that he had damaged his candidacy, relented and said that perhaps once

Chapter V – Enter Great Britain: A Failed Attempt

In April 1814, the Allies entered Paris and Napoléon, left without an escape, was forced to abdicate. War, that terrible struggle that had consumed Europe for the last decade, was finally at an end. Many decided to continue the celebrations across the Channel, and Emperor Alexander I was one of many royalties who arrived in London. Another was Prince August of Prussia, a thirty-five-year-old military officer who had fought in the battle of Auerstadt against Napoléon. During the battle his brother Louis Ferdinand was killed, and the French had captured August and held him captive in Paris until 1807. August's captivity was far from harsh: he developed a taste for fast living and began an affair with the renowned Madame Récamier, a society lady whose salon attracted leading figures of Parisian literary and political circles. The relationship faltered when Récamier turned down August's request that she divorce her husband and marry him. Arriving in London that spring of 1814, August set his eyes on the eligible Charlotte, visiting her and exchanging portraits and jewels. Had her father known of August's intentions he would have been furious: at nearly twenty years her senior and with a tattered reputation, the Prince was scarcely a suitable husband for the future Queen of England. In time, Charlotte learned the truth about her suitor's true character and, realizing that any union was impossible, reluctantly bid him farewell. Or perhaps not quite so reluctantly, for by this time another young man, tall, slender, and attractive, had arrived in London and Charlotte was fascinated. The object of her attraction was Prince Leopold of Saxe-Coburg-Saalfeld.

The youngest child of Duke Franz Friedrich Anton and Duchess Augusta, Leopold had been born in Coburg on 16 December 1790. Nearly everyone agreed that the young Prince was charming, elegant, talented, and extremely attractive: even Napoléon called him *"the handsomest young man I have ever seen."* In Paris with his brother Ernst to protect the future of their duchy, he captivated both the Emperor and his wife Joséphine, and was even rumored to have had an affair with Hortense de Beauharnais, the Empress's daughter and wife of Napoléon's brother, Prince Louis Bonaparte.

Princess Charlotte of Wales.

On returning to Coburg, Leopold completed his political apprenticeship at his brother's little court, acting as regent when Ernst I absented himself from the duchy. Baron Christian Friedrich von Stockmar was soon appointed as Leopold's personal physician, but his influence soon spread far beyond the realm of medicine. Possessing a brilliant political mind, Stockmar became the young prince's political mentor and most trusted counselor at a time when Leopold's fortunes were on the ascent. In 1814, Leopold entered the Russian Imperial Army and became one of the first German princes to join the coalition against Bonaparte. Leopold led his own regiment at the battle of Kulm, and later participated in the French Campaign that again brought him to Paris. During the Congress of Vienna, he had acted as his brother Ernst's representative.

It was a farewell meeting at the Pulteney Hotel that first brought Charlotte and Leopold face to face. By this time, the Princess had turned against the idea of marrying Willem of Orange. Warning that he was also in the hotel, Grand Duchess Catherine urged the Princess to take the rear staircase to avoid meeting him. Charlotte did so, and at the foot of the stairs found a *"tall, dark, handsome officer wearing the all-white uniform of the Russian heavy cavalry."* Although she did not know his name, Charlotte recognized the dashing officer she had occasionally glimpsed at parties during Emperor Alexander I's visit. The young man escorted the Princess and her lady-in-waiting through the crowded hall and safely delivered them to their

Left: Claremont House, in Surrey, was Princess Charlotte and Prince Leopold's country estate. Leopold continued living there after becoming a widower. In later years when his French in-laws needed a home, Leopold let them lodge at Claremont House.

Below: A commemorative medal marking the death of Princess Charlotte of Wales.

carriage. When Charlotte learned his name, she boldly scolded Leopold for not having called on her as most other princes had done. Leopold begged forgiveness and asked for an opportunity to correct his behavior. Thus began the romance between Prince Leopold of Saxe-Coburg-Saalfeld and Princess Charlotte of Wales.

Leopold received Alexander I's permission to stay in England, *"after certain very singular events made me glimpse the possibility, even the probability, of realizing the project we spoke of in Paris,"* wrote Leopold. *"My chances are, alas, very poor, because of the father's opposition, and he will never give his consent. But I have resolved to go on to the end, and only to leave when all my hopes have been destroyed."* He briefly left in July 1814, when his sister Victoire's husband Emich of Leiningen died. The canny Charlotte, aware of her father's feelings for the impoverished and tenuously connected Leopold, pretended that her feelings for Leopold had passed, but many of her relatives, including Prince Edward, Duke of Kent, took up her cause and urged her to let the matter play out over time.

Napoléon's escape from Elba and entry intoFrance in early 1815 temporarily thwarted Leopold's plans to return to England. Once again Europe readied for war and Leopold rejoined his troops. Then, on 15 June, after a reign of only three months, Napoléon met his match at Waterloo and was again exiled. Now Leopold was free to pursue Charlotte.

The romance proved extremely difficult. At one point, after receiving a letter in which Leopold informed the Prince Regent that he was visiting Charlotte, she walked away. George tried to keep Charlotte from seeing the Prince; she ran away from Carlton House, his London residence, and sought protection under her mother's roof. When she finally returned, the Prince Regent sent her to Windsor where, according to her uncle the Duke of Sussex, she was kept under house arrest and isolated from her family circle. The Prince Regent, just as stubborn as his daughter, attempted to revive the Orange scheme. Charlotte was livid. She recognized that because of her birthright her choices were not entirely her own and that she was not free of her obligations to the nation and dynasty. However, she was unwilling to give an inch in the matter of marrying Willem of Orange. *"I remain firm & unshaken, & no arguments, no threats shall ever bend me to marry this detested Dutchman."*

The desperate Princess tried another approach, writing to the Prime Minister and asking that he formally present her wish to marry Leopold to her recalcitrant father. She even threatened to remain a spinster if not allowed to marry the man of her choice. The Prince retaliated by insisting that the unsettled situation in Europe meant any decision would have to be postponed. By late winter of 1815, though, Charlotte had made up her mind. She wrote to one of her ladies, asking *"whether you thought you could by any means send him a hint that his pres-*

ence at this moment in England would be of service to his views if they were the same as 6 months ago." Her decision was aided by a deep belief that "Leo," as she called the Coburg Prince, was a man of high ideals, moral character, elegant, and someone "who certainly did like me." It was a risky move, as Charlotte wanted Leopold to come uninvited. Fearing that this would only further infuriate her father, Leopold refused.

Charlotte finally wrote to her father, insisting that she would have Leopold and no one else. Faced with her intransigence, the Prince Regent relented and asked Leopold to come to England. Months of discreet inquiries about the Prince had resulted in glowing accounts of Leopold's charm and virtues that eventually overcame the Prince Regent's objections. On 26 February 1816, Leopold arrived in England and within six weeks, his engagement to Princess Charlotte was announced.

Leopold and Charlotte were married at Carlton House in London on the evening of 2 May 1816. Some fifty privileged guests, many of them members of the Royal Family, attended the ceremony. To the surprise of many, Charlotte and Leopold were obviously and truly in love. They divided their time between London and Claremont Park, a country house in Surrey, living tranquil, domestic and scandal-free lives that contrasted with those of her parents and most of her royal uncles. A government allowance of £60,000 allowed them to live in immense comfort, and Charlotte happily adopted many of her husband's tastes, joining him in reading, studying, and religious observances. Their exemplary way of life made Charlotte and Leopold tremendously popular among the London crowds.

The country exploded in celebrations when the Princess of Coburg's pregnancy was announced in early 1817. The child, third-in-line for the British throne, would guarantee the dynasty's existence for another generation. Charlotte, already experiencing difficulties with her health, put on weight and felt supremely happy, yet her physicians feared that she would not be able to carry the pregnancy to full term. They attempted to calm her by bleeding her and severely limiting her diet. Not surprisingly, Charlotte began to experience complications while growing increasingly weak. Her physicians' efforts turned her happy pregnancy into a personal Calvary.

The Charlotte Memorial, St. George's Chapel, Windsor Castle. "The monument by Matthew Wyatt was erected by public subscription in memory of the Princess Charlotte, only child of George IV." Her early death led to the Duke of Kent seeking a royal wife, a marriage responsible for producing the future Queen Victoria.

By the beginning of November 1817 the end of Charlotte's pregnancy was rapidly approaching. She had grown very weak as a result of the continued bleedings and malnourishment prescribed by her medical staff. Leopold, worried sick about her wife's excruciating pains, rarely left her side. Her agonizing labor, which continued over two days, began on 3 November. The baby was in transverse position and very large. The medical staff realized that forceps were required, yet they chose not to use them. As the birth took its course, Charlotte's screams filled the house; Leopold was not even allowed to see her. Then came word that the baby, a boy, was born dead. Exhausted and bleeding profusely, Charlotte lingered in agony before finally succumbing. Public grief was enormous. King George III's only legitimate grandchild was dead, and the succession to the British Throne was plunged into a crisis.

A distraught Leopold was shattered. In his mourning he retired to Claremont, shutting away the outside world and living in a world of happy memories. Yet even in his gloom he was soon to play a pivotal role that changed the course of modern history.

CHAPTER VI
Princesses for Export &
Alexandrina Victoria of Kent

Princess Juliane's marriage to Grand Duke Konstantin Pavlovich had merely been the start of a long line of illustrious unions that eventually linked the Coburgs with nearly every other European royal house. Of the three remaining Coburg daughters, one would marry into a distinguished – though scarcely known – aristocratic family; another wed the brother of Empress Maria Feodorovna of Russia; and the third, after marrying into the British Royal Family, gave birth to the girl who one day became Queen Victoria.

Princess Sophie, Countess von Mensdorff-Pouilly (1778-1835)

Although she was the eldest daughter of Duke Franz Friedrich Anton and Duchess Augusta, Princess Sophie was the last to marry. After receiving several proposals from princely candidates as her family's fortunes rose, she eventually settled on the little known Baron Emmanuel de Pouilly (1777-1852), an officer in the Austrian army and a close friend of her brother Ferdinand. Sophie, according to her brother Leopold, met Emmanuel on a visit to Bayreuth. His father, a French Field Marshal, had sought refuge in Prussia during the French Revolution. After having been ennobled in Austria, the family adopted the title of Counts of Mensdorff-Pouilly. Originally from the region of Lorraine, they could trace their roots back some five centuries: one ancestor, Aubertin IV, had lost his life at the battle of Agincourt while fighting against the English.

During the French Revolution Emmanuel emigrated from France and settled in Coblenz. Enrolling in the Austrian army, he participated in the Battle of Valmy in 1793 and later fought in the Napoleonic Wars against the French Emperor, receiving several wounds. Although brave, loyal, and reliable, Emmanuel was drummed out of the Austrian Army at Napoléon's insistence in 1810 owing to his French birth. Pleasant and charming, Emmanuel managed to impress the formidable Dowager Duchess Augusta and duly wed Sophie.

Princess Sophie was never a bastion of health, and her various pregnancies only contributed to her many ailments. *"Sophie is dreadfully ill,"* one of her sisters-in-law reported during one pregnancy. *"Oh, it will be terrible if she should die! She is truly an angel! She is having fearful convulsions, and is paralyzed on one side, we are very worried about her."* Still, she fulfilled her duty and gave birth to six sons: Hugo (1806-1847), Alfons (1810-1894), Alfred (1812-1814), Alexander (1813-1871), Leo Emanuel (1815-1821), and Arthur (1817-1902). It is quite possible that hemophilia, a disease later synonymous with the Coburgs, first made its fearful appearance in Sophie's sons. Both Alfred and Leo Emanuel likely suffered from the dreaded bleeding illness, responsible for wreaking havoc at the Russian and Spanish courts in future years.

Until 1813, Sophie and her family lived in Coburg, where they shared with her family the privations and vicissitudes of war and occupation. During the wars of liberation in 1813, Emmanuel served as military advisor to his brother-in-law Duke Ernst, and after the Congress of Vienna he acted as commander of a cavalry brigade in Bohemia. In 1818 the Habsburgs elevated him to the Austrian nobility, and for a decade Emmanuel commanded the federal fortress of Mainz. In 1834 Sophie followed him when he returned to Bohemia to act as a commanding general. His career advances came as his wife's health declined. In 1831, Sophie had been at her mother's bedside when Dowager Duchess Augusta died. Increasingly unwell, Sophie nonetheless assisted her brother Ernst with preparations for his wedding to their niece Duchess Marie of Württemberg. Shortly after following her husband back to Bohemia, though, on the night of 8-9 July 1835, Sophie died at Tuschmitz.

The widowed Emmanuel continued his impressive career. He was named vice-president of the Austrian Imperial War Cabinet, in charge of the country's military preparations both in peacetime and during conflicts and once again served with distinction. By 1848, exhausted, he retired from his posts. Count Emmanuel of Mensdorff-Pouilly died in Vienna on 28 June 1852.

*Above:
Count Emmanuel of Mensdorff-Pouilly, a distinguished Austrian military officer.*

Right: Princess Sophie, Countess of Mensdorff-Pouilly.

Count Alexander, Sophie's fourth son, made a great impression on his cousin Queen Victoria, who was ecstatic over this handsome, quiet, and able soldier. So retiring was he that he would not address the Queen with the familiar 'du' but instead always used *"Majesty."* When he appeared at court, he did so without a servant and using a hired carriage on such occasion – modest measures that won the young Queen's approval. Even Lord Melbourne praised his hair, insisting that no German could have such nice hair. Created Prince of Dietrichstein zu Nikolsburg by Emperor Franz Joseph in 1868, Alexander married Countess Alexandrine von Dietrichstein-Proskau-Leslie, eldest daughter of the previous Prince of Dietrichstein zu Nikolsburg.

Alexander's youngest son, Count Albert Viktor, later served as Austrian ambassador in London during the reign of Edward VII. Archduke Franz Ferdinand, a stickler for protocol, besides being a difficult man, complained that in England he was placed in the same rank as an Austrian subject, namely the Count of Mensdorff-Pouilly. The British Royal Family assessed rank according to the degree of relationship with themselves, much to the chagrin of sticklers like the Austrian Imperial heir. Even the Kaiser resented that as mere counts, the Mensdorff-Pouilly were so widely feted and influential in London. Although his enemies accused him of being a scheming intriguer, Count Albert Viktor of Mensdorff-Pouilly was a skillful diplomat, and it was extremely painful for him to be Austria's London ambassador when the First World War erupted in 1914.

Princess Antoinette, Duchess Alexander of Württemberg (1779-1824)

Princess Antoinette, the second daughter of Duke Franz Friedrich Anton and Duchess Augusta, married Alexander of Württemberg. The only advantage of this union, and an amazing one at that, was the fact that he was the favorite brother of the impetuous and domineering Empress Maria Feodorovna of Russia, consort of Emperor Paul I. Antoinette and Alexander had first met in 1795, when Augusta took her daughters to Russia, and Maria Feodorovna had decided that one of the impressive Coburg girls should wed her adored brother Alexander. According to Caroline Bauer, who had her own quarrels with the Coburgs, Alexander was shockingly ugly: *"A huge tumor disfigured his forehead, and there was something brutish in his face. Besides, the poor fellow suffered from a sad disease, that of gluttony. When the young bride awoke on the morning after the wedding, horror-stricken she saw her husband besides her gnawing a big hambone with brutish ferocity...a sight the unfortunate princess could never forget. He suffered from another not less odious disease, the most sordid avarice."*

As a younger son, Duke Alexander of Württemberg fulfilled expectation and embarked on a military career. He began service in the Württemberg army and later transferred to Austrian forces, joining them in their fight against the French. In 1798, Alexander relocated to Russia, where his brother-in-law Paul I gave him a commission in Riga. While quartered there, he had Antoinette and their two eldest children join him. In 1804, Antoinette gave birth to a second son, Alexander; three years later a third son joined the nursery, Ernst, named after his Coburg uncle. The youngest son, Friedrich, was born in St. Petersburg in 1810 but died just days before his fifth birthday.

Unlike her more worldly sisters, Antoinette was happiest when at home taking care of her family. She was, as even her family acknowledge, best suited for the traditional role of a 'hausfrau.' Antoinette became a constant presence at Emperor Alexander I's court, and developed a very close friendship with his consort Empress Elisabeth Alexeievna. Both ladies influenced the Emperor on behalf of the Coburgs at every available chance; at one point, Antoinette even tried to arrange the marriage of her brother Duke Ernst I and her sister-in-law, Grand Duchess Anna Pavlovna. The scheme failed, and Anna went on to marry the future King Willem II of the Netherlands, who had previously been engaged to Princess Charlotte of Wales.

Association with the Romanovs greatly influenced Duke Alexander's career. In 1811 Emperor Alexander I made him Military Governor of Bielorussia. The following year Duke Alexander joined Russian efforts against Napoléon's Grand Armée, and participated in the battle of Borodino. In 1813, as the Russian armies swarmed into Europe, Alexander commanded the successful siege of Danzig. Once peace arrived, he returned to his old post in Riga, serving until 1822 when Alexander I asked his uncle to become Head of the Communications Department. In this capacity, Duke Alexander initiated the construction of transportation links and several large-scale waterways across the Empire.

Living in faraway Russia, Antoinette's visits to relations in Coburg, London, Prague, Vienna, and Stuttgart were not easy. She undertook two long journeys in 1808 and 1819, but by then she longed to return to her adopted homeland. In St. Petersburg, she and Alexander occupied a large apartment in the magnificent Yusupov Palace. Yet life in Russia strained her health and, by early 1824, she was seriously ill. On 14 March Antoinette died.

The widowed Duke Alexander continued his career, serving as a member of the State Council until he retired in 1832. That same year, he traveled to Coburg for the 23 December marriage of his daughter Marie to her uncle Duke Ernst I. Some six months later, while still in Coburg, Duke Alexander died unexpectedly. He was buried in the ducal crypt at Schloß Friedenstein. Many years later, Antoinette's remains were brought from Russia and she was laid to rest next to her husband.

Above: Duke Alexander of Württemberg.

Right: Princess Antoinette, Duchess of Württemberg.

Even though Antoinette's marriage was not considered dynastically impressive, it did strengthen the relationship between the House of Coburg and the Russian Imperial Family and established the House of Württemberg. In addition to her daughter Marie, who became Prince Albert's stepmother, her son Alexander later married King Louis-Philippe's daughter Princess Marie d'Orléans. Of Antoinette's other three children, Paul and Friedrich died in infancy, while Ernst made a morganatic marriage later in life and left one daughter, who today has living descendants.

Princess Victoire, Fürstin of Leiningen, Duchess of Kent (1786-1861)

Born in Coburg in 1786, Princess Victoire is said to have been the prettiest of the four daughters of Duke Franz Friedrich Anton and Duchess Augusta. Somewhat plump, good-looking, with fine mischievous eyes, a fresh complexion, and a petite figure, Victoire certainly fulfilled contemporary ideals of beauty. A sister-in-law described her as *"very beautiful, tall and big, very pale with black eyes and black hair; and she is very charming and unaffected."*

The Duke of Kent.

At the tender age of seventeen Victoire married Fürst Emich Carl of Leiningen, a widower twenty-seven years her senior. Born in 1763, Emich Carl was the son of Carl Friedrich of Leiningen and his wife Countess Christiane Wilhelmine of Solms-Rödelheim und Assenheim. An ancient dynasty with origins in the early Twelfth Century, the Leiningens once possessed considerable landed estates in Alsace and Lorraine as well as in the Palatinate. In 1779 they had been elevated to princely status within the Holy Roman Empire, but in 1801 the family lost most of their existing estates on orders of Napoléon. In compensation, they received land in Amorbach, Lower Franconia. This loss was a seriously financial blow that affected the family for generations, though its consequences did not hinder their marriage prospects. In 1787, Emich Carl had married Sophie Henrietta of Reuß-Ebersdorf, Duchess Augusta's youngest sister. Six years later she gave birth to a son, Friedrich Karl, who died in 1800; Sophie Henrietta survived him only by a year, dying in 1801.

Despite his shortcomings, the heartbroken Emich Carl was soon under the protective hand of his sister-in-law Duchess Augusta. Although short on funds, he stood to inherit considerable landed estates. Victoire, it seemed to her mother Augusta, would bring much joy to her former brother-in-law; she was also young enough that she could certainly produce offspring, including the much-desired heir. In 1803, they were married in Coburg.

The marriage between Victoire and Emich Carl was not a great success. Gloomy and morose, he complained of constant ill health, and seethed at the loss of his lands at Napoléon's hands. The relationship between husband and wife was more akin to that between an authoritative uncle and a reverential niece than a love match. Within ten months, Victoire gave birth to a son, Carl Emich, followed by a second child, Feodora, three years later.

Emich Carl died in 1814 after eleven years of marriage, leaving a widow and two young children. *"For dear Victoire and her children his death is naturally a great grief, but not a calamity,"* her mother Augusta wrote. *"His many good qualities were somewhat spoilt by his hasty temper and obstinacy, which made him enemies."* Carl Emich inherited the principality of Leiningen, albeit under a regency as he was still underage. The couple's only daughter, Princess Feodora of Leiningen later married Fürst Ernst of Hohenlohe-Langenburg, inaugurating a long-standing relationship between this house and that of Coburg. Feodora's voluminous correspondence with her half-sister, Victoria, remains one of the most reliable sources on the private lives of these two remarkable and devoted women.

Victoire was overwhelmed at the task of running affairs in Leiningen on her son's behalf. Lacking any practical experience and facing estates in complete disarray, she increasingly secluded herself in Wald Leiningen, near Amorbach, relying on her brother Leopold for guidance and counsel. It was Leopold who now came to his sister's rescue.

The death of Princess Charlotte of Wales had thrown the British royal succession into chaos. None of King George III and Queen Charlotte's seven sons had a legitimate heir. Now, the Prince Regent's brothers made a virtual stampede to Germany, each seeking a young, fertile bride. At nearly fifty years of age, Edward, Duke of Kent stood third in line to the throne after his brothers George and William. Having previously befriended Prince Leopold, he now asked for his help to find a suitable wife. True to family ambitions, the canny Leopold suggested his own widowed sister Victoire, who had already proved her fertility by giving birth to two children.

At the time, Baron Stockmar recalled Victoire was *"of middle-height, rather large, but with a good figure, with fine brown eyes and hair, fresh and youthful, naturally cheerful and friendly, altogether most charming and attractive. She was fond of dress, and dressed well and in good taste. Nature had endowed her with warm feelings, and she was naturally truthful, affectionate and friendly, unselfish, full of sympathy and generous."* As for the proposed bridegroom, the Baron found him *"already inclined to great corpulence; but in spite of the entire baldness of the whole crown of his head and his dyed hair, he might still be considered a handsome man."*

On arriving at Amorbach, the Duke of Kent went straight to Victoire and immediately proposed. Duchess Augusta wrote: *"In a few moons perhaps, Victoire becomes the wife of a man she hardly knows…we had hardly sat down at table when his equerry arrived with the news that the Duke would follow in a few hours…we waited with strained curiosity, and poor Victoire with beating heart. She had only seen him once. The first moment Kent was a little shy, however he must be a man of the world to drop like a bomb in such a large family."*

Although initially suspicious, Augusta quickly deemed him *"a good looking man for his age, engaging and friendly, and with an attractive, good-natured expression about the mouth. His height helps to give an air of nobility, and his simple, blunt soldier's manner combined with the refinement of a man of the world makes his company very agreeable."* Romance took a backseat to political considerations, and on 29 May 1818, the Dowager Fürstin of Leiningen and the Duke of Kent were married in the Hall of Giants (Riesensall) at the Ehrenburg Palace, with a second ceremony celebrated some two months later at Kew Palace, near Richmond, Surrey.

The Duchess of Kent.

A year later, on 24 May 24 1819, the Duchess of Kent gave birth to a daughter, Princess Alexandrina Victoria. Her arrival ensured the royal succession, and greatly enhanced the Duchess of Kent's position at court. Spitefully, many of her British in-laws turned against her, especially the Prince Regent and his sisters. For them she was simply too German and 'hausfrauish,' far too provincial to suit their self-indulgent styles of life. Her customs, difficulty in learning English, and her deep, guttural German accent only served to distance Victoire from her less than commendable English relations.

Victoire tried to ignore it, certain that one day her husband would take the throne as King Edward VII. Then tragedy struck. Searching for weather more salubrious than that found in London, the Kents left the capital and headed to the coast of Devon. They found a house to rent in Sidmouth and the Duke was ecstatic, thinking not only that the weather would improve

their health but also that they would save money by not living in London. The climate, though, proved deadly: the Duke soon caught a chill that quickly deteriorated into pneumonia. Nothing could be done to save him, and he died on 23 January 1820.

Widowed for a second time, and with an infant daughter, the Duchess of Kent retired to Claremont, her brother Leopold's house in Surrey. As the young Princess Victoria of Kent evolved into childhood, Leopold's role became that of a surrogate father for the orphaned princess. Victoria, in turn, came to look on her uncle as *"my second father, my only father."*

Hopeless in financial matters, Victoire was soon in deep debt, and she began to rely heavily on a member of her staff, Captain John Conroy, whose advice eventually supplanted that of her brother Leopold. A handsome man gifted with endless vitality, Conroy became virtual dictator in the Duchess of Kent's household, serving as both her comptroller and private secretary for nearly two decades. He served also in the unofficial roles of public relations officer, counselor, confidant and political agent. Although rumor asserted that their relationship transcended the professional, no evidence supports this widespread belief. What is undeniable, however, is that Conroy's control of the Duchess of Kent quickly led to countless clashes with her brothers-in-law, George IV and William IV, as well as with her own daughter Victoria, who grew to develop an innate, visceral dislike for her mother's advisor.

Top: Kensington Palace, where Queen Victoria was born on 24 May 1819. Immediately above: The Duchess of Kent and her daughter Princess Alexandrina Victoria of Kent.

The young Princess Victoria proved to be a precocious child, mindful of her royal prerogatives and with a tremendous sense of duty. However, she could not ignore the incessant family squabbles between her mother and her late father's resentful siblings. The widowed Duchess of Kent felt little inclination to maintain any contact with her in-laws, and kept her daughter away from court as much as possible. This isolation did nothing to alleviate a gloomy childhood, but worse was to come when Conroy interfered with the Princess's education.

Under Conroy's advice, Victoire raised her daughter in a stiff atmosphere with an absolute lack of foresight, little affection and much misunderstanding. While it is not clear which of the two was more responsible for devising the 'Kensington System' that ruled the young Princess's life, the effect on Victoria's character was inescapable. Described as *"an elaborate and oppressive system of rules regulating every facet of Victoria's life, it kept her in reclusive isolation most of the time, with the goal of making her weak, compliant and utterly dependent upon her mother and Conroy."* After the deaths of George III and then her brother-in-law George IV, only the childless and elderly King William IV stood between Victoire's young daughter and the British throne. The Duchess seems to have believed that she would soon be appointed regent for her daughter, while Conroy anticipated the position of private secretary accompanied by a peerage. The Duchess's own brother Leopold had hoped that, if his niece prematurely came to the throne, he would act as regent – something that only alienated him from his sister. Conroy deliberately appealed to sentiment, painting the Duchess and her young daughter as pure, modest and decorous in contrast to the hedonistic George IV; at the same time, he warned both mother and daughter that certain members of the British Royal Family, especially the dreaded Duke of Cumberland, were so intent on taking the throne themselves that they might well murder the young Princess Victoria.

These strained relations publicly erupted one evening during a dinner at Windsor to celebrate the birthday of William IV. During a toast, the King rose, raised his glass toward his young niece, and expressed his hope that he would live long enough to prevent the Duchess of Kent from wielding any power as regent for her daughter. People were stunned and Victoire was humiliated, though the remarks had not been delivered without reason.

One June morning in 1837, mere weeks after turning eighteen, Victoria was woken and told that her uncle William IV had died. She was now Queen of Great Britain and Ireland. She lost little time building a solid wall between herself and her domineering mother. From morning till dusk the widowed Duchess of Kent found herself unable to approach a daughter whom she had foolishly kept under much control in earlier years. Wearing the royal purple meant for young Queen Victoria a final liberation from both her mother and Conroy.

The Duchess of Kent's loyalty to Conroy ended when Victoria acceded to the throne. Queen Victoria granted him a baronetcy in 1837 on condition that he depart from court, never to return. Somehow, Conroy had managed to get his hands on the fortune of Princess Sophia (1777-1848), one of King George III's youngest children. By the time she died, the court learned that her considerable fortune, under Conroy's management, had dissipated. Whether or not he was guilty of fraud, Conroy's reputation never recovered and he died in 1854, virtually bankrupt and a social pariah.

Young Queen Victoria by Winterhalter.

The relationship between the Duchess of Kent and her only daughter had never been close. In time, though, a detente developed between them. The Duchess had a place at her daughter's court, albeit a small one, and access to her grandchildren. Yet when Victoire died on 16 March 1861 at Frogmore House, Windsor, Queen Victoria was plunged into paroxysms of grief that hinted at the sorrowing despair soon to overcome her with the death of her beloved Prince Albert.

Chapter VII
Enter Belgium
The Uncle of Europe

A political crisis inside the Kingdom of The Netherlands gave birth to the Belgian Royal Dynasty. After the 1830 overthrow of the Bourbons in France, revolutionary fervor spread from Paris to Brussels. Belgian politicians and patriots rebelled against the rule of King Willem I of The Netherlands over their land, and Dutch control of Belgium soon evaporated.

In November of 1830, the European Powers recognized Belgium's independence, and began a search for a new dynasty. The London Conference recognized a provisional government in Belgium, which was placed in charge of finding a candidate for the newly created throne, as well as forming a national congress and writing a constitution. The principle of constitutional monarchy was adopted, and close ties to the government in London were established. Great Britain and Belgium signed a treaty guaranteeing Belgian neutrality, and London was placed in charge of defending the new European country's territorial integrity and sovereignty.

Several candidates for the Belgium throne were proposed. One, the Duke of Nemours, was the son of King Louis Philippe; another, the Duke of Leuchtenberg, was the son of Prince Eugene de Beauharnais, and a grandson both of Empress Joséphine, Napoléon's first wife, and of the dead King Maximilian I of Bavaria. The Belgians chose the Duke of Nemours but the proposal faltered when other European governments objected to the idea of a member of the French Royal Family again wielding power. The candidacy of the Duke of Leuchtenberg also faltered. Finally, a third compromise candidate emerged: Prince Leopold of Saxe-Coburg & Gotha.

At the time Leopold was still living in England. Earlier that year, when Greece won its independence as a new kingdom from the Ottoman Empire, the crown was offered to Leopold. He accepted, but soon international complications convinced him that the shaky throne of faraway Greece was not a prosperous breeding ground for a new dynasty. He refused the throne he had been offered; eventually it was given to Prince Otto of Bavaria, who surprised many of his contemporaries by remaining in Greece for more than three decades.

Belgian emissaries arrived in England and began talks with Leopold about ascending their new throne. Knowing how popular he was in Great Britain, as well as his family ties to the future Queen Victoria, they realized that Leopold would likely play a pivotal role in European politics in years to come. He had remained unmarried since Charlotte's death, and he could wed again and father a new dynasty. This time, the offer a crown was too tempting, and Leopold accepted the invitation.

The new King Léopold I arrived in Brussels on 31 July 1831, and quickly swore allegiance to the Belgian constitution. He faced an immediate threat when King Willem I attempted to reclaim his lost Belgian provinces. Soldiers were dispatched and Léopold fought at the head of his country's troops. Nothing, though, came of the misadventure: realizing that both England and France backed Léopold, the Dutch sovereign was forced to relent and acknowledge the new monarch. Léopold's diplomacy throughout the uncertain period won the respect of Europe's chancelleries.

Léopold needed a wife, and soon he negotiated his betrothal to Princess Louise-Marie d'Orléans, eldest daughter of King Louis-Philippe and Queen Marie-Amélie of the French. An alliance with the French royal family

King Willem I of the Netherlands.

King Willem II of the Netherlands.

gave Léopold's nascent dynasty the respect it needed. Not only did Louise-Marie provide respectability to her husband's court, but she also managed to catch her husband's interest. The wedding took place in 1832 and to a close friend, Léopold confided, *"I'm delighted with my good little Queen: she is the sweetest creature you ever saw, and she has plenty of spirit"*

The royal nursery at the Brussels palace slowly filled up. Three young princes arrived during the couple's first five years together. The eldest of the boys, Prince Louis-Philippe, was born in 1833; unfortunately, he died within a year. In 1835 another baby boy arrived, Prince Léopold, who would later on become the terror of Europe's royal courts and his tormented wife and children. The third boy, Prince Philippe, Count of Flanders, distinguished himself by being everything that his brother Léopold was not. Finally, a little baby girl, Princess Charlotte, arrived in 1840.

Léopold I devoted himself to his new country. He consolidated Belgium's independence, and attained for Belgium respect among Europe's crowned heads. Perhaps the most lasting legacy, though, was in the private realm. Following the example of his formidable mother, Léopold proved to be an inveterate matchmaker, and he filled the courts of Europe with his relatives.

In addition to marrying his nephew into the Portuguese Royal Family, Léopold I also arranged for the marriage of his niece Victoria of Saxe-Coburg-Kohary to Prince Louis-Charles d'Orléans, Duke of Nemours, in 1840. Their eldest son, Prince Louis-Gaston would marry Princess Izabel of Braganza, heiress of the Brazilian imperial throne. Another matrimonial alliance with the French royal family was arranged in 1843 when Prince August of Saxe-Coburg-(Kohary) married Princess Clémentine d'Orléans, sister of both Queen Louise-Marie and the Duke of Nemours. Their youngest child, Prince Ferdinand of Saxe-Coburg-(Kohary), became the reigning Prince of Bulgaria in 1887. In half a century, the Coburgs had thus gained four thrones.

When it came to his own children, Léopold was somewhat less successful. In 1853, his eldest son and heir Crown Prince Léopold married Archduchess Marie-

CHAPTER VII – Enter Belgium: The Uncle of Europe

Henriette of Austria, before either bride or groom had reached the age of twenty. The alliance with the august house of Habsburg was a triumph, yet the marriage soon proved to be a disaster. The 1867 marriage of Léopold's second son Prince Philippe to Princess Marie of Hohenzollern-Sigmaringen was a more successful affair. The couple was suited to each other and they passed marital happiness on to their children. Indeed, there was always a deep contrast between the unhappy brood of Léopold II and Marie-Henriette and the well-raised children of Philippe and Maria.

Another ostensibly glorious union, though, had tragic results. In 1857, Léopold arranged for his only daughter Princess Charlotte to marry Archduke Ferdinand-Maximilian of Austria, brother of Emperor Franz Joseph. This second link with the Habsburgs was prestigious, and Charlotte and Maximilian seemed genuinely devoted to each other. Yet their future years were to be clouded with unhappiness, thwarted glory, and lingering tragedy.

None of the King's romantic endeavors, though, proved to be as momentous as that between his niece Victoria and his nephew Albert. After her 1837 accession to the throne, Queen Victoria flung herself into pleasure, enjoying the luxury and freedom that had previously been denied her. Yet she also wished to marry and break the loneliness of her glittering life of royal isolation. Léopold had arranged the marriage of her parents; now he would arrange that of his niece as well. For Léopold, there was no better candidate to win the mercurial Victoria's hand than his nephew Prince Albert of Saxe-Coburg & Gotha. From his birth in 1819 Albert had been essentially groomed for this role. As a child both he and his brother Ernst had spent long periods of time with their uncle Léopold and Aunt Louise-Marie in Brussels. While Ernst developed into a licentious young man, Albert remained unspoiled, studious and conscientious of his future possibilities. According to his tutor Baron Stockmar, Albert bore *"a striking resemblance to his mother…the same nobility and readiness of mind, the same intelligence, the same over-ruling desire and talent for appearing kind and amiable to others."*

In 1839 Albert and Ernst traveled to London to pay their respects to their royal cousin Victoria. Although initially apprehensive about Albert as a husband, Victoria quickly surrendered to his attractions. She described him as *"very amiable, very kind and good…extremely good looking."* Later her praise grew more exuberant: *"Albert is, in fact, so fascinating and looks so handsome; he has such beautiful blue eyes…his figure is fine, broad at the shoulders and slender at the waist. Albert's beauty is most striking, and he is so amiable and unaffected – in short so fascinating; he is excessively admired here."*

Queen Louise-Marie.

The engagement was announced in 1839 and the following year, on 24 January, Queen Victoria and Prince Albert of Saxe-Coburg & Gotha were married in the Chapel Royal at St. James's Palace in London. No one was more responsible for the union than their jubilant uncle Léopold. Within a generation, the Coburgs had gone from a small, forgotten princely house from the depths of the Thuringian woods to the very heights of royal power.

Left: An artist's rendering of the wedding of King Léopold I and Princess Louise-Marie d'Orléans, eldest daughter of King Louis-Philippe of the French and of his wife, Queen Marie Amélie, née Bourbon-Two Sicilies.

Below: A print of Queen Marie-Amélie, consort of King Louis-Philippe. A true matriarch, she kept abreast of her children and their descendants' doings. Although she served dutifully as Louis-Philippe's consort, Marie-Amélie felt their throne was illegitimate as he owed it to a revolutionary movement.

Without a doubt, Léopold was among the most talented royal matchmakers of his time. Although not every couple he set up found joy and happiness in their union, each alliance served its main goal: the expansion of Coburg influence. The baby born to an impoverished German ducal family in 1790 was now 'the Uncle of Europe,' as his nephews and nieces and their own children introduced Coburg bloodlines into most of Europe's ruling dynasties.

Yet, the success Léopold experienced abroad seemed to elude him at home. Although Louise-Marie adored her husband, she was well aware of the fact that she was yet another piece in his royal chess game. Notwithstanding her marital disappointments, Louise-Marie remained a devoted wife and mother. Her early death in 1850, the same year she lost her father, left her children devastated, while her husband yearned for her company, if not counsel.

The King, a true Coburg to the core, had needs. Yes, he missed his wife – he saw the pain in the faces of his children, but he also needed distraction. Louise-Marie's death left a vacancy, one

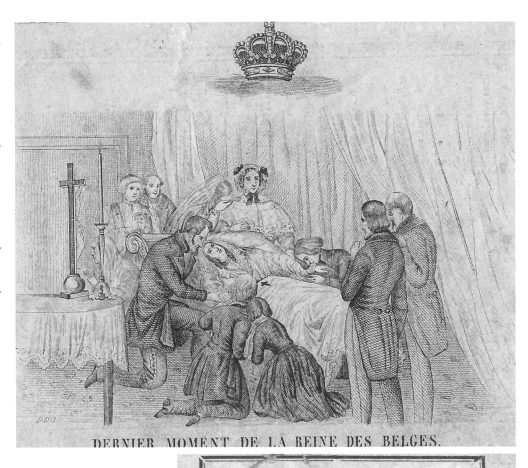

Right: An artist's rendering of the death of Queen Louise-Marie surrounded by her husband and children – Ostend, 11 October 1850. Louise-Marie's reamains were buried inside the royal crypt at the Church of Our Lady of Laeken.

Below: A death card printed at the time of Queen Louise-Marie's passing. Death cards were not only a source of revenue for charities, but they also marked important historical events among all of Europe's ruling families.

that he soon enough filled with the company of ladies surreptitiously brought to the palace to amuse His Majesty. His mistress, a woman by the name of Arcadia Meyer (née Claret), had presented Léopold with a son in 1849, the year before Louise-Marie's death. In 1852, Arcadia presented him with a second son. The boys, George and Arthur, were provided for and in 1862 created Barons von Eppinghoven. Both boys eventually lived in Coburg and worked at the court of their cousin Duke Ernst II. Everyone knew that the Eppinghovens were Uncle Léopold's love children.

To those outside his circle, Léopold seemed distant, manipulating and severe. And yet, he kept a candid correspondence with his niece Victoria, as well as with his mother-in-law Marie-Amélie, his brother Duke Ernst I and also with several of his old friends in England. He may not have been one to show emotion, but that never meant that he didn't care, and when necessary Léopold displayed surprising tenderness. He loved children and animals; he rode his horses until advanced old age prevented him from doing so. While he enjoyed letter writing, studying international affairs and planning the course that best protected his kingdom, he also liked the outdoors.

Old age was merciless to Léopold. His last years were filled with a countless array of personal tragedies, from the death of the Prince Consort and the Portuguese nephews, to the passing of his last siblings. In 1857 died the Duchess of Nemours, in 1859 Queen Stephanie of Portugal, in 1860 Ernst of Hohenlohe-Langenburg and Anna Feodorovna. The following year witnessed an avalanche of deaths: the Duchess of Kent, Prince Albert, and King Pedro V of Portugal, plus his brothers João and Fernando. In 1862 Antoinette of Kohary died. It seemed for quite some time that all around Léopold was death and its merciless sense of loss.

The King was also dealing with personal health problems of his own. When Albert died, Léopold departed to England to keep his niece company during those difficult early days of widowhood. However, his health prevented him from reaching Victoria and instead he languished for several weeks. He was only able to see her briefly before returning to Laeken, where he underwent surgery. Wishing to avoid scandals, Arcadia and their children were sent away to Wiesbaden, while Léopold wrote to the Dean of St. George's Chapel in Windsor to express his wish to be buried next to Princess Charlotte. He survived the surgery, but fell ill with a pulmonary infection. For months it seemed as if the 'Old Coburg Oak' was at death's door. Victoria raced to his side, the King's health improved.

When Maximilian and Charlotte were offered the Mexican throne, Léopold enthusiastically supported

Top left: King Léopold remained a dandy even in old age. The King was always smartly dressed, medals perfectly placed, toupé combed and attached just right!

Left: The death of King Léopold I was an event of national and international importance. Not only was he the architect of Belgium, ensuring that his dynasty would remain deeply attached to the country's fortunes, but he was also closely related to countless other dynasties across the continent.

Chapter VII – Enter Belgium: The Uncle of Europe

the adventure. To help his daughter and her husband along, Léopold had meetings with Napoléon III, Lord Palmerston and even Bismarck. A master schemer to the end, Léopold saw in the Mexican adventure a chance to both increase Coburg influence, as well as expand commercial opportunities for Belgium. In 1864 Maximilian and Charlotte departed from Trieste to the New World. Maximilian would never return. Charlotte would lose her mind and remain hidden from public view for nearly six decades.

Left: A stamp from 1930 commemorating Léopold of Saxe-Coburg & Gotha's acceptance of the Belgian throne.

Immediately above: King Léopold II at about the time of his succession.

Luckily for King Léopold, he did not witness the debacle that consumed and brought down the Mexican Empire. He died on 10 December 1865. At birth in 1790 he was the youngest son of the heir to an impoverished ducal throne lost in the dark forests of Thuringia. By the time death ended his physical ailments, he was widely known as 'the Uncle of Europe' – this being his crowning achievement. Léopold was the king of a revolutionary throne, he had tried his best to imprint his realm, and Europe, with liberal ideas and a style of governing that would bring greater access to a better living to an ever increasing number of people. In nearly thirty-five years of reign, Léopold had managed to solidly establish his dynasty but building alliances with Europe's most respected ruling families. He was, without a doubt, an 'empire builder.' His death signaled the passing of the torch to a new generation of Coburgs who would bring enlightened government, so it was hoped to Europe. His niece Victoria, his true pride and joy, was only too willing to become the Coburg matriarch, a role Léopold wished her to fulfill. At times she felt he was too assertive, complaining that, *"dear Uncle is given to believe thta he must rule the roast everywhere."* No tribute paid to the King better exemplified his life than that published by the *Annual Register*: *"He had one of smallest of kingdoms, yet he was one of the most powerful princes in Europe ... His life was wonderfully calm, yet it is one of the most extraordinary romances in history."*

CHAPTER VIII
Enter Portugal
The Unlucky Promising Brood

Born in 1816, Prince Ferdinand, eldest son of Prince Ferdinand and Princess Antonia, was blessed with tremendous good looks, not to mention a considerable fortune. Tall and slender, his black eyes were wells of intensity. Queen Victoria had been somewhat less impressed, writing that he had *"a slow way of talking through the nose, a singular high singing voice, and a funny habit of shaking hands every time he meets one."* This young man, thought his uncle Léopold, would make an excellent consort, and he knew just who to suggest: Queen Maria II of Portugal who, at the tender age of seventeen years, was already a widow.

Much like its eastern neighbor Spain, Portugal had suffered great political upheaval during Napoleonic times and beyond. The Braganzas, the country's royal family, even packed what they could and sailed to Brazil in late 1807 in an effort to escape Napoléon's onslaught. Faraway Brazil was then Portugal's most prized colonial possession and the absolutist future King João VI, then acting as regent for his deranged mother Maria I, felt protected there. His wife, the former Infanta Carlota Joaquina of Spain and just as conservative as her husband, would become the source of much conflict both in Portugal and Brazil as well as within the confines of the Braganza court.

João and Carlota Joaquina, herself the daughter of King Carlos IV of Spain, had nine children. The eldest, Maria Teresa (1793-1874), was married twice, both her husbands being Infantes of Spain. The second child, Francisco (1795-1801), died an infant. Next came Maria Isabel (1797-1818), who married her first cousin King Fernando VII of Spain. The fourth child was to succeed his father as King Pedro IV of Portugal, but only after leading Brazil's quest for independence from the mainland. Maria Francisca and Isabel followed Pedro, but only the former married, her spouse being a Spanish uncle, Infante Carlos, whose ambition to sit on the throne plunged Spain into the fratricidal Carlist wars. The royal couple's seventh child was Infante Miguel (1802-1866), who tried to do in Portugal what his brother-in-law Carlos had failed to achieve in Spain. Carlota Joaquina's youngest children were both daughters: Maria da Assunção (1805-1834), and Ana de Jesús (1806-1857), who later married Portuguese aristocrat the Duke de Loulé.

João VI succeeded his mother in 1816 but temporarily remained in Brazil. His wife Carlota Joaquina kept herself busy by plotting against Portuguese interests in Brazil; against her own brother's rule in Spanish America; and even against her own husband, having convinced herself that she deserved a kingdom of her own. João VI suffered patiently through his wife's political meddling and, at least in public, always behaved as if there was an absence of tension within the marriage and the royal family.

João's absence from Portugal led to chaos, as the British continually carved away pieces of the King's once vast colonial empire. Fearing a complete loss of power and the declaration of a republic in his homeland, João VI returned to Lisbon in 1821. He left his son Pedro behind in Brazil to serve as regent. The South American country had long pushed for independence, and recognizing the inevitability, João warned his son: *"Pedro, Brazil will soon be separated from Portugal. If so, put the crown on your head before some adventurer grabs it."* Pedro did just that: on 22 September 1822, he proclaimed himself Emperor of a newly sovereign Brazil.

The Portugal that greeted João on his return was torn apart by fights between liberals and conservatives. The former wished the country to embrace the ideals espoused in the French Revolution, while the latter pined for restoration of absolutist rule. Even worse, João faced rebellion in his own family, as Carlota Joaquina and her son Infante Miguel continually pushed against liberal policies and reform. It was no secret that Miguel hoped to depose his father and crown himself as King. The situation was so bad that, at one point – fearful of losing his throne – João even had to side with his rebellious son to maintain his hold on power. Once his position was assured, though, João stripped Miguel of his commands and exiled him to Great Britain, while the quarrelsome donha Carlota Joaquina was placed under house arrest at the Palace of Queluz.

Above left: King João VI, father of Pedro IV and Miguel I. Above right: King Miguel I, who was expected to marry his niece Maria II. Right: Queen Maria II as a youth.

The following year, in an effort to pacify the kingdom, João VI declared a national amnesty. By this time, though, his enemies were unwilling to compromise and they plotted his ouster by whatever means possible. On 10 March 1826, João was found dead in Lisbon. Immediately there were rumors of foul play, but not until 2000 did Portuguese scientists exhume his remains and discover traces of arsenic in his heart sufficient to kill two individuals. Despite the difficult times during which he ruled, King João VI was remembered as *"one of the personalities who had the greatest influence over the formation of the nation....He was an ideal mediator...between tradition – which he incarnated – and innovation – which he welcomed and promoted – during that decisive period for the Brazilian future."*

João's eldest surviving son and heir Infante Pedro learned of his father's death while reigning as Emperor of Brazil. In 1817 he had married Archduchess Marie Leopoldine of Austria, one of the daughters of Emperor Franz I. Their marriage produced six children: Maria II (1819-1853), who succeeded her father as Queen of Portugal; Miguel and João, who died infants; Januária (1822-1901), who married Prince Luigi of Bourbon-Two Sicilies; Paula (1823-1833); Francisca (1824-1898), who married Prince François d'Orléans, Prince de Joinville, through whom she became the ancestor of the present Head of House France; and Pedro II (1825-1891), Emperor of Brazil. The marriage was extremely unhappy. Not only was Pedro I unfaithful to Marie Leopoldine, but he was also callous, distant, and positively cold to her. Despite this, she always treated him with honesty and loved him. Heartbroken and exhausted

by childbearing, the popular first Empress of Brazil died after a miscarriage in December 1826. Pedro was beset with guilt. He dismissed his mistress and banished her from Rio de Janeiro. In a letter, the Brazilian monarch promised that *"all my wickedness is over, that I shall not again fall into those errors into which I have fallen, which I regret and have asked God for forgiveness."*

Pedro decided that he was more interested in Brazil than in Portugal. He renounced the Portuguese crown he had briefly held in favor of his seven-year-old daughter Maria. Hoping to heal the rift that had developed within the Braganzas during the last years of João VI's reign, Pedro offered his brother Miguel – then living in exile in Vienna – his daughter Maria's hand in marriage if he refrained from further revolutionary activities. In 1827 he assumed the regency for the young Maria II and Miguel promised to respect the liberal charter and govern within constitutional bounds. Yet he quickly ignored his promises and began ridding the court and the army of its liberal officials. He dismissed Parliament and refused to call new elections. Adding insult to injury, he overthrew his niece and proclaimed himself King. Once again Portugal was plunged into political and civil strife.

Queen Maria II.

The young Queen Maria II wandered Europe, visiting London and Habsburg relations in Vienna before settling in Paris, where King Louis Philippe received her with open arms and she developed a lifelong friendship with his youngest daughter, Princess Clémentine. As she roamed the continent, her father fumed. Hoping to save the situation, Emperor Pedro finally left Brazil. Traveling by way of the Azores, he finally reached Porto, in northern Portugal and headed an army bound for Lisbon. The conflict was brief, and in 1834 Miguel was deposed and forced to board a British warship for exile. For a time he lived in Rome under the protection of Pope Gregory XVI, who provided him with a small monthly stipend; by the 1850s, he had settled in Baden, after a temporary stay under strained circumstances in London. Although he had lost his succession rights to the Spanish throne, Miguel married Princess Adelheid zu Löwenstein-Wertheim-Rosenberg, whose father, Hereditary Prince Constantin, had married Ernst of Hohenlohe-Langenburg's younger sister Princess Marie Agnes. Adelheid's fatherless brother found in Miguel the paternal figure he so desperately longed for and the Portuguese exile found respite among his in-laws. Miguel and Adelheid eventually had seven children, whose current descendants include members of the Portuguese Royal Family as well as those of the House of Habsburg, the Luxembourg dynasty, and the princely Thurn und Taxis family. Former King Miguel died at Schloß Karlshöhe in Bavaria in 1866.

With his daughter restored to the Portuguese Throne, Pedro returned to Brazil. His first concern – to find another wife – was no easy task given how he had treated his first. Princesses across Europe refused him until the Brazilian envoy in Paris convinced Princess Amélie of Leuchtenberg to accept his proposal. As the daughter of Eugène de Beauharnais, Napoléon's stepson, and his wife Princess Augusta of Bavaria, she was eminently suitable and in 1829 Pedro and Amélie were married. Two years later, their only child Maria Amélia was born. But the war against his brother had left Pedro physically exhausted, and he died of tuberculosis in September 1834.

It now became imperative that Maria II marry as quickly as possible and produce an heir. Finding a suitable consort proved to be an exceptionally difficult task: European courts proposed their own candidates and then opposed those from rival nations, fearing that the precarious balance of power established by Prince Metternich at the Congress of Vienna would be seriously upset. Only a minor prince from an unimportant house would maintain the peace, and so the powers eventually agreed on Prince Auguste de Beauharnais, brother of Prince Eugene, who had once been considered as a future King of the Belgians. Born in 1810, he just happened to be Empress Amélie's brother, and he quickly accepted Maria II's proposal. Prince Auguste was duly shipped to Lisbon and on 26 January 1835, he married Queen Maria. Unfortunately, and to Maria II's chagrin, her consort Prince Auguste suddenly succumbed to physical excess and died on 28 March just two months after his arrival. Maria II was desolate and Europe had another matrimonial crisis in its hands.

Ever canny, King Léopold of Belgium was quick to recognize the possibilities that this sudden death offered, and he now set about finding a suitable new Portuguese consort from within the ranks of the House of Coburg. Chance was on the King's side. European powers blocked any idea of a union with members of the French Royal House; there were no suitable candidates in England; as a Lutheran nation Prussia could offer no eligible princes; and France refused to allow an Austrian Archduke to marry the Portuguese queen. Léopold therefore offered his handsome nephew Prince Ferdinand of Saxe-Coburg-(Kohary) to the Portuguese court. The Queen, a plain girl if there ever was one, fell instantly in love with the painting of young Ferdinand that was shown to her.

There were intense negotiations before Ferdinand could marry Maria. As the eldest son of Prince Ferdinand and Princess Antonia, young Ferdinand was the heir of the fideikomiss that his father had so diligently created to protect his family's vast estates. His proposed marriage into the Portuguese family, as well as his future role as consort of a ruling queen, made it impossible for him to assume control of the fideikomiss at his father's death, and Ferdinand won handsome compensation for this loss of income and position by the Portuguese court. The route to Lisbon took him to Brussels, where King Léopold hosted his nephew for two intensive months of preparation for his role as consort, as well as study in constitutional law. Another stop was made in London, where the Royal Family celebrated and toasted Ferdinand before the young man sailed for Lisbon.

Above: Prince Auguste de Beauharnais, who in 1835 became Queen Maria II's husband.

Right: Prince Ferdinand of Saxe-Coburg & Gotha married Queen Maria II after she became a widow. They were married in Lisbon in 1836.

The nuptials took place in Lisbon on 9 April 1836, and within a year a child was born. The little dynasty of Saxe-Coburg & Gotha had gained its second European throne.

Ferdinand's first few years in Portugal were tempestuous ones. The political instability consuming the kingdom since Napoléon's invasion in 1808 had not abated. If anything, the political class contributed to the climate of uncertainty by taking uncompromising positions that robbed the kingdom of stability necessary to secure industrial, social, and economic progress. Petty disputes became matters of national importance, at least to the politicians, and consequently kingdom and people suffered. During the seventeen years that Maria II and Ferdinand were married, they lived through just as many revolutions, coups d'etat and military uprisings. Meanwhile, a majority of the kingdom's population remained illiterate, the industrial revolution seemed to bypass Portugal, and peasants lived in semi-feudal attachment to the landowners who owned vast tracts of the country's rich soil. It was not a recipe destined to bring much success to a dynasty that never seemed to recover from the loss of Brazil.

Maria II and her husband lived in marital bliss, in spite of the commotion raging outside of their palaces. In 1837, Ferdinand received the title of King Consort and he wielded enormous influence over his wife. Queen Maria II was so taken by her young husband that *"she never received anyone until her king consort had first seen them and arranged with him their affairs. Only then were they presented to her – only to kiss her hand."* In family circles, Ferdinand brought to Lisbon an air of bourgeois respectability never before experienced by the Portuguese Royal Family that had previously seemed consumed by squabbling, scandals and internecine warfare.

King Consort Ferdinand was erudite, possessing vast knowledge of many subjects, while also being able to communicate in several languages. A renaissance man, one of the few of his generation, Ferdinand was also a talented painter, dabbled in sculpting, and collected exquisite porcelains and master paintings that further enriched the royal collections. He also had a passion for building, and castles provided him with particular delight. At Sintra, near Lisbon, and with the collaboration of a German architect, he erected the controversial edifice known as the 'Paço da Pena' (Pena Palace). The result was a conglomerate of disparate architectural styles, from romantic to gothic, with renaissance and rococo tacked on to confusing effect. Perhaps the Paço da

Above left: Queen Maria II toward the end of her life. Motherhood took a tremendous toll on her health. Obesity did not help matters either.

Left: a commemorative medal minted to celebrate the wedding of Queen Maria II and King Consort Ferdinand.

The Necessidades Palace, Lisbon.

Pena represented some memory of Ferdinand's native Thuringia, but it also offered an outlet for his dreams. In this respect, King Consort Ferdinand was much like the extravagant and highly disturbed King Ludwig II of Bavaria, whose passion for building he shared.

In sixteen years Maria II gave birth to eleven children. Pedro was born in Lisbon on 16 September 1837; a year later another boy, Luís, joined Pedro in the nursery. Infanta Maria arrived in 1840, the first of four children who would die at birth. The other three were Leopoldo (1849), Maria da Glória (1851), and Eugénio (1853). The queen's fourth child, Infante João, was born in Lisbon in 1842. Infanta Maria Ana joined the royal nursery the following year; Antónia arrived in 1845; Fernando in 1846; and Augusto in 1847.

These pregnancies, along with several miscarriages, took their toll on Maria's fragile health. On learning that she was again expecting in early 1853, doctors took special care to protect mother and child, particularly since the three previous pregnancies had ended in stillbirths. Making matters more complicated, Maria II had gained a considerable amount of weight and her rotund figure made daily activities extremely difficult. Her medical team recommended that Maria II rest, but she refused to heed their advice and instead continued daily outings on horses, burros or in carriages. *"Tell Dr. Elias,"* she said, *"that I am in optimum condition."* However, she was not, and those around the Queen feared the worst. *"It was necessary to keep one's eyes closed to the queen's physiognomy, how precarious her health was,"* wrote the Marquess de Fronteira, who knew her well. These fears, as it turned out, were well founded.

Trouble began near midnight on 14 November 1853 when Maria II went into labor. Fearing the worst, Empress Amélie pleaded with Ferdinand to call in a priest for confession. *"This is nothing like any of the other times,"*

Pena Palace, above Sintra.

Queen Maria II exclaimed. A baby boy, quickly baptized with the name Eugénio, was extracted from the queen's womb at 10:00am; however, the medical bulletin read, *"Unfortunately, Her Majesty, exhausted by the operation, rendered her soul to God after receiving the Sacraments."* Stunned by the tragedy, Ferdinand could not stop crying. Princess Clémentine d'Orléans wrote to him, saying, *"I sorrowfully cry with you for good, tender, noble Maria, who for so long I have known and loved."* Queen Victoria, not one to let an excuse for mourning and sorrow pass unmarked, commiserated with the King Consort, writing, *"These great afflictions leave behind a terrible void and difficult pain to heal."*

Ferdinand now served as regent for his eldest son, the promising Pedro V, who was sixteen-years-old at the time of his mother's death. The regency lasted two years. While Pedro and his brother Luís traveled around Europe in an effort to provide them with a wider view of continental affairs, Ferdinand led the Portuguese kingdom with aplomb and great care. Widely respected by his son's subjects, Portuguese politicians held his opinion in high regard and Ferdinand offered measured guidance. Preserving constitutional rule, he believed, would provide Pedro V with stability as the regency ended and the young monarch began his reign.

In 1861, Ferdinand lived through the tragic death of three of his five remaining sons. The following year he played an important role in finding his son King Luís a wife, a choice that in later years Ferdinand, very likely, would regret. In 1863, he was considered a possible successor to the deposed King Otto of Greece, but the throne eventually went to the second son of the future Danish monarch, King Christian IX. That same year, and before Maximilian of Austria accepted the offer, Mexican delegates even considered Ferdinand as a viable candidate for their topsy-turvy throne. Years later Ferdinand was also offered the vacant throne of Spain, which he, once again, politely refused, but not before supporting the candidacy of his son-in-law Prince Leopold of

Above: King Ferdinand II and his children at the time of King Pedro V's marriage to Princess Stephanie of Hohenzollern – From left: Queen Stephanie and King Pedro V, Infantes Augusto and Fernando, Infanta Antónia, King Ferdinand, Infanta Maria Ana, Infante João, Infante Luís. Left: A print of King Ferdinand circa 1865. Below: A commemorative medal minted in honor of King Ferdinand II: Fernando II – The Artist King.

Hohenzollern. This candidacy, in fact, was to ignite a major war between France and Prussia, the consequences of which led to the overthrow of Emperor Napoléon III, while planting the seeds of discord that erupted in 1914 with the largest military conflict Europe had ever witnessed.

Not unlike his Uncle Léopold, whose second wife, Queen Louise-Marie, died in 1850, the widowed Ferdinand found consolation in the arms of a young lady by the name of Elise Hensler. Born in 1836, her musical talent had brought her to the royal palace, where she soon attracted Ferdinand's amorous attentions. After several years together, he quietly married Elise in 1869 and his cousin the Duke of Saxe-Coburg and Gotha created her Countess of Edla. Life at court was not easy for Elise, and she was frequently the subject of petty jealousies; only on foreign trips was she treated with respect. In spite of the many insults that Queen Maria Pia, Ferdinand's daughter-in-law, launched against her, Elise always kept her composure. She knew, that above all, Ferdinand would always side with her. In the end, Elise was to come out victorious.

Death came quickly to King Ferdinand. On the evening of 12 December 1885, while attending the opera, he walked out to the royal balcony and stumbled. He had been suffering from cancer on the face, and one of the consequences of the illness was blurred vision and loss of equilibrium. The fall, however, proved fatal, setting off a meningeal hemorrhage. After falling into a coma, Ferdinand died on 15 December.

The Countess of Edla was the main beneficiary of King Ferdinand's will; he even requested that she be allowed to retain her residence in the Necessidades Palace that they had shared. It took nearly four years

Above: King Ferdinand in old age, always dapper.

Left: The Countess of Edla.

to settle the estate; in exchange for real estate and priceless art, Elise received handsome financial compensation. The Countess took her riches and spent the rest of her life with her daughter Alice, the product of an earlier affair with an Italian aristocrat. Elise had the satisfaction of surviving not only all of Ferdinand's children and the disagreeable Queen Maria Pia but also the Portuguese monarchy itself by nearly two decades. The Countess of Edla died in 1929, one day short of her ninety-third birthday, and King Manoel II and his mother Queen Amélie were represented at her funeral.

CHAPTER IX
Enter Great Britain Again
Prince Consort & Mater Familias

In Great Britain, and united through the machinations of their mutual uncle Léopold of Belgium, Queen Victoria and Prince Albert had quickly settled in a happy, agreeable life of domesticity. In a deliberate contrast to the scandalous excesses of the old Hanoverian kings and especially George IV, which had so harmed the monarchy in the eyes of the public, middle-class standards were introduced into the palace, showing *"the bourgeoisie that a king could be a respectable married man as well."* The Victorian Age was born of this situation: a desire to restore morality to the throne and provide the nation with exemplary standards to emulate.

Victoria and Albert had nine children. The first, Victoria, was born in late 1840, and she was to grow into a clever woman. She married the future Kaiser Friedrich III in 1858 and was destined to be the mother of Kaiser Wilhelm II, with whom she did not get along, among others. Three of Victoria's daughters also became consorts. Charlotte of Prussia's husband was Duke Bernhard III of Saxe-Meiningen, who inherited the ducal throne three days before Archduke Franz Ferdinand's assassination in 1914 and ruled until signing an act of abdication on 10 November 1918. Charlotte, it must be noted, was not an easy child, and she gave her mother many headaches with the unfortunate situations she created. Two of Victoria's other daughters, Sophie and Margarete, married King Contantine I of the Hellenes and Landgrave Friedrich-Karl of Hesse-Kassel, respectively. Both were Anglophiles who had the misfortune of having to live long enough to witness the abyss that irreparably damaged relations among Queen Victoria's grandchildren.

In 1841 the Queen gave birth to her first son, Albert Edward, the Prince of Wales. Two years later Alice joined the nursery, followed by a second son, Alfred, in 1844. In 1846 a third daughter, Helena, was born, followed in 1848 by Louise, perhaps the prettiest and most artistic of the royal brood. Arthur, the Queen's favorite son, arrived in 1850. Leopold was born three years later; he became a source of worry to his parents when, from an early age, it became apparent that he was *'ein bluter'* (a bleeder), suffering from hemophilia, the dreaded coagulating deficiency responsible for creating havoc in several royal nurseries. Finally, 1857, the Queen gave birth to her last child, Beatrice, who was to live in her mother's imposing shadow.

Unlike Victoria, who detested pregnancy and did not enjoy her children when they were young, Albert was a loving father, if a bit regimented and austere. His inability to compromise his high ideals in matters of raising children and morality prevented him from understanding those who preferred enjoyment to education. *"He could not bear bad manners,"* the Queen commented, *"and always dealt out his reprimands to the children. A word from him was instantly obeyed."* Albert expected his children to follow the same bourgeois ideals that had dominated the Coburgs since the time of his grandmother Augusta and to set moral examples to the nation. This unbending nature was to have disastrous consequences when it came to his eldest son the Prince of Wales, whom Albert came to view as a dangerous throwback to the immorality of the Queen's Hanoverian uncles.

Armed with a brilliant mind and immense capabilities, Albert struggled to find his place in a nation and a court that centered on his wife. The Queen understood his gifts and appreciated her husband's important political tutelage, yet her difficult and obstinate character often drove him to despair. Marital happiness often alternated with her tendency to overwhelming jealousy, a flaw in her otherwise remarkable character that occasionally left Prince Albert absolutely despondent.

Yet Albert's subordinate position forced him to remain in the background. To his friend, Prince Löwenstein, Prince Albert wrote: *"While I shall be untiring in my efforts and labors for the country in which I shall in future belong...I shall never cease to be a true German, a true Coburg and Gotha."* From Great Britain Albert kept a watchful eye over the various branches of his family. *"To live and to sacrifice myself for the benefit of my new country,"* he wrote, *"does not prevent my doing good to that country from which I have received so many benefits."* Throughout his years of influence, the Prince remained convinced that his native dynasty had an important role to play in furthering constitutional ideals and progress across the continent. Marriages, alliances, and new thrones were matters that consumed his attention, as did his efforts to model Europe into a liberal, democratic region that would become a beacon of hope for the rest of the world. His children, his cousins, his extended family, were therefore tasked with putting into place the institutions that would make his dream a reality. Unfortunately, his vision of a liberal Europe failed when nationalist interests superceded loftier goals.

Constant worry prematurely aged Prince Albert. With the passing years, the dashing young man who had lifted the Queen's heart lost his good looks and hair, and his eyes had lost their brilliancy. He had also become somewhat of a hypochondriac and seemed to have thoughts of death constantly on his mind. The year 1861 was a truly horrible one for Albert and Victoria. First, there was her mother's death. Then, as the year approached its end, news arrived from Lisbon that a typhoid epidemic had claimed the lives of King Pedro V and his brother, the Infante Fernando. Prince Albert, who adored his Portuguese cousins, seemed overwhelmed by events in Lisbon. Within a month Albert himself was prematurely dead at the age of forty-two years from typhoid. The date, 14 December 1861, was to forever remain a black mark in the Queen's yearly calendar. A letter she wrote to her daughter, the Princess Royal, four days after the death of her beloved Albert, best describes the depths of her grief: *"Oh! How I admired dear Papa! How in love I was with him! How everything about him was beautiful and precious in my eyes! Oh! How I will miss all, all! OH! Oh! The bitterness of this – of this woe! I saw him twice on Sunday – beautiful as marble – and the features so perfect, though grown very thin."*

Prince Albert, the Prince Consort.

Widowhood nearly drove Queen Victoria mad; at times her mourning even threatened the very institution to which her husband had dedicated his life. Cocooned in funereal darkness and wallowing in self-pity, she was attacked for absenting herself from public life and questions about the need for a monarchy itself became common. Although the Queen privately continued to work with her Prime Minister, she did so in isolation, abandoning her public duties. A depressing, somber-looking, black-clothed matron replaced the image of the happy monarch. *"She usually carried a white handkerchief so arranged that the lace border showed, and she favored a black silk gown with a small train, the corsage cut in V-shape,"* wrote Princess Louise of Belgium. *"She wore around her neck a locket containing a miniature of Prince Albert, her never-to-be-forgotten husband, on her head a widow's cap of white crepe."* Only when her eldest son the Prince of Wales nearly died in 1871 did the Queen abandon her seclusion and join in the public ceremony of thanksgiving. National rejoicing saved the monarchy and gradually forced Queen Victoria to abandon a decade of isolation.

Not long after her slow return to semi-public life, Queen Victoria astonished her family and inner circle by keeping company with the oddest of men, the gillie John Brown. A rustic Highlander, whose main duty seemed to be keeping the Queen company, he soon became her confidant, combining the office of groom, footman, page and maid all in one. Despite his brusque manners, Brown offered a handsome, manly presence to a woman in desperate search of male companionship. *"I feel I have here always in the house a good, devoted soul whose only object and interest is my service,"* the Queen wrote. *"God knows how much I want to be taken care of."* They passed quiet evenings drinking Brown's peculiar cups of tea. When the Queen once congratulated Brown on how well it tasted, he replied, *"Well, it should be Ma'am, I put a great nip o' whisky in it!"*

However innocent her association with Brown might have been, the friendship made headlines in the foreign press, and soon British papers saucily reprinted articles in italic letters: *"The Queen alias Mrs. Brown!"* Not surprisingly, the Queen felt that her association with John Brown was her own business and excused his more questionable behavior. Many nights he passed out and had to be carried unconscious to his room. *"It must have been the earth tremor,"* the Queen remarked in understanding. Yet most of her family, led by the Prince of Wales, loathed the poor Scotsman. Brown's death in 1883 became another opportunity for the Queen to demonstrate her sorrow, although her scandalized children were thankful when she finally abandoned plans to erect a mausoleum in his memory.

Two new men from the Queen's Imperial domain in India quickly replaced Brown. The Munshis, Abdul Karim and Rafiuddin Ahmed, were Muslim Indians who acted as her constant attendants. Karim even taught her Hindustani. Arrogant and often disagreeable, the pair always drew considerable attention when they traveled with the Queen and caused a good deal of consternation in royal circles.

Queen Victoria and the Prince Consort.

Despite her little idiosyncrasies, by the time death overcame her Queen Victoria had provided her name to one of the greatest eras in human history. German Chancellor Prince Otto von Bismarck, the Queen's old nemesis, once recalled that she was *"a woman one could reason and deal with."* Soon after hearing of her death, a French princess recalled *"in every poignant detail…the last private audience I had with the old Queen-Empress. It was perhaps the only time when I saw the real woman who was so often hidden beneath the necessary pride and ceremony of the Sovereign. She never wholly lost the look of one whose inner mind was busy with national cares and world-important concerns. Her people and their needs came ever first."*

Although not unexpected, Queen Victoria's death on January 22, 1901 shocked the nation. *"DEATH OF THE QUEEN!"* ran one newspaper headline. A local Isle of Wight newspaper read: *"With profound regret and sorrow we announce that at 6.30 o'clock this evening Her Most Gracious Majesty the Queen passed peacefully*

Queen Victoria and Prince Albert's children – From left: Prince Leopold (leaning on a chair as he was recovering from a bout of hemophilia), Princess Louise, Princess Beatrice, Princess Alice, the Prince of Wales, Prince Arthur, the Princess Royal, Prince Alfred and Princess Helena.

away at Osborne." It was a Tuesday, the fourth since the Queen's doctors first announced her weakened condition to the nation.

The previous Saturday, the Queen's physicians, deeply concerned by her failing health, issued bulletins expressing their grave prognosis. In a tidal wave of increasing frequency, various members of the royal family began arriving at Osborne House. The Prince of Wales and Princess Louise, his sister, arrived on the *Royal Yacht Alberta*. They joined Princess Beatrice, always living in her mother's shadow, as well as three of the old Queen's granddaughters: Princess Victoria of Wales, Princess Victoria of Battenberg, and Princess Marie Louise of Schleswig-Holstein-Sonderburg-Augustenburg, the estranged wife of Prince Aribert of Anhalt.

Another wave of worried relations arrived on Sunday. Kaiser Wilhelm II and the Duke of Connaught traveled from Berlin and were met in London by the Duke of York, with whom they journeyed to London. That day, after attending church services at Whippingham Church, more members of the royal family arrived at Osborne: the Duchess of York, the Duke of Argyll, and the Connaught children, Arthur, Margaret, and Patricia. So many relatives came that Osborne House could not hold them: Princess Helena Victoria, Princess Marie Louise's older sister, stayed at nearby Kent House, while Beatrice's children lodged at East Cowes castle, and their uncle Prince Louis of Battenberg, with wife Victoria, slept onboard the *Royal Yacht Osborne*. Day and night, a throng of journalists gathered outside the gates of Osborne House. On Monday, based on bulletins issued by her team of physicians, they reported an improvement in the Queen's condition: *"The slight improvement of the morning has been maintained throughout the day."* However, this was merely a temporary lull before the final storm.

By Tuesday, the mood was ominous. *"The Queen this morning shows signs of diminishing strength,"* read the early bulletin, *"and Her Majesty's condition again assumes a more serious aspect."* Several hours later another bulletin reported no change, but also announced that the Queen *"recognized several members of the Royal Family"* who had gathered around her bed. Touchingly, the Queen asked for her little Pomeranian, "Turi." The Prince of Wales, as the Queen lapsed in and out of consciousness, remained by his mother's side. Death came at half-past six. Her last audible word was "Bertie," Edward's nickname.

At left: The Duchess of Kent, whose death in 1861 began Queen Victoria's (above) death-filled 'annus horribilis.'

In an article published several years ago in the pages of *Eurohistory*, Coryne Hall recalls the public announcement of the Queen's passing: *"Ten minutes later Superintendent Fraser of the Royal Household Police made the announcement of the Queen's death from the steps of the lodge. Outside the gates of Osborne House people stood in stunned silence. She had been on the throne for almost sixty-four years. Only the very elderly could remember a monarch other than Queen Victoria. The Duchess of York summed up the whole nation's feelings: 'The thought of England without the Queen is dreadful even to think of. God help us all!'"*

The following day, 23 January, the new King Edward VII traveled to London to attend his accession council, and Princess Beatrice – who was also the Governor of the Isle of Wight – was left in charge at Osborne House. As a sign of respect toward her late mother-in-law, Queen Alexandra, *"immediately made it known that no one was to kiss her hand or treat her as Queen until after the funeral."* That same day, the household and servants were allowed to pay their respects to the late Queen, who lay in bed wearing her famed widow's cap, *"with her hands crossed and draped with her wedding veil."* The late Queen's Indian servants kept a watchful and silent vigil over the proceedings.

"Queen Victoria had left detailed directions about her funeral. It was to be a white funeral because, after forty years of widowhood, she would be reunited with Prince Albert. In accordance with the Queen's express wishes there were to be no undertakers, so the Kaiser measured his grandmother for her coffin. Sir James Reid placed in it Prince Albert's dressing gown (which Princess Alice had embroidered), a plaster cast of the Prince's hand, the small silver crucifix from above her bed and several family photographs." Among the photographs was one of John Brown, *"diplomatically hidden by some flowers."*

For several days, the Queen's coffin remained inside Osborne House, where a temporary mortuary chapel was fitted in the dining room. The head gardener decorated the room with flowers from the royal gardens, while a large Union Jack hung on a wall; it was afterward given as a memento to Kaiser Wilhelm II, who – much to the surprise of many present – behaved admirably throughout the visit. Covering the coffin was another Union Jack and a white satin pall, *"on* which lay the Queen's robes, a gold and diamond crown and the Order of the Garter." Grenadier Guards stood at each corner, while a small number of officials, tenants and people were admitted to pay their respects. As per the Queen's express command, there was not to be a public lying-in-state.

A cascade of flowers and wreaths surrounded the coffin. An *"immense crown of orchids and lilies-of-the-valley came from King Carlos I of Portugal; a seven foot square wreath of orchids and palms shaped like an angel's wings from Emperor Franz Joseph of Austria-Hungary. Other floral tributes came from Victoria's great friend the Empress Eugenie, the Empress Friedrich (by now too ill to attend her mother's funeral), the German Emperor and Empress and 'her sorrowing and devoted grandchildren Victoria and Louis.'* One poignant tribute from the children of the late Prince Leopold, Duke of Albany, read: 'In Love to dear Grandmama,' and was signed 'Alice and Charlie.'"

Above: Queen Victoria and John Brown were united by a strong bond of friendship. Those who didn't understand the level of comfort he provided the Queen, criticized the friendship by disrespectfully calling her Mrs. Brown.

Right: After the death of the Prince Consort, mourning became synonymous with Queen Victoria. In this image we see her holding a photo of Kaiser Friedrich III, who died of cancer in 1888, while her daughter the Empress Friedrich forlornly looks at her late husband's image.

On Friday, February 1, the weather regaled the late Queen with a fitting adieu. *"It dawned bright, sunny and almost spring-like – the proverbial 'Queen's Weather.' As a religious service was held inside Osborne, a crowd of journalists, tenants dressed in deep mourning, leading public figures on the island and schoolchildren from nearby Whippingham congregated in the grounds of Osborne House. Just prior to departure, while the coffin rested in Osborne's hallway, the Rector of the Parish conducted another brief service and the Bishop of Winchester gave a benediction."*

Shortly after one o'clock, and drawn by eight horses, a carriage arrived at Osborne House. A detachment of the Queen's Highlanders carried the coffin down the steps and placed it on the gun carriage *"to the mournful sound of pipes."* Dressed in glittering uniforms of Admirals of the Fleet, King Edward VII and Kaiser Wilhelm II, accompanied by many others, followed in deathly silence only sporadically broken by the sound of regiments presenting arms and the slow moving horse drawing the gun carriage.

Queen Alexandra, clad in deepest mourning, led the royal women present. Female members of the Royal Family followed, including the Duchess of York, the Duchess of Saxe-Coburg & Gotha, Princess Christian, the Duchess of Argyll, Princess Beatrice of Battenberg, the Duchess of Connaught, the Duchess of Albany, Princess Victoria of Wales, and Princess Maud of Denmark. Not to be excluded, *"behind them came the late Queen's ladies-in-waiting, members of her Household, the clergy, officers from all branches of the services, servants and tenants from the estate. A royal servant carried a large evergreen wreath."*

Dense crowds lined the route of the funeral cortège. Journalists reported that they were eight to ten people deep, while others climbed on chairs and benches to get a glimpse of the historic proceedings. Most impressively, nearly four thousand military troops came from the mainland to provide a fitting farewell along the route from Osborne House down to Trinity Wharf at Cowes, where the Queen's coffin was taken onboard the *Royal Yacht Alberta* for its journey to Portsmouth. Members of the Royal Family boarded the *Osborne* and *Victoria and Albert*, while the Germans followed on the *Hohenzollern*.

As the *Alberta* sailed away from Cowes, "*at the mouth of the river was the guardship, the Australia, which was to give the signal for the fleet's salute. There, stretched away to the eastward from that guardship, the magnificent array of battleships and cruisers lay upon the waters to the distant horizon of Portsmouth. For leagues along the grey wintry waters the line of the British fleet was visible, and far off, near Ryde, could be seen other warships, apart from the regular rank of the floating forts that lay so low and so darkly on the silver tide. These others were the ships of the Germans, and yet another powerful vessel under the command of a gallant French admiral. And then, near the Medina, as the Alberta steamed slowly away from her pier, were a number of sharp, low-hulled, black vessels, the destroyers – the advance guard of the yacht of the Queen of the Sea – which slowly glided from the estuary into the broader waters of the Solent. The long, low destroyers formed in processional order before it. Then from the guardship broke fire and smoke at the cannon's mouth, and loudly, near at hand and lessening in volume of sound as the salute proceeded, came the flash and report from one ship after another along the line of eleven miles, the minute guns answering from ironside to ironside, and then flashing and rolling forth again their thunder from the west to the east in continuous shocks of sound. And then the black hulls in advance sped slowly on down the mighty line, and the silver and grey of the sea was clouded with the smoke, which drifting in a haze that became golden as the sun declined, was brightened by stronger light near*

Above: Queen Victoria frequently hosted visiting members of her extended family. This image dates from the early 1890s and was taken at one of the gatherings of what she called the 'royal mob.' Standing, from left: Princess Alix of Hesse and by Rhine, Prince Henry of Battenberg, Princess Victoria of Battenberg. Front row: Princess Beatrice holding her son Alexander, Queen Victoria and her grandson Leopold of Battenberg, Grand Duke Ludwig IV of Hesse and by Rhine with Princess Victoria Eugenie of Battenberg. One of the Queen's Munshis managed to get himself in the photo.

Left: Queen Victoria with her grandson, the Duke of York and his wife. She was fully supportive of George marrying May of Teck.

Top: A magnificent view of Windsor Castle from the Long Walk.
Above: Queen Victoria's statue outside Windsor Castle.

Portsmouth, whose people, in dense, black, silent masses, fringed all the shore. They saw the dark advance guard of the flotilla coming through the haze. They then made out the little yacht with its bright standard, ahead of the two larger vessels, the Osborne and the Victoria and Albert, which in turn were ahead of the great grey Hohenzollern, the floating place of the German Emperor."

After a mournful procession through London that brought the coffin from Victoria Station to Paddington Station, the arrival at Windsor witnessed an unfortunate contretemps. The gun carriage that was to bring the coffin to St. George's Chapel experienced difficulties, as a witness recalled nearly four decades later: *"It would, perhaps, be more accurate to say that the contretemps was in connection with the so termed gun-carriage than with the horses or their handling by the Royal Horse Artillery. February 2, 1901, was a bitterly cold day with some snow, and the gun-carriage, under the charge of S Battery, R. H. A., [Royal Horse Artillery] and under the independent command of Lieutenant M. L. Goldie, had been kept waiting at Windsor Station, together with naval and military detachments, etc., for a considerable period. I had posted N/R.H.A. which battery I commanded, in the Long Walk ready to fire a salute of 81 guns, commencing when the cortege left Windsor Station for St. George's Chapel, at about 3pm. I placed Lieutenant P. W. Game (now Chief Commissioner of Metropolitan Police) in command, and pro-*

ceeded to the station to ensure that signaling arrangements were perfect. When the Royal coffin, weighing about 9cwt., had been placed on the carriage, drums began muffled rolls, which reverberated under the station roof, and the cortege started. Actually, when the horses took the weight, the eyelet hole on the splinter bar, to which the off-wheel trace was hooked, broke. The point of the trace struck the wheeler with some violence inside the hock, and naturally the horse plunged. A very short time would have been required to improvise an attachment to the gun carriage. However, when the wheelers were unhooked the naval detachment promptly and gallantly seized drag ropes and started off with the load. The gun carriage had been specially provided from Woolwich and was fitted with rubber tires and other gadgets. This was due to Queen Victoria's instructions after seeing a veritable gun carriage in use at the Duke of Albany's funeral, as also was the prohibition of the use of black horses. On February 4, in compliance with the command of King Edward, I conveyed the royal coffin, on another carriage, from Windsor to the Royal Mausoleum at Frogmore by means of the same detachment of men and horses. I may add that a few days later King Edward told me that no blame for the contretemps attached to the Royal Horse Artillery by reason of the faulty material that had been supplied to them." A royal tradition was thus born on the day of Queen Victoria's funeral.

Right: Osborne House, Queen Victoria's home on the Isle of Wight. She died there on 22 January 1901.

Queen Victoria's coffin lay inside St. George's Chapel for two days. Her son King Edward VII and an endless list of her royal descendants attended her funeral service. Accompanying the Royal Family were also several other monarchs, five of them Coburg descendants (Kaiser Wilhelm II, King Léopold II of the Belgians, King Carlos I of Portugal, Grand Duke Ernst Ludwig of Hesse and By Rhine, and Prince Ferdinand of Bulgaria) and a countless array of plumed helmets and uniformed foreign dignitaries, among them King George I of the Hellenes, and the Crown Princes of Prussia, Denmark, Sweden, Greece, Romania, and of Siam; Archduke Franz Ferdinand of Austria-Este (representing Emperor Franz Joseph), Grand Duke Michael Alexandrovich of Russia (representing his brother Tsar Nicholas II), the Duke of Aosta (representing King Vittorio Emanuele III), and countless others. Many of those present were either Coburg descendants or married to a Coburg, exemplifying the dynasty's accomplishment and influence.

The Coburg rise to power owed much to Queen Victoria, who remained a Coburger at heart. She had been a living contradiction. *"Brave and nervous...she was intensely loyal, but loved change. Though she said, 'negotiating by telegraph is a dreadful business,' she made full use of it. She disliked innovations, but once a telephone line was installed between Balmoral and Abergeldie, the apparatus never stopped ringing. She loved carriage rides, disliked electricity, loved tricycles, and is said to have fallen from one in 1881. She was unselfish and inconsiderate...tactful and blunt, sympathetic and hard, patient and fidgety, direct and devious, irresistibly charming and bristling with 'repellent power.' She was stiff and clinging, incurably shy and superbly poised...every ounce a bourgeois and every inch a queen."*

The passing of Queen Victoria not only witnessed the end of an era, but it was most certainly the apex of the Coburg dynasty. The family's meteoric rise, beginning with the Russian marriage in 1796, reached its zenith with the passing of Victoria. In the coming years, King George V would rename his dynasty in an attempt to erase its Germanic roots, and the Coburgs would lose several of the thrones they had so famously achieved.

Chapter X
Return to Coburg & Gotha
A Duke from Great Britain & A Troubled Succession

Ernst II became the reigning Duke of Saxe-Coburg and Gotha at the age of 26. Lord Melbourne praised him for his intelligence, even though he did not show the same scholastic interests and aptitudes as his considerably more studious brother Albert. He had studied in Brussels and at Bonn University before returning to Coburg where, for reasons of state, he married Princess Alexandrine of Baden, the sister of the reigning Grand Duke.

Duke Ernst II showed a complete lack of interest in a wife who bored him to tears. Princess Alexandrine of Baden concealed her shapeless body in shabby black dresses and beneath a cashmere shawl; around her neck she always wore a cameo of her husband. Perhaps her sad and unattractive demeanor stemmed from her husband's maltreatment, yet there was little about her to capture and hold Ernst's imagination and interest, and he quickly sought solace in the company of other women. Ernst was unapologetic about his affairs, in much the same way as his father had been, and Alexandrine suffered through this treatment with resignation.

Women were not Ernst's only weakness. He steadily spent his way through the royal treasury and was constantly short of funds; several times he had to borrow from shady moneylenders, to whom he was then obliged to show a certain consideration. Consequently, his Court became an amalgamation of doubtful gentlemen, second-class actresses, and semi-respectable individuals that markedly contrasted with the staid and scandal-free life of his relations in London. In fact, Ernst's behavior and penchant for trouble shocked the British Royal Family.

Despite these personal shortcomings, Ernst II was an incredibly gifted and intelligent individual. During the Schleswig-Holstein war in 1863, he fully supported Bismarck and the Prussians; he also sided with Prussia in the Seven Weeks' War against his Duchy's old ally Austria. Such was his political acumen that when King Otto was forced out of Athens, Greek politicians briefly considered offering Ernst their throne. Faraway Greece, though, seemed a backwater to the ambitious Ernst, and the lack of an heir made it difficult to consider the offer. In the end Prince William of Denmark, the second son of King Christian IX and Queen Louise, accepted the throne.

Ernst also played an important political role by promoting German unification, though perhaps one based in large part on personal considerations. He supported the idea of a strong Germany that would replace the myriad of existing small states, but he also envisioned himself as a possible candidate for the new imperial throne. Unluckily for him, Chancellor Otto von Bismarck had other ideas in mind and the throne eventually went to Bismarck's overlord, Wilhelm I of Prussia.

An air of amiability did much to keep Ernst in his subjects' good graces. They tended to ignore his dissolute life, and even shared stories about their ruler's peculiar style of life. A story went round that some of the Duke's relatives once visited Coburg and were sur-

Opposite page – A family gathering in Coburg, April 1894. The 'royal mob' flocked there to attend the wedding of Princess Victoria Melita, Duke Alfred's second daughter, to her cousin Grand Duke Ernst Ludwig of Hesse and by Rhine. This image was taken outside the Edinburgh Palais' winter garden. Standing, from left: the Duke of Connaught, Duke Alfred of Saxe-Coburg & Gotha, Kaiser Wilhelm II, the Prince of Wales. Seated: Queen Victoria and the Empress Friedrich.

prised to be greeted familiarly by complete strangers. When they asked about this strange welcome, they were told, *"Oh, they're just a few of der Lieber, Gute Ernst's illegitimates!"*

Ernst played the dandy to the end. In his later years he was described as an old beau, squeezed into a frock coat too tight for his bulk and with a sallow face marred by liver spots. He wore his moustache curled down over the corners of his mouth, its waxed ends turned up. He could be jovial and kind, but was too ceremonious to give free reign to his good disposition. Marie of Romania colorfully recalled her old Uncle Ernst as having *"the jaw of a bulldog, the teeth protruding far beyond the upper and with a pair of bloodshot eyes alive with uncanny, almost brutal intelligence."*

His death on 22 August 1893 left the treasury nearly empty and many of the ladies in Coburg, who had relied on his generosity, had to seek husbands to support them. His long suffering wife Alexandrine did not abandon him, ordering a double sarcophagus built so she could lie next to her husband. This decision raised many eyebrows within the family, who knew how notoriously unfaithful he had been to his wife. However, Queen Victoria regarded the idea as sublime, exclaiming, *"Yes, she was right and the two shall rest side by side, as they slept in life!"* Alexandrine's devotion for the late duke reached a climax when she refused to have a certain country house, scene of many of the duke's escapades, sealed because *"it was there that dear Ernst had passed such happy hours."* Duchess Alexandrine followed her husband to the grave in 1904. Today they lay together in the Glockenberg, the Ducal Mausoleum in the Coburg Friedhof.

Alfred, Duke of Edinburgh and Saxe-Coburg and Gotha (ruled 1893-1900)

Prince Alfred, Queen Victoria and Prince Albert's fourth child and second son, was born at Windsor on 6 August 1844. The Queen,

Top left: Hereditary Prince Ernst of Saxe-Coburg & Gotha as a young man.

Left: Duke Ernst II later in life. He died in 1893, leaving the dual ducal throne to his nephew the Duke of Edinburgh.

Albert wrote to his brother Ernst, *"let us wait a long time, and consequently the child is unusually large and strong."* Christened Alfred Ernest Albert, he was always known in the family as Affie. Ernst was particularly interested in the new arrival, for as it was increasingly likely that his own marriage would be childless, this second nephew would be heir to the German duchy. From early childhood Affie was always interested in geography and the Royal Navy, and at drawing lessons he sketched nothing but ships and naval battles. On his birthday one year his father gave him a ship's clock and barometer, which he always prized highly. With his practical skills, Alfred enjoyed taking mechanical objects apart and reassembling them with some minor improvement, or making small toys for the younger children.

Albert feared that the comparative backwardness of his oldest son Bertie, the Prince of Wales, would have a bad effect on Affie, and decided that, for their own good, the boys should be separated. Although Queen Victoria thought her second son was too young to leave home, Alfred joined the Navy and was appointed to the *Euryalus* a few weeks after his fourteenth birthday in August 1858. His first great journey was to the Mediterranean, South Africa, and the West Indies, from which he returned in August 1861. He was then appointed to the *St. George* for service in the Channel, North America, West Indies, and the Mediterranean.

Sadly, soon after this second departure the Prince Consort fell ill and died of typhoid on 14 December 1861. With the exception of his eldest sister Vicky, Crown Princess of Prussia, Affie was the only one of the children not present at Windsor Castle. Although he was granted compassionate leave in February 1862, Alfred's efforts to appear jovial and smile irritated his grieving mother. He disgraced himself even more soon after rejoining his ship in July 1862, when he had a brief affair with a local girl soon after reaching Malta. The story soon spread throughout the courts of Europe, and the Queen wrote to her eldest daughter Vicky, Crown Princess of Prussia, that she was shocked by his *"heartless and dishonourable behaviour."* It was clear that neither of her eldest sons had inherited their father's high sense of moral virtue.

Duchess Alexandrine of Saxe-Coburg & Gotha (née Baden).

Alfred's 'indiscretion' embarrassingly came at a time when the Greeks had just deposed their unpopular, childless King Otto and were searching for his successor. Of 241,202 votes cast for various members of European royal houses, Affie received 230,016, over 95%, but much to his relief it was contrary to the terms

The Duke of Edinburgh and his wife, Grand Duchess Marie Alexandrovna.

of a treaty signed in London in 1830 for a British prince to accept the throne. He had decided that he wanted to make the Navy his career, and he knew that the volatile Greeks could depose him just as easily if anything went wrong. The Queen told Lord Russell, her Foreign Secretary, that she *"could not understand why people seemed to think there was the possibility of her wishing Prince Alfred to accept the Crown, and she wished it to be contradicted."* His election was declared invalid and Prince William of Denmark reluctantly accepted the throne.

Promoted to Lieutenant in February 1863, Affie was due to return to England for Bertie's wedding to Alexandra of Denmark, elder sister of the new King of Greece, when he fell ill with typhoid. For a few anxious days the family worried that they might lose him; he entered hospital at Malta and missed the ceremony at Windsor, but soon recovered and rejoined his ship. Like his father Alfred tended to be shy and taciturn, but he was a true Hanoverian in his love of life's pleasures. Bored with the funereal gloom of Windsor and Osborne, he preferred to spend his leisure time with amusing society friends like the Duke and Duchess of Sutherland. He got on so well with the Princess of Wales that the Queen worried that he was becoming too fond of her; keen to see him out of temptation's way, she arranged for him to attend Bonn University in 1864. During his time in Germany Alfred regularly stayed with his sister Alice and her husband Ludwig, later Grand Duke and Duchess of Hesse, and met the young Battenberg Princes for the first time. He impressed the eldest, 12-year-old Louis, so much that the boy was determined to join the Royal Navy when old enough. In later years Louis and his younger son, Earl Mountbatten of Burma, eventually held the position of First Sea Lord.

In February 1866 the Queen signed an order-in-council authorizing the Admiralty to promote Affie to Captain, thus bypassing the immediate rank of Commander, and Parliament granted him an annual income of £15,000. On her birthday three months later, she created her second son Duke of Edinburgh and Earl of Ulster and Kent. Shortly afterwards he was appointed to the command of *HMS Galatea*, with orders to undertake an extensive world tour including South America, South Africa, and Australia. The schedule was demanding, and it was little wonder that Alfred sometimes showed impatience with the repetitive ceremonial functions laid out for him.

The tour coincided with the first stirrings of Irish republican agitation at home and abroad: in November 1867 three members of the Fenian Brotherhood were executed in Manchester for shooting a policeman. When the news reached Australia, one Fenian sympathizer found the nearby presence of the Queen's son too good an opportunity for revenge to miss. On 12 March 1868, Alfred was attending a function in aid of a sailors' rest home at Sydney when Irish expatriate James O'Farrell tried to assassinate him. Although shot in the back and wounded, an operation two days later successfully removed the bullet. The rest of the tour was curtailed to allow him time to recover. O'Farrell was tried, found guilty and hanged. Queen Victoria welcomed Alfred with open arms when he returned, hoping he would be *"an altered being,"* but soon she complained that he had become intolerably conceited, and had *"received ovations as if he had done something – instead of God's mercy having spared his life."* In November 1868, fully recovered, Alfred resumed his itinerary and sailed for China, India, and Japan, returning to England in May 1871.

On his next visit to Scotland he walked straight into a major row over John Brown at Balmoral. Like most of the Queen's family, he hated her hard-drinking Highland servant who was blunt to the point of rudeness

The Duke of Edinburgh wearing Russian costume.

with everyone, including Victoria herself. After a quarrel between Alfred and Brown, the Queen's secretary Sir Henry Ponsonby was asked to arrange a reconciliation between them. Affie agreed on condition that Ponsonby was present as a witness, explaining that whenever he saw a man on board his ship it was always in the presence of an officer. The Queen was furious: *"This is not a ship and I won't have naval discipline introduced here."*

Queen Victoria finally decided that the best way to settle her son was to marry him off. Having paid court in his younger days to his cousin Princess Friederike of Hannover, and then the eccentric Princess Elisabeth of Wied, who later became Queen of Romania, Alfred found himself drawn to Grand Duchess Marie Alexandrovna, only daughter of Emperor Alexander II of Russia. One of seven children born to Alexander and his wife Empress Maria Alexandrovna, formerly a Princess of Hesse and By Rhine, Marie had been spoiled and indulged. What she offered in fortune and intellect, Marie lacked in looks. Lady Stanley described her as *"short, dark haired, round faced, inclined to be plump and brusque,"* adding that *"she was lacking in good features."* Yet she also insisted that Marie was *"practical, sensible and without caprice."*

Alexander II had hoped that his only daughter would marry a foreign prince willing to settle in Russia. While the prospect of a union between the Grand Duchess and the son of the Queen of England was undoubtedly illustrious, the proposal was received with numerous objections from both sides. Some suspected that the Duke of Edinburgh was most interested in the large fortune Marie would bring to the marriage. Anglo-Russian relations were far from cordial, and Queen Victoria, a recognized Russophobe, was discomfited by her son's choice, while Alexander II could not stomach his daughter living in a country ruled by *"a silly obstinate old fool!"* However, neither Queen nor Emperor could stop the couple determined to link their future.

The wedding took place in St. Petersburg on 23 January 1874. Marie's refusal to convert from Orthodoxy rankled many, but the Queen had been assured that the Church of England recognized it as a valid faith and deemed the Grand Duchess a more suitable bride for the Duke of Edinburgh than an English subject or a Roman Catholic. Alfred and Marie moved into Clarence House in London, and kept a country house at Eastwell Park, Ashford, Kent. The new Duchess had a difficult time adjusting to life in Great Britain. She disliked most of her British relatives and, always conscious of her imperial background, insisted that – as an Imperial Grand Duchess and the daughter of an Emperor – she should take precedence at court over the Princess of Wales, who was only the daughter of a mere King of Denmark. Queen Victoria positively refused to consider such an idea, though eventually she did grant Marie precedence over her other British sisters-in-law. There were also arguments about Marie's titles: should she be known first and foremost as Grand Duchess of Russia, or as Duchess of Edinburgh, which she regarded as a less distinguished designation? As Ponsonby half-jokingly remarked to his wife, *"Which comes first, a louse or a flea?"*

The Duchess of Edinburgh in the early 1880s.

Marie openly vented her frustrations. She remained very much a Russian, and regularly visited her family in St. Petersburg, where she felt truly at home. *"Even her style of dress,"* commented her daughter Queen Marie of Romania, *"improved in the gold-pillared salons of the Winter Palace. Her gown is deep gentian blue, trimmed with sable, and the rubies she wears are like enormous drops of blood."* Truly, back in England, her appearance set her quite apart from her contemporaries and in-laws, none of whom could understand this unbendingly distant Russian grand duchess. Her mother, Empress Maria Alexandrovna, once wrote: *"Marie thinks London hideous, the air there appalling, the English food abominable, the late hours very tiring, the visits to Windsor and Osborne boring beyond belief."* However, the Duchess of Edinburgh was also appreciated in intellectual circles. Lady Randolph Churchill, a woman of keen intellect herself, commented, *"Marie is a woman of rare intelligence and exceptional education…a fine linguist speaking fluently several languages."*

Alfred and Marie had five children. In October 1874, a son, named Alfred after his father, was born, and four daughters followed over the next ten years: Marie,

The Duke and Duchess of Edinburgh were the parents of five children. Their firstborn, Alfred Jr., arrived during the first year of his parents' marriage, which was celebrated in St. Petersburg in January 1874. He was followed by four sisters born between 1875 and 1884. Top left, from the left: Marie, Victoria Melita, Beatrice, Alexandra and Alfred Jr. Top right: A rare image of Prince Alfred Jr. sitting on a tree branch.

who wed Ferdinand, the future King of Romania; Victoria Melita, who first married Ernst, Grand Duke of Hesse and, after their controversial divorce, Grand Duke Kirill of Russia; Alexandra, who became the wife of Ernst, hereditary prince of Hohenlohe-Langenburg; and Beatrice, who married Prince Alfonso d'Orléans, Infante of Spain. Marie Alexandrovna was devoted to her children, though she was a strict disciplinarian. From an early age they were encouraged to be good conversationalists, and taught to address dialogues to empty chairs in training. *"There is nothing more hopeless than a princess who never opens her mouth,"* she once said. She also believed that women should marry early, *"before strange ideas get in their minds;"* of her daughters only Beatrice waited until she was in her early twenties to wed.

Apart from their love of music, Alfred and Marie had little in common and gradually drifted apart. The Duke threw himself into his naval career. In February 1876, he was appointed to the Mediterranean fleet's ironclad *HMS Sultan*. Two years later, when war threatened to erupt between Russia and Western European powers, Alfred was put in an almost impossible situation as both a senior British naval officer and the Emperor of Russia's son-in-law. He unwitting caused problems when his ship was off the Turkish coast by inviting Alexander of Battenberg, an officer in the Russian fleet, on board for a reunion with his brother Louis, who then happened to be a junior officer under the Duke's command. The Queen and the Admiralty were horrified; when Alfred threatened that he would demand a court martial to clear his name, the issue was dropped and his career continued. In December 1878 he was promoted to Rear Admiral, and in November 1879 he became commander of the Naval Reserve, a post he held for three years. Named Vice-Admiral in November 1882, Alfred commanded the Channel Squadron from December 1883 to December 1884 and in 1886 was made Commander-in-Chief in the Mediterranean Fleet based at Malta, during which time he became a full Admiral. From August 1890 to June 1893 he served as Commander-in-Chief at Devonport; at the end of this post, he was promoted to Admiral of the Fleet.

Shortly after he left Devonport, Alfred's uncle Duke Ernst II died. Marie and her children had already

From left: Hereditary Grand Duke Ernst Ludwig of Hesse & By Rhine, Prince George of Wales, the Duke of Edinburgh and Prince Alfred Jr. of Edinburgh.

decorum permitted from the customs of their more open English cousins.

When the Coburg throne passed to Alfred he faced endless arguments in both England and Germany as to his nationality and privileges as a subject or sovereign prince. At Westminster a Liberal MP asked in the House whether it was *"legally competent"* for the Duke of Saxe-Coburg to continue holding the position and receiving the pay of an Admiral of the Fleet in the Queen's Navy, and to remain a member of the Privy Council. These were ruled as matters of *"nicety, as no practical importance,"* as the Duke was not involved in any executive or administrative work. He could remain on the navy list as an honorary member (without pay or the capacity for active service), as it was thought inappropriate to strike his name from the rolls, but he no longer had a seat or voice in the House of Lords. Similar arguments took place in the Reichstag in early 1894, as nationalistic German deputies, eager to stir up trouble with England, demanded similar clarifications on the Duke's status. Eventually Imperial Chancellor Leo Caprivi ruled that Alfred, as a sovereign German Duke, could not simultaneously be the subject of a foreign power, as in the event of war he could technically be accused of treason.

lived in Coburg for several years; this not only kept her out of the England she detested but also prepared her for her eventual role as wife of the reigning Duke of Saxe-Coburg & Gotha. Alfred and Marie built their own home, the Edinburgh Palais, across the Schlossplatz from the Ehrenburg Palace and next to the Opera Coburg, and it quickly became Marie's favorite residence. There she could once again play a central role without having to share the stage with any bothersome, envious in-laws, while turning her children into good German princelings as far away as

Though Affie was now officially resident in Coburg, he kept Clarence House as his home in England, and visited it annually. He sorely missed the navy, and once admitted to his old friend and colleague Admiral Fisher that he found Coburg *"deadly dull."* Though he was reluctant to speak of it to others, he was also concerned at his nephew Emperor Wilhelm's provocative

Standing, from left: The Duchess of Edinburgh with her daughter Beatrice, Hereditary Grand Duke Ernst Ludwig of Hesse & by Rhine, Prince Max of Baden, Princess Victoria Melita of Edinburgh, Prince George of Wales. Seated, same order: Prince Alfred Jr. of Edinburgh, Princess Alexandra of Edinburgh, the Duke of Edinburgh and Princess Marie of Edinburgh.

behavior towards England, and like many of his contemporaries feared that there would be trouble in the years ahead. In addition to ruling, the new Duke of Saxe-Coburg & Gotha passed his days in a wide variety of interests meant to alleviate the loss of his naval career. As a boy he had been the first member of the family to collect stamps, and he was responsible for beginning the royal philatelic collection, later encouraging his nephew, the future King George V, to take up the hobby. Alfred was also a lifelong friend of composer Sir Arthur Sullivan, and his patronage of musical education helped to establish the Royal College of Music at Kensington. A self-taught violinist, he always enjoyed playing the instrument for relaxation, and while serving at Devonport he participated in concerts with the local orchestra. His niece Princess Alice of Albany,

Left: Schloß Reinhardsbrunn, in Gotha. The estate was one of Duke Alfred's favorite hunting grounds. The property ended as a hotel, but burned down several years ago.

Below left: Prince Alfred Jr. in 1890, three years before becoming the Hereditary Prince of Saxe-Coburg & Gotha. He was raised by abusive tutors. As a young man he suffered from lack of impulse control and consequently found himself in serious trouble. His untimely death was a product of his abuses.

later Countess of Athlone, recalled in her memoirs *"the erratic movements of his bow over the strings, which he fingered with exuberant originality but with little regard for the score,"* though it should be added that she only knew him during his last years when he was in poor health.

Increasingly, Alfred and Marie's only son became the source of much worry. He had joined the German army and fallen into bad company. There are several versions as to what led to his ultimate demise. Some historians have claimed that he had an affair with an Irishwoman, Mabel Fitzgerald, whom he allegedly married. Mabel was carrying his child and his parents, according to this version, were furious. Some historians have doubted whether any ceremony took place, and in any case such a union would have been invalid under the Royal Marriages Act. Again, this is one of the rumors, gossip that was given credibility by historians who accepted it as truth. We simply just don't know.

At the time, Prince Alfred was suffering from a venereal disease and had grown increasingly despondent. One of Duke Alfred's equerries confirmed the ducal staff's frustration with the young man when he told Marie Alexandrovna that "he is absolutely disgusted with Alfred and outraged about his recklessness." At one point, his lack of responsibility made him become "negligent" when performing his military duties. Duke Alfred was forced to travel to Berlin to intervene in his

Chapter X – Return to Coburg: A Duke from Great Britain & A Troubled Succession

Right: Top: Schloß Rosenau, birthplace of the Prince Consort, where Duke Alfred died in 1900.

Middle: The Edinburgh Palais, Coburg (2013).

Bottom: The Château de Fabron, near Nice, Marie Alexandrovna's home on the French Riviera.

son's downward spiral. Alfred Jr. was then interned in a clinic where doctors tried to cure him. His parents were desolate when told that due to the nature of their son's illness, marriage, for the time being, was impossible. This cruel reality did away with his mother's hope of marrying the difficult young man to anyone for at least several years. His behavior had already cost him the chance of marrying one of the daughters of Grand Duchess Vera Konstantinovna. Now, his illness was about to take a turn for the worse.

In late 1898 as they dealt with their son's increasingly worrisome and deteriorating health, Alfred and Marie dispatched invitations to their Silver Wedding Anniversary at Schloss Friedenstein in Gotha. As royal guests began arriving that late January, a terrible drama was playing itself out behind the scenes. Young Prince Alfred hovered between life and death. Either in an attempt to improve his health, or in an effort to conceal what had happened, he was transported to Meran, in the South Tyrol. There, his parents hoped, the clean mountain climate would help improve their son's precarious condition. Sadly, the recovery did not work. Instead, Alfred Jr. found himself at death's door and died on 6

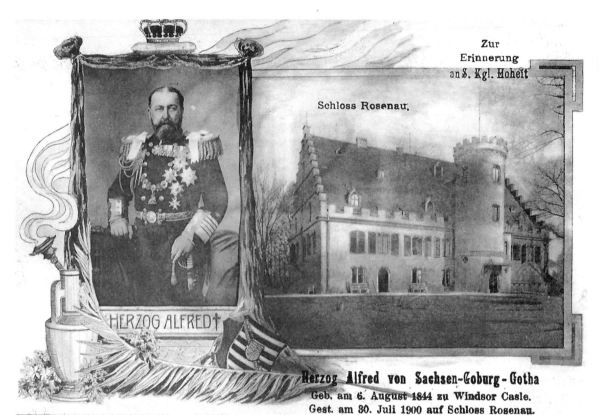

A memorial postcard of the death of Duke Alfred of Saxe-Coburg & Gotha.

February. Officially the cause of death was given as consumption. However, we now know that was not the case. In a letter Marie Alexandrovna wrote to her daughter Marie, the duchess provided a window into the family tragedy. She wrote, *"How could I have born our terrible sorrow if you all had not surrounded me and not let me lead my usual solitary life! The moment I am left longer alone. it all comes back again to me and makes life hard to bear. Our poor, poor Alfred! He gave us only pain and trouble and yet one was always hoping for his better future, one was working for him and had an object in life. And now it all seems too dismal, too empty for words! In what hand will this dear home of ours get later on? People who won't appreciate it, will change everything. I am sometimes very disconsolate."* Marie Alexandrovna's married daughters had immediately traveled to stay with their parents. Marie of Romania, about to get embroiled in a nasty little scandal with Prince Cantacuzene, stayed two months. Victoria Melita, *"who had to go back to such a trying life,"* also remained with her parents for a long visit. Her *"departure was a terrible grief,"* her mother wrote. Alexandra also joined the family. She left to be in Strasbourg, where she fulfilled some duties. Once these were completed, Alexandra returned to Gotha and accompanied her parents on their return to Coburg and the peace of Schloß Rosenau.

Queen Victoria was devastated by the loss of young Prince Alfred. Not only had she lost a grandson in most tragic circumstances, but also his death lay open the succession question in Coburg. To her daughter, the Empress Friedrich, Victoria wrote, *"I know how distressed you are at this awful misfortune – which is so far-reaching. But we must not [lose] heart or courage and God will help us. But oh, the poor, poor parents! To lose their only son, in whom their hopes and life were bound up, is fearful. I have three lines from poor dear unhappy Affie and Marie. Ernie of Hesse went to him and seems most kind and attentive, telegraphing to me several times. He describes poor Affie in a dreadful state on first going to see the dear remains…He telegraphed today: 'I have returned from praying near my dear boy who looks so peaceful. I am broken-hearted, but we start tonight with the remains for Gotha. Funeral on Friday.'"*

The circumstances surrounding the death of young Prince Alfred made his parents choose a quiet funeral rather than the state occasion demanded by protocol. Avoiding a bevy of foreign dignitaries heading to Gotha, Alfred and Marie buried their son under the chapel at Schloss Friedenstein. His remains were later moved to the Ducal Crypt at the Coburg Friedhof where they rest peacefully to this day along with those of his parents, among others.

Both the Duke and Duchess were devastated by their only son's death. Duke Alfred, blaming his wife for his son's death, is said never to have recovered from

The procession at the funeral of Duke Alfred. Behind the bier, in the first row, from left: Duke Carl Eduard, Kaiser Wilhelm II, Hereditary Prince Ernst of Hohenlohe-Langenburg, regent of Coburg & Gotha. Among those behind them are: the Duke of York, Grand Duke Alexis Alexandrovich of Russia, Prince Ferdinand I of Bulgaria, among many others.

this blow, and increasingly he began to drink heavily. His rapidly deteriorating health alarmed family and friends, and the Queen's physician Sir James Reid warned her several times that he *"was in a broken down state from too much drink."* In June 1900 inoperable cancer of the tongue and throat was diagnosed, and the Duke died at the Rosenau near Coburg on 30 July 1900. Queen Victoria had been warned the previous week that his condition was hopeless, but she was still shocked when her daughters broke the news: *"Oh, God! My poor darling Affie gone too! My third grown-up child...it is hard at eighty-one!"* He was buried on 4 August, the funeral taking place at the church of St. Moritz in Coburg. His fellow officers had sometimes found him a demanding, exacting colleague, though they had respected his capacity for hard work and devotion to the service and remembered him with admiration and even fondness. The Times noted: *"It has been truly said that the Duke loved the Navy and the Navy was proud of him."* His remains rest inside the Glockenberg in Coburg's Friedhof.

Widowhood seemed to suit Marie Alexandrovna. With his extra-marital affairs, unpleasant temper, and taste for alcohol, Alfred had been a difficult husband. Now alone, Marie could focus on what she most enjoyed: her children and traveling. Her wealth allowed Marie to maintain residences outside Coburg and Gotha, including a villa in Bavaria and the Château de Fabron, located in one of the most prestigious areas of Nice, which became one of her favorite houses. There, she not only enjoyed the warm weather, but was also in close vicinity to other Romanovs who owned property in the area. The Edinburgh Palais remained her home in Coburg, while Schloß Rosenau served as her country residence until the outbreak of the Great War. In 1914, and given the animosity of the German population to a Russian Grand Duchess living in their midst, it was decided that she was better off vacating the Rosenau. After her death, Marie's children maintained the lease of the Rosenau, but rarely visited. In 1937 the lease was cancelled and the castle was returned to the Coburg State Foundation, which then let it to a Nazi Party labor organization. Today, the Rosenau is a museum dedicated to the Coburgs, while the Edinburgh Palais houses offices.

The Great War was a particularly challenging time for Marie Alexandrovna. A Russian by birth, widow of a German sovereign, aunt of King George V, Tsar Nicholas II, and Kaiser Wilhelm II, and daughter of a German princess, Marie's heartstrings were pulled in myriad directions. She loved Germany and adored Russia, though she maintained her dislike of Great Britain. She was terribly unhappy when Romania, where her daughter Marie's husband now reigned, joined the Allied side. These were dreadful times.

Top left: Grand Duchess Marie Alexandrovna and her grandson Hereditary Prince Gottfried of Hohenlohe-Langenburg. Top right: the Grand Duchess with two of her Orléans grandchildren: Alvaro and Alonso, sons of Princess Beatrice and her husband Infante Alfonso.

War also meant a reduction, a serious one at that, of her income. Not only was the bulk of her fortune held in trust in Russia, but also her British income was stopped. She, who had never experienced penury, now found herself short of funds and unable to meet her obligations. It was, indeed, a terribly painful time. Marie tried, unsuccessfully as it turned out, to keep neutral in what turned out to be a devastating conflict that ripped her family apart.

In old age Duchess Marie lost both weight and conviction. Her hands, formerly plump and sure, had become thin and rather trembling. In the aftermath of World War I, she lost everything. Unwelcome in her beloved Germany for being a Russian, in England for being a German, and in Russia for being a Romanov, she was unable to find in wartime Europe anything that reminded her of days now forever gone. After the Kaiser's abdication in 1918, when Germany became a republic, Marie left Coburg and settled in Switzerland. It was while living there, accompanied by some of her surviving children, that she died a broken woman in 1920. Her remains were brought back to Coburg and she rests in eternal peace in the company of her husband and son, both of whom disappointed her so very much in life.

The Coburg Succession Question

The 1899 death of Hereditary Prince Alfred of Saxe-Coburg and Gotha left the duchy's succession in crisis. By right of inheritance, the next male heir was Duke Alfred's brother, Prince Arthur, Duke of Connaught, followed by his male heir, Prince Arthur of Connaught. After them came Prince Charles Edward, Duke of Albany, only son of the late Prince Leopold, Duke of Albany, Queen Victoria's hemophiliac fourth son. A family council took place at Cimiez, where Queen Victoria was on holiday. Duke Alfred and his mother urged the Duke of Connaught to put forward his dynastic claim to the Coburg inheritance. While the Duke of Connaught was willing, what he did not realize was the rising tide of opposition his candidature created in the more Anglophobic coteries surrounding Kaiser Wilhelm II, his own nephew.

Although the ducal succession in Coburg did not have to be approved by the German Emperor, Kaiser Wilhelm could not refrain from meddling in the business of his English relations. Upon learning of the Duke of Connaught's claim, the Kaiser raised objections to his uncle retaining any of his English military offices, as *"he could not pose as a German prince and still hold his English command."* The Duke of Connaught, an accomplished soldier in his mother's army, categorically refused to give up his life's work. Furthermore, the Kaiser demanded that the Duke of Connaught's heir, Prince Arthur, be transplanted to Germany immediately to be educated as a German prince. Wilhelm's mother, the Empress Friedrich, further expressed her family's frustration with his actions when she wrote to the Queen saying, *"I hope you do not see it fit to write an apologetic letter to William at all and think it would be a great mistake if you were advised to do so. Qui s'excuse, s'accuse…He has nothing to do with the Coburg succession. It is all settled by law."* While Her Majesty's ambassador in Berlin also ignored the Kaiser's posturing as *"ill humor"* for not having been invited to his grandmother's eightieth birthday celebrations, Wilhelm was determined to stand his ground when it came to the future of Coburg.

Grand Duchess Marie Alexandrovna doing needlework. The Great War brought her indescribable pain, worry and suffering as Russia fought Germany, her two favorite countries.

After months of failed negotiations, the Duke of Connaught refused to meet any German demands. Prince Arthur of Connaught himself is said to have told his young cousin the Duke of Albany to accept the Coburg succession. Frustrated by the entire episode, Queen Victoria wrote to her daughter, the Empress Friedrich, explaining the solution the family had reached: *"Coburg is once more a great annoyance especially as Affie [Duke Alfred] seems to resist everything but having young Arthur [in Coburg] and as such pressure is put upon a decision, in England also, there is such agitation as to what Arthur is going to do, that he has to decide that he, and young Arthur also, can't leave England where they are much needed [and will renounce their rights to the Coburg succession]. Charlie (the Duke of Albany) is a remarkably nice boy."* And so the Coburg succession, after a great deal of bickering between the Kaiser and his English relations, went to Carl Edward, Duke of Albany.

Chapter XI
The Kohary Line
Wealth, Position & A New Throne

Born in 1818, Prince August was the second son of Prince Ferdinand and his wife Princess Antonia. Tall and slender, the young man had *"fair hair, small blue eyes, a very pretty nose, and likewise a very pretty mouth."* Queen Victoria, always a good judge of character, said that August *"was like an affectionate child, quite unacquainted with the world, phlegmatic, and talking very little."* Her stepsister, Feodora of Hohenlohe-Langenburg, thought that August was lazy, limited in intelligence, and even less manly than his cousins Ernst and Albert. Yet it was his good fortune that he married exceptionally well, and to a woman with the iron will he himself lacked.

Princess Clémentine d'Orléans, second daughter of King Louis Philippe of the French, had fortitude and fortune. A lovely young woman, she had attracted the favorable attentions of King Charles X during a children's ball when she was only fourteen. *"Monsieur mon cousin,"* Charles told her father, *"if I was forty years younger I would ask for the hand of your daughter to make her Queen of France."* This innocent remark made the rounds of the salons in Paris, and likely filled Clémentine's head with dreams of grandeur and a thirst to be a queen.

Unfortunately for Clémentine, her parents were unable to find her a throne, much less a husband. Many European courts rebuked their inquiries, not wishing to be associated with Louis Philippe's revolutionary monarchy. By age twenty-five, she was still unmarried and considered well on her way to royal spinsterhood. A previous attempt to marry her off to Duke Ernst of Württemberg (1807-1868) had failed. As had so often happened in the past, King Léopold of Belgium now came to the rescue, once again suggesting that there was no need to look beyond the House of Coburg for a suitable consort. He proposed his nephew August, whose status as a junior member of the dynasty was more than offset by the immense fortune he stood to inherit from his parents. There was also precedent for a match between the Coburgs and the House of Orléans: August's sister Victoire had married the charming Duke of Nemours, King Louis Philippe's second son, while Uncle Léopold had married Louise-Marie, the King's eldest daughter.

August first came to Clémentine's attention when she exchanged letters with Queen Maria II of Portugal, who happened to be not only his sister-in-law but also a close friend of the Orléans princess. At the time, some family members suggested that Clémentine should marry Infante Francisco de Asís of Spain, Duke of Cadiz – a union they felt would produce advantageous results for French foreign policy. This Spanish proposal was soon abandoned when the prospective groom was deemed an effeminate slave to fashion; the very idea of marrying such a man, said her sister Queen Louise-Marie of Belgium, filled Clémentine with *"a sense of horror."*

The idea of marrying Prince August, therefore, came when Clémentine was most desperate. The Duke d'Aumâle, one of her handsome brothers, later confided that his sister chose August *"because all the Coburgs became kings."* Otherwise, *"August's taciturn character did not much impress his Orléans in-laws, who profusely, and dismissively one may add, referred to him laughing as 'l'imbecilité d'Auguste.'"*

Once August's proposal was accepted, negotiations over the couple's marriage contract began in earnest. King

A portrait of Princess Clémentine d'Orléans painted by Franz Xavier Winterhalter.

Louis Philippe asked for two guarantees: first, that in Vienna his wife receive the treatment due to the daughter of a French king; and second, that Prince Ferdinand secure his son and new daughter-in-law a yearly stipend allowing for the regal style of life to which Clémentine was accustomed. Although Ferdinand was one of Austria's wealthiest princes, he claimed that he could not provide the desired allowance. His resistance nearly ended the engagement. To her mother Queen Marie-Amélie, Louise-Marie of Belgium wrote: *"Prince Ferdinand [her brother-in-law] wants to marry Prince August to get him away from the rot of the Austrian garrisons. But he does not want to pay anything to do so."*

Clémentine counted on her brothers' support to prevail. Marie-Amélie was lukewarm toward the alliance, while King Louis Philippe and his very influential sister, Princess Adelaïde, were actually against it. A tragedy temporarily brought the negotiations to a halt when Clémentine's eldest brother, the Duke d'Orléans, died in a carriage accident. Perhaps the loss of his heir softened the King's attitudes, for in the end, Louis Philippe relented and authorized the Count de Flahaut to conduct marital negotiations on his behalf in Coburg. *"Only Heaven knows why he [Prince Ferdinand] negotiated this matter directly with Flahaut, squabbling over trifles, for the marriage treaty will not be signed before March* (1843)," King Léopold wrote to Queen Victoria. The pact eventually signed in Vienna on 25 February 1843 provided Clémentine with a huge dowry. In addition to the one million francs Louis Philippe gave to each of his daughters on marriage, Clémentine also received a yearly pension of 50,000 francs; diamonds, pearls, and other jewels valued at 200,000 francs; and a trousseau valued at 100,000 francs. She would also receive her legal share of two inheritances from her Aunt Adelaïde and from the King, to be invested in real estate and annuities. In total, the dowry guaranteed Clémentine the modern equivalent of roughly $150 million, making it one of the largest royal marriage settlements in recent history. Prince Ferdinand finally granted August a yearly pension of 100,000 francs. The couple's property was kept separate, and in the event that Clémentine died without issue, her fortune would revert to her brothers. The Duchess of Dino, a talented memoirist who knew Clémentine, remembered that the marriage gave her the joy of *"acquiring her independence, becoming able to go as she pleased, as well as escaping the boredom of the Tuileries."*

August and Clémentine honeymooned in Portugal, visiting his brother and Queen Maria II, then at Queen Victoria's request traveled to London, where they remained several weeks. *"She is very pleasing and interesting,"* the Queen wrote. *"Fine dark blue eyes, pronounced features and very pretty figure. Very lively and amusing. Her way of speaking is much like Louise's* [the Queen of Belgium], *though she is not like her in the face but the manner reminds me of her. We are already very intimate and I feel what a charming companion she is. She doesn't possess quite the same angelic charm as dear Louise but there is in her such a sense as well, right judgments, good feelings, kindness and cleverness."*

The greeting that awaited the newlyweds on arriving at August's estate, Schloß Ebenthal near Vienna, was truly impressive. Some 300 peasants on horseback, holding green and white banners, welcomed the couple; lackeys held torches on both sides of the entrance route, and young maidens in white dresses extended their welcome by offering the pretty bride bouquets of flowers. In honor of the newlyweds, the Imperial Family hosted a brilliant ball at the Hofburg. Clémentine was ecstatic at her reception into Viennese society, but what impressed her most was touring what seemed as an endless list of castles and estates belonging to her in-laws.

Prince August of Saxe-Coburg. This image comes from a miniature owned by his great-great-great-granddaughter Princess Felicitas of Saxe-Coburg & Gotha.

In Vienna the couple made their home in the Coburg Palais, whose construction August's father had halted in the aftermath of the 1848 revolutions. When Ferdinand died in 1851, August and Clémentine spent five years completing the building, which one relative deemed *"a vestige of the past century."* Viennese wags dubbed the white structure 'the asparagus' after its massive columns supporting the rear portico. Although the exterior was imposing, the interior apparently left much to be desired. Princess Louise of Belgium, August and Clémentine's infamous and scandal-prone daughter-in-law, later wrote of *"massive, old upholstered furniture…all was old, ordinary, somber. Hardly a flower, nothing comfortable, nothing matching. As to a bathroom, there was not a sign of one. There were only two baths in the whole palace; they were far away from each other, and of positively archaic construction. And as for the rest – it is better left unsaid."*

Once the construction bug bit him, August not only fulfilled his father's dream of a residence befitting the Viennese Coburgs, but he also wanted to build a fitting family crypt where his branch of the Coburgs could

The Coburg Palais, Vienna.

Prince August and his sons Philipp and Ludwig August.

rest in eternal peace. In 1856, he financed construction of the Catholic Church of Saint Augustin, located on a small promontory along the rear right side of the Edinburgh Palais, and right up the street from the Burglaßschlößen. Construction of the neo-Gothic style church and crypt took several years before its consecration in 1860. Later, Princess Clémentine assumed the costs involved in expanding the 'Kohary Crypt' to accommodate the remains of fifteen family members beneath the church.

While their Viennese residence was imposing, questions at the etiquette-obsessed Habsburg Court kept them from fully enjoying social life in the capital. Clémentine was a royal highness, while August – as a minor member of the Coburg dynasty – was a 'Durlaucht,' a 'Serene Highness.' Issues of protocol and precedence were finally resolved when Emperor Franz Joseph declared that, as a member of a foreign dynasty living in Austria, August and his spouse would take precedence immediately after the Imperial Family. Later, in 1881, as Vienna prepared for the wedding of Crown Prince Rudolf and Princess Stéphanie of Belgium, Franz Joseph elevated August to the predicate of 'Highness,' as he was the father-in-law of the bride's sister.

August matched his rank as Major-General in the French Army with the same role in the Habsburg

The family of Prince August and Princess Clémentine c. 1865. From left: Princess Clotilde, Prince August, Princess Amelie, Prince Ludwig August, Princess Clémentine, little Prince Ferdinand and Prince Philipp.

Empire; he also served as a Lieutenant-General in the Saxon Army. He received numerous orders, including the Grand Cross of the Saxe-Ernestine House Order, the Portuguese Royal Order of the Tower and Sword, the French Legion of Honor, and the Belgian Royal Order of Léopold. He was a Knight of Honor and Devotion in the Sovereign Military Order of Malta, and in 1862, Franz Joseph granted August of Saxe-Coburg & Gotha the prized Order of the Golden Fleece.

Clever and ambitious, Clémentine's formidable will and her prowess in intrigue earned her the sobriquet of *"Clémentine de Medicis,"* a sure allusion to her own ancestor. By her fortieth birthday, she had grown so deaf that she had to regularly use an ear trumpet. Her daughter-in-law, Louise of Belgium, related: *"I was attracted to her but her deafness, which sadly aggravated her natural dignity, and her spirit of another age, which made her always appear to be living in state of etiquette, often repulsed my natural outbursts of affection."* Another more infamous relation, Crown Princess Louise of Saxony, found the middle-aged Clémentine *"short and fat, but not inelegant, and very much a grande dame. She had piercing blue eyes, a prominent nose, and the brains and judgment of an exceptionally clever man…indeed in our family she was known as Aunt Coffee-Mill and as she possessed an exceptionally mischievous tongue, my brothers declared that she ground the reputation of others to powder in her coffee mill."*

Princess Clémentine and her daughters Clotilde and Amalie.

Prince Philipp.

Prince Ludwig August.

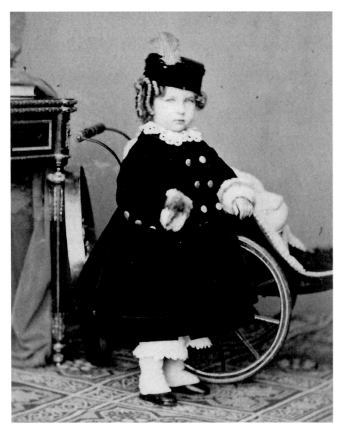
Prince Ferdinand.

Unlike many of her extended relations, Clémentine never developed her husband's interest in hunting. The French Revolution had broken the aristocracy's obsession with the sport, as royals and aristocrats stopped being hunters and instead became the hunted. The Bourbons had revived the sport on their return to the French throne, but Clémentine preferred to concentrate on her voluminous correspondence, while also trying her best to learn German, a language that confounded her. *"Her effort, however, never enjoyed a success. Everybody was speaking French to her and she found the German language rather unpalatable."* She was truly in love with August and enjoyed the moments of solitude they shared, her *"tête-a-têtes with Gusti,"* as she called them. Queen Victoria, however, had a different view of time with her cousin August: *"Clem,"* she said, *"seems very happy and writes that she is happiest when she is tête-à-tête with poor Gusti, which I should not fancy!"*

August and Clémentine had five children. Philipp was born in the Tuileries Palace in Paris in 1844. The following year, Clémentine gave birth to a second son, Ludwig August. A daughter, Clotilde, arrived in 1847, followed by Amalie in 1848. Thirteen years later, while in the midst of menopause, Clémentine unex-

Princess Clotilde.

Princess Amalie.

pectedly found herself pregnant in her mid-forties. The product of this late pregnancy was a third son, Ferdinand, who would one day make history as the ruler of Bulgaria.

Clémentine, like most of the Orléans Dynasty, had a deep sense of family and dynasty. She loved her children, and her letters to countless relations were always filled with news about them: their character, development, peculiarities, and looks were all matters she discussed with a great degree of pride. From their mother the children inherited a love of education, while physically they most resembled their Orléans relatives, having inherited from Clémentine slender and tall bodies, rather aquiline noses, and clear blue eyes plagued by myopia.

The Princess, said one contemporary, was known for her *"shrewd mind and a remarkable understanding of European politics and diplomacy."* Clémentine adored politics and continually gathered information on important questions through both relatives and friends in diplomatic service. She was determined to see one of her sons become a king, using her power and, her critics argued, any means at her disposal, to achieve that which had been denied to her.

Archduchess Clotilde, Archduke Joseph and one of their children, either Elisabeth or Maria Dorothea.

Clémentine more than compensated for what her husband lacked in drive and ambition when it came to their three sons: her machinations eventually saw her eldest son Prince Philipp marry a king's daughter; Prince Ludwig August nearly became consort of the Princess Imperial of Brazil; while Ferdinand achieved his mother's ambitious dreams and became a monarch in his own right.

In early 1881 Princess Clémentine had to abandon plans to travel to Alcsút, a magnificent estate owned by her son-in-law Archduke Joseph, when her husband August fell ill with bronchitis. *"He is very weak,"* she wrote to her brother Louis, Duke de Nemours, *"and eats nothing, sleeps very little and coughs constantly. I am tormented because Braun [the family doctor] still believes there is nothing wrong with his health."* Later that summer, August's condition took a turn for the worse and all the children were called back to Vienna. *"What an awful illness,"* Clémentine wrote to Nemours. *"For days and nights we thought he would leave us at any minute! He has received the last sacraments showing deep faith and beautiful resignation…when the moving ceremony ended he thanked the abbot and took notice of us all. The doctors have lost all hope, his heart stopping seemed imminent."* August rallied one last time, but he had lost the battle and succumbed on 26 July, with Clémentine and his five children at his side. *"His end was an image of his life: beautiful, noble, great, pious,"* his widow wrote to Queen Victoria. *"Every year we loved each other more. He gave me thirty-eight years filled with perfect happiness."*

Widowhood gave Clémentine the time and opportunity to enact her political and dynastic aspirations for her sons. From Schloß Ebenthal, the countryside palace she chose as a dower house, she threw herself into what quickly became her life's ambition: securing a throne for her youngest son Ferdinand. Her sights were set on Bulgaria when the throne of this Balkan backwater became vacant following the ouster of Prince Alexander of Battenberg, and Clémentine used both talk and carefully placed bribes to ensure that the Bulgarian representatives visiting Vienna came away with a favorable view of her youngest son.

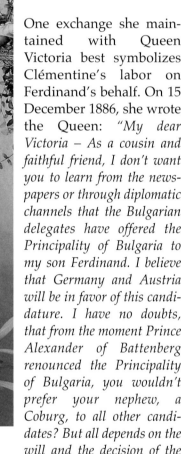
Princess Clémentine later in life.

One exchange she maintained with Queen Victoria best symbolizes Clémentine's labor on Ferdinand's behalf. On 15 December 1886, she wrote the Queen: *"My dear Victoria – As a cousin and faithful friend, I don't want you to learn from the newspapers or through diplomatic channels that the Bulgarian delegates have offered the Principality of Bulgaria to my son Ferdinand. I believe that Germany and Austria will be in favor of this candidature. I have no doubts, that from the moment Prince Alexander of Battenberg renounced the Principality of Bulgaria, you wouldn't prefer your nephew, a Coburg, to all other candidates? But all depends on the will and the decision of the Russian Emperor, and the proposal should remain, for the moment, as a secret between us. I am not writing any more today, leaving you as always as your devoted cousin and old friend."*

To this, Queen Victoria replied: *"My dear Clémentine – I received your letter of the 15th, I must admit, with astonishment. The newspapers already announced Ferdinand's candidature for Bulgaria. So when your letter arrived, it wasn't a secret any more. Knowing how you love your son, I am surprised that you are so willing to listen to this project and in your place I would have been thankful if there were no further question of it. Your devoted cousin and faithful friend for ever – VRI."*

"My son didn't offer his candidature for Bulgaria," the

Princess curtly countered. *"The Bulgarian delegates wanted him earnestly to accept, together with others, who still want him to accept."*

Knowing that Clémentine would brook no opposition, the old widow in Windsor immediately replied: *"My dear Clem, I wish to respond to your nice letter, as I wish to let you know that I understand your cruel uneasiness. What must console you is that it is Ferdinand's great wish to go to Bulgaria. Do not doubt for one instant that my affection for you and my interest in your family has not changed…it is impossible for my government to grant special protection to Ferdinand, for he accepted the throne without the approval of the Great Powers and we must be aware of Russia's animosity. I really pity your poor son in this almost untenable position that he finds himself; and I can only hope that he will escape the dangers that surround it, and that must be a constant preoccupation for you. VRI."*

Clémentine won her battle and saw Ferdinand installed as Reigning Prince in Sofia. Backing his adventure was his mother's incredible fortune. Clémentine visited the Bulgarian capital frequently, and helped Ferdinand establish a respectable monarchy, at least in the eyes of the greater public. She helped him with protocols, uniform designs, court etiquette, and rebuilding decrepit palaces. No challenge seemed insurmountable for this amazing woman, who refused to listen to refusals in her indomitable quest.

In early 1907, Clémentine was visiting Sofia with her sons Philipp and Ludwig August when she fell ill with the flu. Her doctors urged immediate travel to Menton in the south of France, and Clémentine duly set off, stopping in Vienna on 15 February when her strength ebbed. Here she briefly rallied. The following morning, when August visited his mother, she assured him that she was feeling much better and looked forward to continuing her journey. As soon as August left, Clémentine asked a lady-in-waiting to help her move from her bed to a sofa; within a few minutes, the Princess fainted. Doctors were immediately called but nothing could be done. The nearly ninety-year-old Princess Clémentine was dead. Emperor Franz Joseph personally came to the Coburg Palais to pay his respects and express his condolences to the princess' desolate children. Four days later, Clémentine's remains were taken to Coburg, where she rejoined her beloved husband after a quarter century of separation.

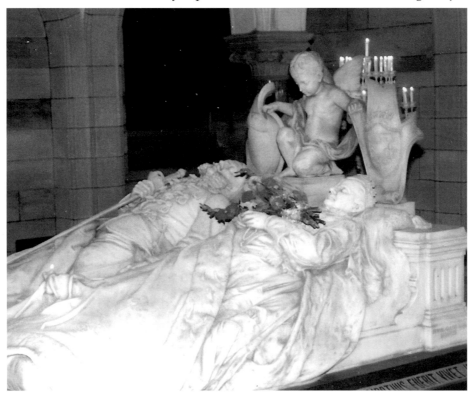

The marble tomb of Prince August and Princess Clémentine, Kohary Crypt, Coburg.

Clémentine was described as a *"remarkable woman…with shrewd counsels…and determination."* She once told a Bulgarian Prime Minister facing tough elections to *"conduct* [them] *with a firm hand."* The daring politician bravely replied, *"It is my belief that it is preferable for the people to express their choice freely,"* which only earned him Clémentine's anger. Sadly for the ambitious Clémentine, she did not live long enough to see Ferdinand crowned Tsar of the throne she had won for him. Ferdinand left his own tribute in the Latin inscription carved on his mother's grave in Coburg: *"A King's daughter, no Queen herself, yet a King's mother."*

CHAPTER XII
Enter Bulgaria
Alas, A Crown at Last

Prince Ferdinand of Saxe-Coburg & Gotha was born in Vienna on 26 February 1861. As a young man he was singularly attractive; even his long nose, inherited from his mother's side of the family, enhanced rather than marred his aristocratic bearing. The imposing Prince Ferdinand cut an elegant figure in Imperial Vienna, where Archduchess Louise of Austria-Tuscany deemed him *"handsome, rich and unassuming."* Ferdinand may have been unassuming, but he also had a taste for luxury, a pronounced fondness for exquisite jewels, and sexual tastes that were quite outside the norm for his times and made him the talk of royal Europe. Early on he learned to lead a double life. To his contemporaries Ferdinand appeared as a proud, erudite, and cosmopolitan Coburg prince; within beat a hearty egoism, accompanied by selfishness and a duplicity that, in time, earned him a lowly reputation among his peers. Ironically, these same traits allowed him to sail successfully between the two empires most threatened by his ambition, Russia and Austria.

Ferdinand became famous as ruler of Bulgaria, a nascent principality and eventually a kingdom in the volatile Balkans. His was no easy task. The disintegration of the Ottoman Empire gave Europe countless headaches, particularly after Russia developed an unhealthy appetite for the formerly Turkish Balkan territories. Greece had been the first to break from Turkey's yoke in the early 1830s; Serbia lived in a state of constant upheaval as two rival dynasties fought for power; and Romania became a state in the late 1850s. In 1861, after a failed experiment with a native prince, the Romanians chose Prince Karl of Hohenzollern as their ruler. Being a second son with no illustrious prospects, he accepted the offer and relocated to Bucharest, taking the name Prince Carol I. Two decades later Carol, who until then remained under the suzerainty of Constantinople, proclaimed his realm a kingdom.

Further Balkan trouble ignited in 1877, when Russia and the Ottoman Empire went to war. Russia had long promoted nationalist aspirations in the Balkans, seeking to extend her sphere of influence into Central Europe. Common Slav ancestry and ties of the Orthodox Church erupted into dangerous ideas of Russian protection and St. Petersburg's increased interference in the region. This Pan-Slavic movement worried most of Europe. In Berlin, Imperial Chancellor von Bismarck recognized the dangers involved in these ambitions; the Habsburg Monarchy in Vienna viewed Russian involvement in the Balkans as a direct threat to its own ambitions; and London worried about losing British domination in the Mediterranean.

The new state of Bulgaria became Emperor Alexander II's pet project. He wanted borders extending from the coasts of the Black Sea to the Aegean and encompassing large areas of Eastern Rumelia and Thrace, as well as Macedonia to serve as a buffer between Greece and Serbia. This was accomplished with the Treaty of San Stefano, which forced Turkey to recognize the independence of Romania, Serbia, and Montenegro, while Bulgaria was left as a suzerain of Istanbul. These terms, extracted from a collapsing Ottoman Empire, horrified Europe, and a conference was quickly called in Berlin to settle the issue. The Powers recognized the independence of Romania, Serbia, and Montenegro, and reduced Bulgaria's size. Although it technically remained a vassal state of the Ottoman Empire, Bulgaria gained its own constitution, flag, anthem, and foreign policy, measures that laid the groundwork for later complete independence.

After the Treaty of Berlin ended the conflict, Bulgarians had to find a new ruler, and Alexander II suggested his nephew, Prince Alexander of Battenberg, as the principality's first head of state. Born in Verona in 1857,

Left: A miniature portrait of Prince Ferdinand c. 1862 – owned by Princess Felicitas of Saxe-Coburg & Gotha.

Below: Prince Ferdinand photographed in Cannes in the 1880s.

Alexander was the second son of Prince Alexander of Hesse and By Rhine and his morganatic wife, the former Countess Julie von Hauke. He had entered military service at an early age and served with distinction. The Prince, said one contemporary, *"possessed much charm and amiability of manner; he was tall, dignified and strikingly handsome."* As the Emperor of Russia's nephew, Alexander seemed perfectly acceptable to Sofia and the Bulgarians duly elected him as their prince in 1879.

Prince Alexander immediately found himself torn. The Russians expected him to follow orders from St. Petersburg; the Bulgarians wanted their ruler to govern with their own national interests at heart. Alexander, unprepared for this difficult role, was caught in the middle of a disconcerting tug of war. His problems intensified in March 1881 when Alexander II was blown to bits while on his way to the Winter Palace. His successor, Alexander III, was not keen on his Battenberg cousin and emphasized that the Bulgarian ruler must tow the Russian line. The Prince, who attended his cousin Alexander III's splendid coronation in Moscow, soon realized that the tides were turning against him. Coincidentally, present at the coronation was Prince Ferdinand, who was representing his branch of the Coburg family. Alexander and Ferdinand met in Russia; although destined to rule over the same country, they would never again meet.

Once back in Sofia, Alexander of Bulgaria soon realized that his position vis-à-vis Russia had changed radically. Alexander III and his representatives increasingly meddled in Bulgarian affairs, and a desperate Prince sought aid in Berlin and Vienna. However, neither chancellery was willing to risk upsetting Alexander III over the fate of a minor Balkan ruler. Chancellor Bismarck even thwarted Prince Alexander's efforts to marry Princess Victoria of Prussia, fearing the possible effect on German-Russian relations. By 1886, Prince Alexander was exhausted, and the Russians took advantage of his weakened state to kidnap him. Although able to return to Sofia with the support of Bulgarian politicians led by the patriot Stefan Stambolov, Prince Alexander accepted that he could no longer remain ruler of Bulgaria. After abdicating in September 1886 he left Bulgaria.

Stambolov and Bulgarian politicians now began the search for a new ruler who would not upset the European Powers. They offered the throne to Prince Valdemar of Denmark, Alexander III's brother-in-law; when he failed to win approval, the Dane walked away from the proposal. Other candidates in Serbia, Weimar, Reuß, and Sweden were approached, but none dared risk the ire of Imperial Russia. The Bulgarians soon realized that the only royal who would accept their offer would be one daring enough to follow his own path and ignore the Powers. They found such a man in Prince Ferdinand of Saxe-Coburg-Kohary.

A Bulgarian delegation traveled to Vienna, where Ferdinand – aware of their intent – entrusted negotiations to intermediaries. After a successful meeting, Ferdinand asked the men to call on his mother Princess Clémentine at Schloß Ebenthal. The ambitious Clémentine welcomed the idea of seeing her favorite son on a throne, though many others were opposed. *"This candidacy is as ridiculous as the candidate,"* Emperor Alexander III said when informed of the proposal. Duke Ernst II of Saxe-Coburg & Gotha approached Bismarck to get a feeling for Germany's views on the candidacy. The Iron Chancellor tried his best to dissuade Duke Ernst II from supporting young Ferdinand because *"the undertaking would be launched against the advice of Austria and against the will of Russia, in my view, then, hopeless; and I fear that it would only increase Bulgarian complications, besides providing our Russian opponents with fresh material to promote the anti-German tendencies of Czar Alexander."*

After further consultations with his mother, Ferdinand demanded that the Bulgarians obtain international recognition, particularly from Russia and the Ottoman Empire. This was impossible: no one wanted to upset the Emperor of Russia, whose disdain for Prince Ferdinand was even more visceral than his dislike of Alexander of Battenberg. Ferdinand then demanded that the Bulgarian parliament elect him unanimously, which was done in July 1887. Diplomats took the election as *"a box on the ear of Russia,"* predicting more doom for Ferdinand. Giers, the Russian Foreign Minister, went as far as declaring: *"We shall never be able to recognize Ferdinand of Coburg."* Alexander III's opinion of the Bulgarian election was written on a report: *"A loathsome business!"*

Ferdinand decided to enter Bulgaria incognito, as Karl of Hohenzollern had done in 1861 when he left Germany for Romania. On 10 August 1887, the Prince boarded a second-class railway carriage and headed to meet his future in Bulgaria. He was dressed in civilian clothes and tried his best to avoid identification. Meanwhile, Vienna noticed his absence and speculation as to his whereabouts spread like wildfire. Everyone predicted Ferdinand's utter demise and the abject failure of his Bulgarian episode as an exercise in utter ambition. Of those close to Ferdinand, only Crown Prince Rudolf of Austria wished him a good journey. Rudolf, unhappily married to Stephanie of Belgium, sister-in-law of Ferdinand's brother Prince Philipp, was also politically frustrated; perhaps Rudolf secretly wished that he had the courage to act as decisively as did Ferdinand.

Prince Alexander of Bulgaria.

One day later, Ferdinand climbed off the train at Orsova, a port city on the Danube in southern Romania. The Alexander, the same vessel Alexander II had gifted to Alexander of Battenberg and which had taken him away from Bulgaria, awaited Ferdinand on the Danube. By this time, most of Europe had learned of Ferdinand's escapade. Some said that sections of the Danube were mined to prevent him from completing his journey. Yet, he ignored all warnings and boarded the *Alexander*, holding his first Privy Council aboard the yacht. Stefan Stambolov, to whom Ferdinand owed much, was among the politicians present.

Once in Bulgaria, Ferdinand headed to Tirnovo, the ancient capital, where on 13 August he swore to uphold the constitution. This was one of the many promises he would be only too willing to break in the future, particularly when his view of the country's interests clashed with those of his government or parliament. Stambolov, who served as prime minister for the first seven years of Ferdinand's reign, soon found out that Ferdinand was not particularly fond of pesky

Left: Schloß Ebenthal, Lower Austria, was Princess Clémentine's favorite country residence. It was from here that Ferdinand departed to embark on the Bulgarian adventure.

Below left: Tsar Alexander III of Russia was one of Ferdinand of Saxe-Coburg & Gotha's biggest detractors. The Tsar simply had no patience for someone of Ferdinand's character and inclination. Yet, in spite of Russian opposition, Ferdinand succeeded in gaining the Bulgarian throne.

and inconvenient legal impediments like constitutions. A Bourbon through and through, Ferdinand of Bulgaria's perception of his role as ruler of Bulgaria was more in tune to the governing style of his mother's French ancestors than that of his constitution-respecting fellow Coburg monarchs across Europe.

Ferdinand's ability to gain the Bulgarian throne was in no small degree a product of his mother's own machinations and personal ambitions. Once he was ensconced in the royal palace in Sofia, Clémentine lost little time before traveling to her son's side. *"The day after her arrival in Sofia, Princess Clémentine already established relations with the civil and military authorities, charity associations and the small group of ladies that formed high social circles of Sofia,"* according to one account. Clémentine's vast fortune allowed her to redecorate the royal palace with *"chandeliers hung from the ceilings; the walls covered with silks and velvets; the floors with Aubusson carpets."* Stambolov rejected this outward display of royal splendor, while some foreign diplomats stationed in Sofia scuffed at the excess of luxurious display. Princess Pauline Metternich once described the court of this Coburg as *"the most refined and exquisitely kept in Europe."* Bulgarians, wanting to see their country and its new ruler achieve European recognition, were awed by this display of wealth by their new prince, and Clémentine's work to better both the image and the lot of Bulgarians, which not coincidentally improved her son's image, proved

Right: The Royal Palace in Sofia was remodeled by King Ferdinand with assistance from his mother's incalculable wealth. By the time they were done, it was a luxuriously decorated residence reminiscent of the past glories of France.

Below right: Archduchess Louise of Tuscany wrote in her memoirs that she was one of Ferdinand's possible brides, but she rejected him. Instead, she married the future King Friedrich August III of Saxony and made a mess of things.

extremely important in Balkan politics.

Ferdinand was ambitious and clever. He took his role to heart and kept his place on the unstable throne using any available means. Archduchess Louise called him *"as cunning as a fox, as wise as a serpent, and strongly attracted to gold as Midas. I always think that in him the theatrical would have lost a fine comic opera king, for he looks as though he ought to be on the stage, singing about himself, and wooing a stage princess in the approved manner…He constantly waved his well-manicured hands, and displayed the costly rings which glittered on his fingers."* At heart, Ferdinand had his success, no matter what the cost would be or who would have to suffer in order for him to achieve those goals.

Whether it was Prime Minister Stambolov, the man to whom Ferdinand owed so much, or his promises to the Vatican, the Bulgarian monarch had no qualms when it came to choosing the most advantageous path. His *"slippery"* personality, along with a penchant for rarely letting anyone know where he stood, earned him the sobriquet of *"Foxy Ferdinand."* A Bulgarian patriot, Stambolov had been one of the founders of modern Bulgaria, and had served in parliament during Prince Alexander's reign. Despite his critical role in bring Ferdinand to the throne, Stambolov often found himself in open conflict with his monarch. *"Stambolov and Ferdinand were ensnared in a power struggle. On one side the politician wanted the ruler to behave within constitutional boundaries, on the other the prince wished to imprint Bulgaria with his own vision."* Ferdinand's desire for more political powers led to numerous confrontations, as Stambolov refused to weaken the Prime Minister's authority. By 1894 Stambolov had enough and resigned the office, becoming one of Ferdinand's staunchest critics. In early July 1895 bullets were fired at Stambolov as he rode in a carriage with a bodyguard and a friend. When the startled men jumped from the vehicle, more assailants attacked them with knives, which the former prime minister fended off using his hands. Stambolov was left mortally wounded, and it was widely believed that Ferdinand had been behind the assassination. As he lay on his deathbed, Stambolov said, *"Bulgaria's people will forgive me everything. But will they forgive that it was I who brought Ferdinand here?"* He would not be the last 'victim' of the Balkan Fox's career.

Finding Ferdinand of Bulgaria a wife proved to be an extremely difficult endeavor. Above all, he needed to marry an eligible princess and father an heir if his dynasty was to last in Bulgaria. Yet much of Europe regarded him as a pariah. There would certainly be no union with a Romanov Grand Duchess given Alexander III's antagonism. The idea of marrying an English princess, Ferdinand believed, would not only be an enormous coup, but it would also earn him British diplomatic support. A visit to Queen Victoria at Balmoral was arranged. Before crossing the Channel, Ferdinand and his mother Clémentine visited her brother the Duke d'Aumâle, who owned the fabulous Chantilly estate, inherited from the last Prince de Condé. Aumâle, who had not seen Ferdinand for several years, caustically greeted him: *"Is that you?...Well, there we are! I am like Europe...I don't recognize you!"* The trip to England proved pointless, as Ferdinand quickly learned that Queen Victoria and her government would not allow any British alliance, if not because of deep religious differences than out of fear over Russia's reaction to such a move.

Ferdinand was also unlucky in Berlin, where the Kaiser did his best to discourage a German alliance. Wilhelm II and his government shared fears that Russia would react badly to any union between a German princess and the Balkan pariah. *"The Imperial Government feels no necessity to adopt a position about the marriage of the Prince,"* the Prussians notified the Viennese government. As if this wasn't laconic enough, Ferdinand was urged not to request meetings with German authorities to spare himself the *"distress of a refusal."*

Prince Ferdinand of Bulgaria.

It soon enough became clear to Ferdinand that most doors were *"closed for fear of Russia."* Frustrated by the unsuccessful search, Ferdinand approached former Imperial Chancellor Otto von Bismarck, who recommended that Ferdinand *"be circumspect...You have shown the world that you can swim; but do not try to swim against the current...Time is your greatest ally...Avoid doing anything that might provoke your enemies...If you do not provoke them, they cannot act against you and in time the world will become used to seeing you on the throne of Bulgaria."* Bismarck was, of course, correct. In time, the great powers had no other option than to extend recognition to Ferdinand, the swimmer who they had turned into a ferocious shark.

The bridal search continued. There was, of course, no point in searching for a princess in France. The Orléans knew about Ferdinand's foibles, while the Bonapartes were not given any serious consideration. On top of this, France was closely allied to Russia and Paris would not risk upsetting St. Petersburg over such a marriage. The Court in Munich received a missive from the Kaiser forbidding the Wittelsbachs from offering Ferdinand a bride. *"A union between a Bavarian princess and the Prince of Bulgaria would be undesirable for the foreign policy of the German Reich,"* the Kaiser's government announced.

Portugal and Spain lacked available brides, while the Scandinavian monarchies, aware of Russian opposition, refused to entertain any proposals. As for Austria, where there were several archduchesses of marriageable age, Franz Joseph was unwilling to risk Russian displeasure. Instead, Vienna suggested that Ferdinand might find a bride from one of the exiled Italian houses then living within the Habsburg Empire.

Princess Clémentine, meanwhile, contacted Duke Robert of Parma (1848-1907). He had lost his throne in 1860 in the Italian reunification and found refuge in Austria. Robert, easily the wealthiest of the petty rulers who succumbed to the Risorgimento and Garibaldi's army, lived in great comfort. Schloß Schwarzau, his castle in Lower Austria, south of Vienna, was near Schloß Frohsdorf, home of his extremely wealthy uncle the Count de Chambord, France's Legitimist claimant. The Duke also had a second home, the Villa delle Pianore, in Camaiore, Tuscany.

In 1869 the Duke of Parma had married his first wife, Princess Maria Pia of Bourbon-Two Sicilies (1849-1882), in Rome, where their first child was born on January 27, 1870, nearly ten months after their wedding. Eleven more children followed over the next twelve years, including several who suffered from mental retardation. Exhausted, Maria Pia died in Biarritz a week after giving birth to a stillborn son.

Princess Marie Louise of Bulgaria.

Duke Robert did not remain a widower for long: in October 1884 he married Infanta Maria Antonia of Braganza, one of the many daughters of former King Miguel of Portugal and of his Löwenstein-Wertheim-Rosenberg wife. Robert and Maria Antonia also had twelve children, but this set enjoyed much better health than their half-siblings. Among the second set of children were Duke Xavier of Parma, Empress Zita of Austria, and Prince Felix of Luxembourg.

Princess Marie Louise, the Duke's eldest daughter from his first marriage, was known as a pious and gentle soul. Although Princess Clémentine described her as *"unhappily not very pretty,"* other memoirs paint a different picture. She had a long, narrow face and the prominent nose of her Bourbon ancestors, yet Anna Stancioff remembered Marie Louise as having *"beautiful blue eyes, and the color of aquamarine, large and transparently clear behind their thick dark lashes."* Slightly built, she was said to have *"a well delineated, sensitive humorous mouth, and a clever expression."* Queen Victoria even praised her *"beautiful English,"* which Marie Louise had learned from a talented and capable English governess, Miss Fanny Fraser.

The fact that her father had lost his throne three decades before did little to reduce the appeal of the Bourbons of Parma. Not only did they have excellent connections with the various Catholic courts around Europe, but Duke Robert was a close friend of Emperor Franz Joseph, who extended these exiles countless prerogatives, as well as welcoming them into Viennese court society. Prime Minister Stephan Stambolov agreed with Princess Clémentine that, given Prince Ferdinand's lack of success with the ruling dynasties, an exiled one would do just as well.

Left: Prince Ferdinand of Bulgaria and his wife Princess Marie Louise.

Below: Princess Marie Louise with her firstborn, Crown Prince Boris.

daughter of the Duke of Parma. He recommends the dear fiancées to your affection." In her journal the Queen conveyed her positive impressions of the announcement *"as Ferdinand has been wanting to marry so long, and as Bulgaria wished it so ardently."* On 20 April 1893, the coupled married at Pianore.

Bulgaria was delighted with Marie Louise's arrival. A national collection raised some 300,000 francs, an astronomical sum at the time, of which two thirds paid for an exquisite tiara with a fleur-de-lis motif in homage of her Bourbon lineage. The tiara was made of *"rubies, emeralds and diamonds, the Bulgarian national colors."* The remainder of the collection, at Marie Louise's request, went to build a maternity hospital.

On 13 January 1894 Marie Louise gave birth to Crown Prince Boris at the royal palace in Sofia. Although the constitution had previously been amended to allow for any children to be raised in the Catholic faith, Ferdinand knew that Bulgarian public opinion would rebel against such a move. When Ferdinand had Boris baptized in the Orthodox Church, Duke Robert was livid and the Pope nearly apoplectic. Ferdinand's perfidy, both ardently believed, knew no bounds. Relations with the Parmas were damaged, while the Vatican lost little time in excommunicating Ferdinand. Neither reaction mattered much to the Prince, who even ignored his own mother's fury on learning that Boris would not be a Catholic. *"Lay low and let time pass"* was a lesson that Ferdinand never forgot. In the end, Ferdinand knew that his dynasty's demands trumped any inconvenience caused to his in-laws or to the Pope.

Stambolov was concerned with Duke Robert's demands that the couple's children be raised in the Catholic faith. Article 38 of the Bulgarian Constitution required that the heir to the throne should be baptized in the Orthodox Church. Fearing that the marriage negotiations would collapse, Stambolov took it upon himself to convince parliament to change the constitution. The prime minister knew that there would be a political price for him to pay, but faced with an increasingly short list of possible brides, Stambolov was willing to take the public blame. With this demand satisfied, Duke Robert gave his approval for the marriage to take place.

Ferdinand and Marie Louise scarcely knew each other when they became engaged at Schwarzau, but a delighted Clémentine telegraphed her cousin Queen Victoria in London: *"Happy to announce the engagement of Ferdinand with Princess Marie-Louise de Bourbon,*

A second son, Kyril, was born in 1895 and also – much to the annoyance of the Parmas, the Vatican, and his own mother – baptized into the Orthodox Church. In early 1898 Marie Louise gave birth to a daughter, Eudoxia, and a year later another daughter, Nadejda, arrived. Four pregnancies in five years compromised the delicate Marie Louise's health, and Nadejda's difficult birth left her mother exhausted. Unable to recover, she died in 1899.

Princess Clémentine served as mother to her son's children, showering them with devoted attentions as she relished the opportunity to be of service to her son and his kingdom. Unfortunately, the elderly Clémentine's death in 1907 robbed Ferdinand's children of yet another maternal figure. Despite his personal inclinations, Ferdinand realized that both Bulgaria and his children needed a consort and a mother. Later that year, after mourning for his mother ended, Ferdinand hosted Grand Duke Vladimir Alexandrovich and his wife, the famed Grand Duchess Maria Pavlovna, who was one of the Prince's close friends. *"He told the Grand Duchess that, 'he wanted a woman who would look after his four children and take an interest in the national charities. He did not want a wife who would expect affection or even get attention.'"* Maria Pavlovna, no stranger to Ferdinand's peculiarities, joined the search and suggested to her friend a Reuß cousin whom she knew would accept the role. Her name was Eleonore and she possessed not only a pleasant disposition but she was also no stranger to personal sacrifices.

Princess Eleonore Reuß zu Köstritz was born at her family estate, Trebschen, on 22 September 1860. She was the daughter of Prince Heinrich IV and of his wife, the former Princess Luise Reuß zu Greiz. Grand Duchess Maria Pavlovna was rather fond of her first cousin Eleonore (Maria Pavlovna's mother was Heinrich's sister). Princess Luise had died in 1875, leaving her widower with three young children, and from an early age Eleonore had dedicated herself to selfless nurturing. She felt a deep sense of accomplishment in giving of herself and took nursing courses, a vocation to which she felt deep devotion. Her Red Cross training, which in Germany was administered by the 'Johanniter' Sisters, led to a position in a Dresden hospital, and she later served as the district nurse for Luben, a voluntary position often given to aristocratic ladies. Eleonore felt medical conditions in the army needed much improvement, and she visited countless hospitals and observed military maneuvers, taking note of the lack of trained medical staff and the poor care regular soldiers received when wounded. Princess Eleonore used her experiences to *"induce the highest military officials to grant several reforms and improvements which had long been desired by the medical branch of the service."* Among aristocratic women, Eleonore was perceived as *"exceptional."* Others considered Eleonore a woman of *"incorruptible integrity."*

King Ferdinand of Bulgaria's children: Crown Prince Boris, Prince Kyril, Princess Eudoxia and Princess Nadejda.

Eleonore twice turned down Ferdinand's offer of marriage. There were worries over his sexual peculiarities; she was also a Lutheran, and he was an estranged Catholic who was raising his sons in the Orthodox faith of his kingdom. Believing that she could be of service to Bulgaria and help raise the Prince's children, she finally agreed to Ferdinand's proposal. There were actually two wedding ceremonies. The Catholic Rite took place in Coburg on 28 February 1908, and the Lutheran service followed at Schloß

The marriage of Prince Ferdinand of Bulgaria and Eleonore Reuß zu Köstritz, Schloß Osterstein, Gera. On the floor, from left: Prince Hermann of Stolberg-Wernigerode, Prince Heinrich XXXIV Reuß, Prince Heinrich XXXIX Reuß, Prince Heinrich XLI Reuß, Prince Heinrich XXXV, the Fürst of Stolberg-Wernigerode. Second row (seated): Prince Heinrich XXXIII Reuß, Prince Heinrich XXVII Reuß, the Fürst Reuß zu Köstritz, Hereditary Prince Heinrich XXVII Reuß zu Schleiz, Duchess Dorothea of Schleswig-Holstein, Grand Duchess Maria Pavlovna of Russia, the Bride and Groom. Third row (standing): Prince Leopold of Saxe-Coburg & Gotha, Prince Hugo zu Dietrichstein, Count Mensdorff-Pouilly, Hereditary Prince Ernst of Hohenlohe-Langenburg, Duke Ernst Günther of Schleswig-Holstein, Grand Duke Vladimir Alexandrovich of Russia, Princess Ida Reuß, the Fürstin of Stolberg-Wernigerode, Prince Philipp of Saxe-Coburg & Gotha, Princess Marie of Saxe-Altenburg, Fürstin Elisabeth Reuß zu Köstritz, Princess Sybille Reuß, Princess Marie of Saxe-Altenburg. Fourth row (in back): Duke Johann Albrecht of Mecklenburg-Schwerin, Princess Feodora Reuß, Princess Sophie Reuß, Prince Heinrich XXXII Reuß, Duke Carl Eduard of Saxe-Coburg & Gotha.

Osterstein in Gera. Existing photos of the wedding ceremonies show Ferdinand and Eleonore staring into the camera with expressionless resignation, and guests noted that during the festivities, Ferdinand showed little enthusiasm, *"but was very affable to his hosts and interested in the long history of the house of Reuß."*

Just in case Eleonore needed a reminder of what life with her husband was to be, Ferdinand brutally reminded her of their arrangement. Soon after the wedding in Gera, the couple traveled to Romania on an official visit to King Carol I. Ferdinand threw a fit on learning that he was to share the guest suite with his bride, and demanded that they *"be given separate quarters."* Ferdinand's unkindness toward Eleonore eventually led to many rumors. Whether true or just malicious gossip, such was Ferdinand's reputation that many accepted their veracity. It was said that he notified Eleonore that she was only required to join his dinner table at official banquets; on other occasions, she could have her meals alone in her own apartments at the royal palace. On smelling the odor of food in a palace hallway, went another story, Ferdinand allegedly insisted: *"In future, if the Queen dines in her apartments, she is to be brought cold meals."*

Several authors have questioned whether the marriage was ever consummated. Eleonore was nearly fifty and Ferdinand had four children. Then there was the issue of Ferdinand's sexual orientation; his interests lay more in the company of tall, slender, blonde young men than in the marital bedchamber. His royal guard was famous for boasting some of the best looking specimens of Bulgarian masculinity. While many historians have accused Ferdinand of being a homosexual, he was quite likely a bisexual with homosexual tendencies. He is reported to have been oversexed and indiscriminate when it came to sexual partners. In Vienna and Paris Ferdinand could find easy outlets for his sexual escapades, but such was not the case in Sofia, where he had to be discreet. Ferdinand was extremely conscious of his royal persona: once, after a banquet in Potsdam, Kaiser Wilhelm II, who had a tendency to cause untoward episodes, smacked Ferdinand's ever enlarging behind and laughed loudly. The Bulgarian ruler was not only livid but he demanded an immediate apology for the transgression. The Kaiser, known for his bullying sense of humor, refused, insisting it had merely been *"a joke."* Only when a furious Ferdinand left and tempers calmed did Wilhelm II express his regret. Ferdinand exacted the ultimate revenge when he gave an arms contract to a French firm instead of the Krupp arms factories in Essen. Princess Radziwill reminisced: *"I fear Germany's Balkan policy is going to feel this blow on the backside."*

King Ferdinand and his children, from left: Princess Eudoxia, Crown Prince Boris, King Ferdinand, Prince Kyril and Princess Nadejda. He was a demanding and prickly father who the children feared.

Queen Eleonore proved to be a great success with her stepchildren and the Bulgarian people, much to Ferdinand's shock. Boris, Ferdinand's eldest son, was very fond of Eleonore and *"liked and respected her."* It is said that at times Boris was deeply embarrassed by Ferdinand's abusive treatment of Eleonore. One such episode happened in 1911. While he was out of the country, Eleonore invited Queen Elisabeth of Romania to stay for a short visit at Euxinograd, the Bulgarian royal summer retreat on the Black Sea coast built by Ferdinand after the French palace of St. Cloud. In an unkind telegram to Boris, Ferdinand protested this visit of *"two half-mad royal women, who concocted this affair together, taking advantage of my absence."*

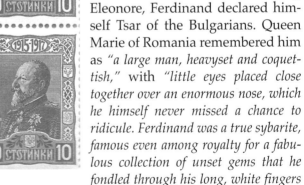

Eleonore's nursing training allowed her to reform Bulgaria's medical services, and she played an important role in *"organizing hospital work with efficiency and genuine compassion."* Ferdinand, who had a phobia about hospitals, blood, germs, and infections and was something of a hypochondriac, was suspicious of such interests and happy for his wife's passion for what he called *"these abominations."*

In 1908, months after marrying Eleonore, Ferdinand declared himself Tsar of the Bulgarians. Queen Marie of Romania remembered him as *"a large man, heavyset and coquettish,"* with *"little eyes placed close together over an enormous nose, which he himself never missed a chance to ridicule. Ferdinand was a true sybarite, famous even among royalty for a fabulous collection of unset gems that he fondled through his long, white fingers like worry beads."* Ferdinand spent great energy in securing his role among the other crowned heads of Europe, many of who scorned his existence. This led to hilarious incidents in which the Bulgarian ruler went to great efforts to remind his royal peers of his position. In 1910, while on his journey to the funeral of his second cousin, King Edward VII, a near-diplomatic confrontation broke out over where his private railway carriage would be positioned in relation to that of the heir to the Austro-Hungarian throne, Archduke Franz Ferdinand. The Austrian Heir won out, having his carriage positioned directly behind the engine, and Ferdinand's was placed directly behind. Realizing the dining car of the train was behind his own carriage, Ferdinand obtained his revenge on the Archduke by refusing him entry through his own carriage to take his meals. This forced Franz Ferdinand and his entourage to exit his carriage at a scheduled stop and run along the station platform to board the dining car, then wait until the next stop to return to their own compartment. Franz Ferdinand was not amused, nor was Kaiser Wilhelm II, who sided with the Austrian over his Bulgarian cousin.

During the funeral in London, his fellow sovereigns made light of Ferdinand's penchant for protocol, uniforms, and what they considered his out-dated adherence to precedence. His Portuguese cousin King Manoel II baited Ferdinand and teased the Bulgarian Coburg much to the hilarity of those around him. Without a second thought, Ferdinand turned around and icily told Manoel off: *"Laugh, laugh away my dear cousin, I am indeed a King of yesterday, but are you quite certain of being a King of tomorrow?"* This proved prescient: by year's end, Manoel II found himself living in exile in London, his throne replaced by a republic.

Ferdinand never quite overcame the sense that much of Europe disliked him, yet he craved acceptance by the Great Powers, particularly his beloved Austria, land of his birth. While he disliked Archduke Franz Ferdinand, Ferdinand had a deep veneration for Emperor Franz Joseph and sought his support. Obtaining the venerable Order of the Golden Fleece from the august Habsburg ruler became a raison d'être for the Bulgarian upstart. As the years passed and the decoration was not forthcoming, Ferdinand grew more irascible when discussing what he saw as an affront from the Habsburg imperial court. Ferdinand's fury knew no bounds when he learned that Crown Prince Ferdinand of Romania received the decoration before him: How could *"that useless incompetent who has never done anything receive the Golden Fleece, which they refuse to give me after twenty-one years on the throne, a reign which has been by no means an easy one – I am not one of those who are born with a crown attached to their umbilical cord."* Ferdinand's ire abated when Emperor Franz Joseph finally made him a Knight of the Golden Fleece.

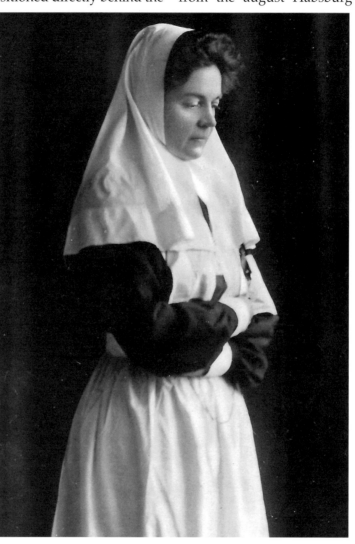
Queen Eleonore of Bulgaria wearing nurse's uniform, 1915.

In her book *Victoria and the Coburgs*, Dulcie Ashdown best summarized Ferdinand's accomplishments: *"Foxy Ferdy they called him, and not only because his long, sharp nose and his pointed ginger beard lent him a remarkable resemblance to a caricatured fox: he had also proved the characteristics traditionally ascribed to that animal, in his guile in Bulgarian politics, his wily persuasion of influential powers, his soft wooing turning without warning into a pouncing attack. Yet he was still a man to be admired. Had he not transformed a backward, unstable satellite into an industrialized, firmly governed, independent nation, of which he himself was indubitably the leading statesman? Had he not won recognition from the Great Powers that had formerly derid-*

ed him? His Coburg forebears might quail at his methods, for he had not the Coburg morality, but the results were only what they themselves had sought to achieve elsewhere. It was Ferdinand's misfortune, as much as his fault, that coming events would deprive him of the throne he had worked so hard to fill."

The First and Second Balkan Wars plunged Bulgaria into a crisis. Eleonore worked indefatigably as a nurse, and her presence in field hospitals was a source of great comfort to countless injured and dying soldiers. A noted biographer once deservedly described Eleonore as a *"capable and kindhearted"* woman whom her husband had *"always neglected so shamefully."* Bulgarian losses were heavy, and the peace lasted a mere year before the outbreak of the Great War. Ferdinand made a fateful decision that summer of 1914, joining Germany and Austria-Hungary in the conflict against Great Britain, France, and Russia.

Right: Grand Duchess Maria Pavlovna and her very good friend, Ferdinand of Bulgaria.

Below: King Ferdinand and Emperor Karl during the Great War. Besides being Austria-Hungary's ally, Ferdinand was firstly married to a half-sister of Karl's consort.

Eleonore again threw herself into wartime work, and her attention *"in the Clémentine Hospital in Sofia had been unstinting."* An observer, in awe of her delicate touch and attention to the welfare of those under her care, believed that she had *"a special gift for relieving suffering."* Countless obligations, though, left her exhausted and ill, and Eleonore's physical condition steadily declined. By summer 1917, it was obvious to all around her, even to Ferdinand – who had finally come to realize what an amazing asset his wife was – that the end was near. Eleonore died at Euxinograd on 22 September 1917. Not wishing to detract from Bulgaria's war efforts, she asked that her remains be quietly buried in the cemetery of a medieval church near Sofia. She rested there until

1946, when Bulgaria fell prey to the Communists. Her grave was desecrated, her corpse robbed of jewels, and the gravestone was destroyed and bulldozed to the ground. It was not until Bulgaria overthrew the Communist yoke that the grave of this beloved and self-sacrificing queen was restored to its original state.

For all of his canny political acumen, Ferdinand could not fight the tide of history, and in October 1918 he was forced to abdicate the throne in order to save the dynasty. In leaving the crown to his son Boris, he pompously declared, *"I am becoming your subject, but I remain your father."*

Ferdinand left Bulgaria, and eventually settled in Coburg, living at the Burglaßschloßen, the small town palace that had once served as home to the most famous Coburg military figure, Prince Friedrich Josias. As the situation in Austria worsened and the Habsburgs seemed headed toward the abyss, Prince

Left: Prince Ferdinand of Bulgaria enjoying the outdoors.

Above: Euxinograd, Ferdinand's French-style castle.

Below: A photo of King Ferdinand signed in exile in 1920.

Philipp, Ferdinand's remaining brother, also relocated to Coburg and shared the same residence.

In exile Ferdinand spent time trying to rebuild his image. He dedicated photos, signing them: *"Le vieil Exilé! J'expie tout le bien et le bon de mon passé"* ("The old exile! I expiate all the good in my past!"). Exile, however, seemed to suit him as he could now dedicate his attention to myriad hobbies, travel being one of his favorite pastimes. He was able to follow his whims because, despite the abdication, Ferdinand remained very wealthy. He had left vast amounts of money in London banks. When the British government declared these deposits forfeit as enemy property, Ferdinand craftily proved that the money was initially deposited by his mother and thus managed to regain it. He also used the courts to force the German government to pay him large sums promised him by the Kaiser's government if he joined the Central Powers. Vilified in the German press for this legal process, Ferdinand ignored all criticism and won the lawsuit.

Ferdinand enjoyed natural history and kept large aviaries in his Coburg residence. He also traveled extensively to South America and various regions of Africa to conduct studies. He remained a lifelong devoté of Wagner and was a frequent visitor to his widow Cosima, as well as a regular attendee to the festivals yearly held in Bayreuth, not far from Coburg.

Once, when interviewed by an English writer, Ferdinand summarized the outcome of post-war history, saying, *"Is not France tiresome? She is most tiresomely drunk with victory, forgetting she might have been annihilated if America had not come in. And how France hates me. Like my ancestor Philippe Egalité, my papers are not quite in order. You must understand I refuse to meddle in politics; as a political power I am completely negligible. I went into the Monarchy to benefit mankind, but I was too progressive for Europe. My relative, the late King Léopold II of Belgium, who also worked for*

Royal visitors to the Vatican, 1925. From left (surrounded by Vatican officials) are Infante Alfonso and Infanta Beatrice of Spain (Orléans), King Ferdinand of Bulgaria, Monsignor Canali, Duchess Nadejda and Duke Albrecht Eugen of Württemberg.

the advancement of his country, did not receive adequate recognition during his lifetime – but his domestic discords did much to alienate popular sympathy."

Always conscious of protocol and his role in history, Ferdinand could embarrass his extended family. While attending the wedding of his son King Boris III to Princess Giovanna of Savoy, third daughter of King Vittorio Emanuele III and Queen Elena of Italy, he had a run-in with Princess Françoise of Greece, wife of Prince Christopher and daughter of the Duke de Guise, Head of House France. *"I have always felt more Orléans than Coburg,"* Ferdinand giddily said to Françoise. Bitingly, she replied, *"So, Uncle, you have already forgotten the war!"* Two years later, *"gaily attired in black breeches, a shimmering gold tunic and a large black beret surmounted by a gold and jeweled aigrette,"* Ferdinand attended the wedding of Sibylla of Saxe-Coburg & Gotha to Prince Gustav Adolf of Sweden. Using his walking stick, *"something between a scepter and a field marshal's baton,"* he brushed aside anyone who dared take precedence over him. Among his victims was Grand Duchess Victoria Feodorovna, his particular rival on matters of precedence, whose derrière had a terribly disconcerting encounter with the dreaded walking stick Ferdinand managed with such efficacy and ease.

King Ferdinand of Bulgaria later in life.

The Second World War was responsible for destroying the life Ferdinand built for himself in quaint Coburg. While his cousin Carl Eduard had been an enthusiastic supporter of National Socialism, Ferdinand resented Hitler's persecution of Jews and Catholics. He was most disturbed by the difficulties his daughter Nadejda experienced for raising her children as Catholics. In 1943 Ferdinand lost his son Boris, while two years later Prince Regent Kyril also met an untimely death. The old Tsar died in 1948, two years after the fall of the throne he had painstakingly built. He was buried at the foot of his parents' marble sarcophagus inside the Kohary Gruft, under the Church of Saint Augustin in Coburg.

Chapter XIII
Duke Carl Eduard
Fortune and Position Withered

Born in 1853, Prince Leopold – youngest son of Queen Victoria and Prince Albert – suffered from hemophilia and occasional epileptic fits. His delicate health resulted in a sheltered childhood, where Leopold was overprotected against any small bumps or exertion that might lead to tragedy. Leopold strained against this lonely existence, which kept him shielded from the activities of other boys his age. He compensated by arguably becoming the smartest of the Queen's four sons. He attended Oxford, and in 1876 received an honorary doctorate in civil law. During this time, he developed a friendship with Alice Liddell, daughter of Oxford's Vice-Chancellor and the girl for whom Lewis Carroll wrote *Alice's Adventures in Wonderland*. He later became godfather to Alice's second son, a boy named Leopold in his honor.

Hemophilia made it impossible for Leopold to follow a military career, and instead he was tasked with the unenviable duty of serving as his mother's secretary. She rewarded him with the title of Duke of Albany, but the funereal gloom of the Queen's court only enhanced Leopold's desire to escape. He was particularly close to his sister Alice and her husband Ludwig, who became reigning Grand Duke of Hesse and By Rhine in 1877, and often spent time with the family in Darmstadt. Married life, Leopold believed, would offer the independence he craved. Queen Victoria opposed the idea, hating the notion of sharing her son with someone else and potentially exposing him to new risks, but in the end Leopold won.

Finding a willing bride, though, was fraught with difficulty. Many eligible princesses balked at the thought of marrying the queen's son only to act as his nurse, and Queen Victoria agreed that he could wed an English wife. At one point, Leopold considered Daisy Maynard, an heiress nearly eight years his junior; this idea collapsed when Leopold learned that his friend Francis Greville was interested in her. In 1893 Greville succeeded his father as the 5th Earl of Warwick, and Daisy went on to great fame as mistress to Leopold's brother the Prince of Wales, the future Edward VII.

The next potential candidate was Princess Friederike of Hannover, youngest child of Queen Victoria's first cousin, the blind, exiled King Georg V. The Hanovers had lost their throne in 1866 when Prussia annexed their realm as punishment for Georg V's support of Austria during the Seven Weeks' War. Friederike resisted Leopold's courtship as she was already in love with Baron Alfons von Pawel-Rammingen, whom she married in 1880 against the wishes of her family, who expected a more suitable husband. Leopold also courted Princess Victoria of Baden, but her parents – especially her mother – had a far grander alliance in store for the young woman: in 1881, Victoria married Crown Prince Gustaf of Sweden. Leopold made unsuccessful overtures to his cousin Princess Karoline-Mathilde of Schleswig-Holstein-Sonderburg-Augustenburg, whose sister later married the future Kaiser Wilhelm II. Karoline-Mathilde, who was a granddaughter of Fürstin Feodora of Hohenlohe-Langenburg, Queen Victoria's beloved half-sister, politely ignored Leopold and later married a distant cousin, Friedrich Ferdinand of Schleswig-Holstein-Sonderburg-Glücksburg by whom she had several children, three of them destined to marry descendants of Queen Victoria. Yet another prospective bride was Princess Elisabeth of Hesse-Kassel, eldest daughter of Landgrave Friedrich and of his second wife the former Princess Anne of Prussia. This attempt also floundered and the young princess instead married another Leopold, the Hereditary Prince of Anhalt. Ironically, her Leopold also died unexpectedly before the age of thirty-one while visiting Cannes.

Opposite page: A new duke arrives. Carl Eduard greets well-wishers at Sonnefeld near Coburg. With him is Hereditary Prince Ernst of Hohenlohe-Langenburg, who acted as regent of Coburg and Gotha during Carl Eduard's minority.

Left: Prince Leopold, Duke of Albany.

Below: Princess Helene of Waldeck-Pyrmont, who in 1882 married the Duke of Albany.

Although Queen Victoria remained skeptical about her youngest son marrying, she now suggested that a sturdy German wife might be best. Her choice, Helene, was one of the daughters of Fürst Georg Viktor of Waldeck-Pyrmont and his wife, the former Princess Helene of Nassau. The Queen had once described their offspring as *"enormous, fine children but with…literally no noses!"* Although the Waldeck-Pyrmont children grew sturdy at Schloß Arolsen, a large, beautiful XVIII century baroque castle, their snub noses marred their looks. The daughters, though, were healthy, strong, and seemed quite fertile. Emma (1858-1934) became the second wife of King Willem III of the Netherlands in 1879 and mother of the future Queen Wilhelmina. Another daughter, Pauline (1855-1925), married Hereditary Prince Alexis zu Bentheim und Steinfurt in 1881; while Marie (1857-1882) wed the future King Wilhelm II of Württemberg.

Leopold initially resisted the idea of marrying the young Princess Helene. *"What is to be done about the Waldecks'"* he wrote to his brother-in-law Grand Duke Ludwig IV of Hesse and By Rhine in the summer of 1881. *"I'm so dreading meeting the princess."* Perhaps Leopold feared yet another refusal, but his mother insisted. A short visit to the Fürstin of Waldeck-Pyrmont and her two daughters, Leopold noted, left him *"much pleased."*

Months went by with no public mention of any engagement, but behind the scenes negotiations were furious. A report about Leopold's health seemingly satisfied the Waldecks, and in November the Duke of Albany returned to Arolsen, where for the first time he was allowed to spend time alone with Helene. On 18 November 1881, after a private talk with Fürst Georg Viktor, Leopold went to his daughter and, *"after luncheon, being alone with Helen, the great question was settled, to my intense happiness."* News spread quickly and congratulatory letters soon reached Arolsen. Queen Victoria, however, was *"after a moment of agitation quite calm, & I only hope she will remain so,"* wrote Princess Beatrice. It took the queen a full week before bringing herself to write *"a very kind and welcoming letter"* to her future daughter-in-law.

Once resigned to the idea that her youngest son had escaped her grasp, Queen Victoria arranged for the wedding to take place at Windsor Castle on 27 April 1882. It was a cool and cloudy day, yet crowds gathered enthusiastically to watch the procession. Leopold rode with his supporters, his brother the Prince of Wales and their brother-in-law Grand Duke Ludwig IV of Hesse and By Rhine. The groom, recovering from a bout of hemophilia, had to use a cane throughout the day, but according to a reporter from the *Illustrated London News* few noticed. The bride's arrival was spectacular as *"the sun broke through the clouds…[and] the ceremony was conducted in a blaze of light and colour."*

The couple received an impressive array of wedding gifts. The Queen gave Princess Helene *"a pearl and diamond necklace, an amethyst and diamond necklace, a parure of coral cameos, an old enamel and diamond brooch and earrings, [and] a portrait of the bride."* The Prince of

Wales gifted his brother a beautiful piano, much to Leopold's delight, along with *"a diamond fleurs-de-lis and a Russian silver-gilt tea service."* The Empress Eugénie, a great favorite of Leopold's, was not outdone and gave the couple *"a set of silver plates and a diamond ring."* The Duke and Duchess of Edinburgh's gift was *"a ruby and diamond bracelet and a Russian liqueur service,"* in addition to the beautiful jewelry Marie Alexandrovna had already given to Leopold's fiancée. The bride's parents gave the couple *"a necklace and sun rays in diamonds, as well as a silver-gilt breakfast service."* From the King and Queen of the Netherlands came *"a large diamond spray and a Deventer carpet,"* while Helene's brother gave them *"a bronze tazza and cigar lamp."* Helene's sister Marie and her husband Wilhelm of Württemberg regaled them with *"a pearl and diamond butterfly,"* while her sister Pauline and her husband presented them with *"a large china jardinière."* There were countless other gifts, many precious, some functional. Leopold's beloved cousin Friederike of Hannover, always in precarious finances, gave them "silver-gilt candlesticks."

Right: The Duchess of Albany and her children in 1884.

Below: The Duchess of Albany and her children circa 1888.

The Duke and Duchess of Albany settled at Claremont House, the former home of King Léopold I of the Belgians, which the Queen had given to Prince Leopold so that he would have his own establishment. Parliament voted a stipend of £10,000 to renovate the building, while Prince Leopold was given a yearly stipend amounting to £25,000. If widowed, the Duchess of Albany would receive a yearly pension of £6,000. Although not huge sums by royal standards, these amounts were enough to keep the Albanys in some luxury and eliminate financial worries.

Ten months after their wedding, Leopold and Helene welcomed their first child, a baby girl whom they named Alice. She would grow up to become an institution all her own within the Royal Family, as well as Queen Victoria's longest-lived grandchild. Alice, who carried hemophilia, married Prince Alexander of Teck, brother-in-law of the future King George V. In 1917, when the British Royal Family swept away their former German titles, Alexander became Earl of Athlone. Enjoying a successful military career, as well as serving as Governor-General of the Union of South Africa and of Canada, Athlone became a beloved uncle to the children of both of his brothers-in-law.

By early 1884 Helene was again pregnant, much to her husband's delight. Leopold's happiness, however, was short-lived. Cold winter water wreaked havoc on his health, causing rheumatism and extreme pain from *"swelling of the smaller joints."* When Helene fell ill, she could not accompany him to Cannes, where it was hoped that the mild weather would improve Leopold's condition. As his health improved, Leopold left his rooms at the Villa Nevada and began planning his attendance at the coming wedding of his niece Victoria of Hesse and By Rhine to his friend Prince Louis of Battenberg. One day, though, he fell and badly struck his knee. Heavy doses of morphine could only help assuage the pain as he hemorrhaged. Whether due to the fall or the medication, Leopold's condition did not improve. In the early hours of 28

March he went into convulsions. Nothing could be done, and Leopold died, ten days shy of his thirty-first birthday.

Helene was stunned on receiving the telegram saying that her husband had died. The Prince of Wales traveled to Cannes to retrieve Leopold's body and bring it back for interment at St. George's Chapel, Windsor. The Queen was devastated. In a letter to her daughter Victoria, she wrote: *"This is an awful blow. For him we must not repine; his young life was a succession of trials and sufferings though he was so happy in his marriage. And there was such a restless longing for what he could not have."* She traveled to Claremont and from there wrote her eldest daughter another letter in which she expressed her admiration for Helene's stoicism: *"After the short service, at which we all the family were, we drove up to the Castle. Dear Helene…so touching resigned and calm…bore it like an angel. Her whole behaviour is beyond praise."*

Nearly four months later, and a few weeks before the baby was due, Helene gave birth to Leopold's long awaited son. *"God has granted you a son of consolation in your great sorrow and I pray that the little child I was so happy to welcome into this world may grow up to be a comfort and support to you,"* wrote Sir William Harcourt, the cabinet minister tasked with certification of the birth. Christened with the names Leopold Charles Edward George Albert, the boy would always be known as Charles Edward, perhaps a late tribute to his father's passion for the Stuarts. Within the family he was also referred to as *"Charlie."* Queen Victoria later reported on the baby, writing to her granddaughter Victoria of Battenberg – who had loved her late uncle dearly – that *"Charlie"* was a *"pretty healthy looking baby – very like Uncle Leopd. – his eyes quite remarkably so."*

Princess Alice of Albany (later Countess of Athlone).

The Albany children were brought up at Claremont, *"an attractive place,"* said Princess Alice, who recalled her *"affectionate memories"* of life there. The Duchess of Albany's finances, although somewhat constrained given Leopold's will and her annual allowance of £6,000, still allowed her to hire a full staff, including nannies, footmen, ladies-in-waiting, a comptroller, a butler, an under-butler, a housekeeper, cooks, and maids, and even a horse master. When not at home, where the children were tutored, they could be found visiting Queen Victoria at her various residences, as well as the Duke and Duchess of Connaught's children, their cousins closest in age. The Duchess frequently took the children to visit her parents in Arolsen and Pyrmont, as well as her sisters in the Netherlands and Germany, establishing relations with many of their continental cousins. There were, though, few friends outside the family circle. While Alice was gregarious, Charles Edward was a highly-strung, nervous, tiresome, and delicate boy lacking his sister's mettle.

Helene, said her daughter Alice, *"was wonderful with children, who all adored her as we did. At the same time she was a strict disciplinarian, sometimes too domineering in her anxiety to bring us very ordinary little urchins up as perfect beings. My brother even feared her, which was a great handicap, as it tended to make him evade independent decisions as he grew up."* This fear of his mother, coupled with the presence early on of a nanny who found Charles Edward a difficult child, marred his early development.

The death of their cousin Alfred Jr. of Saxe-Coburg & Gotha, Alice recalled, *"brought a dramatic change to our lives."* Suggestions that the Duke of Connaught or his son be offered the succession came to nothing. *"The Queen is rather overwhelmed by her family and the Coburg succession problems, endless discussions, some of them rather stormy,"* wrote Marie Mallet, one of her Maids-of-Honor. After much squabbling and several frayed egos, the succession was settled on Charles Edward. *"Poor Aunt Marie and Uncle Alfred's wishes about young Arthur, I fear are an impossibility wh. Ernie (Ernst Ludwig of Hesse and By Rhine) will be able to tell you,"* the Queen wrote to her granddaughter Princess Victoria of Battenberg. *"The whole family is united in thinking it must be Charlie. But Uncle A. has got* [it] *into his head that it must be young Arthur. I will not here dwell on the almost if not quite insuperable difficulties of that & all the advantages of the other arrangement."*

After attending a preparatory school at Lyndhurst, Charles Edward had gone on to Eton, and it was there that he first learned of his possible nomination as heir to the Coburg throne. Queen Victoria wrote to her grandson Kaiser Wilhelm II: *"Respecting the Coburg affairs, I will surely say that I entirely agree with Arthur and his views, which he will communicate to you."* Newspapers, citing an "old Etonian" who was

The Duke of Connaught.

related to both Charles Edward and the Duke of Connaught's son Prince Arthur, claimed that the latter had confronted his cousin over the succession: *"Look here,"* Prince Arthur said, *"You have heard, I suppose, that they want me to go off to Germany and be Duke of Coburg? Well, I am going into the British Army, and I am not going to turn German."* If Charles Edward refused to accept the Coburg inheritance, Arthur warned that he would have to *"look out for squalls, and take care I don't kick you jolly well all around the school yard."*

While the Kaiser insisted on Charles Edward's immediate relocation to Germany, both the Duchess of Albany and Queen Victoria felt it would be best for the boy to remain at Eton. Wilhelm II, however, was unbending and demanded that a future German ruler had to be educated in Germany, where he was also expected to begin military service in earnest. Unwilling to separate herself from her son, who happened to be just fourteen-years old, the Duchess of Albany, with Princess Alice in tow, duly took Charles Edward to Germany; from this point on, the boy was known as Carl Eduard.

When Duke Alfred met the trio at Reinhardsbrunn, he told his sister-in-law that he would like Carl Eduard to attend a school at Schnepfenthal in the Thüringen forest, which was the alma mater of Prince Heinrich of Battenberg. Helene, however, refused to let her son attend a *"horrid scruffy place."* Instead, she and her children went to live with her brother-in-law Wilhelm, who in 1891 had become King of Württemberg. She also ignored recommendations from her sister-in-law Empress Friedrich, who suggested a reputable school near Frankfurt *"supposed to be very modern but...mainly attended by the sons of rich Jews."* This anti-Semitism displayed by the Albanys was perhaps an omen of events to come. After much dithering on the matter, in no small way com-

Duke Carl Eduard at the time of his accession.

Hereditary Prince Ernst of Hohenlohe-Langenburg and his wife Princess Alexandra of Saxe-Coburg & Gotha.

pounded by Duke Alfred's unwillingness to provide Helene and her children with living quarters, the Duchess of Albany accepted the Kaiser's offer to enroll Carl Eduard at the Lichterfelde Military Cadet Academy in Potsdam, *"the German equivalent of Sandhurst."* Helene was also given a residence, the Villa Ingenheim on the Havel River not far from Lichterfelde. There the family lived for several years and, Princess Alice recalled, *"My brother and I spent some of the happiest days of our teenage life."*

Duke Alfred's death in July 1900 was followed by the accession of Carl Eduard to the ducal throne of Coburg and Gotha. As he was still a minor and lived in Potsdam, the duchy was placed under a Regency led by the late Duke Alfred's son-in-law, the Hereditary Prince Ernst of Hohenlohe-Langenburg, husband of Princess Alexandra. Carl Eduard was lucky not only in that his late uncle had begun the long process of placing the duchy's coffers in order, but also that he was one of the beneficiaries of Queen Victoria's will. Judicious handling of the finances of the ruling ducal family ensured that Carl Eduard would have a considerable income.

While in Potsdam, Carl Eduard and his sister became close to their cousin Kaiser Wilhelm II's children, particularly Crown Prince Wilhelm, Prince Eitel Friedrich, and Prince August Wilhelm. *"Much of our spare time was taken up with the Imperial Family, because the Neues Palais was close by and not a week passed without our going there,"* Princess Alice recalled. Unlike most of their English cousins, Alice considered Wilhelm II *"naturally kind and generous,"* while she deemed his wife Empress Augusta Viktoria to be *"delightful."* Proximity to their Prussian cousins led Carl Eduard and his sister to think that they were *"like another brother and sister to them."* All however was not well, for under the bullying Kaiser's aegis Carl Eduard became a target for *"his rather sadistic behavior toward the young Duke."* A member of the Kaiser's household, Count Robert Zedlitz-Trutzschler, recalled one such incident: *"The little Duke of Saxe-Coburg had a bad time the other evening in the library. The Emperor loves to make him the butt of his jokes. The end of it is generally that he pinches and smacks him so hard that it is hardly an exaggeration to say that the little Duke gets a good beating."* Already wanting in self-confidence, exposure to this sort of bullying did little to build Carl Eduard's character, instead reinforcing his self-perception as someone weak of character and easily swayed.

As part of his education, beginning in the spring of

Chapter XIII – Duke Carl Eduard ... Fortune and Position Withered

The Duchess of Albany in coronation robes.

Kaiser Wilhelm II at Schloß Rosenau in Coburg.

1902, Carl Eduard began a course of study in the Prussian Ministry of the Interior and the Royal Wealth Management office. Later, he traveled to Geneva, where for a few months he studied French. His studies also included a stint in Gotha, where he was instructed on the internal workings of the ducal government. Then, beginning in May 1903, and for three semesters, Carl Eduard studied law and political science at the University of Bonn. While there, he joined the exclusive Borussia Corps, a fraternity reserved for men of his background.

In 1904, as Carl Eduard celebrated his twentieth birthday, pressure mounted for the Duke of Saxe-Coburg & Gotha to find a wife and settle down. There were unsubstantiated rumors that the Duke's interest focused on men, not women. Years later, Maximilian Harden, an influential journalist who published the journal *Die Zukunft*, best known for destroying the reputation of Fürst Philipp zu Eulenburg (the Kaiser's best friend), announced that he possessed *"evidence"* against Carl Eduard and several other suspected homosexuals, among them Prince Aribert of Anhalt and the Grand Duke of Hesse and By Rhine. Some authors consider the rumors about Carl Eduard were true yet no evidence of his alleged homosexuality has

Grand Duke Ernst Ludwig of Hesse and By Rhine.

ever been put forward. Harden, in spite of all his threats and success in uncovering Eulenberg's private peccadilloes, never published his *"evidence."* What we know is that Carl Eduard, weak of character, was easily inclined to follow *"stronger personalities than his own."* Born an English prince, raised from his teenage years to forget his past and become German, he adopted the bombastic militarism so prevalent in Wilhelmine Germany. Carl Eduard would find it difficult to find a place where he felt he belonged. This aspect of his life he could not control, yet it was to play a devastating role in his future, particularly after the fall of the German Empire.

Whether the rumors played a part in Carl Eduard's decision, he did indeed marry early. Worries over the Coburg succession were also at work: if Carl Eduard had no sons of his own chaos would once again erupt. The Connaughts did not want the throne, and decades earlier the Prince of Wales had renounced any rights for himself or his descendants. If Carl Eduard died childless, the throne would pass to the Catholic descendants of Duke Ernst I's next brother, the late Prince Ferdinand, and the house laws in Coburg stipulated that the ruling Duke must be Lutheran. Furthermore, of Ferdinand's three sons,

A commemorative postcard of the wedding of Duke Carl Eduard and his bride, Princess Viktoria Adelheid of Schleswig-Holstein.

Empress Augusta Viktoria (née Schleswig-Holstein).

two had left legitimate progeny but only the line of Prince August could possibly succeed as his elder brother Ferdinand had renounced his rights upon marrying Maria II of Portugal. If it proved impossible to recognize the succession rights of Prince August's sons and their legitimate descendants, there was a chance that the duchy would be subject to extinction and its lands redistributed.

Aware of the size of the Coburg inheritance, Empress Augusta Viktoria sought to find Carl Eduard a wife within her own family. As he joined the Empress and her children on many voyages, Carl Eduard saw Augusta Viktoria as a surrogate mother and fully trusted her decisions and respected her opinions. Hence, when she suggested her own niece as a possible bride, Carl Eduard did not resist and willingly met the woman. Born Princess Victoria Adelheid of Schleswig-Holstein-Sonderburg-Glücksburg at Grünholz on 31 December 1885, she was, coincidentally, the daughter of a woman once courted by Carl Eduard's father and – like the Duke – a descendant of the Duchess of Kent, Queen Victoria's mother.

Carl Eduard visited the Schleswig-Holsteins at their North German properties in Glücksburg and Grünholz. The couple liked each other immediately and their destinies were soon settled. Victoria Adelheid's private photo albums document the endless picnics, sailing trips, and family outings surrounding the beginning of her relationship with Carl Eduard. The alliance that began in the Empress' boudoir turned out to be a love match, one that brought the couple enormous happiness, and their engagement was announced in Berlin in February 1905. Carl Eduard's choice of a bride also sent a clear message: not only was Victoria Adelheid of unquestioned German stock, but she was also the niece of Kaiser Wilhelm II. How could anyone ever question his allegiance and devotion to his adopted country?

Right: Duke Carl Eduard and Duchess Victoria Adelheid traveling in Turkey.

Below: The ducal family spent long periods at Schloß Callenberg, outside Coburg. In this image are their three oldest children, seated: Prince Hubertus and Hereditary Prince Johann Leopold, while behind them is Princess Sibylla.

Carl Eduard and Victoria Adelheid were married on 11 October 1905 in her family's ancestral home in Glücksburg. Surrounded on three sides by the waters of the Flensburg Fjord, the Renaissance castle was tremendously picturesque but unable to accommodate all of the wedding guests. Among those attending were Kaiser Wilhelm II and his wife, accompanied by most of their children, with only the Crown Prince being absent. Prince Arthur of Connaught, the groom's first cousin and one-time candidate to succeed in Coburg, represented the British Court. The German Imperial Family stayed overnight onboard the *Hohenzollern*, the Kaiser's massive yacht that had sailed from Kiel. Outside the castle, a large crowd gathered and cheered the couple once the marriage ceremony had concluded. Those present also toasted the Kaiser's second son, Prince Eitel Friedrich, whose engagement to Duchess Sophie Charlotte of Oldenburg was announced the same day from Glücksburg. After the wedding, Carl Eduard and Victoria Adelheid went on their honeymoon, making their official entry into the duchy in early November.

Carl Eduard and Victoria Adelheid had five children. Hereditary Prince Johann Leopold was born on 3 August 1906, at Schloß Callenberg, nearly ten months after his parents' wedding. On 18 January 1908, Princess Sibylla (Sibylle) was born at Schloß Friedenstein in Gotha, while the family's third child, Hubertus, was born at Schloß Reinhardsbrunn on 24 August 1909. Nearly three years later Caroline Mathilde, born at Schloß Callenberg on 22 June 1912, joined the nursery. The last of the children, Friedrich Josias, was also born at Schloß Callenberg in 1918. These disparate locations reflected the movements of the ducal court: from December to April the family resided at Friedenstein, while the remainder of the year was spent in Coburg, with short visits to Greinburg and Hinterriß.

When Carl Eduard assumed the throne as reigning Duke in 1905, the German press grumbled openly about "an Englishman" inheriting such an important

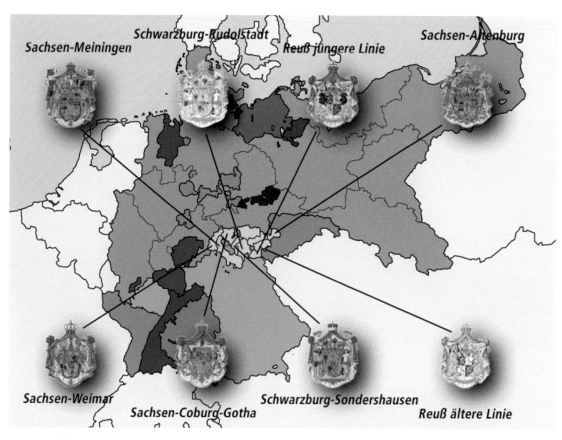

Left: A map of Imperial Germany showing the various Thuringian duchies and principalities.

Below: Service plaque given by Duke Carl Eduard of Saxe-Coburg & Gotha. These were usually attached to canes, umbrellas and the like.

German heritage. It seemed, as it would appear in later years, that no amount of effort made by Carl Eduard to become 'Germanized' was enough for his detractors. Notwithstanding his critics, he became an effective administrator. He signed important agreements with his largest neighbors, Bavaria and Prussia, and moved many of the remaining administrative dependencies to Gotha, a larger political entity than Coburg. What remained in Coburg, much to the duke's delight, was the administration of his personal fortune, and Carl Eduard worked hard to continue his uncle Duke Alfred's cleansing of the troubled ducal finances, which had been mismanaged since the XVIII century. There was a bruising negotiation with Gotha over ownership of ducal lands, in which the duchy received 3/7 of the ducal property while the ducal house retained 4/7 of these domains. Gotha, inhabited by feistier citizens than was Coburg, would always remain the most difficult part of the duchy to govern.

This property included tens of thousands of hectares, most of them covered with pristine forests. Besides several palaces and castles peppered around Thüringen, the Duke of Saxe-Coburg and Gotha also owned considerable property in Austria. In Coburg, starting in 1909, Carl Eduard invested large sums in restoring the Veste Coburg, turning one of the bastions into an inhabitable structure for his private use. No other ruler had lived at the Veste Coburg for three-and-a-half centuries. He was not just interested in architecture, however. The Duke also provided his support to the University of Jena and, following the taste of his mother, who had instilled in him the same love for the arts that she had shared with his late father, he became an important patron of the Coburg Theater, contributing a handsome yearly stipend from his private funds. Through his auspices Richard Strauss came to Coburg and conducted, and the Duke was one of the most prominent supporters of the nearby Bayreuth Festival. Carl Eduard was also fascinated by modern technology and enthusiastically promoted the nascent automobile industry as well as aviation. He once flew aboard an airship from Frankfurt to Gotha, and established Zeppelin hangars and even an airfield in Coburg.

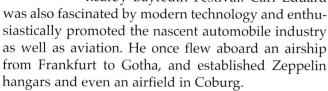

Chapter XIII – Duke Carl Eduard ... Fortune and Position Withered

Before the Great War, the Bulgarian princes visited their Coburg family. From left: Prince Leopold, Crown Prince Boris of Bulgaria, Dowager Duchess Marie Alexandrovna, Duke Carl Eduard and Duchess Victoria Adelheid, Prince Philipp, Prince Kyril of Bulgaria.

Above: A view of Claremont House now. The house should have been inherited by Duke Carl Eduard after his mother's death. However, because he fought on the German side during the Great War, the British government disallowed the inheritance and confiscated the estate. It was sold several times and finally acquired by a school.

Left: When news of the Sarajevo assassination reached Great Britain, Duke Carl Eduard was visiting his mother. Fearful of the seriousness of the situation, he left and returned to Germany. Within a month, Europe was at war. In this image, we see Duke Carl Eduard and the Duchess of Albany.

Above: Duke Carl Eduard in military uniform.

Below: Medal given by Duke Carl Eduard for distinguished service. It was customary for German rulers to hand out various medals for civic service and war bravery. Today, collecting these historical pieces is a big business.

As the summer of 1914 approached, Carl Eduard traveled to England to visit his relations. He was still there when the news of the assassination of Archduke Franz Ferdinand arrived. Fearful that war was imminent, Carl Eduard made a hasty return to Germany, where he learned that war had been declared. Fighting against the country of his birth was anathema, and so Carl Eduard asked that he be sent to the Eastern Front. He made countless troop inspections and visits from military headquarters in Galicia, near the Russian border, but by 1915 the strain and anxiety of war, combined with difficult living conditions, exacerbated his rheumatism, and his stays in Coburg grew longer.

Carl Eduard was not immune from the virulent and xenophobic attacks that became widespread as the war lengthened. In Germany, his detractors openly questioned his loyalties to their land, while on the Allied side many politicians eagerly criticized King George V's cousins fighting for the Kaiser. *"The outbreak of war shattered his life,"* his sister Alice wrote, *"for he was denounced in Germany for being English and in England for being German."* In 1917 King George V, afraid of mounting Germanophobia, changed his dynasty's name from Saxe-Coburg & Gotha to the far more English sounding name of Windsor. Other reprisals included both German royals being deprived of their membership in the Order of the Garter and of their British titles, among them the Duke of Cumberland and the Duke of Albany. This decision was later certified by an order of the King in Council in March 1919 that removed from the roll of Peers those *"having adhered to the King's enemies."* Thereafter, Carl Eduard's British title would remain in abeyance.

As America entered the war and 1917 turned into 1918, Germany's military situation increasingly worsened, fanning the flames of social, labor, and political unrest. Food and fuel shortages only made matters worse. The war that was to have ended in a Christmas 1914 victory had now entered its fourth year and the German Reich's social and political structures disintegrated. On 8 November 1918 unrest began in Gotha; that same day sailors in Kiel mutinied. Within hours the tide of revolution engulfed the Kaiser's empire as rebels took over railroad stations and postal offices, while many civil servants joined the revolt. Fearing the same kind of revolutionary chaos that had engulfed Russia the previous year, Imperial Chancellor Prince Max of Baden urged the abdication of a stunned and unconvinced Kaiser Wilhelm II. Dithering and wasting precious minutes, Wilhelm II, once bullying and bombastic, blamed everyone but himself for his misguided actions. The following day, left without any other pathway to prevent Germany from falling into civil war, Baden announced the Kaiser's abdication. Germany and its rulers had lost all political power.

News of the outbreak in Gotha soon reached Coburg, where the authorities waited for the air to clear. The ducal government asked military authorities for help to fight the outbreak, but the request could not be fulfilled as there were no reliable troops and no one wished to risk bloodshed. News from the other German states was no different. In several, the revolutionaries had declared a republic and calls for Bolshevik-style governments sent deathly chills up the spines of many palace occupants. The situation in Coburg and Gotha was complicated as both duchies were never unified, but were placed as separate entities under a personal union represented by the reigning duke. While Gotha was more industrial, Coburg was more agricultural. In Gotha revolution spread wildly, while in Coburg the authorities, deeply respectful of the ducal family, awaited further developments. November 8 and 9 were rather quiet days, then in Gotha workers and firebrands formed a new government, while in Coburg *"old social democrats, several honorable people, as well as representatives from the reserve infantry regiment"* joined with *"both city magistrates and officers from the ducal offices willing to act as a kind of supervisory body."* Meanwhile, Duke Carl Eduard remained at Schloß Callenberg, where his wife was weeks away from delivering their fifth child.

Several politicians in Coburg tried to retain the old political structure by granting concessions and demonstrating a willingness to listen and address the demands of the revolutionaries. Even though there were some small revolutionary parades through the streets of the sleepy town, it was all very orderly and basically peaceful. Such was the devotion of his State Council in Coburg that it *"went a step further and made*

Duke Carl Eduard inspecting trenches during the Great War.

preparations to defend the ducal throne if necessary." Yet, without any military assistance from the outside, any such maneuver was completely impractical given the country's precarious political situation. On 14 November, almost a week after revolution began, Duke Carl Eduard of Saxe-Coburg and Gotha voluntarily signed an act of abdication and freed his officials from their oath of office. Two weeks later Victoria Adelheid gave birth to their youngest child and third son, Prince Friedrich Josias, whose father was now a private citizen.

The settlement of the ducal family's properties proved a somewhat difficult affair as it involved negotiations with two governments. Coburg, where a staid middle class was in ascendance was easier to deal with; socialists in Gotha, however, made the process extremely difficult. As expected, one state was more generous than the other. In all, Carl Eduard received more than 20,000 acres of land, along with several castles and other real estate, among them Schloß Friedenstein, Schloß Reinhardsbrunn and Schloß Callenberg. The Ehrenburg in Coburg, considered state property, was lost to the republican authorities. The Veste Coburg also remained within the family control and Carl Eduard stayed there often. The settlement also included an impressive collection of art, great portions of which were returned to the ducal family. Once the property was transferred to him, Carl Eduard smartly placed most of it in a foundation to protect it from excessive taxation and further expropriation. Shareholders in the foundation included members of various branches of the Coburg family, both within Germany and abroad. This shrewd legal act later ensured for his descendants the recovery of considerable property after German unification.

Left: The last photo taken of the Duchess of Albany with her son. She was visiting him at Schloß Hinterriß in the Tyrol. She died three days after the photo was taken. By her own request, to be buried where she died, the Duchess of Albany was laid to rest in a chapel nearby.

Below: A photograph of Schloß Hinterriß taken by Duke Carl Eduard.

In 1921, Carl Eduard was allowed to travel to England to visit his mother the Duchess of Albany, whom he had not seen for some time. The following year, Helene and her daughter Alice came to stay with Carl Eduard and his family at Schloß Hinterriß in the Austrian Tyrol. Here, in September 1922, Helene died of a massive heart attack. Following Helene's request that she be buried wherever she died, her earthly remains were interred near the chapel at Hinterriß.

In 1930, Carl Eduard and Victoria Adelheid celebrated their silver wedding anniversary: among their guests were King Ferdinand of Bulgaria, who had lived in Coburg since his abdication, as well as the couple's five children. Sibylla, the eldest daughter, was involved with a young man, as Victoria Feodorovna reported to her sister Marie of Romania, who did not meet the requirements for an equal marriage. Hoping to prevent scandal, her parents sent her off to stay with her aunt Princess Alice in South Africa. *"I like to think the six months' liberal education of sharing our lives there fitted her,"* Alice wrote. In October 1931, Sibylla attended the wedding of her cousin Lady May Cambridge, Princess Alice's only surviving child. While in England, she met Prince Gustaf Adolf of Sweden, eldest son of Crown

Right: Schloß Friedenstein, Gotha. Upon the division of the ducal properties, Friedenstein, with its contents, was returned to Duke Carl Eduard. When Soviet-ruled East Germany expropriated private property, the Coburgs lost it again. Upon reunification, lengthy negotiations followed, leading to a final settlement between the State of Thuringia and the Saxe-Coburg & Gotha Family Foundation. Instead of assuming ownership of Friedenstein, the Coburgs were compensated with lands and forests.

Prince Gustaf Adolf and his first wife, the former Princess Margaret of Connaught, eldest child of the Duke of Connaught. Sibylla and her Swedish cousin, to the delight of all involved, hit it off and their wedding took place in Coburg a year later.

In late 1931, Princess Caroline Mathilde married Count Friedrich-Wolfgang zu Castell-Rüdenhausem; their first child, Count Bertram, was born the following summer and was Carl Eduard's first grandchild. Caroline Mathilde and her husband had two more children before divorcing in 1938, the same year she remarried a German commoner by the name of Captain Max Schnirring, by whom she had another three children. Her parents were terribly displeased with "Calma's" marital challenges and treated her accordingly. Both her former spouse and Captain Schnirring died in air crashes during the war. She later married a third time, but this union lasted only a few months before ending in divorce. As was the case with her older brother, "Calma" never really found happiness and was considered a black sheep by many of her close relations. She died in 1983.

Trouble was also brewing with Hereditary Prince Johann Leopold, who was involved in a liaison with Baroness Feodora von der Horst. *"I was told that my uncle was trapped into marrying Feodora,"* said a relative, *"however their first child was not born until nearly two years later. Whether Feodora had a miscarriage or not, that is something I don't know for sure, but it is a possibility and perhaps the reason why I was told he was forced to enter into this unequal marriage."* As Johann Leopold's bride lacked the ancestry necessary to qualify as an equal, their March 1932 marriage was morganatic and all their children lacked succession rights. They had three children, a daughter Caroline Mathilde, and two sons, Ernst-Leopold and Peter Albert, born in 1935 and 1939 respectively. Johann Leopold divorced Feodora in 1962. The following year, he married Maria Theresia Reindl, and lived quietly at Grein, where he died in 1972.

In these years Carl Eduard, like many of Germany's former rulers, struggled with the loss of his political power and enforced anonymity. Some adjusted to the new political reality brought about by the Weimar Republic, while others, perhaps the overwhelming majority, had considerable trouble adapting to life as mere wealthy landowners and private citizens. While local populations often treated their former rulers with admiration and respect, the days of militaristic pageantry and court life had vanished. The fact that the Treaty of Versailles, a

Left: Duke Carl Eduard, Duchess Victoria Adelheid, Princess Sibylla, Hereditary Prince Johann Leopold and Prince Hubertus skiing in the hills behind Schloß Callenberg.

Below left: Duke Carl Eduard and his wife, who loved dogs, with a new litter of dachshunds.

vengeful international agreement imposed on the Central Powers, attempted to rob Germans of their glorious past and penchant for public displays of military order, only further exacerbated the senselessness in which the general population and the former ruling families were now condemned to exist. The financial and social dislocation pervasive across the former empire only contributed to the radicalization of the masses and a yearning for the orderly existence of yesteryear.

The Weimar Republic tried its best to attract the support of the social, economic and aristocratic elites, but these efforts failed and it was just a matter of time before its end came. Paramilitary groups soon arose and many soldiers, officers, and imperial military leaders lent their support, as did members of the former ruling dynasties. The most prominent paramilitary organization was the *Stahlhelm, Bund der Frontsoldaten* (Steel Helmet League of Frontline Soldiers). Several of the Kaiser's sons were active and enthusiastic supporters of the Stahlhelm, including Carl Eduard's friends Princes Eitel Friedrich, Oskar, and August Wilhelm. From Italy, Fascist dictator Benito Mussolini saw in the Stahlhelm a sister organization and sent his support. *"Those days,"* wrote August Wilhelm in a letter to his sister the Duchess of Brünswick, *"were wonderful, so exalting...we were on the march for two hours, nine stationary on the way on Sunday...Alexander* [his son] *stood for four hours in the stadium and for seven hours on Sunday without food! The population, too, were greatly enthusiastic. Charlie [Carl Eduard], too, stayed for seven hours."* The Stahlhelm quickly became a rallying point for Germans convinced that the Allies had treated their country

Right: The Coburg ducal family – From left: Prince Hubertus, Princess Sibylla, Duchess Victoria Adelheid, Duke Carl Eduard, Prince Friedrich Josias, Hereditary Prince Johann Leopold, and Princess Caroline Mathilde, c. 1927.

unfairly, and who, truth be told, longed not only for the glories of the empire, but also for revenge. Nationalism impregnated these organizations with a fervor not seen for many years as the majority of members longed for a return to the Imperial regime and restoration of the Hohenzollern monarchy. Many within the Stahlhelm were also convinced that Imperial Germany's defeat was caused by a *"stab in the back,"* perpetrated by power hungry Socialists and Jewish radicals intent on imposing a Bolshevik-style regimen on the German people. This provided the radicalized elements a rallying cry that, in the hands of a demagogue of the caliber of Adolf Hitler, was to bring untold destruction to millions of innocent people.

"Although the Stalhelm was officially a non-party entity and above party politics," wrote one historian, *"after 1929 it took on an open anti-republican and anti-democratic character. Its goals were a German dictatorship, the preparation of a revanchist program, and the direction of local anti-parliamentarian action."* Among their demands were the establishment of a Greater Germanic People's Reich, and struggles against Social Democracy, the *"mercantilism of the Jews,"* and the general liberal democratic worldview. They promoted candidates favorable to the politics of a renewed German expansion to the East, the *"lebensraum"* (living space) responsible for later Nazi expansionism into areas of Eastern Europe with high numbers of ethnic Germans. Duke Carl Eduard, encouraged by his Hohenzollern cousins, soon began attending paramilitary gatherings of the Stahlhelm. The Duchess of Brünswick described the *Stahlhelm* as *"an organization of front-line soldiers whose members maintained that order and discipline should be their way of life, and which increasingly interfered in political affairs."* By 1928 Carl Eduard not only supported the organization, but he also served as one of its board members until 1933.

Hitler rose to power against this political and economic vacuum. Back in 1926, seeking approval from the Hohenzollerns, Hitler had paid a visit to Crown Prince Wilhelm at his Potsdam home, Schloß Cecilienhof. During the meeting, Hitler expressed to Wilhelm that his *"goal was the restoration of the monarchy."* The Crown Prince declined political involvement, but remained open to contact, although he later called Hitler *"a demagogue and a little philistine."* It was this penchant for a restoration that brought many German royals into close contact with the Nazi leadership. Hitler smartly used the sentiments expressed in the Stahlhelm to not only gain a following but also eventually rise to become Germany's leader. Among the Hohenzollerns, none was more enthusiastic about the Nazis than Carl Eduard's close friend Prince August Wilhelm. Both had spent time together as young men in Potsdam and were close in age. August Wilhelm was also Carl Eduard's brother-in-law: in 1908, when a young officer in the imperial army, August Wilhelm had married Princess Alexandra Victoria of Schleswig-Holstein-Sonderburg-Glücksburg, a younger sister of Duchess Victoria Adelheid. Never happy, the couple had one son,

The silver wedding anniversary of the ducal couple, Coburg 1930. Seated, from left: Countess Caroline-Mathilde of Solms-Baruth, Duchess Marie Melita of Schleswig-Holstein, King Ferdinand of Bulgaria, Duchess Victoria Adelheid and Duke Carl Eduard, Princess Helena of Denmark, Prince Friedrich Josias, Fürstin Adelheid of Solms-Baruth. Standing in back, same order: Fürst Friedrich of Solms-Baruth, Prince Harald of Denmark, Count Hans of Solms-Baruth, Prince Hubertus, Princess Sibylla and Hereditary Prince Johann Leopold, Princess Feodora of Denmark, Princess Caroline Mathilde, Count Friedrich-Wolfgang of Castell-Rüdenhausen and Duke Friedrich of Schleswig-Holstein.

Princess Sibylla in the late 1920s.

Alexander Ferdinand, born in 1912, and divorced in 1920. August Wilhelm's enthusiasm for the Nazis cost him dearly after Germany's collapse. He died, a virtual social pariah, in 1949.

Many historians claim that Carl Eduard was one of Hitler's early financial supporters, as apparently was his cousin Grand Duchess Victoria Feodorovna of Russia, second daughter of Duke Alfred and his Russian wife Marie Alexandrovna. Victoria Feodorovna lived in Coburg after escaping the Bolsheviks with her husband Kirill and their children. Countless Germans, from industrialists and bankers to royalty and common folk lent such early support; in fact, it was a group of German magnates who recommended Hitler to Hindenburg as a viable interim Reich Chancellor. Perception of the Hitler of the late 1920s, however, was quite different to the Hitler who later embarked on a reign of terror. Many – including prominent British figures – saw Hitler and the Nazis as the saviors of Europe, guarantors of peace and bulwarks against Communism who would also free Germany of chaos and lift the oppressive restraints imposed by the Treaty of Versailles. The market crash of 1929 had caused a major disruption to an already wavering economy burdened by war reparations. Privation, economic and social anxiety, as well as high unemployment, were the order of the day. Even Theodor Heuss, who later served as President of the Federal Republic of Germany, praised Hitler at the time. Heuss believed that *"Hitler was a volunteer in 1914 and served bravely, indefatigably and faithfully...He was very impressive. No one could deny the perseverance of the man who, just released from prison, was so painstakingly and persistently aware, and who understood how to fit the broken fragments of his party together again...One is conscious, perhaps, when he talks about the historical development of the people and the State, that he is trying to clarify a pedagogic theory."* What Carl Eduard and countless others failed to see in their blind enthusiasm for Hitler's false promises, was that the man who portrayed himself as Germany's savior was a sociopath only interested in gaining power to carry out his own murderous agenda. Their serious error in judgment was to have dire consequences, not just for Carl Eduard and many of his peers, but for the entire world.

By 1933, Duke Carl Eduard had become quite open in his support of the rising Nazi star. The previous year, Hitler had run for the office of German Chancellor but had been defeated by Paul von Hindenburg. The old hero of the Great War, though, proved incapable of governing, and in 1933 several politicians and industrialists urged Hindenburg to appoint Hitler as leader of a caretaker government, *"independent from parliamentary parties."* Initially, Hindenburg resisted the suggestion and called for further elections. Twice Germans headed to the polls, but neither election produced a governing majority or a coalition. Left without options, Hindenburg asked Hitler to form a

Right: The wedding luncheon of Princess Sibylla and Prince Gustaf Adolf of Sweden. From left: Prince Hubertus, Crown Princess Louise of Sweden, Duke Carl Eduard, Princess Alice (Countess of Athlone, the Bride, King Ferdinand of Bulgaria, the Groom, Princess Margaretha of Denmark, Crown Prince Gustaf Adolf of Sweden and Prince Sigvard of Sweden.

Duchess Victoria Adelheid wearing a family heirloom.

Left: Princess Sibylla and Princess Caroline Mathilde in the late 1920s.

Below left: Princess Caroline Mathilde married Count Friedrich-Wolfgang of Castell-Rüdenhausen, a young aristocrat she had been dating for some time. Their wedding took place on 14 December 1931, the seventieth anniversary of the death of the Prince Consort. One wonders if the family realized the significance of the date before choosing it. Sadly, the couple divorced in 1938 after three children and only seven years of marriage.

government and on 30 January 1933 his new cabinet was sworn in; soon Nazi operatives were appointed to important positions, and Hitler began his suppression of political opposition.

Taking full advantage of the revanchist desires within the Stalhelm, the National Socialists had built their own paramilitary organization, the *"Sturmableitung,"* better known as the SA or the *"Brownshirts,"* who became Hitler's crack troops and intimidated Germany into submission. In 1934, fearing that SA were too powerful, Hitler obliterated their leadership and all public policing power fell to the SS (Schutzstaffel – Protection Squadron). Under the ferocious leadership of Heinrich Himmler, one of Hitler's most merciless henchmen, the SS was transformed from a small paramilitary organization to one of the most powerful, and feared, organizations of the Nazi regime. When, in August 1934, Hindenburg died, his presidential powers were merged with the office of the Reich Chancellor. Hitler's takeover of Germany was now complete.

Although concrete evidence is lacking to show that Carl Eduard believed in the political credo of the Nazi Party, particularly in their noxious racial policies, his decision to publicly meet with Hitler in the late 1920s had given the party much needed prestige and lent it an air of legitimacy. Here was a grandson of Queen Victoria, a first cousin of both King George V and of Kaiser Wilhelm II, a man who not only had close and intimate connections with the Hohenzollerns but was also related to countless European royal families, publicly expressing his enthusiasm for Hitler's movement. For Carl Eduard, Hitler and the Nazis represented a direct link to a movement and man whom he saw as the future of

Right: A beautiful photo of Duke Carl Eduard and Duchess Victoria Adelheid in 1933. That year, Germany gained a new leader, one the Duke of Coburg supported wholeheartedly. He hoped, no doubt, that Hitler's promises of restoring Germany to its former glory would end the nightmare that began in November 1918. The Duke never wavered both in support and enthusiasm for the country's new ruler. For this monumental error, he paid dearly.

Germany. Not only was Hitler willing to bring back the empire and restore Germany to its pre-1914 grandeur, Carl Eduard mistakenly believed, but also he saw in a strong Germany a dependable international partner for his native England. Furthermore, in his mind, Carl Eduard saw himself as a bridge between Berlin and London. During the 1930s he used his contacts with Hitler and the Nazis to further this international rapprochement that was so very important to him, his family and his two countries, Great Britain and Germany. He was a small actor in a large play, one that he failed to fully appreciate and understand, but perceptions of his influence in Nazi Germany were destined to bring Carl Eduard untold misery in the aftermath of the Second World War.

The former Duke of Saxe-Coburg & Gotha's meetings with Hitler were not as frequent as were those with other leading Nazis. Once in control of the government, the Nazis kept Carl Eduard busy with minor offices and tasks designed to portray him as having closer contacts with the leadership than he actually enjoyed. Hence, in 1933 Carl Eduard became the honorary leader of the Nazi Motor Corps as well as President of the German Automobile Club. He was also appointed "Gruppenführer" in Hitler's staff and given small offices in Berlin, and became a member of the Reichstag (parliament), a puppet body that rubber-stamped Hitler's decisions.

Carl Eduard's thirst to help Germany, this desire to play a larger public role, a self-vision perhaps, was to be better realized in his position as President of the Red Cross. Already in 1934 he had represented Germany at an International Red Cross gathering in Japan. On the way there, he made a visit to the United States, where one of his responsibilities was to present to *"John Barton Payne, chairman of the American Red Cross, the highest decoration of the German Red Cross."* This was not to be the only visit he made to both countries. Two years later he made a very public visit to Italy, during which he pinned on Mussolini the Order of the Red Cross of Germany, which Hitler had conferred upon the Italian dictator.

It is clear, given Hitler's wish to polish his regime's international reputation, that the dictator took advantage of the Duke of Saxe-Coburg & Gotha's enthusiasm to achieve that goal. It seemed ideal to the Nazis' agenda then that Carl Eduard, born in England, was tasked with leading a new Anglo-German Fellowship. In London, where many politicians wanted to avoid another European-wide conflict, these efforts received considerable attention and even support from those who had experienced the nightmare of the trenches during the Great War and wished to avoid a complete breakdown in diplomacy. Many politicians, businessmen and aristocrats saw the Nazis as a barrier to Communism's expansion; even within the Royal Family there were those who privately hoped that Hitler would bring order to a crushed Germany. Most prominent among those in Britain suspected of being

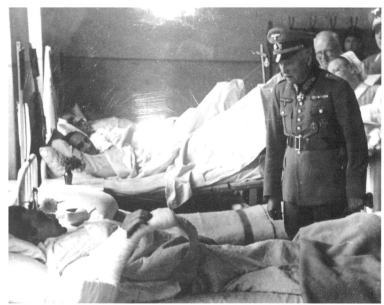

Left: Duke Carl Eduard visiting wounded soldiers in his role as President of the German Red Cross.

Middle: Another image of Duke Carl Eduard fulfilling his responsibilities with the German Red Cross.

Bottom: Duke Carl Eduard and Italian dictator Benito Mussolini.

pro-German was none other than the Prince of Wales, who renewed his contacts with Carl Eduard in the early 1930s as the Duke's visits to England increased.

Hitler and his henchmen did not impress King George V, nor was he at ease with his son's new-found friendship with Carl Eduard. For the old King, the Nazis were deplorable in their tactics, while he worried about Germany's *"needless and provocative scale of rearmament,"* policies that he believed were destined to plunge Europe into war. He also rejected both the Nazis' efforts to lay blame on Jews, as well as their fondness to use violence to carry out their schemes. Wanting the Prince of Wales to have as little to do with Germany's rising overlords, he had forbidden his attendance at the wedding of Princess Sibylla, an event the Nazis used to stage a show of might in Coburg. In a note sent to Carl Eduard through their Swedish relations, the Prince of Wales excused himself for not attending: *"George* [the Duke of Kent] *and I are very disappointed we cannot accept your kind invitation. So sorry not to have let you know definitely before … love to all from us both, David."*

In Berlin, the British Embassy was skeptical of the Anglo-German Fellowship and feared that its supporters, among them British industrialists had *"swallowed all they saw"* when touring German industrial sites in 1934. The Foreign Office echoed these sentiments and was deeply suspicious of the organization and Carl Eduard's role in it. The Anglo-German Fellowship, they feared was an *"admirable vehicle for German propaganda…the Duke of Saxe-Coburg-Gotha is…President of the Fellowship."* At the launch of the organization, attended by many notable personalities in London, Carl Eduard expressed his wish that the Fellowship would become a vehicle to demonstrate the *"widespread sympathy in Germany for the English people, the depths of which was not fully understood in England."* The British government's discomfort increased after the Prince of Wales gave a troubling speech at the annual conference held by the Royal British Legion. In it, he suggested that the time might be approaching when Great Britain should *"stretch forth the hand of friendship to the Germans."* The King was livid with his son's speech and chastised him for expressing opinions that ran counter to the British government's policies. On the other side of the Channel, Berlin looked with great expectation to the passing of King George V as the future seemed to promise better Anglo-German relations during the reign of King Edward VIII.

King George V's death at Sandringham on 20 January 1936 offered a further opportunity for talks. Carl Eduard was among the members of the German delegation to London and it was hoped that they would take advantage of *"the contacts they will make in the next few days – perhaps not so flamboyantly as did the Kaiser, but nevertheless as effectively, if not more so – to promote such rapprochement as Germany evidently has at heart."* Carl Eduard, who sported Nazi uniform and steel helmet as he walked behind George V's casket, claimed to have had several conversations with King Edward VIII. In a memorandum to Hitler, he reported that Edward VIII was interested in improving Anglo-German relations. *"I myself wish to talk to Hitler, and will do so here or in Germany,"* Carl Eduard quoted the new King. *"Tell him that please."* Carl Eduard also wrote that the King had asked him to visit London frequently to ensure that their conversations on

Duke Carl Eduard as a member of the Stahlhelm.

these confidential matters continued. Whether Carl Eduard exaggerated the content of these conversations or not, his memorandum to Hitler was clearly designed to promote his own image as an international goodwill ambassador of the Third Reich. These efforts were brought to an end later in the year when King Edward VIII was forced to abdicate so he could marry the woman he loved, American-born Mrs. Wallis Simpson. As an addendum, Edward did get his wish to meet Herr Hitler in late 1937, when in the company of his wife he visited Nazi Germany where both were fêted and given royal treatment. However, Edward did so as the powerless Duke of Windsor, no longer as King Edward VIII. It was a pointless meeting that further damaged the Duke of Windsor's image while achieving nothing concrete for Hitler.

The United States feared the idea of a new European conflict, and the majority of Americans hoped to avoid yet another war. Experiences in the Great War had tempered opinions, while major American corporations also looked to a strong Germany with a thriving economy, an expanding middle class and a solid consumer base, to enrich themselves. *"Some of the primary and more famous Americans and companies that were involved with the fascist regimes of Europe,"* wrote one historian, *"were William Randolph Hearst, Joseph*

The Duke of Saxe-Coburg & Gotha and the Führer.

Kennedy [father of President John F. Kennedy], Charles Lindbergh, John Rockefeller, Andrew Mellon [head of Alcoa, banker, and Secretary of Treasury], DuPont, General Motors, Standard Oil [now Exxon], Ford, ITT, Allen Dulles [later head of the CIA], Prescott Bush [father of President George H. W. Bush], National City Bank, and General Electric."

War broke out in Europe as the United States readied for another presidential campaign. President Franklin Roosevelt, first elected in 1932 and then reelected four years later, was running for an unprecedented third term in office. While he wished to embroil the United States in the European conflict, Roosevelt also knew that there was no desire in America for such a course of action, at least not yet. During the presidential campaign in 1940 the President promised to keep the United States out of the conflict. Hitler and his government were well aware of these promises. To take advantage of the quandary Roosevelt found himself in, they dispatched Carl Eduard on yet another goodwill tour of the United States.

The Duke of Saxe-Coburg and Gotha arrived in the United States in March. Soon after his arrival, he had meetings with Norman H. David, President of the American Red Cross, ostensibly to confer on *"means for improving cooperation between the two organizations with reference to relief in Poland and other parts of the Reich."* Prominent financiers, industrialists and society figures flocked to the various luncheons and dinners hosted to fete the visiting royal. Even the Swedish Minister organized a reception in honor of Carl Eduard, *"whose daughter is the wife of the heir presumptive to the throne."*

In 1938 Duke Carl Eduard visited London as President of the Anglo-German Fellowship.

The visit created quite a stir among American newspapers, as well as the country's political elites. It was meant to raise goodwill, but Carl Eduard's comments on the German invasion of Poland caused great concern and bewilderment: *"Everyday life in Poland is back to normal,"* the Duke said. He argued that since the German campaign invading the country was so short, *"and German relief aid after the war so quick and so effective, that today the people of Poland are back to normal so far as their everyday lives and their immediate needs are concerned."* Perhaps he honestly believed that Poles were now better off than before German panzer units obliterated their nation. He did concede that *"the political effects of Germany's invasion of Poland...would take some more time to wear off."* Carl Eduard met with President Roosevelt on 18 March during which he reassured the American leader of Germany's goodwill.

From Washington DC, Carl Eduard continued to New York City where several receptions and dinners were held in his honor. At a dinner hosted by the Board of Trade for German-American Commerce, Carl Eduard heard words that were music to his ears when Senator Ernest Lundeen urged *"absolute neutrality in the quarrels of Europe and trade with all...The American people are not going to ignore the great trade market of the Greater German Reich with its population of 105.000.000!"* Furthermore, the senator argued, *"There are millions of Americans like myself, not of German blood, who want to do justice to those who have received little justice in the past."* It was clear to those in the elegant halls of the Waldorf-Astoria that Senator Lundeen believed that Germany had been mistreated after the Great War and what Hitler and the Nazis sought was owed to them:

justice. The senator was well known in American pro-German circles and had close ties to a leading German agent, who often used his office, and *"sometimes dictated speeches for Lundeen, openly using the Senator's telephones to obtain material from Hans Thomsen at the [German] embassy."* The good Senator Lundeen, however, was unable to do much to further his German sympathies. He died in an airplane crash just a few months after giving the infamous New York speech.

By the time Carl Eduard arrived in Tokyo, six weeks after his visit to the United States, American newspapers were referring to him as *"Hitler's Duke."* His every move when in the United States was amply reported, as was his *"mystifying"* visit to Tokyo, his second in 1940. Officially he was in Japan as Hitler's envoy to commemorate the 2600th anniversary of the founding of the Japanese empire; unofficially he was there to assuage Japanese fears over the Soviet-German pact negotiated by Hitler earlier in the year. Undoubtedly, the groundwork for future German-Japanese cooperation was being laid down. The New York Times reported: *"The Duke is not a political personality and the absence of an official suite precludes the idea that he has come to submit political proposals, but it is undoubtedly hoped that he will improve the atmosphere...but the policy of no involvement is too deeply rooted in national interest to be shaken."* Encouraged by German military success in Europe, Japan threw caution to the wind and pursued their *"Greater East Asia policy, formally allying Tokyo with Berlin and Rome...They gambled on Germany's winning the war before the United States is ready."* The alliance Japan signed with Germany and Italy was meant to send a clear message to the international community in general, and the United States in particular. On 7 December 1941, about eighteen months after Carl Eduard's Tokyo visit, the Japanese Empire bombed Pearl Harbor.

Duke Carl Eduard later in life. Below his right eye one can see the cancer that ultimately killed him after several years of serious health complications.

Carl Eduard and Victoria Adelheid worried as their three sons fought in the war. Hubertus, the ducal couple's second son, was a *"very special type of person,"* said his nephew Count Bertram. *"I liked him very much. He was kind and nice, a soft-type of man, a funny person. He had a difficult time with his parents, like all the children did in fact...in his case I think it was because he was gay. So to please his parents he would do things that were not true to his nature, but he desperately wanted to please them. Even going to fight in the war, a decision that ultimately cost my uncle his life...even that I believe he did to appease his parents and gain their approval. It is sad, very sad indeed."* In November 1943 word came that Prince Hubertus, heir to the Coburg dynasty, had been killed in action near Mosty, Romania. His remains were returned to Coburg and buried in a plot on a hilltop where other family members were destined to later join him.

On 20 July 1944 Hitler miraculously escaped an assassination attempt. It was not the first such effort, but it was the one that came closest to killing the dictator. The plot, Operation Valkyrie, carried out by Count Claus von Stauffenberg, called for a bomb to be planted inside a conference room used by Hitler at one of his headquarters in Eastern Prussia. For the plot to work, Hitler had to be killed, thus freeing soldiers from their oath of allegiance and allowing the plotters to take over the armed forces. Hitler, although hurt, survived the attack, and his reaction was swift and bloody. As many of the plot leaders were aristocrats, the SS rounded countless titled Germans as suspects. Count Hans Georg zu Solms-Baruth, father-in-law of Carl Eduard's youngest son, was among those arrested. Gestapo officers visited both Crown Prince Wilhelm and his son Prince Louis Ferdinand, though neither was arrested. Hitler, though, died convinced that the Hohenzollerns and other royals were involved in the plot. Their former influence with the

Left: *The funeral of Duke Carl Eduard. Duchess Victoria Adelheid is accompanied by her daughter Sibylla and son Friedrich Josias. The other ladies in mourning include Princess Alice, Princess Denyse (Friedrich Josias' second wife) and Princess Caroline Mathilde.*

Nazis had evaporated, yet for Carl Eduard the sobriquet of *"Hitler's Duke"* remained.

Germany's defeat in May 1945 devastated Carl Eduard. Coburg had fallen to the American army and those suspected of Nazi involvement were quickly detained. Carl Eduard and Victoria Adelheid were living in the Veste Coburg when he was arrested on 8 June. General George Patton allowed the broken man to remain at home while the authorities decided what to do with him. In November, American military authorities announced that Carl Eduard was *"under arrest, and his estates have been confiscated."* He was transferred to a prison camp where he experienced serious privations that threatened to complicate his perennial fight against arthritis and rheumatism. Conditions were so dreadful that prisoners had to scamper about for grass to add to their meager, tasteless soup.

"Prison was physically and mentally not easy for poor Uncle Charlie," recalled Carl Eduard's daughter-in-law Viktoria-Luise, *"who was not at all well, and had never been a strong willed person. He had been spoiled all his life with every comfort possible...Eventually he was transferred to a prison hospital, where it was found, that among other problems, he had skin cancer between his right eye and the bridge of the nose* [the illness that would kill him in 1954]. *I felt very sorry for him. Not only had his world fallen apart...but he was sick and all alone in prison. I never understood how this cultured, well-educated and gentle man could believe in an animal like Hitler and his horrific empire! I often tried to talk to him to find out what he thought about certain things that had happened, but he always put it off as advertising smears of the anti-Nazi movement. There was no convincing him that things were all wrong."*

Months after his arrest, Carl Eduard was released and with Victoria Adelheid went to live in a small cottage near the stables at Schloß Callenberg. Since the castle was filled with refugees, Carl Eduard had to do with what the authorities allowed him. Victoria Adelheid was forced to ride a bicycle about ten miles, the distance between Callenberg and Coburg, to purchase what food she could find. When Princess Alice visited the couple in 1948, she described their living condition as *"all so sad and sordid."* With her husband, Alice did *"all we could to persuade the American and, later, the German authorities, to provide them with better quarters. They were all odious, though I confess it was most difficult to find anywhere for people to live at that time."* In the end, Carl Eduard was allowed to move into a house he owned in Coburg since his physical ailments made living in Callenberg impossible.

As a former Nazi Party member, Carl Eduard had to face a denazification tribunal. The answers Carl Eduard provided to his captors were dumbfounding *"by their ignorance, lack of contrition, and by American standards, unbridled arrogance."* Carl Eduard was convinced, and maintained, that Germany was attacked by Poland, not the other way around. In his view, because the Poles attacked first, they deserved what they got. Germany's ultimate defeat shocked the

CHAPTER XIII – Duke Carl Eduard ... Fortune and Position Withered

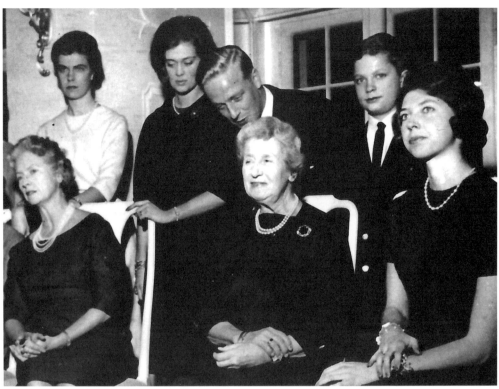

Right: Seated, from left: Princess Sibylla, Duchess Victoria Adelheid, Princess Désirée of Sweden. Standing: Princess Margaretha of Sweden, Princess Birgitta and Prince Johann Georg of Hohenzollern and Crown Prince Carl Gustaf of Sweden.

duke, who claimed to have believed to the very end that his country would triumph. As for National Socialism, Carl Eduard still, in 1945, believed it was a *"wonderful"* idea. When confronted with proof that human experiments had been conducted under cover provided by the German Red Cross over which he had presided, Carl Eduard claimed ignorance of any such atrocities. As for the concentration camps, the Holocaust and National Socialism's treatment of Jews, he refused to believe the accusations and insinuated that they were fabrications at worst, misinformation at the very least. Was he that obtuse, one must wonder, or perhaps naïve? Throughout the interrogation, the officers noted, his wife, present most of the time, unsuccessfully tried to convey to Carl Eduard that his answers were getting him into deeper trouble. "*Uncle Charlie had never been a man with a strong moral fiber, that is, he was easily influenced by others and often indecisive,*" his daughter-in-law (and niece) Viktoria-Luise recalled. "*Aunt Dicky* [Victoria Adelheid] *was definitely the strong leader in the marriage and in every other place.*" Viktoria-Luise also remembered that Carl Eduard believed that Japan's attack on Pearl Harbor guaranteed that the United States would not be able to continue aiding England, therefore securing German victory. He was, of course, proven wrong as the United States' victory in the Battle of Midway, six months after Pearl Harbor, was the beginning of the end for Japan. As Admiral Yamamoto, Japanese commander of the battle group sent to bomb Pearl Harbor, allegedly commented, *"the sleeping giant had been awakened."*

Viktoria-Luise further illustrated her uncle's enthusiasm for Hitler and the Nazis by recalling that while "*Aunt Dicky was pro-German, she was not too comfortable with Uncle Charlie's support of the Nazi regime.*" Furthermore, "*Uncle Charlie wanted to make up for the fact that he was a British subject and so to say had adopted Germany as his new fatherland. He had to prove his loyalty to Germany more so than any other German citizen.*" As for Carl Eduard and the Führer, "*he felt that Hitler was the man who could get Germany back on its feet and make it a strong and proud country again.*" This, of course, served Hitler masterfully, as he could use Carl Eduard's connections and prestige to enhance the Nazis' international image.

For his active and public support of Hitler, Carl Eduard was condemned for being a Nazi "*camp follower*" and heavy fines were levied against his property. Carl Eduard died a sad, forgotten and broken man. Wrecked by cancer and arthritis, his death took place in Coburg on 6 March 1954. The funeral was held a few days later and his remains were buried in the same plot occupied by his son Hubertus since his death in 1943. Victoria Adelheid survived until 1970, dying in her mid-eighties. In Coburg they were both celebrated and remembered for their endless dedication to the town and the welfare of the citizenry, and Carl Eduard's former subjects seemed willing to excuse his faults, missteps, and shortcomings. Perhaps this was because, just like their former duke, so many Coburgers had enthusiastically welcomed Hitler's rise while naïvely failing to realize that they were not supporting their fatherland's rise to glory, but its ultimate destruction.

Chapter XIV
The Coburgs of Windsor
A Dynasty's Name Changed

Edward VII, who ascended the throne on the death of his mother on 22 January 1901, was to rule the United Kingdom and the British Empire for the following nine years until his death in 1910. Edward had waited nearly six decades to inherit his legacy, a legacy that his parents had feared he would be incapable of managing. As the first British monarch of the House of Saxe-Coburg and Gotha, King Edward VII proved Victoria and Albert wrong. He was, without a doubt, the best of the Coburg dynasty's twenty-one rulers descended from Duke Franz Friedrich Anton and Duchess Augusta.

Albert Edward was born on the morning of 9 November 1841 at Buckingham Palace, the eldest son and second child of Queen Victoria and Prince Albert. His christening, celebrated on 25 January 1842 at St. George's Chapel, Windsor Castle, was a joyous and solemn occasion. He was to be the first of many of Albert and Victoria's descendants to receive his father's name, while the second, the more traditionally English Edward, was given in remembrance of his late grandfather the Duke of Kent and Strathearn. Within the family circle, and between the Coburg extended web of cousins he was known as "Bertie." Just a month after his birth, Queen Victoria created her eldest son Prince of Wales, a title reserved for the sovereign's heir apparent; on birth he also became Duke of Cornwall and Rothesay, after the duchy created in the Fourteenth Century by King Edward III for his son Edward, later called the "Black Prince" either owing to his temperament or to his heraldic shield. The Duchy of Cornwall, with its vast properties, guaranteed the financial independence of the heir apparent, and Bertie remains the longest holder of the titles of Prince of Wales and Duke of Cornwall and Rothesay.

The Coburgs believed that the role of the monarch was to defend constitutional government, a lesson learned after the French Revolution, the Napoleonic Wars, and the rise of self-determination. The monarch, Prince Albert fervently believed, was not to play an active role in politics nor support one party ideology over another. Queen Victoria liked to think that she was following the Prince Consort's philosophy, although at times she failed to do so as she favored one politician over another. Hence, and to avoid their son making missteps in the future, Prince Albert determined that their eldest son should have an education that prepared him to be a model constitutional monarch. At age seven, Edward embarked on a rigorous educational program devised by Prince Albert, with the support of his Uncle Léopold I of the Belgians and Baron von Stockmar, and supervised by his parents. However, unlike some of his siblings, Edward was a disappointing pupil, and his listlessness and proclivity to self-indulgence drove his parents to suspect his future abilities. Prime Minister Benjamin Disraeli described him as *"informed, intelligent and of sweet manner."* Queen Victoria, far less kind than her beloved Disraeli, was convinced that Edward could not be trusted and kept him from involvement in governmental affairs. Ironically, this isolation became a self-fulfilling prophecy, leaving Edward idle and with ample time to pursue the very interests his parents abhorred.

Edward was not close to his parents, and there was little warmth between them. Victoria and Albert always treated him as something of a failure, someone whose shortcomings made him fade in the shadow of his far more intelligent elder sister Victoria. Lessons with private tutors failed to make much impression, and Edward was eventually sent to the Continent in an effort to widen his overall education. Upon his return from Rome in 1859, he spent some time attending the University of Edinburgh before matriculating as an undergraduate at Christ Church, Oxford. This newfound freedom from excessive parental supervision allowed Edward to

Left: The Danish Royal Family. From left: Princess Dagmar (Empress Marie Feodorovna), Crown Prince Frederik, Prince Valdemar, Queen Louise, King Christian IX, Princess Thyra (Duchess of Cumberland), King George I of the Hellenes and Princess Alexandra (Princess of Wales – Queen of Great Britain).

enjoy his studies and his overall performance witnessed much improvement. After Oxford, he also attended Trinity College, Cambridge, where professors and lectures alike inspired him.

In 1860, Edward made an extremely successful, four-month visit to Canada and the United States, where he was greeted with great enthusiasm everywhere he went. He carried out many public functions, including the inauguration of the Victoria Bridge across the St. Lawrence River in Montreal. While in Washington DC, he was the guest of US President James Buchanan and stayed at the White House for several days. At Mount Vernon, with Buchanan by his side, Edward paid respects to George Washington, while in New York's Trinity Church prayers for the Royal Family were said for the first time since the American Revolution. The visit, which Queen Victoria felt gave her son too much attention, was in fact a huge success not only diplomatically, but also in helping Edward's self-confidence.

Victoria and Albert had decided that once of age Edward was to have his own establishment. The revenues of the Duchy of Cornwall, which Prince Albert masterfully administered during his son's minority, provided the financial settlement that allowed for such a move. By the time the Prince of Wales gained access to his fortune, his father had managed to save £600,000, an astronomical sum at the time (equaling nearly $740 million in today's currency). On top of that, the yearly revenues produced by the Prince of Wales's properties provided him with an income of nearly £60,000 to pay for his living expenses. Queen Victoria designated Marlborough House as her son's London residence and Parliament voted for

Above left: The Prince of Wales (future King Edward VII) – Right: The Princess of Wales.

Chapter XIV – The Coburgs of Windsor ... A Dynasty's Name Changed

Right: Sandringham House in Norfolk, the country estate of the Prince of Wales.

Below right: Marlborough House, the epicenter of London's social life when Edward VII was Prince of Wales.

its refurbishment. Wanting a country estate for his son, Prince Albert arranged the purchase of the Sandringham estate in Norfolk, a huge property now some 8,000 hectares and open to the public.

The Prince of Wales was considered one of the most eligible bachelors of his time, but his parents worried that he would fall prey to temptations of the flesh. *"An early marriage was regarded by his parents...as the best panacea for the character of the Prince of Wales, and public opinion insisted that he must marry within the royal caste,"* one of his biographers wrote. Unfortunately, there were few available princesses from which to choose. Princess Elisabeth of Wied, eldest child of Fürst Hermann and his wife, the former Princess Marie of Nassau-Weilburg (whose brother Duke Adolph of Nassau-Weilburg later became the Grand Duke of Luxembourg) was put forward as a talented, well-educated young lady. Albert and Victoria believed that she was a perfect choice, but Edward thought otherwise, refusing *"to look a second time at photographs which probably failed to do justice to her charms."*

Soon, attention turned to the modest Yellow Palace in Copenhagen, where the beautiful, long-necked, and svelte seventeen-year-old Princess Alexandra lived. Known as Alix, she was the eldest daughter of future King Christian IX and of his wife, the former Princess Louise of Hesse-Kassel, beloved cousin of Queen Victoria's Cambridge cousins. At birth, Prince Christian had been a minor prince, but on the death of King Christian VIII in 1848 and the succession of his childless son Frederik VII, a new heir to the Danish throne had to be found. After endless negotiations, the Powers gathered in London and agreed on Prince Christian. A new home, Bernstorff, was provided for him though his income was negligible and the entire family, along with their minute court, learned to live without luxuries. The luck experienced by these poor relations of wealthier royals is astounding, particularly when one realizes that four of Christian and Louise's six children would sit on thrones, either as rulers or consorts. Their son Frederik succeeded his father in 1906 as King of Denmark; in 1863 William ascended the Greek throne as King George I; Dagmar, first engaged to marry Tsesarevich Nicholas Alexandrovich, instead wed his younger brother, the future Emperor Alexander III, after his untimely death; Thyra married the Duke of Cumberland, only son of former King Georg V of Hannover; and Valdemar married Princess Marie d'Orléans, eldest daughter of the Duke and Duchess of Chartres.

Victoria and Albert disliked Louise's family, believing

Above: The Princess of Wales with her two eldest children, Prince Albert Victor and baby Prince George.

Right: The Princess of Wales surrounded by her five surviving children, late 1870s.

Diplomatic considerations also made Alexandra's candidacy a source of considerable concern owing to Prussia's designs on the duchies of Schleswig and Holstein, which the Danish monarch held as personal fiefs. Denmark, however, wished to incorporate these border duchies into its territory, an act that the Prussians considered an affront to German territorial integrity. Having Alexandra, the daughter of the Danish heir and a Hesse-Kassel princess, marry the Prince of Wales, opponents of the alliance believed, would be the source of untold international complications. The young princess, though, was stunning and once Edward laid eyes on her, nothing could stop him. Unfortunately, and unlike Elisabeth of Wied, Alexandra, although among royal Europe's most beautiful ladies, also happened to be rather dim – bright light emanating from an empty bulb – and her education had suffered from her parents' lack of funds.

Victoria, the Princess Royal, who since 1858 lived in Berlin, was sent by her parents to inspect her brother's future bride. Defying Prussian concerns, the couple traveled to Strelitz where Grand Duchess Augusta, a Cambridge by birth as well as Princess Louise's first cousin, provided the private venue for the visit. Victoria was deeply impressed and wrote her parents glowing descriptions of lovely Alix of Denmark, which Albert quickly shared with his son. Their first meeting took place *"before the altar of St. Bernard in the cathedral at Speyer on the morning of 24 September 1861."* To his anxious parents, Edward wrote: *"We met Prince and Princess Christian, and the young lady of whom I had heard so much; and I can now candidly say that I thought her charming and very pretty."* Of his future in-laws, the Prince of Wales thought: *"Princess Christian seems a very nice person, but is, unfortunately, very deaf. The Prince is a most gentlemanlike and agreeable person."* The meeting was a success and Victoria reported to her parents that *"the reverse of*

that they had become *"addicted to a fast and frivolous life"* in the Eighteenth Century castle of Rumpenheim on the Main, near Frankfurt. Princess Louise's mother and her siblings inherited their estate from their father *"with the expressed wish that they should assemble there and amuse themselves as often as possible ... Rumpenheim became a center of anti-Prussian sentiment and intrigue. Furthermore, and much to the utter shock of Queen Victoria and her prudish husband, Rumpenheim was reported to be a scene of gossip, lounging, gambling and unseemly practical jokes which offended the earnest spirit of the age."*

indifference on both sides soon became quite unmistakable…Alix has made an impression on Edward, though in his own funny and undemonstrative way. He said to me that he had never seen a young lady who pleased him so much." The Queen was charmed by Victoria's report, and even more so when her son spoke to his parents on returning from Germany. The Prince Consort was delighted with the news, writing: *"We hear nothing but excellent accounts of the Princess Alexandra; the young people seem to have taken a warm liking to on another."* More caustically, the Queen wrote: *"Bertie is extremely pleased with her, but as for being in love, I don't think he can be, or that he is capable of enthusiasm about anything in the world."*

The marriage was nearly derailed by a sexual scandal involving Edward and an actress named Nellie Clifden. The Prince of Wales and the young woman had a series of encounters while he attended military maneuvers in Ireland. When news of the dalliance reached his parents, Albert and Victoria were nearly apoplectic. Albert, exhausted and ill, traveled to Cambridge to mete out a reprimand to his wayward son; he caught a chill during the visit and two weeks later was dead. Victoria, disconsolate, irrational, and deeply depressed, held Edward responsible. To her daughter in Berlin, the Queen expressed her distaste for Bertie: *"I never can, or shall, look at him without a shudder."*

Prince Christian and Princess Louise were duly informed of Edward's transgression, though this was not enough to prevent their daughter's marriage to the future king. Nearly a year after Edward met Alexandra, the Queen, draped in black widow's weeds, headed to Coburg on a pilgrimage to her beloved Albert's birthplace. She arranged for Uncle Léopold I to invite Alexandra and her parents to visit Laeken Palace, outside Brussels, where she met them on 3 September 1862. Later that afternoon, the Queen and Alix, *"in a plain black dress, without jewels, and with her hair hanging in curls over her shoulders,"* spent some time alone. Queen Victoria's impressions of her future daughter-in-law were glowing, as she tried to think of what Albert's reaction to Alix would have been: *"How he would have doted on her and loved her."* Exquisitely polite, charming, unpretentious and lovely, Alix had gained Queen Victoria's support.

The Prince of Wales and Crown Prince Frederik of Denmark, elder brother of Wales' wife. In the early years of his marriage, Edward visited Denmark frequently, but as he grew older, he found his Danish in-laws utterly boring and stayed away as much as elegantly possible.

The Prince of Wales and the beautiful Alexandra of Denmark were finally married at St. George's Chapel, Windsor Castle, on 10 March 1863. Three weeks later, Alexandra's brother was elected King of Greece, and on November 15, her father finally acceded to the Danish throne. The newly married couple moved into Marlborough House, originally designed by Christopher Wren and his son and built for Sarah, Duchess of Marlborough, which the Crown had acquired in 1817; previously Queen Adelaide, William IV's widow, had lived there until her death in 1849. As the London residence of the Prince and Princess of Wales, Marlborough House became the venue for countless, lavish parties, the theatrical stage on which Edward and Alexandra played the role of society's leaders to perfection and where their circle of friends found great enjoyment characterized by frivolity, consumption and 'fast' living. Queen Victoria, appalled by rumors of life within Marlborough House, tried her best to control her son's life, but as she failed to provide Edward with any constructive role, her efforts were unsuccessful.

Queen Victoria was not the only one who viewed Edward and Alexandra with deep suspicion. The

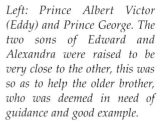

Left: Prince Albert Victor (Eddy) and Prince George. The two sons of Edward and Alexandra were raised to be very close to the other, this was so as to help the older brother, who was deemed in need of guidance and good example.

Wilhelm I were convinced that the Danish Royal Family's influence on the Prince of Wales would cause a rift between Great Britain and Germany. Caught in the middle, Queen Victoria worried about Alexandra's influence, yet nothing could stop the German Confederation taking the duchies from Denmark. The Marlborough House set, however, never forgot the affront inflicted on Denmark and Alexandra raised her own children to be deeply suspicious of Prussia.

Despite her beauty, elegance, and absolute devotion, Alexandra could not maintain her selfish husband's interests. Soon after his marriage, thirsty for the sort of dalliance he had enjoyed with Nellie Clifden, the Prince of Wales began what became a long list of extramarital entanglements that brought him, his spouse and children, and the monarchy itself, into disrepute. At the time Alexandra had just given birth to her first child, and her pregnancy had not been easy. *"She was consumed by anxiety"* due to her brother's destiny in Greece. *"I am very sad for that,"* Alexandra wrote on hearing the news William had become King of the Hellenes. *"God give him strength and patience, to stand up to what the future might bring."* The baby was born premature, two months before he was due. Queen Louise fearfully wondered if the early birth of her grandson would give Queen Victoria cause to *"say it is all weakness in Alix?"* Queen Victoria was most displeased by the early arrival, which she blamed on the Wales's frenetic rounds of merriment and entertaining. Alexandra had been out all day watching some of her friends skate on a frozen lake and had to rush back to Frogmore House at Windsor, where on 8 January 1864 she gave birth to a son. The parents had little say in the baby boy's names, for the Queen assumed that she, not her son and his wife, held that right. The Prince of Wales seems to have learned through his sister Beatrice, then seven-years-old, that their mother

The Wales sisters: Victoria and Louise, Maud between them.

Prussians considered Marlborough House a hive of plotters and schemers focused on planning Berlin's downfall, and when Alexandra's father became King of Denmark, their suspicions heightened. This perception was only accentuated when war erupted between Prussia and Denmark over the duchies of Schleswig and Holstein. Alexandra and her husband openly supported Denmark and criticized Prussia's expansionist foreign policy. In Berlin, Bismarck and

had chosen the names Albert Victor, in honor of his paternal grandparents. Since there was nothing that could be done, Edward and Alexandra added "Christian" and "Edward" to the roster, but the child was always referred to as "Eddy."

The Princess of Wales's slow recovery after her first child did not prevent a second pregnancy. It was again a boy, this time born at Marlborough House on 3 June 1865, who also arrived a month before his expected due date. *"It seems that it is not to be that I am present at the birth of your children, which I am very sorry for,"* the Queen wrote to Edward. In fact, she was never to be present at the birth of any of the Wales grandchildren. Whether that was because Edward and Alexandra lied about the expected due date, which Prince Alfred believed to be the case, or not, Alexandra did not have to deal with her meddlesome mother-in-law during such intimate moments.

Motherhood did not affect Alexandra's beauty, although it increased her deafness, a condition that she quite possibly inherited from her mother. Louise was born at Marlborough House in February 1867, and the delivery left Alexandra greatly weakened. At one point her condition was so serious that her parents came from Denmark as the end seemed imminent, but luckily the princess recovered and the following year she gave birth to another daughter, Victoria, who was also born at Marlborough House. The family home also saw the birth of Maud in November 1869, but not that of Alexander, a sickly baby born in 1871 at Sandringham who only lived for a day. All five surviving children were devoted to their mother, but afraid of their father, whose temper at times made walls shake and thunder. Alexandra, in turn, adored her children and refused to treat them as adults, even after they had left the nest to form families of their own.

While Edward was a caring husband, by no means was he a loyal one, and his cavalier approach to marital fidelity tarnished his image and the reputation of the monarchy. It reminded his mother of her lecherous Hanoverian uncles, who had inflicted such disheartening harm to the institution. Consumed by her unseemly and worrisome devotion to the dead Albert, Queen Victoria took her heir's wayward manner as evidence that he was indeed immature, irresponsible, selfish, and untrustworthy, unworthy of his father's legacy of marital devotion, moral probity, and self-sacrifice. How could this immature, reckless young man be trusted with the heavy burden Queen Victoria stoically carried? The Queen's condemnation further fated the Prince of Wales to the empty life of endless merriment for which she constantly chastised him.

Alexandra kept her beauty for a long time. Yet, this was not enough for her husband who constantly sought illicit enjoyment in the arms of others. Alexandra, who had a deep influence on her children, raised them to be anti-German. Perhaps it was her ultimate revenge against her wayward Coburg husband.

Within a decade of their marriage, Edward and Alexandra were increasingly spending time apart. In the meantime, in 1868-69, they toured the Mediterranean and Egypt, and called on Alexandra's brother George and his wife, the former Grand Duchess Olga Konstantinovna, who became one of Alexandra's confidants. Edward genuinely liked his brother-in-law, and followed Alexandra's lead in promoting the interests of Greece and Denmark in London. Unfortunately, such actions only enhanced perceptions in Berlin that the Prince and Princess of Wales were anti-German, despite the fact that Edward and Alexandra personally liked Crown Prince Friedrich and his wife Victoria.

While her husband led an active social life both at home and abroad, Alexandra liked nothing more than

The Princess of Wales, still beautiful in her mid-forties.

visiting her Danish family with her own children in tow, where she could enjoy the carefree and rambunctious world of her youth. Christian IX and Louise of Denmark looked forward to opening their various homes to this growing swarm, but Edward tried to avoid accompanying his wife and children on their journeys to Denmark. He didn't dislike his in-laws; they simply bored him – the high jinks, pranks, endless jokes in which the visitors engaged were not something he appreciated or tolerated.

Edward's numerous dalliances contributed to his image as a reckless bon vivant. *"You know,"* a princess friend of mine once said, *"fidelity, that is such a bourgeois concept…the aristocracy, royalty included, do not marry expecting their husbands to be exclusive, we expect them not to leave us for a mistress, but what the eye cannot see, the heart ought not to bother with, like Edward VII…look how many mistresses he had, but he was always discreet!"* Prudence always ruled Edward's infidelities: to this day there are no recognized illegitimate descendants, despite several rumors. His paramours were plenty, some well-known, some members of the aristocracy, and some married, but they were all beautiful, cosmopolitan women who knew their place as royal favorite and usually made no fuss. Among his mistresses were actresses Lillie Langtry and Sarah Bernhardt and American Jennie Jerome, Winston Churchill's mother. Two, however, stand out: Daisy, Countess of Warwick, and Alice Keppel, great-grandmother of the present Duchess of Cornwall. Daisy was a rich heiress who married a good friend of the Duke of Albany and went on to have a relationship with the Prince of Wales that lasted more than a decade, finally ending in 1898. Neither was loyal to the other, as both had other dalliances during their sexual friendship. That was not the case with Edward's last "official" mistress, Alice Keppel. Born Alice Edmonstone, child of a prominent Scottish aristocratic family, in 1868, she married the Honorable George Keppel, a younger son of the 7th Earl of Albemarle. *"I do not mind what she does as long as she comes back to me in the end,"* Keppel once said of his wife. Alice's husband also engaged in several affairs of his own, but the couple's union remained, as one of their daughters later recalled, *"a marriage of companionship of love and laughter."* Alice was Edward's trusted, discreet and intimate confidante and mistress until his last breath.

As Prince of Wales, Edward led a hollow existence accentuated by his mother's lack of trust in him. Although constitutionally the Queen was not commanded to find her heir a proper role to play, her not doing so condemned the Prince of Wales to a life of frivolity and a frustrated Prince of Wales had to create his own role within the monarchy. As his mother retreated further from the public eye to a world consumed by longing for Albert and the construction of the fanatic myth around his image, Edward smartly stepped into the void, becoming the public face of the British monarchy. He established the modern principle of public appearances, bringing the monarchy out from the high walls surrounding their palaces while allowing the masses more access. This, in turn, helped restore reverence and respect for the institution. Alexandra, who had a natural gift in presenting herself to an adoring public, also carried out an increasingly large number of appearances. Feelings for the couple intensified when the Prince of Wales nearly died of typhoid fever in the winter of 1871, and his recovery led to national rejoicing.

The political class took notice of Edward's popularity. They worried that his mother's unwillingness to prepare him for the burden he was to inherit would undermine his success as future king. With this in mind, several cabinet members privately supplied the Prince of Wales with government dispatches and eventually cabinet papers were made accessible to him. Edward's bonhomie allowed him to build and cultivate friendships with politicians from all political parties, even those who opposed the monarchy, only enhanced his likeability, while also providing a solid excuse for his missteps and peccadilloes.

In 1875 Edward achieved a life-long dream of visiting India, though without Alexandra, who was forced to remain behind. The journey lasted nearly nine months and the Prince of Wales reveled in the beauty of Great Britain's most important colonial possession. While there, he was fêted by many of the subcontinent's ruling families, who incurred great expense in entertaining the future monarch. Hunts and dinners, balls and visits, followed one another, and at every turn Edward treated all whom he met, whether royals or paupers, the same. This made a deep impression not only on his companions but also among Indians. The prince quickly noticed the high level of disdain used by British officials when dealing with the natives, complaining, *"because a man has a black face and a different religion from our own, there is no reason why he should be treated as a brute."* This is the same approach that Edward took when welcoming Jews into his inner circle, particularly financiers who helped him with his finances. Among them two were particularly close, Baron Moritz von Hirsch and Sir Ernest Cassel. He also kept close contact with members of the Rothschild and Sassoon families. Edward did not see why Jews, particularly rich and successful ones, ought to be excluded from the highest echelons of society, but few other royals and aristocrats, harboring their own anti-Semitic prejudices, followed his lead.

The Orléans settled in England during their various exiles. While there, one of their biggest supporters was the future King Edward VII, a Francophile to his dying day. Here he is with the Duke d'Orléans.

A tireless traveler, the Prince of Wales frequented various continental courts as well as several well-heeled spas, where he conducted diplomatic relations with other royals and the most important politicians of the time. He often visited the French Riviera and was a constant presence at Marienbad and Carlsbad, two of the most exclusive spas on the continent. He also spent considerable time hunting at the estates owned by his Belgian, Portuguese, and Kohary Coburg cousins, who viewed him as the 'paterfamilias' and respected his senior role. Interested in the political destiny of his Coburg cousins, Edward helped shape their futures through written communication and personal visits, public and private, to Brussels, Coburg, Vienna, and even Portugal.

Although Edward mismanaged his wealth, and several times found himself in dire financial straits, his fortune allowed him to engage in expensive sports. His exquisite stud farm produced several winners, including Persimmon, Diamond Jubilee, and Ambush II. The Prince of Wales not also enjoyed the thrill of competition on the turf, but he was also an avid sailor, a sport in which he played a major role with a plethora of ships that were the envy of many other monarchs and millionaires. Among the most jealous was his troublesome nephew, Kaiser Wilhelm II, who remained a thorn in his uncle's side.

The relationship between Edward and Wilhelm II was neither easy nor healthy. Edward had very little patience for his nephew's troublemaking and abusive behavior toward his parents. Wilhelm always felt that his uncle was Prussia's most prominent enemy, a schemer bent on isolating the German Empire and turning it into Europe's pariah. Wilhelm, one can certainly agree, was a very complicated young man, the product of a court

Above: The Prince and Princess of Wales onboard the Royal Yacht Osborne. With them are their five children. From left: Maud, Louise, Albert Victor, Alexandra, Edward and George. On the floor by her father's side is Princess Victoria.

Left: Wilhelm II and his English uncle had a troublesome relationship, consequently diplomatic relations between their realms suffered.

filled with power struggles and intrigue. While his parents sought to guide the German state toward a more pro-British, pro-democratic position, his grandfather and Imperial Chancellor von Bismarck feared that Wilhelm's parents were misguided tools of London's efforts to dominate the world. Caught in the middle, the highly-strung young man became an important piece in the monumental chess game played by his elders. Consequently, while loving Great Britain and the way of life of his cousins across the Channel, he also resented them for treating him coldly. Edward saw in his nephew a belligerent, spoilt, worrisome and selfish egotist whose goal was bringing misery to his parents. Wilhelm II was a bully who used his wealth and position to mask his inadequacies. Edward had no time for such unseemly behavior and the countless run-ins that Wilhelm's behavior and personality caused. Envious of his uncle's popularity, Wilhelm tried to outshine Edward, whether playing diplomat on a grand scale or purchasing larger and faster yachts to defeat his uncle's boats. Both men failed to realize that, sadly, their inability to enjoy a working relationship tainted the diplomatic relations between their countries, and played a significant role in the mistrust between London and Berlin that fueled the naval race and eventually plunged the world into the 1914 conflict.

Edward undoubtedly loved Alexandra and their children, but he failed to provide them with the warm atmosphere that his own parents had denied to him. The fact that both his sons were clearly not as intelligent, cosmopolitan, and well educated as their father was a source of great disappointment to Edward. The plainness of his three daughters confounded Edward since their mother was such a beauty. And yet, in his own peculiar way, he cared for them all deeply. In 1871, in fact, as he put Prince Alexander's remains inside the coffin, the Prince of Wales did so with *"tears rolling down my cheeks."*

These paternal feelings became apparent in 1892 when Edward's eldest son, Prince Albert Victor, Duke of Clarence and Avondale, contracted pneumonia and died within days. The young man, the source of much worry to his parents and grandmother, had vacillated between several prospective brides, among them Princess Hélène d'Orléans, the exquisitely beautiful daughter of the Count of Paris. Back in 1887, Eddy, who had known Hélène since childhood (their parents were good friends), asked her for a photograph. This was the start of what would culminate in an impossible love affair that could have threatened the foundation of the throne. This was mainly due to religious differences as the princess was Catholic and her family refused permission for her to be received into the Church of England. Informed of what was happening, Queen Victoria warned Clarence: *"you had been thinking and talking of Princess Hélène d'Orléans! I can't believe this for you know that I told you (as I did your parents, who agree with me) that such a marriage is utterly impossible. None of our family can marry a Catholic without losing all their rights..."* At one point, the Duke seems to have countenanced renouncing his succession rights if not allowed to marry Hélène, but he categorically rejected this suggestion. On 30 June 1891 the Queen had a conversation with the Count of Paris, who was visiting her at Windsor Castle. She, in no uncertain terms, told Hélène's father that marriage to Clarence was out of the question as the Act of Settlement impeded such a choice and even if Hélène changed religion, the prime minister demanded that they wait some time before marrying, *"to enable us to be assured of the sincerity of her conversion."* The Queen concluded that *"we must not delude ourselves and we cannot keep up the delusion of these young people."* In the end reason prevailed and both lovebirds reluctantly walked away from the other.

Queen Victoria took the time to write to Princess Hélène. In her touching letter, the Queen conveyed to the princess her sadness for *"the annihilation of your hopes and those of my poor grandson,"* while also recognizing that *"the difficulties of this marriage...would be insurmountable."* She ended her letter by expressing to Hélène her *"feelings of true affection for you."*

Clarence and Hélène parted ways. She married the Duke of Aosta and went on to have a colorful life as a member of the Italian royal family, as well as an enthusiastic supporter of Mussolini. Clarence, however, had to find a suitable bride. Shortly after, he was engaged to marry his cousin Princess Mary (May) of Teck, a daughter of Princess Mary Adelaide

Top: *Prince Albert Victor, Duke of Clarence.*

Above: *Princess Mary (May) of Teck.*

Left: *Princess Hélène d'Orléans.*

of Cambridge and her German husband the Duke of Teck, and a morganatic descendant of Duke Alexander of Württemberg. *"To lose our eldest son,"* the Prince of Wales wrote to his mother, *"is one of those calamities one can never really get over...[I would] have given my life for him, as I put no value on mine."*

The death of Clarence had one clear consequence. From then on, Edward became much closer to his one surviving son, Prince George, who Queen Victoria made Duke of York. The young man, a sailor, was unprepared to assume the burden awaiting him, and Edward attempted to correct these shortcomings.

A royal gathering at Windsor Castle, 1907. Front row (seated), from left: King Edward VII, Infanta Isabel of Spain, Grand Duchess Maria Pavlovna (Sr.), Queen Amélie of Portugal, the Duchess of Aosta, Princess Johann Georg of Saxony. Standing in back, same order: The Princess Royal, the Duke of Connaught, Queen Maud and Crown Prince Olav of Norway, Kaiser Wilhelm II, the Princess of Wales, Princess Patricia of Connaught, the Prince of Wales, King Alfonso XIII of Spain, Empress Augusta Viktoria, Prince Arthur of Connaught, Queen Alexandra, Grand Duke Vladimir Alexandrovich of Russia, Queen Victoria Eugenia of Spain, the Duchess of Connaught, Princess Victoria of Great Britain and Prince Johann Georg of Saxony.

The Prince of Wales's eldest daughter, Louise, married the Earl of Fife, Alexander McDuff, a great-grandson of King William IV. Two days after the marriage, Queen Victoria elevated Alexander to the title of Duke of Fife, and in 1901, her father created Louise the Princess Royal. Although she was talented and intelligent, Princess Victoria of Wales remained unmarried; this owed less to her own desires than to her mother's controlling personality and desire to keep her at home as a companion. At one point, King Luís of Portugal sought her hand for his son Carlos, but Queen Victoria denied the request on the basis of religious differences. Then there was Maud, who in 1896 married her first cousin Prince Carl of Denmark, second son of the future King Frederik VIII. Carl, an officer in the Danish navy, lacked financial means, and the couple lived off his salary and the allowances they received from their parents. The Prince of Wales gave Maud a home, Appleton Cottage, on the Sandringham Estate, where she could stay during her frequent visits to her parents. In 1905, the couple's situation dramatically improved when Norway dissolved its political union with Sweden. The Storting (encouraged by the European Powers) offered the throne to Prince Carl of Denmark. Edward VII actively supported his son-in-law and urged Carl to accept. Once established in

King Edward VII and Queen Alexandra.

Oslo, Carl became Haakon VII, while his wife retained her name. Their only son, Prince Alexander, became Crown Prince Olav; Norway's present king, Harald V, is their grandson.

The decade of the 1890s was a challenging time for the British branch of the Coburg dynasty. Most of these problems were caused by a worsening international situation that slowly led to Great Britain's

Right: The Russian Imperial Family's visit to the Isle of Wight, 1909. Seated, from left: The Princess of Wales, Tsar Nicholas II, King Edward VII, Empress Alexandra Feodorovna, the Prince of Wales, Grand Duchess Maria Nikolaevna. Standing, same order: Prince Edward of Wales, Queen Alexandra, Princess Mary of Wales, Princess Victoria of Great Britain, Grand Duchesses Olga and Tatiana Nikolaevna. On the floor: Tsarevich Alexis Nikolaevich and Grand Duchess Anastasia Nikolaevna.

isolation from other European countries, even those who in the past had been her allies. The colonial race in Africa caused many confrontations between London and Berlin, Brussels, Lisbon, Rome, Paris and even Madrid. The Congo, where Great Britain believed, rightfully, that King Léopold II of the Belgians was responsible for unimaginable atrocities, caused a rift between London and Brussels. British control over South Africa and the protracted fight with the Boers soured the already tense relations between London and Berlin, particularly after Kaiser Wilhelm II made untoward and bellicose comments against Great Britain's handling of the conflict. Then, as if the situation was not difficult enough, the end of Queen Victoria's long reign seemed imminent as her physical condition deteriorated and caused much worry across her vast empire and in the chancelleries of Europe's powers.

The Prince of Wales became King Edward VII on 22 January 1901. His reign, destined to last a little over nine years, was to bring Great Britain out of diplomatic isolation and a damaging insular approach to international affairs. Edward VII helped Great Britain build new alliances, and his sociability, judiciousness, and esteem improved his kingdom's standing among the European powers. He was also one of the moving forces behind the two international alliances destined to end London's isolation. A Francophile at heart, Edward VII played a major role in Anglo-French Entente Cordiale, which bound

From the left: King Edward VII and Queen Alexandra, the Prince and Princess of Wales.

London and Paris and provided both countries with increased security against a belligerent Germany. Also, his strong connections with the court in St. Petersburg made it possible for Edward VII and his nephew Tsar Nicholas II to smooth over Anglo-Russian differences and improve diplomatic and commercial relations. The Anglo-Russian Convention signed in 1907 was a masterful diplomatic coup. Berlin, which had allowed its alliance with Russia to lapse, now found itself surrounded. His uncle's various diplomatic coups sunk Kaiser Wilhelm II into paroxysms of mistrust, persecution, xenophobia and Anglophobic vile. The King may not have been the architect of the end of Great Britain's splendid isolation, but he was certainly among the most avid supporters of a change in course.

The King's intricate web of family connections allowed him a unique position to better work for his empire's benefit. Through his parents, he was uncle to an amazing numbers of rulers, chief among them Kaiser Wilhelm II, but the list also included Crown Princess Sophie of Greece; Grand Duke Ernst Ludwig of Hesse and By Rhine; Empress Alexandra Feodorovna of Russia; Crown Princess Marie of Romania; Crown Princess Margaret of Sweden; Duke Carl Eduard of Saxe-Coburg & Gotha; and Queen Victoria Eugenia of Spain. The King of Norway was his son-in-law, while on his wife's side Edward VII was the brother-in-law of King Frederik VIII of Denmark and King George I of the Hellenes, as well as the uncle of Tsar Nicholas II. Extended Coburg cousins included the Kings of Belgium, Portugal, Bulgaria, and Saxony, as well as Princess Napoléon and the Fürst of Hohenzollern.

An image, taken shortly before his death, of King Edward VII and Queen Alexandra at his last opening of Parliament.

Edward VII also had close relations among the Orléans, Hannover and the Habsburg families.

King Edward VII had a passion for diplomacy, but abhorred politics. Unlike his mother, though, Edward VII found himself less attracted by the Conservative Party. Holding somewhat liberal opinions and being deeply critical of anti-Semitism, the King was also deeply bothered by the treatment of blacks and the use of pejorative words when referring to them. He believed universal suffrage was necessary, but he did not believe that women ought to have the right to vote. He liked some social reform, which he saw as a necessity with changing times and the continued demands of expanding technologies.

At issue in the last years of the King's reign was the excessive power held by the House of Lords, a non-elected, hereditary chamber that increasingly opposed the reforms proposed by the government of Prime Minister Asquith. The government wanted to pass the "People's Budget," which would increase the tax burden of the landed aristocracy and the business, industrial and financial elites. The Lords had usually passed such bills, but this time they refused to follow the Prime Minister's requests. This opposition opened a constitutional crisis that eventually led, after King Edward's death, to the House of Lords losing its veto power. The King saw in this conflict the incipient beginnings of class warfare and he rejected such governmental action. He believed that radical reform would lead to the people questioning the very foundation and role of the monarchy, something he could not possibly countenance. Such was his despondency and depression over the quarrel that once he introduced his son George to a Cabinet minister as *"the last King of England."* For the House of Lords it was a losing battle – an un-elected and hereditary body having the power to veto a bill passed by a government supported by the electorate. Edward VII did his best to urge the House of Lords to find a compromise. It was all to no avail and as the King's health deteriorated, the kingdom headed toward a collision.

The 'Royal Mob' at the royal funeral in 1910. Among them one can identify several guests: King Alfonso XIII of Spain, King Manoel II of Portugal, King Ferdinand of Bulgaria and Archduke Franz Ferdinand of Austria.

A heavy smoker for decades, Edward VII was also a passionate gourmand. Between cigarettes and cigars, the consumption of alcohol and his affinity for the dinner table, Edward VII had gained enormous weight. His physical condition, compounded by the absence of exercise, only served to further compromise his health. Already in 1909 while visiting Berlin, Edward VII had lost consciousness. A year later, he collapsed while convalescing in Biarritz. In late April 1910, the King's condition was worrisome and by the time he returned to London, he was suffering from severe bronchitis. Queen Alexandra, who had been visiting her brother George in Greece, returned to London to be by her husband's side. He died the following day. Urged to slow down and rest, Edward VII replied, *"No, I shall not give in; I shall go on; I shall work to the end."* After suffering several heart attacks, King Edward VII died at Buckingham Palace at 11:45pm on 6 May 1910.

King Edward VII and his beloved 'Caesar,' who walked behind his master's coffin, much to the crowds' satisfaction.

Tributes to the dead monarch poured into London. From St. Petersburg Alexander Izvolsky, Russia's Imperial Foreign Minister, said, *"We have lost the mainstay of our foreign policy."* An English peer, Lord Morley, declared: *"The feeling of grief and a sense of personal loss throughout the country, indeed throughout Western Europe, is extraordinary, and without a single jarring note. It is in a way deeper and keener than when Queen Victoria died nine years ago, and to use the same word over again – more personal. He had just the character that Englishmen, at any rate, thoroughly understand, thoroughly like, and make any quantity of allowance for. It was odd how he managed to combine regal dignity with bonhomie, and strict regard for form with entire absence of spurious pomp."*

Two weeks after his death, Edward VII was buried at St. George's Chapel, Windsor. His funeral marked *"the greatest assemblage of royalty and rank ever gathered in one place and, of its kind, the last."*

One of Edward's nieces once described him as not having *"an easy character, and he could be rather frightening. But when one was courageous, bold enough to stand up to him, and did not allow oneself to be intimidated by his manner, then there was no kinder or better friend than Edward VII."* She further reminisced about the glorious reign that ended in 1910, writing that Edward's name has gone down in history as *"'The Peacemaker;' viewing his reign in retrospect, with its carefree life of wealth and enjoyment, I think it may truly be described as the lull before the storm."* Yet, no one missed the beloved King Edward VII more than his only son and successor, King George V, who wrote that he had lost his *"best friend and the best of fathers…I never had a [cross] word with him in my life. I am heart-broken and overwhelmed with grief."* Sadly, the new king's relationship to his own children did not mirror the one he had successfully managed to build with his own father.

The late King's short reign witnessed the height of the *"Edwardian era,"* named after him. This prosperous decade overlapped not only the start of a new century, but was also a harbinger of transcendental societal and technological changes experienced by Europe, in particular, and the world at large. Across the world, Great Britain's influence shone as a beacon of calm and order; across the Atlantic, the United States began making its presence felt in international affairs; and across the Channel, a restless Germany's grumbling pushed Europe toward the brink of war. The Edwardian era also witnessed amazing changes in how humans lived, from automobiles becoming more commonplace and technology improving people's daily existence, to the beginnings of air travel. It was an era of great privilege and elegance, just as it was a time when workers across Europe and America began questioning their role in society amid the rise of socialism. While Edward, as Prince of Wales and later monarch fostered European peace, he also supported the expansion of the British Empire's naval superiority, fostered new alliances, and isolated an increasingly belligerent German Empire. Unfortunately, his own role in protecting the British Empire from Germany's militarism only accelerated the arms race between both countries, which ultimately plunged the continent into war just four years after his death.

Below: Flanked by Kaiser Wilhelm II and the Duke of Connaught, King George V rides behind his father's coffin.

The widowed Queen Alexandra struggled to adapt to her changed circumstances, and even postponed moving out of Buckingham Palace; her husband's funeral had been delayed for several days when she refused to part with his body as she asked the nation to *"give me a thought in your prayers which will comfort and sustain me through all I still have to go through."* Alexandra's sister, the Dowager Empress Marie Feodorovna, who was among the first foreign guests to arrive in London after Edward VII's death, contributed much to Alexandra's difficult behavior. In Russia, the Dowager Empress took precedence ahead of the Emperor's wife, and Marie Feodorovna, seeing no reason why this rule should not apply in Great Britain, encouraged her sister to demand her "rights." Queen Mary, who usually displayed endless quantities of tact, acknowledged the difficult situation when replying to her aunt Grand Duchess Augusta of Mecklenburg-Strelitz: *"I understand every word, expressed or not and have feared what you so justly allude to. May the pernicious influence soon depart, then I hope all will come right."* In the end, all did

Left: Queen Alexandra and the Dowager Empress Marie Feodorovna riding in a carriage at the funeral of King Edward VII.

come out "right," but Alexandra put up a good fight, even trying to keep for herself some of the jewels that by tradition she had to cede to the new queen. There is no doubt that with age Alexandra had become more selfish and difficult. Accustomed to having Edward VII fulfill her every whim, *"Motherdear,"* as her children affectionately called her, had become an egotistical old lady.

In widowhood, Queen Alexandra moved back to Marlborough House, which remained her London residence until her death, and she enjoyed hosting her many relations, particularly her Russian and Greek family. She continued traveling, particularly to Denmark, where after her father's death in 1906, Alexandra and the Dowager Empress purchased an elegant seaside villa, Hvidøre, outside of Copenhagen. It was their home away from home and both sisters loved spending extended periods in their native country, but in their own home, not as guests of their difficult and aloof sister-in-law Louise, the wife of Frederick VIII.

In 1912 Alexandra suffered two deep losses. In January she received news of the unexpected death of her son-in-law the Duke of Fife, who with his family had been shipwrecked off the coast of Morocco the previous month. The Fifes survived the shipwreck, but the Duke contracted pleurisy and died some weeks later after arriving in Cairo. Five months later, another death caused the Dowager Queen of Great Britain deep distress. Her brother Frederick VIII died suddenly while out for a stroll in Hamburg, where he was staying with some family members on their way to Copenhagen. The Danish Royal Family experienced frantic hours caused by the King's disappearance and it was not until the following day that the authorities realized that the unidentified corpse in the city morgue was that of the Danish King. The family traveled to Copenhagen to attend the funeral, but then tragedy struck again. Driving through Prussia on his way to the Danish capital, Prince Georg Wilhelm of Hannover, Alexandra's nephew, was killed in a motoring accident. As if these losses were not enough, on 18 March 1913, King George I of the Hellenes was assassinated while on a stroll in Salonika, a city the Greek army had recently conquered during the latest Balkan war. Alexandra deeply felt the death of her favorite brother.

While still mourning her brother, Alexandra witnessed Europe erupt into the war that her husband had tried to avoid. Alexandra encouraged King George V to remain steadfast in his efforts to defend Great Britain and the Empire, while finally putting ambitious Prussia in its place. She did not realize that the conflict would consume her Russian and Greek family, while bringing untold destruction, as well as pain and loss, to millions of people. In 1917 Tsar Nicholas II's abdication ended the Russian monarchy, and that same year Constantine I, King George I's heir, was forced out of Greece. The Greeks fared much better than the Russians, who lost everything in the ensuing revolution that engulfed their once proud realm. By early 1919, nearly twenty Romanovs had fallen victims to the butchery of the Bolsheviks. Those who managed to escape Russia were impoverished and confronted a life completely alien to the world of their birth. The Dowager Empress, a ghost of her old self, was among those who escaped Russia with British help. She reached England and stayed with Alexandra for some time before settling in Denmark. By then, Queen Alexandra, nearly deaf and but a memory of the beautiful woman she once was, slowly approached her own passing. Both her memory and speech suffered impairment, while her deafness kept her isolated from the outside world.

The British public loved Queen Alexandra, who had invested her efforts in various charities, some of which survive today. An avid photographer, the Queen published some of her photographs in a book sold to the general public, the proceeds of which went to fund her charitable work. Whenever her adopted country found itself at war, Alexandra was among the first royal ladies to labor tirelessly raising funds to assist the wounded and ensure better medical care. One of her schemes sought to provide *"home comforts"* to American soldiers fighting in Europe during the Great War, for which she was widely praised in the US press. Lacking any concept of the value of money, she spent freely on others. Anyone who wrote to her seeking help received it. This caused her advisers several headaches, for *"her generosity was a source of embarrassment"* to them as they tried unsuccessfully to manage her troublesome finances.

A heart attack finally freed Alexandra from her earthly sufferings: King George V and Queen Mary, as well as other members of Alexandra's family, were at her side when she died at Sandringham on 20 November 1925. Although she had requested a small funeral, it became a glittering event, attended by the British Royal Family; King Christian X of Denmark; King Haakon VII of Norway; and King Albert I of the Belgians. Both Queen Maud of Norway and Queen Victoria Eugenia of Spain were also present at the service in Westminster Abbey on 27 November. As the coffin entered the Abbey, said one onlooker, *"the bowed heads

Above: Prince George of Wales c. 1885.

Left: Prince George and his cousin Hereditary Prince Alfred of Saxe-Coburg & Gotha.

of Britain's illustrious living and the silent tombs of her illustrious dead"* paid tribute to Queen Alexandra and her legacy. Swirling snow outside Westminster did not deter a crowd of over 60,000 who stood *"silent, reverent, and shivering in a last homage to the best beloved of Britain's long line of Queen consorts."* Alexandra rests next to her beloved husband in St. George's Chapel, Windsor Castle.

King George V (1865-1936)

When the future King George V was born in 1865, no one expected that this premature, puny baby one day would succeed to the mighty throne of his forebears. *"At half-past three in the morning,"* his august grandmother wrote in her diary, *"was quite startled by being brought two telegrams which they said I must have. They were from Bertie, announcing that dear Alix had been taken ill and then she had been safely delivered of a boy at half-

past one this morning." This was perhaps the only startling act in George's long life, for he developed into a dependable, conventional, dutiful man whose life was ruled by *"precedence and punctuality."*

The baby's name caused a stir between his parents and the Queen. Wanting to preempt Queen Victoria imposing her will on them, the Prince and Princes of Wales notified her that they had chosen *"George, as we like the name and it is an English one."* They also chose Frederick in homage to the mother's Danish ancestry. The Queen was not amused with the choices and let her son know it in no uncertain terms: *"I fear I cannot admire the names you propose to give the Baby. I had hoped for some fine old name. Frederick is, however, the best of the two and I hope you will call him so. George only came in with the Hanoverian family. However, if the dear child grows up good and wise, I shall not mind what his name is. Of course you will add Albert at the end, like your brothers, as you know we settled that all dearest papa's male descendants should bear that name, to mark our line, just as I wish all the girls to have Victoria after theirs."* In the end, the baby boy was christened George Frederick Ernst Albert on 7 July 1865 at St. George's Chapel, Windsor.

Although Edward loved his children, they feared his short temper and punctiliousness and were much closer to their mother, who doted on them and treated them as possessions even when they had become adults. Alexandra had a particular weakness for her sons, who were usually dressed alike and entered the navy together. As Albert Victor seemed a bit slower than George, the parents believed that the one could help the other. Consequently, both brothers were very close, just as were their three sisters – always dressed alike, always together, always in their mother's wake. Alexandra contributed to this frozen maturation by writing sugary letters in which she expressed her unbound motherly feelings. *"With a great big kiss for your lovely little face,"* she wrote George when he was in his mid-twenties. Not to be outdone by his mother's excess, George would reply with equally syrupy sentences: *"My own darling sweet little beloved Motherdear … Your loving little Georgy."* One can but imagine how the Prince of Wales reacted to such sweetness.

The Prince of Wales and his son Prince George. The image was taken while they were on vacation in Cannes, France. This copy was sent by the Prince of Wales to his brother the Duke of Saxe-Coburg & Gotha.

Along with his brother, George embarked on a naval career at an early age. Neither brother was a paragon of intellectual activity, being rather simple in their scholarly pursuits. *"They are such ill-bred, ill-trained children,"* Queen Victoria once recalled. *"I can't fancy them at all"* was her final verdict. The fact that the Wales children tended to be a sickly bunch further diminished them in her eyes. *"Most wretched, excepting Georgie, who is always merry and rosy,"* the Queen wrote. Albert Victor being rather lethargic and odd, it fell on George, urged by his worried parents, to provide his elder brother with better examples. This, the young prince sometimes succeeded in doing, although not all the time as he was prone to get himself in trouble more often than not. *"Prince Albert Victor, requires the stimulus of Prince George's company to induce him to work at all,"* a report informed the Queen. *"The mutual influence of their char-*

Prince George, Duke of York.

Princess Mary, Duchess of York.

acters on one another is very beneficial. Difficult as the education of Prince Albert Victor is now, it would be doubly or trebly so if Prince George were to leave him."

As the "spare," not much was expected of young Prince George. He shared the same tutor with his brother, and both princes entered the Royal Navy, which the Prince of Wales believed provided *"the very best possible training for any boy."* While intellectually disappointing, George's naval career seemed to be the best course for the young prince to follow, and the scheduled, orderly, and regimented life of a sailor perfectly suited him. The princes' naval years also included three years aboard *HMS Bacchante*, a 4,000-ton fully rigged corvette that took them around the world.

While the naval experience was designed to toughen the young princes, it sacrificed their schooling. Queen Victoria, like Prince Albert, fervently believed that royalty had to be educated and intellectually stimulated, and worried that neither prince was able to speak any language other than English. Due to this lack of linguistic mastery, the princes were sent to Switzerland to learn another language, but these efforts failed and they returned to London with little knowledge of either German or French. *"You and your sisters spoke German and French when you were five or six,"* the Queen disappointedly reminded Edward. The Princess of Wales provided little help or encouragement, as she did not wish her children to learn what she called *"that old Sauerkraut, the German language."* Years after, and while attending the University of Heidelberg, Prince George expressed his own utter contempt for the language of his forebears: *"Well, I am working here very hard with the old Professor Ihne at this rotten language which I find very difficult and it certainly is beastly dull…I really can't remain here much longer than two months and miss all my shooting and hunting in England."*

Chapter XIV – The Coburgs of Windsor ... A Dynasty's Name Changed

Upon their return from Switzerland, Albert Victor and George were separated, the elder prince continuing to Trinity College, Oxford, while his younger brother returned to the Royal Navy where he served until 1892. While serving in the Mediterranean, Prince George was under the command of his Uncle Alfred, who was stationed in Malta along with his wife and four daughters. George regularly visited his uncle and aunt, and developed a sincere and devoted attraction to their eldest daughter, Princess Marie, who was developing into a stunningly beautiful, albeit conceited, young woman. Although both George and Marie's fathers approved the young couple's fledgling romance, their mothers were opposed. The Princess of Wales thought the Edinburghs, destined to relocate and live in Coburg since Alfred was the heir of their old Uncle Ernst II, was too pro-German, while the Duchess of Edinburgh, who detested Great Britain – where she was expected to play second fiddle to her Danish-born sister-in-law – dissuaded Marie from accepting George's approaches.

Four generations of British royalty: Queen Victoria holding her great-grandson Edward of York; behind her are the Prince of Wales and the Duke of York.

While George searched for a bride, his brother found a willing candidate in their cousin Princess May of Teck, but the Duke of Clarence's unexpected death in early 1892 put an end to the engagement. Soon voices within the Royal Family, led by Queen Victoria, wondered if sensible, dutiful, cosmopolitan May would willingly take George instead. *"Have you seen May and have you thought more about the possibility or found out what her feelings might be?"* Victoria wrote to her grandson. Dutiful as ever, George followed entreaties and soon called on her family during a visit to the French Riviera, having asked her if it was possible for him to *"see you then."* Alexandra feared losing her son: *"There is a bond of love between us, that of mother and child, which nobody can ever diminish or render less binding – and nobody can, or ever shall, come between me and my darling Georgie boy,"* she wrote. The Prince of Wales, though, encouraged his son. *"It is hard,"* he said, *"that poor little May should virtually become a widow before she is a wife."* In addition, there was a family precedent: in 1865, Tsesarevich Nicholas Alexandrovich, then engaged to Alexandra's sister Dagmar, had died, and the Emperor had urged his second son, Alexander, to pursue her. They married in 1866 and grew to become deeply in love and amazingly suited to the other.

After months of pursuit, George finally proposed on 3 May 1893 and May, who had always been sincerely fond of her Wales cousins, dutifully accepted. At the beginning it was awkward for both. *"I am very sorry that I am still so shy with you,"* May once wrote to George, *"I tried not to be…but alas failed, I was angry with myself! It is so stupid to be so stiff together…there is nothing that I would not tell you, except that I love you more than anybody in the world, and this I cannot tell you myself so I write it to relieve my feelings."* George, who received the title of Duke of York from his grandmother, answered in equally reticent terms: *"Thank God we both understand each other, and I think it really unnecessary for me to tell you how deep my love for you, my darling, is and I feel it growing stronger and stronger every time I see you; although I may appear shy and cold."* The couple married at St. James's Palace, London, on 6 July 1893.

Above: The Duke of York with two of his children, Prince Edward and Princess Mary.

Right: Prince Edward of York, who in 1936 succeeded his father as King Edward VIII, only to abdicate eleven months later.

known as "Bertie". Victoria Alexandra Alice Mary, born at York Cottage and called Mary in the family, joined the nursery two years later. In 1899, Henry William Frederick Arthur arrived at York Cottage; George Edward Alexander Edmund was born in 1902, while the youngest child and fifth son, Prince John Charles Francis, arrived two years later.

George and Mary were distant parents at best. *"My father was frightened of his mother, I was frightened of my father, and I am damned well going to see to it that my children are frightened of me,"* George once said. Randolph Churchill, Winston's father, was the source for this quote, which was apparently made to the Earl of Derby. Whether he actually made the statement, George was certainly a terrifying father, aloof and distant. Mary, a devoted wife like no other, always sided with her short-tempered husband and urged her children to follow in lockstep. As a result, David became self-centered and egotistical; Bertie developed a stammer and lacked self-confidence; Henry became heavily reliant on spirits; and George dabbled in sexual adventurism and recreational drug use, both the source of much worry to all who cared about him. As for Prince John, he suffered from epilepsy and as his condition worsened, his parents kept him away from the public eye. When it came time to find young Princess Mary a husband, she married an English peer fifteen years her senior and who had an unfortunate attraction to the bottle. Luckily Bertie, Henry, and George married spouses of boundless integrity who provided them with the care and attention denied them in childhood and urged them to realize their potential.

Parliament allocated the Duke of York a handsome yearly stipend, while Queen Victoria granted the couple use of York House, St. James's Palace. The Prince of Wales also gave his son York Cottage, a quaint, small, and uncomfortable house on the Sandringham Estate that remained the family's home until 1926, as Queen Alexandra refused to leave the larger house after her husband's death. Children soon followed. Prince Edward Albert Christian George Andrew Patrick David of York, called David in the family, was born at White Lodge, Richmond Park, on 23 June 1894. The following year, while at York Cottage, Mary gave birth to a second son, Albert Frederick Arthur George,

George was an incredibly insular Briton. He did not find in traveling the same child-like joy expressed by his father every time he sailed away from Great Britain. In 1900, during the waning months of his grandmother's long reign, George was tasked with representing his family at the coming-of-age ceremonies for Crown Prince Wilhelm of Prussia in Berlin. His utter disappointment with this journey was clearly expressed when he wrote: *"I hate going of course, but am always ready to do what the Queen wishes."* His life was devoted to two hobbies, philately and hunting. Not interested in physical exertions, the taciturn George much preferred long hours with his stamps, transforming it into one of the world's most important collections. Hunting was his only other passion, a solitary activity that provided him with untold joy. *"He may be all right as a young midshipman and a wise old king, but when he was Duke of York…he did nothing at all but kill [i.e. shoot] animals and stick in stamps,"* recalled one of George's most respected biographers.

Upon his father's accession George became Duke of Cornwall as heir to the throne, though not until November 9 did King Edward VII create him Prince of Wales. As heir, George, who now had full access to the considerable revenues of the Duchy of Cornwall, moved his family from St. James's Palace to Marlborough House and was allowed use of Frogmore House at Windsor for weekend stays. He refused, however, to abandon York Cottage at Sandringham. If anyone expected Marlborough House to continue as society's epicenter they were disappointed, as George and Mary led a retiring life. Parsimonious, intellectually unimpressive, a traditionalist and a paragon of upper middle-class family values and morality, George stood in sharp contrast to his grandmother and his father. While Edward VII relished his role of *"paterfamilias"* of the Coburg dynasty's various branches, George's connections to his extended European family were timid at best, uninterested at worst. Unlike his father, a cosmopolitan and bon vivant polyglot, George was happiest playing the role of a country squire.

Shortly before Queen Victoria's death, George and Mary were asked to represent her at the opening of the first parliament of the Commonwealth of Australia. Although Edward VII tried to deter the government from sending his son away in the first months of the new reign, the Prime Minister demurred and insisted that the visit could not be cancelled. For George and Mary it was an opportunity to travel around the globe, a unique chance for them to see unimaginable lands

Above: Queen Victoria holding Prince Henry of York. Next to her is Prince Edward, while seated on the chair is Princess Mary. Prince Albert is on the ground.

Right: York Cottage in the Sandringham Estate.

The children of King George V and Queen Mary. Standing from left: Prince Albert, Prince Henry, the Prince of Wales. Seated, same order: Prince John, Princess Mary and Prince George.

and exotic destinations. She thoroughly enjoyed the experience, while George – never eager to travel – did his best, as always, to carry out his responsibilities. The journey took them to South Africa, Australia, New Zealand and Canada. The royal entourage traveled *"for eight months…covering 45,000 miles, laid 21 foundation stones, received 544 addresses, presented 4,329 medals, reviewed 62,000 troops and shook the hands of 24,855 people at official receptions alone."* When Queen Alexandra urged the travelers to slow down, George replied: *"It is all very well for you and Papa to say we mustn't do too much but it is impossible to help it. Our stay at each place is so short that everything has to be crammed into it, otherwise people would be offended and our great object is to please as many people as possible."* Among the most pleased, however, were the couple's children who stayed with their indulgent grandparents during their parents' absence. In later years, the Duke of Windsor recalled this carefree stay with Edward VII and Alexandra as one of his happiest childhood memories.

More journeys followed. There were visits to the Continent, where Mary enjoyed visiting her German relations, something her husband found less appealing. In late 1905 the couple boarded a naval vessel and sailed to India, where George was appalled by the living conditions of the majority of Indians. He rightly believed that the lack of native involvement in running the sub-continent presaged troubling times ahead, and warned his father of the danger. Two months after returning from India, George and Mary attended the wedding of King Alfonso XIII of Spain and Princess Victoria Eugenie of Battenberg, George's first cousin. Miraculously, all the royalties attending the magnificent celebration escaped an assassination attempt that left scores dead and the bride's wedding dress splattered with the victims' blood. Barely a month after escaping the Madrid terrorist attack, George and Mary were among the royal guests at the coronation of King Haakon VII and Queen Maud of Norway.

George became King of Great Britain, Emperor of India on 6 May 1910. The loss of his father, to whom he referred as *"my best friend and the best of fathers,"* was a devastating blow. In his journal, the new monarch confided a foreboding sense of doom: *"I am heart-broken and overwhelmed with grief but God will help me in my responsibilities and darling May will be my comfort as she has always been. May God give me strength and guidance in the heavy task which has fallen on me."*

King Edward's funeral provided the opportunity for George to host one of the most impressive gatherings of royalty ever witnessed. Not only was it an opportunity for the world to bid farewell to "the Peacemaker," but the assembly also provided George V with an opportunity to renew links to his many royal cousins from abroad. This, however, was not a role he relished, for George V was increasingly insular and "British," while distancing himself from the prominent role played by Queen Victoria and King Edward VII as leaders of the "royal mob."

George V's reign witnessed great national and international challenges. At home the political establishment headed toward a monumental clash between the power of the electorate and that of hereditary peers. The Liberals won this mammoth struggle and began the long process of ridding the House of Lords of its power to veto bills approved by the majority of the House of Commons, the people's chamber. George V, reluctantly, one must add, sided with the Liberals to avoid plunging the realm into further constitutional strife. Had the decision been left to him, it is quite likely the traditionalist monarch would have left the status quo in place. The other great pressing national issue, home rule for Ireland, also gave George V many headaches. The King tried to navigate these perilous waters to prevent Eire from plunging into civil war. His efforts were frozen, at least for the time being, by the biggest crisis George V faced as monarch, the Great War.

Kaiser Wilhelm II's bellicosity had not abated after the passing of his hated Uncle Edward. During the first years of George V's reign, Wilhelm II was responsible for further alienating Great Britain and securing the German Empire's isolation. It seemed to diplomatic observers as if the Kaiser's grandiosity was geared toward further making his realm Europe's pariah, yet deep down he envied his English cousins. In 1913, the

Above: King George V and Queen Mary with their eldest sons, the Prince of Wales and Prince Albert.

Left: The Prince of Wales wearing the ceremonial clothes of his investiture. At school, Edward was teased mercilessly because of wearing this attire.

Kaiser invited King George V and Tsar Nicholas II to attend the wedding of his daughter Viktoria Luise to their first cousin Prince Ernst August of Hannover. George and Mary traveled to Berlin, as did Nicholas II; the Russian Empress feigned a diplomatic illness to avoid being in the same room as the Kaiser, whom she disliked intensely. Sadly, the goodwill Wilhelm II tried to build failed to stop the war machinery the following summer. This was so after the impulsive Kaiser made statements claiming that *"I don't care a fig for your hundred thousand* [an agreement London and Paris had signed to send British troops to help France in case of war with the German Empire]. *There you are making alliances with a decadent nation like France and a semi-barbarous nation like Russia and opposing us, the true upholders of progress and liberty."*

On 28 June 1914 several shots fired by an anarchist in

Sarajevo set in motion the military machinery that soon plunged the Continent into chaos. The victims of the heinous act carried out by Gavrilo Princip, a Serbian terrorist, were Archduke Franz Ferdinand of Austria and his morganatic wife, Duchess Sophie of Hohenberg. The volatile-tempered Habsburg being the heir to the multinational empire ruled by his old Uncle Franz Joseph, news of his assassination sent a chill through the chancelleries of Europe and inflamed passions in Vienna.

The Kaiser, who had been among Franz Ferdinand's closest friends, saw the Austrian heir's assassination as an affront by the lesser humans of the Serbian nation against a higher caste. As such, this outrage should be met with the harshest reaction. If Austria-Hungary wished to punish Serbia militarily, Vienna could count on Berlin's support. This blank check the Austrians used to extract as much humiliation from Belgrade as they could. Serbia, however, was unwilling to meet Vienna more than half way. The assassins' activities were supported by elements within the Serbian government and military. Yet, Belgrade pleaded innocence. Consequently, and in spite of Wilhelm II and Nicholas II's minimal efforts to avoid a major conflict as well as George V's shock, by the first week of August the world was at war. It all was a sad comedy of errors with unimaginable consequences. Europe, the world, in fact, would never be the same.

The various governments, who saw in this hot-blooded policy a golden opportunity to gain wider popular enthusiasm for the war, exploited nationalist sentiments. Both sides were equally guilty in exploiting jingoism to denigrate the opponent, while using petty nationalist arguments to excuse the enormous demands imposed by a long and protracted conflict that failed to bring the troops home by Christmas. By early 1917 the war had turned into a nightmare, depleting resources and leaving millions dead and opinion turned ugly, with such "patriotic" suggestions as the elimination of all dog breeds perceived to be "German." This idiocy soon gave rise to inexcusable demagoguery that questioned the Royal Family's allegiance to the nation. Even some of the most talented intellectuals of the day fell victim to this faux nationalism, among them H. G. Wells, who referred to George V's *"alien and uninspiring court."* The King, livid at the accusation, famously replied, *"I may be uninspiring, but I'll be damned if I'm alien!"*

This sort of sentiment was indicative of a wider malaise among George V's subjects. As irrational charges rose, the King acted. Official word came on 17 July 1917: *"We, out of our royal will and authority, do hereby declare and announce that as from this date of our royal proclamation our house and family shall be styled and known as the House and Family of Windsor and that all descendants in the male line of our grandmother, Queen Victoria, who are subjects of these realms, other than the female descendants who may marry or may have married, shall bear the said family name of Windsor."* He added a clear break with the dynasty's German ties: *"And we do hereby declare and announce that for ourselves and for,*

Above: King George V and Queen Mary c. 1911.
Right: A medal minted to commemorate the 1911 Coronation.

and on behalf of our descendants and all other descendants of our grandmother, Queen Victoria, who are subjects of these realms, relinquish and enjoin the discontinuance of the use of degrees, styled dignities, titles and honors of the Dukes and Duchesses of Saxony and the Princes and Princesses of Saxe-Coburg and Gotha and all other German decrees, styles, dignities, titles and honors and the appellation to us or to them heretofore belonging or appertaining."

George V's proclamation in the Privy Council suddenly ended the rule of the Coburg dynasty in Great Britain. The Kaiser, never one to mince words, reacted to King George V's decision mockingly, saying that he planned to see *"Shakespeare's play The Merry Wives of Saxe-Coburg-Gotha."* The King's decision also made irrevocable the change of last names and titles to other branches of his family, among them the Battenbergs, Tecks, and Schleswig-Holsteins. While the first two became Mountbattens and Cambridges, the latter dropped their territorial designations and became simply *"Princess Victoria and Princess Marie Louise"* of nowhere.

A final break with the Royal Family's German relations came at year's end. In Letters Patent published on 11 December 1917, George V restricted the use of the title of *"Prince (or Princess) of Great Britain and Ireland to the children of the Sovereign, the children of the sons of the Sovereign and the eldest living son of the eldest living son of a Prince of Wales."* Furthermore, relatives of the Royal Family fighting on the German side, namely the Duke of Cumberland and Teviotdale, who actually never joined the war effort but whose son was the Kaiser's son-in-law, and the Duke of Albany (Duke Carl Eduard of Saxe-Coburg & Gotha) were cut off, as was the Duchess of Edinburgh, Grand Duchess Marie Alexandrovna, then living in Germany.

George V's decision severed ties between London and Coburg, while bringing to an end the rule of the House of Saxe-Coburg & Gotha's British branch. Relations between George V and his cousin Carl Eduard never truly recovered, even though the Duke's sister was married to the King's brother-in-law. Relations between the British cousins and the Austrian Coburgs did not survive the aftermath of the Great War either. Sadly, most of these links remain broken.

King George V.

King George V died on 20 January 1936. His beloved May lived long enough to witness their eldest son, King Edward VIII not only renounce the throne, but unthinkingly use his contacts with Duke Carl Eduard of Saxe-Coburg & Gotha to arrange a meting with Adolf Hitler. Queen Mary survived her husband by nearly two decades, becoming the most respected, admired, and beloved member of the Royal Family. When she died at Marlborough House on March 24, 1953, it was the end of an era. Many paid tribute to the old matriarch, but none were more to the point than Sir Henry "Chips" Channon, who wrote that she was *"above politics...magnificent, humorous, worldly, in fact nearly sublime, though cold and hard. But what a grand Queen."* Less than three months after her death, following her request that there be no interruption to the proceedings, Mary's granddaughter was crowned as Queen Elizabeth II.

Chapter XV
The Coburgs of Brussels Despised & Beloved

Born in Brussels on 9 April 1835, although Léopold was the second son, he was destined to inherit the throne his father had won after monumental efforts. Maternity did not suit the young Queen, for *"it hardly rejoices me,"* she wrote to her mother. Louise-Marie's delight with her children began once she gave birth to them. She described her son as having *"the same eyebrows and mouth as Léopold. He has the same nose. He is very nice and very pretty child."* Her mother agreed wholeheartedly with her daughter, praising her first surviving grandchild: *"He is delicious, lovable, spiritual, conversing without timidity equally in French and in German; in short I am crazy about him."*

The young prince was raised in a new court to which his father had imparted the formalities observed in some of the continent's oldest royal families, along with considerable luxury. As Belgium's first king, Léopold I knew that the outward signs of royalty were extremely important in providing his subjects with the appearance of a reliable, stable, and lasting monarchy. Thus, when his son was nine-years-old, King Léopold devised a new title for the heir, Duke of Brabant.

As a child, the Duke of Brabant's health and physical condition were the source of much worry to his parents, who had lost their first son before the baby's first birthday. *"The rumor was that he was tubercular,"* wrote one of his biographers, who added, *"Unhappily he was afflicted with a distressing limp, the result it seems, of sciatica, an infirmity particularly painful to a prince destined to wear the uniform and to fill a public role all his life."* Because he was viewed as *"a symbol of reconciliation between the parties"* that fought each other during the struggle for Belgian independence, Brabant's health, at least until there was a spare in the royal nursery at Laeken Palace, was of great importance.

The education provided to the future King of the Belgians was extremely important for the dynasty's future success. With this in mind, and once childhood ailments were conquered and overcome, King Léopold I developed a program designed to prepare his son for the crown. Léopold I, the architect of his family's meteoric rise to power and European prominence, also realized that post-Napoleonic monarchs could only grow old on their thrones if they respected the constitutional charters governing their realms. Kings who chose otherwise, Léopold I firmly believed, would go the way of the French Bourbons, who learned nothing, forgot nothing, and no longer ruled. Queen Louise-Marie, also the product of parents who had invested great efforts educating their offspring, *"followed the education of her children closely – correcting their homework herself, and lavished on them the treasure of a generous nature and highly cultivated mind."*

The Duke of Brabant showed *"seriousness above his age,"* no doubt due in great part to the loss of his beloved mother in October 1850. Louise-Marie had been a stabilizing influence in her son's development and she always managed to find a way to calm the young prince, who *"had inherited the sarcastic wit"* of his father and had a tendency to use it on those around him, his siblings being particularly regular targets. This irritability, Brabant would later heap not only on his family, but also on those who dared love and serve him as king.

For Belgium's first monarch building a dynasty was of immense importance. Of Louise-Marie's four children, three survived. In addition to Brabant, there was Philippe, Count of Flanders, born in 1837, and Maria Charlotte, born at Laeken Palace – like her closest brother – in 1840. Their father considered that their future

marital alliances would strengthen the Belgian royal dynasty and Coburg prestige, and determined that Brabant's marriage could neither be left to chance nor put off for a later date.

In 1851 Léopold I had hoped that his eldest son would make a grand alliance with one of Europe's most prestigious royal clans, the Berlin Hohenzollerns. In April of that year, the Belgian Royal Family hosted Prince Wilhelm of Prussia, heir to his brother Friedrich Wilhelm IV, and his family, hoping that sixteen-year-old Brabant would be drawn to twelve-year-old Princess Luise and develop feelings that could later be cultivated. Brabant, nursing a cold during the Prussian visit, failed to ingratiate himself to Luise. Although Léopold convinced the young princess's mother to consider such a match, the militantly Protestant Princess Augusta could not support her necessary conversion to Catholicism and the idea collapsed.

The Duke of Brabant.

Many in Europe viewed Brabant as heir to a monarchy born in the barricades of revolution; Léopold I was determined to marry him to a princess from one of the continent's major powers to erase that perception. The King's advisor Baron Stockmar agreed that Brabant's bride must come from one of Europe's most prestigious ruling families. With this in mind, in 1853 the King and his heir toured Europe's courts. *"The purpose of the expedition,"* Léopold informed Queen Victoria, *"was to find a wife for the eldest son, but please say nothing of the one chosen."*

To confuse observers, Léopold I and his retinue first visited Coburg, where Duke Ernst II received his Belgian relatives with great enthusiasm before they traveled to Dresden and then Berlin. The choices offered by both royal families were paltry; Léopold I's desired prize was in Vienna, where the Habsburgs, after nearly facing extinction in the early Eighteenth Century, had quickly replenished the imperial nursery with Empress Maria Theresa's sixteen children and their descendants. By the time Léopold I and Brabant arrived in Vienna, the Habsburg Dynasty had several branches including the descendants of Emperor Franz I; the Palatines; Tuscany; Modena; and the line from Archduke Rainer. Léopold I and Stockmar had carefully flipped through the pages of the *Almanach de Gotha* and discovered the perfect bride: Marie Henriette, youngest daughter of the late Archduke Joseph, Palatine of Hungary, and of his third wife the former Duchess Marie Dorothea of Württemberg (whose brother was the grandfather of May, George V's wife).

Marie Henriette met her future husband only once before he proposed, at a ball in the Hofburg, Vienna's impressive imperial palace, where the sixteen-year-old Archduchess was presented to two elegantly uniformed men, Léopold I and the Duke of Brabant. *"Nothing,"* Brabant complained to his brother Philippe, *"is more embarrassing than arriving at a court where one knows not one person and add to that the Austrian etiquette, you can well imagine what sort of evenings we have to endure here."* However, three days after their arrival in Vienna, Brabant wrote his brother another letter expressing his surprise at developments: *"I have important news to share with you which will have to pass on to Charlotte. Papa has chosen for me the companion that he wanted; it's the Archduchess Marie, daughter of the Palatine, and sixteen-years-old. I was quite surprised when informed of this choice. But I will submit to the supreme will; she is of medium height, a bit plump and not very attractive without being ugly."*

Chapter XV – The Coburgs of Brussls ... Despised & Beloved

"Do not trust new kingdoms," a fortuneteller once supposedly warned the young Archduchess Marie Henriette. *"They will provide you with riches, but will also cover your and your loved ones in unhappiness. You will reach the zenith of a throne, but nor it or anyone will make you happy. All those you love will suffer tragic ends. You will be accused of not caring for your people and they will be against you."* Whether true or not, this warning presaged the miserable existence Marie Henriette was destined to live in Belgium. Initially she resisted the Duke of Brabant's marriage proposal, but pleading and tears were irrelevant when it came to dynastic marriages, and her mother insisted.

News of the engagement shocked Vienna. Not only did Léopold and Marie Henriette barely know each other, but also they were children. Observers at court later recalled that both groom and bride were, as expected, timid and nervous in each other's presence. Princess Metternich, not one of King Léopold I's admirers, commented with horror when discussing the coupling as that *"of a stable-boy and a nun, it being understood that the nun is the Duke of Brabant."* Marie Henriette loved riding and found immense joy when surrounded by her beautiful stallions; considered a tomboy, she had little interest in frivolous matters. Léopold of Brabant was tall, serious, studious, morose at times, and not a friend of physical activity. Lady Westmoreland, who had met Brabant, described Léopold as *"a large asparagus with a narrow chest and no shadow of a beard whatsoever."* Even Queen Victoria was surprised, writing to her cousin: *"I wish you could wait another year before you get married, you're still so young, a wedding imposes many duties, a lifetime of them, it is a very serious thing. It is not only your own happiness, but also that of those who consecrate their life and affection to you."*

Archduchess Marie Henriette of Austria.

Yet, marriage with the Habsburgs was a major diplomatic coup for King Léopold I, for not only did it guarantee Belgium's entrance in the royal marriage market but also provided the Coburgs of Brussels with Vienna's prestigious acceptance and recognition as an equal. A proxy wedding ceremony took place at Schönbrunn on 10 August. Archduke Karl Ludwig, Franz Joseph's brother, stood for the Duke of Brabant and *"played the groom, but I was promised not to be forced to keep her for me."* Two weeks later Léopold and Marie Henriette were married in Brussels. This was but the first of several alliances between Habsburg and Coburg, alliances that may have seemed grandiose but were usually rather unsuccessful. A second alliance was established in 1857 when Léopold's sister married Archduke Maximilian, Emperor Franz Joseph's brother. Both families contributed something unique to each other's success: Habsburg prestige and Coburg new blood and family connections.

No one within the core of the Belgian Royal Family was as excited about the bride's arrival as Princess Charlotte, the only female in the family since Queen Louise-Marie's death. She hoped that in her sister-in-law she would find the source of attention and affection that her distant father and shy siblings could not provide. Much to Charlotte's delight the two girls became quite good friends quickly. *"One cannot know her without loving her,"* Charlotte wrote to her nanny. *"If Léopold is not happy with her, then that is his fault as she is quite worthy of his affection."*

Léopold did not like his wife. Although he accepted his father's choice, once married Léopold made little effort to learn how to love his wife, viewing her as an impediment to his freedom, which he defended at all

King Léopold II of the Belgians c. 1865.

Queen Marie Henriette in full court dress.

costs. He was inflexible and pedantic and Marie Henriette suffered greatly in a strange country with a distant husband incapable of demonstrating his feelings. From London, Queen Victoria entreated the Duke of Brabant to become a better husband. *"I worry about you because you are the children of that loving soul who was like a sister to me,"* she once wrote to her cousin. Soon after their wedding, Léopold brought his wife to London under the guise of introducing her to his relations. The visit had other purposes, as King Léopold I had expressed to his niece Queen Victoria his deep worries about the couple's ability to coalesce, or even consummate their marriage. The Queen was convinced that Marie Henriette remained a virgin and she reassured her uncle that *"I can explain to Marie what her obligations are with her husband, but I assure you that she is quite well aware of what is expected of her...It is impossible to submit her to a youngster of eighteen-years, who physically is four or five years younger than her and unquestionably less instructed than she is about certain matters. Marie, I will not deny saying to you, does not love him right now and if there is something a woman detests above all in a man, is the absence of virility in his character and behavior."* Furthermore, Queen Victoria told her Uncle Léopold that young Léopold *"looks prepubescent, so quite young and incapable (I must tell you this frankly as a woman) of inspiring love or otherwise respect. I am always next to Marie, while Albert spends time with Leo, as we try to help them and hope for an improvement."* She added: *"Leo [Brabant] does not manifest the least sentiment of love or admiration for Marie, or any other woman."*

After a rocky and difficult start, Léopold and Marie Henriette learned how to at least tolerate each other long enough to procreate. A daughter, Louise, was born in 1858, followed the next year by a boy, Léopold, destined to be the next Duke of Brabant. Five years later, Marie Henriette gave birth to a third baby, Stéphanie, at Laeken Palace in 1864. By then, however, the couple's intimacy was at an end.

The Duke of Brabant succeeded as Belgium's second monarch on 10 December 1865. In tribute to his father, the new King of the Belgians chose to retain his birth name and reigned as Léopold II. The new king's inauguration was celebrated on 17 December, the day following his father's magnificent state funeral. It was a historic moment for Belgium, for *"the accession of the son gave, in effect, to the work of the father, the sole consecration which it still lacked – that of time."* The tranquil transition that followed the passing of one king and the inauguration of his successor was further proof that Belgium had gained national cohesion and integrity as well as international respect. *"The death of the King, lamented as it was by the country, had not shaken the solidity of the edifice,"* wrote one of Léopold II's biographers. This became the late King's lasting legacy.

Members of the extended Coburg family and crowned relatives joined their cousin as he took the oath prescribed by the constitution, including King Luís of Portugal and his brothers-in-law Prince Georg of Saxony and Hereditary Prince Léopold of Hohenzollern; the Prince of Wales and the Duke of Connaught; Prince August of Saxe-Coburg & Gotha; Queen Victoria's sons-in-law the Crown Prince of Prussia and Prince Ludwig of Hesse and By Rhine; Archduke Joseph, Queen Marie Henriette's brother; Prince Nicholas of Nassau; the Duke of Cambridge; and Prince Wilhelm of Baden. It was a day, the new King said in his accession speech, when *"the unanimous homage which the nation pays his memory* [Léopold I's] *corresponds worthily with the sentiments she pledged him in his life...Succeeding today a father so honored in life. So regretted in death, my first promise to the representatives of the nation is to follow religiously the precepts and examples which his wisdom has left me."*

Léopold I had been a nation builder; his son became an empire builder. Since his days as heir, young Léopold had been allowed entry to the Senate and had urged Belgian politicians to secure the nation's future by looking forward. This, he believed, would grant Belgium access to a higher level of importance among other European countries while also providing for a stronger presence among the community of nations. Greatness, he believed, could only be achieved through colonial expansion. In 1855, for example, Léopold exhorted Belgium *"to be bold, always progressive and confident in itself. Our resources are immense, I am not afraid to say...To dare is to thrive."*

Queen Marie Henriette and her son, the Duke of Brabant.

As King of the Belgians, Léopold II lost little time in "daring" to create a stronger, larger realm. Back in 1839, as a condition for settling the conflict with the Netherlands, Belgium lost the provinces of North Limburg and Luxembourg, a loss the nation had not forgotten. When Prussia defeated Austria in 1866, France accepted Bismarck's suggestion and offered to purchase Luxembourg from the Netherlands. Doing so, Napoléon III believed, would provide his empire with a further buffer against any further Prussian expansion. *"The offer was made, and caused, as Bismarck possibly hoped it would, an uproar in Europe."* Léopold II tried to intervene and suggested that Belgium buy Luxembourg instead. To further his plans, the Belgian monarch – not for the last time – secretly backed a virulent press campaign supporting his offer. The Luxembourg offer was rejected as well and instead the province was declared a grand duchy with the King of the Netherlands as its ruler.

These were trying times for Léopold II, who felt that Belgium deserved a grander future. A year after the Luxembourg fiasco, he witnessed the collapse of his brother-in-law's reign in Mexico, which caused his sister Charlotte's madness. For some time she was housed at Miramare Castle near Trieste, and later her Belgian family retrieved her. After psychiatric examination, doctors determined that the Empress of Mexico was insane and Léopold II had her isolated at

Empress Charlotte of Mexico.

the Château de Bouchout, a Fourteenth Century castle that served as her home and prison until death freed her tortured mind and soul in 1927. As her guardian, Léopold II was also the administrator of Charlotte's large fortune, which he would put to good use when financing his legacy, the Belgian Congo.

Charlotte's madness was but one tragedy suffered by the Belgian Royal Family. An even bigger heartbreak was visited on Léopold II on 22 January 1869 when his only son died. The child, named Léopold in honor of his father and grandfather, had been styled Count of Hainaut at his birth, and become Duke of Brabant in 1865. His sister Louise remembered him as *"handsome, sweet, sincere, tender and intelligent."* Léopold was also considered a very sensitive child who loved ponies. Unfortunately, little Brabant *"fell into a pond and caught pneumonia."* This in turn caused the child to develop a heart condition and none of the country's best doctors could save him from an early death. Léopold and Marie Henriette were devastated by their loss. The father's despondency was plainly visible: when *"the body was about to be lowered into the crypt, the King, sobbing bitterly fell to his knees and leaned his head on the coffin. The terrible sound of his crying could be heard throughout the hushed stillness of the church."*

The untimely passing of the young Duke of Brabant raised a serious problem for the royal succession. As Léopold II only had two daughters, whom Salic law denied succession rights, his heir was his brother Philippe, Count of Flanders. This studious prince had married Princess Marie of Hohenzollern in 1867, but at the time of Brabant's death the couple were still childless, although Marie was in her first pregnancy. The absence of a successor in the next generation forced the King to reconsider resuming intimate relations with his estranged wife. It took some time for this to happen, and even though the Flanders' first child was a boy born in June 1869, Léopold II and his queen tried once more to produce a son. Much to his utter disappointment, Marie Henriette gave birth to a third daughter, Princess Clémentine, her parents' last child, in 1872. It was the end of their marriage.

Today, the world remembers Léopold for his sagacity and audacity, as well as the brutality involved in building a colonial empire in the heart of Africa. He wanted Belgium to become an imperial and colonial power. In 1866 he tried to convince Queen Isabel II of Spain to cede the Philippines to Belgium. The King fervently believed that energetic Belgium was better suited to administer this faraway colony than Spain, a kingdom he believed to be ill suited to rule its remaining overseas possessions. Isabel II, not surprisingly, ignored Léopold II's audacious requests.

As Europe's exploration of Africa continued, Léopold II saw an opportunity and he daringly went after a piece of the unknown, but resource-rich, continent. To mask his ulterior motives, Léopold II organized *"a private holding company disguised as an international scientific and philanthropic association, which he called the International African Society, or the International Association for the Exploration and Civilization of the Congo."* To those who did not know his goal, Léopold II's interest seemed a philanthropic endeavor. Feigning such goals, Léopold II supported and financed explorer Henry Morton Stanley, a Welsh-American journalist dedicated to investigating Africa. Stanley obtained from his employer, an American newspaper magnate, the necessary funding to travel to Africa and find David Livingstone, a Scottish missionary and explorer who had gone missing in the heart of

Africa while searching for the source of the Nile River. While exploring Africa, Livingstone witnessed the unimaginable atrocities slave traders inflicted on the natives. *"We passed a slave woman shot or stabbed through the body and lying on the path,"* he recalled. *"[Onlookers] said an Arab who passed early that morning had done it in anger at losing the price he had given for her, because she was unable to walk any longer."* His writings stirred the abolitionist movement, particularly as the world learned of the atrocities traders committed. It is shocking to realize, then, that Léopold II's support of Stanley's explorations, who was motivated to go to Africa by Livingstone's disappearance, led to the establishment of Belgian control of the Congo, perhaps one of the most nightmarish tragedies ever heaped on any region of the African continent.

Initially, Léopold II tried to obtain his government's support for further exploration of the Congo, as well as the establishment of a Belgian colony in the region. When state support failed to materialize, Léopold II used his own fortune, and that of his mad sister, to finance the adventure responsible for the creation of the "Congo Free State." Although the Belgian government did not want the Congo, it did loan the King funds to finance further exploration and his ultimate acquisition of the vast territories that eventually became his personal private property.

Crown Prince Rudolf of Austria and Princess Stéphanie of Belgium.

From the Congo Léopold II extracted untold riches including ivory and rubber. His mercenaries used these resources to line his bank accounts with unimaginable wealth and enslave the native population. Administrators of the Congo Free State resorted to ruthless practices. Workers who failed to meet quotas, for example, suffered grave physical punishment, including the amputation of hands. Studies of the atrocities committed during Léopold's involvement in the Congo point to the stunning fact that anywhere from 2 to 15 million natives perished at the hands of his administrators. One missionary, who witnessed the carnage, was so shocked by what he had come across that he wrote to Léopold's chief agent in the Congo, saying, *"I have just returned from a journey inland to the village of Insongo Mboyo. The abject misery and utter abandon is positively indescribable. I was so moved, Your Excellency, by the people's stories that I took the liberty of promising them that in future you will only kill them for crimes they commit."* Reports of these human rights violations eventually reached the European and American press, who lost little time bringing them to light. The brutality shocked the world and the resulting clamor forced Léopold II to sell the Congo Free State to the Belgian government, the same entity that had helped finance his adventure. This divestment took place in 1908, a year before the King's death.

Unfortunately, the brutality in the Congo – and the King's role in it – obscured his many positive achievements as monarch. Brussels was rebuilt as a "modern" European capital with large public areas, wide boulevards and all the necessities to improve public health. In 1879 a law passed by the government created free, secular and compulsory primary schools financed by the government, while it withdrew state financing of Catholic primary schools. In 1893 universal suffrage was adopted, while the King encouraged military expenditure to protect the nation from invasion by its larger, and more powerful, neighbors. He lobbied for an universal conscription law, but it was not until his last days that he managed to get it approved.

Queen Marie Henriette concentrated on raising her three daughters. She was said to have been an unbending

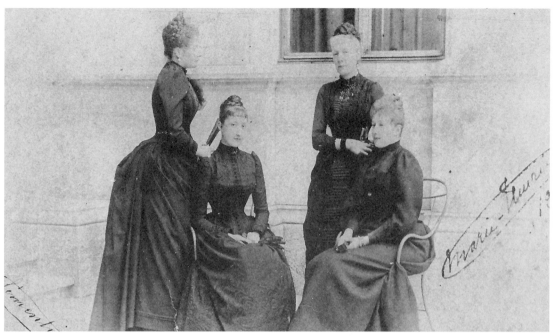

From the left: Princess Louise of Saxe-Coburg & Gotha, Princess Clémentine, Queen Marie Henriette and Crown Princess Stéphanie of Austria.

disciplinarian, causing Louise, Stéphanie, and Clémentine considerable unhappiness. Perhaps mirroring her own fate, Marie Henriette failed to dissuade her two elder daughters from entering marriages for which they were completely unsuited. Ultimately, both princesses were thoroughly miserable with their husbands and proved to be failures as mothers. Clémentine, who fell in love with a man her father would not countenance her marrying, was the luckiest. She waited for Léopold II's death and, once free from parental oppression, wed Prince Victor Napoléon.

Princess Louise's marriage to her cousin Prince Philipp of Saxe-Coburg & Gotha was utterly disastrous. Although she made Léopold II and Marie Henriette grandparents in 1878, there was very little else that the parents appreciated in their self-involved eldest child. As for Princess Stéphanie, her marriage to Crown Prince Rudolf of Austria was her father's greatest dynastic accomplishment. Here was the granddaughter of Belgium's "revolutionary" King Léopold I uniting with the future Emperor of Austria and King of Hungary. Unfortunately, the marriage brought untold misery to the couple, as well as unfathomable disappointment to their parents.

Throughout Léopold II and Queen Marie Henriette remained miserable. He was somber, horrid, and fragile, while she was willful, blunt, and boisterous. Extremely rude and domineering to his wife, Léopold II tried to impose his will on her with unkind criticisms and frequent infidelity. There is no question that the aloof and goal-driven Léopold II was far less popular with his subjects than his wife, whose natural charm was endearing. His estrangement from Marie Henriette led to liaisons with various women from all strata of society. These unorthodox entanglements, not uncommon among his Coburg generation, caused a stir among his people. The King's villa in Ostend was rumored to be the venue of licentious scenes that scandalized his church-going subjects, and rumors of the King's predilection for prostitutes and ill-reputed ladies were rampant. Once, a parish priest was pressured by his flock to bring these rumors to the King's attention. *"The word has gone round,"* the mortified priest told Léopold II, *"that Your Majesty has a mistress."* Léopold, shocked by the question, composed himself and retorted questioningly, *"Could you believe such a thing? Well Monsieur le Curé, I was told the same story about you yesterday, but I refused to believe it!"* In 1895, tired of her husband's affairs and boorish behavior, Queen Marie Henriette left the capital and retreated to Spa, a renowned resort near Liège. It was there that the Queen, better remembered for her love of horses and pets, died in 1902. Belgium barely shed a tear for this forgotten queen.

Critics of Léopold II's scandalous private life mockingly referred to him as *"King of the Belgians and the Belles."* None, however, were prepared to hear that the sixty-five-year-old monarch had fallen in fallen with a seventeen-year old Parisian prostitute better known as Caroline Lacroix. Born in 1883, Blanche Zélia Joséphine Delacroix, moved in with a gambler who, when short of money, pimped her out. King Léopold II first saw Caroline in the corridor of a Parisian hotel. After meeting the young lady, Léopold II arranged another liaison at Bad Gastein, an elegant Austrian alpine resort. *"She was pert, she was coarse, she was quick-tempered, but there was something about her that*

Princess Clémentine of Belgium.

The Baroness de Vaughan – "The Queen of Congo."

appealed to the old man...There was talk of depraved sexual tastes...of her ability to give him the illusion of youth and vigor." Whatever Caroline's wiles entailed, she captivated Léopold II, and the King lost little time showering her with riches from his Congo profits. Because of this, many called her *"The Queen of the Congo,"* and none disliked her more than Marie Henriette's daughters.

While he tried to legally disinherit his daughters, particularly Louise and Stéphanie, Léopold II bestowed upon Caroline unbelievable wealth. Critics of the King argued that he was feeble-minded and under the control of a *"rapacious and ambitious woman."* Some even argued that he was no longer fit to rule the country. He brought Caroline to live in the royal domain of Laeken and even built a pedestrian bridge to ease his ability to visit her villa there. He also presented her with the Villa Leopolda, an estate he owned in the resort town of Villefrance-sur-Mer on the French Riviera. Eventually, Caroline presented her lover with two sons: Lucien, Duke of Tervuren, and Philippe, Count of Ravenstein. After Lucien's birth, Caroline was created Baroness de Vaughan. To add insult to injury, five days before dying, King Léopold II married the baroness in a religious ceremony performed by his personal chaplain. The marriage, although recognized by the Vatican, lacked civil validity. Still, once Belgians heard of the latest outrage Caroline became the target of popular discontent. She was so vilified that at one point an infuriated populace even stoned her carriage.

Old and decrepit, suffering from *"intestinal blockage,"* King Léopold II died at Laeken Palace on 17 December 1909, forty-five-years to the day since he swore the oath of office. The man President Theodore Roosevelt had once called a *"dissolute old rake"* was laid to rest a few days later in the royal crypt. Baroness de Vaughan made her exit from Belgium soon after. Along with her two sons came the fortune Léopold had showered upon her. Although the King's daughters sued Caroline, the King's financial advisors had protected his mistress so well that Caroline retained most of her wealth although she did lose the Villa Leopolda as well as the home she had at Laeken. A few months later, she remarried her old pimp. The marriage did not last long, but his silence was bought

King Albert I leading the funeral procession of King Léopold II. Among those behind him are: Archduke Leopold Salvator of Austria-Tuscany, the Duke of Connaught, the Duke of Oporto, Prince Johann Georg of Saxony, Duke Ernst Günther of Schleswig-Holstein and Prince Leopold of Saxe-Coburg & Gotha.

with a considerable settlement. Caroline settled in Paris where she had many suitors but she never remarried. She died in 1948 and was survived by her eldest son, who lived a long and quiet life comforted by his inherited millions.

Five days after Léopold II's death, his nephew and successor presided over his state funeral. Behind the late king's corpse walked a plethora of plumed royal guests, many of them his cousins. Pomp and circumstance did not rule the day, however. What interested Belgians even more than the royal mourning display, was the salaciousness of the pamphlets *"dealing with the King's private life, that were being sold like hot cakes all along the funeral route."*

Albert I (1875-1934)

Presiding over the impressive galaxy of spectacularly uniformed royals following Léopold II's coffin was a bespectacled thirty-four-year-old man who succeeded the old rake as Belgium's third king. At birth, Prince Albert of Belgium was not expected to inherit his grandfather's throne. Born at his parents' home in Brussels in 1875, he was the fifth child of his German-born mother and Prince Philippe of Belgium, Count of Flanders.

Unlike Léopold II and Marie Henriette, Philippe of Belgium and Marie of Hohenzollern were suited for each other. Born in 1837, Philippe possessed a studious disposition and enjoyed nothing more than the quiet of his private library, a collection numbering more than 30,000 books housed in his Brussels mansion on the rue de la Regence near the Place Royale. In 1866, he had been offered the throne of Romania, but Philippe declined and instead it went to his future brother-in-law, who ruled the country with the name Carol I. Princess Marie of Hohenzollern, born at Schloß Sigmaringen in 1845, was the youngest child of Fürst Karl Anton and of his wife, the former Princess Joséphine of Baden. Two of her siblings had already married into the Coburg clan: her eldest brother Léopold was the husband of Infanta Antónia of Portugal,

King Léopold II and his nephew Albert.

while their sister Stephanie was the wife of King Pedro V.

Philippe was very taken with the plump, healthy-looking princess he met in Germany, and before long she accepted his proposal. Queen Victoria hoped that they would not marry in May, warning that *"it is so unlucky. In Scotland nobody would marry in May and you know Uncle Léopold and Princess Charlotte married in May, Grandmama and my poor father, the Duke of Orléans and Helene and Pedro and Stephanie. I never would let one of our children marry in that month. I have quite a feeling about it."* Instead, Philippe and Marie married in Berlin on 25 April 1867.

Crown Princess Victoria of Prussia, one of the guests, reported to her mother that she *"had the satisfaction of seeing the perfect happiness written unmistakably on the beaming faces of dear good Philippe and his dear young wife."* Victoria also told her mother that *"the marriage ceremony was very splendid,"* although, *"the church is one of ugliest I ever beheld."* The bride *"looked very pretty though I thought her dress heavy, tasteless and unbecoming – her pretty manner and expression quite made one forget that."* Victoria had also witnessed the proxy wedding of Marie's sister Stephanie and *"it made me quite sad when I thought of sweet Stephanie."* Marie, Victoria complained, lacked her sister's *"sweet touching expression; she is much livelier and has rather a roughness in her manner…She is a dear girl. Her features are much more regular than Stephanie's – her profile is faultless – but she has not the charm of her sister nor the lovely eyes and skin."*

Prince Philippe, Count of Flanders.

At least for the first few years of their marriage, Marie was quite able to retain her husband's fidelity. Although never as outrageous a philistine as his older brother, Philippe had an eye for pretty women and had several discreet liaisons. As a wife, Marie was perfect for Philippe, and Victoria of Prussia wrote to her mother that *"she rules Philippe entirely."* A talented painter and sculptor, she had received an exemplary education. On 3 June 1869, she gave birth to a boy named Baudouin, whose arrival seemingly secured the third generation of Coburg princes. Twins named Henriette and Joséphine arrived the following year, but the latter died two months after her birth. In 1872 the Countess of Flanders gave birth to a

From the left: Princess Henriette, the Countess of Flanders with Prince Albert, Princess Joséphine and Prince Baudouin.

Princess Isabelle d'Orléans.

fourth child whom the parents also named Joséphine in memory of their dearly departed daughter. Then in 1875 the succession was reassured when Marie of Flanders gave birth to a second son, Albert.

Albert's early years were spent in the company of his siblings, and the four Flanders children were very close to each other as well as to their parents, in contrast to the unhealthy environment in which Léopold II and his wife brought up their daughters. Philippe's children received exemplary educations and were deeply respectful to their parents. The family suffered a devastating misfortune when in 1891 both Baudouin and Henriette fell ill. She contracted influenza and unfortunately passed it to her brother when Baudouin came to see her. The young prince, already feeling unwell, could not recover and died within days. It was rumored that Baudouin was about to become betrothed to his cousin Clémentine, thus uniting both branches of the Belgian Coburgs, but his death ended the proposal. Belgians mourned their beloved prince and parliament and commerce were closed for days, not reopening until after his heartbreaking funeral.

Most Belgians assumed that Albert, nearly forty years younger than his father, would be Léopold II's successor in place of the elderly and frail Philippe. While Léopold II seems to have liked his nephew Baudouin very much, he did not enjoy the same rapport with Albert, who closely resembled his father's bookish and quiet nature and preferred study to physical displays of princely virility. Yet throughout the remaining years of his Uncle Léopold II's reign, Albert quietly prepared for the heavy burden that was to fall on his shoulders and developed a deep concern about the living conditions of the working classes in Belgium.

In his early twenties, Albert started the search for a bride, and met her at a funeral. On 4 May 1897 a rapidly expanding fire consumed a charity bazaar in Paris. Among the countless victims, who were either burned alive or suffocated by the fumes, was the Duchess d'Alençon, née Sophie, Duchess in Bavaria. She was one of Empress Elisabeth's peculiar sisters and in 1868 had married Prince Ferdinand d'Orléans, Duke d'Alençon, and first cousin of Léopold II. In fact, the Alençons were doubly related to the Belgian Coburgs. Ferdinand was the second son of Prince Louis, Duke de Nemours, a brother of Queen Louise-Marie, and of his beautiful wife Princess Victoire of Saxe-Coburg & Gotha, only daughter of Prince Ferdinand and Princess Antonia. Furthermore, Albert's sister Henriette was the wife of Prince Emmanuel, Duke de Vendôme, the only son of the Dukes d'Alençon. With these close connections, Albert attended

Elisabeth, Duchess in Bavaria.

Sophie's funeral on behalf of his family.

During the days spent in the company of his Orléans cousins, Albert renewed a friendship with a stunningly beautiful cousin whom he had not seen for several years, Isabelle, next to youngest daughter of the late Count of Paris and of his wife Infanta Isabel of Spain. Born at the famed Château d'Eu, a picturesque red brick palace in Normandy, Isabelle was three years Albert's junior. Her deeply clear blue eyes were characteristic of her Orléans lineage, while her svelte physique and height made the princess one of the most desirable "partis" available to any prince. Albert was smitten with Isabelle, whose older brother the Duke d'Orléans was not only the Head of House France, but also had been a close friend of Baudouin.

Albert kept his feelings to himself, but his father the Count of Flanders quickly learned the truth and had his wife visit Isabelle's mother at the Château de Randan, her country residence outside Paris, to discuss a possible marriage. The Countess of Flanders returned to Brussels filled with enthusiasm over Isabelle's many attributes: *"Isabelle is a distinguished young lady, perfectly raised, intelligent and seems to have a very good character, without a doubt she is the woman who will make our son happy. Along with her sisters, she enjoys excellent health. She is used to living with seriousness. Besides the fortune inherited from her father, she will also inherit a portion of her mother's fortune as well."* Albert and his parents all went to Léopold II to obtain his permission.

Prince Albert and Princess Elisabeth of Belgium.

Léopold II, however, rejected the idea, claiming that Albert's marriage into the Orléans family would poison Belgium's bilateral relations with the French Republic, since her brother was not only Head of House of France but also forced to live outside the country by the law of exile that banished both the Orleanist and Napoleonic pretenders and their firstborn sons. Léopold II had already expressed his concerns about an Orléans-Coburg alliance when Isabelle's brother the Duke d'Orléans had expressed interest in marrying Princess Henriette, the eldest Flanders daughter. Hence, his decision to deny permission to Albert and Isabelle, as stunning as it was, should not have surprised anyone

From the left: Prince Albert, Prince Léopold, Princess Elisabeth and Prince Charles-Théodore.

Three Duchesses in Bavaria. From the left: Marie Gabriele (who married Crown Prince Rupprecht of Bavaria), Sophie (who married Count Hans-Veit of Törring-Jettenbach), Elisabeth (Queen of the Belgians). Photo courtesy of Count Hans-Veit of Toerring-Jettenbach – Sophie's grandson.

involved in the failed betrothal. Although unable to become husband and wife, Albert and Isabelle remained lifelong friends.

Yet it was at the funeral of Sophie d'Alençon that Albert of Belgium also met Elisabeth, Duchess in Bavaria. Born at Schloß Possenhofen near Munich, she was one of the daughters of Karl Theodor, Duke in Bavaria, and his wife Infanta Maria Josepha, one of the many German-born daughters of former King Miguel I of Portugal. Karl Theodor was socially active, having founded several medical institutions that provided health services to the needy, while Infanta Maria Josepha supported her husband's philanthropy. The couple also pursued cultural activities, as both the Duke and his Portuguese wife were talented painters and musicians, traits inherited by their children.

A year younger than Albert, Elisabeth was one of six children: Amalie (1865-1912) married the Duke of Urach; Sophie (1875-1957) married Count Hans-Veit zu Toerring-Jettenbach (1862-1929); Marie Gabriele (1878-1912) married Rupprecht, later Crown Prince of Bavaria; Ludwig Wilhelm (1884-1968) married Princess Eleonore zu Sayn-Wittgenstein-Berleburg; and Franz Joseph (1888-1912), who died of polio and was unmarried. These unions produced further royal ties as Elisabeth's nephews and nieces included Count Karl Theodor zu Toerring-Jettenbach (who married Princess Elisabeth of Greece, sister of Marina, Duchess of Kent, wife of King George V's youngest surviving son) and Duke Albrecht, Head of House Bavaria after the death of his father, Crown Prince Rupprecht. Elisabeth was also a first cousin of Crown Prince Rudolf of Austria (husband of Albert's own first cousin Stéphanie); Fürst Albrecht of Thurn und Taxis (who in later years provided protection and solace to several dispossessed royals, among them Dorothea of Schleswig-Holstein, a granddaughter of King Léopold II); the Duke of Braganza (Duarte Pio); Princess Elisabeth of Liechtenstein (mother of Prince Franz Joseph, father of the present ruler of the Alpine principality); Grand Duchess Charlotte of Luxembourg; and Empress Zita of Austria.

Undoubtedly, the Bavarian ties to most of Europe's Catholic dynasties made Elisabeth an attractive royal bride. She came to know Albert at the Parisian home of Emmanuel, Duke de Vendôme; Elisabeth was Emmanuel's first cousin while Albert was the Duke's brother-in-law. This time, King Léopold II consented to the marriage and the wedding was celebrated in Munich in October 1900. A few days later, the newlyweds made their official entry into Belgium, where the citizenry received them with honest enthusiasm. Throughout their exemplary married life, Albert and Elisabeth emulated the example set by his parents, in contrast to Léopold II's thoroughly dysfunctional family.

Although she loved her children, Elisabeth did not enjoy pregnancy; as a free spirit, raised in a culturally rich environment created by her talented parents, she felt imprisoned and constrained. However, once the babies were born, she was loving, committed, and very involved in their education and development. The first child arrived in 1901 and received the traditional Belgian Coburg name, Léopold. Nearly two years later, Elisabeth gave birth to a second son, Charles Théodore, named to honor her own father.

Elisabeth frequently returned to her beloved Bavaria, several times with her husband and children but often alone, attempting to escape from the conservative, oppressive atmosphere of court life in Brussels.

Prince Albert, tasked by King Léopold II with official business both within Belgium and abroad, was an indefatigable representative of the Royal Family. His allegiance to the difficult King was undisputed, but Albert did not share his uncle's licentious behavior nor did he allow Léopold II to treat him disrespectfully. His position within the line of succession was further strengthened in 1905 when Albert's father died and he became the King's direct heir. The loss of his father was ameliorated the following year when Elisabeth gave birth to their third and last child, a girl born at their summer villa in Ostend and baptized Marie-José in honor of her grandmother. Marie-José was a talented free spirit like her mother, adored by her father and siblings, although she knew that Elisabeth favored her sons.

A year before succeeding Léopold II, Albert visited the Belgian Congo. By then Belgium had gained possession of the area after buying Léopold II's stake in the enterprise, and Albert was shocked by both the poor conditions and also by the abuse inflicted on the natives. Incensed by the mismanagement he witnessed, upon returning to Brussels the prince lost little time in recommending reforms to safeguard the natives. He also asked that the government invest in technology to further improve production and the safety of workers.

King Albert was drawn to reform, a fact emphasized when he succeeded Léopold II and gave the accession oath in French and Dutch, thus recognizing the duality that made Belgium such a unique nation. His grandfather and uncle had read the oath only in French. His innovations also included his family life. For the first time since the country was founded, Belgium had a King and Queen who were deeply in love with each other. Unlike his predecessors, Albert's family life was cordial and unpretentious, and his disposition friendly and democratic. With his svelte wife by his side, Albert portrayed a new image of royalty, one resembling a bourgeois family. These were changing times and the new King of the Belgians wanted his monarchy to become more accessible to the people, more open to national and international culture, more an entity of gradual changes. He further implemented new reforms in managing the Belgian Congo. A devout Catholic, the King believed that the natives deserved his protection from abuse and oppression. He did not seek the independence of the Congo, for this would have been a radical statement at the time, but he understood that the atrocities previously committed there could never again take place.

King Albert and Queen Elisabeth with their children. From left: Prince Charles-Théodore, King Albert with Princess Marie José on his lap, Queen Elisabeth and the Duke of Brabant.

The Belgian royal couple suffered an "annus horribilis" in 1912. The year seemed to be a promising one as the weddings of two of Queen Elisabeth's cousins were scheduled to take place. Firstly, Prince Georg of Bavaria married Archduchess Isabella of Austria on 10 February, a happy event that soon turned sour as the couple realized that they had little in common. The marriage was annulled the following year. Georg eventually became a priest, while Isabella, perhaps shocked by the experience, remained unmarried. Two

Left: King Albert I wearing the uniform used in the trenches during the Great War.

Below, left: Cousins and Allies – The Duke of Brabant, the Prince of Wales and Prince Charles-Théodore of Belgium.

days later, Elisabeth received news that her Uncle Guillaume IV of Luxembourg had finally passed away after years as an invalid. Then, while the court was in mourning for both Guillaume and Duchess Amalie of Urach, who died on May 26, Elisabeth's nephew, the sickly, cherubic and diabetic three-year-old Prince Rudolf of Bavaria succumbed to illness on 26 June. Less than two weeks later, Prince Franz, son of the future King Ludwig III, married Princess Isabella of Croÿ on 8 July. This time, the couple remained married for nearly forty-five years. Unfortunately the losses continued. On 23 September the family was doubly shocked by the deaths of Infanta María Teresa, wife of Prince Ferdinand of Bavaria, who died a week after giving birth to her fourth child, and of Duke Franz Joseph, Queen Elisabeth's brother, who died from complications caused by polio. Racked by tuberculosis, Princess Marie Gabriele, Elisabeth's, sister passed away at Sorrento on 24 October, and a month later Albert's mother, the amiably rotund Countess of Flanders, died of pneumonia, leaving her son bereft with grief. Then, on December 12, Prince Regent Luitpold, who had ruled Bavaria since 1886, passed away aged ninety-one. The birth on November 20 of Archduke Otto, first son of Elisabeth's cousin Zita, passed nearly unnoticed amid this melancholy string of tragedies.

As if all these personal losses were not enough, conversations King Albert had with his cousin Kaiser Wilhelm II weighed heavily on his mind. The two sovereigns had spoken during the German state visit to Brussels and the reciprocal Belgian state visit to Berlin. The Kaiser, never one to refrain from bombastic and shocking comments, warned Albert of imminent war, blaming French revanchism for any conflict and excusing Germany's arms race as a reaction to France's malevolent designs against the Reich. Princess Marie-José remembered that there was *"a theatrical side in him, worthy of a ham cooked to please children."* Her father, she later remembered, was *"exceedingly annoyed by the bluster and intentional gaffes"* the Kaiser carelessly dispensed. Wilhelm II sought to reassure his Belgian cousin concerning Germany's future intentions when he said that *"he had no intention of annexing Belgium because he would gain nothing,"* since he found Belgians *"an intractable people."*

Right: King Albert was keenly interested in new technologies. He was among the first royals to take to the air as flying with airplanes became safer and widespread.

Notwithstanding the Kaiser's reassurances concerning Belgium's integrity, King Albert realized that his kingdom was wholly unprepared to resist the German juggernaut. At a court ball during Albert's visit to Berlin, the Kaiser provided him with an inkling of what was to come, pointing to General von Gluck and describing him to Albert as the man who was *"to lead the march on Paris."* During another conversation with General von Moltke, the Chief of Staff, Albert was shocked as the military leader said, *"This time we must make an end of it. Your Majesty cannot imagine the irresistible enthusiasm which will permeate the entire German nation on 'The Day.'"* One historian convincingly presents these conversations as a clear attempt by the Germans to cajole and frighten King Albert. Their ultimate goal, outlined in a strategy known as the Schlieffen Plan, called for Germany's defeat of France in a matter of weeks. To do so German troops expected to swarm through Belgium on their way to the French border. While France focused on defending the German border, Germany's plan entailed hitting France's northwest and trapping her armies along the Rhine in a deadly blow. For the plan to work, however, Belgium was expected to *"allow German troops to pass through her territory unhindered."* That, of course, was impossible since allowing such an action was tantamount to renouncng his kingdom's sovereignty. That, King Albert simply would never do.

Upon returning to Brussels, a deeply concerned Albert contacted the prime minister and the Belgian General staff. In a memorandum, Albert clearly stated his position in the event of the violation of national sovereignty: *"We are resolved to declare war at once upon any power that deliberately violates our territory; to wage war with the utmost energy and with the whole of our military resources, whenever required, even beyond our frontiers, and to continue to wage war even after the invader retires, until the conclusion of a general peace."* Among diplomats, King Albert's warning was not given much weight. It seemed impossible to them that the Belgian king would risk the annihilation of his small kingdom to defend its neutrality. Even the British were told in clear terms that if they landed a force to attack Germany, Belgium would not hesitate to fire upon them. Albert's position was unshakeable and he was convinced that as monarch, rightfully so, he was ultimately responsible for defending the territorial integrity of his realm. Unless the menacing powers changed their military strategy, Belgium would use force to defend itself.

This is exactly what happened in 1914, when Germany mobilized and troops headed toward the Belgian border. On the evening of 2 August, the German Minister delivered an ultimatum to the Foreign Minister in Brussels, alerting the country that the Kaiser's troops intended to violate Belgium's neutrality to reach the border with France. The Belgian government was given twelve hours to reply. Belgium rejected the German demands. Instead, King Albert stood his ground and called his people to arms against the invader. Seeking to remind Great Britain of its obligations as guarantor of Belgian independence, Albert sent a telegram to his cousin George V. In it, the Belgian monarch stated: *"Remembering the numerous proofs of Your Majesty's friendship and that of your predecessor, of the friendly attitude of England in 1870, and the proof of friendship which she has just given us again, I make a supreme appeal to the diplomatic intervention of Your Majesty's Government to safeguard the integrity of Belgium."*

Albert blurted, *"What does he take me for?"* To preempt the German juggernaut, Albert ordered the immediate destruction of strategic bridges on the Meuse near Liège, as well as railroad infrastructure leading to Luxembourg. Belgium, Germany was about to discover, could also roar.

On 4 August, when German troops entered Belgium, Albert's subjects were unwilling to cooperate with the invaders. Over the following weeks the nation's *"anti-German feeling"* became *"intense."* Patriotism spread wildly and even Belgian Boy Scouts joined the struggle against Germany. The royal palace was turned into a makeshift hospital and Albert and Elisabeth rallied their subjects behind the national banner.

Germany's hope of surprising France and dealing it a deathblow failed owing to Belgium's heroic stand. The Belgians even managed to inflict the Germans a defeat near Liège; although only a temporary respite, this delayed the German advance and allowed the French to further prepare. German fury over Belgium's actions took form in daily atrocities committed against the invaded population. There was nothing Albert could do for his suffering people. Although he tried to resist, his armies retreated toward the coast and eventually most major cities fell to the advancing Germans, who were less than civil when dealing with the defeated. The countryside also suffered grave losses and widespread destruction. Albert, who had retreated to Antwerp, continued the fight as he awaited the arrival of Allied troops, but by then his efforts were meaningless. The world observed in dismay as Germany raped Belgium. A political cartoon published in the magazine Punch best exempli-

Above: A gathering of Coburg cousins after the Great War. Seated: Princess Marie José and the Duke of Brabant. Standing, from left: Queen Elisabeth, Queen Mary, Princess Alice, Countess of Athlone, and her husband the Earl of Athlone.

Right: King Albert and Queen Elisabeth out for a stroll.

Albert, with Elisabeth's help, also sent a personal appeal to the Kaiser, hoping that Wilhelm II would listen to his pleas for a diplomatic solution. However, the Belgian monarch was to be completely disappointed. In an unappealing and concise telegram, the Kaiser reiterated Germany's position, surrender or perish. *"As the conditions laid down made clear,"* the Kaiser wrote, *"the possibility of maintaining our former and present relations still lies in the hands of Your Majesty."* Not amused by his cousin's unwillingness to negotiate, a frustrated

fied this reality: it showed the Kaiser and King Albert standing face to face over a ruined Belgium. *"You see,"* the Kaiser said, *"you've lost everything." "Not my soul!"* the gentleman king replied. Germany's forces headed toward Antwerp, forcing Albert and the remnants of the Belgian army to retreat to the coast. At one point the King was asked to depart Belgium or risk capture, but refused and promised to fight to the end. *"It is for you,"* Albert told his troops, *"to maintain the reputation of our arms by the tenacity and bravery of which you have already given such ample proofs…Our national honor is at stake!"* It was his unwillingness to forsake his people that provided Albert with monumental prestige and made him the kingdom's most respected historical figure.

Although war raged across Europe for the next four years, the Belgians retained control of a sliver of territory on the coast, where the King remained for the duration of the conflict. The Queen, distraught at the destruction her fatherland had inflicted on her beloved Belgium, dedicated herself to medical services. The fact that so many of her German relations were involved in the war, chief among them her brother-in-law Crown Prince Rupprecht, pained Elisabeth gravely. German agents tried taking advantage of this and spread malicious rumors about Elisabeth's sympathies. Not unlike her British relations, the Belgian Coburgs were accused of German sympathies,

Queen Elisabeth in Egypt.

attacks generated not by Albert's adoring subjects but by the Germans hoping to rouse the Belgians against their royals. *"My husband and I are one,"* Elisabeth had once told the Kaiser. Her tireless work and sacrifice during the war years served as proof of her devotion to Belgium.

To guarantee the safety of their children, Albert and Elisabeth decided to ship them off to Britain. There, Léopold and Charles-Théodore attended Eton, while Marie-José spent time at the home of her father's cousin, Princess Alice, Countess of Athlone, who was close to the Belgian royal couple and visited their sparse wartime home at La Panne. Shocked by the simplicity, Alice asked Elisabeth *"how she could bear to live in such surroundings."* Elisabeth refused to consider improving their living conditions, thinking that doing so would signal that they accepted the house in La Panne as home and had given up their fight to regain the kingdom. Simplicity and self-sacrifice remained the order of the day until liberation arrived.

Toward the end of the war, a conflict that Albert had unsuccessfully tried to end through diplomatic overtures, he received command of the Army of Flanders, consisting of Belgian and Allied divisions. The King led this multinational army as it forced the German retreat across Belgium. He refused to annex any German territory and always claimed that his sole goal was the defense of Belgium's neutrality and the restoration of its national territory. He wished for a peace without victors, thus avoiding future hatred. Once when someone accused the Germans of being cowardly, the King quickly replied, *"Barbarians yes, but in the mass not cowards. They have been misled, shamefully misled, but they die as bravely for their country as my men die for theirs, and I myself have seen some magnificent examples of heroism – heroism that has made me wish with all my heart it were in a better cause."*

In October 1918, King Albert entered Ostend. Each day brought news of yet another German defeat and, as the

King Albert I shortly before his death.

their sons Léopold and Charles-Théodore. Prince Albert of Great Britain, the future King George VI, had earlier welcomed his Belgian cousin as the King entered Brussels. It was a moving, proud day, proof that all the sacrifices suffered to defend an ideal and retake the nation were worth the unmentionable pain experienced by all Belgians. *"Throats were hoarse, arms were limp, faces were wet with tears,"* commented one biographer. Another witness noted how Albert allowed his feelings to show, while Elisabeth was *"plainly overwhelmed by their reception…she sat erect and motionless on her white horse, her face piteously grave in the midst of so much rejoicing, and her eyes stonily fixed on the road ahead."*

The path ahead was a difficult one for a small nation ravaged by war and years of brutal occupation. The King's first act once in control of the political situation was to form a government of national unity comprised of the country's three largest political parties. He also lobbied for absolute universal suffrage, different from the one sponsored by his Uncle Léopold II, which accorded the number of votes one person held based on their worth.

At the Versailles Peace Conference, Belgium, encouraged by Albert I, was among the least vindictive participants. While France wished to blame the conflict solely on Germany and Austria, Albert believed that a less harsh stand would prevent German revanchism and end the vicious cycle of war that had consumed Europe for the last century. He wished to have Belgium's security strengthened, while promoting better relations with the Grand Duchy of Luxembourg, now ruled by one of Queen Elisabeth's first cousins. The Belgian monarch was also deeply skeptical of the new regimes that replaced the ousted imperial structures in Berlin and Vienna. He believed that restoring the German and Austro-Hungarian monarchies would provide Europe with the stability needed to avoid falling into yet another abyss of political and economic dislocation, responsible for furthering social upheaval. He was right in thinking so, but the French delegates, not surprisingly, ignored their Belgian ally's requests and blame was heaped upon the defeated. Huge war reparation payments were imposed and Germany would suffer great economic

Army of Flanders marched toward Brussels, war seemed at an end. Then followed a triumphant entry into Bruges where, with Elisabeth and their three children, Albert rode through streets filled with wildly acclaiming people. It was while staying at the Château de Lophem, outside Bruges, that the King learned that Germany had signed the armistice at Spa on November 11, the same resort where Albert's Aunt Marie Henriette had once lived. A jubilant Belgium prepared to welcome the Coburgs home to Brussels.

On 22 November Albert made a triumphant entry into Brussels. The capital's streets and wide boulevards were packed with people who wanted nothing more than to welcome their beloved king. For them, Albert was a gentleman, a "chevalier," who had sacrificed nearly everything to defend his people and their nation. The King rode a magnificent stallion; immediately behind him came Queen Elisabeth, followed by

Right: The death of King Albert caused nationwide mourning in Belgium. Stunned by the loss of their beloved king, hundreds of thousand of his subjects lined the streets of Brussels to witness his funeral procession. In this image we see the King's lying-in-state.

dislocation that contributed to the financial chaos that consumed the world in 1929 and eventually to the rise of Adolf Hitler.

In 1919 Albert and Elisabeth traveled to the United States, where they were received with glorious enthusiasm. During the six weeks that the Belgian royal couple remained in the United States, they were fêted as heroes by a population cognizant of the great sacrifices this unprepossessing couple had incurred. When they returned to Belgium they focused on rebuilding a country devastated by the German occupation. With Belgium's infrastructure nearly ruined, Albert led efforts to rebuild railroads, expand workers rights, reform socio-political institutions, and restore the heavily battered national defenses. He also went to great efforts to support the granting of rights to Belgium's large Flemish population, so much so that nearly all their demands were met. By 1926, in contrast to the rest of Europe, Belgium had managed to achieve astounding progress in its plans for rebuilding the country. Belgium also faced serious challenges caused by the economic debacle of the late 1920s, as well as the instability caused by political squabbles. In all, the King tried his best to remain above the fray, while providing the political class with guidance when necessary.

As life eased, the King was able to continue enjoying his many favorite pastimes, chief among them climbing, which he had been passionate about since his youth. In this difficult sport, he found the equation to obtain great satisfaction while challenging himself with ever more daring feats. The King also loved traveling and whenever possible combined both pursuits. On 17 February 1934, Albert left the royal palace and headed to Ardennes, where he was to spend the day on some of his favorite peaks. Accompanied by his valet, Albert spent the early afternoon climbing the *"towering Roche du Bon Dieu….When the King, usually so punctual, did not return…*[his valet] *began to worry."* Hours were spent frantically searching for the King in the evening's frigid darkness. Queen Elisabeth ignored what was happening and believed her husband was at an award ceremony scheduled for the evening. His lifeless body was found lying on its back while still dangling from a rope, *"a gaping wound"* on the side of his skull. It seems he had fallen and been slammed against the side of the mountain. Elisabeth was devastated for months, and Belgium was plunged into a deep abyss of despondency and national mourning. Their beloved king, only fifty-eight, was no more.

"The real peak of Albert I's achievement," wrote a historian, *"was that he was the best constitutional monarch who has ever reigned on the Continent of Europe."* Perhaps a more fitting tribute was that Albert I was the best king ever produced by the Coburg dynasty, one who quickly realized that being a good king meant sacrifice. Above all, Albert also understood that the defense of national integrity and fraternity trumped dynastic allegiance. He was a Belgian before he was a Coburg.

Chapter XVI
The Coburgs of Vienna
Debacle and Ruin

Born in 1844 at the Tuileries in Paris, Prince Philipp was the eldest child of Prince August and Princess Clémentine. He was raised in Austria, where his family settled after the death of his grandfather Ferdinand, and brought up to inherit the two Fideikommiss established by his father, a legacy that made him among the richest and most prominent members of the Habsburg court. Today, though, he is perhaps best remembered as the most famous royal cuckold of Nineteenth Century Europe.

Philipp was educated by private tutors at his family's Viennese palace, and later attended the University of Bonn before entering the Austrian Imperial Army. The Battle of Sadowa, during the Austro-Prussian War of 1866, emphasized to him the futility of armed conflict, and Philipp escaped death when a bullet lodged itself in his helmet. He later entered the Hungarian Hussars Regiment, receiving the rank of Lieutenant Field Marshal, and used his linguistic talents when he traveled around the world in 1872. He recorded his impressions in a book, *Voyages and Hunts Across the World*, published under the pseudonym "Cariudo" ("the Hunter" in Japanese). Philipp also used his travels to amass one of the world's most extensive collections of rare coins; when finally sold after his death it fetched a princely sum.

Prince Philipp's legacy was enormous. The two Fideikomiss he would inherit included nearly a hundred villages, along with mines, sawmills, dairy and stud farms, foundries, factories, arable fields, pastures, and forests. This complicated enterprise was managed from three locales: the Central Chancellery was located in Vienna, while the Forestry Direction was in Jolsva (Jelsava, Slovakia) and the Iron Works Management in Pohorelá (Slovakia).

The varied estates were rich in possessions and disparate incomes. Prized merino sheep were raised in the lands around Schloß Ebenthal in Lower Austria, a large castle first acquired by the Kohary family in 1732 and used by Princess Clémentine as her country home. It was here, in 1887, that Prince Ferdinand had accepted the Bulgarian throne. Nearby lay the estate of Walterskirchen, acquired by the Kohary family in 1733 and including a castle and neighboring village. After World War II, the Coburgs restored Walterskirchen and used it after most of their Vienna palace was rented out to various business enterprises. Although Walterskirchen is now closed, one can still see on the wrought-iron railings the initials "SCG." Kleinhadersdorf, near Walterskirchen, contains a small Kohary crypt where several members of the family rest, among them six-year-old Franz, whose premature death made Princess Antonia her father's sole heir. The estate of Dürnkrut, dominated by its ancient, towered castle and bought by the Kohary family in 1781, was also located in Lower Austria. It contained a factory that processed sugar beets grown on Coburg and Kohary lands and, like other properties, included prosperous hunting grounds.

Located in Hungary, the estate of Puszta Vacs was a profitable agricultural endeavor; some lands were leased, while others were home to merino sheep. In 1844 Prince Ferdinand founded a stud farm there that raised horses for riding and coaches, and the Vacser studs were highly sought after. The estate also included a distillery and a liquor factory. Regarded by Hungarians as the geographical center of the country, Puszta Vacs featured a commemorative 11-meter high pyramid; although burnt in 2001, it was rebuilt three years later.

The Fideikomiss properties in what became Czechoslovakia included estates such as Füllek, which included

Left, top: A map of the former Austro-Hungarian Empire placing Sankt Antal in relationship to Budapest and Vienna. Schloß Sankt Antal, the main Coburg residence in the region where the majority of the non-Austrian Coburg and Kohary Fideikomiss estates were located, was a great favorite of Prince Philipp and of his brother King Ferdinand of Bulgaria.

Middle and bottom: Views of Schloß Sankt Antal (now known as Sväty Anton). The estate was lost through expropriation and later confiscation. Today, the castle houses a museum dedicated to its history, and that of the Kohary and Coburg former owners.

hunting lodges as well as the ruins of a castle that played an important role in Hungarian history, having figured prominently in the wars against the Turks. The estate of Balloghvar, now in Czechoslovakia, had a splendidly designed one-story castle of thirty rooms and a chapel, surrounded by an English-style garden. Not far away, perched on a hill, are the ruins of Ballogh Castle, which gave the estate its name. The property, purchased from the Counts von Erdödy, boasted merino sheep, deer, and wild boar.

Since 1622 the Koharys owned an estate at Szitnya (Sitno), now in Slovakia, which formed part of the title Antonia's family had received from the Emperor. The estate lay below the ruins of an ancient castle of the same name. The Schemnitz River runs through the main valley and its strong current powered mines, mills, brickworks, and the production of charcoal. Sankt Antal Castle, the main Coburg residence on the estate, was surrounded by a vast, finely kept park. The castle and park were rebuilt in 1759 by Antonia's great-grandfather, Count Andreas of Kohary, who died there eight years later. Its size and magnificent contents made this property a princely residence. Today it is a well-visited museum dedicated to the Coburg and Kohary families; the Kohary Archive was once housed there.

Coburg and Orléans cousins gather at Claremont House. From left: The Duke de Penthièvre, Prince Ludwig August of Saxe-Coburg & Gotha, the Prince de Condé, the Duke d'Alençon, Prince Philipp of Saxe-Coburg & Gotha, the Count d'Eu. Just a few years later, d'Eu and Ludwig August embarked on a futeful journey to Brazil.

Yet another important estate, located at Murány, was perhaps larger and more profitable than the others. Named after a ruined castle that had played a major role in Hungarian history, the Kohary family acquired it in 1720. Murány encompassed three villages and twenty-six hamlets, large ironworks, mills, sawmills, breweries and distilleries, and some twenty inns. The estate was enriched by the Garam River, which begins at the foot of the Konigsberg and after taking numerous tributaries builds into a powerful channel. Mountains and pastures dominated the geography, and the valleys produced rich grain harvests and fed the considerable stock of cattle.

In Pohorelá, located in the Slovakian region of Banská Bistrica, the Garam Valley made the area particularly fertile and rich. The Coburgs owned an estate there, dominated by a fairly large and well-equipped castle surrounded by a handsome park, which they used for summer stays. From Pohorelá the prince could not only hunt but also visit the nearby ironworks. Administration of this aspect of the Coburg fortune lay here, where Princess Antonia's father had purchased numerous mines in the region. In the Upper Garam valley he built ironworks in the Lordship of Murány. Prince Ferdinand paid particular attention to this estate and he also regulated, surveyed and better cultivated the healthy forests located there. Under his administration the ironworks were modernized and

Prince Philipp of Saxe-Coburg & Gotha c. 1858.

expanded through the purchase of more mines. In the late 1830s a furnace, the Ferdinandhütte, was built there and a foundry was established as well.

chamois as well as more exotic trophies from his world tour. Although his eventual wife's memoirs painted him in a negative light, Philipp was something of an intellectual with a number of interests. In addition to hunting and coin collecting, he was – like his friend and cousin the Prince of Wales (later Edward VII) – a gourmand who loved good wine and cigars. True to his Coburg heritage, he was also a sensual man, with a predisposition to engaging in the pleasures of the flesh.

Princess Clémentine, who had grand ambitions for her children, wished her son Philipp to make an illustrious marital alliance, preferably with the daughter of a king. With this goal in mind, Philipp was dispatched to Brussels to woo King Léopold's eldest daughter, the barely nubile Princess Louise. Philipp and the young girl were closely related: he was a grandson of King Louis Philippe, while she was his great-granddaughter. They were also great-grandchildren of Duke Franz Friedrich Anton and his wife Augusta. Fourteen-years younger than her prospective groom, Louise had been brought up in an atmosphere of cold distrust, by parents who seemed to loathe each other and who took little notice of their daughters. In fact, an observer later recalled that Louise enjoyed Parisian visits with her great-uncle the Duke d'Aumâle, her late grandmother Louise-Marie's extremely rich brother, because he liked Queen Marie Henriette and always made her laugh, conditions missing from her home in Brussels.

Above: The Duke d'Aumâle, the extremely rich and and erudite brother of Princess Clémentine (right).

Technological improvement continued throughout the Nineteenth Century and under Prince Philipp's administration, production tripled. Despite his constant travel, he remained devoted to managing the estates under his care. Not only were the Coburgs innovators in the industrial production of iron, but the Fideikomiss also developed the infrastructure required to bring it to the marketplace. Consequently, the Coburgs were responsible for the system of roadways in this remote part of the Habsburg Empire.

Prince Philipp of Saxe-Coburg & Gotha, said one author, was *"an unattractive, squat, myopic, coarse-natured creature."* Despite his myopia, he was an excellent shot, adorning the walls of his many residences with deer and

For several years Léopold II refused to allow the union: not only was Louise too young, but he also hoped that his eldest daughter would make a more substantial alliance. When other suitors failed to appear, though, the King relented. In February 1875 Louise, two weeks shy of her seventeenth birthday, wed the nearly thirty-one-year-old Philipp. Philipp was deeply fond of his wife; perhaps he even loved her, for she was undoubtedly a very pretty young lady. She was also completely ignorant of the physical side of married life, and her wedding night presaged the dangers ahead. Louise was so shocked as to what was taking place in the intimacy of their room that she ran away in distress. For several hours she was missing, only to be found hiding under a fountain of the royal gardens at Laeken Palace. It took much effort to calm the poor girl and convince her to return to Philipp's presence, if not his embrace. Louise was a sacrificial lamb to the duty of royal alliances, yet while her childhood had undoubtedly left her emotionally fragile, as an adult she failed herself, her children and her house. In fact, Louise's sad legacy was an absolute inability to accept accountability. Her memoirs, fraught with self-serving inaccuracies, testify to her shallowness and lack of character. One chapter in her highly exaggerated biography, titled, *"My Beloved Belgium; My Family and Myself; Myself – As I Know Myself!"* reveals something of her egotistical approach to life.

Louise's willful character frustrated Philipp, and discovering that he sexually repulsed her was deeply hurtful. When he tried to provide Louise with direction, she accused him of being authoritarian. When he brought to Louise's attention the damage her reputation was suffering, she ignored his pleas. Hurt and jealous, Philipp became distant and spent longer periods away from his difficult wife. His mother, livid when informed of Louise's behavior, could barely set eyes on her Belgian cousin. Yet, nothing seemed to restrain the young princess as marriage, instead of providing her with boundaries, unleashed a wild mare.

Both Philipp and

Above: Prince Philipp in his thirties, while his wife, the former Princess Louise of Belgium, is at left.

Louise's parents hoped that children would save the situation. A son, Prince Leopold, was born on July 19, 1878, at Sankt Antal, where his parents had gone for the summer. The arrival of a boy guaranteed the Fideikomiss succession, but as many royal and princely families knew, a spare, although not required, offered welcome assurance in case tragedy struck. In late 1880, Princess Louise found herself pregnant again, but disappointingly a daughter, Princess Dorothea, arrived at the Coburg Palais on 30 April 1881. Although a healthy baby, Dorothea was not a particularly pretty one, having inherited the pouty lips

Left: Prince Philipp and Princess Louise with their firstborn child, Prince Leopold.

Below, left: Princess Louise and her daughter Princess Dorothea.

sported by several Coburgs and the Orléans nose. Her blue eyes graced a face that at times could be described as chubby, with full cheeks and a chin that barely made its presence. As she aged, Dorothea's long blonde flowing mane became one of her most attractive features, as did her height and uncanny predisposition to thinness. Her father, fonder of children than his wife, welcomed his daughter joyfully; while a second boy would have been wonderful, a daughter could also provide many benefits, particularly in older age. Despite their rather traumatic childhoods, both Leopold and Dorothea remained deeply attached and loyal to their father. Relations with their mother, though, were entirely different.

Louise, happy to be done with what would be her last pregnancy, was quite frustrated that her recovery would keep her from partaking in the Austrian Imperial Court's most important event of that year, the wedding of Crown Prince Rudolf and her sister Stéphanie, scheduled for 10 May. Her one consolation was the presence of her parents at Dorothea's christening, which took place the day before Stéphanie's wedding. Louise welcomed her sister Stéphanie's arrival in Vienna, as the latter recalled: *"My sister Louise and I became close chums, having no secrets from one another."* She also recalled that prior to marrying Rudolf, he *"was on intimate terms with my brother-in-law…*[and] *greatly admired my sister Louise."* Louise was convinced that Rudolf was interested in a liaison with her, though whether such an affair happened is not known. Once installed in Vienna, Stéphanie relied on Louise, her *"ray of sunshine."* Had the sisters been smarter, they could have had Vienna at their feet. However, a frivolous, fluttering butterfly with a propensity for self-inflicted damage was in no position to provide guidance to a child who was wholly unprepared for the role marriage catapulted her into.

In 1883, Louise became an aunt when Stéphanie gave birth to a daughter, Elisabeth, destined to be her only child. Later in life, Elisabeth and Dorothea were to be great friends, both commiserating about the marital disasters of their respective parents. After Elisabeth's birth, Rudolf and Stéphanie parted ways. He was restless while she was unable to help her unstable, if talented, husband. Philipp and Louise, having serious problems of their own, spent time with the Crown Prince and his wife, and the two men, through separated by fourteen years, became friendly, sharing a love of hunting and, if truth be told, illicit distractions away from the Belgian sisters. When Rudolf fell under the spell of Baroness Marie Vetsera, Philipp was aware of the liaison. Once, attending a reception at the German Embassy in Vienna, Rudolf left Stèphanie's side to confide in Louise that *"She [Vetsera] is there, ah, if somebody would only deliver me from her!"* Louise believed that Rudolf was completely under Vetsera's spell, *"an imperial sultana, one who feared no other favorite, so sure was she of the power of her full and triumphant beauty, her deep black eyes, her cameo-like profile, her throat of a goddess, and her arresting sensual grace."* Tragedy and scandal hung over the Imperial Court and Philipp was about to witness one of the most traumatic episodes in the Emperor's long life.

Right: Crown Prince Rudolf of Austria.

Below, right: Baroness Marie Vetsera, the teenaged mistress of Crown Prince Rudolf. She pursued him with a vigor that left witnesses astonished. Her infatuation with the continually despondent Rudolf had dire consequences, not only for them, but also for the empire. Rudolf's death is one of those events that "changed history."

Rudolf's oppressive existence began unraveling in 1888. Although aware of what was happening, neither Prince Philipp nor any of Rudolf's close friends could stop the Crown Prince from spiraling into an abyss of depression. In Rudolf's case, mental instability was also hindered by repercussions caused by venereal disease, *"morphia addiction, to say nothing of an excessive dependency on alcohol. These factors would account for his restlessness, irritability, moodiness, tension and outbursts of rage."* Rudolf was a walking time bomb.

By early January 1889, Baroness Vetsera had become Rudolf's mistress. She gave him a gold cigarette case fortuitously engraved, *"With gratitude to a kind fate."* This Rudolf showed to Prince Philipp. It is quite possible that by then Rudolf had made the decision to end his life. A willing Baroness Vetsera made it much easier to accomplish. Rudolf and Vetsera arrived at Mayerling on 28 January. The Crown Prince had acquired the hunting lodge from the Heiligenkreuz Monastery in 1886, made extensive renovations, and in 1887 *"ceremoniously opened"* the estate. Rudolf asked Prince Philipp, whom he jocularly called "Fat Boy," to join him and Count Joseph Hoyos for a hunt on the 29th. In Vienna, alarmed by the disappearance of their daughter, the Vetseras began inquiring as to her whereabouts.

When Prince Philipp arrived in Mayerling, he had breakfast with Rudolf and Count Hoyos. Former Prince Alexandr of Bulgaria was invited, but declined.

Left: Mayerling Jagdschloß, site of the tragedy that shook the Austro-Hungarian empire to its foundations. A witness to the events surrounding the death of Crown Prince Rudolf, Prince Philipp remained silent about the untimely death of his friend and brother-in-law.

Everything seemed normal, though the Crown Prince did excuse himself from going out hunting, claiming a cold that the wintry weather outside would only worsen. That evening, the Emperor was giving a family dinner to celebrate the engagement of Archduchess Marie Valerie, Rudolf's sister, to Archduke Franz Salvator. Rudolf was expected, but instead sent a telegram to Stéphanie, asking her to write to his *"papa that I ask his pardon most obediently for not appearing at dinner."* Rudolf claimed that *"because of a heavy cold I wish to avoid the journey this afternoon and stay here with Josl Hoyos."* During tea with the Crown Prince, Rudolf asked Philipp to tell the Emperor that he *"respectfully kissed his hands."* With this, Philipp left Mayerling, traveling by carriage to Baden and then by train to Vienna to attend the dinner.

Prince Philipp's elite position at court was evident that evening, when at the Hofburg he dined at the "All-Highest Table" occupied by the Emperor and Empress, the Crown Princess, eight Archdukes, five Archduchesses, Prince Reuß (German Ambassador), and Count Meran. He confirmed Stéphanie's telegram and told the Emperor that Rudolf was indisposed. Archdukes Albrecht and Wilhelm said they hoped that Rudolf would soon recover. The Emperor had apparently wished to take advantage of the happy occasion and speak to Rudolf and Stéphanie with the goal of a reconciliation that, if all went well, might lead to further children and a secure succession.

That same evening, Count Hoyos and Rudolf enjoyed dinner together at Mayerling. Hoyos later recalled that Rudolf seemed in better spirits, eating heartily and not consuming copious amounts of alcohol. They discussed hunting and praised the cook's wonderful dishes before Rudolf excused himself and retired to his quarters. It was the last time Hoyos saw him alive.

Baroness Vetsera's grave at Heiligenkreuz, near Mayerling.

Prince Philipp returned to Mayerling early the next morning, expecting to have breakfast with Rudolf and Hoyos, only to learn that something was amiss. Johann Loscheck, Rudolf's worried valet, informed Hoyos that at 6:30am the Crown Prince had asked him to call on him an hour later. When the valet knocked on the door no one answered, and he found all entrances to Rudolf's bedroom locked. When Count Hoyos gave the order to break Rudolf's door, Loscheck revealed that his master was not alone: Baroness Vetsera had been in the bedroom all along. *"The worst was now to be feared,"* Count Hoyos later wrote. *"The responsibility which I had to bear was crushing."*

As Hoyos deliberated about forcibly opening the bedroom door, Prince Philipp arrived. Learning what had happened, Philipp sided with Hoyos and had the door broken in, only to be met with a ghastly scene. Loscheck confirmed that *"there was no trace of life in the two bodies, that the Crown Prince was lying bent over the edge of the bed with a large pool of blood before him."* Ambassador Prince Reuß later confided to Chancellor

Viktor telegrammed Mayerling asking if Rudolf would be back in Vienna to attend a second family dinner. Philipp, not wanting to reveal anything, telegrammed back saying that Rudolf was still indisposed, adding that *"further details would follow later."* Prince Philipp remained at Mayerling until the body was removed in the early hours of 31 January, then he went to meet the Emperor. The content of their discus-

Princess Louise in the 1890s, when trouble was around the corner.

Prince Philipp some time after the Mayerling tragedy.

von Bismarck that *"I now know for certain that Count Hoyos and the Prince of Coburg saw the two bodies immediately after breaking down the door."* In a panic, Hoyos, who believed the death of the Crown Prince was caused by poisoning, left Mayerling immediately and headed straight to Vienna to report to the Emperor.

The grisly task of guarding the bedroom fell on Prince Philipp's shoulders as he awaited instructions from the Hofburg. After more closely examining the body, Philipp and the staff discovered that Rudolf had shot himself; how Loscheck failed to hear the gunshots remains a mystery. Later that day, Archduke Ludwig

sion was never revealed. The Prince, in fact, never wrote a word about the events he had witnessed in Mayerling, respecting the Emperor's wishes that he take these secrets to the grave. For this sign of both loyalty and respect Franz Joseph was forever in debt to his son's friend, and later protected him during Philipp's marital troubles.

Those troubles soon became apparent to nearly everyone. Throughout, Philipp kept silent as his wife vilified and maligned him. From her arrival in Vienna, the irrepressible Belgian princess had gained the attention and friendship of one of the most dangerous tongues in the imperial capital, that of Archduke Ludwig Viktor, the homosexual youngest brother of Emperor Franz Joseph. Known by the sobriquets of "Bubi" and "Luzivuzi" to his intimates, the young man was a walking train-wreck who went from one frivolity to the next, leaving in his flimsy wake a stellar collection of scandals for the imperial secret police to clean up. At one point this unattractive duckling was rumored a candidate for the hand of Emperor Pedro II's eldest daughter, though luckily for her the plans never came to fruition.

The friendship that developed between Ludwig Viktor and Louise, both great flirts who loved gossip, eventually contributed to her downfall. Louise would later write that their enmity emanated from her turning down his efforts at *"vanquishing the citadel of my virtue,"* insisting that *"he laid his devotion at my feet."* Unfortunately, Louise claimed, *"Louis Victor, jealous of the worthy sentiments with which another, who was not a prince, had inspired me, lost his patience, and from being the object of his love I became the object of his hatred. I own that I had a taste for satirical repartee, which I had inherited from the King and which made me many enemies. Was the Archduke offended at a little plain speaking? Wounded vanity is prompt to avenge itself. I had henceforth in him an open enemy. He swore that he would force me to leave the Court."* Apparently, at least according to Louise, Ludwig Viktor told his Imperial brother that he saw Louise in a compromising situation, and in public of all places, with an Uhlan officer. The ensuing scandal was tantamount to a fall from grace. Louise, who claimed her innocence, was personally asked by Emperor Franz Joseph not to appear at Court and instead to embark on *"a trip somewhere."*

Of a flirtatious nature, Louise was bored with married life and soon enough got herself into trouble. Her family ended her first known affair, but not long after Louise was driving in her carriage around the Vienna Prater when she saw an attractive young officer, Geza Mattachich. Soon their relationship developed into a full-blown affair. Her indiscretions won Louise a private interview with Emperor Franz Joseph who, tired of her escapades, exiled her from the Viennese court. Undaunted by this official reprimand, Louise simply left Vienna with her lover in tow. Separated from her husband, Louise did not abandon her access to his inestimable fortune and incurred huge debts.

Archduke Ludwig Viktor, one of Vienna's most poisonous gossips.

Louise had taken her daughter Princess Dorothea with her when she fled Vienna. Living with her scandalous mother and her lover threatened to damage her reputation, and Philipp and Princess Clèmentine decided that the best way to protect Dorothea's reputation was to marry her off immediately. Their choice fell on a distant cousin, Duke Ernst-Günther of Schleswig-Holstein-Sonderburg-Augustenburg, only brother of Empress Augusta Viktoria, Kaiser Wilhelm II's first wife; his grandmother, Fürstin Feodora zu Hohenlohe-Langenburg, also happened to be a Coburg descendant. Louise reluctantly consented and Dorothea married Günther in August 1898 at Coburg in a ceremony attended by a bevy of royal relatives.

Emperor Franz Joseph, outraged at Philipp's inability to control his wayward wife, insisted that the Prince seek retribution from Louise's lover in a duel organized at the Reitsaal of the Spanish Riding School in Vienna. Both men drew pistols: Philipp's shot went astray, while Mattachich fired his into the air. They were then handed swords. Mattachich, more agile than the middle-aged prince, brought the farcical episode to an end when he nicked Philipp lightly on the right hand. Louise soon took her revenge. Short of funds, she made the mistake of forging the signature of her sister Stéphanie, widow of Crown Prince

The wedding of Princess Dorothea of Saxe-Coburg & Gotha and Duke Ernst Günther of Schleswig-Holstein-Sonderburg-Augustenburg, Coburg, 2 August 1898. Standing from left: Prince Ferdinand of Bulgaria, Prince Philipp and Prince Ludwig August of Saxe-Coburg & Gotha, Crown Prince Ferdinand of Romania, Duke Philipp of Württemberg, unknown, Princesses Feodora and Louise of Schleswig-Holstein, Duke Siegfried in Bavaria, Princess Caroline-Mathilde of Schleswig-Holstein, unknown, the Groom, Prince Albert of Schleswig-Holstein (Glücksburg), Prince Leopold of Saxe-Coburg & Gotha, Hereditary Prince Alfred of Saxe-Coburg & Gotha, Prince Friedrich Leopold of Prussia, Princess Beatrice of Saxe-Coburg & Gotha, Hereditary Prince Ernst and Hereditary Princess Alexandra of Hohenlohe-Langenburg, Grand Duke Ernst Ludwig of Hesse and by Rhine, Prince Christian of Schleswig-Holstein and Duke Alfred of Saxe-Coburg & Gotha. Seated: Princess Henriette of Schleswig-Holstein, Duchess Marie of Saxe-Coburg & Gotha, Duchess Adelheid of Schleswig-Holstein, the Bride, Princess Marie Louise of Bulgaria, Crown Princess Marie of Romania and Grand Duchess Victoria Melita of Hesse and by Rhine.

Rudolf of Austria. Philipp used this act to have her committed to a mental institution for several years, including the Lindenhof Sanatorium in Saxony. Mattachich was thrown in jail for having abandoned his military obligations, charged with embezzlement, lost his title, and was sentenced to six years in prison without any evidence. Four years later, with the support of a Socialist parliamentarian, he was finally released and rehabilitated.

For seven years, Louise remained locked away and of her family only Dorothea, urged by her Aunt Flanders, once paid her mother a visit. Louise always hoped that once free, Mattachich would retrieve her. She was not to be disappointed. Mattachich traveled to Saxony and began planning Louise's escape. While on a supervised visit to Bad Elster, a spa near the border with Austria-Hungary, Mattachich spirited Louise away. Eventually, they reached the safety of Paris, where they lived like bohemians with little money.

At one point, Emperor Franz Joseph asked Léopold II to assume responsibility for Louise's expenses. The Belgian king, who had not spoken to Louise in years, replied that she was dead to him. *"You also have to pay for a dead daughter,"* was the Emperor's prickly reply. At the time, Louise and her sisters were owed the share of their inheritance from Queen Marie Henriette, but Léopold II refused to extend any disbursements to his daughters. Louise and Stéphanie went to court and sued for half of the estate. Although they lost, their father was accused of having a heart of gold *"harder than stone."* Wishing to stop the public flogging his actions had rightfully earned, Léopold II offered Louise a settlement: an estate near Cologne plus 50,000 francs per year, as long as she abandoned her lover. Louise refused. In 1907, her marriage to Prince Philipp was dissolved, finally exempting the long-suffering husband from her mounting debts. The dissolution of Louise's marriage, viewed as a slander to the family name, was the last coup and her father, as well as her sister Stéphanie, cut off all contact with her.

"The divorce did not solve all of Louise's problems; she and Geza still were in a difficult financial situation and had to move frequently," one author wrote. The death of King Léopold II brought Louise further financial complica-

tions since he left her and Stéphanie not a penny. What his second wife did not get, Léopold II had transferred to a foundation he created with the specific purpose of providing the Royal Family financial independence. The princesses lost little time in starting legal proceedings against their father's will. Stéphanie, along with Clèmentine, eventually settled with the Belgian government. Since she was desperate to fend off her creditors, Louise required more than the government offered and thus continued the lawsuit. In due course she lost in court. In 1913, the government gave permission to pay the princesses six million francs, but by then Louise and her lover had moved to Germany. The outbreak of hostilities in 1914 prevented Louise from receiving the settlement and she had to wait a further five years for it.

Besides bringing Louise financial uncertainty, the outbreak of war also disrupted her household. As a Croat, the German police considered Mattachich suspect of holding Allied sympathies and he spent two years in prison. The couple then moved to Budapest, where they were living when the Habsburg Empire fell. *"Here lives a Princess who is poorer than I am,"* said one of the Communists who searched her home. Instability in Hungary forced Louise and Mattachich to move once again, this time back to Paris, where she wrote her memoirs, a vehicle she used to settle old scores with many of her husband's closest family members. While in Paris, Mattachich's health deteriorated and in 1923 he died. Without the support of her protector, Louise relocated to Wiesbaden, Germany. It was there that death released her from worry and the difficult life her selfishness had caused. *"I knew much misery, humiliation and physical pain,"* she wrote shortly before her death in 1924. *"But I also know love, and whatever adversities I faced, when you have had real love in your life you can say you truly lived."* Her escapades had cost Louise her family, fortune, and position. The famous Theodor Herzl, seeing her at the theater, turned to a friend and remarked, *"Eve after the fall!"*

After paying off his wife's incredible debts with the help of his friend Emperor Franz Joseph, Prince Philipp retired from public life and spent his remaining years traveling around his various properties, to Primkenau, Coburg, Bulgaria, and other European destinations, his spirit broken by his wife's behavior. No one, though, was more affected by Louise's actions than her son Leopold, who never spoke to her again and treated her as if she was dead; Louise, in turn, regarded her son with disdain, never accepting that her own actions had led to the break. A dissipated young man of disagreeable character, Leopold, said a contemporary, *"had big lips, the lower slightly protruding, his nose was large and his nostrils sensual...he had small eyes, perhaps placed too low in his expressionless face, he wore glasses due of his myopia."* Prince Leopold had entered military school, graduated in 1897, and served as a lieutenant in an Austrian Imperial Hussar regiment, but his myopia made it difficult for him to have a successful career, though he could still sport the dashing uniform expected of any prince. In 1905 he finally left the military and joined the reserves. One of his friends, Baron Lafaurie, described him as *"of heavy character, lacking in joviality, often annoyed and only interested in people for the entertainment they could provide."* A Germanophile mainly interested in the army and the emperor, Leopold could be personable when he wanted, but seemed cynical, proud of his heritage and rank, and an altogether emotionally damaged young man. Close to his father and sister, he also developed a strong bond with Grand Duchess Marie Alexandrovna, whom he frequently visited in Coburg. Both shared a love of horses, apparently finding in them the peace, comfort and calm that human relations had denied.

Princess Louise a prelude to her troublesome times.

As heir to the fortune held in trust by his father, Leopold possessed a considerable yearly stipend that allowed him to live in considerable comfort and luxury. He visited his German and Austrian family frequently, particularly during the hunting season. Myopic as he was, Leopold also happened to be a very good shot. He adored his sister and liked his brother-in-law, often staying at Primkenau, their Silesian estate, and joining them on travels across the Continent. His relations with the Belgian side of the family were minimal at best and although he was Léopold II's first grandson, he only saw his grandparents infrequently. He was much closer to his Coburg grandmother, who cared deeply for him while also trying to shield Leopold from the embarrassment caused by the marital collapse of his parents.

Right: A 1904 photo of Prince Leopold while in Port Said, Egypt. The photograph was sent by him to Grand Duchess Marie Alexandrovna. Due to their frequent visits to Coburg, Leopold and his father maintained close relations with the senior line. These relations continued with Duke Carl Eduard as well.

On leaving active service, Leopold traveled for nearly two years, taking in Asia and the United States. Once back in Europe, he continued leading an active social life. Leopold lived in his own set of rooms in the Coburg Palais and was a frequent presence at court. He was also fond of opera and theater, with a predilection for singers and actresses that contributed to his demise.

For dynastic purposes, as well as for the safeguard of the Prince Ferdinand and Counts Kohary Fideikommiss, it was imperative to find Leopold a proper wife. The young man, however, resisted these approaches, even though there were a few archduchesses willing to marry him. Instead, he found solace in the embrace of women who could never have been presented at court. In 1907, while taking the cure at Marienbad Leopold met a young actress named Mila Rybicza. Born in Prague in 1886, her father had been a functionary at the imperial court. Mila began her acting career in 1905, first appearing in Meran and later transferring to the theater in Regensburg.

Leopold quickly became infatuated with Mila, who in 1908 was hired by a theater in Berlin. Mila, who used the stage name Lotte Gregowicz, was once described as *"a brunette with admirable hair, green-eyed, amber-skinned, slim, impeccably dressed and with charming feet. Her voice was enrapturing, as were her grace and charm."* However, and in spite of all her physical attributes, the young woman lacked the necessary social background to enter the rarefied world of the Coburg dynasty.

Lotte Gregowicz was an ambitious woman and pos-

Prince Philipp and his children, Dorothea and Leopold. This image was taken at one of Prince Philipp's hunting lodges and remained unknown for decades since it was pasted in a long-forgotten photo album.

sessed an iron will. Once she had Leopold in her tentacles, she was unwilling to release him. At one point, she became convinced that Leopold loved her so deeply that he would marry her and fulfill her ultimate goals of social acceptance and unimaginable wealth. When the affair was revealed in 1911, the Coburgs were stunned. Leopold's brother-in-law, having heard rumors of the liaison, summoned the manager of Lotte's theater to Primkenau, where the poor man confessed knowledge of the romance. Armed with this information, Günther confronted Leopold, who admitted to the affair. Prince Philipp, mortified by this development, quickly offered a princely sum to Lotte if she left Leopold, a suggestion she indignantly rejected as she continued to hold out for a marriage that could never be.

From left: Prince August Leopold, Prince Philipp and Prince Leopold just before the Great War.

Prince Philipp and his cousin Philippe, Duke d'Orléans.

The following year, Lotte abandoned her theatrical career and returned to Vienna, where Leopold installed her in an apartment. Convinced that Leopold would defy his father and marry her, she did not realize that such an action would deprive him of his inheritance rights to the two Fideikomiss forming the bulk of his family fortune. She apparently told one of Leopold's friends that all would be well as soon as her lover settled matters with his recalcitrant father. The couple traveled around Europe, later visiting Palestine and Egypt, but her ambition and his dilettantism were a flammable mix and many witnessed their ferocious arguments. Once, a friend of Leopold's recalled, a quarrel was so heated that Lotte yelled at her lover, *"Seriously Leo, with your awful personality you should consider yourself lucky to be loved by a woman like me."* The prince did not think twice about his response: *"F... your heart, what I love is the rest of you."*

Leopold, with Lotte in tow, first heard of the news of Archduke Franz Ferdinand's assassination while staying at Paris's famed Hotel Majestic. Livid and convinced that the Serbs were malevolent schemers responsible for the murder, Leopold immediately returned to Vienna, leaving Lotte behind as he expected to return after attending the Archduke's funeral. Lotte, concerned about her own interests, seems to have asked Leopold to provide her with guarantees, including a promise to marry her within six months, making her the universal legatee of his will, as well as asking Prince Philipp to pay her an astronomical sum should her lover prematurely die. The start of the war prevented Leopold's return to Paris; instead, and with the help of some of his friends, Lotte later met her lover in Budapest, where he resided during the conflict.

The war uprooted the couple's plans. While Leopold's visual impairment made it impossible for him to fight, he received a commission as an officer in the Austro-Hungarian Red Cross. When Lotte again tried, unsuccessfully, to have Leopold formalize their relationship, the Prince informed her that his father not only opposed such a move but was also pressuring him to find a suitable bride. Philipp suggested one of the many daughters of Archduke Friedrich, or his first cousins Archduchess Elisabeth, daughter of Philipp's sister Clotilde, or Princess Eudoxia of Bulgaria, eldest daughter of King Ferdinand. By then, Leopold's ardor for Lotte had begun to subside. Settling down with a proper bride would solve all his problems and guarantee his succession to the Coburg fortune. To get Lotte to release him, Leopold offered her a sizable settlement, but she declined the compromise. She would either marry her prince or take matters into her own hands.

Fearful that she was about to lose her lover, Lotte – in the throes of depression – lured Leopold to her apartment on the afternoon of 17 October 1915 after sending her servants away. He arrived at 5pm, asking his chauffeur to return in about two hours. An hour later passersby heard the sound of gunshots from the apartment. When they managed to open the door a ghastly scene met them: Lotte had committed suicide after throwing acid on Leopold's face and shooting him four times. Lying on the floor near Lotte's lifeless body and in extreme pain, the unfortunate prince murmured incessantly, *"I am blind, I am blind."* Rushing to Vienna, Dorothea and Günther were devastated by Leopold's precarious condition. Prince Philipp tried to censor newspaper reports, but in the end had to accept the fact that all of Vienna knew of his son's sad tragedy.

Prince Leopold's memorial card.

Over the next few months, Leopold underwent several procedures in an effort to restore his health. One of the bullets had perforated a lung and he suffered serious complications. Dorothea continued her frequent visits to Vienna *"due to the terrible accident suffered by my brother…my father rejoices as he is very lonely."* By Christmas Leopold's condition was critical, but he rallied, although the pain he experienced was at times simply unbearable. Worse still, Leopold used alcohol to ameliorate his pain. Depressed by his future, he underwent yet another surgery to restore his vision on 27 April 1916, but unfortunately his heart stopped during the procedure and Leopold died.

In his last will, Leopold thanked his father for *"the kindness he demonstrated to me all my life and I beg him to forgive me."* Dorothea became Leopold's sole beneficiary, while his mother was not mentioned at all. Of her son Louise had nothing but acidic comments: *"Leopold died in such a frightful way that I cannot even mention it, he had not belonged, in my belief, for a long time to this world, but it was not I who was affected by this terrible punishment which terminated the lineage of the eldest scion of the House of Saxe-Coburg."*

The death of his only son robbed Prince Philipp of any wish to live. He seemed to age overnight and became a recluse as dark shadows descended upon the Coburg Palais. When political unrest toppled the Habsburgs, Philipp left Vienna and settled with his

Left: Prince Philipp and his brother King Ferdinand of Bulgaria. This image was taken after the Great War. The brothers were spending time in one of their properties in Czechoslovakia.

brother Ferdinand in Coburg. By then the elderly prince had become an invalid and was only rarely seen in public. Gone were the resplendent and plumed helmets, the elegant uniforms layered with medals and orders. Also consumed by the end of Habsburg rule was a considerable part of the Coburg and Kohary fortune. Without any incentive to continue living in a world that seemed foreign to him, Philipp passed away in Coburg's Burglaßschloßen on 3 July 1921. His funeral, three days later, was attended by several Coburg relations, among them Duke Carl Eduard and King Ferdinand of Bulgaria.

Earlier in the year Dorothea, whose financial situation had become precarious after her husband lost the yearly pension disbursed to him by the Kaiser, lost Günther. His health had suffered greatly due to the stress caused by his overwhelmingly tenuous financial situation. Primkenau, the estate to which Günther had dedicated his life, consumed more revenues than it produced. Without the Kaiser's funding Günther's debts skyrocketed. At Primkenau, Günther's dental infection led to septicemia and nothing could be done to save him. On 22 February Dorothea became a widow at forty. The couple remained childless, and the bulk of Günther's debt-laden estate passed to his cousin Albert, the only remaining son of Queen Victoria's daughter Helena, who in 1866 had married Christian of Schleswig-Holstein, Günther's uncle. Since Albert did not have any heirs either, it was clear that the Augustenburg line was destined to become extinct.

Prince Philipp shortly before his death.

Later in life Dorothea received the lion's share of her father's private fortune, as well as several large legacies, as a granddaughter of Léopold II, from her Belgian family. Primkenau consumed considerable revenues, but she would not consider abandoning the enterprise. She adopted two children of Günther's distant cousin, but as they grew older her relations with them soured. Dorothea also provided her mother some financial support, but relations between them were never fully re-established. She surrounded herself with an odd menagerie of companions and servants, several of whom obtained large benefits from her. Relations with her Coburg cousins in Austria were always fraught with bitterness as she sued them, and they counter-sued, to obtain a larger share of the Coburg and Kohary Fideikomiss. Later, when National Socialism overtook Germany, Dorothea was an enthusiastic supporter, much like her cousin Carl Eduard; she believed that Hitler would restore the empire.

In February 1945, with the Red Army an hour away from Primkenau, Dorothea and her entourage quickly left, leaving behind many of her most prized possessions. Everything was lost when her home was burned. Dorothea first headed to Blankenburg, where her niece, the Duchess of Brünswick, welcomed the refugees. Later, when Blankenburg was placed under Soviet control, Dorothea and her remaining companions traveled to Bavaria, where she enjoyed the hospitality of her Thurn und Taxis cousins. Fürst Albrecht, whose wife Margareta of Austria was Dorothea's first cousin, sheltered her in one of his castles. Dorothea quietly lived under Thurn und Taxis protection until her death at Schloß Taxis in Baden-Württemberg on 21 January 1967. By then the world had forgotten all about Dorothea, her parents and brother, and the sad fate this princess born to such privilege had suffered.

The Descendants of Prince Ludwig August

A bronze commemorative plaque given by Prince Philipp of Saxe-Coburg & Gotha to those attending his 70th birthday party.

Sorting out the Coburg and Kohary Fideikomiss was a monumentally complicated venture. The vast landholdings owned by both entities were now located in three countries: Austria, Czechoslovakia, and Hungary. Abolished in some countries, the elimination of this institution exposed wealth to taxation and divisions caused by inheritance rights and wreaked havoc on the Coburg fortunes. Also affecting the succession was the fact that Philipp died without a direct heir: a new "head" had to be chosen among the descendants of his two younger brothers.

Prince Philipp's next brother was Prince Ludwig August, the most pleasant looking of Prince August and Princess Clémentine's sons. At nineteen, he had been sent with his first cousin Prince Gaston d'Orléans, Comte d'Eu, when his aunt the Princess of Joinville suggested the two handsome princes, both children of Coburg-Orléans marriages, as candidates for the daughters of the Brazilian emperor. *"August would be most suitable for Izabel, whereas I see Gaston ideal for our little Leopoldina,"* she wrote to her brother. Princess Clémentine was naturally intrigued by the idea of a possible union of her son to the heiress of the Brazilian throne. *"Almost at the sight of the debonair young suitors,"* wrote one chronicler, *"whose tongues were as glib as their manners were delightful, the Princesses felt themselves willing captives."* However, the princesses played a trick on their self-assured aunt. Izabel chose Gaston, while Leopoldina fell in love with Ludwig August and married him in December 1864.

The marriage between Leopoldina and Ludwig August was extremely happy but short lived. A few months after the birth of their fourth son Leopoldina contracted typhoid fever in Vienna and died suddenly before the age of twenty-four. Devastated, Ludwig August never countenanced marrying again. Although he retained close contact with his Brazilian in-laws, Ludwig August remained in Austria, enjoying the life guaranteed by his wealth and position. Ludwig August also visited Ferdinand in Bulgaria but rarely attended royal events. At the wedding of his niece Dorothea to the Duke of Schleswig-Holstein, he stood in naval uniform next to his brothers, Philipp and Ferdinand. As a widower, Ludwig August relinquished the care of his sons to his mother and relocated to Paris.

Without the responsibility of raising his sons, exempted from residing in Brazil, and the recipient of a large appanage, he attended various hunts throughout Europe. While in Paris, his circle of friends included

Prince Ludwig August, Princess Leopoldina and their firstborn son Prince Pedro Augusto.

Prince Ludwig August in naval uniform.

wealthy aristocrats who owned extensive hunting grounds, including a rich and passionate man by the name of Gustave de Vernouillet. He often hunted on an estate in Schladming owned by his friend Johann Rudolf Ritter von Gersdorff, a wealthy mining entrepreneur in Styria, and soon Prince Ludwig August came to the area. Soon he purchased land and in 1884 built a hunting lodge in Schladming to serve as his summer residence. As years passed, the prince acquired even more lands, reaching as far as Gröbming; after building several additional hunting lodges, Prince Ludwig August had a large castle constructed in Schladming. These estates not only provided the prince with excellent hunting grounds full of chamois and blackcock to hang on his walls but also with some 15,000 acres of forests that he exploited. The bulk of Ludwig August's Styrian properties went to his second son, whose descendants own them today. Ludwig August died while in Karlsbad in 1907. His remains were interred in the Kohary Crypt, St. Augustin's Church, Coburg.

Ludwig August had four children: Peter August (Pedro Augusto), August Leopold, Joseph Ferdinand, and Ludwig Gaston. As all were dynasts and their Aunt Izabel was unlikely to have any children, they stood to inherit the imperial crown of Brazil. The two eldest sons returned to Brazil to live under their grandfather's care. Born in Rio de Janeiro in 1866, Pedro Augusto was a sensitive young man and Emperor Pedro's favorite grandson. For several years Prince Pedro Augusto was the Heir

Prince Pedro Augusto while in Paris in 1887.

Presumptive, but the 1875 birth of Pedro d'Alcantara, Izabel's son, displaced him. He had once been considered as a possible groom for the infamous Archduchess Louise of Austria-Tuscany, who remembered him as *"quite a nice boy, though we did not fulfill the matrimonial hopes of our relations...Poor Dom Pedro! Three years after our meeting he went mad, and he is now under restraint in a castle somewhere in Austria."* In late 1889, Pedro Augusto witnessed the overthrow of his beloved grandfather in Rio de Janeiro and his nerves were so shattered that he suffered a complete mental collapse. Soon after his return to Europe his eccentricities and fits of madness forced his internment in an asylum. Pedro Augusto, who never married, died in Austria in 1934.

Right: Prince Ludwig Gaston, Princess Mathilde and their son Prince Antonius.

Below right: Princess Anna with her daughter Joséphine and step-daughter Maria Immakulata

Ludwig August's other three sons led much quieter lives. While Joseph Ferdinand had died in his teens in 1888, both his brothers August Leopold and Ludwig Gaston married and left descendants. Ludwig Gaston served in the Austrian imperial army, where he reached the rank of captain in the Tyrolean Shooters Regiment. In May 1900 he married the rather weak Princess Mathilde of Bavaria, one of the daughters of future King Ludwig III. She bore him two children, Antonius and Maria Immaculata, before dying in 1906. A widower with two small children to care for, Ludwig Gaston married again the following year to Anna, a daughter of Fürst Karl von Trauttmasdorff-Weinsberg and his wife, the former Joséphine Margravine Pallavicini. In 1911 Anna gave birth to a daughter, Joséphine. The family resided at Schloß Vogelsang in Styria, Austria, which Ludwig Gaston had purchased at the turn of the century and spent enormous sums restoring. The expenses, though, drove him to penury and in 1928 Ludwig Gaston was forced to sell the

Left: Schloß Vogelsang, also known as the "Villa Coburg." It was acquired by Prince Ludwig Gaston, who retained it until his financial collapse in the late 1920s.

estate and most of its contents. He purchased a smaller home in Innsbruck, where he died in 1942. Princess Anna eventually left Austria and settled in Coburg, where she died in 1948.

Ludwig Gaston's three children had equally difficult lives. Maria Immaculata never married and died in Varese, Italy, in 1940. In 1937 Joséphine married Baron Richard von Baratta-Dragono, by whom she had two children before their marriage ended in divorce. Joséphine never remarried and died in Stockdorf, Bavaria, in 1997. Both her children, Maria-Carolina and Richard-Pedro, remained unmarried and had no descendants.

Prince Antonius lived at Vogelsang until his father's financial collapse. Those who remembered the prince thought him somewhat odd. He became an enthusiastic supporter of National Socialism and at one point in 1934 Austrian authorities investigated him after he claimed membership in the SS. Suffering from mental instability, he had to be interned several times. He later claimed to have opposed Hitler and National Socialism. Family members believed he *"had a sinister character, with the instinct of a rapist."* In 1938 Antonius married, in contravention of Coburg House laws, a young lady by the name of Luise Mayrhofer, daughter of an Austrian postal employee. The couple remained childless. At one point, Antonius joined forces with Dorothea of Schleswig-Holstein and sued for a share of what remained of the once gigantic family fortune. Nothing came of this other than high legal bills. His death in 1970 ended this cadet branch of Coburg descendants.

Prince August Leopold in 1892.

Leopoldina's second son, August Leopold, was arguably the most successful of her children, serving in the Brazilian imperial navy. Once exiled from Brazil, August Leopold returned to Austria, where Emperor Franz Joseph provided him with a commission in

Left: Standing: Archduchess Blanca, Archduchess Carolina and Archduchess Marie Valerie. Seated: Archduke Leopold Salvator (husband of Blanca of Spain), Archduke Albrecht Salvator and Archduke Franz Salvator, the latter was married to Marie Valerie, Emperor Franz Joseph's youngest child. The three archdukes were Carolina's brothers.

the Austro-Hungarian imperial navy. A sailor at heart, August Leopold's naval career was very successful. He also achieved a great coup when he married Archduchess Carolina of Austria-Tuscany, whose brother had married Franz Joseph's youngest daughter Marie Valerie. The fourth child of Archduke Karl Salvator and his wife, the former Princess Immaculata of Bourbon-Two Sicilies, Carolina was born on 5 September 1869 at Alt-Bunzlau Castle, one of her family's many estates. For a year she had served as Abbess of the Convent for Noble Ladies in Prague.

August Leopold and his wife were closely related. He was the grandson of Teresa of Bourbon-Two Sicilies, one of the daughters of King Francesco I of the Two Sicilies. His maternal grandfather was also a Habsburg descendant as his mother was Leopoldine of Austria, a daughter of Emperor Franz I. Clémentine d'Orléans, August Leopold's paternal grandmother was also a descendant of the House of the Two Sicilies and the Habsburgs, her maternal grandparents being King Ferdinand I of the Two Sicilies and his Austrian wife, the former Archduchess Maria Carolina, Emperor Franz I's aunt. Maria Carolina was also a great-aunt of Grand Duke Leopoldo II of Tuscany, Archduchess Carolina's paternal grandfather, while her maternal grandmother, Antonietta of Bourbon-Two Sicilies, was also the daughter of a Habsburg.

Prince August Leopold, his wife Carolina, and her brother Archduke Franz Salvator.

The couple married in Vienna in May 1894 and after their honeymoon settled in Pola, where Prince August Leopold was stationed. Pola, under Austrian control since Napoléon's defeat, was the Habsburgs' main naval base and major shipbuilding center on the Adriatic. It was at Pola that Carolina gave birth to four of her eight children. August Clemens was born there in 1895 (he died in 1909) and Klementine followed two years later. In 1899 the Archduchess gave birth to a second daughter who was her namesake. One year later, a second son joined the nursery, Rainer.

August Leopold, after serving in the Austrian imperial navy for several years, left his commission and joined the naval reserve, where in 1912 he attained

Left: Standing: Prince August Leopold and Archduchess Carolina with four of their children. From left: Klementine, Maria Karoline, August Leopold, Carolina holding Rainer, and August Clemens. This image dates from 1900 and is among several acquired by the author from the couple's descendants.

Archduchess Carolina and her daughters Princess Theresia and Princess Klementine c. 1913

Prince August Leopold, accompanied by his wife, while at one of his hunting lodges in the Alps.

The silver wedding anniversary of August Leopold and Carolina of Saxe-Coburg & Gotha.

Standing from left: Prince Philipp-Josias, Prince Rainer, Princess Klementine, Princess Leopoldine, Princess Maria Karoline.
Seated, same order: Prince August Leopold, Prince Ernst, Archduchess Carolina and Princess Theresia. Prince August Clemens, who suffered from infirmities, had died at Schloß Gerasdorf in 1900.

Right: Schloß Walterskirchen was once one of the most commonly used Coburg country palaces in Austria. Still in family hands, the building is now closed. Repairs and upkeep are too costly.

Below right: Jagdschloß Schladming, the hunting castle built by Prince Ludwig August. His descendants sold it and today it serves as the City Hall of Schladming.

the rank of corvette captain. After the birth of the couple's fourth child, August Leopold relocated his family and spent the year between several family properties. In Vienna they used the vast Coburg Palais. When in the Alps, they lived at a castle in Schladming (Styria), or the smaller Villa Coburg in nearby Gröbming. He also had access to three other castles in Lower Austria owned by the Coburgs: Schloß Walterskirchen, where Carolina gave birth to Philipp-Josias and Theresia, in 1901 and 1902, respectively; Schloß Gerasdorf, where Leopoldine and Ernst were born, in 1905 and 1907, respectively; and Schloß Ebenthal, old Princess Clémentine's favorite country home.

Sadly, three of August Leopold and Carolina's children were mentally retarded: August Clemens, Marie Karoline, and Leopoldine. While it is possible that this was a product of the high degree of consanguinity shared by the prince and his wife, one of their great-grandchildren believed that August Leopold had suffered a venereal disease that attacked the mental capabilities of some of his children. Lacking any proof, though, the reduced gene pool must remain the chief suspect.

August Leopold was close to his Uncle Philipp and after Prince Leopold's death in 1916 he knew that he was heir as holder of the Coburg and Kohary Fideikomiss. The complication, of course, came when the Habsburg Empire collapsed and the multinational monarchy splintered into several countries. Czechoslovakia, where the Coburgs owned large estates, was among the most viciously anti-aristocratic states to succeed the Danube monarchy. Although Philipp was not a member of the Habsburg dynasty, and in fact for legal purposes was a foreign prince living in Austria, the new government in Prague sought to expropriate as much land as possible as Coburg lawyers fought them.

When Philipp died, his will named Prince Philipp-Josias as the universal heir to the inalienable estates protected by the Coburg and Kohary Fideikomiss, while charging him with the thankless task of *"disbursing contributions as necessary to other members of the House, allowing them to continue living according to their rank."* Philipp's personal property was divided among various family members: Dorothea received half, along with the right in perpetuity of residence at the Coburg Palais when in Vienna. The remainder of the late prince's personal estate was divided in equal parts between Philipp-Josias and his cousin Kyril of Bulgaria. For Philipp-Josias it was to be the start of decades embroiled in legal disputes with other members of his family.

Prince August Leopold died in October 1922. Rainer, his eldest surviving son, was not interested in inheriting the unenviable position of "head" of family and willingly "sold" his rights to Philipp-Josias. In 1930, Rainer married a minor noblewoman, Johanna Károly de Károly-Patty, and fathered a child, Johannes Heinrich. He found the responsibilities of fatherhood too demanding, though, and divorced Joanna in 1935. She managed to escape from Hungary and lived the remainder of her life in Austria, dying in Innsbrück in 1992.

In 1940 Rainer married a Hungarian woman, Edith de Kózol, daughter of the director of the National Bank of Hungary. Born to an upper middle-class Hungarian family in 1913, Edith spent most of her youth on her family's country estate. Rainer and Edith remained childless, though he seemed very taken with her. They spent most of the Second World War in Budapest and were there in March

Prince Philipp-Josias, fourth Fideikommiss holder.

Left: An intimate moment with their mother. While on a drive, Princess Theresia and Prince Philipp-Josias help braid their mother's long, flowing white hair. Archduchess Carolina eventually moved to the Coburg Palace in Budapest. The cost of living in the vast Coburg Palais in Vienna was too exhorbitant and economies had to be made.

1945 when tragedy struck. Hungarian communist partisans arrested Rainer, took him away, and no one ever saw him alive again. Most likely executed by his kidnappers, Rainer was finally declared dead in 1961, his death retroactive to 31 December 1945.

Princess Edith remained in Hungary until 1949 when, disguised as a peasant, she managed to escape to Austria. She lived in a monastery near Graz for one year, eventually settling in Salzburg, and later became an interpreter for the American forces as well as a partner in a jewelry business. Princess Edith regularly visited Coburg, maintaining strong attachments as demonstrated by her membership in both the Coburg Historical Society and the Prince Albert Society, and tried to rebuild the family record of the Catholic Saxe-Coburgs, which was lost in Vienna during the Second World War. Princess Edith died in 1997.

Prince Philipp-Josias spent most of the two decades after the death of Prince Philipp involved in constant legal quarrels, mainly with Kyril of Bulgaria and Dorothea of Schlewsig-Holstein. Czechoslovakia finally abolished the institution of the fideikomiss in 1924. Kyril then sued Philipp-Josias for a share of the family's Czechoslovakian landholdings. The cousins settled out of court and Philipp-Josias relinquished 42% of the property to Kyril, retaining the remaining 58%. Then Dorothea sued them, alleging that she was owed a share, even though she had signed away her succession rights upon marrying Günther and had received a sizable dowry. The ensuing legal wrangling, to this day, is held responsible for financially devastating the Coburgs of Vienna. Legal bills reached insurmountable levels. As the family's internecine warfare exhausted their bank accounts, the successor governments of the Danube monarchy continued the land graft that

One of the last known photographs of Archduchess Carolina.

Right: Since such a large number of Coburg and Kohary estates were located on the Hungarian side of the empire, and the Kohary were a Hungarian dynasty, the Coburgs owned several homes there. The Coburg Palace at Andrassy utca 96, served as their Budapest residence until the late 1930s, when Philipp-Josias acquired another one.

Princess Klementine and her dog.

Prince Ernst of Saxe-Coburg & Gotha.

further decreased the family's revenues. On top of all these problems, the world's financial collapse only made a horrific situation worse. By the late 1920s, alleging financial challenges, Philipp-Josias began eliminating the appanages he had to pay to other members of the family. This in turn forced the bankruptcy of his Uncle Ludwig Gaston.

Yet life continued and the family grew. In 1925 Princess Klementine surprised the family when she announced her intention to marry Eduard von Heller, a wealthy businessman of Jewish extraction. She settled in Switzerland where she gave birth to three children: Marie-Amelie, Helene, and Athlone, named in honor of his godfather the Earl of Athlone. Marie-Amelie was the only one of the Hellers to marry and have children. In 1949 she wed Carlo-Felice Nicolis of the Counts de Robilant and Cereaglio, by whom she had three children. The late Countess of Paris, Isabelle, once told me that when she met her distant Coburg cousin, Marie-Amelie told her, *"Je suis vôtre cousine, la demi-Gotha, demi-Ghetto,"* ("I'm your cousin, the half-Gotha, half-Ghetto one!") an obvious allusion to the von Heller background. Princess Klementine died in Lausanne in 1975, surviving her husband by five years.

At the beginning of 1930 Princess Theresia married Baron Lamoral Taxis von Bordogna und Valnigra, a nobleman related to the Thurn und Taxis princely family. Among the children of August Leopold, Theresia was the one who enjoyed the closest ties with the children of Carl Eduard and Viktoria Adelheid, and she frequently visited them on holidays in Coburg. Theresia and Lamoral had four children, all born in Europe but naturalized as Brazilian citizens with the last name "Tasso de Saxe-Coburgo e Bragança." Her eldest son, Carlos-Eduardo (Carl Eduard), returned to the "fold" when in 1969 he married Archduchess Walburga of Austria-Tuscany, by whom he had eight children. Baron Lamoral died in 1966; Princess Theresia survived until 1990.

Lacking an imperial court in Vienna, remaining there was of little interest to August Leopold's family. In widowhood, Carolina returned to the capital and lived with her three unmarried sons and youngest daughter. When Rainer divorced, he returned to the family fold. By then, Philipp-Josias had moved to Budapest with his mother and siblings. In the Hungarian capital the Coburgs owned a splendid palace at Andrassy útca 96, an elegant street on the Pest side. It not only served as residence, but also housed estate administration offices. Then, in 1937 the Coburgs moved to a newly acquired town palace located at Uri útca 43, on Castle Hill. It was while living in Budapest that the Coburg brothers met the women with whom they were destined to share the remainder of their lives.

Prince Philip-Josias married as he approached his mid-forties during the Second World War. His wife, Sarah Aurelia Hálasz, was born in 1914 to an old Hungarian family with distant ties to the nobility. Her father is said to have been a river captain on the Danube, while her family had Russian origins. In her memoirs, Sarah's sister remembered Philipp-Josias as *"having a friendly personality and abundantly modest,"* saying that he *"lived for my sister and their son, Philipp-August. His days were consumed with the management of this property. He provided a livelihood to a large number of agricultural workers."* Their marriage took place several months after the birth of their only son, Prince Philipp-August.

As the war neared its tragic end, Hungary fell under the control of the German army and a pro-Nazi government was imposed. Persecution of Jews became the order of the day and terror spread throughout the country. At great risk, the Coburgs provided refuge to a Jewish lady and her son. Philipp-Josias, by then in his mid-forties, was conscripted and sent to work on a naval transport in the Mediterranean, while Sarah and their son remained in Budapest, where her mother-in-law Archduchess Carolina also lived with her daughter Princess Leopoldine. The two ladies resided in the Coburg palace in Budapest and were still there when the city fell to the Red Army. Carolina died in Budapest in May 1945; the Communists, as some historians have claimed, did not kill her. Instead, terrorized by the events she witnessed and believing that *"Marx had finally won,"* she died of natural causes.

Prince Philipp-Josias on a hunt.

Princess Leopoldine, who remained in Communist Hungary, later recalled that she made the mistake of letting her domestics know where the family silver and gold, precious stones and jewelry, porcelain and paintings, were hidden. In the ensuing confusion caused by the fall of Budapest, nearly everything was stolen. Sarah's family, informed of the misfortune raining on the Coburgs, moved quickly to help them save what was left in the palace. Important artwork, tapestries and porcelain found their way out of the Coburg residence and into the homes of trusted friends of the Hálasz family.

With the war at an end, Philipp-Josias returned to a Budapest in ruins. Destruction was rampant and little remained of the world he had left behind. Two years later, fearful of what further misfortune life would bring if they remained in Communist Hungary, Philipp-Josias organized their escape to Austria. He left alone, while Sarah traveled with their son. No one could find out who they were and the travelers remained strictly incognito. After weeks of depending on the goodwill of strangers, they reached Vienna, where the Coburg Palais had fallen under Russian control. With the help of one of his estate administrators, the prince and his family were able to depart Vienna for the safer, and warmer, Lisbon, where many

Prince Philipp-Josias in traditional Austrian hunting gear.

of their royal cousins had also settled. Along with him, the prince brought some precious objects, which once sold, allowed them to live simply, but without worry.

The future seemed dark and deeply uncertain. Once Czechoslovakia and Hungary fell under the oppressive yoke of Communism, all Coburg properties were lost. In Austria, where the Coburg family was considered German, all their properties were sequestered. For a time it seemed as if all was lost, until when in the first years of the 1950s the situation within Austria changed for the better. Most of the prince's domains were returned to him, particularly the estates in Walterskirchen, Dürnkrut and most of those in Styria. The property restored to him also included the Coburg Palais. Philipp-Josias, with Sarah and their son in tow, returned to Austria and spent the remaining three decades of his life managing what was left of the family's once vast fortune.

Prince Philipp-August of Saxe-Coburg and Gotha.

Misfortune was never far away from the descendants of Prince August Leopold. Philipp-Josias had witnessed the spoliation of his family's fortune and lived long enough to begin its reconstruction, but the war cost him dearly, and not just in the loss of property. Besides Rainer's assassination, they lost their mentally handicapped sister Maria Karoline, who was gassed by the Nazis in 1941. The end of the war reduced the family to Philipp-Josias, his brother Ernst, and three of their sisters. Leopoldine, who was also slightly handicapped, remained in Hungary where the Hálasz family took care of her until her death in 1978.

Of Prince Rainer's son, Johannes Heinrich was a slender, good-looking young man who carried the heavy legacy of his name. He and his mother lived simply, as without an inheritance he had to build a life for himself. Johannes Heinrich married Baroness Marie-Gabrielle von Fürstenberg in 1957 and the following year she gave birth to their daughter Felicitas. Unfortunately, the baby's parents were soon at odds and the couple eventually separated and divorced. Marie-Gabrielle, who was a talented portraitist, settled in Munich and raised her daughter alone. In 1987, Felicitas married Sergei Trotzky, an Austrian with Russian ancestry. They had several children and brought them up beween Gröbming and Salzburg. The family visited Munich frequently and Felicitas always enjoyed good relations with royal relations, particularly Princess Gisela of Bavaria, wife of the current Margrave of Meißen. Princess Marie-Gabrielle lived in Munich until old age forced her to move to Salzburg, where Felicitas spent most of the year. She died there in October 2007. Princess Marie-Gabrielle once said that she eventually understood what difficulties her former husband lived through: *"just imagine, you are a Coburg, one of the most powerful clans in Europe ... you are a cousin of The Queen, but you have nothing to your name. Nothing, of course, is relative, but when compared to what my husband's family once owned, he had nothing. He belonged to a world to which he felt he didn't belong."*

Prince Johannes Heinrich, a successful businessman, remarried in 1968. His second wife was Princess Mathilde of Saxony, youngest daughter of Margrave Friedrich-Christian of Meißen and his wife, the former Princess Elisabeth Helene of Thurn und Taxis, only daughter of Fürst Albrecht and his Austrian wife. Mathilde, in fact, is a Coburg descendant through both her parents. Friedrich-Christian's father, King Friedrich August III of Saxony, was the son of Infanta Maria Ana of Portugal, one of the daughters of Queen Maria II and King Consort Ferdinand. Elisabeth Helene's mother was the daughter of Archduke

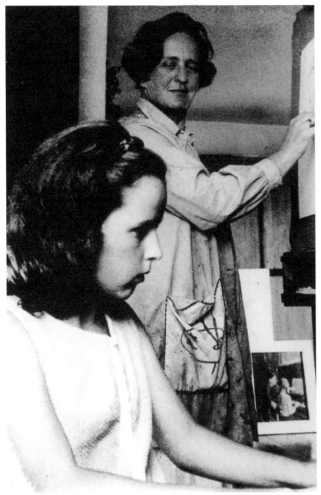

Left: Princess Marie Gabrielle was a talented painter, her Munich apartment serving as her attelier. This photograph shows her at work, while Princess Felicitas sits by her side.

Above: Princess Felicitas married Sergei Trotzky in 1987. No relation to the Bolshevik leader, even though some newspapers claimed so, he was born in Austria and worked in tourism for a long time.

Joseph of Austria and of Princess Clotilde of Saxe-Coburg & Gotha, a daughter of Prince August and Princess Clémentine.

A year after their wedding, Mathilde gave birth to a son, Johannes Albert, who was to remain their only child. The family settled in Innsbruck, where Johannes Heinrich managed his enterprises and his wife practiced medicine. Their son, who had an adorable face topped by a mop of blond hair, was the mortar holding the family together. Johannes Albert was a restless sportsman and, much like his kinsman Albert I of Belgium, loved nothing more than climbing the surrounding peaks. It was this passion that brought him to his untimely end. On 21 August 1987, the young man told his parents he was off to climb a nearby peak. The prince, however, headed to a much steeper mountain. By day's end he had not returned home and, alarmed by their son's absence, his parents sounded the alarm. Search parties scoured the area but not until a few days later was his lifeless body found in a ravine. He was three months short of his eighteenth birthday. Johannes Heinrich and Mathilde were overwhelmed with pain and, unable to find support in each other, their marriage collapsed, ending in divorce in 1993. They remained friendly and in time even attended several events together. Johannes Heinrich and his daughter Felicitas were not close, unfortunately. He died in April 2010. Mathilde, who now lives in Munich, survives her ex-husband and son.

Surrounded by the peace provided by the Austrian countryside, Philipp-Josias remained focused on the management of his remaining estates. In the 1950s he divided one with his youngest brother Ernst, who in 1939 had married a commoner, Irmgard Röll. Ernst was an enthusiastic early supporter of National Socialism, a fact that in later years he sought to erase. His inherited properties centered on Schladming and Gröbming, but Ernst was a less efficient manager than his older brother. He and Irmgard were childless and at his death in 1978, his estate was divided between Prince Philipp-August and Princess Felicitas, whom he had adopted earlier.

Left: Princess Felicitas and Prince Johannes Albert, the children of Prince Johannes Heinrich.

The same year that witnessed the death of his brother Ernst, Philipp-Josias sold the Coburg Palais. The once-magnificent residence of the formerly wealthy Coburgs had fallen into disrepair and Philipp-Josias refused to pour endless sums of money into restoring the structure. A real-estate developer purchased the building, but never paid the Coburgs what he owed them, having sold off the building and later filed for bankruptcy. Prince Philipp-August once told me that his parents were not even paid a third of the selling price. The prince and his wife moved to a smaller apartment in Vienna, but visited the countryside frequently.

Philipp-Josias lived long enough to witness the marriage of his only son, Prince Philipp-August, to Bettina von Pfretschner in 1968. The following year she gave birth to their first child, Isabella. In 1972 a second child joined the family, a baby boy named Maximilian, while a third, Alexander, was born in 1978. Bettina died in 1989, leaving a widower with a broken heart and three young children. The lonely Philipp-August remarried in 1991. His second wife, the former Rosemarie Jäger, gave birth to their only child, Christina, in 1995.

Prince Johannes Heinrich, Innsbruck (1986).

Prince Johannes Albert, Innsbruck (1986).

Philipp-Josias died ten years before the birth of his fourth grandchild. Had circumstances been different, it is quite likely that the jovial and contented prince would have been just as excellent an administrator of the family fortune as was his Uncle Philipp. It was Philipp-Josias's great misfortune that the world of privilege into which he was born was inevitably headed toward an abyss. Nothing could be done to avert its ultimate collapse and spare his family losing the majority of their wealth and their position. Princess Sarah survived her husband by nearly a decade, dying in Vienna on New Year's Eve 1994.

Princess Felicitas and her mother Princess Marie-Gabrielle, Munich (2002).

As his father's only child, Philipp-August inherited his estates and remaining assets. His properties include land and forests in Lower Austria and Styria, although not the castle in Schladming, which Philipp-Josias had sold in 1940. Today it houses Schladming's town hall, but glass sheets protect some of the rooms, left intact as if the Coburgs had just departed but are expected to return at any moment. A few years ago, Philipp-August traveled to Coburg and met his cousin Prince Andreas, renewing contacts between these two branches of the once powerful Coburg dynasty that had lapsed.

Separated from his second wife, Philipp-August lives in Ebenthal, while his eldest son Maximilian manages the family's estate in Walterskirchen, where the costs of restoring the vacant castle are prohibitive. In 2005, Maximilian married Christina Schnell, and they have one daughter, Franziska. Princess Isabella, now divorced, is the mother of three children with whom she lives not far from her father. His siblings, Alexander and Christina, remain unmarried. On Alexander's shoulders rests the responsibility, whether he appreciates it or not, of producing the next generation of the Coburgs of Vienna.

Prince Johannes Heinrich and Princess Mathilde attending the opening of the "Queen Victoria Exhibition," Schloß Callenberg, Coburg – April 2001.

CHAPTER XVII
The Coburgs of Lisbon
An Unsurprising End

King Consort Ferdinand became the founder of a new Portuguese royal dynasty. All monarchs ruling in Lisbon, until King Manoel II was ousted in 1910, were his descendants.

Ferdinand and Maria's eldest son, King Pedro V, ruled Portugal between 1853-1861. Queen Victoria had considered him a good candidate for the hand of their cousin Charlotte of Belgium, future Empress of Mexico, calling him *"out and out the most distinguished young Prince there is, and beside that, good, excellent and steady according to one's heart's desire – all one could wish for an only and beloved daughter."* In a conversation with the Count of Lavradio, one of Pedro V's closest advisors, the Queen even told the Portuguese courtier: *"When it comes to intelligence and tastes, I am sure that there is much in common between the King and the Princess Royal."* Pedro V, who had visited Victoria and Albert and made a deep impression on them, was very fond of their eldest daughter Victoria. The Princess Royal was but fourteen at the time; while the Queen was profoundly flattered that her carefully educated cousin would demonstrate any interest in her daughter, she and Albert had other dynastic plans for her, and the issue of religion was something on which the Queen would not compromise. *"I would give any of my daughters to him were he not Catholic,"* she wrote. Although her opinion was quite clear on the matter, she sent Pedro V a portrait of her daughter; replying to Prince Albert, Pedro V asked him to *"thank the Queen for sending me the portrait of Vicky* [The Princess Royal], *which I have sent to get framed and will hang in my room."*

Charlotte of Belgium, already showing promising signs of budding intelligence and will, therefore seemed an ideal consort for the young King of Portugal. Queen Victoria tried further to convince her Uncle Léopold, writing, *"I hope Charlotte has not finally made up her mind, as we both feel so strongly convinced of the immense superiority of Pedro over any other young prince…beside which, the position is infinitely preferable."* Uncertain about Charlotte of Belgium's feelings, Portuguese officials also inquired about the Princess of Asturias, eldest daughter of Queen Isabel II, which might unite the two Iberian crowns. Whether the European powers would have allowed such an alliance is unknown, and as the princess in question was not yet eight-years old, the idea was quickly abandoned.

Pedro V felt slighted by Charlotte's reaction to him. *"As much as I liked Charlotte in 1854,"* he wrote two years later, *"I felt that her coldness was not very pleasant for one so closely related."* Later, Pedro V wrote to his cousin Albert about an encounter he had with Charlotte a year later: *"In 1855 it seemed quite different, but maybe she was annoyed with my lack of grace."* All through 1856, Pedro harbored hopes that Charlotte would agree to marry him. When a letter from King Léopold I on the issue arrived, Pedro enthusiastically wrote to Albert: *"My father gave me an agreeable surprise with a letter from Uncle Léopold that discussed the project I had already considered lost."* A few months later, however, Charlotte, who refused to enter an arranged marriage, instead chose Archduke Maximilian of Austria to be her husband. It was, as it turned out, a tragic choice. From Portugal, a nearly despondent Pedro V did not receive the news well: *"In the meantime, Charlotte has become Archduke Maximilian's fiancée…and that to me is a subject in which I have played an unintentionally unpleasant role. It seems that happiness has passed before me…it seems to me that although happiness in this world always comes to those who despise it, but it fools me."*

Although Pedro V's hopes to marry Charlotte were dashed, Victoria and Albert actively continued seeking a

King Pedro V.

Queen Stephanie.

bride for him. *"The queen must be young, beautiful, pure, well educated and raised, not overly pious, or spoiled,"* Prince Albert wrote. *"We believe to have found someone with these requirements in the oldest daughter of the Prince of Hohenzollern-Sigmaringen, who abdicated in 1848. She belongs to the House of Prussia, and habitually lives in Berlin, and for now she resides with the Princess of Prussia (the Princess Royal's mother-in-law), who praises her. I have never met her; Vicky shared with your father everything we have found about her. What makes me bring her to your attention is the circumstances that she is practically the only Catholic princess who has the conditions required for your future spouse – also, in fact, Prince Plon-Plon* [Napoléon III's nefarious cousin] *is, apparently, in the process of asking for her hand in marriage."* Choosing a bride sooner rather than later, Albert believed, *"would give your Court and home, the completeness and normality that cannot be expected of a bachelor."* The princess' name was Stephanie and her future pointed toward Portugal.

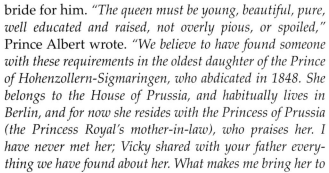

Armed with such glowing descriptions, Pedro V's emissaries contacted Stephanie's father. Negotiations began and within months all seemed close to reaching a settlement, though fearful that the discussions with the Hohenzollerns would become public knowledge before being settled, the King asked the President of the Council of Ministers to keep them a secret, *"as I lead the life of a hermit with my books – my best and most loyal friends in this country; and as my father finds enjoyment in a manner that I cannot either approve or imitate, for it is entirely against my principles…"*

Finally, in June 1857 the Chambers of Parliament were informed that marriage negotiations were nearing completion. Entrusted with leading the Portuguese delegation, the Count of Lavradio opened talks with the Prince of Hohenzollern-Sigmaringen. Pedro V's request to marry Stephanie was made on 20 October, and two months later the kingdom learned of the engagement.

Stephanie, accompanied by her family, visited several German courts early in 1858 to introduce her as the future Queen of Portugal. Pedro V and Stephanie married by proxy in Berlin on April 29, 1858. Three days later the young bride began her journey to Lisbon, where Pedro V awaited her arrival with baited breath. Stephanie and her retinue, including her father and eldest brother, visited

Infante João.

Infante Fernando.

Stuttgart, Brussels, and London on their way to Lisbon, and while in England, Queen Victoria received them at Windsor Castle. *"You may treat me as a second mama and ask me anything,"* the Queen effusively told Stephanie.

On 11 May, Stephanie departed Plymouth onboard the *Bartolomeu Dias*, a corvette specifically acquired by the Portuguese Royal Navy to transport her to her new country. A French naval vessel, along with three British and three Brazilian ships, escorted the travelers. When the flotilla reached the mouth of the Tagus River, Lisbon came into sight. Upon meeting his wife, Pedro V was taken by her manner and beauty: *"We said nothing, we held hands, she kissed my forehead, I cried, she was teary-eyed. We looked at each other for a long time without much to say, but understanding each other."* Witnesses who saw her disembark took in her white dress adorned with exquisite lace, orange blossoms, and myrrh, admired her deep blue eyes, and *"the four-thousand brilliants in the tiara Pedro V gifted her shining under the spring sun."* The thunderous acclamations nearly drowned the sounds of the artillery salvos fired from the capital city's defenses.

The religious wedding took place at the Church of S. Domingos on 18 May and was officiated by Cardinal-Patriarch Guillherme Henriques de Carvalho. King Pedro V's subjects were enthusiastic in welcoming their new Queen and crowded the streets along the procession. Indeed, the crowds were so thick that the royal carriages arrived late at the Necessidades Palace, which was to serve as the couple's home. The Duchess of Terceira, appointed the Queen's highest lady-in-waiting, later recalled that after helping Stephanie prepare for bed, *"Pedro arrived to spend the night and I could not shut my eyes. I felt a little embarrassed as I don't think that the custom of spouses sleeping together is very nice."*

Stephanie's first days as Pedro V's wife were filled with happy and private moments spent in each other's company. They went for walks, prayed, and came to know each other. Stephanie became accustomed to sleeping with her husband every night as *"a duty to God and the purity and delicacy of Pedro sensitizes me and makes me very happy…without it there would be things that would make it all very difficult."* To the public at-large, the spouses seemed to be an image of marital happiness, virtue and purity.

By July 1859 no children had arrived. None would. Stephanie complained of discomfort and fever soon set in: she had contracted diphtheria. On 13 July a medical bulletin revealed the Queen's delicate condition. There was nothing that the royal medical staff could do to save her life. As she lay dying, Pedro softly whispered, *"my beloved wife, trust in God."* She

A portrait of King Pedro V.

King Luís.

looked at him and comforted Pedro by saying, *"I always have."* In her last moments, Stephanie wanted those in the room to let her mother know that she had been happy in Portugal. Her last words were a plea to *"console my Pedro."* Four days after first informing the population of the young Queen Stephanie's illness, the royal court mourned her passing.

Surprisingly, when the doctors conducted an autopsy, before embalming the Queen's body, they were shocked to discover that she was still a virgin. Apparently, Pedro's *"virtue and purity"* were not conquered during the couple's brief marriage, as a doctor revealed to the Duchess of Terceira, who cloaked her mistress's body in a white dress. On Stephanie's head, she placed a crown made with orange blossoms, the sign of virginal purity.

His wife's untimely death aged Pedro V prematurely, and no one could lessen his pain. Having finally found a woman he loved, Pedro had tragically lost her. He would never remarry. As a widower, he found what little pleasure life had in store in work and contemplation. A devout Catholic, Pedro V's faith convinced him that slavery was a social illness that had to be eradicated. He continued a long correspondence with Prince Albert, who inspired him to change his backward and underdeveloped kingdom. The King lobbied for the government to rebuild Portugal's infrastructure, and his reign witnessed an increase of the country's roads, railway systems, and telegraphs. Recognizing that Portugal's public health was seriously lacking, Pedro V also supported improvements, and founded a Lisbon hospital in memory of his beloved wife.

Then, tragedy struck again when the King, accompanied by his brothers Augusto and Fernando, visited several towns in the undeveloped regions of Alentejo and Ribatejo, northeast of Lisbon. The King's brothers contacted typhoid. When Infante Fernando died on November 6, Pedro felt responsible, as the visit to the inland regions had been his idea. Dejected and melancholy, Pedro V also fell ill. He died five days after his brother.

From London, Queen Victoria acknowledged the effect the Portuguese tragedy had on her husband, writing to King Léopold: *"Albert is a little rheumatic."* Victoria and Albert were *"shocked and startled by the news."* Later, Queen Victoria effusively wrote to King Léopold: *"I hardly know how to write, for my head reels and swims, and my heart is sore! What an awful misfortune this is! How the hand of death seems bent on pursuing that poor, dear family! Once so prosperous…Poor Ferdinand, so proud of his children – his five sons – now the eldest and most distinguished, the head of the family, gone, and also another of fifteen, and the youngest still ill!…It is an almost incredible event! A terrible loss for Portugal, and a real European loss! Dear Pedro was so good. So clever, so distinguished! He was so attached to my beloved Albert, and the characters and tastes suited so well…He is happy now, united with Stephanie, whose lose he never recovered!"*

King Pedro V had been the kind of man the Prince Consort wished he had sired. In a letter to King Wilhelm I of Prussia, Albert expressed his sorrow: *"The death of poor good Pedro has affected her [the Princess Royal] deeply. It has shaken me in an extraordinary way, for I loved and valued him greatly, and had great hopes that his influence might contribute towards setting on its legs a State and nation which had fallen low. It is to be hoped that fruits of his government may long outlive his short span. For it was his desire to establish sound principles and implant roots in his people's minds, which might eventually grow of themselves. Louis [Luís] will be a poor substitute to his brother, although he is a good and honest soul, and has the advantage of having seen something of the world before being called upon to bear the burden of government."* This tragedy greatly weakened Albert's already fragile constitution, and within a month he would himself be dead.

At the time of Pedro's death, his brothers Infantes Luís and João were away, having sailed from Lisbon on the ship carrying their sister Antonia and her husband Leopold of Hohenzollern-Sigmaringen, who had wed in the Portuguese capital on 12 September 1861. News of Fernando's death was kept from Luís and João when, on their return, they reached London. Queen Victoria wrote to King Léopold in anticipation of receiving the young men: *"Two others at sea, and will land tomorrow in utter ignorance of everything and poor dear, good Louis [Luís] (whom I thought dreadfully low when I saw him and Jean [João] for an hour on Sunday) King!"* Not until their Brazilian steamship docked in Belem on 14 November and heard the number of cannon salvos fired did Luís realize he was now King of Portugal. *"What a fatality!"* he exclaimed in shock.

The Royal Family's tragedy did not end with the deaths of Fernando and Pedro V. On reaching Lisbon, Infante João also fell ill and died at the end of the December. By then, believing that the royal deaths were the product of a malevolent conspiracy, the Portuguese were ready to rise against the authorities and palace staff. It took quite some effort to calm the despondent crowds gathered outside Necessidades. Luís had to agree to the crowd's demand to leave Necessidades and stay at the Caxias Palace, where the capital's citizens believed he would be safer.

King Luís.

Born at the Necessidades Palace on 31 October 1838, Infante Luís Filipe Maria Fernando Pedro de Alcántara António Miguel Rafel Gonzaga Xavier Francisco de Assis João Augusto Júlio Amélio had been destined for a naval career, not the throne. Luís's birth assured the dynasty, as King Léopold wrote from Brussels: *"The news of the good fat Queen are satisfactory…it seems that they made a good impression, Portugal to have a reinforcement of the Royal Family in the shape of a little Prince, though Princesses ought at all times to be greatly preferred."* As he had an older, and more importantly, healthy brother, Luís's parents believed that given the kingdom's long sea-faring tradition, their second son ought to become a sailor. It was lucky for all involved that the young boy found in the solitude and ferocity of the ocean such incredible joy.

Family life at the Necessidades Palace was characterized by both a desire for simplicity and an absence of excessive luxury. Coburg ideals demanded that princes be educated to serve the kingdom, not live off it, and learn to sail the ship of state from obscurantism to the safety of port guaranteed by a liberal, constitutional, and somewhat democratic regime supported by a thankful populace. These were lofty ideals indeed, although not always easily attained as King Luís and his descendants would eventually discover.

Within the family circle, Luís was called "Lipipi." His adoring mother once wrote to Queen Victoria: *"Luís is very strong and begins to be very sweet...I believe that his teeth are about to come out as anything he holds in his hands goes directly into his mouth and he is constantly biting everyone's fingers until it hurts, but it is both the source of much pain and pleasure."* Several years later, as she complained about the demands of her younger children, Maria II only had praise for Luís: *"Lipipi I believe resembles our dear Ferdinand."*

Luís was introduced to the sea at an early age and by the age of five had learned how to swim. Pedro was more fearful of the water, but their mother believed that *"this will pass with time."* Coupled to the children's physical development was an arduous academic program: they were woken at 7:00am and had German lessons; at 9:45am came ethics and history and, time permitting, a rest; luncheon at noon was followed by music practice; at 2:00pm time was spent in the garden; at 4:00pm there were lessons in English and mathematics; and at 7:00pm, they had dinner. At the end of the school year the children had to present exams in front of teachers and palace functionaries as their parents watched. While Luís was physically stronger, Pedro always obtained higher grades.

Infante Luís entered the navy in 1846, having been given the title of Duke of Oporto [Porto] by his mother. He began as a seaman recruit, but was soon elevated to the rank of seaman, and remained on active naval service until 1861. His first long sea voyage away from Portugal took place in 1854 when accompanied by Pedro, Luís sailed to England and then on to the continent. The brothers visited London and Windsor, Ostend and Brussels, as well as the Netherlands, Germany, Austria, and France; the following year there were visits to royal cousins in England, France, Germany, Belgium, Italy, and a tour of Switzerland. These journeys were designed to introduce the brothers to other cultures as well as the Continent's main royal courts, and they established close links with their cousins Victoria and Albert, as well as their Uncle Léopold in Brussels. They also met other important rulers, among them Emperor Franz Joseph and Emperor Napoléon III, Willem III of the Netherlands, and Vittorio Emanuele II, with whom Luís later developed a closer connection.

King Luís I.

In 1851 Luís became a Second Lieutenant; three years later, he was made Lieutenant-Captain; became Frigate Captain four years later; and became War and Sea Captain in 1859. Two years earlier he assumed command of the brig *Pedro Nunes*, on which he sailed along the coast and reached as far as Gibraltar. In 1858, as Corvette Captain of the *Bartolomeu Dias* was tasked with retrieving Prince Georg of Saxony, transporting him to Portugal to collect his new wife, Luís's sister Maria Ana, and took them to England to meet Queen Victoria. Other commissions took him to the Azores, Angola, and Tangiers, and he escorted Hereditary Prince Leopold of Hohenzollern-Sigmaringen to Lisbon for his wedding to Antónia and afterward sailed with them to Antwerp.

Since his late teens, Luís, typical Coburg that he was, had found enjoyment in the arms of various ladies. His first mistress seems to have been a young Portuguese lady named Maria Oliveira. The *"pretty girl was the daughter of a cobbler from Belém"* and Luís was so fond of her that he got Maria a small house where their encounters could take place. When Pedro

V was informed of his brother's audacity, he lost little time in sending Luís overseas on various journeys as commander of the *Bartolomeu Dias*. Pedro V wrote to Prince Albert, expressing his worry: *"In any case, the journey will separate him from some dangers to which he was exposed."* While Luís sailed away, Maria Oliveira was married off to a cousin and five months later, much to the consternation of her husband, the young lady gave birth to a full-term baby boy who shared an uncanny resemblance to Luís.

As King, Luís I was acclaimed on 22 December 1861, the second Coburg to rule the Portuguese throne. One of his most pressing problems, especially after the family's tragedies, was finding a wife. His heir was his brother Augusto, then only fourteen-years old. *"Today I have one brother close to me…but who cannot substitute the King and my brother João,"* Luís wrote. *"Pedro…not only was a brother, for me he was my best friend, my second father."* His two sisters, having married foreign princes had, as custom demanded, renounced their succession rights, and if Luís did not have heirs the throne might pass to former King Miguel and his descendants.

The King's search began within his own extended family, particularly the English branch that had been so very supportive of him, his parents and his siblings. During his many visits to her court, he had established a close friendship with Queen Victoria's second daughter, Princess Alice, and Luís felt that she might make an admirable consort. In March 1862, he wrote to Queen Victoria: *"If possible, the marriage that would make me happiest is one with an English princess that I know well and love as a sister."* Victoria, again, alleged religious differences and declined her cousin's offer: *"While I thank you for the good and amiable manner*

King Luís I and Queen Maria Pia.

with which you mention our daughters, religious differences impede our daughters from marrying a Catholic…But I am touched that you think of them." Besides, dear Albert had already settled Alice's future before he died: she was to marry the future Grand Duke of Hesse and By Rhine, and thus help her elder sister Victoria move Germany toward a more constitutional form of government.

Queen Victoria suggested several other candidates, including the very talented Princess Marie of Hohenzollern-Sigmaringen, Stephanie's sixteen-year-old siser. Her parents, however, having already lost one daughter in Portugal, were unwilling to risk losing another, and in 1867 Marie married the Count of Flanders, Luís's first cousin-once removed. Not ready to give up, Queen Victoria next suggested Archduchess Maria Theresa, eldest daughter of the extremely rich Archduke Albrecht, Duke of Teschen. Besides having inherited vast properties in Bohemia and Silesia, Albrecht was one of Austria's most respected military leaders as well as a close friend of his cousin Emperor Franz Joseph. He had married Princess Hildegard of Bavaria, a daughter of King Ludwig I and Queen Therese, née Saxe-Hildburghausen. Maria Theresa was quite an attractive young lady, but when presented with the prospect of leaving the comforts of her father's magnificent palaces for life in insalubrious Lisbon, she rejected the offer. Archduke Albrecht, also, was unwilling to let his daughter go to Portugal, and she instead married Duke Philipp of Württemberg, a grandson of Princess Antoinette, the Coburg aunt of Luís's father.

Next came Princess Maria Pia of Savoy. Born in 1847 at the stifling royal palace in Turin, she was the sixth of eighth children of King Vittorio Emanuele II, an unapologetic womanizer, and his pious wife Archduchess Adelheid of Austria, who also happened to be his cousin. Exhausted from giving birth to eight children in a dozen years, she died in 1855 just twelve days after the birth of her last child. Both Luís and Maria Pia had lost parents and siblings, and both of their widowed fathers had taken up with commoners – perhaps not the most promising of similarities, but the Portuguese government expressed its satisfaction. Maria Pia's father, responsible for leading the effort to unify Italy, was a "liberal" monarch, and it was believed that a Savoy was a much better choice than an excessively religious Habsburg or an unhealthy Bourbon. Some, like Luís's friend Prince Oskar of Sweden, were delighted at the choice; Queen Victoria, on the other hand, was suspicious of the Savoyard monarch and felt that her late husband would have thoroughly disapproved of Maria Pia if for no other reason than her father's lineage.

King Umberto I of Italy, Maria Pia's eldest brother.

Luís eventually appealed to King Vittorio Emanuele II for help, asking that the Italian King would grant him his daughter in marriage, thus joining the destinies of two "liberal" nations. *"I have made my choice,"* he said, *"I lack only your consent to my request."* Unwilling to loose the opportunity, Vittorio Emanuele accepted. *"I will marry him if this is the request of my father,"* wrote Maria Pia when informed of her fate. Vittorio Emanuele II replied to Luís that the request had *"touched"* his heart – Maria Pia had agreed to the proposal and now he announced *"my consent to the marriage."*

Not one to mince words, upon hearing the news of the Portuguese-Savoy engagement, Queen Victoria wrote to Luís: *"Naturally the change so sudden…in your opinion astonishes me greatly. But since you have made your choice, I have nothing more to say…what I regret is the extreme youth* [of Maria Pia] *…hardly of an age to be useful to you."*

There are some curious letters Luís and Maria Pia exchanged before their wedding as they attempted to learn about each other. The King describes himself as a smoker with a tendency to become stout, whose passions include hunting and music, but accepts that he is *"a mediocre dancer."* Maria Pia insisted that she did not mind the smoking for she rather liked the smell; after all, her father and brothers were smokers as well. She did not mind his stoutness as it revealed in his face *"how much you are sweet and good."*

The Duke of Aosta, Maria Pia's brother, who briefly ruled Spain after the fall of Queen Isabel II.

On September 27, 1862, Luís of Portugal and Maria Pia of Savoy were married by proxy in the chapel of the royal palace in Turin, in a ceremony officiated by the Archbishop of Genoa. Witnesses remembered that her crown was so large that it dwarfed the bride. The weight ended up giving the poor child a headache as she was publicly serenaded; once all festivities concluded ice had to be applied to her head.

Two days later, Maria Pia boarded the *Bartolomeu Dias* in Genoa for the voyage to Lisbon, escorted by a squadron of Italian and Portuguese vessels. The Marqués de Loulé, an aristocrat and politician who had married one of Pedro IV's sisters, accompanied her; Luís later elevated him to the title of "Duke." After sailing along the Mediterranean through the Straits of Gibraltar and up the coast, the flotilla anchored in the calm waters of the mouth of the Tagus, in front of the Belém Palace, on October 5. Luís, eagerly awaited his bride's arrival, was very impressed with her, while she thought that his pictures did him little justice. Their marriage was celebrated the following day in the Church of S. Domingos, where four years earlier Pedro V had married Stephanie.

Adapting to life in Portugal was no easy task for Maria Pia. Not yet knowing Portuguese, she used French and felt isolated in a court consumed by mourning. Her ladies-in-waiting, chosen for their position and rank, failed to keep her entertained. She found life at court boring, monotonous, and suffocating, and always longed for open spaces and physical exercise, riding being one of her favorite pastimes. Unaware of the value of money, she seemed consumed with acquiring increasingly striking and elaborate costumes. Not infrequently, her extravagance got the royal couple in financial trouble, and the King had to resort to Parliament for increases of the royal budget.

Maria Pia drew her conception of what a husband ought to be from her family. Her thin and handsome brothers were sportsmen and hunters; for her, education, culture and refinement did not rank highly. Luís was everything her father and brothers were not, studious and artistic. Both King Consort Ferdinand and Queen Maria II had believed that a well-educated prince needed to play a musical instrument. In Luís's case, he took up the violoncello at an early age under the tutelage of a talented virtuoso named Manuel Inocêncio Liberato dos Santos, who had been recommended to Maria II by her aunt Infanta Isabel Maria, Pedro IV's unmarried sister. In Luís, the maestro found a gifted youngster from whom he *"obtained the best results."* By 1849, Luís's talent with the instrument was appreciated by the commission in charge of testing the educational progress of the Queen's children. In time, Luís also learned to play the piano, often doing so during family soirées to the accompaniment of his father's tenor voice. Even as sailor and king, Luís continued perfecting his mastery of the violoncello, as in music he *"found a refuge and repose in the midst of the obligations and responsibilities destiny condemned him to fulfill."*

King Luís I.

The King was also a talented artist. He had begun his training under the guidance of one of his tutors while still quite a young boy, and used his allowance to acquire several Old Masters, including works by Holbein and Bosch. These paintings were added to the royal collection and the general public was provided with access. Luís also added superb sculptures and porcelain that he purchased with his own funds. Today, the overwhelming majority of these marvelous pieces is owned by the Portuguese government and displayed in countless royal residences and museums across the country.

Another passion Luís shared with his Coburg contemporaries was numismatics. His parents had instilled a love of collecting in their children, and Luís began acquiring coins and medals during his early voyages. These pieces served as the foundation for a collection that by the end of his life was considered among the best in Europe. Luís also added collections assembled by prominent numismatists that sold their treasures to him. In 1867 Luís's collection was displayed at the Universal Exposition in Paris, for which he received the accolade of "Honorary President of the French

Queen Maria Pia.

Society of Numismatics and Archaeology." Two years later, King Luís ordered his collection open to the public on every Sunday.

In addition to painting, music, sculpture, and collecting, Luís could translate Shakespeare to Portuguese. In all, Maria Pia found the contrast to her own masculine family members disappointing. During one of her darkest moments, she impudently carved on a palace window, *"Luís does not please me."* Yet, she apparently never stopped to wonder if she pleased her husband. She was selfish, immature, ignorant, and above all, uneducated. Queen Victoria had been right: Maria Pia was far too young to be of any real service to King Luís. In time, though, they developed a friendship based on understanding and companionship, as Luís tolerated his wife's outbursts and she came to terms with his personality. To Queen Victoria, Luís wrote, *"My happiness is each time greater with my dear Marie."*

Despite their differing personalities, Maria Pia was soon pregnant, and on 28 September 1863, she gave birth to a son at the Ajuda Palace. He was baptized Carlos, a new name for the Portuguese Royal Family but one apparently chosen by Maria Pia in honor of her beloved brother Carlo, who had died in infancy. As heir to the throne, Carlos became Duke of Braganza. The young Queen of Portugal, who was weeks from her sixteenth birthday when she became a mother, was fascinated with her baby. She described him in glowing terms as having *"great blue eyes like his father, and he has blond hair...white and pink."* She watched over him, noting his every development, and it was not uncommon for palace staff to find her on the floor, crinolines spread across the carpet, as she played with her baby boy.

In late 1864, Maria Pia, pregnant a second time, brought Carlos with her to Turin. Luís, worried that his second child might be born in Italy, urged her father to send Maria Pia back to Portugal. The baby, another boy, was delivered on 31 July 1865 at the Ajuda Palace, up the hill from Necessidades. The baby, christened Afonso, received the title of Duke of Oporto, the same title King Luís previously bore.

Both sons, although fond of each other, were quite different. Whereas Carlos grew into an artistic young man, Afonso preferred the outdoors. The heir enjoyed sciences and letters, and found intellectual pursuits much to his liking; the spare preferred physical labor and sports, areas in which he could take advantage of his uncharacteristically "Herculean strength." However, the birth of both sons gave Luís I's family an air of domesticity and traditionalism that sat rather well with the Portuguese. As a father, the King was severe and strict when the boys' shenanigans got them in trouble, but also caring and dedicated to guiding Carlos in his preparation as future monarch.

The family enjoyed a number of palaces spread across the beautiful country. In Lisbon, bordered to the north by pine-covered mountains, the Braganzas owned several magnificent properties. In Santa Maria de Belém and Ajuda there were four palaces a stone's throw from each other: Necessidades (inhabited by King Consort Ferdinand and his second wife), Pedrouços, Ajuda, and Belém. Queluz, Cascais, and Caxias lay just outside the capital, while in the mountains, the Braganzas owned palaces in Sintra and the intricate masterpiece at Pena built by Luís's father. In Porto, Luís acquired the Palace of Carrancas, which he used whenever his visits took him to the northern provinces.

Hunting, a sport practiced by royalty since time immemorial, seemed synonymous with the Coburgs. Luís had been taught to shoot as a boy, and small hunts were organized in the gardens of the Necessidades Palace, where he hunted partridges using a miniature gun specifically designed for his use. Later, Luís and his brothers hunted rabbits and birds. This was not indiscriminate butchery, as their educational plan also demanded that the royal children learn botany and *"observe nature"* while accompanied by their tutors. As king, Luís hunted in fall and winter, traveling to Mafra near Guimarães, a massive monastery also housing a royal palace, or to Vila Viçosa, a large agricultural estate near the Spanish border, or staying with prominent Portuguese aristocrats. Nearly all of his foreign travels included time specifically added so the King could hunt, whether it was with his Coburg Belgian, Austrian, or English cousins, his Savoy in-laws, or other royal families. Under Luís's tutelage, both of his sons learned to hunt, and Carlos in particular became a sharp shooter in spite of his unusual corpulence.

Besides being a talented painter, King Luís was also a man of considerable renown in science. He admired technological progress and wished to see Portugal gain advantage from it. As steam engines were improved, he led efforts to reform the Portuguese navy and, using his own knowledge as a sailor, the King designed new artillery grenades that he sent to France for testing. Emperor Napoléon III recognized the King's invention by granting him a medal. Further experiments carried out in Luís's laboratory focused on increasing the accuracy of projectiles, preventing them from going astray while also making them more lethal (and thus saving waste).

The Duke of Braganza.
(Future King Carlos)

Political stability, "Portuguese style," allowed King Luís the ability to become a renaissance man. He invested part of his time in scientific studies. The king also pursued his artistic inclinations, all the while gathering one of the Continent's most prized coin collections. He was a learned man, a scientist, an artist.

During the first four decades of the Nineteenth Century Portugal had suffered military action, occupation and civil war, which gravely delayed the country's development. During the reign of King Luís a rotating process (Rotativism) was developed by the country's two major political groups, Históricos and Regeneradores. The first, the Históricos, upheld a more liberal program, while the latter supported a gradual "regeneration" of the kingdom's institutions and laws. Eventually the two movements joined forces and became one party as both basically shared the same goals, differing only on the speed of reforms. A new political party, the Reformistas (Reformers), also emerged. When Históricos and Regeneradores separated, the former joined the Reformistas and founded a new party, the Progressistas (Progress Party). In the cities, other political movements criticized Rotativism and demanded further institutional change, yet no one dared ask for the overthrow of the monarchy, at least not yet. This virus later spread as it became more difficult for the Portuguese to join the middle class, particularly as the aristocracy and high bourgeoisie assumed a smaller percentage of the taxation required to finance progress and infrastructure. In the countryside, many small farmers, poor and illiterate, felt forgotten by the government, and many later emigrated, robbing Portugal of labor and talent. Although the monarch's role in running the country was constrained by the constitution, eventually some of the malaise created by the corrupt political classes attached itself to the king, and would lead to disaster.

In 1868, a revolution overthrew Queen Isabel II. Luís's father, in retirement and dedicated to his own pastimes, was invited by the Spanish parliament to succeed her. Ferdinand considered the offer, but in the end turned it down. Instead, Luís's brother-in-law, Leopold of Hohenzollern-Sigmaringen, was offered the Spanish throne. France overreacted to being surrounded by Germans ruling along her Eastern and Western borders. War with Prussia ensued, Napoléon III lost his throne and the republic was proclaimed. Leopold's candidacy for the Spanish throne was unsuccessful, yet another candidate quickly emerged, Maria Pia's brother Prince Amedeo, Duke of Aosta.

The second son of King Vittorio Emanuele II, Amedeo of Savoy was born in Turin in 1845. At the age of twenty-two he married a wealthy Italian aristocrat, Maria Vittoria del Pozzo, Princess della Cisterna. What the bride lacked in lineage she more than made up in fortune. When Spain offered Amedeo the throne, Maria Pia was thrilled at the prospect of one of her adored brothers ruling Portugal's only neighbor. The road to Madrid, however, was fraught with danger; although Amedeo had the best intentions, his reign was short. It did not help that Amedeo's subjects viewed him as particularly uneducated and lacking in culture. Legend has it that the King once drove past the house where Cervantes had lived; when his secretary pointed out the building, Amedeo retorted, *"Well, if he is so famous, even though he has not come to see me yet, I'll pay him a visit soon."* Cervantes had been dead for nearly three centuries. By February 1873 Amedeo knew the end was near. He abdicated, proclaiming the Spanish people *"ungovernable."*

Ungovernable, in fact, was Amedeo's proclivity for infidelity. Maria Vittoria constantly complained that her husband's sexual escapades were a source of deep pain. It was a dilemma Maria Pia also understood. Although very fond of his short-tempered wife, Luís seems to have had several affairs during their twenty-seven years of marriage. Once, according to legend, Maria Pia recognized one of his mistresses and charged at her while on horseback. Courtiers heard the Queen's furious outburst when she returned to Ajuda. Even after Luís's death, at least one lady, demanding payment in exchange for compromising love letters the late king had written to her, approached the new king.

King Luís I.

The 1870s were a trying time for the Portuguese Royal Family. Once overthrown, Amedeo returned to Italy where in 1876 Maria Vittoria passed away at the age of thirty. Two years later, Maria Pia lost her father. On New Year's Day the Italian monarch caught a cold that quickly turned into pneumonia. His medical staff's rudimentary and barbaric treatment of the malady hastened his demise, and Vittorio Emanuele II died on 9 January 1878.

In Portugal, the King and his family were dealing with a different illness – the Countess of Edla. Maria Pia, a puritan when it came to such matters, had always treated Ferdinand II's second wife with outright disdain. The feud deepened between both women to a point where each was openly malicious when speaking of the other. Since her arrival in Lisbon, Maria Pia made it known that the Countess of Edla was not welcome in her presence. King Consort Ferdinand was none too happy with his daughter-in-law and repeatedly expressed his fury to King Luís, who was caught in the middle. The row between Maria Pia and the Countess did not end with Ferdinand's death on 15 December 1885. As he had left most of his estate to his wife, the Countess had the last laugh.

By the time his father died, Luís had aged prematuly. Like his siblings he did not enjoy a strong constitution; indeed, four had died immediately after birth, and three others fell ill with typhoid in 1861. Luís's two sisters had settled in Germany. In Dresden, Maria Ana found life at Court oppressive and stifling, and found her Saxon in-laws prudish and humorless. Her husband Georg proved to be a domineering, religious martinet. Maria Ana, however, fulfilled her wifely duties and gave birth to eight children. In February 1884 as she nursed her youngest son, Prince Albert, who had contracted typhoid, she also caught the disease and died.

Death, never far away from the various branches of the extended Coburg dynasty, then set its course toward Portugal. Infante Augusto, Duke of Coimbra, Luís's lone surviving brother, had remained unmarried, serving in the army and becoming a Division General. Augusto's health was also compromised and his condition deteriorated quickly. King Luís was also suffering from worsening health. It seems that he had contracted syphilis years before, and the illness ate away at his constitution. He had gained a considerable amount of weight, and suffered from rheumatism and gout. Consequently, the King had become an invalid and even walking was out of the question. Further complicating his condition, the King's excessive smoking only worsened his circulatory system. Both Luís and Augusto were taken to Sintra in the hope that a change in climate would improve their condition, but it was too late. Augusto passed away on 26 September 1889. King Luís's last illness proved that, even after all the troubles he had experienced with Maria Pia, both still had tender thoughts for the other, as he gazed *"at his wife who had never abandoned her post at his sickbed, had captured her hands and bringing them to his lips, kissed them touchingly."* King Luís I died at the Citadel, in Cascais, on 19 October.

Queen Maria Pia.

His funeral took place a week later, and the King's remains were deposited at the royal necropolis inside the old Monastery of São Vicente de Fora. A witness recalled the funeral as quite an impressive spectacle of royal pageantry: *"The procession was led by a platoon of cavalry. They were followed by six heraldic ensigns bearing heraldic banners; all the corporations which wished to join the procession; a great number of ladies mourning for the King; carriages of the presidents of the Cortes; the carriages of the municipal council of Lisbon; high officers of the Court; the foreign princes who had come to attend the ceremony, among whom were the Duke of Edinburgh, the Duke de Montpensier, [and] the Prince of Hohenzollern."* Not surprisingly, as it usually happens at these events, one of the very first problems the new King had to solve was one of protocol. The question arose about who would have the right of precedence between the Duke de Montpensier [representing the Spanish Regent] and the Duke of Aosta [Maria Pia's brother]. King Carlos's mother argued that it should be her brother, while Carlos's consort lobbied for her uncle Montpensier. King Carlos solved the prickly question by giving the right of precedence to Aosta for, as former King of Spain, Montpensier had been Amedeo's subject.

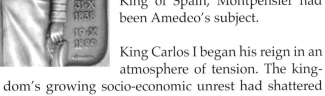

King Carlos I began his reign in an atmosphere of tension. The kingdom's growing socio-economic unrest had shattered relations between the working classes, bourgeoisie, and aristocracy. The political classes seemed unwilling to carry out the reforms necessary to further open the electoral system and grant a larger franchise. Increasingly frustrated by the kingdom's many prominent and corrupt statesmen, King Carlos made the monumental error of becoming embroiled in politics. This misstep was to cost the King his life and his son the throne.

Following the precepts established by his grandparents, Carlos had received a good education at the hands of private tutors and could speak with erudition on many topics. He was also, like many of the Coburgs, a gifted linguist: in addition to his native Portuguese, he read and spoke English and French extremely well, and also knew some Italian and German.

In personality, Carlos most resembled his mother. Shy and timid by nature, his reserve sometimes seemed tantamount to cold, haughty reserve. His subjects never saw him as the affable private man, but instead viewed him as distant, hostile, intellectually deficient, and lacking affection. Yet photographs with his family and friends reveal that King Carlos was jocular and jovial, smiled and teased, and demonstrated great affection toward his sons. King Carlos recognized his shortcomings, once confiding to a courtier: *"I have great imperfections as a man and a King. My defects come from two sources: the first, the heredity in the gestation of my being; the second, the influences exerted by the atmosphere in which I was born and raised."* A reporter for The New York Times described Carlos as *"a young man with an active mind and quite the reverse of a self-effacing disposition,"* someone *"greatly under the sway of Orleanist and Russian influences…credited with a desire to make himself felt in European politics. It will be much better for all concerned if he leaves the rest of Europe alone and sets himself to bringing Portugal itself forward out of its medieval sloth and stupor into something like a progressive condition."*

Carlos and Amélie.

Like their father, Carlos and Afonso were introduced to the sea at a young age. The Count of Mafra, one of the King's friends, later remembered that their greatest joy was *"the beach where ships were built."* Here, they mingled with sailors and fishermen, watched them work and listened to old sea tales. It was, in fact, on a beach in Cascais where Carlos and his brother almost met early deaths. The Queen and her sons were walking along a rocky shore when a rogue wave hit them and swept both boys out to sea. Maria Pia jumped in the ocean immediately, as did a young António de Almeida Neves, the assistant lighthouse keeper. Carlos and Afonso survived the ordeal, but their love for the sea never diminished, and as an adult, Carlos always looked forward to holidays in Cascais.

Queen Maria Pia was a strict mother, and the royal couple insisted that no special privileges be extended to their sons. Maria Pia even forbade tutors to kiss her sons' hands, as had been the custom. While Carlos always proved an adept student and obtained excellent grades except in mathematics, such was not the case with Afonso. The younger brother was happy-go-lucky, naughty, constantly tried to avoid homework, and at every chance indulged in dangerous pranks like climbing onto the palace roof. Yet Maria Pia apparently admired her younger son's love for adventure.

Carlos and Afonso were not completely isolated from their contemporaries. Sadly, the royal children did not have cousins living nearby with whom they could play and interact. Instead, their friends were the children of the aristocracy, the Court and military functionaries, government officials, and the diplomatic corps. Several times a year, the King and Queen hosted a tsunami of children on Christmas, Carnival, or for birthdays. The Count of Mafra later recalled that when *"a wave of children invaded the halls with fury, they were initially astonished, but eventually they renewed their deafening shouting."*

As a child, Carlos traveled outside Portugal frequently. Most of his journeys were to Italy, where Maria Pia enjoyed spending long periods with her father and siblings. In 1878 he attended the funeral of King Vittorio Emanuele II. That same year Carlos swore the oath as heir presumptive, and within a few months Luís gave his son a military commission. The King also gifted the schooner *Duke of Braganza* so that Carlos could embark on countless seafaring explorations that made him an oceanographer of note.

At the age of twenty, Carlos served as Regent during his parents' state visit to King Alfonso XII in Madrid, the first of several occasions that provided the heir with the practical training he would one day require as monarch. In 1884, following royal custom, Carlos embarked on a long journey to several European courts, designed not only to introduce him to his royal contemporaries but also to search for marriageable princesses.

The Count of Paris.

Great Britain, of course, was off limits given Queen Victoria's recalcitrance when it came to the Catholic faith. Sweden and Denmark could not offer anything, nor could The Netherlands. In Belgium, Carlos knew of his cousin Clémentine, but she was still too young; religion also put Prussia and most of Germany out of the running. That left Austria, the former ruling dynasties of Italy, some German Catholic dynasties, and Spain.

Carlos briefly considered Archduchess Marie Valerie, youngest daughter of Emperor Franz Joseph and Empress Elisabeth. Born in 1868, she was only five years younger than Carlos and seemed in excellent health. Another possibility, more closely related, was Archduchess Maria Dorothea, eldest surviving daughter of Archduke Joseph and of his Coburg wife, Archduchess Clotilde; Maria Dorothea's sister, Margarethe, who later married the Fürst of Thurn und Taxis, was too young. Neither suggestion brought results nor were there any suitable princesses among the Coburgs of Vienna.

In Dresden Carlos met his cousins Mathilde and Maria Josepha of Saxony, daughters of his Aunt Maria Ana. He moved on quickly as one was unsightly, while the other was excessively pious. Marrying into any of the deposed Italian dynasties would have been complicated, given that his grandfather had been responsible for their dispossession, and Carlos passed on Tuscany, Parma, the Two Sicilies, and Modena, which was well on its way to extinction.

From Sigmaringen, Carlos's aunt Antónia busily looked through the Gotha in search of a bride for her nephew. She turned her attention to France, and toward an Orléans princess of whom everyone spoke extremely highly. Princess Marie Amélie Louise Hélène d'Orléans was born at York House, a historic stately home outside of London, on 28 September 1865. She shared a birthday with her future husband, but their lives could not have been more different, for Amélie was born in exile. In 1848, her great-grandfather, King Louis Philippe, had been overthrown and landed in England, where Queen Victoria extended to her Orléans friends every courtesy possible.

Amélie's father, Prince Louis Philippe, Count of Paris, was born in 1838, eldest son of the Duke d'Orléans who died suddenly in 1842. From childhood, the Count of Paris was his grandfather's successor. His long tenure as Head of the House of France began on the 1850 death of the exiled King Louis Philippe. Although he had spent long periods of time in Germany (his mother was a Princess of Mecklenburg-

Schwerin), the Count eventually settled in England, as France was inhospitable to the Orléans. Here he acquired several vast estates, among them York House in Twickenham and Stowe House in Buckinghamshire, and his family's immense fortune allowed him to live in semi-regal style.

In 1864 at Kingston-on-Thames, the Count of Paris married his first cousin Infanta Isabel of Spain, the sixteen-year-old daughter of the fabulously wealthy Duke de Montpensier and his wife, the pious Infanta Luisa Fernanda of Spain, whose vast Andalusian estates wielded great riches. Amélie was one of eight children. Her brother Philippe (1869-1926), Duke d'Orléans, married Archduchess Maria Dorothea; sister Hélène (1871-1951) married King Carlos's first cousin Emanuele Filiberto, Duke of Aosta; brother Charles was born and died in 1875; Isabelle (1878-1961) married her cousin Prince Jean, Duke de Guise; Jacques, born in 1880, died the following year; Louise (1882-1958) married King Alfonso XIII's former brother-in-law Infante don Carlos of Spain; and her brother Ferdinand (1884-1924) married a Spanish aristocrat.

Queen Amélie.

The Count of Paris's long exile ended in 1870, when Emperor Napoléon III was defeated and captured by the Prussians. Shortly after the fall of the Second Empire, Louis Philippe's descendant crossed the Channel and made a triumphant return to France. It had been nearly a quarter of a century since they had set foot on their motherland. Many in France had expected the Count of Paris to assume the throne left vacant by Napoléon III's overthrow. The Count was certainly ready and willing to do so, but he required the support of the Count de Chambord, the childless last Legitimist claimant to the throne of St. Louis. Chambord had hesitated. He wanted the new French kingdom to recognize the wrongs committed by the country since the beheading of Louis XVI and his family, a ridiculous stance given the immense social and political changes that had taken place since the Revolution. A historic moment was thus lost and the restoration never occurred.

Now, hoping to arrange a family alliance, the Duke d'Aumâle, richest son of the late King Louis Philippe, invited Carlos to hunt at Chantilly, his impressive estate outside of Paris. He also asked his nephew the Count of Paris and his eldest daughter, the tall, slender and ravishing Princess Amélie, to join the party. Having heard unfavorable reports about Carlos, the Count of Paris was skeptical, and refused to force his daughter to marry against her will. Before accepting the invitation, the Count sent an emissary to the Hôtel Bristol in Paris *"where the prince [Carlos] was to stay, to bid him welcome from him, and to say – according to the impression the Prince made on him – what he thought best; either that the Comte de Paris would be glad to meet him next day in Chantilly, or that he extremely regretted that he could not meet him, all his arrangements being made for leaving for Cannes that evening."*

There was no departure to Cannes. Instead, the Orléans, en masse, headed to Chantilly where the Duke of Braganza was to spend the day with Aumâle and his extended family. *"The Duke of Braganza arrived, enthusiastic over the short time spent in Paris and enchanted with the beauty of Chantilly. He saw the Princess and thought her more delightful than anything he had seen in France. Placed next to her at table, he told her so; his manner was gentle and delicate; she felt that she made him shy, and thought him very attractive."* That day Carlos's search for a bride ended. Having found *"the most bewitching of Princesses, he intended to marry her, and wished the necessary overtures to be made as quickly as possible."*

After alerting his parents, Carlos remained at Chantilly and spent time with Amélie. He was thoroughly charmed and *"made no secret of the admiration her grace and daring excited in him."* Amélie was equally taken: *"He gave satisfaction; the Princess thought he looked good and true; she was delighted with his talk. When she tried to look deep into her heart, she found there a mixture of 'gladness, agitation, and perplexity.'"* Amélie confided that she *"was truly happy."*

On February 23, *The New York Times* announced: *"The Duke of Braganza had time here to look for a wife in the Orléans family. Some days ago he informally declared himself a suitor of the Princess Amélie...Yesterday the Portuguese Minister waited on the Comtesse de Paris to present her a letter from the King and another from the Queen formally asking them to consent to the marriage of the Duke of Braganza with Princess Amélie. The request was made at the Hôtel de Galliera, in the rue de Varennes, where the head of the house of France occupies a floor, placed at his disposal by the Duchess de Galliera. As agreed beforehand, the request was complied with, and when the Minister left the royal suitor arrived and was received in the character of fiancé...the marriage was one of affection...the Duke simply on meeting the Princess fell in love with her, and she reciprocated his sentiments. This certainly is true, but it was arranged before the heir to the Portuguese Crown visited Paris that he should propose for the Princess Amélie if he found they suited each other."*

Carlos followed Amélie and her family to the majestic Château d'Eu, the Count of Paris's country estate in Normandy. Amélie shared her happiness with a friend: *"The Duke of Braganza is here, and to tell you the truth, I find him more and more after my own heart."* When Carlos left, she wrote: *"The more I know of him, the more certain I am that ours will be a happy life."* Although happy, she was somewhat daunted by her future in a strange country. *"I am very anxious about the duties awaiting me there; but there and everywhere, with God's help, I will seek for the right road,"* Amélie wrote.

Carlos returned to Lisbon at the beginning of May, and on the fifteenth of the month the Count of Paris hosted an extravagant fête in honor of his daughter and her fiancé. Thousands were invited to the salons of the vast Hôtel Galliera, but the French government was indignant and saw the celebration as nothing more than a political provocation. For his lack of vision, the Count of Paris would pay dearly.

Two days after her father's ill-fated gala, and accompanied by a large retinue of family, supporters and wedding guests, Amélie boarded a naval convoy and sailed to Lisbon. Again she worried about what awaited her in a country that seemed somehow savage. *"You do not know Jane [de Polignac] what it is to leave one's country and friends,"* she confessed. When, a few days later, the naval convoy anchored in the Tagus estuary, Amélie emerged wearing a striking dress composed of Portugal's national colors of blue and white and a matching hat. Seeing her tribute, the crowd went wild. The Duke of Braganza broke all protocol and kissed her. Amélie had won the hearts of the Portuguese.

Carlos and Amélie with their firstborn, Luís Filipe.

The wedding ceremony took place on 22 May. Correspondents wrote that the Portuguese capital's euphoria was unprecedented and that *"the French and Portuguese colors floated from every house in Lisbon, and general gladness prevailed."* Large crowds greeted the royal wedding procession as it snaked from the Ajuda and the Necessidades, where the Orléans stayed, to the Church of S. Domingos. *"Princess Amélie,"* reported one journalist, *"whose charm and grace were much admired, was greeted as she entered the church by the plaudits of the throng...The Duke of Braganza stood at the door of the church, and only took his place beside the bride as she*

Queen Amélie with her two sons, Luís Filipe and Manoel.

seated herself in the armchair opposite the high altar. Then the choir commenced a chant and the priests intoned the actions de grace." When the Archbishop asked Carlos if he desired *"to take for wife the Princess Amélie d'Orléans,"* the groom *"rose, went up to the King and Queen and kissed their hands, thus to prove, in the presence of the Court, that he wedded Princess Amelia* [sic] *with their Majesties' authorization."* When asked the same question, Amélie went to her parents, embraced them and returned to give her affirmation to the Archbishop. As the ceremony ended, just before a Te Deum was sung, Lisbon's calm air was overwhelmed as the sound of *"cannon salvos* [and] *rockets rose in the air."* When the wedding procession moved back to the palace of Belém for a sumptuous luncheon, *"ovations and cheers marked the progress of the procession from first to last."*

The joy experienced by Amélie during her wedding celebrations was soon replaced by incomparable sadness. By the time Carlos and Amélie announced their engagement, France's republican authorities were ready to strike against the increasingly popular Count of Paris. His reception at the Hôtel Galliera on 15 May 1886 offered them their chance. The Duke d'Aumâle had counseled against such a display of monarchist might, but his nephew ignored the warnings. No major members of the French government were invited to the festivities. A red flag was waved and the French parliament moved quickly. On returning to France from Portugal, the Count of Paris learned that the government meant to pass a new law of exile. On 22 June, President Jules Grévy signed the bill. The Count of Paris and his eldest son the Duke d'Orléans, as well as Plon-Plon and his eldest son Victor (in their case as representatives of the Napoleonic tradition), were given a few weeks to depart from France. This abusive demonstration of governmental overreach, besides being a violation of its victims' rights as citizens of the French Republic, touched the Portuguese Royal Family. Not only did it banish Amélie's father and brother from France, but it also meted the same punishment to Maria Pia's Bonaparte brother-in-law and her nephew. To a friend, the Duchess of Braganza sent a desperate letter expressing her utter sadness: *"You don't know what I suffer at feeling myself so far away, at thinking that while I was happy here my father was going into exile…I, too, know what exile means, all the pain and bitterness contained in that word."* The French claimant gained himself a future king as a son-in-law, but lost the possibility of ever wearing a crown himself.

The Duke and Duchess, once all the wedding celebrations subsided, moved into the Palace of Belém, and Amélie quickly set about disposing of the ancient rituals and protocols that had long governed Portuguese royal life. Considering herself a fairly modern woman, she simply could not tolerate ostentation and oppressive etiquette. During those first halcyon days of their marriage, Amélie *"liked breakfasting tête-à-tête with the Duke of Braganza, and riding with him in the Picadeiro, the riding-school near the Palace…They both painted scenes, read the same books, went incognito to the opera in the evening; and after they got back delighted in serving themselves at supper."* Their bourgeois domesticity surprised a general public accustomed to excessive royal display. Amélie, however, provided a much-needed breath of fresh air, especially when compared to her somewhat difficult mother-in-law. She did not mind domestic work and used to say that *"no one was better at polishing a pair of shoes or tucking up a bed than she was."*

Chapter XVII – The Coburgs of Lisbon ... An Unsurprising End

On 21 March 1887, Amélie gave birth to a boy at the Palace of Belém, seemingly securing yet another generation of Coburg rule in Portugal. Amélie was delighted with her child, reporting that: *"He is adorably pretty and very strong."* Not surprisingly, the child was given the name Luís Filipe after both of his grandfathers. When Carlos and Amélie represented Portugal at Queen Victoria's Golden Jubilee, they stayed with the exiled Count and Countess of Paris.

As soon as she had recovered from giving birth, Amélie again found herself pregnant. Nearly nine months after the birth of her first child, the Duchess of Braganza gave premature birth to a daughter, Maria Ana, at Vila Viçosa. That day, a small fire inside the palace threatened to consume Prince Luís Filipe's room. His mother saved him, but the stress induced labor, and the premature baby died the same day, much to her parents' grief. On 15 November 1889, Amélie gave birth to a second son, Manoel, at Belém. By this time, King Luís had passed away and Carlos had succeeded his father. Two brothers assured the succession. Whether marital relations between the increasingly corpulent Carlos and his wife ceased, Amélie would have no more children.

King Carlos was an expert shot, as were so many of his Coburg cousins around Europe.

The new reign began with the country in the midst of a somber time. Riddled by economic and financial difficulties, the kingdom again seemed quite unstable. Nearly 70% of the population was poor and illiterate. A prominent Portuguese historian once said: *"It was a crown of thorns that the King placed on his head…alone, he was left helpless by men who abandoned the throne…with parties disjointed in the hour of most need, resigning while confessing their impotence…the wrongs of society were confused with the responsibility of the Crown, dooming the salvation of the monarchy."* Portugal was also under pressure beyond its borders. While the political situation was the source of considerable unease, more so was Europe's hunger for the kingdom's remaining colonies. Unable to defend the remnants of her once thriving empire, Portugal – whether she liked it or not – was at the mercy of the continent's more rapacious colonial juggernauts.

The royal couple tried their best to build a comfortable oasis of domestic peace to protect their family from the winds of unrest ripping Portugal apart. Despite his tendency to corpulence, Carlos joined his wife rowing, sailing, bathing in the sea, hunting, and traveling. The children, fast growing up, followed their parents on their annual progresses from Belém to Cascais, Mafra, Vila Viçosa, and to Sintra, where Amélie grew to love the Pena Palace. *"We are at Cintra, which I used not to love,"* Amélie said, *"but which I find delightful this year. Everything is exquisitely green. We go for long walks among the mountains…I ride horseback a great deal."*

While Carlos tried to find solution to the kingdom's worsening situation, Amélie saw a need for her increased involvement charity work. Unlike her mother-in-law, *"elegant, richly dressed, always distant,"* Amélie was *"more concerned with charity."* She founded a children's hospital and constantly raised funds to pay for her charities. Whether lottery, raffles, or donations, the Queen was tireless in her efforts to fund various social welfare projects that she inaugurated. In France, many of Amélie's aristocratic friends also organized events with the specific purpose of funding her charities. Once when receiving funds collected by her French friends, Amélie wrote to them, *"I was deeply touched at seeing that I was remembered in France, and that such a kind way of proving it to me was taken."*

In late 1889, before Carlos swore the oath, the Portuguese Royal Family received news that Brazil had overthrown the Emperor Pedro II. Within weeks of leaving Rio, the Emperor and his family arrived in Lisbon, where Carlos tried his best to console his uncle. Empress Teresa Cristina, already deathly ill, died on the same day that Carlos officially became King of Portugal, 28 December 1889. Pedro II, not wishing to cause more worries, left Portugal and settled in Paris, where he died in December 1891. Barely recovered from the death of their Imperial aunt, Amélie lost her dearly loved grandfather the Duke de Montpensier, who passed away near Sanlucar de Barrameda, one of his fantastic estates in Andalusia. The loss of her grandfather *"brought back to her all the memories of her childhood in the most melancholy fashion; the domain of Eu had fallen back into silence and desolateness since the exile of the Comte de Paris; Villamanrique, and her travels in Spain when she was a little girl...all that could never live again."*

In early 1890 Carlos also lost his Uncle Aosta. Former Spanish King Amedeo never changed his ways. Even though in 1888 he remarried – this time to his niece Letizia Bonaparte – the irrepressibly irresponsible Duke of Aosta continued cavorting as if he had not a care in his life. Fast living finally overtook him and Amedeo died on 18 January.

More worrisome for Portugal was a festering conflict with Great Britain, which had long-standing diplomatic bonds with Lisbon. At the time, the European powers were busily carving out chunks of Africa for colonial exploitation. Portugal, wishing not to be left behind in the race for colonialism, claimed parts of the continent, arguing that these territories belonged to her based on historical discovery. Portugal had effectively controlled two coastal cities and several outposts in Angola, with large holdings in Mozambique where, in the second half of the Fourteenth Century, Lisbon had tried to bring the Zambesi River valley under its control. Other Portuguese-led expeditions came perilously close to rubbing shoulders with the British, a situation London found intolerable. Africa was a hornet's nest and from its adventure Portugal would come out severely bruised.

Seated: King Carlos and Queen Alexandra. Standing in back: Princess Victoria, Queen Amélie and the Duchess of Fife.

In January 1890, Lord Salisbury, the English Prime Minister, demanded the withdrawal of Portuguese troops from Mashonaland and Matabeleland, in modern-day Zimbabwe, and Shire-Nyasa, in today's Malawi. The Ultimatum demanded swift action: *"What Her Majesty's Government require and insist upon is the following: that telegraphic instructions shall be sent to the governor of Mozambique at once to the effect that all and any Portuguese military forces which are actually on the Shire or in the Makololo or in the Mashona territory are to be withdrawn. Her Majesty's Government considers that without this the assurances given by the Portuguese Government are illusory. Mr. Petre* [British Minister in Lisbon] *is compelled by his instruction to leave Lisbon at once with all the members of his legation unless a satisfactory answer to this foregoing intimation is received by him in the course of this evening, and Her Majesty's ship Enchantress is now at Vigo waiting for his orders."*

Unable to fight Britain, Portugal acquiesced, and acceptance of the British demands became a source of grave national humiliation. Was not Portugal Great Britain's oldest ally? Republicans in Portugal, now a growing segment of the political spectrum, vehemently denounced the government and held King Carlos responsible for the debacle. The government, not surprisingly, fell and the King had to name a new Prime Minister, who was out of office by year's end. These were ominous developments and as Portuguese politics fractured, the King seemed abandoned by the ruling class.

Chapter XVII – The Coburgs of Lisbon ... An Unsurprising End

Since Ferdinand of Saxe-Coburg married Maria II, the Portuguese Royal Family had maintained close ties with their cousins in Great Britain. When Luís succeeded Pedro V, he relied on Queen Victoria's guidance in the same way as his brother had done with the late Prince Albert. King Carlos was no stranger to the Court of St. James's: *"I like him very much and so do we all,"* Queen Victoria wrote. Yet little did the Portuguese know that, during the Ultimatum crisis, Carlos's friend the Prince of Wales had tried to mediate with Lord Salisbury. However, the Prince of Wales was unsuccessful. To Carlos, he wrote a letter explaining how precarious his position was, adding, *"You must understand that we have also a public opinion to deal with which, though better instructed, is equally exacting."*

Then an insurrection exploded when Portugal's Republicans gathered for a congress in January 1891. Although divided between those who wanted an immediate revolution and those who believed that the climate was not yet ripe, the Republicans staged a coup in Porto on 31 January and proclaimed a republic. Government forces raced to quash the insurrection, and a dozen people died during the dangerous hours that ensued. Finally, the government succeeded in pushing back the revolutionaries.

The Prince of Wales understood how the Ultimatum had damaged Carlos's position, while also realizing that the quarrel with Great Britain was greatly to blame for the Porto uprising. Albert Edward was well versed in Portuguese matters, as one of his closest friends was the Marquis de Soveral, the kingdom's minister in London. Years later, and to lessen his Portuguese cousin's state of despondency, Albert Edward convinced Queen Victoria to confer the Order of the Garter upon King Carlos, who accepted the honor. When Carlos visited England to be invested, he was also Albert Edward's guest at Sandringham, where he enjoyed a good shoot. Unfortunately, nothing King Carlos did assuaged his virulent critics, and Republican charges that he lacked patriotism further eroding his public image.

When in 1892 Portugal was forced to declare bankruptcy, King Carlos decided to play a larger role in guiding the country's destiny. He tried to find solutions outside the two mainstream parties that dominated the kingdom, relying on some patriotic leaders to front interim governments. Without political backing, the King's men were unable to govern. The political parties returned and Rotativism began again. As the years passed, the country's problems only deepened.

In 1902 Portugal again declared bankruptcy. The politicians who had returned to power with Rotativism had done little to correct the institutional ills responsible for Portugal's financial chaos and the people grew more frustrated. The King,

Luís Filipe, Duke of Braganza.

Infante Manoel, Duke of Beja.

Queen Amélie.

equally frustrated by what he believed was absence of leadership, feared the country was headed toward an abyss of absolute socio-political dislocation. What should he do?

The politicians seemed concerned only with retaining power; when dissident leaders abandoned the major parties their complaints were ignored. To keep dissidents from regaining power the electoral laws were changed, but these measures only inflamed opinion. As the Republicans gained strength, a frustrated Carlos finally intervened. To Prince Albert of Monaco, he wrote: *"I decided to start a complete revolution of the process of governing…done from the top, organizing a liberal and honest government, with modern ideas, so we can prevent that tomorrow a revolution from the bottom destroys everything, securing the ruin of my country."*

With students rioting in the streets, strikes disrupting the economy, and instability rampant, Carlos called on João Franco, one of the dissidents, to form a new government. Franco believed that adopting liberal concepts would provide salvation, copying the Republican platform so the revolution would come from the top rather than the bottom and cast the King, not his enemies, as reformer. Franco established alliances with liberal reformers while implementing some press freedoms. He even called for transparency in the royal civil list, but his measures only succeeded in uniting the critics against the throne.

On 9 May 1907, King Carlos authorized the dissolution of the parliament without calling for a new election. It was an institutional coup d'etat. The two majority parties, both of which asked the King to take this road when they were in power, now criticized him and Franco. The Republicans were livid and called for a revolution, and even some former supporters of the monarchy abandoned the King as insurrection spread across Portugal. Franco responded by restricting freedoms. Leaflets, newspapers, and books deemed against public order were banned. On 23 June, Carlos wrote Franco, encouraging the "dictator" to remain steadfast: *"Our campaign has started, and it seems to me it's going quite well. During this serious phase avoid provocation. We must remain calm and cold-blooded, but without ever losing our strength, since this all came about due to lamentable alteration of the public order."* The King, supported by Franco, firmly believed that the suspension of the institutional order had already improved Portugal, and *"without my constant supervision, the situation would return to where it was."*

In an interview the King granted to a French journalist, Carlos shed light on his actions: *"It was necessary that the confusion, the mess, if you will, end. That just could not last. We were headed nowhere…they speak of a dictatorship, but the parties yelling the loudest also asked me to do this when they were in power."* By December 1907, Carlos and Franco believed the situation had normalized enough for elections to be called for the following April. It was the first indication that the "dictatorship" had achieved the normalization the King wanted.

In November Queen Amélie headed to England to attend the wedding of her youngest sister Princess Louise to the Infante don Carlos of Spain, widower of King Alfonso XIII's eldest sister Maria de las Mercedes, the Princess of Asturias, who had died in childbirth. Left with three children, Infante Carlos wished to find a royal bride who could be his partner as well as mother to his offspring. Carlos and Louise went on to have four children, among them Princess María de las Mercedes, who in 1938 gave birth to the future King Juan Carlos of Spain. Amélie was also among the large royal contingent invited by King Edward VII to spend a weekend en famille at Windsor Castle. Several are said to have expressed to Amélie their *"fears for the Crown of Portugal,"* but she dismissed them, having *"so much belief in the loyalty of her subjects that she smiled at these fears, reassuring every one about her."*

Still, the regime's enemies continued their conspiracies unabated. In late January 1908 some Republicans were jailed when the authorities uncovered a plot to assassinate Franco. This led to convulsions within the movement and another uprising that was quashed before it began. In this atmosphere of unrest, Carlos, who was spending time at Vila Viçosa with the Queen and their sons, decreed that anyone suspected of disorder would be banished, without trial, to one of Portugal's foreign possessions. By so doing, the King had signed his death sentence.

Given the perilous times, Carlos decided on a hasty return to Lisbon. Along with the Queen and Crown Prince Luís Filipe (Manoel had already returned to the capital), they boarded a morning train from Vila Viçosa on 1 February. The royal passengers arrived in Lisbon Praça do Comercio, on the Tagus estuary, later that afternoon and were met by Infante Manoel, Franco, and Infante Afonso. Hoping to give the impression of normality, the King – attired in a colorful uniform – joined the princes and his wife, her face shaded by a large hat and hands clutching a large bouquet, in an open carriage for the drive to the palace. Armed police and a mounted cavalry officer surrounded the vehicle, while another carriage held Infante Afonso, the Prime Minister and assorted officials.

At Vila Viçosa, fives days before the regicide, the Portuguese royals enjoy a day in the country. From left: the Duke of Braganza, King Carlos, Queen Amélie and the Duke of Beja.

As the royal carriage rounded the eastern part of the wide, colonnaded square, shots rang out. A bearded assassin used his Winchester carbine rifle to take aim at the King from a distance of some 24 feet. The bullet struck the King's neck, killing him instantly. Another assassin ran into the street and began firing at the Royal Family. Additional bullets hit the King's body as Crown Prince Luís Filipe, who was carrying a revolver, stood and took aim at the attacker who had lunged atop the carriage step. Although he apparently fired four shots, none stopped the assassin whose bullet now tore through the Crown Prince's skull. Wielding her bouquet, the Queen managed to repel an attack on her youngest son, who escaped with only a wound on the arm. Arm tied with a handkerchief bloody with his family's blood, young Manoel was now King. Both of the assassins, Manuel Reis Buíça and Alfredo Costa, were killed, death providing protection

The site of the regicide, the Praça do Commercio.

A memorial for the victims of the regicide.

to any larger involvement in the grisly deed.

Shocked and gloomy, Edward VII could not believe the tragedy that had befallen his Portuguese cousins. Yet, he also realized that constitutional monarchs had limitations: *"Yes, it is horrible – horrible. But I'll tell you something: a constitutional King must not do such things."* Later when Soveral returned to London after attending the royal funeral and voting to dismiss Franco, a bewildered Edward VII asked his friend: *"Well, what kind of country is that, in which you kill the King and Prince, and the first thing to do is ask for the resignation of the Prime Minister? The revolution has triumphed, isn't it true?"* Soveral later said that it was then that he realized the magnitude of the error committed by the new King, for one of the traumatized King Manoel's first acts as monarch was to demand Franco's resignation.

Queen Amélie took swift action to protect both her remaining son and the throne. A government of National Unity was appointed, but this was later seen as an encouraging sign that the monarchy had weakened beyond salvation. The general amnesty declared to calm the kingdom was viewed as a further sign of royal infirmity. Had Manoel II, with his mother's advice and guidance, pursued the conspirators and implemented tough measures, his enemies may have been cowered into submission. While the general population extended him deep sympathy, Republicans – who after all had gotten away with the regicide – were emboldened by his feeble reaction to their deed.

Manoel II's reign was to be of short duration. In an effort to reestablish a connection with his subjects, Manoel and his mother traveled around Portugal, visiting countless communities, towns, and cities. He made a good impression and the people showed him, and Amélie, heartfelt compassion. The Republicans, busily planning his overthrow, reacted sarcastically to Manoel II's efforts and one of them said, *"Your Highness arrives too young into a very old world!"*

For a time the situation stabilized. In February 1909 Manoel hosted King Alfonso XIII, who drove his own automobile over the border and paid his Portuguese cousins a visit at Vila Viçosa. Later that year, Manoel II visited Madrid, where his Aunt Louise and his Grandmother the Countess of Paris were among those who greeted him at the Oriente Palace. From Madrid Manoel II continued to Cherbourg, where the *Victoria and Albert* transported him to Portsmouth, where the Prince of Wales (George V) received him. Manoel II continued on to Windsor Castle where he celebrated his twentieth birthday on 15 November, and the following day, Edward VII invested him with the Garter.

While in England, it was rumored that Manoel II was exam-

King Alfonso XIII of Spain and King Manoel II of Portugal.

Chapter XVII – The Coburgs of Lisbon ... An Unsurprising End

Left: King Manoel II in Garter robes. He always remained close to his English cousins – even in exile he was a frequent guest of King George V.

ining potential brides. One, Patricia of Connaught, born in 1886, was the youngest daughter of the Duke and Duchess of Connaught. Flattered though she was by the attention, Patricia had no interest in either marrying a King, much less one who sat on such a shaky throne, or abandoning her faith. The other royal ladies were the Fife Princesses Alexandra and Maud, granddaughters of Edward VII. Neither, however, was interested. Queen Amélie later confided that she wanted Manoel II to pursue Princess Louise of Battenberg, who eventually married the King of Sweden.

From England, Manoel II sailed across the Channel to France. Here, in addition to official government receptions, Manoel had ample opportunity to indulge in more pleasing distractions. *"I have found out through gossip that Manoel is involved in an affair with a little Parisian diva named Gaby Deslys,"* Amélie wrote. Manoel II was enthralled with la Deslys and in due time showered her with presents. Gaby even traveled to Lisbon and visited Manoel II at Necessidades.

In May 1910, King Manoel was back in England to attend the funeral of King Edward VII. King George V, flanked by his cousin Kaiser Wilhelm II, led the cortege, followed by King Haakon VII of Norway, King Alfonso XIII of Spain, and King George I of the Hellenes. Behind them came Manoel, marching in the same row as King Ferdinand of Bulgaria and King Frederik VIII of Denmark, and followed by Albert of Belgium, Archduke Franz Ferdinand, and the Hereditary Prince of the Ottoman Empire. Only two of the Coburg monarchs present would survive the debacle caused by the Great War.

Legislative elections were held in Portugal on 28 August. The results gave the government eighty-nine deputies, including forty-five monarchists and fourteen Republicans. Despite nearly doubling their numbers, the Republicans were still a small minority. Then, on the evening of October 3, having played host to the Brazilian president, the King faced a full revolution. As rumors of a plot spread across around Lisbon, the Chief of the General Staff summoned troops to the city. At the time Amélie and Maria Pia were away at Sintra; Manoel II immediately tried to reach the President of the Council and members of the cabinet, but telephone lines were cut and the King was isolated at Necessidades Palace.

By the following morning no loyal troops had yet arrived at the palace; the King did not know that increasing numbers of his army and navy had already joined the revolt. As deadly combat erupted on the streets of Lisbon and several vessels in the royal navy had opened fire on the palace, the King's military staff urged him to flee the capital. The King took their advice, traveling to Mafra, where he followed events as monarchist forces fought for control of Lisbon. By the morning of 5 October the cause was lost and the monarchy fell. Most people in Lisbon had no idea that a republic had been proclaimed until the following day.

Manoel II, accompanied by his mother and grandmother, boarded the royal yacht *Amélia IV* and left Portugal at Ericeira. The King hoped to head to the northern provinces, where the monarchy enjoyed more support, but

Above: The wedding of King Manoel II and Princess Auguste Viktoria of Hohenzollern, Sigmaringen, 4 September 1913. From left: The Prince of Wales, the Duke of Aosta, Dowager Grand Duchess Luise of Baden, Infanta Louise of Spain, Queen Amélie, the Duchess of Aosta, King Manoel and Queen Auguste Viktoria, Prince August Wilhelm of Prussia (between them), Prince Johann Georg of Saxony, Grand Duke Friedrich II of Baden, Infante Carlos of Spain, the Duke of Oporto (nearly hidden), Fürst Wilhelm of Hohenzollern and Hereditary Prince Friedrich of Hohenzollern.

Right: Fürstin Adelgunde of Hohenzollern, Hereditary Prince Friedrich of Hohenzollern, King Manoel II and Queen Auguste Viktoria.

en route the course was changed and the Portuguese exiles instead went to Gibraltar, where they learned the devastating news. Porto had fallen to the revolution and nothing could be done. Manoel had become the first Coburg king to lose his throne.

In exile, Manoel settled in England, where his mother's family owned several vast estates near London. At first money was short, as the Royal Family had not been able to bring many possessions out of Portugal. Amélie's wealth, though, was considerable, and she expected to receive a share of her mother's fabulous fortune. One report alleged that when the Portuguese government began paying Manoel a pension it was done so at London's prompting. This monthly stipend helped resolve Manoel's finances and allowed him to purchase Fulwell Lodge, a stately home in Fulwell Park that served as his residence for nearly two decades between 1913-1932. Although he remained deeply concerned about Portugal and followed political developments with interest, the King understood that his monarchy had passed into history.

Manoel's relationship with la Deslys did not survive the revolution by long. In 1911 she left Europe and settled in the United States, and Queen Amélie used her departure to push her son to find a respectable bride. During a spring 1912 visit to Switzerland, he met the blonde, blue-eyed, twenty-two-year-old Princess Auguste Viktoria, eldest child of Wilhelm of Hohenzollern, himself the eldest son of Fürst Leopold and of his Portuguese wife Infanta Antónia. Although first cousins, Manoel and Auguste Viktoria were taken with each other and on 4 September 1913, they were married at Sigmaringen in the presence of numerous royal relatives. The Prince of Wales (the future King Edward VIII) stood as Manoel's supporter, watched by Prince August Wilhelm representing his father the Kaiser; the Duke and Duchess of Aosta; the Duke of Genoa; the Grand Duke and Grand Duchess of Baden; the Infante Carlos and Infanta Louise of Spain; the Duke of Vendôme; the Duke of Saxe-Coburg & Gotha; Prince and Princess Johann Georg of Saxony; and many others, including representatives from Romania. The bride's grandmother, who died the following December, lived long enough to see her descendants joined to the line of her Coburg ancestors. It was her last satisfaction.

Queen Auguste Viktoria.

Manoel dedicated much of his time in exile to assembling his extensive library. A respected bibliophile, Manoel used his book and manuscript collections to write historical treatises on Portuguese literature. During the Great War, he joined the Red Cross and in this capacity visited the Western Front, where he always sought out Portuguese soldiers, doing what he could to bring them supplies and help lift their morale. This show of patriotism gained Manoel recognition, not just among the Portuguese, but also among his British hosts. In July 1919, when the victory parade streamed through the streets of London, Manoel and Auguste Viktoria stood next to the British Royal Family. For his wife, the conflict was the source of grave worry as her family fought on the German side, while the overwhelming majority of Manoel's closest relations sided with the Allies. Queen Mother Amélie, no friend of Prussia, carried out countless charity events, often attended by members of King George V's family, to raise funds for Allied war casualties.

At war's end, Manoel and Auguste Viktoria traveled to Germany, visiting Sigmaringen and other estates. After nearly a decade, though, the couple still had no children; since the Duke of Oporto had married morganatically in 1917 and died childless in 1920, Manoel worried about the succession. With this in mind, he resumed relations with the descendants of King Miguel.

King Miguel's only son, Infante Miguel (1853-1927), had three sons from two marriages. His eldest son, Miguel (1878-1923), renounced his rights to marry an American lady, Anita Stewart; although the couple had three children, none were royal. Miguel's second son, Infante Francisco José (1879-

King Manoel II in exile.

Infante Afonso, Duke of Oporto.

Queen Amélie of Portugal in later life.

1919) was a notorious homosexual best known for the string of scandals he left across Europe, and he died childless. Then there was Duarte Nuño, Infante Miguel's only son from his marriage to his first cousin Princess Marie Therese zu Löwenstein-Wertheim-Rosenberg. Born in 1907, Duarte Nuño represented the future of the dynasty if Manoel died childless. Although Manoel was never able to negotiate the succession in his lifetime, Duarte Nuño was unopposed when he styled himself Duke of Braganza. Unlike his father and grandfather, who fathered children in old age (Miguel I was fifty-one when he fathered his son Miguel, who in turn was fifty-four years of age when he fathered Duarte Nuño), the Duke of Braganza married in hs thirties. His bride was Princess Maria Francisca d'Orléans-Braganza, a great grand-daughter of Emperor Pedro II of Brazil. Interestingly, Maria Francisca carries the blood of Coburg in her veins as her paternal grandfather was the Count d'Eu, whose own mother was Princess Victoire, King Consort Ferdinand of Portugal's only sister. Maria Francisca, as was King Manoel, was a great-great grandchild of Princess Antonia Kohary. The bloodlines shared by Maria Francisca and King Manoel also included two Braganza connections. Her great-grandmother Pedro II was the brother of Queen Maria II, Manoel 's great-grandmother. Also, Maria Francisca and Manoel both were descendants of King Pedro IV. Infante Duarte Pío, Duarte Nuño and Maria Francisca's eldest son, is the present Head of the Royal House of Portugal.

Former King Manoel II died unexpectedly at Fulwell Park on 2 July 1932. He developed an abnormal swelling in the vocal folds of his larynx that led to suffocation. The Portuguese government, led by António Oliveira de Salazar (who ruled Portugal for decades), authorized Manoel II's burial in Lisbon. The *HMS Concord* transported the King's remains and on August 2, Manoel finally returned to the capital. He rests surrounded by his family inside the cold peace of the royal crypt in the Monastery of São Vicente de Fora.

In the early 1920s Amélie dismantled her English home, Abercorn House, and returned to France, where she acquired a lovely, turret-roofed château, Bellevue, near Versailles. She was devastated at Manoel's death. Her trusted valet recalled later that upon being handed a silver tray with a telegram, even before opening the missive, Amélie exclaimed, *"I know, my son is dead!"*

Beginning in the late 1930s Amélie renewed contact with the Portuguese government, and she corresponded with Salazar for many years. She also began donating many historical artifacts that had once belonged to the Royal Family to the Portuguese Government. Amélie was in France when World War II erupted. Although several times she searched for a

Chapter XVII – The Coburgs of Lisbon ... An Unsurprising End

safer residence, she always returned to Bellevue. When the Germans requisitioned it as a home for officers, she insisted on remaining in her old rooms. Even though Portugal invited her to return, she declined the offer and remained undisturbed at Bellevue. In 1945, though, Amélie did visit Portugal for nearly six weeks – her first time on Portuguese soil since departing from Ericeira in 1910. On 19 May, the fifty-ninth anniversary of her arrival in Portugal as a bride, Amélie visited São Vicente de Fora and prayed for her husband and their children.

Amélie spent her remaining years at Bellevue, devoting herself to charities. One of her last acts was to make Infante Duarte Pío the principal beneficiary of her movable and immovable property in Portugal. With that Queen Mother Amélie ensured that Portuguese monarchists knew where her loyalties rested. She died on 25 October 1951, four decades after her mother-in-law, who had returned to live in her native Italy. The Portuguese government had already decided that Amélie was to rest in São Vicente. Her remains were taken by ship to Lisbon where more than 400,000 filed past her bier. It was an incredible homecoming for a Queen chased away by revolution forty-one years earlier.

Widowhood in England proved lonely for Auguste Viktoria. Unable to overcome the pain she felt due to her husband's loss, she closed Fulwell and returned to Germany, where she built a house in Umkirch. Seven years after Manoel's death, she married a landed German aristocrat of Swedish ancestry, Count Robert Douglas. He died in 1955; Auguste Viktoria survived him eleven years, dying in Münchhöf on 26 August 1966.

AUGUSTA VIKTORIA
GRÄFIN DOUGLAS
GEB. PRINZESSIN VON HOHENZOLLERN
VERW. KÖNIGIN VON PORTUGAL

geb. am 19. August 1890 in Sigmaringen
gest. am 29. August 1966 in Münchhöf

Memorial card for Queen Auguste Viktoria.

Very little remains of the time the Coburgs of Lisbon spent in England. Fulwell Lodge was sold, razed, and the site later redeveloped for housing. Visitors paying close attention, though, can still see Manoel Road, Lisbon Avenue, Augusta Road, and Portugal Gardens. They stand as fitting tributes to a dynasty that tried, but in the end failed to achieve lasting success.

The Duke and Duchess of Braganza, Duarte Nuño and Maria Francisca.

Chapter XVIII
King Albert I's Descendants
Tragedy, War & Redemption

The tragic death of the patriotic King Albert of Belgium presaged the country's years of trouble under his son's rule. Dark and ominous clouds were gathering, clouds that would challenge not only the Coburg dynasty's hold on the throne, but would threaten the kingdom's very existence.

During the Great War, young Prince Léopold, Duke of Brabant, had worn the uniform of a private and served in his father's army, struggling to defend the small territory King Albert had managed to keep. The experience not only initiated Léopold into service to his country, but also offered Belgians a visible and potent symbol of the future for which they were fighting. As part of his education, Léopold had journeyed to other European countries as well as Belgium's overseas territories, and in 1919 he joined his parents when they became the first Belgian monarchs to visit the United States. During long hours spent on trains, the young Prince learned – as had his Bulgarian cousins – to drive a locomotive. After watching a show put on by Native Americans and cowboys in Albuquerque, New Mexico, the young heir expressed his satisfaction with the performance, but wished *"there had been more lassoing."* Léopold was also taken with California, saying that he wished he could stay and study, perhaps engineering.

A few years later, the Duke of Brabant visited Egypt, traveling as far as Khartoum, before journeying on to Belgium's African colonies. Appalled by what he saw there, Léopold gave a speech asking for improved sanitary conditions of Africans living under Belgian rule. This early advocacy hinted at Léopold's eventual reign. Unlike his father, he would be active in political affairs and seek to lead, not merely reign. This tendency worried his mother, who cautioned against excessive candor: *"Always be prudent on your judgment of politicians and the parties,"* she wrote. *"Be a Sphinx in politics and be amiable to all. Don't allow anyone to label you!"*

When it came to finding Léopold a bride, King Albert believed that as long as she was royal the search ought to be left to his son. Albert's marriage to Elisabeth had not been an arranged one, and he intended to extend to Léopold the same freedom to wed. However, both King and Queen kept a close watch over the process, and when needed exerted their influence.

Rumors over Léopold's choice of bride filtered through Europe. In 1921, as his parents prepared to visit Italy, several newspapers in Europe and in the United States announced that an engagement between the Duke of Brabant and Princess Jolanda of Savoy, eldest daughter of King Vittorio Emanuele III, was imminent. The Belgian visit passed without any such announcement, and two years later Jolanda married Italian aristocrat Count Giorgio Calvi di Bergolo, whose sister Mathilda was wed to Prince Aage of Denmark. Later, Léopold was asked to consider Giovanna, Jolanda's sister, but he deemed her too young, and she went on to marry another Coburg.

Prince Carl of Sweden, one of the sons of King Oscar II and his wife Sophie of Nassau – whose family ruled neighboring Luxembourg – had three elegantly beautiful, blue-eyed, and educated daughters. Their pedigree was impeccable: their mother, Princess Ingeborg of Denmark, was a daughter of King Frederik VIII and Queen Louise. Although the eldest daughter, Margaretha, had wed Prince Axel of Denmark, the two youngest, Märtha and Astrid, remained unmarried. There is a story that Brabant first met Astrid at the christening of one of the children of Axel's sister Margrethe and her husband Prince René of Bourbon-Parma, brother of Empress Zita.

Above: The wedding of the Duke of Brabant and Princess Astrid of Sweden. Seated, from left: Princess Feodora of Denmark, Princess Marie José of Belgium, Princess Märtha of Sweden, the Groom and the Bride, Princess Ingrid of Sweden and Ms. Alfhild Ekelund. Standing, same order: Prince Carl and Prince Gustaf Adolf of Sweden, Crown Prince Olav of Norway, Ms. Margareta Stähl, Count Claes Sparre, Ms. Anna Adelswärd, Prince Charles Théodore of Belgium, Count Folke Bernadotte, Baron Sigvard Beck-Friis, Ms. Anne Marie von Essen and Baron Carl Strömfelt.

Left: Queen Astrid of Belgium at home.

Another claims that Brabant's friend Axel of Denmark may have first introduced him to his future wife through him. Others cite a letter Brabant wrote to his mother as proof that Queen Elisabeth, and her husband, played a larger role directing their son to the chosen princess: *"My present happiness, I owe to you,"* Brabant wrote to his mother. *"Truthfully, you could not have found me anyone better."* Although King Albert and his wife had publicly proclaimed that they had little to do with finding Brabant a bride, now we know that the exact opposite was true.

The Duke of Brabant was captivated by Astrid, and soon headed incognito to Stockholm to become better acquainted with her. In 1926, on one of his visits, Queen Elisabeth joined her son, and before long Brussels and Stockholm announced the engagement of the Duke of Brabant and Princess Astrid of Sweden. In Belgium there was great interest in this beautiful Scandinavian princess; in time, it is arguable, Belgians came to love Astrid more than they did her husband.

Léopold and Astrid married civilly in Stockholm on 4 November 1926. Four days later, the "Snow Princess," as

Astrid was popularly called, arrived in Brussels, which *"surrendered itself to the spirit of festival as it has not done since the first joyous days of the liberation in 1918."* Earlier in the day, when the ship carrying the Swedish royals arrived in Antwerp, Astrid was *"moved by singing of children."* The effusive greeting she gave Léopold pleased the crowd immensely, while conveying to Belgians the image of a fresh new approach to royal lifestyle and behavior. Some journalists compared the reaction to Astrid's arrival tantamount to London's 1863 greeting of Princess Alexandra of Denmark.

Right: King Léopold III and Queen Astrid with their three children: Joséphine-Charlotte, Baudouin and Albert, 1934.

Below left: Princess Joséphine-Charlotte and her brother Baudouin, Duke of Brabant.

The royal wedding took place on 10 November in Brussels' majestic Cathedral of SS Michael and Gudule. The imposing building, *"dating chiefly from the Thirteenth Century, with massive gray pillars, high pointed arches, and great carved figures of saints on the columns of the nave,"* seemed to float on a sea of flags and banners displaying the colors of Belgium and Sweden. *"The sun shone brilliantly all day, blazing through the old Sixteenth Century windows of the south transept, the prevailing tone of which is bright blue and gold, as if in happy augury, those being the national colors of the bride."* Inside the cathedral, a throng of guests witnessed the service, conducted by the Archbishop of Mechelen, *"who made a short address to the young couple before the actual ceremony from the liturgy."* Since Astrid was not a Catholic (she converted in 1930), *"there could be no nuptial mass,"* though the glittering guests, covered in priceless jewelry, and resplendent in military uniforms layered with sashes and orders, compensated for the lack of religious pageantry. In addition to the families of the bride and groom, the King and Queen of Denmark, the Grand Duchess Charlotte of Luxembourg, Crown Prince Olav of Norway, Prince Henry of Great Britain, Prince Sixtus and Prince René of Bourbon-Parma with their spouses, and countless others attended the service. Surrounding the cathedral and lining the route of the wedding procession as it snaked toward the royal palace, more than a quarter of a million people roared with applause as they saw the newlyweds, particularly as the Duchess of Brabant waved *"greetings to the people with her bouquet with that same spontaneity and unaffectedness which she has shown ever since her arrival in Belgium."*

Upon returning from their honeymoon, Léopold and Astrid settled at the Bellevue Palace, where they led a very simple, bour-

King Léopold III and Queen Astrid.

geois existence that greatly pleased Belgians. On 11 October 1927 Astrid gave birth to a baby daughter who received the name Joséphine Charlotte. The people of Brussels were pleasantly surprised when Astrid was seen, very frequently, wheeling the baby's pram along the paths of the park across from her home. Although *"for Astrid this was a natural thing to do,"* Belgium had never before witnessed such simple and unaffected royal behavior. Three years later, while living at Stuyvenberg Palace, Astrid again gave birth. This time, and to the kingdom's delight – not to mention that of the baby's father and grandfather – the child was a boy. His parents named him Baudouin in honor of King Albert's long-deceased older brother. It was also at Stuyvenberg that Queen Astrid gave birth to a third child, Albert, born nearly four months after the death of his Belgian grandfather. Albert later received the title of Prince of Liège.

In these years the Duke and Duchess of Brabant carried out an increasing number of royal duties. Foreign travel continued and along with her husband, Astrid visited faraway lands in Asia and Africa. In 1933 they visited the Belgian Congo, and again Léopold was deeply bothered by what he witnessed. He was appalled at the backward state of agricultural technology used there and worried that this lack of development only worsened the living conditions of the natives. His outrage was such that, upon returning to Brussels, Léopold gave a speech in the Senate in which he openly criticized the unscrupulous practices of the colonial authorities and the colonists: *"A colony must safeguard the natives,"* Léopold said, *"and must not be limited to simply enrich a minority."* Throughout his life, Léopold would return to Africa with frequency, a continent that had made a deep impression in him.

On 23 February 1934, six days after the tragic death of his father, Léopold III swore the oath and his reign officially began. His speech provided a window into the new King's deep love for Belgium: *"I give myself completely to Belgium. The Queen will assist me with all her heart in the execution of my responsibilities. We will raise our children to love the Nation."* Although deeply fond of her late father-in-law, Astrid had little time to mourn his passing as she assumed the burdens of being Queen. She supported organizations and institutions dedicated to improving childcare, cultural activities, and raised the nation's conscience about the plight of the poor. Her many activities across Belgium allowed the people to see their Queen, which genuinely enhanced her public role and the country's perception of her. In 1935, Astrid started an organization commonly known as "The Queen's Appeal," a National Relief Committee to raise funds and collect food and clothes to be distributed to the poor. It was an extremely suc-

King Léopold, injured, walking behind his wife's coffin.

cessful endeavor and it brought much needed relief to those affected by the country's troubling economic situation.

Then, tragedy struck. After attending the Stockholm wedding of their cousins Crown Prince Frederik of Denmark and Princess Ingrid of Sweden in May of 1935, Léopold III and Astrid had paid their first official visit to his mother's cousin Empress Zita, who had relocated from Spain to Belgium several years earlier, in an effort to mend the rift caused between the two royal families by the Great War. In August, the King and Queen went on holiday to Switzerland, along with their two eldest children, and spent their days swimming, going on excursions, playing golf, and driving through the scenic countryside. After sending their children back to Brussels the couple remained for a few extra days. On 29 August, Léopold and Astrid set out on an excursion, with the King driving a Packard convertible and their chauffeur sitting in the back seat. As they reached a picturesque spot in Küssnacht am Rigi and the Queen pointed out something to her husband, he lost control of the vehicle and it careened off the road and down a steep slope. The Queen was thrown out of the car and her body slammed into a tree, as the Packard continued down the slope and plunged into a lake. The King, who was also thrown from the car, escaped with minor injuries, as did the chauffeur, but Astrid died from her injuries in her husband's arms at the scene.

Above: A striking pose of King Léopold III on horseback.

Léopold's grief was unfathomable, and news of Queen Astrid's death fell on Belgium like a mind-numbing thunder strike. The kingdom was in shock and would remain so for years to come. Queen Elisabeth, who was visiting her daughter Marie José in Italy, departed with her immediately to Brussels, while Astrid's parents chartered an airplane and also flew to the Belgian capital. Once again, Brussels played host to a bevy of royalty, this time for a much sadder gathering. The Queen's funeral was held on 3 September, as King Léopold, his arm in a sling and bandages covering part of his face, walked behind her coffin. It was an emotional image. The King tried to keep his composure, but during the funeral mass, *"for an instant...as he tried to rise from pride he faltered and those nearest him stepped forward to help him. When at last the body was laid in the royal crypt at Laeken he covered his face with his uninjured hand and broke down."* Four days later, Baudouin celebrated his fifth birthday.

The King and his country were forever marked with a sense of loss and a sense of unfulfilled potential. The

Below: King Léopold III and Queen Astrid's children: Joséphine-Charlotte surrounded by Albert and Baudouin.

King Léopold III with Baudouin and Albert in Switzerland.

King Léopold III and Princess Lilian c. 1945.

death of his closest advisor and companion robbed Léopold III of much needed counsel and guidance during events that were destined to change his life, and his kingdom, forever.

Outside the walls of the royal compound at Laeken, a gathering storm increased its fury, and Belgium bitterly felt the financial chaos caused by the near collapse of the world economy. Unemployment and penury threatened to consume the country, just as political division created incredible challenges to the institutions binding Belgium together. While other European nations fell under the aegis of fascism and totalitarianism, Belgium tried its best to remain neutral and find lasting solutions to the deepening socio-economic crisis. In addition to this crisis and the loss of his adored wife, Léopold III was inevitably compared to his legendary and heroic father. Success seemed elusive; though the King attempted to overcome these obstacles, in the end he failed.

Astrid's death left a void in the King's life, and soon the press began to speculate on whether he would remarry. There was talk of Maria of Savoy, the youngest daughter of King Vittorio Emanuele III; Eudoxia of Bulgaria, a sister of King Boris III; Feodora-Louise of Denmark, and even Adelheid of Austria, Empress Zita's eldest daughter. There were also rumors that the King traveled to Paris to fulfill his sexual needs. Though broken hearted at Astrid's death, the King was not interested in a monastic way of life, and he soon met the woman who would both conquer his heart and complicate his existence.

Mary "Lilian" Baels, whom Léopold III met in 1938, was born in London in 1916 to Henri Baels, the Governor of West Flanders. She was very pretty, intelligent, charming, and seductive. *"Her vitality was exceptional...she was devoted to sport; she swam, she drove, she played golf. It was in fact through a game of golf that Léopold first came to know her."* Léopold felt an uncontrollable attraction to her natural looks and *"Latin charm,"* and she encouraged his pursuit. Two years later, Léopold met Lilian again when Queen Elisabeth, *"who as a mother wanted to see her son happy,"* encouraged the relationship and invited them both to join her for lunch.

On September 1, 1939, in the midst of this romance, Germany invaded Poland, unleashing international condemnation and igniting the Second World War. By Spring of 1940 Belgium's politics were bordering on chaos. The King had refused to accept the prime minister's resignation, alleging that given the storm gathering over the border, *"it was not the time for a ministerial crisis caused by internal politics."* Seizing the moment, on May 10, 1940, Germany invaded the kingdom.

Léopold III spent the first few weeks of the German invasion dealing with military matters. Despite Belgian resistance, the Germans were able to cut through the country and after nine days reached the French coast, creating a corridor that went from the Ardennes to the Channel. After conferring, the Belgians and French decided to attack, the former striking southward and the latter in the north, but the plan was never carried out as Allied forces along the German corridor were too weak. In an effort to capture the British Expeditionary Force (BEF) located around Dunkirk, the Germans began advancing northward along the coast, which led to mass evacuation. Léopold III and his forces remained at Bruges, occupying an area barely one-eighth the size of the kingdom. *"It was an area crammed with panicky refugees and strafed almost continuously by the German air force,"* said one historian. As if this situation was not chaotic enough, the Germans began dropping leaflets designed to destroy whatever was left of Belgian morale. *"The war is over for you,"* these read, *"Your leaders are going to escape by airplane. Lay down your arms."* To minimize the effect of this campaign, Léopold III promised, *"Officers and Soldiers, whatever happens, I should share your fate!"*

King Léopold III signing the act of abdication while King Baudouin looks on.

By 24 May the situation seemed untenable. The BEF were readying a retreat across the Channel, along with remaining French and Belgian troops. It was then that the final break between Léopold and his ministers took place. The King, who had had a rocky relationship with most Belgian politicians, believed himself singularly suited to make decisions. Since his father's death, there had been nearly ten different, largely ineffective governments, which did nothing to improve the King's trust of politicians. Léopold III granted a last audience to the few remaining cabinet members, including Prime Minister Hubert Pierlot, who reminded the King that under no circumstance should he be personally associated with the capitulation. The King was also urged to depart and join the Allied effort in London, instead of remaining behind in occupied Belgium. *"The Government unanimously shares this opinion,"* Léopold III was told. Violating his constitutional oath, the King refused to follow the Prime Minister's recommendations. He argued that leaving his troops was tantamount to desertion and believed that it his duty to remain in Belgium. *"That is what I have chosen,"* Léopold III told Perliot. The ministers were even more horrified when they heard the King say that he intended to

Prince Albert, Princess Lilian with Marie Esmeralda, King Léopold with Marie Christine.

Princess Lilian with Baudouin and Joséphine-Charlotte.

"*remain and reign.*" He would form a new government, "*in opposition to them – the elected government.*" These words came through as pure treason to the Prime Minister and his colleagues. "*The horrible words dishonor, desertion, betrayal…[fell] from our lips in the very presence of him who was going to commit this act,*" one of the ministers present remembered. The King bid them farewell before the remnants of the Belgian government fled to exile, from where they intended to carry on the business of government.

The King resisted the German onslaught for another three days. The Germans broke through Belgian defenses and surrounded the area, trapping 3 million people. To force their capitulation, the Germans bombed mercilessly, cut off all supplies, contaminated the water supply, and inflicted widespread carnage. The King, who had previously informed the Allies that he could not hold on indefinitely, then made a momentous decision. On 28 May, left without other options, Belgium capitulated. Reaction from the Allies was immediate. The French Prime Minister, in an unusually misleading demonstration of vitriol, accused the King of having abandoned the Allies "*without any consideration, without a word for the French and British soldiers who, responding to his anguished appeal, had come to the rescue of his country.*" This, Prime Minister Paul Reynaud argued, was "*an event without precedent in history.*" The Belgian Government-in-Exile lost little time in making its voice heard. Assembled in Limoges, they unanimously declared the King lacked the legal and moral right to reign. Prime Minister Pierlot expressed his shock by claiming "*the errors of one man cannot be blamed upon the Nation.*" From London, Prime Minister Winston Churchill led the British attack on Léopold III. "*Shame, treachery!*" cried irate parliamentarians. David Lloyd George, Great Britain's World War I leader, went a step further in describing Léopold III's decision, calling him "*a reprobate…a sample of perfidy and poltroonery.*"

Léopold III's decision to ignore his government consequently caused a vituperative avalanche. Queen Wilhelmina of the Netherlands, who was in the same predicament, chose to follow her government into exile, thus being able to eventually return as a liberator and heroine. Léopold III's decision to ignore his government's pleas and remain in Belgium was used as proof of his betrayal. As a constitutional monarch, the King should have departed. Not doing so created a constitutional crisis, an action responsible for many of the later problems he faced.

King Baudouin, Prince Alexandre and Prince Albert.

What is undeniable is the fact that Léopold's decision to continue fighting the Germans during those crucial days slowed their race toward Dunkirk and allowed the evacuation of French, Belgian, and British troops facing certain annihilation by the far superior German army. Between 27 May and 4 June, nearly 340,000 troops boarded 933 vessels and reached the safety of England; many would later take part in the Allied landing in Normandy.

During the occupation, the King and his family lived at Laeken Palace under German surveillance. They were not imprisoned, but they were also not free to come and go as they pleased. Lilian, too, had moved in, providing Léopold III with great comfort. In a way, Lilian received a losing hand. She may have won the heart of a man, but winning the nation's acceptance, much less love, was an entirely different endeavor. She had little trouble in gaining the love of the King's children, particularly that of Baudouin and Albert, who accepted her as the mother they had lost. Joséphine Charlotte, though, proved more difficult.

The situation was exacerbated by worries that Lilian might become pregnant. The King realized that, unless they were married, any such child would be illegitimate – a situation to be avoided at all costs in conservative, Catholic Belgium. The King, without the consent of his government and in secret, married Lilian in a small, private Catholic ceremony. Aside from the officiating priest, the only other witnesses were Queen Elisabeth and Henri Baels. The bride received the title of Princess de Réthy. To the public, the couple later claimed they had married on 11 September 1941; in fact, several historians have suggested that the wedding took place on December 6, after Lilian learned that she was pregnant. In July 1942, she gave birth to a son, Alexandre, who did not possess succession rights.

King Léopold III and his sister Queen Marie José of Italy.

Right: King Baudouin, Princess Marie Christine, Princess Lilian with Princess Marie Esmeralda, Prince Albert, Princess Paola and King Léopold III.

King Léopold III and Princess Lilian.

The pregnancy forced Léopold and Lilian to make their union public. In December 1941, with Cardinal Van Roey's support, a pastoral letter was read from every pulpit across Belgium, in which the King's second marriage was revealed to his subjects. Belgians were aghast at the news, and Léopold III's critics argued that Lilian was the real reason he had decided to remain in Belgium. The news soon erased sympathetic public perceptions of a lonely, heartbroken Léopold III, living under guard and experiencing the trials and tribulations of the German occupation. *"Sire,"* a furious journalist wrote, *"We thought you had your face turned toward us in mourning; instead you had it hidden on the shoulder of a woman."*

Lilian was no Astrid, and never could be. *"Kings marry princesses,"* Lilian had told the King when he proposed, and she was right. In 1940s Belgium, that was what the people expected. Many of his former supporters felt that Léopold III's remarriage was an affront to Astrid's memory. Had he wed a royal princess, all might have been forgiven, but the people could not stomach a commoner, a bourgeois like them, *"pas du tout."* Lilian was condemned as an adventuress, a social climber, and an "arriviste." The fact that her father spent the remainder of the war living in comfort in the South of France, and her brother ignored the call to military service (for which he was later prosecuted and sentenced) did very little to help Lilian's public image. While Belgians never warmed to Lilian, she, in turn, never made much effort to be discreet. Beautiful, adored, and a caring maternal figure to the King's children though she might be, Lilian also exerted considerable – and questionable – influence over her besotted husband, whose life belonged to Belgium.

The Prince of Liège.

Princess Paola Ruffo di Calabria.

When the Allies landed in Normandy, Léopold III was deported from Belgium. His family in tow, the King was kept under house arrest in Hirschstein-sur Elbe, a locality near Meißen, Saxony. Later, they were relocated to Strobl, Austria, where conditions were severe. He was liberated on 7 May 1945. Until then, his whereabouts had been unknown to all but a few high-ranking Nazis. Three days later a delegation of Belgian politicians demanded that he agree to certain conditions before returning home; the King refused. Prime Minister Spaak, a delegate who despite many differences wanted the King's return, expressed his frustration when he wrote: *"The misfortune of the man is not trusting those who are his natural counselors, who he profoundly dislikes, and that he does not respect those with whom he has to live, politicians."*

Léopold III, whose future seemed uncertain at best, announced that he would return to Laeken. The Belgian government, those same politicians whose advice had he ignored in 1940, now declined his request. His decision to form a monarchist government only worsened the political crisis, known to Belgians as the "Question Royale." In retaliation, the government then ceded to Parliament, where an anti-Leopoldist majority held sway, the responsibility of deciding the King's fate. While these negotiations were taking place, the King left Austria and crossed the border into Switzerland, where he remained for the next few years. He and Lilian lived in an elegant villa in Prégny and enjoyed a hedonistic round of parties and indulgences, behaving as if they had not a care in the world as Belgium hovered on the brink of civil war.

During the King's absence, his brother Prince Charles-Théodore, Count of Flanders, led the regency. Queen Elisabeth, who argued for Léopold III to be more decisive and not trust the politicians whom she blamed for many of the country's ills, also provided him with constant counsel: *"You should use the radio to reach the public who do not understand why the silence and hesitation,"* she recommend. *"The people will side with he who speaks to them,"* she recommended. In 1946 a commission had exonerated the King of treason, and some 70% of his subjects wished him to return, yet the government demanded that a debate concerning the King's constitutional powers take place in Parliament.

King Léopold III later in life.

For the next few years there was complete stagnation in the negotiations between the government and the King, who remained in Switzerland. There were suggestions that the only possible solution was Léopold III's abdication in favor of his son Baudouin – advice Léopold, his inner circle, and Queen Elisabeth rejected. Finally, a plebiscite to decide the Royal Question took place on 12 March 1950. The results were mixed. The King won the popular vote by 58%, while also winning in seven of the nine provinces. However, regionally, while he won Flanders, he lost Wallonia and Brussels. In July, as the cabinet voted to remove the Government-in-Exile's decision concerning the King's inability to reign, Léopold III prepared his return. He arrived in Belgium on 27 July 1950. That same day a strike was called affecting the entire kingdom, but Wallonia in particular, and politicians began demanding Léopold's abdication. By the 31st the situation was so perilous that Prime Minister Jean Duvieusart asked the King to delegate his powers. The police, trying to keep the public peace, killed three protesters, which only added more fuel to the fire. With Belgium on the brink of civil war, Léopold III decided to capitulate, abdicating on 1 August. The most turbulent reign in Belgium's history had come to an end.

Badouin succeeded his father. On 3 August he swore the oath in front of Parliament, becoming "Prince Royal" and enjoying all the prerogatives of King. Not until 17 July 1951 did he finally become King Baudouin I of the Belgians.

In February 1951 Princess Lilian gave birth to a second child, Marie-Christine, and a third, Marie-Esmeralda, was born in 1956. Léopold III and his family, King Baudouin included, continued living at Laeken. One wonders why the politicians demanded Léopold's abdication but allowed him not only to remain in Belgium but also to reside under the same roof as his successor. Eventually, Baudouin was suspected of being under the aegis of his father and stepmother, which caused considerable worry. Those who criticized the living arrangement argued that Belgium had become a diarchy, a kingdom with two monarchs, father and son. King Léopold III never seemed to learn the lessons life had taught him, and he had difficulty relinquishing his power. His influence over his two sons began to wane in the late 1950s, not because they wanted independence, but because the government and the women the sons married forced it.

In 1952, when King George VI died, Baudouin sent his brother Albert, not yet eighteen-years-old, to represent him. The press criticized this action as an attempt by King Léopold to settle a score with the British. Whether Léopold had anything to do with his son's decision, Baudouin believed he had a duty to clear his father's name and reputation, even if it meant insulting his cousins in London.

King Baudouin and the Duke of Edinburgh.

One year later, the Belgian Coburgs celebrated the wedding of Princess Joséphine Charlotte to Hereditary Grand Duke Jean of Luxembourg. This was to be the last "state" marriage, thus far, contracted by a member of the Belgian Royal Family. It is now known that the young couple was urged to marry, even though her romantic interests lay elsewhere. However, she knew what was expected of royalty, and married Jean on 9 April 1953. They had five children, among them the current head of state, Grand Duke Henri. They also grew to become extremely close and loving; when Joséphine Charlotte died of cancer in 2005, Jean was absolutely devastated.

The first crack in the protective shield Léopold built came in 1956. Baudouin revered his father and, not wishing to disappoint him, adopted a cold and distant stance toward those politicians who had been responsible for the abdication. The former King, again, had learned nothing. The hostility Baudouin demonstrated when in the presence of these men frequently created tension. Baudouin avoided former Prime Minister Perliot like the plague and at one ceremony completely ignored him. The situation finally came to a head when the current Prime Minister pressured Baudouin to invite Perliot to a celebration in honor of

Queen Elisabeth. Baudouin resolutely believed that, out of respect for his father, he had to join in the settling of Léopold's political debts.

The second rupture came in 1959, when without the government's authorization, Léopold III took it upon himself to ask Pope John XXIII to officiate at the wedding of his second son. Doing so, he believed, would exempt the young man and his bride from first obtaining a civil marriage, the law for all Belgians. Léopold firmly believed that as Head of State, any marriage conducted by His Holiness was both civil and religious. The government of the day raised serious objections and some politicians were actually livid with the former King's constant meddling in affairs no longer in his province. Further complicating the matter, Cardinal van Roey sided with Léopold and supported the idea that a Vatican marriage was both civil and religious. The controversy became so heated that eventually the Pope backed down and told the parties involved that in his opinion the marriage ought to take place in Brussels given Albert's proximity to the throne.

The wedding of the Prince of Liège and Italian-born aristocrat, Princess Paola Ruffo di Calabria.

This latest extra-constitutional meddling infuriated the government. Prime Minister Van Acker, listening to the rising roar coming from Parliament, finally intervened. The former King and the Princess were told to vacate Laeken Palace and find their own home. In 1960, the couple moved to a large property called the Domaine d'Argenteuil. This relocation, many Belgian historians argue, marked the beginning of King Baudouin's independent reign.

Léopold spent his remaining years pursuing his varied passions. He was a talented photographer and traveled the world, documenting his visits to remote areas with his camera. He was also an avid anthropologist and entomologist. Léopold died in 1983 after a long period of quiet and solitude away from the public eye. One of his daughters, Marie-Christine gave her parents countless headaches while leading a chaotic, bohemian life. She remains estranged from the family and is rarely seen in Belgium. Prince Alexandre, who suffered from heart trouble early on, eventually married when nearly fifty-years old. His bride, Léa Wolman, already had two children from previous marriages and the couple remained childless. He died in 2009, seven years after the passing of Princess Lilian. Princess Marie-Esméralda, who is devoted to propagating her late father's scientific and photographic work, married a pharmacologist from El Salvador, Salvador Moncada, with whom she has two children, the only grandchildren of Léopold III and Princess Lilian.

The search for Baudouin's wife was a matter of great national importance. Most Belgians expected their King would choose one of the many princesses who seemed to visit Brussels with frequency. Among the names put forward were those of Infanta María del Pilar, eldest daughter of the Count of Barcelona; Princess Maria Gabriella of Savoy, the King's first cousin; Isabelle of France, the eldest daughter of the Count of Paris; Birgitta of Sweden, one of the sisters of future King Carl XVI Gustaf; and Cecile of Bourbon-Parma, a niece of Empress Zita. Baudouin, had he wanted to find a princess to marry, had an unbelievably large number of candidates to choose from inside the pages of the *Almanach de Gotha*. And yet he chose an aristocrat, much like his brother Albert had done.

In 1958, Brussels hosted the Universal Exposition and

welcomed countless visitors, one of whom – according to the accepted version of events – was Fabiola de Mora y Aragón, a Spanish aristocrat born in 1928. Her father, the Marquess of Casa Riera, who had died the previous year, had been a close friend of King Alfonso XIII and his wife, who served as Fabiola's godmother. Hence, Fabiola had the social credentials necessary to enter the rarefied world of royalty. Another more recent account suggests that Baudouin asked a trusted religious confidant, Sister Veronica O'Brien, to help him find a suitable Catholic bride. Sister Veronica headed to Madrid where she met Fabiola, who had studied nursing and had worked at the military hospital. Fabiola's intense Catholicism had, at times, brought her close to considering the convent. Much to King Baudouin's joy, and future happiness, she chose otherwise.

When reporting to the King, Sister Veronica is said to have described Fabiola as *"good looking and striking."* The young lady received an invitation to visit Brussels and there met the King. Baudouin and Fabiola maintained frequent correspondence and their friendship blossomed. Both were deeply Catholic and their devotion to Rome provided yet another common bond. They both enjoyed going on pilgrimages to Catholic shrines; indeed, according to one author, it was at Lourdes that *"their engagement was sealed."* The news, announced by the Prime Minister soon after the declaration of Congo's independence, not only surprised the overwhelming majority of Belgians, but also members of the Royal Family. Albert and Paola first learned of it, and Fabiola, during a telephone call from the King while in Italy. No one knew the identity of this mysterious, thin, tall, long-necked, smiling brunette, nor did they have any inkling that this relationship even existed. Little did they know, either, that she possessed an indomitable will and was to become the mainstay of her shy husband until his last day. *"Fabiola is full of enthusiasm, of fire, and of an explosive imagination…while also showing flexibility and humility when I ask her to be prudent,"* King Baudouin wrote.

The wedding of King Baudouin and Fabiola de Mora y Aragón.

The wedding took place in Brussels on 15 December 1960. Once again SS. Michael and Gudule opened its heavy doors to welcome the marriage of yet another Belgian Coburg. The Belgian Royal Family hosted a sumptuous dinner the night before, attended by 350 guests, many of them members of European royal, princely and aristocratic families. An elegant court ball for 2,000 guests followed. Fabiola was said to have set the tone of the evening as she wore *"a yellow silk gown…a golden crown ornamented with jewels presented to her in the name of the Spanish people."* Princess Margaret, representing her sister the Queen, wore *"a diamond-studded tiara and a gown of lilac silk."* Belgians, as they had done when the groom's parents married, were extremely enthusiastic about the latest royal wedding, lining the procession route and enthusiastically cheering as the couple passed by in a glass-topped limousine. The honeymoon was spent in Spain.

The year of his marriage was a busy one for King Baudouin. Earlier, he had traveled to the former Belgian Congo to participate in the independence ceremonies. The political situation within the colony had worsened considerably as the decade

King Baudouin and Queen Fabiola with his brother and sister-in-law, the Prince and Princess of Liège.

advanced. Rioting in 1959 precipitated events, and little doubt remained that to avoid a major bloodbath, independence had to be granted. Baudouin had visited the Congo several times and tried to keep the entire territory as one country. Later, when the Congo disintegrated in a vicious civil war, he blamed local politicians for the failure.

Queen Elisabeth, who at eighty-four was still going strong, caused several controversies, particularly around her enthusiastic visit to the Soviet Union. She died in 1965. Queen Fabiola had played an important role in distancing her husband from Léopold and Lilian. Truth be told, there was not much in common between the self-composed and aesthete Spanish aristocrat and the glamorous former Belgian commoner. Once she was in command at Laeken Palace, Fabiola quickly worked to cut off whatever remaining strings still bound her husband to his stepmother. The Queen knew that if Baudouin was to enjoy a successful reign, then his independence had to remain unquestioned. Consequently, relations between Laeken and the Domaine d'Argenteuil were rarely warm.

One thing was missing: Baudouin and Fabiola were very concerned about the Queen's inability to carry pregnancies to term. It is accepted as a fact that Queen Fabiola had at least five pregnancies during the first years of marriage. All ended early. By 1970, both the King and his consort had resigned themselves to childlessness, which they saw as God's will. Their deep Catholic faith provided them with the inner strength necessary to face the many disappointments and challenges they encountered.

In 1976, to celebrate the Silver Anniversary of his reign, the King formed "The King Baudouin Foundation." Its purpose was to improve the living conditions of the Belgian people, while also changing society for the better through investments in inspiring projects and individuals. In 2012, for example, the Foundation provided nearly €22 million in support to 1,700 organizations and individuals. The Foundation also organizes debates on important social issues, enters into partnerships, and encourages philanthropy. Both King Baudouin and Queen Fabiola worked tirelessly to make sure the Foundation was an absolute success, and it remains one of the King's lasting legacies to Belgium.

Belgians also remember King Baudouin for his strict adherence to Roman Catholicism. Not only was he a devout believer, but he also participated in the Catholic Charismatic Renewal movement and went on pilgrimage every year. It was his deep faith that in 1990 put the King on a collision course with his government. When a law liberalizing abortion in Belgium was submitted to Parliament and subsequently approved, the King refused to give his Royal Assent. The impasse was solved after the King asked the Prime Minister to declare him temporarily unable to reign and allow him to

King Baudouin with Queen Sofía of Spain.

abstain from signing the bill into law. The government acquiesced: with the King temporarily unable to execute his prerogatives, constitutionally, the government could do so in his stead. The measure became the law of the kingdom and the following day Baudouin's prerogatives were restored.

King Baudouin died on 31 July 1993 while on vacation in Motril, Spain. He had suffered from cardiopulmonary illness, but an operation the previous year had seemed to work. He suffered massive heart failure at his vacation home, Villa Astrida, and nothing could be done to save his life. His funeral was an immense affair as nearly 500,000 people came to pay their respects at the King's Lying-in-State. Queen Elizabeth II, who rarely attends such events, traveled to Brussels to honor her Coburg cousin. He rests at Laeken.

In widowhood, Queen Fabiola remained tremendously busy. In addition to her work for the Foundation, she carried out many royal duties, lending her support where needed, and was actively involved in social work in the Third World. As dowager, she moved to Stuyvenberg Palace and was particularly masterful at receding from public life. At the age of eighty-five, Queen Fabiola is now wheelchair-bound, but she still manages to appear at royal events throughout the year.

The funeral of King Baudoin.

Albert II succeeded King Baudouin as the sixth Belgian monarch. As children, Baudouin and Albert, though devoted to each other, had been complete opposites. While Baudouin was studious and devout, Albert was more hedonistic, a bit irresponsible and, although a practicing Catholic, he rarely showed the high levels of outward devotion that characterized his brother. Albert enjoyed parties, fast cards, boats, motorcycles, and amorous dalliances. In 1993 the highway police stopped a lone speeding motorcyclist near Charleroi. It was not until he presented his license that the officers realized that the speeder was none other than Albert. *"Do your duty,"* he told the officers. People found it difficult to chastise the blond, handsomely athletic man with blue eyes and a winning smile.

In 1958, attending the coronation of Pope John XXIII at the Vatican, Albert met a stunning Italian principessa. Born in 1937, Paola was the seventh and youngest child of Fulco, Prince Ruffo di Calabria, 6th Duke of Guardia Lombarda (a First World War flying ace) and the former Countess Luisa Gazelli di Rossna e di Sebastiano. Paola had been brought up strictly, constantly reminded to behave according to her position in society while at the same time warned against affecta-

Queen Fabiola at the wedding of the Prince of Asturias.

tion. To assist in the latter, the children were expected to even use public transport, a novelty for members of the Roman aristocracy at the time. As the youngest child, Paola was somewhat spoiled, with a mischievous smile, a contagious laugh, and an irrepressible thirst for fun.

For several months Albert and Paola conducted their relationship in complete anonymity to avoid intrusive press photographers as they came to know each other. When certain of his feelings, Albert asked Paola to visit Brussels, where he introduced her to his family. The blond, ravishing Italian aristocrat made quite an impression and King Baudouin approved. The engagement was announced and the couple married on 2 July 1959.

While Albert felt that *"marriage has liberated me…my wife has forced me to open up to others and live as normally as possible,"* Paola found great enjoyment, perhaps not in marriage, but in children and in running her home. In 1960 she gave birth to a son, Philippe, followed in 1962 by Astrid and by Laurent in 1963. Palace staff later recalled that Paola loved spending time with the children and was often found helping

Albert and Paola with their children: Laurent, Phillipe and Astrid.

Prince Philippe, Duke of Brabant.

King Albert II and Queen Paola with Queen Sofía of Spain (2004).

The Duke and Duchess of Brabant, Copenhagen (2004).

them with homework. At day's end, she liked nothing better than walking with the children, Laurent in particular, around the palace grounds with the family dogs jumping and cavorting around them. She tried to introduce a variety of Italian dishes to the royal kitchen; however, when the change in diet began showing on her husband's waistline, the experiment was abandoned. The royal chef once recalled that, as he was leaving on a day off to attend a soccer match, Paola informed him that they had unexpected guests for dinner later that night. He promised to return in time from the stadium but a traffic jam delayed his arrival. Worried that she would be irritated, he entered the palace kitchen and found Paola and Albert, joined by Baudouin and Fabiola and their guests, attempting to prepare the meal themselves. *"The heat,"* he recalled, *"was insufferable since they forgot to open the vents, the refrigerator was left wide open. They had already drunk the aperitif in the kitchen. Paola gave me the evil eye, but Baudouin quickly understood the situation. He wanted to know who won the match and who were the scorers."*

Paola later said that she and her husband were *"too shy to talk to each other"* when they first met. In the 1960s, their marriage experienced serious challenges when Albert fathered an out of wedlock child with a girlfriend, Baroness Sybille de Selys Longchamps. The child's existence remained a "state" secret for the next thirty-one years and was only publicly revealed when Flemish writer Mario Daneels published an unauthorized biography of the Queen. The press managed to trace the alleged daughter, Delphine Boël, who initially kept her silence as the Royal Palace dismissed the matter as gossip. However, that Christmas the King opened up about what he considered a private matter. *"This Christmas feast is also the occasion for each of us to think of one's own family,"* he told the nation, *"to one's happy periods but also to one's difficult moments. The Queen and I have remembered very happy periods, but also the crisis that our marriage experienced more than thirty years ago. Together, and a long time ago, we surpassed those difficulties and rediscovered a deep understanding and love. This period has been recalled to us just a short time ago. We don't wish to dwell on that subject, which belongs to our private lives. But, if certain people who meet today similar problems could find reason to hope from our life experiences we would be so happy."* During the reign of King Baudouin, Albert was tasked with leading commercial and trade missions abroad and Paola accompanied her husband on innumerable voyages. This led Albert to create The Prince Albert Foundation, dedicated to the promotion of expertise in foreign trade. Albert and Paola also regularly joined her family in Italy for holidays, particularly at Forte dei Marmi near Lucca, where she had been born. Throughout her life in Belgium, Paola has often returned home and visited her mother, who died in 1989, as well as her surviving siblings.

Observers have always believed that King Baudouin constantly encouraged Albert and Paola to resolve their marital differences, and by 1984, when Princess Astrid married, the couple had worked through past difficulties. A shy, private lady, Astrid had attended the University of Leiden and taken courses at a prominent school in Geneva before volunteering for some time at an American hospital in Michigan. *"One did not know of any of her passions, or failures, or hidden loves,"* a Belgian journalist wrote. *"Unlike other members of the family, she did not feel as the soul of a rebel, but she always knew well what direction she wanted her life to take."* At a ball given by her parents to mark her eighteenth birthday, she had fallen in love with Archduke Lorenz of Austria-Este, eldest son of Archduke Robert and his wife, the former Princess Margherita of Savoy-Aosta. Astrid and Lorenz were distantly related through both of his parents, as they are Coburg, Orléans and Braganza descendants, though the closest link was Astrid's great-grandmother Queen Elisabeth, who was a first cousin of Lorenz's grandmother Empress Zita. On 22 September 1984, inside Brussels' Nôtre Dame du Sablon Church, Astrid and Lorenz married in the fourth alliance between a Belgian Coburg and a Habsburg. This time it worked, as it was not an arranged marriage but a love match. Today, along with their five children, they form a very united family, and Astrid remains one of the Belgian Royal Family's greatest assets.

Throughout the 1980s, most Belgians believed that Prince Philippe was to succeed his Uncle Baudouin. In 1978 Philippe entered the Belgian Royal Military Academy and for the following three years he served in the armed forces. Later, he attended Trinity College, Oxford and afterward completed a Master's degree in political science at Stanford University, graduating in 1985. Returning to Belgium, the Prince followed other military courses earning his fighter pilot's wings as well as certificates as a parachutist and a commando. By 2001 he was appointed to the rank of Major General in the Land and Air Components, and also a Rear Admiral in the Naval Component. A few days after his father's succession, Philippe was appointed Honorary Chairman of the Belgian Foreign Trade Board and embarked on an endless round of foreign travel to promote investment and business in his country.

Dutch state visit. From left: Queen Beatrix, the Duchess of Brabant, Queen Fabiola, the Princess of Orange, Queen Paola and King Albert II.

As Duke of Brabant, much attention focused on Philippe's potential bride. Among candidates mentioned in the press were the daughters of King Juan Carlos of Spain, Infantas Elena and Cristina; Princess Alexia of Greece; Princess Tatiana of Liechtenstein; Mathilde of Württemberg; several granddaughters of the Count of Paris; and a posy of Archduchesses. As he approached his fortieth birthday, it became an even more pressing matter for Brabant to find a woman who shared his goals, expectations, education, and ability to perform the difficult tasks that would come with the throne.

That woman turned out to be a Belgian aristocrat named Mathilde d'Udekem d'Acoz. Born in 1973, Mathilde was the eldest of five children of Jonkheer (Esquire) Patrick d'Udekem d'Acoz and his wife, the former Countess Anna Maria Komorowska, an aristocrat with ancient roots in Poland. Mathilde attended school at the Institut de la Vierge Fidèle in Brussels before studying at Louvain University, and speaks French, Dutch, Italian, and English; she graduated magna cum laude and began working as a speech therapist in Brussels in 1995. In 1997 Mathilde suffered a family tragedy. On her way to a reunion, Mathilde volunteered to ride with Princess Zofia Sapieha, her grandmother, but instead her sister Marie-Alix entered the car. On the freeway between Aachen and Brussels, there was an accident and both Mathilde's grandmother and sister were killed. Driving some distance behind the first car were Mathilde, her parents and siblings. Not until they reached the accident did they realize what had happened.

Philippe and Mathilde met at a time when both were still grieving the loss of close family members, and their shared experiences led first to friendship and then to romance. When, in the summer of 1999, a photographer spotted them walking and holding hands in Havana, the image unleashed a torrent of journalistic speculation. On July 22, the Prime Minister

Princess Astrid and Archduke Lorenz, Copenhagen (2004).

announced the government had approved Philippe's request to marry Mathilde.

The imminent wedding of the Duke of Brabant to a beautiful young Belgian lady gave a country in the midst of a series of national scandals a cause to rejoice. The government hoped the marriage would revive national pride and *"perhaps halt what many observers see as the slow fragmentation of Belgium."* A journalist expressed this hope when he said: *"The monarchy is one of the few institutions widely accepted by both the Dutch-speaking Flemings in the north and the French speakers in the southern Wallonia region and the French-speaking enclave of Brussels. The reasoning is that anything that strengthens the monarchy also strengthens the tenuous bonds between north and south. But at the same time, Belgium's bipolar tensions are being highlighted by the country's fourth major institutional revision since the 1960s, which began this month."*

Before her wedding, Mathilde was made a Princess of Belgium in her own right, effective on her marriage, and her father and his two brothers were elevated to the rank of Count. On 4 December 1999 the Duke of Brabant married Mathilde d'Udekem d'Acoz at the Cathedral of SS Michael and Gudule. The weather was incredibly cold and a typical Brussels' drizzle threatened to ruin the day, but the skies remained closed until the wedding procession had reached the Royal Palace and newlyweds and guests were all under shelter. Not until then did the sky open and unleash cold rain, hail, and even snow over the Belgian capital.

In the early 1990s, Belgium changed the succession. Until then, the succession favored males over females. The new law created absolute cognatic primogeniture, with inheritance rights to the firstborn child irrespective of gender. Thus, when Mathilde gave birth to a baby girl, Elisabeth, in 2001, Belgium welcomed its future monarch, as well as its first future queen regnant. In 2003, as Mathilde and Philippe were touring the San Francisco Bay Area, they announced that she was expecting a second time. Prince Gabriel was born in August 2003. Two more children joined the family, Emmanuel and Eléonore, born respectively in 2005 and 2008. Other than their eldest daughter, all of Philippe and Mathilde's children have first names never before used by the Belgian Coburgs.

While Philippe's work kept him busy promoting foreign trade and investment, Mathilde, besides her obligations with her children, has been actively working on behalf of the poor, not only in Belgium, but also worldwide. She has been involved with UNICEF and served as the World Health Organization's Special Representative for Immunization. In 2001 she set up the Princess Mathilde

Prince Laurent and Princess Claire, Copenhagen (2004).

Fund to promote care of the vulnerable. The Fund awards an annual prize for good works in a particular field, and each year the chosen sector changes. She also presides at the ceremony awarding the King Baudouin International Development Prize.

Months before Mathilde gave birth to the couple's second child, Prince Laurent finally settled down and began a family. Prince Laurent is a warm-tempered man who more resembles his maternal relations than the Coburg side of his family. His devout uncle King Baudouin apparently never understood his nephew's "laissez faire, laissez aller" approach to Catholicism, and Laurent's support of environmental causes and animal charities remains unique. He shares his father's passion for speed: Laurent was once stopped at the entrance to Laeken Palace after police had clocked him doing 220kph. The royal guard protected him, but when Baudouin learned of the incident, he demanded that Laurent face consequences. As a result the Prince was fined and had his driver's license suspended for some time.

When it came time to marry, Laurent chose a commoner named Claire Louise Coombs who, although born in England, had lived in Belgium since childhood. The couple married at the Cathedral of SS. Michael and Gudule on 12 April 2003. The night before the wedding, a concert in honor of the couple was held in Brussels, but although a galaxy of royals attended the ceremony, the event was not as significant as the marriage of Philippe and Mathilde four years earlier. Prince Laurent and Princess Claire, who live in the vicinity of Brussels, are the parents of three children: Louise, born in 2004, and twins Nicolas and Aymeric, born in 2005. Prince Laurent remains a controversial figure within the Royal Family and he is not circumspect when dealing with those who attack his actions. In a way, he is his worst enemy – his irascibility, at times, has made him a target of the press, but the attacks he suffers, which he considers unmerited, are often fueled by his intemperate behavior. If there is a member of the family today who dislikes the press intensely, it is Prince Laurent. The marriages of their children have provided Albert and Paola with twelve grandchildren.

Right: King Philippe, Queen Mathilde and their children. From left: Princess Eléonore, Prince Gabriel, the Duchess of Brabant and Prince Emmanuel.

On 3 July 2013 King Albert II revealed to the Belgian government that he intended to abdicate. The King had informed his ministers several times that his increasing age made him feel unable to carry the burden of the throne. Continuing problems over the paternity of Ms. Boël did not help matters either. She has a lawsuit to establish that Albert II is her biological father. Yet, as he neared his eightieth birthday, Albert II needed rest. On 21 July, Belgium's National Day, King Albert abdicated the throne, and King Philippe succeeded immediately.

The seventh Coburg has become the King of the Belgians. Much hope surrounds Philippe and Mathilde. He has the preparation; she has the vocation. The kingdom wishes to see in Philippe I a monarch who can sacrifice his personal needs and desires for the country's good, and in Mathilde he has someone who can help him achieve their goals.

Chapter XIX
The Coburgs of Sofia
"Tantamount to an Invitation"

King Boris III was just twenty-four when he succeeded to the Bulgarian throne. Boris was courageous, intelligent, and modest, and made himself extremely popular by his openness and eagerness to please. Democratically inclined, he loved nothing more than driving a train through the countryside. Today, history remembers Boris III more for the difficult choices he faced, his forceful relations with Bulgarian politicians, the dilemma forced by the Second World War, and for his mysterious death.

King Ferdinand's fall was a terrible shock to his family. Boris and his siblings had been brought up to believe that their father was infallible: a distant figure, nearly perfect in his god-like sagacity, and incapable of error. His fatal miscalculation of Bulgaria's ability to fight in the Great War ultimately led to calls for his abdication. *"Your Majesty, the Council of Ministers, which is in uninterrupted session, believes that every hour is being wasted and that it can no longer wait,"* wrote Minister Stamboliyski. *"News from the front attests that the routing of our army is complete. We are threatened by catastrophe. If Your Majesty does not accept the Council of Ministers' decision to seek immediately an armistice and then peace, it will refuse to take further responsibility. The acting commander-in-chief informs me that the situation is hopeless, that disaster is inevitable. He wants an immediate decision."* That evening, Bulgaria's emissaries, carrying a peace initiative, departed for Salonika, while Alexander Stamboliyski left the capital and headed to *"the tumultuous center of the soldiers' mutiny."*

King Boris III began his reign amid the chaos of 3 October 1918, as his defeated and disconsolate father left Bulgaria to begin a long exile, joined aboard an elegantly decorated private train by his other three children. Facing the immediate problem of mutiny by the armed forces, Boris demobilized the Bulgarian Army. This action served several purposes. It dismantled the insurrection threatening the country's fragile stability; sent a message to the Allies that Bulgaria's peace overtures were genuine; began the long process of gaining Bulgaria respect from its enemies; and sent a chilling message to Vienna and Berlin. The war was lost – it was time to adopt positions more favorable when peace arrived. It also conveyed to those around the King that he was willing to do what was necessary to secure the country, defend the throne, and provide Bulgaria with a fresh start.

Several weeks later, Boris III received in audience a correspondent of *The New York Times*, who noted that three of the Balkans' major kingdoms were now ruled by young men: Alexander as regent of Serbia, Alexander I of the Hellenes, and King Boris III, a generational change presaging a new type of monarchy. During the interview, Boris III came across as *"agreeable and frank…good nature*[d]*…Looks at you straight in the face with a pleasant, straightforward and natural expression."* Boris talked about his hopes and goals, while also praising the British and their Allies, particularly their airplanes: *"I have several times had an excellent opportunity of appreciating their efficiency in dropping bombs,"* he recalled. *"We used to see the British machines coming toward us on the Vardar, where you had the mastery of the air, and we always knew that we were in for a mauvais quart d'heure [a bad quarter hour!]"* Boris III also proclaimed his positive views of Great Britain, which *"has always been well disposed toward Bulgaria. Gladstone was one of the first to raise the question of the emancipation of the Bulgarian people. Here we have always counted the British among the liberators of Bulgaria."* The King also emphasized his own views of Great Britain, for *"the sympathies which the Bulgarian nation has felt and will continue to feel for the English people, as you have been able to witness during your visit here, could not but be shared by its sovereign."*

The "good faith" campaign Boris III directed toward the Allies failed to gain its desired effect. Devastated by

King Boris III in 1920.

Princess Giovanna of Savoy.

the war, the Treaty of Neuilly-sur-Seine, signed in November 1919, further eviscerated the kingdom. Bulgaria lost considerable territory, including Western Thrace to Greece and thus access to the Aegean, as well as some borderlands to Serbia and Romania. On top of these losses, the Bulgarian Army was reduced to 20,000 men and the country was condemned to pay $100 million in reparations. It also was forced to recognize the creation of a larger Kingdom of Serbs, Croats and Slovenes along its Western border.

Earlier that year, Alexander Stamboliyski gained the majority in parliament and was asked to form a government. Behind this astute politician stood the forces of the left, mainly the marginalized peasant class. The bourgeoisies and the aristocracy were deeply suspicious of the new Prime Minister and at every turn possible sought to undermine him. The four years he served King Boris III were fraught with danger and instability, while at times it seemed that the country's internal problems were about to degenerate into a civil war.

In 1923, as the kingdom swung from Left to Right, ominous clouds gathered over Sofia. On June 9, a coup d'etat overthrew Prime Minister Stamboliyski and Bulgarian Communists were in retreat. The seditious forces were composed of right wing factions, disgruntled military, nationalists, and parties of the Right. Army officers arrested Stamboliyski, who was following events and trying to organize a counter coup from his village, Slavovitsa. He was interrogated, tortured and executed; the hand he used to sign an unpopular treaty with Serbia was cut from his mutilated body. Another coup, this time led by opponents of the new government, failed the following September. Bulgaria had quickly degenerated into one of the Balkans' most unstable countries.

Brief respite from the country's internal chaos came in early 1924 with the wedding of Princess Nadejda to Duke Albrecht Eugen of Württemberg, a distant Coburg and Orléans cousin. The couple had met in Germany, where Nadejda lived with her father. The groom was the second son of Duke Albrecht and Margarete Sophie, Archduke Franz Ferdinand's sister. Duke Albrecht's grandfather, Duke Alexander (1804-1881), son of Princess Antoinette of Saxe-Coburg-Saalfeld, had married Princess Marie d'Orléans, a sister of Princess Clémentine, Nadejda's paternal grandmother. Unlike her siblings Kyril and Eudoxia, Nadejda rarely visited her brother Boris III in Sofia. The couple eventually had five children, all born in Württemberg.

The wedding could not conceal Bulgaria's worsening internal situation. Failure to quash opponents of the government only emboldened their actions. Bulgarian Communists wanted the King deposed, the monarchy abolished, and the "people's republic" proclaimed. They believed that the strong-arm measures used by the government amounted to acts of terrorism. *"Terror should be met with terror,"* they insisted, and embarked on a violent program that ultimately led to two 1925 assassination attempts on King Boris's life. On 14 April the King's car was ambushed. "As his car was passing through a narrow stretch of road between high banks, a volley of shots rang out," read a report. *"Mr. Iltcheff* [one of the King's companions] *and the servant collapsed. The windshield flew to pieces, and the chauffeur, who was also struck by the bullets, almost fell out of the car."* One of the bullets was so close that it clipped the King's mustache. That same day, General Gheorgieff was assassinated in Sofia.

Another and potentially deadlier attack was the bombing of the Cathedral "Sveta Nedelia" in Sofia in an attempt to assassinate the King, an event that scarred Boris deeply. *"You can't imagine what's going on here,"* he wrote. *"The horrors that have happened and are still happening. Yes, of course you know what's been in all the papers: the series of killings and attempted killings – they just missed me – the carnage at the cathedral, all those people crushed under the dome. All that is*

The wedding of Princess Nadejda of Bulgaria and Duke Albrecht Eugen of Württemberg.

dreadful enough. But it's a vicious circle. The horrors have been going on for a long time. Repression in the villages, vengeance – personal vengeance, party vengeance – ever since they murdered the poor man, the poor great man [Stamboliyski], who stood by me…Yes…he did go too far. But they didn't just kill him, they cut him up, they made butcher's meat of his body. It was barbaric."

Bulgaria suffered through a reign of terror during these troubled times. One newspaper article pointed out that nearly forty political assassinations had taken place between 1924 and 1925. The Right assassinated Communists, the Left assassinated government officials, while Macedonian nationalists attacked both. King Boris III tried to put an end to the violence when he signed into law *"the Defense of the State Act, and since this*

King Boris III and Queen Giovanna exit the Church at Assisi after their wedding. Behind them are Prince Gaetano and Princess Enrichetta of Bourbon-Parma, while the Duchess of Parma looks on from Boris' left. She was the second wife of his maternal grandfather, Duke Robert of Parma.

has become known, extraordinary measures have been taken for his protection." However tragic the attack at "Sveta Nedelia" was, it turned the country against the terrorists. They had overreached and by the early 1930s internal peace was restored.

Repeated attempts on the King's life also underscored the perilous situation over the succession. As neither the King nor his brother Kyril were married or had legitimate children, finding them spouses was a matter of great national importance. In 1922 it was rumored that the King would marry Princess Jolanda of Savoy, the same Italian royal gossip also suggested was the Duke of Brabant's choice for wife. Boris, one newspaper report claimed, *"has his own ideas as to a proper choice, and when the selection is made it is sure to be his own and not that of a statesman flipping a coin."*

By 1924, *"young, handsome and single,"* King Boris III was *"in the market for a wife."* The press in Bulgaria and abroad conjectured and reports abounded as to whom the King was looking at, what princess was "certain" to become his bride, and when an engagement would be announced. Yet, nothing happened. In 1926 as Boris III journeyed out of Bulgaria for the first time since 1918, the rumor mill went into high gear. Prime Minister Liapchev did not help quiet matters when he *"intimated that King Boris might be going abroad to sue for the affections of some fair lady."* A long list of names of eligible candidates was shuffled, including Princess Ileana of Romania (a daughter of neighbor King Ferdinand, who later was firstly married to Archduke Anton of Austria-Tuscany); Princess Françoise of France (a daughter of the Duke de Guise, future wife of Prince Christopher of Greece); and Grand Duchess Kira Kirillovna (a daughter of Grand Duke Kirill and of his wife, the former Princess Victoria Melita of Edinburgh, neighbors of exiled King Ferdinand in Coburg).

Princess Giovanna of Savoy, a younger sister of Jolanda, was first mentioned in 1926. The fourth child of King Vittorio Emanuele III and Queen Elena (née Montenegro), Giovanna was born in 1907 and thirteen years younger than Boris. Though continually reported by newspapers, nothing happened until the fall of 1930, when Boris's engagement to Giovanna was suddenly announced. Due to the couple's different faiths a Vatican dispensation was requested so the wedding could proceed. The Pope, not wishing to cause a diplomatic quarrel, granted the request.

Queen Giovanna in Bulgarian costume.

The wedding, at central Italy's famed Cathedral of St. Francis of Assisi on 25 October, occurred amidst a raging storm, as driving rain and hail peppered the stained glass windows of Giovanna's favorite church. The ceremony's simplicity only enhanced the solemnity of the ritual. *"Princess Giovanna, on her way both to and from the church appeared a picture of happiness,"* read one report. Many royals from across the continent attended the wedding. Their number included not only the bride's family and the groom's father, who had left his Coburg exile to join this important dynastic event, but also the couple's siblings, Duke Albrecht Eugen of Württemberg, and Queen Elisabeth of Greece, by then estranged from her husband and living also in exile. Mussolini, along with several of his ministers, also made an appearance, though he had the good sense to wear diplomatic, not military, uniform.

The couple's honeymoon took them from Brindisi along the Adriatic, the Aegean, and into the Black Sea. On reaching Bourgas, the largest Bulgarian port on the Black Sea after Vrana, Queen Giovanna first set foot on her new homeland's soil. An enormous crowd of Bulgarians cheered this first glimpse of their new queen's arrival. Also awaiting them were Prince Kyril and Princess Eudoxia. *"The crowds broke through the cordon of soldiers and police, and scores of enthusiastic citizens poured water over the magnificent carpets in front of the rather surprised queen. 'An old custom,' explained Boris. 'May everything run smoothly like floating on water.'"* From Bourgas the royal party continued by train to Sofia, where the reception was even more spectacular. For a fleeting moment, it seemed as if all the pain, tragedy, and worry of prior years had disappeared.

Both Boris III and Giovanna enjoyed traveling, and the easing situation within Bulgaria made it easier for them to go abroad. Early in 1933, Giovanna delivered their first child, Marie Louise; a few months later, Boris and his consort embarked on another extended journey that took them to London. In 1927 King George V had invited Boris to join in a hunt – the first time that the Sofia and London Coburg branches had been in contact for more than a decade following the outbreak of the Great War. Boris had always been very fond of Great Britain, unlike his exiled father, who was far more Germanic in character, demeanor, and inclination. Boris's first visit led to further political discussions, not just with King George V, but also with members of his government, paving the road, so King Boris III hoped, for closer relations between London

King Boris III and Queen Giovanna with their children: Princess Marie Louise and Crown Prince Simeon.

and Sofia. In 1933 Boris held discussions with George V and presented his wife to his cousins. Throughout the decade, it was common for the King to visit Great Britain as a guest of George V and later George VI, with whom Boris also enjoyed a good relationship. These contacts with the Windsor cousins also included King Edward VIII, who ruled in 1936. In fact, that year Edward VIII briefly visited Bulgaria on his return journey to London, after a controversial Mediterranean tour with Mrs. Simpson, his twice-divorced American paramour.

After the birth of their first child, Queen Giovanna had trouble becoming pregnant again. Several doctors in various European countries saw and treated her, as the couple wondered if their daughter would be their only offspring. Finally, in October 1936, Queen Giovanna announced that she was expecting. Boris III was ecstatic; although he adored his blue-eyed daughter, he hoped that his prayers to secure the succession with the birth of a son would come true. The King's hopes were fulfilled on 16 June 1937 when the Queen gave birth to a son amid indescribable national rejoicing. To further tie the dynasty to Bulgaria's once royal past, the baby received the name Simeon. He was to be their last child, as well as Europe's last child-King to date.

King Boris III hunting, one of his favorite hobbies. He also enjoyed driving locomotives, which he did every time he could.

Unfortunately the country's fragile political stability faltered and left the King deeply worried. In 1934, the military backed a coup d'etat and the King, without another politically viable option, as well as frustrated by the recklessness of the country's largest political parties, recognized the new government. He agonized about the perilous international situation. Bulgaria had isolated herself from the neighboring Balkan countries when Ferdinand sided with the Central Powers. Serbia, now known as Yugoslavia, led a movement to unify other Balkan Powers in an international alliance to protect the region from Bulgarian revanchism. Greece and Romania, both having recently fought the Bulgarians, felt this alliance gave their countries further protection and security; Turkey agreed. Aware that suspicious neighbors surrounded Bulgaria, Boris began extending olive branches.

In Yugoslavia, King Alexander had succeeded his father Peter I in 1921; the following year, he married Princess Marie of Romania, a granddaughter of Duke Alfred of Saxe-Coburg & Gotha. Alexander ruled with an iron fist. His kingdom was a patchwork quilt of conflicting nationalities. Serbs now ruled Croats, Slovenes, Montenegrins, Macedonians, and ethnic Bulgars, a dangerously flammable mix that could ignite at any moment. To prevent the disintegration of his polyglot realm, Alexander resorted to force, making the monarch the unifying mortar that kept the structure together. It would later cost him his life. As he was Queen Giovanna's first cousin, Alexander welcomed Boris's overtures. When the Bulgarians visited Yugoslavia the two royal couples spent time together and Boris later repeated these diplomatic efforts with neighboring Romania, establishing cordial relations with King Carol II.

With the end of the 1930s, as many European leaders expected, came another devastating war. On 1 September 1939 Germany invaded Poland. War declarations ensued, with France and Great Britain once again joining forces to put Germany in check. In Bulgaria the beginning of the Second World War was welcomed with deep foreboding. The Allies were incapable of providing any protection to the Balkan kingdoms, and instead Italy, Hitler's ally, made inroads in the region. London urged Boris III to declare his support for the Allies, but the King worried that doing so would invite Russo-German retaliation. Instead, he opted for neutrality. His Windsor cousin George VI assured Boris that Britain would respect Bulgaria's neutrality if *"it was not violated by others."* And so the final scene of King Boris III's tragic life began.

Above: King Boris III with his cousins King George V and the Duke of York.

Right: King Edward VIII, with King Boris III and Prince Kyril, during his brief visit to Bulgaria in 1936.

A year before the war began, Bulgarians were granted an election to restore constitutional rule and on 22 May 1938 King Boris opened a new Parliament. The King sought to calm the nation when he *"stressed the amelioration of Bulgaria's international position…*[He] *stressed the new friendship with Yugoslavia and the good relations with Bulgaria's neighbors, Turkey, Romania, and Greece."* This latest exercise in Balkan democracy faltered as soon as war exploded in Europe. By the end of 1939 another ministerial crisis forced the government's fall and Boris III had to appoint yet another cabinet. A report in the *New York Times* referred to Bulgaria as *"Europe's Cinderella,"* for her *"hopes have been dashed repeatedly"* by her inability to find *"a good fairy,"* meaning a major ally. The 1930s had witnessed greater German investment in the Bulgarian economy, to the detriment of the influence of London and Paris. The British government had tried to convince the Bulgarians to join the "Balkan Entente," yet as this entailed forsaking *"territorial claims"* stemming from the Treaty of Neuilly-sur-Seine, Sofia refused. Hence, Boris III and his government found themselves trapped at the outset of war. Theirs was an unenviable position, and as international threats increased, the political situation within Bulgaria only worsened.

In an interview with *Time Magazine*, conducted in early 1941, King Boris expressed in very clear terms the predicament he was caught in. Bulgaria was running out of options. The Italian adventure in Greece was not going as planned and Mussolini needed German aid. Romania was already under German control, mostly due to its dictator Antonescu's compliance woth Hitler's demands. Yugoslavia was on the brink: cooperate or face invasion. Bulgaria, located on the path the Germans wanted to take into Northeastern Greece were on the path of destruction. In the interview, King Boris told the American reporter that he wished to remain neutral, but his government wanted to join the Allies, while his queen wanted him to come to the aid of her father's battered trrops.

As war raged across Europe and Germany seemed to be the Continent's undisputed master, pressure on the Balkan countries to take sides increased. In Romania, King Carol II had left the previous year and the country was under the control of Antonescu, a virulent fascist. Yugoslavia, under the regency led by Prince Paul, feared that both German and Italian armies were about to ransack the country. Greece, at the very tip of the Balkan Peninsula, had already tasted the bitter consequences of Italy's cannons. Since October 1940, the Greeks were involved in a valiant struggle against

In September 1937, accompanied by his wife, King Boris III visited London. Here they are photographed at the Bulgarian Legation, where they were attending a reception given to the Bulgarian colony in London.

Mussolini's troops, which had invaded the country through Albania. However, with enough time to prepare its defenses, tiny Greece managed to derail Italy. Doing so, on the other hand, caused Germany to increase pressure on the remaining Balkan countries to allow it safe passage to come to Italy's aid. In Sofia, the cabinet wondered, *"Can we oppose the inevitable German passage through Bulgaria? Should this passage follow a preliminary agreement with Bulgaria? Is it necessary and in the interest of our country to sign the Tripartite Pact?"* The answers to these serious questions made all parties involved realize that in order to safeguard Bulgaria from annihilation, it would have to sign the Tripartite Pact with Germany and Italy, thus becoming a non-combating ally of Berlin and Rome. King Boris III's goal was to keep his army from joining the fight, preserve his country's territorial integrity, and spare Bulgarians further sacrifices. The Americans sent an emissary to conduct last minute talks with the King and his ministers and presented him with the quandary at hand: if Bulgaria publicly opposed a major Power's decision to cross the country, this would be a provocation. If Bulgaria said that they would allow it, then *"it was tantamount to an invitation."* Despite the Allies' virulent attacks, Boris decided to sign the Tripartite Pact to gain his country extra time. On 1 March 1941 the agreement was sealed; unbeknownst to Boris, had he not done so, Hitler had already decided to invade Bulgaria.

This was the position that Prince Regent Paul tried to adopt in neighboring Yugoslavia. On 25 March, weeks after Bulgaria joined the Central Powers, Yugoslavia signed the Tripartite Pact as well. Two days later, military officers unhappy with the decision overthrew the regency and arrested Prince Paul. The British supported the coup d'etat and King Peter II seized power. That same day, Hitler ordered the invasion of Yugoslavia. King Peter II, faced with the German onslaught, was forced to depart Belgrade. He never saw his homeland again.

Witnessing these events from the position of relative prosperity enjoyed by his subjects, Boris III realized that signing the pact saved Bulgaria from the same fate as Yugoslavia. And yet, as it always seemed to happen during the reign of this luckless monarch, the Japanese

King Boris III and Queen Giovanna, with Princess Eudoxia and Prince Kyril behind them.

Princess Marie Louise and her brother Crown Prince Simeon. *Princess Eudoxia of Bulgaria.*

attack on Pearl Harbor forced the United States's entry into the conflict. In Sofia, news of the Japanese attack was seen as potentially catastrophic, as indeed it turned out to be. A despondent Boris III now believed that Germany was destined to lose the war, allowing thus for the Soviet Union to gain increased control, if not total domination, of the Balkans. The King, in fact, predicted the *"bolshevization of Bulgaria."* Tormented by anguish, fear and worry, Boris III pondered what best to do: continue, abdicate, or commit suicide?

One of the King's most important legacies was his stand against Germany on the Jewish predicament. While inside Bulgaria the Jewish community experienced increased persecution after 1941, the King played an important role in preventing their deportation to extermination camps. Both Boris III and Giovanna felt deep revulsion toward Nazi treatment of Jews and other minorities, and counted many Jews among their friends. When in March 1943 the Nazis, acting through Bulgarian local governments, ordered the arrest of all the country's Jews, the order was rescinded with minutes to spare. *"It is more than certain that the interior minister was instructed from the 'highest place' to suspend the execution of the planned deportation of the Jews,"* one Bulgarian contemporary of the King wrote. King Boris tried his best to protect as many of his Jewish subjects as possible. Years later, Pope John XXIII's secretary revealed that while he was Apostolic delegate in Istanbul, His Holiness, who was a friend of the King, had received his help in saving thousands of Slovakian Jews, *"who had first been sent to Hungary and then to Bulgaria and who were in danger of being sent to concentration camps."* The King, according to the Pope's secretary, had signed transit visas that allowed these persecuted people safe passage to Palestine. Bulgaria, most uncharacteristically and unlike many other European countries, did not surrender its Jewish population to the Nazis, and King Boris III deserves great praise and recognition for guaranteeing their survival.

Hitler summoned King Boris to several meetings between 1941 and 1943. Their last encounter took place inside the Wolf's Lair, the dictator's underground bunker near Rastenburg, East Prussia. The meeting did not go well as apparently the King looked somber and dejected when he departed. Hitler, desperate for more troops and disappointed with Bulgaria's stand on the Jewish Question, had had enough of Boris III's evasions and had drawn a line on the sand. When the King said farewell, such was Hitler's frustration with his guest that *"the Führer, looking particularly grim, hardly looked at King Boris when he mumbled an icy goodbye."* They never saw each other again.

Boris III returned to Bulgaria on August 15. Thirteen days later, following several days of physical and medical complications, he died. Those around him decided to keep the King's worsening health a secret from the country, believing that Bulgaria had enough worries. Even the Queen was kept uninformed until the situation worsened and she had to rush to be by her dying husband's side.

A view of the lying-in-state of King Boris III.

Those around the King later recalled that he had been exhausted and depressed. Already suffering from various illnesses, Boris III's last month was fraught with unimaginable stress as he worried about his family, his country, and what lay ahead for both. He had trouble sleeping and complained of a terrible sense of foreboding. At times he seemed listless and short-tempered, defeatist and crestfallen. He had complained of feeling chest pains, identified as angina pectoris, and on 23 August, following a grueling day of work, the King began *"vomiting violently."* His doctors were summoned again and initially thought the King was suffering a severe gallbladder attack. As his condition worsened, further examination led the medical team to say that he had suffered a thrombosis, *"or coagulation of blood in the heart."* Several German specialists were flown in for observation and consultation and agreed with the diagnosis. Several days passed before Prince Kyril informed their sister Eudoxia of Boris's condition. *"Boris is not well, I don't like it,"* the prince said. *"Could he have been poisoned?"* asked Princess Eudoxia. In and out of consciousness, King Boris III died on 28 August. Giovanna was in a state of shock, as was Prince Kyril. Princess Eudoxia addressed the Prime Minister and cautioned, *"Now, Mr. Filov, you must hold firmly."* That evening Bulgarians heard on the radio that their beloved King had died. His funeral, which witnessed crowds filing past his coffin, was followed by burial at Rila Monastery in a simple grave marked by a wooden cross.

Rumors of all kinds surrounded Boris III's death. Among the first to raise the specter of poisoning was his own sister Eudoxia, who believed the Nazis were behind her brother's downfall. She was an early opponent of Bulgaria's proximity to Berlin, although later some in the Western press accused her of being a Nazi-sympathizer. Her criticism of the King's decisions regarding Germany had led to more than a few regrettable scenes between them. She was not the only one who believed the King was murdered: many suspect-

Prince Regent Kyril.

ed that he had been poisoned, though not by Germans. Hitler, in fact, thought that the Italians poisoned Boris III, the King's sister-in-law, Mafalda of Hesse, having played an important and maleficent role in the dastardly deed. Perhaps, others thought, it was the Communists, or the military, or politicians, or the Allies…When confronted with such tragic loss, one attempts to make sense out of a nonsensical event.

King Simeon II's reign began in the midst of national mourning and despondency. Prince Kyril took over as regent of Bulgaria during the child-king's minority. Internally, the situation worsened as Communists, taking advantage of Boris III's, death prepared to take over. Just a year after King Simeon succeeded to the throne, the country hovered on the brink of the abyss. By then, the Red Army had crossed through Romania and reached the Bulgarian border. The government had already severed ties with the Germans and was seeking aid from the Allies. It was then that a Communist-supported coup d'etat overthrew the government. Prince Kyril and the other two regents serving with him were eventually arrested, as were countless politicians. The Kingdom of Bulgaria was now under Stalinist control.

In 1954, Queen Frederica of Greece organized a cruise on the Aegean Sea. It had a double purpose: promote Greek tourism, while providing young royals with an opportunity to meet each other and perhaps find spouses. King Simeon was among the guests.

While Queen Giovanna and her children were allowed to stay together, not so other family members. Kyril fell to the bullets of a firing squad organized by Bulgarian Communists in February 1945, accused of treason and sentenced to death. Also in the same mass grave were the bodies of the other regents, as well as those of leading politicians and friends of the late King. Those who escaped the firing squad were imprisoned and tortured, among them Princess Eudoxia, who was miserably treated by her jailors and tormentors.

By 31 August 1946, three years after Boris's death, Giovanna expected to join her family in exile. Eight days later, in a plebiscite policed by the Soviet Army, 97% of Bulgarians "voted" for the abolition of the monarchy. The popular "consultation" did not reflect the people's will. The results were manipulated and the plebiscite was anything but democratic. Instead, the former kingdom became the "People's Republic of Bulgaria." The reign of Communist terror began in earnest and it would consume Bulgaria as a cancer from within even beyond the fall of the Berlin Wall in 1989.

On 9 September King Simeon, along with his mother and sister, was expelled from Bulgaria. Princess Eudoxia was also allowed to leave. The small group, carrying

Queen Giovanna and Princess Alexandra of Hohenlohe-Langenburg visiting El Quexigal (near Madrid), the splendid home of Princess Piedita of Hohenlohe-Langenburg.

King Simeon at Valley Forge Academy.

barely their basic necessities, left Bulgaria and headed to Istanbul. There they boarded a Turkish ship bound for Egypt, where Giovanna's family had settled after the fall of the monarchy earlier in the year. The Savoys and the Coburgs, also joined by King Zog and his family, were guests of King Farouk, who opened his kingdom and gave shelter to these royal refugees. Queen Giovanna and her children were still living in Egypt when her father, King Vittorio Emanuele III died on 28 December 1947. His fortune, plus the legal settlement the King received from the new Italian republican authorities, guaranteed that his descendants would enjoy a comfortable exile.

The Bulgarians were still living in Egypt when old King Ferdinand passed away in Coburg on 10 September 1948, nearly two years to the day his grandson was forced into exile. The poor man had lived long enough to witness the destruction of everything he held dear: Bulgaria, his sons, his fortune, and his privileged world. Even his properties in Czechoslovakia were gone. Ferdinand left little of his once considerable fortune behind. King Simeon once told me, *"I never met my grandfather…the war first, then exile in Egypt… died before we took the first trip from Egypt to Europe."*

After her father's death, Queen Giovanna's mother decided to leave Egypt, where the situation was turning sour. Queen Elena settled in Montpellier, where she died in 1952. Giovanna contacted General Franco, Spain's dictator, and requested his hospitality. In July 1951 Giovanna, accompanied by her children, settled in Madrid. As her brother King Umberto II had settled permanently in Estoril, Portugal, Giovanna and her children began spending holidays in that paradisiacal "royal" enclave, where so many other members of the European Gotha found the respite their homeland denied them. The Count of Barcelona led the "royal" community in Estoril from his villa, La Giralda, trying his best to build the political will for a restoration of the Spanish monarchy. His Italian and Bulgarian cousins were to be less successful.

In Estoril, according to Spanish author Ricardo Mateos, Simeon and his sister Marie Louise usually lodged with the Count and Countess of Paris, whose eleven children, along with visiting nephews, nieces, other relations and staff, formed a veritable tribe. *"As my Mother lived there from 1963 to her death, we would often visit her, with our children and later with grandchildren too. We all have wonderful memories"* of Estoril, King Simeon told me. The Bulgarians, because of these visits, developed deep friendships with their Orléans cousins, as they did with the children of the Barcelonas. Not surprisingly, these close relations with other exiled royals led to press rumors concerning the identity of Simeon's future bride. Some newspapers alleged that he was going to marry

King Simeon and Queen Margarita's wedding, Vevey, 1962.

Isabelle, the eldest child of the Count of Paris. He was also paired with several of her sisters, as well as with Infanta María del Pilar, eldest daughter of the Barcelonas. He was among the guests of Queen Frederica's famed royal cruise onboard the *Agamemnon* and attended countless royal events along the Continent. Simeon, however, was in no rush to settle down.

In 1957, Princess Marie Louise married Prince Karl Wladimir of Leiningen, who was several times her cousin through their shared Coburg links. Born in Coburg in 1928, Karl was the second son of Fürst Karl and of his Russian wife, Grand Duchess Marie Kirillovna, the eldest daughter of Grand Duke Kirill Vladimirovich and his wife Victoria Melita. Fürst Karl was also a great-grandson of Queen Victoria's half-siblings, Carl of Leiningen and his sister Feodora of Hohenlohe-Langenburg. Dynastically, Karl and Marie Louise's marriage was a splendid one. However, it only lasted eleven years, the couple divorcing in 1968 after having two sons. The following year, Princess Marie Louise married Bronislaw Chrobok, by whom she had a further two children.

Burg Hohenzollern, 1963 – King Simeon and Queen Margarita attending the silver wedding anniversary party for Prince Louis Ferdinand and Princess Kira of Prussia. Kira Kirillovna, at one point, was rumored to be under consideration for marriage by King Boris. Both Kira and Boris had a Coburg parent.

Nevertheless, two years after his sister's marriage, King Simeon II arrived in the United States to complete a one-year course at Valley Forge Military Academy. Several American newspapers conducted interviews with the King, who was quite emphatic in his hope to return to Bulgaria. King Simeon II also urged the West to *"put more emphasis on freedom and less on peaceful coexistence."* He did support the reestablishment of diplomatic relations between Washington and Sofia since this would *"give the United States an additional window into the Iron Curtain."*

The following year, King Simeon, now one of royal Europe's most prized bachelors, was among a distinguished group of eligible royals invited to attend a magnificent ball hosted by King Gustav VI Adolf of Sweden. Ostensibly, the main purpose of the splendid gathering was to introduce the King's unmarried granddaughters to their

In 1972 King Simeon and Queen Margarita posed for a family photo with their children. Their youngest, Princess Kalina, was born earlier in the year.

Standing, from left: Duke Ferdinand of Württemberg, Queen Margarita and King Simeon II, Queen Giovanna, Princess Eudoxia, Princess Marie Louise and Mr. Bronislaw Chrobok. Seated, same order: Princess Kalina, Prince Konstantin, Prince Kubrat, Prince Kyril, Crown Prince Kardam, Prince Boris and Prince Hermann of Leiningen, and Alexandra-Nadejda and Paul Chrobok.

King Simeon II and Queen Margarita.

"Gotha" cousins. The girls' mother, the former Princess Sibylla of Saxe-Coburg & Gotha, hoped that the ball would stir the hearts of the new generation and encourage them to look within royal circles for spouses. However, King Simeon, along with Crown Prince Constantine of Greece, Crown Prince Harald of Norway, the Duke of Kent, Prince Max Emanuel of Bavaria, Prince Ludwig of Baden, Princes Moritz and Karl of Hesse, Hereditary Prince Kraft of Hohenlohe-Langenburg and Hereditary Count Hans-Veit zu Toerring-Jettenbach – all of whom were present – looked elsewhere when it came to finding a bride.

Upon completing his courses in America, King Simeon returned to Madrid, where he studied law and business administration. Soon after he entered the business world, serving as chairman of a French defense and electronics company for many years. He also acted as adviser in the *"banking, hotel, electronics, and catering sectors."*

It was in Spain that King Simeon met his future bride, doña Margarita Gómez-Acebo y Cejuela. *"We met at a dinner party,"* King Simeon told me. She was a granddaughter of the wealthy Marqués de Cortina and her parents had been killed during the Spanish Civil War. Margarita possessed endless grace and a winning smile while boasting an excellent educa-

In 1993 King Simeon and Queen Margarita joined their Württemberg cousins for the wedding of Duke Friedrich of Württemberg and Princess Marie of Wied. With them is the Countess of Paris, the groom's grandmother. Behind King Simeon is Infanta Elena of Spain and behind her is Prince Laurent of Belgium.

tion and a considerable inheritance. Simeon II and Margarita married at Vevey, Switzerland, in 1962. However, not everyone was happy with the King's choice. King Umberto II was a martinet when it came to matters of marital equality, and he was so displeased at the match that he ordered his children not to attend their Bulgarian cousin's wedding. King Simeon, however, believed that change was a necessity if royals were to remain relevant, and as Head of House he saw nothing wrong or lacking with his bride.

On returning to Madrid from their honeymoon, Simeon and Margarita settled in his mother's large villa, while Queen Giovanna relocated to Estoril, where she would be closer to her brother Umberto. Giovanna died there in February 2000. Her sisters-in-law had long predeceased her: Nadejda died in Stuttgart in 1958, Her husband having predeceased her by four years. Eudoxia died in 1985 at Friedrichshafen, a beautiful Württemberg palace on the shores of Lake Kontanz. When once I asked King Simeon about press reports alleging that Princess Eudoxia held Nazi sympathies, the King said, *"As to Princess Eudoxia being pro-Nazi, I would use the British expression…rubbish!"*

Simeon's Madrid residence was described as *"a palacio* [palace], *and the atmosphere inside suggests a family tradition that takes itself very seriously indeed. Portraits of ancestors grace the spacious entrance hall, through which a servant in white uniform escorts a visitor, sharp left into an imposing study. A signed portrait of King Juan Carlos is on the table, alongside one of Hassan II of Morocco. Don't lose hope, all this seems to say, yet Simeon is cautious about his prospects."* It was in this comfortable atmosphere that Simeon and Margarita raised their five children. Crown Prince Kardam was born in 1962, followed by Prince Kyril (1964), Prince Kubrat

King Simeon II and Queen Giovanna.

The Margrave and Margravine of Meißen with King Simeon II and Queen Margarita attending a royal event in 1996.

(1965), Prince Konstantin-Assen (1967), and Princess Kalina (1972). All were born in Madrid and all are married to Spaniards.

When Crown Prince Kardam was born in Madrid, his father gave him the title of Prince of Tirnovo. He studied at Penn State in America, graduating with a Master's degree in Agricultural Economics. Although Simeon's eldest son, Kardam was the last to marry. In 1996 he wed Miriam de Ungría, born in 1963. They have two sons: Boris (1997) and Beltrán (1999).

Simeon granted his son Kyril the title of Prince of Preslav. Prince Kyril graduated from Princeton and on returning to Europe became the darling of the pink press, constantly gracing the pages of weekly magazines like *Hola/Hello*. In newspapers and magazines he was paired with many an available princess, including the daughters of King Juan Carlos and Queen Sofía of Spain, with whom the Bulgarian Royal Family has long maintained close ties. In the end Prince Kyril chose a beautiful woman named Rosario Nadal y Fuster-Puigdorfila (born 1968), daughter of a Spanish industrialist. Her mother is a descendant of the Counts de Olocau, a title created in 1628, and Rosario also happens to be a descendant of Emperor Montezuma II, the last Aztec ruler. Kyril and Rosario, who married at Palma de Mallorca in 1989, are the parents of three children, all born in London: Mafalda (born in 1994), Olimpia (1995), and Tassilo (2002). Recently the Spanish press announced that the Prince and Princess of Preslav had decided to separate, although no decision has apparently been made regarding a divorce.

Prince Kubrat, born 5 November 1965, received the title of Prince of Panagjuriste from his father. He studied medicine and has worked as a doctor since graduating. In 1993 he married Spaniard Carla María Royo-Villanova, born in 1969. The Prince and Princess of Panagjuriste are the parents of three sons, all born in Madrid: Mirko (1995), Lucas (1997), and Tirso (2002).

On December 5, 1967, Queen Margarita gave birth to her fourth son, Konstantin-Assen, created Prince of Vidin by his father. Konstantin of Bulgaria studied business and has worked in the area for some time. Several years ago, when his father was elected Bulgaria's prime minister,

In 2002, King Simeon and Queen Margarita were among hundreds of members of the Gotha who convened in Vienna to celebrate the 90th birthday of Archduke Otto of Austria. This photo was taken by the author at the evening gala at Schönbrunn Palace.

From left: Crown Prince Alexander of Yugoslavia, Queen Margarita and King Simeon of Bulgaria, Crown Princess Margarita and Prince Radu of Romania.

Konstantin worked to attract foreign investors to the Communist-ravaged country his family had once ruled. The Prince of Vidin married María García de la Rasilla (born in 1970) in 1994. Through her mother Princess María is a descendant of the Counts of Superunda, a title King Fernando VI of Spain granted in 1748 to don José Antonio Manso de Velasco, Viceroy of Perú; her mother is also a descendant of the Ybarra family, a prominent dynasty of Spanish industrialists and politicians. Five years after her marriage, Princess Maria gave birth to twins, Prince Umberto and Princess Sofía.

Princess Kalina, the King's youngest child, was born in 1972. Kalina studied in France and is a gifted linguist, speaking Bulgarian, Spanish, French, English, Italian, and German. She has always been, and remains, an unconventional princess, often expressing her personality through a very unique sense of fashion. Kalina possesses an artistic personality and has a true passion for art, furniture restoration, painting, and animal rights. Kalina is also the only one of King Simeon's children to convert to Catholicism. In 2002, she married Antonio (Kitín) Muñoz, a noted Spanish adventurer and humanitarian who was born in Morocco in 1958. Their wedding took place in Bulgaria and was attended by a number of royals. Their son, Simeón Hassan Muñoz y de Bulgaria, was born at Sofia in 2007; he was the first member of the King's family born in Bulgaria since King Simeon in 1937.

As the years passed and Europe abandoned the old rancor caused by the Second World War, King Simeon II, who remains extremely well liked by his Coburg and other royal cousins, renewed contacts with the House of Windsor. *"I called on Her Majesty some time in the 1950s,"* the King told me. Contacts have continued uninterrpted since then. In 1981, Simeon II and his wife were honored with an invitation to the wedding of the Prince of Wales to Lady Diana Spencer. In Spain, King Juan Carlos never fails to invite his Bulgarian cousin to attend every major royal event in Madrid.

In 1990, after the fall of communism, Simeon was issued a new Bulgarian passport. Six years later, half a century after the abolition of the monarchy, Simeon returned to Bulgaria and was met in many places by crowds cheering, *"We want our King!"* He did not, at that point, make any political announcements or moves. Finally, and in a thoroughly Balkan turn of events, King Simeon became the Prime Minister of Bulgaria in July 2001 after his political movement obtained the majority

The Prince and Princess of Tirnovo with their sons Boris and Beltrán.

The Prince and Princess of Tirnovo followed by the Dukes of Braganza, the Princes of Naples and Prince Georg Friedrich of Prussia. The four men in this photo are Coburg descendants, Copenhagen (2004).

in the country's parliamentary elections. When I asked him what prompted him to enter politics, he said that *"My sense of duty and responsibility."* He served as prime minister until 2005, and has remained active in national politics. King Simeon and Queen Margarita now reside in Sofia, although they frequently visit Spain and attend royal events across the continent. Most recently, they were among the large number of Gotha members present at the wedding of the Hereditary Prince Hubertus of Saxe-Coburg & Gotha. King Simeon was asked, not long ago, why he continued living in Sofia instead of in Madrid where his sons resided. The king calmly told the reporter that he was a Bulgarian, first and foremost, and kept from his country for as long as he lived in exile, he felt it his duty to be among his people. Crowned or not, Simeon remains the nation's most fervent servant. Personally, he is soft-spoken, elegant and unassuming. Deeply interested in his Coburg past, he always refers to his cousin Andreas as *"the Head of Our House."* Greatly respected by all who know him, Simeon has avoided any negative comments about his personal life or his role as father, husband and King-in-exile.

On a sad note, Crown Prince Kardam and Princess Miriam suffered a tragic automobile accident in August 2008 as they approached the outskirts of Madrid. Prince Kardam suffered severe brain-skull trauma and serious injuries to his hands, while Miriam broke several ribs, her elbow, and had a collapsed lung. A spokesperson for the Bulgarian Royal Family, confirming the accident, announced that Crown Prince Kardam had undergone surgery the following evening. He was kept in an artificial coma for several months. After several weeks of intensive care, Miriam recovered and left hospital. Crown Prince Kardam's recovery has been long and slow. The King told me that, *"Alas his condition has not changed since his accident on 15 August 2008. This is a source of much pain for all of us."*

The Prince of Preslav, Madrid (2004).

King Simeon's one lingering struggle is his legal battle against the Bulgarian government over his private property. Back in 1946, the Communist Prime Minister Georgiev ordered an inventory of all royal property and the following year it was taken from Simeon II by the *"Act for nationalization of the Property of Kings Ferdinand and Boris and Their Successors."* The expropriation was done arbitrarily and in a blatant effort to rob the Royal Family of much needed funds to live in exile. Having left Bulgaria with only a few possessions crammed into suitcases, Giovanna and her children have relied on her Savoy inheritance to finance the family's life in Egypt, Spain, and later Portugal. In 1998, the Bulgarian Constitutional Court decided that the nationalization of the King's private property was an unconstitu-

CHAPTER XIX – *The Coburgs of Sofia ... "Tantamount to an Invitation"*

The Prince and Princess of Panagjuriste, Madrid (2004).

The Prince and Priness of Vidin, Coburg (2009).

tional act and announced that several estates must be returned to him immediately. These properties included Vrana and Tsarska Bistritsa Palaces, along with a third of the land that once surrounded these estates; other properties returned included a house in the town of Banya and a forest in the region of Samokov. None of the expropriated properties had originally been obtained with government funds and had, in fact, been purchased using the Royal Family's private resources. Succeeding governments, though, have tried to recover the restituted properties, as if determined to ignore the rights of one Bulgarian, King Simeon. Their unexplainable efforts to illegally deprive the royal family of these lands are but an echo of the abuse Bulgarians suffered under the tragic abuses of the Communist era.

King Simeon, in spite of it all, remains positive and hopeful for the future of his country. Today, despite the challenges his political enemies have placed in his path, King Simeon is poised to embark on what seems a larger role in the political life of a Bulgaria that continues to awaken from the ghastly specter of Communism. For this, the King must be commended for as was the case with his father, Simeon II remains Bulgaria's number one patriot.

Princess Kalina and her husband, Mr. Kitín Muñoz, Madrid (2004).

CHAPTER XX
The Women of Coburg
A Most Interesting Club

I believe that the 'women of Coburg' are far more interesting than the men," Prince Andreas of Saxe-Coburg & Gotha once told me, *"and by 'women of Coburg' I mean the princesses from my House. Look at the marriages they made and the many links they provided to our House. It is through their descendants that we are related to the majority of Europe's ruling and formerly ruling dynasties. Their story deserves a book, or at the very least some type of mention in yours."*

Looking at the dynasty's family tree, it is clear that Prince Andreas has a point. Coburg women have married extremely well since the time of Duke Franz Friedrich Anton's daughters. These alliances are responsible for establishing strong bonds among the various families that form the European Gotha. And yet, studies of royal personages tend to focus on paternal relations, disregarding in many instances the far more interesting maternal half. Consider how many of the myriad family trees found in royal biographies follow the intricacies of maternal ancestry? How many of these ancestors' charts actually bother with showing the close bonds brought into a family by the women that marry into it?

Composing a family tree of paternal descent is a far more common, and easier, enterprise. Yet maternal lines often provide closer family bonds. It was through female lines of descent that Kaiser Wilhelm II, Queen Sophie of Greece, King George V, Queen Maud of Norway, Empress Alexandra Feodorovna, Queen Marie of Romania, Crown Princess Margaret of Sweden, and Queen Victoria Eugenia of Spain were first cousins. All were grandchildren of Queen Victoria and Prince Albert, a double Coburg ancestry.

Archduke Otto of Austria and his wife, the former Princess Regina of Saxe-Meiningen, were both distant Coburg relations. Otto's paternal grandmother, Maria Josepha of Saxony, was the granddaughter of King Consort Ferdinand of Portugal, a grandson of Duke Franz Friedrich Anton. Regina's great-grandmother, Feodora of Hohenlohe-Langenburg, was a granddaughter of the Duchess of Kent, a daughter of Duke Franz Friedrich Anton. Hence, Otto and Regina were fifth cousins through shared Coburg ancestry.

Another interesting example, as well as a more current one, is that of King Simeon II of Bulgaria and three fellow Balkan royals: King Constantine II of the Hellenes, Crown Prince Alexander of Yugoslavia and King Michael of Romania. Simeon II is, of course, a Coburg by birth. Constantine, Alexander and Michael are all Coburg descendants through female lines.

One of the images chosen to illustrate this book presents us with a perfect example of how intricate Coburg female lines are among today's royals. The image, taken by the author at the wedding of Crown Prince Frederik of Denmark and Ms. Mary Donaldson, shows for Coburg descendants walking into the church: the Prince of Tirnovo, the Duke of Braganza, the Prince of Naples and Prince Georg Friedrich of Prussia. Tirnovo, of course, is the eldest son of King Simeon II of Bulgaria, a male line Coburg. Immediately behind him walk the Duke of Braganza and his wife Isabel. Duarte is the grandson of Pedro d'Alcantara of Brazil, the son of Count d'Eu, who was the son of Victoire of Saxe-Coburg & Gotha, a sister of Tirnovo's great-great-grandmother. The Prince of Naples is the son of Princess Marie José of Belgium, a Coburg of Brussels. At the very end comes the Head of House Prussia, Georg Friedrich, who happens to have five Coburg lies of descent. Both his paternal grandparents, Louis Ferdinand of Prussia and Kira Kirillovna of Russia, are descendants of Queen Victoria and the

Prince Consort. Furthermore, Louis Ferdinand's great-great-grandmother is Fürstin Feodora of Hohenlohe-Langenburg, née Leiningen, Queen Victoria's halfsister.

Princess Astrid of Belgium and her husband Archduke Lorenz of Austria are both "Coburgs." Astrid, a male line Coburg, is a great-great-granddaughter of the Count of Flanders, a grandson of Duke Franz Friedrich Anton. Lorenz, a female line Coburg descendant, is the great-grandson of Maria Josepha of Saxony, a granddaughter of King Consort Ferdinand, who was a first cousin of the Count of Flanders and a grandson of Duke Franz Friedrich Anton.

Fürst Andreas and Fürstin Alexandra of Leiningen, whose children have seven lines of descent from Duke Franz Friedrich Anton of Saxe-Coburg-Saalfeld and his wife Augusta.

Also, Prince Guillaume of Luxembourg, a maternal line Coburg, married Sibilla Weiller, a distant "Coburg" relation. Guillaume's mother was Joséphine-Charlotte of Belgium. Sibilla's maternal grandmother was the Infanta Beatriz of Spain, whose maternal grandmother was Princess Beatrice, youngest daughter of Queen Victoria and Prince Albert.

An additional alliance between Coburg descendants was that of Princess Cécile of Hohenlohe-Langenburg and Count Cyril de Commarque, who are now divorced. Cécile's grandmother was Princess Margarita of Greece, a maternal granddaughter of Princess Victoria of Hesse and By Rhine, who was also a maternal granddaughter of Queen Victoria and Prince Albert. Cyril is one of the grandsons of Princess Marie Clotilde Napoléon, the daughter of Princess Clémentine of Belgium.

Interestingly, Fürst Andreas of Leiningen and his wife Alexandra of Hannover are both Coburg descendants through female lines. Andreas descends from the three children of the Duchess of Kent. This unique circumstance was provided by the marriage of his Leiningen grandparents, Karl of Leiningen and Marie Kirillovna. Princess Alexandra has three Coburg lines of descent, as she descends from Prince Albert, Queen Victoria and her halfsister Feodora. The couple's children, in fact, possess seven lines of descent from Duke Franz Friedrich Anton. One could easily say that Andreas and Alexandra are their own Coburg cousins.

As for the mainline Coburgs, Prince Andreas' parents were both Coburg descendants. Prince Friedrich Josias's parents, Carl Eduard and Viktoria Adelheid, were related through the Coburgs. Carl Eduard was a grandson of Queen Victoria and the Prince Consort, while Viktoria Adelheid's maternal grandmother, Adelheid of Hohenlohe-Langenburg, was a granddaughter of the Duchess of Kent. Andreas' mother, Viktoria-Luise of Solms-Baruth, was a granddaughter of Karoline-Mathilde of Schleswig-Holstein-Sonderburg-Augustenburg, a great-granddaughter of the Duchess of Kent.

Examples of these high levels of consanguinity through female lines abound among Coburg descendants. Piecing their ancestry together, although at times a mind numbing exercise, provides the genealogist with a visual demonstration of why Prince Andreas believes the 'Women of Coburg' are of such great interest and importance, while also helping explain the family's intricate web of relations within the Gotha. To analyze every alliance would require its own book. To simplify matters, I have chosen to provide brief vignettes of the lives of twelve Coburg women who married monarchs, crown princes or heads of mediatized dynasties: the Empress Friedrich, Grand Duchess Alice of Hesse and By Rhine, Queen Maud of Norway, Queen Marie of Romania, Grand Duchess Victoria Feodorovna of Russia, Fürstin Alexandra of Hohenlohe-Langenburg, Crown Princess Margaret of Sweden, Princess Maria Ana of Saxony, Fürstin Antónia of Hohenzollern, Princess

Clémentine Napoléon, Queen Marie José of Italy and Grand Duchess Joséphine-Charlotte of Luxembourg.

Victoria, The Princess Royal, Empress Friedrich (1840-1901)

Born at Buckingham Palace on 21 November 1840, Victoria was the eldest child of Queen Victoria and Prince Albert. In 1841 her mother created Victoria Princess Royal, a title sometimes conferred on the sovereign's eldest daughter.

Early on, Albert and Victoria realized that their daughter was precociously intelligent and sought to maximize her intellectual gifts by closely supervising her education. As a child, Victoria learned not only English but also German and French. Tutors taught her science, literature, Latin and history, while Prince Albert tutored his daughter in politics and philosophy. Victoria, in time, became the over-achieving and sharp individual that her brother the Prince of Wales was not. Victoria rarely disappointed her parents, while her brother did so constantly.

The Princess Royal first met her future husband, Prince Friedrich Wilhelm of Prussia (1831-1888), when Queen Victoria invited him and his parents to visit the Great Exhibition, Prince Albert's crowning achievement. The seeds of love and admiration were first planted then, but not until 1855 did London and Berlin announce the official engagement. The couple married at the Chapel Royal, St. James's Palace, on 25 January 1858. By then, and given the childlessness of King Friedrich Wilhelm IV of Prussia, his nephew Friedrich Wilhelm was expected to one day inherit the throne. Through his daughter's marriage to the heir of the mighty Prussian throne, the Prince Consort sought to democratize Prussia, the leading German power. It was a carefully constructed plan, but it failed miserably.

Friedrich Wilhelm and Victoria were the parents of a large family. In January 1859, Victoria gave birth to a son, the future Kaiser Wilhelm II. It was a difficult birth and both mother and son were at risk of dying. Unfortunately, the baby's leftt arm was damaged at birth and thus was never able to fully develop. This accident played an important role in shaping Victoria's eldest son's troublesome character.

Besides Wilhelm II, seven other children eventually joined the Prussian royal nursery. Charlotte was born

Crown Prince Friedrich Wilhelm of Prussia and his wife Victoria.

Standing from left: Princess Heinrich of Prussia, Princess Henry of Battenberg and Victoria. All surrounding Queen Victoria.

At her home, Schloß Friedrichshof, the Empress Friedrich is surrounded by family members. Standing from left: Princess Irene of Prussia, Crown Princess Sophie of Greece, Hereditary Princess Charlotte of Saxe-Meiningen, Empress Augusta Viktoria, Victoria, Princess Victoria of Schaumburg-Lippe and Princess Margarete of Hesse. The Children: Alexander, Helen and George of Greece. Seated: Prince Adolf of Schaumburg-Lippe, Prince Friedrich Karl of Hesse, Prince Heinrich of Prussia, the Kaiser, Crown Prince Constantine of Greece, Prince Albert of Schleswig-Holstein and Grand Duke Ernst Ludwig of Hesse and By Rhine.

at the Neues Palais in July 1860. Next came a second boy, Heinrich, born at the Neues Palais in 1862. Two years later Victoria gave birth to a third son, Sigismund, who unfortunately died of meningitis two years later. To her mother, Victoria lamented the loss of the boy: *"My pride, my joy, my hope, is gone, gone."*

In 1866, the same year Prussia defeated Austria becoming the undisputed German power, Victoria gave birth to her fifth child and namesake. Two years later Victoria gave birth to a fourth son, Waldemar, whom his mother adored and found *"quick to learn and to teach."* Sadly, in 1879 Waldemar fell victim to diphtheria and his broken-hearted mother mourned him as *"the dearest, nicest and most promising"* of her four sons. A sister followed Waldemar, Sophie, who one day was to become the consort of King Constantine I of the Hellenes. Lastly, Victoria gave birth to a fourth daughter, Margarete, born in 1872. As the youngest child, she was to remain her mother's closest companion. Two of Victoria's children, Wilhelm II and Heinrich, married other Coburg descendants, Princess Augusta Viktoria of Schleswig-Holstein-Sonderburg-Augustenburg and Princess Irene of Hesse and By Rhine respectively. A larger number of Victoria's grandchildren married Coburg descendants.

Victoria's four daughters all made, as expected, good dynastic marriages, although of these only two were arguably love matches. Charlotte, who died in 1919, was a known troublemaker and relished stirring turmoil. She seems to have been tainted with porphyria and passed it on to her daughter, who had a miserable life plagued by illness. Charlotte married the future Duke Bernhard III of Saxe-Meiningen, who survived her by nearly a decade. Their only daughter left no descendants.

Princess Victoria of Prussia, Friedrich III and Victoria's second daughter, also had a difficult life. Her mother insisted that she marry Prince Alexander, who was chosen as the first ruler of a liberated Bulgaria. The young couple liked each other, but international complications made match their diplomatically impossible. She later agreed to marry Prince Adolf of Schaumburg-Lippe, and not surprisingly they remained childless. After his death in 1916, Viktoria remained unmarried until in 1927 when, consumed by loneliness, she married a swindler by the name of Alexander Zoubkov. She died in 1929 in Bonn, where she had lived for years. Zoubkov had spent all her money and she was a pariah to most her family.

Sophie and Margarete fared better. Sophie married future King Constantine I of the Hellenes and by him had six children. She cared deeply for him, but Constantine was not always faithful to his wife. He succeeded to the Greek throne in 1913 upon the assassination of his father, only to be ousted in 1917 and accused of being pro-German, which he was not. Their son Alexander ruled in his stead until he died of a monkey bite in 1920. Constantine and Sophie, along with their family, returned to Athens. Unfortunately, two years later he was forced to abdicate as a consequence of a military disaster suffered by Greece at the hands of the Turks. He had not started the war, yet as monarch, Constantine received all the blame while the politicians responsible for the debacle washed their hands. Broken-hearted, Constantine died in Palermo, Sicily, in January 1923. Sophie survived him by nine years, dying in Frankfurt-am-Main in 1932. Through her the Coburg bloodline first entered the Greek royal family.

As for Margarete, she married Prince Friedrich Karl of Hesse, whose family the Prussians dethroned in 1866. It was a love match and they remained very close to her mother, from whom Margarete inherited Schloß Friedrichshof, still in the hands of her descendants. Margarete is unique among royal ladies for giving birth to six sons, among them two sets of twins. Friedrich Karl died in 1940; his wife survived him until 1954.

Unfortunately, the Prince Consort's grand plans for his daughter were never realized. Her husband finally succeeded as Kaiser Friedrich III in 1888. However, he was already deathly ill with cancer and his reign lasted ninety-nine days. Once her husband was gone, Victoria's difficult eldest son lost little time in isolating his mother completely and was, at times, vicious toward her.

In her widowhood, Victoria retired to the Taunus Mountains above Frankfurt. There she built a magnificent palace, a large part of the financing coming from an inheritance she received from a friend, the Duchess of Galliera. The structure, which she named Friedrichshof, was built in English style, a reminder to all those who maligned her that she was, above all, a British princess. Victoria died at Schloß Friedrichshof on 5 August 1901.

The Grand Duke and Grand Duchess of Hesse and By Rhine.

Alice, Grand Duchess of Hesse and By Rhine (1843-1878)

The third child of Queen Victoria and Prince Albert, Alice was born at Buckingham Palace on 25 April 1843. Precocious, inquisitive and a woman of great talent, Alice was to be more than a match for her mother, with whom she fought many a battle. As was the case with all her siblings, Alice's father chose her tutors and played an active role in her education.

When Prince Albert fell ill in 1861, Alice nursed her father and rarely left his bedside. His death was a sorrowful loss, but her efforts to restore his health led Alice to continue a lifelong interest in nursing. She was an early "feminist," if such a word could be applied this early in history, and was very supportive of Florence Nightingale.

Alice was very close to her Portuguese cousins and although she would have been an excellent choice for King Luís, destiny took Alice to Germany. Prince Albert had already "settled" his daughter's marriage to Prince Ludwig (1837-1892), who one day was expected to inherit the Grand Duchy of Hesse and By Rhine. Given the advantageous geographical location of Ludwig's country, as well as his family's excellent connections to Berlin and St. Petersburg, Albert wished his daughter to enter the family. They married at Osborne House on 1 July 1862. The Queen, in mourning for her husband, watched the lugubrious proceedings from behind a screen.

In time Alice's relationship with Ludwig became strained. Alice, far more intellectually inclined than her husband, found the petty mindedness of Darmstadt stifling. There she invested her energy in social causes and sought to bring reform to the grand duchy. She founded the "Frauenberein," a society for the training of women, as well as a guild to train nurses. It was hard, strenuous, and thankless, but although she never wavered, Alice was constantly exhausted. To her sense of hopelessness were added the constant squabbles she had with her mother. Whether it was about rearing children, requesting more funds for her Darmstadt home, or insisting her mother return to the world of the living, Alice, Queen Victoria believed, was a nuisance.

Ludwig and Alice had a large family of two sons and five daughters. Alice gave birth to her first child, Victoria, in 1863, at Windsor Castle under her mother's supervision. Victoria of Hesse and By Rhine was destined to become the grandmother of the Duke of Edinburgh, Queen Elizabeth II's husband. A year later, Alice gave birth to a second daughter, Elisabeth, who later married her cousin Grand Duke Serge Alexandrovich. Along with several other Romanovs, Elisabeth died in tragic circumstances at Alapaievsk, victims of Bolshevik butchery.

In 1866, Alice gave birth to a third daughter, Irene, who later married her cousin Prince Heinrich of Prussia. Two years later, Alice's fourth child, Ernst Ludwig, was born in Darmstadt. With his birth the succession was assured. He married twice, his first wife being his first cousin Victoria Melita of Saxe-Coburg & Gotha and Edinburgh. Friedrich Wilhelm, Alice's fifth child, was born in 1870. Suffering from hemophilia, he died after suffering a fall in 1873. Alice's youngest children were both girls. Alix was born in 1872, while Marie followed two years later. Alix went on to marry Tsar Nicholas II of Russia and the story of her tragic life is well known.

Ludwig succeeded his uncle in 1877. The following year tragedy struck the family. In November, diphtheria descended on the family. Victoria was the first to fall ill, and all the other children except Elisabeth caught the disease; even Grand Duke Ludwig IV fell ill. Indefatigable to the end, Alice nursed her family to health. However Marie died on 16 November. *"Oh it is agony,"* Alice told her mother when writing to inform her of the child's death. Unfortunately, Alice's weakened condition made her vulnerable and she caught the disease. Nothing could be done to save her and she died on 14 December 1878, the seventeenth anniversary of her father's death. Ludwig IV survived his wife until 1892, when he died at the relatively young age of fifty-four years.

Grand Duchess Alice and her six children: Victoria, Elisabeth, Irene, Ernst Ludwig, Alix and Marie.

In 1884 Victoria married her father's first cousin, Prince Louis of Battenberg, who served with great distinction in the Royal Navy. They had four children: Alice (1885-1969), who married Prince Andrew of Greece – they were the parents of the Duke of Edinburgh; Louise (1889-1965), who was destined to live in Sweden; George (1892-1938), who married Countess Nadejda de Torby, a Romanov morganaut; and Louis, better-known as the Earl Mountbatten of Burma.

Irene married her first cousin Prince Heinrich of Prussia. They had three sons, two of them hemophiliacs. Their middle son, Sigismund, relocated to Central America and lived in Costa Rica for nearly five decades with his wife Charlotte Agnes of Saxe-Altenburg. Heinrich died in 1929, while Irene survived him until 1953.

As for Ernst Ludwig, he succeeded as Grand Duke of Hesse and By Rhine in 1892. His second marriage compensated for the unhappiness of the first, and rumors have always abounded about his sexuality.

Whatever his sexual orientation may have been, Ernst Ludwig was an incredibly talented artist and patron, and turned Darmstadt into a veritable artistic and cultural center. In February 1905 he married Princess Eleonore of Solms-Hohensolms-Lich and by her had two sons, Georg Donatus and Ludwig. Ernst Ludwig died in 1937, just as the family prepared for Prince Ludwig's wedding. A month later, his widow, accompanied by their eldest son, his wife Cecile of Greece (a daughter of Andrew and Alice), their two sons and several companions, boarded an airplane and took off to England to attend Ludwig's wedding to Margaret Geddes. They never arrived. There was an air crash over Belgium and there were no survivors. Left behind was Georg Donatus's youngest child, Princess Johanna, but she died in 1939 from a childhood illness. Ludwig and Margaret, who were dearly loved and respected members of the European Gotha, were childless. He died in 1968, the last of the long line of Hessians who ruled over Darmstadt for centuries. Princess Margaret, who was very close to their English cousins, died in 1997.

Prince Carl of Denmark and Princess Maud of Wales.

The fate of Alice's children and their descendants remains to this day one of great tragedy and sorrow, all while giving testimony to the strength of the human spirit.

Queen Maud of Norway (1869-1938)

Youngest daughter of the future King Edward VII and Queen Alexandra, Maud was born at Marlborough House, London, on 26 November 1869. She was the couple's third and prettiest daughter, though in truth none of the girls seems to have inherited their mother's ravishing looks. Maud, at least, was more refined than her sallow, heavily eye-lidded sisters. All were shy and tended to be reclusive, never having developed a taste for the grand social scene ruled by their father. Behind their backs, the sisters were mockingly called *"Their Royal Shynesses."*

If given her choice, Alexandra would probably have kept her daughters unmarried. As a matchmaker, she left much to be desired. Maud's sisters, it is true, were a mixed bag when it came to finding husbands. Louise, the eldest, escaped the maternal birdcage by marrying the immensely wealthy Earl of Fife, a Scottish peer. Victoria, the middle daughter, was less lucky and remained the unmarried companion to their increasingly dependent and selfish mother. Maud, not wanting to suffer the fate of Victoria and realizing early on that their mother was unlikely to promote her marriage, took matters into her own hands. She developed an attraction to the handsome Prince Francis of Teck, her sister-in-law May's younger brother. However, Francis had two blotches against him: he was reckless and perennially broke. Other suggestions included the highly suitable Prince Max of Baden, though Maud rejected him, aware that her mother would never approve of a German husband. However, it was in Denmark that Maud found her husband. He was Prince Carl, the second son of future King Frederik VIII and Maud's first cousin.

Maud never wanted to be a queen, nor did she seek a life in the public eye. She preferred leading a domestic existence away from crowds and publicity. Marrying the second son of the future Danish king, she believed, would guarantee her the anonymity she craved. The wedding took place in the private chapel at Buckingham Palace, with her grandmother the Queen among the witnesses. The couple spent a long honeymoon at Sandringham and not until months later did Maud accepted the unavoidable and travel to

Denmark, where her husband's naval career awaited. Seven years after their wedding, Carl and Maud had their only child, a son Alexander, who was born at Appleton House, Maud's home on the Sandringham estate.

In 1905 the couple's life changed radically when Norway ended her union with Sweden and began searching for a king. The Norwegians eventually settled on Prince Carl, as his father was Danish and his mother Swedish. It seemed the perfect fit for the new Scandinavian kingdom. Neither Carl nor Maud truly desired a throne. In Denmark they led a quiet, domestic, comfortable and very private existence. Carl demanded that Sweden, Denmark and Great Britain endorse him, while also asking the Norwegians to hold a referendum on the royal question. When all involved agreed and the Norwegians overwhelmingly voted for the monarchy, Carl accepted the throne. He became Haakon VII and his son Alexander became Olav, while Maud refused to change her name. In June 1906 King Haakon and Queen Maud were crowned at Trondheim, in a ceremony witnessed by several royals who had traveled to this picturesque northern location for the event. The Princes of Wales wrote to a close relation that the affair had been conducted in *"a dignified manner."*

Since Norway lacked an aristocracy and court life was non-existent, Haakon and his small family led a relatively quiet and uneventful life. In public, Maud's shyness sometimes made her appear stiff, distant, and perhaps a bit uninterested. Those who knew her always lauded her cheery, compassionate, witty personality. As Queen of Norway, Maud was a vigorous supporter of women's rights. Her work on behalf of unwed mothers and their offspring was necessary to better the life of these people, but it raised many an eyebrow.

In 1929 Crown Prince Olav married Princess Märtha of Sweden, the daughter of a first cousin of his paternal grandmother. Olav and his wife were deeply in love and provided a warm home for their three children, Ragnhild, Astrid, and Harald. Queen Maud was delighted with her daughter-in-law, for until then the Norwegian Royal Family consisted only of Haakon VII, Maud and Olav.

Queen Maud of Norway.

Maud never lost her love for England, and made frequent use of Appleton House, which her father had given to her. She visited her family as often as she could and enjoyed a close bond with her siblings. It was while in England in 1938 that Queen Maud died unexpectedly. Her remains were transferred to Norway and she rests inside the royal mausoleum at Akerhus Castle.

King Haakon VII never remarried. In 1940 confronted with a German juggernaut, Haakon VII departed Norway and took refuge in England. While there, Haakon VII and Olav joined the Allied war effort and lobbied for Norway, where they returned in triumph on 7 June 1945. In 1957, nearly two decades after the death of his wife, King Haakon VII died in Oslo. He was eighty-five years old.

Queen Marie of Romania (1875-1938)

If the Twentieth Century witnessed a queen of legend, surely that accolade referred to Marie, consort of King Ferdinand I of Romania. Marie was boisterous, narcissistic, dazzling, egocentric, and extreme; she was also passionate, devoted, irreplaceable, inimitable, and courageous.

Princess Marie of Edinburgh was born on 29 October

1875 at Eastwell Park, her parents' country estate. Her childhood was spent in several European spots as her father's naval demands, and later Coburg obligations, kept the Edinburghs on the move. Marie once described her upbringing, writing, *"I grew up an exceedingly royal little person, full of my own importance, and in the belief that our glory, like that of the sun, was an unquestioned reality."*

Marie developed into a beautiful young girl and several suitors vied for her hand, including her cousin George of Wales. Marie's mother did not want her children to marry in England and George's suit was discouraged, much to her father's displeasure. Instead, her mother, who believed that girls ought to marry before developing ideas of their own, found Marie a husband in Prince Ferdinand, heir to his uncle King Carol I of Romania. Ferdinand had a Coburg mother, Infanta Antónia of Portugal, and was Marie's third cousin.

Their wedding took place in Sigmaringen in January 1893. Marie was not even eighteen-years old, while Ferdinand was twenty-seven. *"I must have looked exactly what I was,"* Marie later wrote, *"an innocent little fool with a head stuffed full of illusions and dreams."* The ill-suited couple quickly found out that Marie was expecting, becoming pregnant during their honeymoon. In October, Marie gave birth to a son, who received the name Carol. In later years, Carol, both as crown prince and king, became his mother's tormentor. A daughter arrived nearly a year later, receiving the name Elisabeth in honor of Queen Elisabeth, Carol I's childless wife.

Throughout the 1890s, Marie experienced countless disagreements with her husband's family. These were caused by the young woman's indiscretions fed by the boredom governing her life in Bucharest. Ferdinand's ability to capture Marie's attention was, at best, lacking, and the careless woman found enjoyment in shocking her entourage. Soon Marie's infractions were the talk of the capital and beyond. Her mother admonished Marie, who only listened when she was deep in trouble. As a result, it is rumored that men other than her husband fathered several of Marie's later children. Her cousin Grand Duke Boris Vladimirovich, who possessed a rapacious appetite for nubile women, has always been alleged as one of her lovers. Romanian Prince Barbo Stirbey also seems to have had more than a friendship with Marie.

Princess Marie of Edinburgh on her wedding day.

In January 1900 Marie gave birth to a daughter, her namesake. The child was born in Gotha under the protection of Marie's indomitable mother, who although deeply critical of her daughter's flightiness, never vacillated in coming to her defense. Three years later, Marie gave birth to a second son, Nicholas, at Castle Pelesch. In 1909 Marie gave birth to a third daughter, Ileana, who was to become her companion. Marie's last child, Mircea, was a cherubic little boy born in Bucharest in 1913. He died of typhoid fever in 1916.

Much like their Belgian cousins, Ferdinand and Marie suffered gravely the losses faced by their ransacked country during the Great War. King Carol I died in October 1914 and Ferdinand, prodded by Marie, later declared his support for the Allies. This led to Germany, Austria and Bulgaria attacking Romania. Marie gained enormous popularity through her Red Cross work and photos of the Queen clad in nurses' uniform were common. When war ended and the fate of Europe was left in the hands of the peace conference, Marie lost little time traveling to France and successfully lobbying for Romania. Her country fared exceedingly well and gained territories and a large compensation.

Left: King Ferdinand, Princess Ileana, Prince Nicholas and Queen Marie.

Above: Marie with her three eldest children: Carol, Elisabeth and Marie.

Below left: Queen Marie and her grandson Michael.

Crown Prince Carol, frankly a horrific human being, turned into a chimera. He first eloped with a Romanian commoner named Zizi Lambrino and illegally married her, only to abandon her and their non-dynastic child. He then married Princess Helen of Greece and turned her life into a veritable inferno. Both Carol and Helen were Coburg descendants, as her mother was a daughter of Empress Friedrich. The only good Carol ever brought Helen was their child, Michael (who interestingly has five Coburg lines of descent). Carol then divorced Helen and ran away with a disreputable virago named Elena Lupescu.

In February 1921 Elisabeth married Crown Prince George of Greece, but the marriage, besides bringing the spouses untold misery, remained childless. In 1922 Marie married King Alexander of Yugoslavia. Only Nicholas and Ileana remained unmarried, though in 1931 Nicholas contracted a morganatic marriage while later that same year Ileana wed Archduke Anton of Austria-Tuscany.

By this time, Queen Marie had become a widow. Ferdinand died in 1927, his grandson Michael succeeding him. Three years later Carol returned and staged a coup d'etat. Queen Marie had to do her best to function under the aegis of her unstable son, a selfish villain who ran the kingdom into the ground and robbed it of as much as he could before abdicating and departing Romania. King Carol II and Madame Lupescu eventually settled in Estoril, where other exile royals treated them with open coldness.

In the intervening time, Queen Marie gained worldwide recognition as the face of the Romanian monarchy. Her dealings with the United States were highly successful and her public image reached mythical levels. In private though, she suffered countless humiliations at the hands of her son Carol II. Death finally freed her from his abusive control in 1938.

Grand Duchess Victoria Feodorovna of Russia (1876-1936)

Among Queen Victoria's granddaughters, Victoria Melita holds a unique position: consort in Hesse and By Rhine and consort to Russia's Emperor-in-exile. Born November 25, 1876, at the Palace of San Antonio in Malta, where her father was stationed at the time, her second name paid homage to her birthplace. Victoria Melita, although not as pretty as her sister Marie, was tall, svelte, and statuesque, with piercing violet-blue eyes and a controlled, rather imperial manner. In many instances, she was far more Romanov than Coburg, and always cut an imposing presence.

Childhood was spent between Eastwell Park and London. Marie and Victoria Melita were particularly close, both sharing the same interests and even dressing alike. This bond was broken when Marie married and left for Romania. Queen Marie of Romania once referred to her shy, sensitive and serious sister as a *"passionate child…often misunderstood."* In time, her personality tended toward being unbending, uncompromising, one who had trouble forgiving. And yet, among her contemporaries, Victoria Melita was the rare conscientious, loving, compassionate parent. There is a reason why her children did not turn out to be a disappointment like so many of her Romanian nephews and nieces.

The Grand Duke and Grand Duchess of Hesse and By Rhine.

Victoria Melita missed her sister dreadfully and the solution found was for her to marry quickly. It was a grave error on the part of all involved. Since 1889, Victoria Melita's family had lived in Germany because of her father's obligations in Coburg. She was far more Germanic in her upbringing than English. Like her mother, Victoria Melita felt at ease in the rarefied atmosphere of the petty courts peppered across the German Empire. Hence, when marrying her cousin Grand Duke Ernst Ludwig of Hesse and By Rhine was suggested to her, Victoria Melita reluctantly accepted. There were, however, problems: the groom seemed to have no inclination to marry, while the bride may have had feelings for someone else. A large royal contingent, led by Queen Victoria, descended on Coburg to attend the 1894 wedding. It was there that the groom's sister, Alix, became engaged to the future Tsar Nicholas II.

"The jolliest, merriest house party to which I have ever been in my life" was how Prince Nicholas of Greece once described a visit to the newly married couple. Victoria Melita, though, quickly realized that once guests left and parties ended, she and her husband – left to themselves – had little in common. In 1895 she gave birth to a daughter, Elisabeth, and soon afterward the couple drifted apart. The families intervened; several attempts were made to reconcile Ernst Ludwig and Victoria Melita; and even though she became pregnant a second time (a baby she lost during the pregnancy), the marriage was doomed to fail. Divorce followed soon after Queen Victoria's death in 1901.

"Now that I am calmer I see the absolute impossibility of going on leading a life which was killing her and driving me

Left: Grand Duke Kirill Vladimirovich and his wife Victoria Melita soon after their wedding, Coburg, 1906.

Above: Victoria Melita with her children: Maria, Kira and Wladimir, while exiled in Finland, 1918.

nearly mad," he wrote to his elder sister Victoria of Battenberg. Unfairly Victoria Melita was treated as a virtual pariah after her divorce while most regarded Ernst Ludwig as the victim. Both shared much blame in the collapse of their marriage, but at the time it was women who usually bore the brunt of criticism. After the divorce, Victoria Melita returned to her mother's protection, staying with her at the Château de Fabron, Marie Alexandrovna's home on the Riviera. A further blow was the untimely death in 1903 of Victoria Melita's daughter Elisabeth, who succumbed to typhoid while staying at the Emperor of Russia's hunting lodge in Poland. Yet it also freed Victoria Melita as it cut the last remaining links to Darmstadt.

By this time, Victoria Melita's liaison with her first cousin Grand Duke Kirill Vladimirovich was well known, although still confined to murmurs. Kirill, who served with distinction in the Russo-Japanese War, asked his cousin Nicholas II for permission to wed their mutual cousin Victoria Melita. Nicholas II, vacillating at best and spineless at his worst, gave no definitive answer, only advising caution. Tired of waiting Kirill finally married Victoria Melita at her mother's Bavarian villa at Tegernsee on 8 October 1905. Reaction from St. Petersburg was immediate and furious. Kirill was stripped of his prerogatives, blocked from accessing his money, expelled from the Imperial Navy, and exiled from Russia. The confrontation that ensued between Nicholas II and his Uncle Vladimir Alexandrovich was legendary.

Two years later, Victoria Melita, who earlier converted to Orthodoxy and adopted the name Victoria Feodorovna, gave birth to a daughter. Marie Kirillovna (1907-1951) later married her Coburg cousin, Hereditary Prince Karl of Leiningen in 1925 in Coburg. In 1909, a second daughter, Kira Kirillovna, was born. Particularly close to her cousin Ileana of Romania, at one point she was considered a possible bride for her Coburg cousin the King of Bulgaria. However, Kira went on to marry Prince Louis Ferdinand of Prussia, a great-grandson of Queen Victoria and Prince Albert.

Rapprochement with Nicholas II took place in 1910. Kirill, with his wife and daughters, returned to St. Petersburg, where he eventually acquired a small city palace. There the couple led an active social life, much in contrast with the secluded existence led by Nicholas II and Empress Alexandra Feodorovna. When war broke out in 1914, Victoria Feodorovna plunged into relief efforts, working tirelessly as a Red Cross nurse and organizing a mobilized ambulance unit known for its efficiency. Victoria Feodorovna clashed with her mother-in-law over the issue, believing that Grand Duchess Vladimir did it for selfish reasons, and instead of helping actually hindered relief work.

In 1917 as the Russian Empire collapsed, Victoria Feodorovna discovered that she was again pregnant. In the midst of the revolution Kirill swore loyalty to the Duma in an effort to restore peace, but many who had failed considered his actions treasonous in preventing Nicholas II from attempting to further plunge the Romanovs into chaos. Later that year, Kirill obtained permission to move his family to Finland and it was in the relative peace and security found there that Victoria Feodorovna delivered the long-awaited heir, Vladimir Kirillovich.

As civil war raged across Russia, the family eventually reached the safety of Coburg. Kirill and Victoria Feodorovna were at the sides of both their mothers, who died within weeks of each other in September and October 1920, returning to Coburg where they lived for several years. From Coburg Kirill published a proclamation in which he assumed Headship of the Imperial House, as by then most accepted that Nicholas II, Tsesarevich Alexei Nikolaievich and Grand Duke Michael Alexandrovich had been executed in Russia. This decision splintered the Russian monarchist community, a division that survives to this day.

In due course Kirill and Victoria Feodorovna moved to France, keeping an apartment in Paris and purchasing a villa in St. Briac-sur-Mer, Brittany. Both were very active in Russian monarchist circles, and Victoria Feodorovna even visited the United States to raise awareness of the plight faced by Russians living in exile, as well as husband's political activities. Her last years were marred by both illness and sadness. Victoria Feodorovna suffered from poor circulation and felt constantly exhausted. She also discovered that Kirill, a true Romanov to the core, had taken his vows of fidelity lightly, and never forgave him for his betrayal, which seemed to nullify all of the sacrifices and heartache she had endured to be with him. In early 1936 she suffered a stroke while visiting her daughter Marie Kirillovna, who had recently given birth to her fifth child. The family immediately flocked to her bedside, including Queen Marie. "*It makes all the difference,*" said Victoria Feodorovna when asked if her sister's presence comforted her. Grand Duchess Victoria Feodorovna of Russia died at Amorbach, Germany, on 2 March 1936. Her husband followed her to the grave in 1938, the same year he witnessed the marriage of his second daughter Kira to Prince Louis Ferdinand of Prussia.

From left: Princess Alexandra, Fürstin Alexandra and Hereditary Prince Gottfried of Hohenlohe-Langenburg, the Duke of Kent and Hereditary Princess Margarita of Hohenlohe-Langenburg.

In death, Kirill and Victoria Feodorovna rested in a side chapel inside the ducal mausoleum, Glockenberg, in Coburg, which held the coffins of her parents and brother. For decades they remained there, where visitors could come and pay their respects. That changed after the fall of the Soviet Union, when their remains were transferred to Russia and buried inside the Grand Ducal Vault next to the Cathedral of SS. Peter and Paul.

Fürstin Alexandra of Hohenlohe-Langenburg (1878-1942)

In a family of beautiful and striking daughters, Alexandra of Edinburgh was the ugly "duckling." Never as pretty as Marie, as distinguished as Victoria Melita, nor as striking as Beatrice, Alexandra passed through life wishing to be someone she was not. Alexandra was destined to lead a far less brilliant existence than her sisters. At times she seemed to resent this, and never understood how lucky she was sharing life with a man who adored her and stayed true to their marriage.

Above: Fürstin Alexandra, Grand Duke Wladimir Kirillovich, Grand Duchess Victoria Feodorovna, Grand Duke Kirill Vladimirovich and Hereditary Prince Gottfried.

Left: In back: Fürstin Alexandra, Princess Alexandra and Princess Irma. Seated: Princess Marie Melita, Hereditary Prince Gottfried and Fürst Ernst.

Below left: Fürstin Alexandra in later years.

Alexandra, known as "Sandra" to her family, was born in 1878 in her grandfather Prince Albert's birthplace, Schloß Rosenau in Coburg. The town, cradle of her dynasty, was to retain a permanent place in the princess' life. Her cousin Ernst of Hohenlohe-Langenburg, also a Coburg descendant, began pursuing Alexandra. In a letter written from Schloß Reinhardsbrunn, her mother shared the news with daughter Marie: *"But what I feared has happened: would you believe that Ernie Hohenlohe had fallen madly in love…with…Sandrichen! What do you think of it! I, who only dreaded a flirtation more on her part, was soon obliged to see very plainly, that he was getting more and more devoted to her…He was so miserable to leave, that I thought every moment he would ask to talk to me. But it seems he was far too 'bien élevé' to put in a word himself and never made any allusion of his 'attachement' to Sandra."*

Ernst did not abandon his suit, and soon had his close friend Prince Max of Baden write to Alexandra's mother, attesting to his *"honest and deep character."* Her mother tried to dissuade the lovebirds and even went as far as discussing the matter with Ernst's father, Fürst Hermann, first cousin to Alexandra's father. He relayed to Marie Alexandrovna that his son was devoted to Alexandra; having turned down a proposed marriage to Helena Victoria of Schleswig-Holstein and rejected suggestions about the Wales sisters, Ernst insisted, was proof of his son's attachment to Alexandra. The conversation ended with Alexandra's mother arguing that her daughter was *"far too young."* She also demanded time, so her daughter could mature, and hopefully find a more *"brilliant parti."*

Writing from Castle Pelesch, Marie expressed a positive opinion of Ernst to her mother: *"What a pity that he is not someone else as he is such a nice young man, not that I think Sandra would remain attached to him, if she saw someone else she is a little flirt who likes to amuse herself, but I hardly think that she looks upon those little flirtations as anything serious, though she ought to take care. But it would not be a position for her I quite agree…it is all very well as long as they are at home, but the moment they were to go anywhere, Sandra would soon notice the difference of position and who knows if she would not be disappointed."* The *"difference of position"* Marie referred to was the fact that the Hohenlohe-Langenburg, despite possessing exquisite bonds to other dynasties around the continent, was mediatized – *"a formerly ruling family who had ceded their sovereign rights to others while (in theory) retaining their equal birth."* Alexandra could marry him, but whenever protocol intervened, he would always rank behind her.

In the end, Alexandra's parents, principally her mother, relented and Ernst was allowed to propose. Queen Victoria, surprisingly, was most displeased with the news, believing that despite the accolades surrounding the young man, her granddaughter could have found a better husband – by which she really meant a richer one. Nonetheless, the wedding took place on 20 April 1896 in Coburg's Schloß Ehrenburg. Again myriad royal relations, most of them Coburg descendants, arrived to partake in the festivities, including Kaiser Wilhelm II and his wife; the Duke and Duchess of York; Crown Prince Ferdinand of Romania and Marie; Ernst Ludwig and Victoria Melita; Grand Duke Paul Alexandrovich; Max of Baden; and assorted Hohenlohes, Reuß, Leiningens, Saxe-Meiningens and Coburgs. Prince Philipp of Saxe-Coburg & Gotha and his wife Louise were also present, just as she was about to become the protagonist of the scandal that ruined their marriage. Queen Victoria, otherwise engaged, remained away.

Princess Margaret of Connaught.

The following year Alexandra gave birth to a son, Gottfried, and a daughter, Marie Melita, arrived in 1899. Three other children followed: Alexandra in 1901; Irma in 1902; and in 1911, after a long hiatus from pregnancies, Alfred, who died two days after birth. Of the Hohenlohe-Langenburg children only the two eldest married. Gottfried, after an eyebrow raising dalliance with Gloria Morgan Vanderbilt, finally settled on Princess Margarita of Greece, a granddaughter of Victoria of Battenberg, Alexandra's first cousin. Marie Melita also married another royal with Coburg connections. Her husband was Prince Wilhelm Friedrich of Schleswig-Holstein, a nephew of Empress Augusta Viktoria, as well as the only brother of Duchess Victoria Adelheid of Saxe-Coburg & Gotha.

Ernst succeeded his father as Fürst of Hohenlohe-Langenburg in 1913 and his personal finances improved considerably. He had already served as Regent of Coburg and Gotha during the minority of Duke Carl Eduard; now as head of house, he was tasked with the administration of the various landed estates that formed the family fortune. During the Great War, Alexandra worked as Red Cross nurse, while her husband supervised several relief and military posts, but never on the Western Front due to logical circumstances.

In later life, Ernst and Alexandra focused on Schloß Langenburg, their family seat. She missed the bygone days of Imperial Germany; he was consumed by the demands of keeping the family's finances afloat. As a couple, they experienced challenges, as Queen Marie suspected her sister would, but they rekindled their vows and remained together. Both Ernst and Alexandra, just as their son had done earlier, joined the Nazi Party, a blotch on otherwise exemplary lives. Alexandra saw Hitler's movement as the foundation for an eventual restoration of the monarchy. No proof

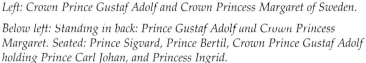

Left: Crown Prince Gustaf Adolf and Crown Princess Margaret of Sweden.

Below left: Standing in back: Prince Gustaf Adolf and Crown Princess Margaret. Seated: Prince Sigvard, Prince Bertil, Crown Prince Gustaf Adolf holding Prince Carl Johan, and Princess Ingrid.

exists, really, to accuse either spouse of anti-Semitism.

Alexandra died during the war in 1942. Ernst, who missed her dearly and retired to the privacy of his estates, survived his wife until 1950. Their descendants remain one of the leading aristocratic families of modern-day Germany.

Crown Princess Margaret of Sweden (1882-1920)

Princess Margaret of Connaught was the first child of the Duke and Duchess of Connaught. Margaret, a plump, healthy, and beautiful blue-eyed baby was born at Bagshot Park, a large residence some eleven miles from Windsor Castle that her parents called home. Queen Victoria had ceded the house to Arthur, who razed the structure and replaced it with a 120-room pile of red brick that he moved into in 1879.

Margaret, who was confirmed in 1898, grew into a beautiful young woman. Classically elegant, her dreamy look and an endearing manner made her one of the most attractive available princesses. In 1905 the Connaughts, who enjoyed a happy family life, visited Lisbon, Cadiz and Seville before continuing to Egypt and the Sudan. In Cairo, they met Prince Gustaf Adolf of Sweden, eldest son of Crown Prince Gustaf and of his wife Victoria, née Baden. The meeting had been arranged so that the prince might consider Margaret's sister Patricia as a possible bride; instead, he was drawn to Margaret. Their romance was intense: both fell deeply in love and soon enough they were engaged. Tall Gustaf Adolf was handsome and had an excellent education. He enjoyed nothing more than archeology; was a good dancer; and an even better shot. Their wedding took place in St. George's Chapel, Windsor Castle, on 15 June 1905, much to the delight of her uncle Edward VII, who wished for all his remaining nieces to marry well.

Once established in Sweden, Margaret had to contend with her mother-in-law's pro-German opinions. Victoria, whose husband became King Gustaf V in 1907, was a granddaughter of Kaiser Wilhelm I, her mother Luise being Friedrich III's only sister. Even though Margaret's own mother was a Prussian by birth, the Duchess of Connaught had become quite Anglicized after living in Great Britain for three decades. Gustaf Adolf found his wife's more relaxed and natural approach much to his liking. Margaret was a talented artist. She enjoyed photography, did lovely paintings that were sold to raise funds for various charities, and created beautiful gardens. Learning Swedish was an arduous process, but she eventually mastered the language. The longer she lived in Sweden, the more comfortable and relaxed Margaret became. She played tennis and golf in summer; in wintertime she indulged in skiing, ice-skating, and hockey.

In April 1906 Margaret gave birth to a boy, named Gustaf Adolf after his father and grandfather. The following year a second boy, Sigvard, joined the family; daughter Ingrid arrived three years later. Ingrid, to whom Margaret became very attached, went on to become the wife of King Frederik IX of Denmark and thus mother of both Queen Margrethe II and Queen Anne Marie of Greece. Two years after Ingrid's birth, Margaret gave birth to a third son, Bertil, to the great delight of her Swedish in-laws.

The outbreak of the Great War in 1914 posed family difficulties. The King's consort was pro-German, their son's wife pro-Allied. To keep family peace, and to protect the kingdom from international entanglements, Gustaf V opted to remain neutral. Margaret, who had relations fighting on both sides, *"devoted herself to maintaining an open line of communication between the warring factions, not only from her own relatives, but also from prisoners-of-war on both sides."*

In 1916 Margaret gave birth to her fifth child, and fourth son, Prince Carl Johan. Four years later, and while she was carrying her sixth child, Crown Princess Margaret died suddenly after undergoing an operation for mastoiditis. She left behind a stunned Sweden and a devastated family. Gustaf Adolf, who had to wait until 1950 to succeed his father, missed his wife dearly, as did their children. He later remarried Lady Louise Mountbatten, a close relation of his first wife. Louise tried her best to be a mother to her stepchildren, although relations with Ingrid at times were, understandably, difficult. Gustaf VI Adolf survived his first wife until 1973; Louise had predeceased him in 1965.

Princess Maria Ana of Saxony.

As for their sons, only the eldest, Gustaf Adolf, married a fellow royal, his cousin Princess Sybilla of Saxe-Coburg & Gotha. With her he had five children before dying in an air accident in 1947. Sybilla survived him for a quarter of a century and died in 1972, a year before her son Carl Gustaf became King of Sweden. Sigvard and Carl Johan renounced their succession rights to marry commoners. Bertil, who maintained a long relationship with a Welsh-born commoner, was able to marry her equally in 1976, and in Sweden she was known as Princess Lilian. Bertil and Lilian were to be like grandparents to the children of King Carl XVI Gustaf. Bertil died in 1997; Lilian followed him in 2013.

Princess Maria Ana of Saxony (1843-1884)

If the Portuguese Royal House remains little known to most English reading history enthusiasts, the daughters of Queen Maria II must seem even more obscure. Of the eleven children born during her marriage to Ferdinand, four were girls. Maria and Maria da Glória died at their births in 1840 and 1851; the other two, Maria Ana and Antónia, survived infancy and were in due time shipped off to do their duty in Germany.

Infanta Maria Ana, her mother's eldest surviving daughter, was born in Lisbon on 21 August 1843. As was the case with her brothers, Maria Ana's education was placed in the hands of tutors supervised by her father. She was a pretty blond girl, with deep blue eyes, a well-shaped mouth and a nose that evoked her

Above – Standing: Prince and Princess Johann Georg and Father Maximilian. Seated: Princess Mathilde, King Friedrich August III and Archduchess Maria Josepha of Austria.

Left: King Georg of Saxony.

Coburg ancestry. She was a dutiful daughter, a talented amateur artist, and very Portuguese. Raised a Catholic, she was not the type infatuated with religious obscurantism. She loved open spaces, the blue skies of Portugal, and the scents of her country. It was to be her great tragedy that in adulthood, all these things she so dearly loved would be lost to her.

Maria Ana's fate was decided at an early age when King Consort Ferdinand selected Prince Georg of Saxony as her future husband. Born in 1832 at Schloß Pillnitz, a beautiful riverside palace on the banks of the Elbe not far from Dresden, the kingdom's capital, Georg was the child of King Johann of Saxony and of his wife Amalie, née Bavaria. At the time of Georg's visit to Lisbon in 1858, during which he became officially engaged to Maria Ana, it was assumed that at some future date he would become King of Saxony. His older brother, Crown Prince Albert, who had married Princess Carola Vasa (from the deposed Swedish dynasty), seemed destined not to have children. Albert was delighted at the news, writing, *"You can imagine with what heartfelt joy I received the news of your happy engagement. My dearest wish is to see you perfectly happy, hopefully this is now fulfilled. Too bad, that I do not have the joy of loving a bride who is pretty to look at. I cannot imagine you in this state!"*

Georg returned to Lisbon a year later. The wedding took place at the Palace of Belém on 11 May 1859 and was attended by Maria Ana's family, among them her sister-in-law Stephanie, who would die in two months. Two weeks later, Georg and Maria Ana arrived at Schloß Moritzburg, an impressive castle owned by the Saxons that sits in the middle of an island deep in the forests outside Dresden, and in a few days made a triumphant entry into Dresden.

A little over year after her arrival in Saxony, Maria Ana, not yet seventeen-years old, gave birth to her first child, Marie Johanna. The little princess, however, was not a strong baby and she died before her first birthday. Nearly a year after losing her first child, Maria Ana gave birth to another daughter, Elisabeth, who also unfortunately died an infant. Two months before the death of her second daughter, Maria Ana gave birth a third time, to yet another daughter, Mathilde. Finally, Maria Ana gave birth to her fourth child, the long-awaited heir and future King Friedrich August III, on 25 May 1865. Another sister, Maria Josepha, was born in Dresden on 31 May 1867. Maria Josepha later married Archduke Otto of Austria, a nephew of Emperor Franz Joseph, and produced two sons, one being Austria-Hungary's last ruler, Karl I. Maria Ana's three youngest children were all sons: Johann Georg, born in 1869; Maximilian, born in 1870; and Albert, born in 1875. None of these three boys left descendants. Johann Georg, although married twice, remained childless; Maximilian became a priest; and Albert died in a traffic accident caused by, of all people, Infante Miguel of Braganza, a grandson of King Miguel, the nemesis of Maria Ana's mother.

Life in Saxony was very difficult for Maria Ana. She felt suffocated, constrained, and trapped. The Saxon Royal Family's religious fervor was much too much for a girl raised by a family that was religious but not obsessed with Catholicism. The oppression inflicted on Saxon royal ladies would later cause Maria Ana's daughter-in-law, Louise of Austria-Tuscany, to elope and consequently result in the ruin of King Friedrich August III's marriage. Maria Ana however, did not live long enough to witness such dire and sad happenings. She died of typhoid fever on 5 February 1884. Her husband survived Maria Ana twenty years, dying in October 1904. Her son was the last King of Saxony.

Fürstin Antónia of Hohenzollern.

Fürstin Antónia of Hohenzollern (1845-1913)

Much like her older sister Maria Ana, Antónia of Portugal remains shrouded in the mists of history. She was born in Lisbon on 17 February 1845, and since childhood enjoyed painting, which her father always supported. Antónia, who some had said to be among the *"great beauties of her time,"* had a Grecian profile, classic features, her hands *"long and delicate, her feet very small and useless."* She also *"somehow could not fit in with the clothes of the day, there was a disproportion between the bust and the legs…Superbly aristocratic, she moved slowly with a curious swinging of the hips. She loved fine clothes and jewels and, though leading almost an invalid's life, was very smartly dressed."*

Antónia first met her future husband when he accompanied his sister Stephanie to Portugal in 1858. Hereditary Prince Leopold of Hohenzollern, ten years her senior, cut an imposing figure in his Prussian uniform, and Antónia was smitten with the handsome soldier. However, since she was not yet a teenager, matters had to be put on hold for a few years. Finally, on 12 September 1861, Leopold and Antónia were married in Lisbon. Her brother Luís commanded the ship that took her from Portugal and it was upon his return that he learned of his succession to the throne.

Leopold was once described as *"one of the most charming princes of his day. Clever, cultivated, good-looking…the most perfect homme du monde."* Shy, modest, and unselfish, he dutifully took care of those around him, whether it was Antónia, who always suffered weak health, or his *"adorable old, and very deaf mother whom he dearly loved."* Antónia's life at Sigmaringen, the Hohenzollern family seat, was idyllic. Years later her daughter-in-law wrote: *"Sigmaringen, with its cozy little town nestling like a flock of well-fed geese beneath the shadow of the old castle, was a perfect picture of the Germany of that time; a self-sufficient, self-sufficing little place, living in happy respect of its Fürstliche Familie which was the centre, the pride, the very raison d'être of the whole country."* She displayed items including *"some beautiful old Spanish and Portuguese objects from her father, furniture, china, glass, ancient statuettes and some magnificent old silver. She had great taste and had set up her treasures to their best advantage."*

Three years after arriving in Germany, Antónia gave birth to her first child, a boy named Wilhelm; a second son, Ferdinand – future King of Romania – was born the following year. Finally, in 1868, Antónia gave birth to the family's last child, Karl Anton, at Sigmaringen. All three boys were devoted to their mother and respectful of their father. However, as one writer noted, *"Ferdinand was her favorite son, there was a great affinity of character between the two; besides, as is often the case, distance had minimized his faults and magnified his good qualities."*

Antónia had *"an interesting, if not altogether a lovable personality. She was profoundly artistic, an excellent painter, and deeply learned on certain subjects, such as botany, biology and natural history."* However, her daughter-in-law Queen Marie also thought, *"in other ways she had remained very narrow and her religion cramped instead of widening her heart, mind and sympathies…She was a curious mixture of dignity and childish futility, vain, self-centered, small in her judgment of others; she had no wider sympathies. Life, with its broader human understanding, lay outside her field of comprehension. She lived in a small circle of rules, prejudices and conventions which she considered perfection."* One wonders, however, knowing the sort of consternation that Marie's behaviors heaped on her in-laws, if her recollection of Antónia's character was more a settling of debts, than an honest description. I tend to think it was more the former than the latter. Marie, beautiful and self-centered, was not an easy human being to deal with.

In 1889, Antónia's son Wilhelm married Princess Maria Teresa of Bourbon-Two Sicilies (1867-1909), only daughter of the Count of Trani and his wife Mathilde, a sister of Empress Elisabeth of Austria and Karl Theodor, Duke in Bavaria. Wilhelm and his wife had three children, the eldest being Auguste Viktoria, the wife of King Manoel II of Portugal. Their two remaining children, who were twins, both married Coburg descendants: Friedrich married Princess Margarete of Saxony, a granddaughter of Infanta Maria Ana; while Franz Joseph married Maria Alix, Margarete's sister. After Maria Teresa's death in 1909, caused by multiple sclerosis according to several accounts, Wilhelm remarried Princess Adelgunde of Bavaria, one of the many daughters of King Ludwig III.

Fürst Leopold of Hohenzollern.

Karl Anton, who lived at Schloß Namedy, a beautiful castle and estate near the Rhine River, married his cousin Princess Joséphine of Belgium, one of the sisters of King Albert I. During the Great War, Joséphine set up a military hospital in the Hall of Mirrors at Namedy. Karl Anton died in 1919, relatively young, while his widow survived him nearly four decades, dying in 1958. By then she had joined the Benedictine order and become a nun.

Antónia became a widow in 1905. By then an invalid, she survived her husband until late December 1913. She had already suffered several strokes that left her unable to communicate. Her sons were devastated for it was *"the final breaking up of the old home."* Queen Marie, who at the time of her mother-in-law's death was visiting her own mother at Tegernsee, immediately left for Sigmaringen. In her memoirs, she recalled a funny conversation shared by Wilhelm II and the King of Saxony during the meal after the funeral, a time when, *"those not overwhelmed by grief occasionally have a tendency to expand rather too much under the comforting influence of food and drink."* The Kaiser and the King of Saxony, who typically spoke a few decibels too loud, sat next to the other at luncheon. Friedrich August III, Marie of Romania recalled, was louder than normal that afternoon, *"Spreading out his napkin with a sigh of content he leaned over towards my brother-in-law William, who was, so to say, chief mourner and exclaimed in a cheerful tone:*

'Well, William my boy, it's a good thing your church ceremony did not last any longer or your mother would not have been the only corpse!' This was an allusion to the freezing temperature of the family crypt." As if this infringement of politesse was not enough, the tipsy King turned to the Kaiser, who was headed from there to a hunt with Archduke Franz Ferdinand, and asked him what he intended to wear during his visit, plain clothes or uniform. *"The Kaiser demurred for a moment and then voted for uniform. 'Right you are!' exclaimed the cheerful guest. 'Right you are, because you look hideous in plain clothes!'"*

Princess Clémentine Napoléon (1872-1955)

She was born at Laeken Palace on 30 July 1872. Her names were Clémentine Albertine Marie Léopoldine. She was an unwated child. With the death of their only son the Duke of Brabant, the unhappily married King and Queen, desperate for an heir, had briefly resumed marital relations, hoping for a son. Much to their disappointment a third daughter, Clémentine, arrived. *"I cannot say how much I envy those children who know a mother's love,"* Clémentine once said.

Clémentine was raised in a home where father and mother detested each other, and it is remarkable – given the circumstances and the lives of her two sisters Louise of Saxe-Coburg & Gotha and Stéphanie of Austria – how well she developed. Unlike her sisters, Clémentine got along with their father and in due time, particularly after her mother left Brussels, would act in her stead. For her father's subjects, it was not uncommon to see the tall and svelte princess standing by her father's side at various engagements throughout the year. In fact, the more she witnessed her sisters' predicaments and failings, the more upstanding Clémentine became.

In due time, Léopold recognized in his daughter a level of maturity absent in her sisters, and in late 1889 granted her private apartments at Laeken. She was ecstatic, as this would give her some independence to continue with her studies, her needlework, as well as playing ballads on her piano without distractions. In wintertime she enjoyed skating, and Clémentine, much like her mother, loved riding for hours. Sadly, this joyful independence was short-lived for a violent fire consumed the left wing of the palace and in the conflagration Clémentine's governess lost her life. The princess was brokenhearted since her closest confidantes had been those ladies who tended to her.

Clémentine, Princess Napoléon.

Interestingly, Clémentine first met her husband in 1888 when Prince Victor Napoléon paid a visit to the Belgian Royal Family. Born at the Palais Royale in Paris in 1862, he was the eldest of Prince Napoléon Joseph, better known as Plon-Plon, and of his long-suffering wife, Princess Clotilde of Savoy. At the time of his birth, Victor was third-in-line to the imperial throne, behind the Prince Imperial and his father. Since Napoléon III's son died in 1879 and his will by-passed Plon-Plon, Victor then became the Head of the Imperial House. His father, livid with the situation, essentially cut off contact with his son. Nevertheless, in 1886 both were exiled from France by the same law that banned the Count of Paris and his eldest son.

By then, King Léopold II was actively preparing his nephew Baudouin for his future obligations as king. Clémentine, three years her cousin's junior, had always been very fond of the dutiful prince. *"Every time that I see him,"* she wrote to Stéphanie, *"I love him a little more; he is very handsome."* Her father, upon hearing the news, was hopeful that at least through a daughter his bloodline would continue on the throne. Unfortunately, Baudouin died during an influenza epidemic in 1891 and Clémentine was deeply touched by the loss of her first love. Again, to her sister Stéphanie, she wrote: *"How can I express the sorrow my heart feels and that overwhelms me when I think that I will never again hear his lovely voice, that I will never see his*

Above: Prince Napoléon, Princess Marie-Clotilde and Princess Clémentine.
Below: Princess Clémentine and her son, Prince Louis Napoléon.

seductive smile, no it's impossible...I will go mad. I suffer cruelly, more so than I can say."

Given the disastrous marriages of Louise and Stéphanie, Léopold II did not try to push Clémentine into a dynastic alliance. Finding a husband, as it turned out, was left up to her, and she enjoyed more marital freedom than her sisters. This became a problem when Clémentine developed feelings for Baron August Goffinet, one of the King's aides-de-camp. *"This is a choice unfit for a princess,"* was her father's reaction, who refused to consider any such marriage.

Victor Napoléon, despite rumored liaisons with other women, remained hopeful that his interest in Clémentine would be reciprocated. Although not particularly wealthy, he stood to inherit part of Empress Eugénie's fortune. Gossips accused the prince of being interested in Clémentine solely for her wealth, since after all she stood to receive considerable settlements from her parents and her old Aunt Charlotte, still mad but locked inside the lonely halls of Bouchout. When Clémentine brought up Victor's name to her father, the King categorically rejected the idea, telling her, *"Royal princesses are unlike other women. They can only love their country, just as nuns only love God."*

Still, Clémentine did not completely give up on marrying Victor. By then in her early thirties, she convinced her father to grant her a home, Château de Belvédère, inside the Laeken Palace complex. There at least, she had peace of mind and she would not have to see her father's mistress. Also, after her mother's death in 1902, Clémentine became the kingdom's *"unofficial queen,"* as protocol demanded.

On Léopold II's death in 1909, Clémentine was free to marry Victor, as her cousin King Albert would not impede the union. The couple's wedding took place on 14 November 1910, at Moncalieri Castle outside Torino, where Victor's mother resided. The groom was then forty-eight, the bride ten years younger; she was a great-granddaughter of King Louis-Philippe, the groom a cousin of Emperor Napoléon III, and their marriage united the bloodlines of France's two last monarchs. A journalist who witnessed the wedding in Moncalieri reported that, *"Public rejoicing marked the occasion. The streets were decorated profusely, bands played in the squares, and flags waved from the castle...All members of the Savoy and Bonaparte families were present, including Prince Louis Napoléon, the younger brother of the Pretender, who for some time had not been on good terms with the bridegroom, but who agreed to a reconciliation on this occasion, chiefly through the efforts of his mother."* Other royals attending the wedding included the Duke of Aosta, the Prince de Ligne (representing King Albert) and Archduke Friedrich of Austria.

On 20 March 1912, Clémentine gave birth to a daughter, Marie Clotilde, and in January 1914 the long-awaited heir, Louis Jérôme Victor Emmanuel Léopold Marie, arrived. Both of Clémentine's children were born in Brussels, where the couple settled after their wedding. As Victor could not enter France, Belgium became their permanent home.

Clémentine sued the Belgian government in an effort to share in her father's huge fortune. A rascal to the end, the King had disinherited his three daughters, while leaving most his money to his second wife and to a foundation he created to hide his fortune. After several lawsuits and intense negotiations, Clémentine accepted an offer from the Belgian government.

During the Great War, Victor volunteered to serve in the French Army, but his offer was rejected due to the law of exile. Clémentine had hoped to remain in Brussels during the conflict, but that ceased to be an option when Germans poured over the border. Instead, the Napoléons left for England, where they remained during the war. Clémentine, who enjoyed close relations with King Albert and Queen Elisabeth, kept an eye over their children on their arrival in England. During her exile there, Clémentine became involved in countless charities to aid fellow Belgians affected by the war. In recognition, Clémentine was asked in 1920 to inaugurate the monument Belgium built in London to thank the English for their hospitality during the war.

Once back in Belgium, Victor and Clémentine settled at the Château de Ronchinne, near Namur. His health was giving concern, while in the countryside she could engage in one of her favorite pastimes, gardening. When in 1920 Empress Eugénie died, she left a colossal fortune estimated at $10 million (at the time). Both Victor and his son Louis were in her will, as was Princess Marie Clotilde, Eugénie's godchild. Victor's sister, the Dowager Duchess of Aosta also received a portion of the estate, as did the Fitzjames descendants of her sister: the Duke of Alba and Berwick; the Duke of Peñaranda; and their sister, the Duchess of Galisteo and Tamames.

Princess Clémentine Napoléon.

Sadly, Victor Napoléon died suddenly in 1926. Clémentine's joyful marriage had lasted not even fourteen years. She had once said: *"My husband is good, gentle, adorable, loving, intelligent, fine connoisseur of people and things. He is very handsome, good-looking, good manners, and has interesting conversations. Napoléon is my love, I adore him, and my days are spent looking for things to please him. As to evenings…they are exquisite, and I did not believe IT could be so good."*

Although Clémentine missed her husband profoundly, she dedicated herself to the children. Marie Clotilde gave her much trouble, and Clémentine was not particularly thrilled when she married an obscure Russian by the name of Count Serge de Witt. She would have preferred a better "parti" – but times were changing. As for Louis, he was his mother's pride and joy, attending school in England and showering her with satisfactions. Louis grew to become a giant towering at 6'4". In 1940, he volunteered to fight for France under an assumed name, since the law of exile was still in effect. His war service earned Louis the Légion d'honneur, the prestigious decoration created by Emperor Napoléon. De Gaulle later said that, *"Prince Napoléon, himself, abrogated the law of exile."* This was a testament to the prince's heroism. In 1949, Louis, Prince Napoléon, married Alix de Foresta, a French aristocrat. They had four children. Their grandson Jean-Christophe, who carries the bloodline of Coburg, is the present Head of the Imperial House of France.

Princess Clémentine died in Nice on 8 March 1955. Her remains were later transferred to the Imperial Chapel in Ajaccio, Corsica, the island that gave Napoléon to Europe, and the world.

Queen Marie José of Italy (1906-2001)

As a child, Marie José's father lovingly called her *"la petite"* – the little one. *"He rejoiced seeing her frolic, grow, loved to hear her laughter,"* one author wrote. Marie José corresponded this devotion and adored her father, whom she *"loved best when he wears his uniforms. I loved playing with his epaulettes…"*

During the Great War, Marie José accompanied her siblings to exile in England, where she was a pupil at the Brentwood Ursuline Convent High School. During this time, she also stayed with Lord Curzon, whose three daughters provided Marie José with company during her lonely days away from home and her family. Queen Elisabeth visited the children whenever demands on her time permitted, while the princes and princess were able to spend vacations in the little corner of Belgium left under their father's control. When in La Panne, Marie José oftentimes went along with her mother on hospital visits. There, the young girl was confronted with the brutality of war when *"the screams coming from the wounded when their dressings were changed, impressed me horribly."*

In 1917 Marie José was sent to a school in Firenze. She later recalled that while there she heard that her mother had lost a baby: *"I was simply told that my mother was ill, because in spite of my eleven years, I still believed that children were born out of cabbages,"* she later recalled. Albert and Elisabeth wanted Marie José to learn Italian, as this would make their future plans much easier to achieve. *"From my childhood, I was raised with the idea that one day I would marry Umberto, the heir to the Italian throne. This knowledge made me fantasize about life as a fairytale. My mother simply encouraged it. She spoke about Prince Charming, describing him in attractive ways, making me feel he was the incarnation of perfection. The Italian sovereigns, on their part, also wanted this union."*

The Prince and Princess of Piedmont.

Marie José later remembered that during her Italian stay, she was invited to visit the Italian Royal Family. Much to her surprise, upon arriving at the palace, she discovered that her parents were there as well. Both families then visited Venice, where Marie José reminded everyone of her penchant for mischief. She brought as a small snack, a mandarin and some nuts, and hid them in her garters. Unfortunately, visiting St Mark's Cathedral, mandarin and nuts fell out and rolled on the tiled floor. Although Umberto laughed hilariously, Queen Elisabeth was not as amused.

Umberto, Prince of Piedmont, heir to the Italian throne, was born in 1904 at Racconigi Palace, an estate owned by the Savoy dynasty in the province of Cuneo. They had acquired it in the Sixteenth Century and in 1630 Duke Carlo Emanuele I granted it to his nephew the Prince of Carignano, from whom the present Savoy dynasty descends. The Savoys were one of Europe's oldest dynasties, going back to the year 1000. They traced their lineage to one Umberto Biancamano, Count of Aosta, an early ally of Emperor Konrad II; Aosta's second son, Oddone, brought the family considerable wealth and power through his marriage to Adelaide, heiress of Torino, whose vast properties in the region gave the family a seat in "Italy." Through countless dynastic alliances, the Savoy power grew and the family gained continental prestige; for nearly seventy years, they had ruled a unified Italy.

King Vittorio Emanuele III also had four daughters, two older, two younger than Umberto. As the only son of the King of Italy, a monarchy in which only males could ascend the throne, Umberto was raised with great self-perception that at times he deployed to excuse his deeply self-indulgent and egotistical character. Hedonistic, artistic, and sensual (to both sexes), Umberto went about life in true Italian fashion, without a care in life. *"Que sera, sera,"* seemed to be his motto, as long as there was always enjoyment little accountability. Yet he showed no disregard for his position; to the Italian people he was the personification of royalty, always exquisitely dressed, debonair, caring, and cosmopolitan.

Once reestablished in Belgium after the war, Marie José was sent to a boarding school run by the Sisters of the Sacred Heart in Linthout. It was a strict environment specifically designed to teach pupils discipline and self-reliance. Marie José later remembered having enjoyed her time there and the company of other young women – something missing with her two brothers at the palace. A newspaper described her as having a *"certain natural haughtiness that becomes her tall figure and anything but delicate build."* Vivacity and liveliness, as well as her penchant for pranks, distinguished her from her siblings. *"She is very tall,"* reported one newspaper. *"She has luxurious dark hair, cut short…[she is] regal, rather and appealing and elusive. She is a person, in addition to being a princess."* She also possessed great intellectual appeal, vast imagination, and *"a strong sense of the dramatic."* Marie José was a passionate and talented musician with a deep interest in the plight of the poor and unfortunate, for she *"approaches human misery like a true queen, offering a hand that is skilled in giving comfort."*

In October 1929 the engagement of Umberto and Marie José was finally announced. That same day, while in Brussels where he was placing a floral arrangement at the Tomb of the Unknown Soldier, an antifascist protester fired at Umberto. The bullet missed the Italian Crown Prince, but the attempt on his life provided an inkling of how many Belgians felt about their princess marrying a Savoy, the dynasty that tolerated, if not outright supported, Mussolini's fascists.

Marie José married Umberto, Prince of Piedmont, on 9 January 1930 in Rome. A galaxy of royalties witnessed the wedding. In addition to the Savoy and Belgian dynasties, nearly one hundred members of the Gotha were present, including King Boris III of Bulgaria, King Manoel II of Portugal, Queen Sophie of Greece, Prince Kyril and Princess Eudoxia of Bulgaria, Infante Fernando of Spain, Prince Paul and Princess Olga of Yugoslavia, the Duke of York, as well as members of the Greek, Scandinavian, Romanov and French dynasties, and several representatives of German former ruling dynasties.

The Princess of Piedmont's return from Abyssinia in 1936. While there, she performed nursing duties at various military hospitals.

The wedding was a grand affair, with the ladies all wearing *"court dresses of pale, pastel colors, with long cloaks falling from their shoulders to form trains trailing on the ground and veils of exquisite lace on their heads and extending to their feet and diadems with brilliant jewels on their heads."* Not to be outdone, *"princes, diplomats and officials at the wedding wore the uniforms of their office and rank. The brilliant colors of their tunics a background for flashing medals and decorations."* During the ceremony, when asked if he wanted to marry his bride, Umberto, *"after turning to indicate a formal request for consent of the King and Queen of Italy, which was given with a nod of the head, replied in a firm, clear voice: 'Yes!' When the Cardinal officiating the wedding asked Marie José the same question, she gave a resounding, 'Yes,' forgetting to turn until afterward to ask her parents' consent."*

The streets of Rome were choked with well-wishers, and the wedding procession took a long time to reach the Quirinal Palace, home of King Vittorio Emanuele III and Queen Elena. Once inside, Umberto and Marie José *"appeared on the balcony over the main entrance of the Quirinal Palace, where they received a tremendous ovation from the enormous crowd that had gathered in the piazza below. They were greeted with such great enthusiasm that they were obliged to appear on the balcony again and again as the crowd never seemed to tire of feasting its eyes upon them and called them back with loud shouts every time they disappeared into the palace."* Marie José, with her usual frankness, years later described her wedding day as *"a scene out of Hollywood!"*

Life with Umberto was no bed of roses for the Belgian princess, pas du tout. On returning from their honeymoon, during which a large number of his friends had joined them, Marie José soon discovered that her husband, far from renouncing the pleasures and temptations indulged during his bachelor years, continued to enjoy them. The unsavory scenes eventually led Marie José to find peace in turning a blind eye to her husband's dalliances.

Another point of contention was their position vis-à-vis Mussolini and the fascists. Umberto, conscious of what was expected of him, avoided political entanglements and remained neutral. Marie José, far less tactful, never concealed her feelings when it came to the dictator and his 'sicarii' – she despised them. Once when the fascists banned women from wearing pants, Marie José lost little time in breaking the law.

Standing, from left: King Umberto II, Princess Maria Gabriella, Princess Maria Pia and the Prince of Naples. Seated: Princess Maria Beatrice and Queen Marie José.

Marie José was friendly with her husband's cousins Amedeo and Aimone, Dukes of Aosta and Spoleto, and gossips later insinuated something unsavory about her friendship with the Aosta branch of the Savoy dynasty. Some even argued that Amadeo, Duke of Aosta, fathered some of her children. The charges were nonsense, but Mussolini's son later said he had letters in his possession proving his father and the Princess of Piedmont had been intimate. He never produced a shred of evidence to support his outrageous claim.

It is true, however, that within a few years of marriage Marie José and Umberto were already leading separate lives. They usually took separate holidays, with Umberto disappearing to seek out the most enjoyment possible while Marie José often traveled to Belgium to visit her parents. In February 1934 she traveled to Brussels on her beloved father's death and there learned that she was expecting. On 24 September, Marie José delivered a baby daughter, Maria Pia, in Naples, where her husband was stationed. Everyone was delighted for it meant that Umberto and his wife could in fact produce children. No one realized how the baby came to be. The Neapolitan gynecologist, during an unfortunate university lecture, *"revealed the royal secret...his experiments with artificial insemination."* The poor man was summarily dismissed from service at the palace, *"which did not harm his reputation, nor help the prince's."* Three years later, a second child arrived using the same method. This time it was a boy, named Vittorio Emanuele in honor of his grandfather the King. Parenthood seemed to settle some of Umberto's restless character, and he devoted more time and attention to his wife and their children. Before Princess Maria Gabriella, their third child was born in 1940, Marie José confided to Count Galeazzo Ciano, Mussolini's son-in-law, that the baby to come was conceived *"without the intervention of physicians and syringes."* The couple's last child was a third daughter, Maria Beatrice, born in Rome in February 1943.

The Second World War plunged Italy into the conflict. The Italians had always hoped that Germany would actually do all the fighting, but Mussolini harbored imperial dreams over the Balkan region. Marie José worried that, yet again, Germany was planning to invade and obliterate Belgium, and used her friendship with Count Ciano to secure promises that she would be warned in advance. True to his word, Ciano confided the plan to attack Belgium and she immediately conveyed the news to her brother at Laeken.

By 1940, Marie José and Queen Elena were fully invested in the war effort. They donned nurse's uniform and went to work helping in various hospitals. In her work Elena found a Jewish doctor who helped her, she protected him from Nazi persecution and was responsible for saving his life and that of his family.

In 1943 the war began turning against the Axis Powers, particularly once Allied troops landed on the beaches of Sicily. Vittorio Emanuele III had already begun planning Mussolini's ouster and the Allied landing only accelerated the outcome. Marie José was also working, surreptitiously, against Mussolini. She had been *"facilitating seditious contacts among liberals of pre-Fascist times,"* and the last pre-Mussolini Prime Minister. When the King discovered Marie José's activities, he was furious, banishing her to the royal estate in Val d'Aosta. *"I made her understand clearly,"* he said, *"that in the House of Savoy women must absolutely never enter into affairs of State."* Marie José, accompanied by her children, left Rome. In Val d'Aosta she was relieved to be near the Swiss border, just in case a quick escape to a neutral country needed to be arranged. Her daughter, Princess Maria Gabriella recalled: *"She was an independent woman against Fascism, she saw the disaster, tried to help but they would not let her. The war years were terrible."*

With the situation crumbling by the hour, Vittorio Emanuele III summoned Mussolini to a meeting, during which he dismissed the dictator, who was arrested as soon as he left the audience. Italy, and the Savoys, was free of Mussolini, yet their support for the Fascists and their decision to plunge the country into war had damaged the monarchy. On 8 September 1943, the King publicly announced an armistice with the Allies. The army was not informed in advance and chaos ensued. The King and his government took refuge in Brindisi, but German retaliation was swift and brutal. Among its victims was Marie José's sister-in-law Princess Mafalda of Hesse, who was trapped by Nazi agents, transported to Germany and after interrogation imprisoned in Buchenwald, where she suffered great privations. In 1944 the Allies bombed the concentration camp and she suffered severe burns to her arms, which had to be amputated. Infection and loss of blood caused her death in the night of 26-27 July 1944. Her family did not learn Mafalda's fate until after the end of the war.

King Umberto II and Queen Marie José. Behind them are their son-in-law Prince Alexander of Yugoslavia, Princess Maria Pia and the Prince of Naples.

That same year, realizing that he was compromised, Vittorio Emanuele III transferred all his prerogatives to his son Umberto, who as Lieutenant General of the Realm was then tasked with the arduous labor of restoring the tattered image of the monarchy. At the beginning, it was not uncommon for him to hear catcalls, while feeling about to be assaulted by the countless Italians who blamed his father for Mussolini's rise to power. Yet Umberto persevered and by 1946 he had managed to regain the support of millions of Italians. In an effort to lend support to Umberto, his father abdicated on 9 May 1946, a month before a scheduled plebiscite to decide on Italy's future form of government, monarchy or republic. It was too late.

Umberto II and Marie José were monarchs for a month. They tried their best to secure, through good deeds, a different outcome. Sadly, the monarchy lost the plebiscite, held on 2 June. A few days later, the republic was proclaimed and nearly a millennium of Savoy rule came to an end. The King's last words to Italians before departing for exile were: *"Italians...I believe it is my duty to do all I can to spare the people, who have already suffered greatly, further pain and tears...Not wanting to oppose force to the abuse of power, nor render myself an accomplice to the illegality committed by the Government, I take leave of my country's soil...Performing this sacrifice in the supreme interests of the Fatherland, I feel it my duty as an Italian, and as King, to raise my protest against this violent act...With my heart filled with pain, but with my conscience serene in having made every effort to fulfill my duty, I leave the Fatherland. The oath of obedience to the king may be considered dissolved..."*

King Umberto II and Queen Marie José.

In exile, Umberto II settled in Cascais, where his French and Spanish cousins, among others, had found solace. He eventually purchased a large home and called it 'Villa Italia' – it faces the Atlantic and has marvelous views. The first years were financially challenging as Umberto had no fortune outside of Italy and his father's estate took years to settle. Once in exile, however, it was no longer necessary for Marie José to remain with her husband. She left Cascais and traveled to Switzerland to visit her brother Léopold III.

In 1947, Marie José experienced serious health problems that nearly caused her death. Her eyesight, however, was permanently damaged and she felt the sun of Portugal was simply too much for her. She left Umberto II for good and in Switzerland bought a large home in the locality of Merlinge. Along with her came their son Vittorio Emanuele, while the couple's three daughters remained in Cascais under Umberto II's supervision.

The marital difficulties, not to mention the separation, affected the children deeply. In 1955 Maria Pia married Prince Alexander of Yugoslavia. During the couple's marriage, 'Pia' gave birth to two sets of twins. However, by the time the second twins arrived, the marriage was already foundering. The younger children had an uncanny resemblance to Prince Michel of Bourbon-Parma, one of the couple's close friends and neighbors; Alexander certainly seized on the issue, moving out of the family home and years later informing his father-in-law that he was divorcing his wife as her relationship with Michel was vox populi. *"Savoys do not divorce,"* replied the King. *"Karageorgevichs do,"* insisted Alexander. "Pia," a rather nice lady, simply married too young. Her relationship with Michel has lasted nearly six decades and they finally married in 2003. In 1966 he had separated from his wife, Princess Yolande de Broglie, but she took thirty-three years to grant him a divorce. Alexander and his second wife, Barbara of Liechtenstein, remain friendly with Michel and "Pia," able to ignore the unsavory past.

Vittorio Emanuele, Prince of Naples, had a difficult relationship with his father and his sisters. When he fell in love with a Swiss lady named Marina Doria, who was two-years his senior, Umberto II categorically rejected any idea of marriage. The couple married civilly in Las Vegas in January 1970, and in October of the following year there was a religious ceremony in Tehran, of all places, where the Shah gave them his protection. They had one son, Emanuele Filiberto, Prince of Venice, whose escapades became the fodder of Italy's press. In 2003 he married Clotilde Courau, a French actress several years his senior. As they have only two daughters, and the Italian throne precluded female succession, a growing number of monarchists are shifting their support to the Dukes of Aosta, who do have a male heir.

King Umberto II did not approve Princess Maria Gabriella's marriage to a wealthy businessman. For years, she was rumored to have been the love interest of the Prince of Asturias; however, her Coburg bloodline cousin Sophie of Greece won the hand of the man now reigning as King Juan Carlos I. Maria Gabriella, an erudite and deeply cultured lady, is – like her mother – an expert in the history of the Savoy dynasty. She had one child with her husband, Robert de Balkany.

Princess Maria Beatrice gave her parents great worry. After many years of unbalanced living, in 1970 she married Luis Reyna Corvalán, an Argentine diplomat, and had two children, Raffaelo and Azaea. The family settled in Cuernavaca, Mexico. All seemed to go well until April 1994, when Raffaelo plunged from the seventh-floor window of his apartment at Boston University. It has never been established if this was accident or suicide. The loss of their son was a devastating blow, and Maria Beatrice and Luis separated, and she began spending longer periods in Florida and Switzerland. Then, and as if they had not suffered enough, Luis Reyna was found dead in his bathroom. The scene was shocking, and several men, among them his chauffeur, were arrested and accused of the bizarre crime.

King Umberto II did not live long enough to witness these tragedies, which would certainly have accelerated his end. His last days were plagued with loneliness and cancer before his death in Geneva in March 1983.

In 1988, after four decades of living abroad, Queen Marie José was allowed to set foot in her husband's former kingdom. Her poor eyesight did not impair her erudite work on the history of the Savoy dynasty. She wrote several books on the Savoys, as well as a fascinating memoir of her parents. At one point, she left Switzerland and settled in Cuernavaca, where her youngest daughter resided, and the climate and relaxed way of life seemed to improve her health. However, old age compelled her to return to Switzerland, and she died in Geneva in January 2001. Both Umberto II and Marie José rest in the Savoy crypt in Hautecombe, France.

Several years ago, I asked Prince Dimitri of Yugoslavia to reminisce about his Italian grandparents. *"Do you think people care,"* he asked me in his New York office. *"Of course they do,"* I replied. *"Well, in that case,"* he said, *"give me a few days and I will write a small tribute to these two most peculiarly fascinating people."*

Prince Dimitri of Yugoslavia recalls:

"My grandmother was wonderfully eccentric and funny. She lived in her own world and was always so vague. She looked at me once and very sweetly introduced herself as Aunt Marie Jose!!! I, of course, burst out laughing and told her 'No, you are my grandmother!' 'Oh,' she replied, 'then you are the son of...?' And I replied, 'PIA!' 'HAAAAA, yes of course,' she then said, and we ended up roaring with laughter as she announced that she thought she was a little gaga!

"Nobody made me laugh more than her; she just had the funniest sense of humor. I loved going to visit her; she was so soft, cozy and kind, always surrounded by interesting people. The most delightful powdery scent floated around her.

Queen Marie José and the Prince of Naples.

"As a child I loved the piano and she used to teach me how to play. She herself was an accomplished concert pianist and it was a delight to listen to her. Her conversation was fascinating, she knew everything about music and knew all the great musicians, she always had the latest books on everything, always told us stories about her life...such as her trip to Libya and Morocco in the 1930s, her visit to Israel, then to China with her mother in the 1960s, as well as the USSR.

"She also always told us how she loathed Mussolini, how frightening it had been to meet Hitler, an experience that she remembered with horror to the end of her life!

"She was very energetic and used to go out for long walks with or without us. As a way to exercise she used to saw big logs of wood at the end of her garden! She adored her grand children; we could storm into her room screaming at any time and she would just burst out laughing when we did that. It was always very sad to leave that enchanted place. I always admired her profile and her hands and especially that majestic allure she had that was so natural and unassuming. The funny thing was that with all that she was always dressed like a 'bag' lady, which was the cause of endless giggles.
"Her house was equally as untidy, with piles and piles of books and music scores everywhere, knick-knacks of all sorts cohabitated with the precious silver frames and antique bibelots, hordes of ugly dogs running around, and

destroying something. She always had these strange looking mutts that she adopted from the local dog shelter…she always used to say that she 'much preferred animals to humans.'"

"We, the brothers, always kissed her hand; my mother, my aunts and my sister always curtsied very deeply, after kissing her hello and goodbye – She was a queen to the end! My grandfather, on the other hand, was the opposite of my grandmother, very precise, very organized. He was extremely spiritual and one of the most erudite men in the world and it was very impressive to listen to him. We loved going to stay with him in Portugal; he was very kind to us and always made sure we were happy and had something fun or interesting to do.

"We always stood up in his presence until given permission to sit and always bowed at him when saying hello or goodbye. We loved him dearly because he was so attentive to us and so generous too. He was like that with everyone and everyone adored him. He was kindness, simplicity and dignity personified. He too had a wonderful sense of humor. I was always impressed by his ability to make everyone feel comfortable in his presence. It was very sad for us to see all the horrible petty things the Italian government did to him. I am convinced that he would have been one of the greatest kings of European history. He really embodied all the great qualities you expect from a king!"

The baptism of Princess Joséphine-Charlotte of Belgium, 27 October 1927. From left: Princess Margaretha of Denmark, Princess Ingeborg of Sweden, Princess Märtha of Sweden, Prince Axel of Denmark, Prince Carl of Sweden, the Duke and Duchess of Brabant, Princess Joséphine-Charlotte and her nurse.

Grand Duchess Joséphine-Charlotte of Luxembourg (1927-2005)

H.R.H. Princess Joséphine-Charlotte Ingeborg Elisabeth Marie-Jose Marguerite Astrid of Belgium was born at Stuyvenberg Palace on 11 October. Stuyvenberg Palace, which is situated one mile from Laeken Palace, was at the time her parents' residence. The infant Princess was baptized at the Church of St. Jacques-sur-Coudenberg. Her godmother was Grand Duchess Charlotte of Luxembourg (her future mother-in-law), while her godfather was her uncle Prince Charles-Théodore, Count of Flanders.

The Princess spent her early childhood at Stuyvenberg, enlivened by long holidays in Sweden at the home of her maternal grandparents Prince Carl and Princess Ingeborg of Sweden. The Princess studied at first with a governess then joined a class with several companions (the class took place on the second floor of the Royal Palace in Brussels, to which the Princess and her fellow students traveled every day). The Princess spent several periods of time at Noordwijk in the Netherlands to perfect her knowledge of Flemish.

Between 1935 and 1940 the Princess accompanied her father King Léopold on several occasions to official events and presided over numerous patriotic and charitable ceremonies. The loss of her mother always weighed heavily on Joséphine-Charlotte, who was almost eight-years old at the time of Queen Astrid's death.

In May 1940, following the invasion of Belgium by German troops, the Princess and her brothers left

Belgium by road, taking refuge first in Normandy and then, due to the unstoppable German advance, at the Château de Montal in Lot, placed at the family's disposal by the French Government. In June 1940 the Princess and her brothers went on to Spain, remaining until their August return to their father at Laeken Palace. At the end of 1940 the Princess entered a boarding school, "de la Vierge Fidele," in Brussels, and in 1942 she continued her studies at Laeken under the care of private tutors.

Much like her siblings, Joséphine-Charlotte enjoyed a close relationship with her father; her relationship with Princess Lilian, however, was strained. While Baudouin and Albert were too young to remember their mother, that was not the case with Joséphine-Charlotte, who at times saw Lilian as an usurper. Eventually matters improved between them.

On 7 June 1944, following the D-Day landings in Normandy, members of the Waffen SS escorted the King, Princess Joséphine-Charlotte, and other members of the Royal Family to Germany. Here, they were imprisoned in Schloß Hirschstein on the banks of the River Elbe until the end of winter 1944. At this time the whole Belgian Royal Family was transported to Strobl in Austria, where the captives passed two distressing months in a little villa on Lake Wolfgang, again surrounded by fences and under SS surveillance. Captivity ended suddenly when on 7 May 1945 a detachment of the American 7th Army, commanded by General Patch, liberated King Léopold III.

Because of political difficulties the Royal Family remained for some time at St. Wolfgang, where the American Army put a villa at their disposal. In October 1945 they moved to "Villa du Reposoir" at Prégny near Geneva. Princess Joséphine-Charlotte continued her private studies before enrolling at the "Ecole Supérieur de Jeunes Filles" in Geneva, where she later also attended university lectures, developing an interest in child psychology and social problems. While at Prégny, Léopold III received a visit from the Grand Ducal Family of Luxembourg, accompanied by Hereditary Grand Duke Jean. He told Joséphine-Charlotte captivating stories about his experiences in the war, *"the escape to Portugal, exile in the United States, his studies in Canada, his service in the Irish Guards, as well as his triumphant entry into Brussels with the Allied armies."* Both families hoped that the pair would find in the other shared interests that would lead to marriage, and there were further visits to the Luxembourgs, in the grand duchy or sometimes in Italy, where Prince Félix of Luxembourg owned an estate.

The Hereditary Grand Dukes of Luxembourg.

In April 1949 Joséphine-Charlotte returned to Belgium for the first time since the deportation in June 1944. She started the journey from Fischbach in Luxembourg, where she had been the guest of the Grand Ducal Family. She only stayed for a few days in Belgium, receiving an enthusiastic welcome that encouraged her father to make his own eventual return. Once her father and brothers were back in Brussels, Joséphine-Charlotte spent more time in the capital, fulfilling many official engagements and taking an interest in social and artistic fields.

Hereditary Grand Duke Jean of Luxembourg was a frequent visitor. A strapping young man whose moustache made him look much older, he had an excellent education, spoke several languages, and was destined to inherit the grand duchy, along with his family's considerable fortune. He also had close family ties to Joséphine-Charlotte. Her grandmother Queen Elisabeth was a first cousin of both Prince Félix and Grand Duchess Charlotte, all three being children of daughters of King Miguel of Portugal. Furthermore, an alliance between both dynasties, it was thought,

A group photo taken at the wedding of Hereditary Grand Duke Jean of Luxembourg and Princess Joséphine-Charlotte of Belgium. From left; Archduke Otto of Austria, unknown, Count Knud Holstein Ledreborg, King Baudouin and King Léopold III of the Belgians, Prince Alexandre of Belgium, Princess Astrid of Norway, the Princess de Réthy, Prince Félix of Luxembourg, Princess Maria Pia of Savoy, Princess Ingeborg of Sweden, Prince Michael of Bourbon-Parma, Grand Duchess Charlotte of Luxembourg, Queen Marie José of Italy, Princess Maria Teresa of Bourbon-Parma, the Duchess of Braganza, the Prince of Naples and Prince Charles of Luxembourg.

would serve the "economic and financial life within the Belgo-Luxembourg Economic Union." Although the families wanted the couple to marry willingly, it was purely and simply a dynastic alliance. Luckily Joséphine-Charlotte and Jean were fond of each other, and as years passed their bonds only became stronger.

The wedding of Hereditary Grand Duke Jean and Princess Joséphine-Charlotte was celebrated in Luxembourg on 9 April 1953. The civil ceremony took place in the "Salle des Fêtes" of the Grand Ducal Palace, and was immediately followed by a religious ceremony in the majestic Nôtre Dame Cathedral. The previous evening Grand Duchess Charlotte and Prince Félix gave a gala dinner at the Palace, attended by members of both families, royal guests from all over Europe, officials from the Belgian and Luxembourg Governments, and members of the Diplomatic Corps.

The Hereditary Grand Duchess gave birth to her first child in 1954, a daughter baptized Marie Astrid. One year later a son and heir, Prince Henri, was born. Twins Margaretha and Jean were born in 1957, while Guillaume, the couple's last child, arrived in 1963. In addition to bringing up a young family, the Hereditary Grand Duchess undertook many public engagements, particularly those of a social and cultural nature.

In November 1964 Grand Duchess Charlotte abdicated in favor of her son Jean, and the new Grand Duke and Grand Duchess eventually moved into the Sovereign's official residence, the Château de Berg. As Grand Duchess, Joséphine-Charlotte carried out many official duties and accompanied the Grand Duke on State Visits abroad. Interested in family and health issues, she served as President of the Luxembourg Youth Red Cross from 1959 until 1970, and from 1964 on was President of the Luxembourg Red Cross. The Grand Duchess's favorite leisure occupations were gardening and horticulture, though she also liked hunting, fishing, skiing, and water sports.

After the abdication of Grand Duke Jean in favor of his eldest son Henri in October 2000, Grand Duke Jean and Grand Duchess Joséphine-Charlotte retired to the Château de Fischbach. The Grand Duchess was diagnosed

Clockwise: Grand Duke Jean of Luxembourg, Princess Alix Napoléon, the Prince of Liège, Grand Duchess Joséphine-Charlotte of Luxembourg, Prince Louis Napoléon and the Princess of Liège. Prince Louis Napoléon remained close to his Belgian cousins and it was not uncommon to see him attending royal events in Brussels and Luxembourg.

with cancer in 2003, but despite her illness was able to make a valuable and amusing contribution to a Danish-produced documentary film on the descendants of King Christian IX. One of the funniest memories she shared was that of an elderly Prince George of Greece pulling his teeth out and using them to get shrieks out of the children during family gatherings. She passed away peacefully at Fischbach on 10 January 2005.

Those who knew her remember the late Grand Duchess Joséphine-Charlotte, known as Jo to her friends, very kindly. One princess, who attended the state funeral on 15 January, described her as *"simply wonderful, such an amusing person…a great shot and such a true friend. When I suffered the same illness that took her, she always kept in touch with me, came to see us here at home. Whenever in our city, Jo always called and we had marvelous dinners incognito, she was one of our dear friends."*

The funeral service for Grand Duchess Joséphine-Charlotte of Luxembourg was held at Nôtre Dame Cathedral on 15 January. As the coffin left the Grand Ducal Palace, borne by military pallbearers, trumpeters played a salute, church bells tolled, and a 21-gun salute sounded. The coffin was followed by the family and a group of royal mourners, among whom were the Archduke Otto and Archduchess Regina of Austria (accompanied by a bevy of Habsburgs); the Count and Countess of Paris; the Duke and Duchess of Braganza; the Prince and Princess of Naples; the Duke of Parma; the Duke of Calabria; Princess Napoléon; the Margrave and Margravine of Baden; Dukes Franz and Max Emanuel of Bavaria; Princess Margarita of Romania and her husband, Prince Radu; Prince Kyril and Princess Rosario of Bulgaria; the Fürst of Sayn-Wittgenstein-Sayn; the Fürst and Fürstin of Löwenstein-Wertheim-Rosenberg; the Fürst of Oettingen-Spielberg; and Princess Tatiana Radziwill and her husband Dr. Fruchaud, along with countless other members of the European Gotha.

At the entrance of the cathedral Grand Duke Jean awaited the coffin with the mortal remains of his wife. The Cathedral was decorated with white roses, honoring her favorite color and flower. Within, even more royal guests awaited to bid farewell to of one the most-liked members of the Gotha. The funeral mass was sublimely touching and emotional. Grand Duke Jean looked devastated by the loss of the woman to whom he was married for more than half a century. The grand duchess's body was cremated and the ashes interred in the family crypt at the cathedral, during a private service attended by close relatives, at the end of five days of national mourning in the wealthy but tiny country.

Joséphine-Charlotte was rather traditional about royal marriages, and was delighted with the unions of her two daughters. In 1982 both Marie Astrid and her sister Margaretha made spectacular alliances. Marie Astrid

From left: Grand Duchess Joséphine-Charlotte, Grand Duke Jean, Hereditary Grand Duchess María Teresa and Hereditary Grand Duke Henri attending the 50th birthday of King Carl XVI Gustaf of Sweden, a Coburg cousin. Grand Duchess Joséphine-Charlotte also had strong Bernadotte bonds with the Swedish royal family, her mother being a first cousin of King Carl XVI Gutaf's grandfather.

married her cousin Archduke Carl Christian of Austria (of Coburg descent). The groom's great-grandmother was Duchess Maria Antónia of Parma, née Braganza, while the bride descended not only from the Duchess of Parma, but also from her sisters the Duchess in Bavaria (Maria José) and Grand Duchess Maria Ana of Luxembourg. All three sisters were daughters of King Mighel of Portugal. Margaretha's groom was Prince Nikolaus of Liechtenstein, son of Prince Franz Joseph II. Both groom and bride also descended from King Miguel of Portugal. Surprisingly, the Liechtenstein remain among the few dynasties without genealogical lnks to the Coburgs. The union of Margaretha and Nikolaus is also of particular interest as, to date, it was the last between children of reigning sovereigns. One can bet safely, that given changes in succession laws and customs, mariages between ruling royals will likely become a thing of the past.

The sons of Grand Duke Jean and Grand Duchess Joséphine-Charlotte followed a different path. In 1981 Henri married Cuban-born María Teresa Mestre, daughter of a wealthy exile whom he had met while studying in Geneva. Henri is said to have obtained his parents' permission to marry María Teresa by threatening to renounce the throne and thus create a constitutional crisis. His Grandmother Charlotte was not pleased and it was not until the couple baptized their first son that she became reconciled to the union. Henri, who succeeded his father in 2000, has five children and several grandchildren.

Prince Jean, having renounced his succession rights in 1986, married the following year Hélène Vestur, a commoner he had been dating and with whom he had fathered a daughter. The couple settled in Paris, where both worked, and it was there that their five children were born. Jean and his first wife divorced several years ago. In 2009 he remarried, his second wife being Diane de Guerre. Jean's children, by grand ducal decree issued by Henri, became Prince or Princess of Nassau in 2004, though they do not have succession rights in Luxembourg.

Guillaume married King Alfonso XIII's great-granddaughter Sibilla Weiller at Versailles, where her parents

From the balcony at Buckingham Palace – Princess Margaret, Grand Duke Jean and Grand Duchess Joséphine-Charlotte of Luxembourg, the Duke of Edinburgh and Her Majesty, Princess Michael of Kent (partly obscured), Lady Gabriella Windsor, the Queen Mother, Prince Michael of Kent, the Duke of Kent (partly obscured), the Prince of Wales and Prince Edward of Great Britain and Northern Ireland.

lived. Her father, Paul-Annik Weiller, was one of France's richest men, while her mother was Olimpia Torlonia di Civitella-Cesi, daughter of Infanta Beatriz of Spain and her husband Alessandro Torlonia, the Prince di Civitella-Cesi. With this ancestry, it is not surprising that the marriage was recognized as equal and their children granted succession rights in Luxembourg.

Grand Duke Jean, her five children, twenty-one grandchildren, and several great-grandchildren all survive Grand Duchess Joséphine-Charlotte of Luxembourg.

Grand Duke Jean and Grand Duchess Joséphine-Charlotte in their rose garden.

Chapter XXI
A Return to Coburg
" ... and I Smiled"

Prince Friedrich Josias, last child of Carl Eduard and Victoria Adelheid, was born in 1918. Although the youngest of the couple's three sons, in time he would become the heir of the Coburg name and tradition, a heavy burden the young prince was wholly unprepared to carry.

Unlike his father and older brothers, Friedrich Josias never joined the Nazi Party, although like millions of other young German boys, he participated in the Hitler Youth (Hitlerjugend). Twenty-one when the Second World War erupted, he entered the German Army. By 1941, he was serving in a tank unit and training facility near Stahnsdorf, some 20 kilometers outside Berlin and close to Lichterfelde, where his father had once attended cadet school. He often spent weekend leaves at the nearby home of his aunt Caroline-Mathilde of Schleswig-Holstein-Sonderburg-Glücksburg, who in 1920 had married Count Hans Georg zu Solms-Baruth, and came to know their eldest child, Viktoria-Luise, who had grown into a rather attractive, happy-go-lucky young lady with exquisite manners and suitable background. *"These visits seemed to become more and more frequent,"* Viktoria-Luise recalled, *"and Fritzi [Friedrich Josias] became more and more flirtatious,"* and soon things turned serious.

Viktoria-Luise eagerly accepted her cousin's marriage proposal, though she later regretted her haste. *"When Fritzi finally asked my father for my hand,"* she remembered, *"my father gave his consent to the engagement, but asked us to postpone the marriage until times were less uncertain and it was possible for us to have a normal family life together."* Another concern, of course, was that they were first cousins, and although the Solms-Baruths had brought new bloodlines into the mix, the possibility of consanguinity causing birth defects was a real concern. In Coburg, Carl Eduard and Victoria Adelheid were ecstatic with the news. Having lost one son to a morganatic marriage and with another disinterested in settling down with an acceptable bride, Friedrich Josias embodied the dynasty's future.

When Viktoria-Luise expressed her misgivings to her Aunt Victoria-Adelheid, she *"could see her expression of shock and disappointment."* Friedrich Josias' mother begged her niece not to break the news to him while the young man was in the field. *"I knew Fritzi had a very sensitive personality and often became easily depressed,"* Viktoria-Luise said. *"Although Aunt Dicky [Victoria Adelheid] was a very strong woman, and was able to handle most any situation, Fritzi was more like his father's temperament. Uncle Charlie [Carl Eduard] was a highly cultured, gentle man who liked books, poetry, classical music, good food and conversation."* Friedrich Josias also shared his father's innate dislike for conflict: *"Uncle Charlie did not like difficulties with anyone and would try to avoid awkward situations as much as he could, always saying: 'Oh Dicky, you can handle this so much better than I.' Most of the time she would take over, but sometimes she made him handle his own battles."*

In December 1941, Carl Eduard and Victoria Adelheid asked their niece to visit them at Reinhardsbrunn, where Friedrich Josias was expected to arrive after serving in Yugoslavia. Much to her surprise, he had already returned from his posting by the time Viktoria-Luise joined the Coburgs. *"I still can feel the sensation I had when I saw him in the doorway to greet me,"* she remembered. *"Frankly, I thought at the time that he had a premonition of what I was going to tell him. Our embrace was certainly not one of two people who are in love. There was a shyness about it."* Several times she tried to express her feelings but could not find the right words. Then, news of the Japanese bombing of Pearl Harbor made it impossible to discuss the issue. After spending Christmas in Coburg, Viktoria-Luise prepared to return home, and Victoria Adelheid was *"very encouraging and persuasive*

Above: Princesses Alexandra and Irma of Hohenlohe-Langenburg, Grand Duchess Kira Kirillovna of Russia and Princess Sibylla. In front are Grand Duke Wladimir Kirillovich and Prince Friedrich Josias. The photo was taken at the wedding of Grand Duchess Maria Kirillovna and the Hereditary Prince of Leiningen, Coburg, 1925.

Right: Grand Duke Wladimir Kirillovich and Prince Friedrich Josias at Schloß Callenberg.

Below: Prince Friedrich Josias in 1938.

about the fact that once Fritzi and I were married, we would grow together and learn from each other, even though we might not always have the same interests."

Prevented from fleeing an engagement for which she lacked enthusiasm, the skeptical Viktoria-Luise married the newly promoted 1st Lieutenant Friedrich Josias on 25 January 1942. The ceremony, held in the church at the bride's family home of Schloß Casel, was a winter wedding and snow was piled high as the couple and their guests walked along a path from the schloß through the park to the chapel and back. Organizing such an event during times of rationing was no small feat, but her parents did as best they could given the country's situation. "Wine and champagne arrived in crates," the bride recalled. "Some of the white wine had frozen and broken the bottles during transport and had to be reordered. All of this was involved with the greatest of complications due to the irregular availability and transport of such goods. It is amazing how savvy one gets in such abnormal times."

Guests were housed in several of the family's castles in and near Casel, mainly in Baruth and Golssen, which were both part of their estates. The night before the wedding the bride's parents gave a beautiful buffet dinner, but there was no dancing as Count Hans Georg did not believe that such frivolity was proper *"during the war, when so many young men were out in the field fighting and being killed and maimed."* Viktoria-Luise later recalled that the weather was so bitterly cold that *"under my wedding dress I wore my Father's hunting underwear, top and bottom, and a pair of white thick felt riding boots."* A borrowed thick white lamb's wool coat provided further warmth. *"I was definitely dressed for the North Pole!"* she recalled. *"My lacy veil flowed over my polar bear figure, and I am sure Fritzi had to chuckle when he saw me like that, and maybe he even had second thoughts at the sight."*

From Casel the newlyweds were taken to Golssen, where they boarded a train headed for Berlin and their stay at the prestigious Bristol Hotel. From there they continued to Oberhofen, a resort area in Thüringen then owned by the Coburg estates. Along with the couple came Viktoria-Luise's white-haired terrier Truxa, *"who immediately made friends with everybody, guests and hotel personnel, except the drummer of the little dance orchestra that played in the bar every night. Truxa would sneak away from us and try to take the drumsticks away from the drummer, and if he could not get one, he would bark at the drummer! Naturally, that did not go over well with the manager of the hotel."*

Princess Viktoria-Luise and Prince Andreas.

After visiting Coburg, Friedrich Josias and his wife settled in Berlin and close to Stahnsdorf, where he was still stationed. She recalled that the apartment was not very cheery, but as they expected him to be transferred any day it made no sense to seek better lodgings. From their home they could hear the sirens blaring from the *"rumbling bombs and anti-aircraft fire from the German guns. On occasion this would happen twice a night. Thank goodness these attacks were not as severe as they would become in the following years. Nevertheless, it is scary when you are on the receiving end, and are so totally unable to defend yourself."*

A few months after her wedding, Princess Viktoria-Luise realized that she was pregnant. She had been feeling unwell for weeks and believed that she was merely suffering from some vague ailment. A trip to the family doctor in Berlin confirmed the pregnancy. *"Everyone was absolutely elated, especially Fritzi's parents, who were hoping for an heir to the Coburg family name and their large estates,"* the prospective mother reminisced many years later.

Soon after discovering that he was to become a father, Friedrich Josias received notice that he was to serve in North

Prince Friedrich Josias during the Second World War.

Prince Hubertus in the early 1940s.

Africa, where his tank division was to bring needed reinforcement and supplies to Field Marshal Erwin Rommel's Afrika Corps, then successfully fighting the Allies. Much to the frustration of her in-laws, who wanted her to give birth in Coburg, Viktoria-Luise returned to her parents in Casel, but new orders sent Friedrich Josias to Stahnsdorf. Wanting her family doctor in Berlin to deliver her child, Viktoria-Luise returned to the capital and, with her mother, settled at the Bristol Hotel. The situation, however, had worsened considerably and bombings were now one of the daily certainties faced by all Berliners. One night, Viktoria-Luise recalled, *"many of the asphalt streets were burning, not to say anything about the buildings. The Bristol Hotel was hit several times with firebombs and burned down to the fourth floor [their rooms were on the third floor], while we were all huddled in the cellar of the hotel. I was sitting near the bottom of the elevator shaft, when suddenly there was a loud noise like a crash right behind me. I jumped up, fearing that the whole elevator was crashing down behind me. We could not go upstairs while the raid was going on, and we were all afraid that the basement would fill up with water, and we would drown like rats down there."* After this, Viktoria-Luise and her mother returned to Casel.

It was there that, on 21 March 1943, Viktoria-Luise gave birth to a healthy baby boy. Her labor was long and filled with anxiety, as her obstetrician could not reach Casel and she had to use one from Luckau Hospital. *"After a long, hard day,"* she recalled, *"at eight-thirty in the evening my little baby…BOY was finally born. When the doctor picked him up and gave him a couple of little spanks to make him cry, he did not only cry, but a little fountain turned on at the same time. We all laughed and the doctor said: 'Well we know that works!'"*

Friedrich Josias reached Casel a few days after the birth and was *"thrilled with his little son."* The baptism, scheduled for 27 May, provided the excuse for another large gathering in Casel, where the ceremony took place in the same castle church where his parents had married. *"All of Fritzi's family were there, including his brother Hubertus who was an air force officer and his sister Sibylla, who came from Sweden for the occasion,"* Viktoria-Luise recalled. *"The baptismal fount was decorated with roses, and the altar was surrounded by peonies in big copper containers … Fritzi's mother held the baby over the fount while Bishop Boelke* [a family friend] *sprinkled the christening water on his head saying the words: 'I christen you in the name of the Father, of the Son and the Holy Ghost, Andreas-Michael, Armin-Siegfried, Hubertus, Friedrich-Hans.'"*

This last happy family gathering was followed by unforeseen tragedy, misery, and devastation. Germany's war effort was seriously curtailed by the arrival of massive numbers of American troops, materiel and supplies, and Rommel and his Afrika Corps were defeated. He tried to explain to Hitler that the United States' entry into the war had changed the situation irreversibly, but the dictator would not hear of it. Germany's invasion of Russia had also failed, though Berlin ignored reality and continued pouring indispensable supplies into the suicidal effort. Nearly two months after Prince Andreas's baptism, Benito Mussolini was arrested on the orders of King Vittorio Emanuele, who welcomed the landing of Allied troops in Sicily. In the Balkans, the situation was no better, while in Coburg Carl Eduard and Victoria Adelheid mourned the death of their second son and heir, Prince Hubertus, in 1943.

In 1944, Friedrich Josias received a commission to the staff of Army Group B, serving under Field Marshal Rommel. He was stationed in France along the channel coast near the Pas-de-Calais, where Hitler and his military leaders expected an Allied invasion. When the actual landing took place on the beaches of

Normandy, the surprised Germans were unable to prevent the massive Allied invasion from gaining a foothold in France. Seven weeks later Paris was liberated. Friedrich Josias was transferred to serve in the staff of General Hermann von Hanneken, supreme commander of German occupation forces in Denmark. It was here after the bungled Operation Valkyrie that Friedrich Josias learned his father-in-law had been arrested. The family tried every option available to free Count Hans Georg, and even Friedrich Josias took leave from his post in Denmark to plead for his release, but to no avail.

Germany's situation increasingly worsened. From the East, the Soviet Army gained strength as it rumbled into across the country, leaving nothing but anguish and desolation in its wake. No one was safe from the Red Army's ravenous hordes, and Viktoria-Luise realized that she had to leave Casel. With baby Andreas in her arms, she was driven to Torgau and reached Coburg after a few days. *"When we finally arrived in Coburg it was in the late evening,"* she recalled. *"Andreas and I were dead tired from the strain of the long day, and although Andreas of course did not realize the magnitude of the events that surrounded him, I did and was exhausted and devastated."* Soon the American Army surrounded it and demanded the town's capitulation. Viktoria-Luise later remembered that Hitler had given an order *"to defend the town to the last, and troops were ordered to bring explosives to the cellars of the ancient fortress* [Veste Coburg] *to blow up in case of a defeat in the last battle."* Luckily, the town's mayor informed Carl Eduard of the plan, but Victoria Adelheid refused to leave the Veste Coburg. To be safe, Viktoria-Luise, Andreas, her mother and brother were relocated to a nunnery nearby.

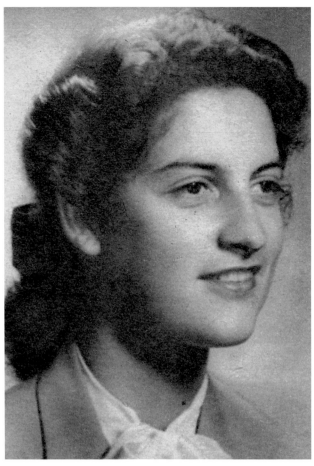

Princess Denyse of Saxe-Coburg & Gotha.

Hitler's suicide in his Berlin bunker, and Germany's unconditional surrender a week later, finally ended the war. Count Hans Georg gained his freedom as the regime collapsed, and he laboriously made his way to the safety of Coburg. Once recovered, he started organizing his family's move to a property he owned in Austria, Steinwändt, located along the Salzach River near Werfen, which he

The 60th birthday of Prince Friedrich Josias of Saxe-Coburg & Gotha. Standing in back: Gion Schäfer and Prince Andreas. Seated: Princess Carin, Princess Claudia, Princess Katrin, Prince Friedrich Josias, Prince Adrian, and Princess Beatrice with her husband Prince Friedrich of Saxe-Meiningen.

Above – In 1981, to commemorate the Sesquicentennial of Léopold I's accession, the Coburgs of Brussels traveled to Coburg, where Prince Friedrich Josias and his son Andreas hosted their cousins. In this image we see Queen Fabiola with Prince Friedrich Josias and Princess Katrin.

Left: Prince Friedrich Josias of Saxe-Coburg & Gotha.

had inherited from one of his Pleß uncles, Count Conrad von Hochberg, a bachelor without descendants. Hans Georg and his wife, with their son Hubertus, left Coburg and eventually reached the safety of Steinwändt. Viktoria-Luise wished to follow them, but before doing so she had to secure travel papers for herself and baby Andreas.

Before Viktoria-Luise departed Coburg, Friedrich Josias, who had been initially arrested by the British, arrived in town. Their reunion was tense. They had not seen each other in nearly a year and during this time there had been only minimal contact, and the only thing they had in common, their son Andreas, could not keep them together. Upon seeing her husband, Viktoria-Luise recalled not knowing *"what to say to each other. He was obviously happy to see Andreas. I think that the fact that his father had been imprisoned, which he learned when he came home, and the circumstances under which he lived, depressed him even more than he would admit. But after all, we Germans were the losers of the war, and had to bear the consequences…Fritzi was not one to pick up the pieces very easily."* Not knowing what else to do, Friedrich Josias focused all his attention on a sports car once owned by his late brother Hubertus; it was easier to fix the car than it was to repair his marriage. When he went to visit his brother Johann Leopold, Viktoria-Luise warned her husband that she was leaving and taking Andreas with her. He did not believe her, and gone she was by the time he returned.

Deciding that her marriage was at an end, Viktoria-Luise wished to find a man who would take the lead and not merely be a follower, as her mother-in-law had done with Carl Eduard. The Coburgs were deeply worried about Andreas leaving their care and wanted to retain control of the boy who one day would inherit the family's remaining estates. Knowing that, in their present circumstances, her in-laws could not raise her son, Viktoria-Luise denied their requests and took Andreas with her to Austria. As her father had lost Casel and their estates in the Baruth area to the occupying Soviets, Steinwändt was to serve as their family home.

The divorce proceedings took some time. Viktoria-Luise would not risk a trip to Coburg for fear that Friedrich Josias and his family might take Andreas from her. *"According to Fritzi's belief,"* she recalled, *"Andreas belonged to the Coburg family, and therefore should be given to him to raise."* At one point the couple met at the German-

Austrian border to discuss matters, but Friedrich Josias refused to cede control over his son. Carl Eduard had also made Andreas heir to the Coburg estates to lessen the family's tax liability when the old duke died. Still, Viktoria-Luise stood her ground and didn't budge. *"When I confronted Fritzi with the fact that his future was certainly not looking settled, his answer was: 'Well, Andreas would be better off in Sweden with Sibylla and her children than with you in the unsettled conditions in Austria.'"* She was certain that Andreas *"had had enough traumas in his short life! I was not going to let that happen!"* In the end Viktoria-Luise won, and Andreas remained with her for the next two decades. The bond between mother and son was intensely strong, loving and sincere.

Prince Friedrich Josias's tombstone located on a hill behind Callenberg.

The divorce decree became official on 19 September 1946. Disillusioned with life in Germany while also seeking to avoid involvement in rebuilding his family's decimated fortune, Friedrich Josias left Coburg and traveled to be with his sister Sibylla in Stockholm. While staying with the Swedish Royal Family, he met a young lady, Denyse Henriette de Muralt, born in Basel in 1923 and then working for his sister. Although the couple's attraction was immediate, it also forced them to leave Sweden because as Sibylla's brother, Friedrich Josias could not possibly be allowed to marry a member of her staff. With the help of his Swedish relatives, Friedrich Josias obtained a position working for the Johnson Shipping Line, which led to a job in the San Francisco offices of WR Grace & Company. It was in San Francisco that Friedrich Josias and Denyse married on 14 February 1948. Carl Eduard, apparently, considered the marriage equal and all children were born members of the Saxe-Coburg & Gotha dynasty. They had three children, the first, Maria Claudia, was born in San Francisco. Beatrice was born in Bern, while Adrian was born in Coburg.

By 1951 Friedrich Josias had gone to work at the headquarters of SANTOS, the Brazilian shipping giant, which later became the Mediterranean Shipping Company. The following year he was transferred to the company's shipping offices in Hamburg. Once back in Germany, Friedrich Josias was convinced by his father to quit his job and return to Coburg to work on the restructuring of the family fortune, which was in dire need of effective administration. Lost were all the properties in Thüringen as that region was now in Eastern Germany, while Soviet authorities controlling the country sequestered the estates in Austria. Once in Coburg, Friedrich Josias and his family lived at the Veste Coburg. It was also in Coburg that Prince Adrian was born in 1955: the last prince of Saxe-Coburg & Gotha born in Coburg was his father, nearly four decades earlier.

When the Austrian property was returned to the Coburg Family Foundation in 1958, their finances improved considerably. That same year Friedrich Josias left Germany and relocated to Buenos Aires, where he once again worked for the Swedish Johnson Line. His marriage to Denyse was also entering a difficult period, certainly worsened by his liaison with a Berlin-born young lady by the name of Katrin Bremme, who was twenty-two years his junior. In September 1964 Friedrich Josias and Denyse divorced and the following month he married Mrs. Bremme.

Friedrich Josias spent the remaining years of his long life dedicated to the administration of his family's estates. He was rarely seen attending royal events and his visibility as the Head of House Saxe-Coburg & Gotha was nearly non-existent. During much of his tenure, it was as if the Coburgs had disappeared from among the ranks of the German Gotha. There were no children from his third marriage and as he grew older, Friedrich Josias found living in Schloß Greinburg suited him perfectly. Away from the public eye, he could do as he pleased and live completely unnoticed. His participation in "royal" events was reduced to being present in Coburg whenever prominent family members (his nephew the King of Sweden, his cousins the Grand Dukes of Luxembourg and the King and Queen of the Belgians, to name a few) visited the town.

Prince Friedrich Josias died in Grein on 23 January 1998. His funeral took place in Coburg and he was buried with his parents and brother in the family plot overlooking Schloß Callenberg. Princess Katrin, who continued living at Greinburg, was often seen in Coburg attending events organized by her stepson Andreas. I met her there several times and she always came across as a nice, yet quiet and painfully private, lady. She died in Grein in 2011 and is buried with her husband.

Of Friedrich Josias's three children with Denyse Henriette de Muralt, in 1971 Maria Claudia married a Swiss named Gion Schäffer. They had two children before divorcing in 1998. She now lives in Chile with another man. Beatrice married in 1977 Prince Friedrich of Saxe-Meiningen in what was, thus far, the last marriage between Wettins. They had two children, a boy and a girl. Beatrice's son, Prince Friedrich Constantin is the only Saxe-Meiningen prince of

Prince Andreas' sisters, Victoria Whitten and Princess Beatrice of Saxe-Coburg & Gotha. Although both are Coburgs, the two ladies are not siblings, although they share Prince Andreas as a brother. Victoria is his maternal sister, while Beatrice is his paternal sibling.

his generation. His Uncle Konrad, however, the Head of House, refuses to extend the young man recognition as a dynast because his father's mother was of unequal birth. Still, once Konrad dies, Friedrich Constantin, if he survives his difficult uncle, will be the only male Saxe-Meiningen alive. Both Konrad and his nephew are unmarried.

Prince Adrian, said his brother Andreas, *"was never interested in being a Coburg...as he was raised by his mother in Switzerland, he has very short roots in Coburg."* Adrian was a complicated man who held most peculiar progressive ideas and views. He married twice. His first wife, Lea Rinderknecht, was the mother of his two sons: Simon and Daniel. It appears that these young men were born without dynastic rights. The reason behind this decision has always confounded me given that their grandfather had personally relaxed marriage rules for family members. In 1997, four years after divorcing his first wife, Adrian married Gertrud Krieg, by whom he had no descendants. Adrian committed assisted suicide in 2011. Although holders of stakes in the Coburg Family Foundation, Adrian's sons grew up without contact to their Coburg roots.

As to Friedrich Josias's first wife, in 1947 Viktoria-Luise met an American army officer, Captain Richard Whitten, whom her brother Count Friedrich-Hans encountered at a party in Salzburg hosted by a Russian aristocrat. Richard and Friedrich-Hans hit it off and became fast friends. After his first visit to Steinwändt, Captain Whitten became a constant presence at the Solms-Baruth home; in him, Viktoria-Luise found the strong, decisive man that she had failed to discover in Friedrich Josias. They were married in Steinwänd on 6 November 1947. The following year, Captain Whitten received orders to return to the United States. Viktoria-Luise and Captain Whitten, along with Andreas and Victoria, the couple's baby daughter, sailed from Bremen to build a new life in America. Viktoria-Luise Whitten passed away in 2003 in Louisiana, where she had lived for many years. Captain Whitten predeceased her by two years. Three years before his death they celebrated their golden wedding anniversary. As for Princess Denyse, she remained unmarried after divorcing Friedrich Josias. Her contact with the Coburgs was minimal at best, as she focused on raising her three children. She died in Möhling, Switzerland, in 2005.

Prince Andreas of Saxe-Coburg & Gotha, Head of House

I first met Prince Andreas about two decades ago. At the time, his father was very ill and led a retiring life at Schloß Greinburg. Prince Andreas had succeeded as administrator of the Coburg estates at an early age and when we first met he was battling German authorities in Gotha. Since Thüringia had recently been incorporated into the Federal Republic of Germany, Prince Andreas was among the many who asked for the return of property stolen by the communists after the Second World War. It was an arduous and costly process, but Prince Andreas assured me, on our first meeting, that he was intent on recovering as much as possible of what he believed German communists had unlawfully taken from his family. The property not only included valuable real estate and woodlands, but also invaluable art collections.

Prince Andreas posing in front of a bust of the Prince Consort, Schloß Callenberg, October 2001.

Prince Andreas, who was brought up in the United States, shares some parallels with his grandfather Carl Eduard. Both were brought up in countries other than the one in which they were destined to live. Prince Andreas once told me: *"I went to the U.S. with my mother and her husband and my sister and there I stayed until my early twenties. I think I must have been twenty-one or perhaps twenty-two when I returned to settle in Germany. I returned to Coburg as an American who did not really know how to speak German. It was very similar to my grandfather if you think. My mother never spoke to us in German you see…my stepfather did not understand the language and, well, she did not want him having the feeling that we were talking about things he did not understand. My mother was always very thoughtful about such things. So, consequently, I had to attend a language school in Germany for two years. It is funny though, when you think about it. As a child my first language was German. When I went to the United States at the age of five I had to learn English…and then when I returned to Germany in the 1960s I had to learn the language, again!"*

As Andreas reached the age when young men had to do military service this presented a complication. As both an American and a German, Andreas could choose to serve either country. One, at war in Southeast Asia, seemed far less appealing than the other, at peace with Europe. Off to Germany the youngster flew. He remembers that at the beginning it was difficult to follow orders, not because of his personality, but because he had trouble understanding the language. Prince Andreas recalled that *"sometimes it was funny because I did not understand the language, at times also very awkward as people tried giving me orders and I would shove my shoulders not knowing what it that I was supposed to do."*

Prince Andreas's education brought him back to the United States, where he attended university to study business administration. He left without finishing his degree and returned to Germany to do complete work and internships in the timber industry. Between 1969-1971 he also completed an apprenticeship in Hamburg working for a logging company doing overseas timber business with various regions around the planet. Prince Andreas described his life in Hamburg as *"an interesting time and I even worked for a Japanese company while living in Hamburg, where I also met my wife. We were married in Hamburg in July 1971 and even though she did not come*

The Belgian royal visit to Coburg in 1981 – Touring the Veste Coburg, from left: the Prince of Liège, Queen Fabiola, King Baudouin, the Princess de Liège, Prince Laurent (obscured), Princess Astrid, Prince Friedrich Josias and his son Prince Andreas. Relations with the Coburgs of Brussels have continued during Prince Andreas' tenure as Head of House.

from an aristocratic background, my father, as Head of House, recognized our union as equal. He felt that times had changed and that if we as a family, and a dynasty, maintained old forms and laws, we would guarantee our disappearance in the end. It was time to change and adapt to modern and exciting times, and, that, we certainly did." Prince Andreas and his wife, the former Carin Dabelstein, have three children: Stephanie and Hubertus, who arrived in Hamburg in 1972 and 1975 respectively, and Alexander, born in Coburg in 1977, who is the last male Saxe-Coburg & Gotha to be born there. Breaking family tradition, Prince Andreas is also very close to his children. Princess Stephanie, who lives in Coburg, worked in her father's office for quite a few years. She now is involved in her own projects and dedicates endless energy to her equestrian interests. Her brother Alexander manages the estate at Greinburg and of the three children he is the least seen in Coburg.

Andreas lost his Coburg grandmother in 1970. By then, the family's presence in the town was almost invisible. Friedrich Josias was spending greater periods of time in Grein and it seemed as if the Coburgs had abandoned their former capital. This was one of the reasons why Andreas and his young family relocated to Coburg, where he and his wife were destined to play prominent roles, not only socially, but also as upstanding members of local society. Andreas also felt that his family's absence from royal and aristocratic events had lasted far too long. *"Since I knew so few of my relations,"* he says, *"I slowly started reaching out to them and introducing myself. It took time and effort, of course, but I feel we have regained much of our former presence. You see, my grandfather made a huge mistake during the Nazi times, terrible mistake, without a doubt. He allowed himself to believe that Hitler's goal was to restore the princes, but he was fooled. He was not a bad person, but he made a horrible mistake and that basically cost us contact with our English cousins and many other dynasties. My father was also caught in this terrible ordeal. When he returned from the war he found a country completely in ruins. His marriage had collapsed and he just left. As he could not face life here, he wanted to rebuild it somewhere else, faraway and he found that place in California….After some years there, he was relocated to Brazil where he remained for some time. In the 1950's he returned to Germany for a brief time,*

Above: Prince Andreas and Princess Carin in 1998.

Right: Prince Andreas during a television interview conducted the day before the opening of the "Queen Victoria Exhibition" at Schloß Callenberg in 2001.

Below: Hereditary Prince Hubertus, Princess Stephanie and Prince Alexander at the reception following the opening of the "Queen Victoria Exhibition" at Schloß Callenberg in 2001.

but was soon sent away again, this time to Argentina in 1958. When he returned to Europe in the mid-1960s he had lost contact with many of his relations, and sincerely, he was not very interested in restarting these contacts either. So, after decades of the family being 'away' from our social circles, leading the Coburgs re-entry in the Gotha was left to me. It has not been an easy task, but I am satisfied of where we stand and hope that my son Hubertus will continue with these contacts. I am sure he will do us very proud."

For nearly four decades, Prince Andreas served as administrator of the Coburg Family Foundation. Under his wise and business-like guidance, the family's wealth has improved exponentially. To his land holdings in Western Germany and Austria were added thousands of acres of forestland recovered in settlements reached

Right: Guests arriving at the wedding of Hereditary Prince Hubertus and Ms. Kelly Rondesvedt. From left: Queen Silvia and King Carl XVI Gustaf of Sweden, Prince Andreas greeting Prince Georg Friedrich of Prussia, Queen Margarita and King Simeon of Bulgaria, St. Moritz Church, Coburg, May 2009.

Below right: Hereditary Prince Hubertus and Hereditary Princess Kelly on their wedding day posed for photos inside Schloß Ehrenburg.

with the state government of Thüringia. The negotiations were lengthy and complicated but the family's position was certainly improved by the fact that Duke Carl Eduard had placed all the family's real estate into a foundation. Another foundation was created to hold the artwork. Members in the foundation belonged to all branches of the Coburg family, and this, Prince Andreas believes, *"gave us a stronger hand when dealing with the authorities as some of the property was not taken from my grandfather, but from a foundation that included foreign citizens among its members. I was allowed to purchase some real estate under my name, as well as some under the foundation's name. Finally, the agreement reached with Thüringia returned to us more forests amounting to several thousands of hectares. We ceded the art collection and Schloß Friedenstein and its contents, but we retained some say. Surely, had we continued fighting we could have obtained more, but it seemed to me that what we received allowed us to save money and time, while being able to put these lands to work faster. It was far more important to look to the future and the creation of wealth and employment for the local communities, than endless battles that would only benefit our very efficient lawyers. Our landholdings are now 19,000 hectares"* His approach to business, in fact, is quite American and the prince prefers to focus on what is, rather than what could be.

Prince Andreas has a deep passion for his family's prestigious past and has served as patron of many

Chapter XXI – A Return to Coburg ... "and I Smiled"

Above: Prince Andreas, accompanied by his children Alexander and Stephanie, attending the wedding of Prince Georg Friedrich of Prussia, Potsdam, August 2011.

Right: A commemorative marker for the Duchy of Saxe-Coburg.

exhibitions about the history of the Saxe-Coburg & Gotha dynasty. All the exhibitions, whether hosted at Schloß Callenberg or the Veste Coburg, have attracted positive attention and been extremely successful, and members from other branches of the family, among them the Belgians, Bulgarians, Luxembourgs, Swedes, and even the British, have traveled to Coburg to attend. In 2001 I spent time in Coburg helping the Callenberg staff arrange an exhibition about Queen Victoria, to which I also loaned and donated some items for display. Prince Andreas was extremely welcoming and helped me establish links with other German dynasties such as Prussia, Bulgaria, Hesse, Baden, Hohenlohe-Langenburg, and Solms-Baruth. In due time these contacts that began in Coburg turned into friendships that contributed greatly to providing access to private archives across Germany.

The prince has always loved automobiles. He used to be an avid hunter, as was his grandfather Carl Eduard, who at one time served as Honorary President of the German Hunters' Guild. Today, Schloß Callenberg, besides serving as a family museum, also houses a hunting museum funded by this national organization. Prince Andreas is unique for his age in that he absolutely loves technology. In fact, during one of our last meetings, he spent a great deal of time showing me how he was taking fantastic photographs using a drone. He also showed me how to best utilize some file transferring systems that I had previously ignored.

The last few years have been physically challenging for Prince Andreas. He managed to recover from serious illness and hand over to his son, Hereditary Prince Hubertus, the administration of the family's vast forestry holdings and investments. Prince Andreas' wife, who suffers from a debilitating disease, has also battled illness, and sadly Princess Carin has not appeared in public for several years. Prince Andreas enjoys living in Coburg, where the townspeople treat him with enormous deference and kindness. He hopes his children will continue family traditions and revere the past they carry in their bloodlines.

Hereditary Prince Hubertus spent many years preparing to assume the role destiny had saved for him. His studies took him from to Coburg to Munich and then on to the London School of Economics. He has worked in banking both in Europe and the United States. It was while working for a bank in New York City that he met an American lady, Kelly Rondesvedt. They were married in a splendid ceremony at Coburg's beautiful St. Moritz Church. Countless members of the European Gotha were present and the people of Coburg were amazingly enthusiastic about their "royal wedding." Illness prevented me from attending, but from a distant California I realized that the Coburgs had returned ... and I smiled!

Above: Prince Andreas is the godfather of Princess Madeleine of Sweden. Her godmother is Princess Benedikte of Denmark. Andreas and Benedikte are first cousins of King Carl XVI Gustaf of Sweden – His father was the King's uncle, her mother was his aunt. On 8 June 2013, Prince Andreas attended in Stocholm the wedding of Princess Madeleine to an American banker.

Right: Hereditary Prince Hubertus and Hereditary Princess Kelly accompanied Prince Andreas to Stockholm. While there, she wore this interesting tiara, which many coomentators had not seen before. What many royalty watchers did not know, is that the heirloom was worn by Duchess Victoria Adelheid, Hubertus' great-grandmother. A photo on page 133 shows Duchess Victoria Adelheid weating the tiara, along with matching earrings, necklace and stomacher.

EPILOGUE

A Roundabout Way to Coburg

My interest in the Coburg dynasty began in a roundabout way, for in fact it was through the Hessians and Prussians that I first developed a curiosity for Queen Victoria, the Prince Consort and, consequently, the Coburg Dynasty.

As the reader may know, Princess Irene of Hesse and By Rhine married her first cousin Prince Heinrich of Prussia. They had three sons, two of them hemophiliacs. Their middle son, Sigismund, relocated to Central America and lived in Costa Rica for five decades. His home was Finca San Miguel, an agricultural estate perched on a rain forest-covered mountain some distance from the nearest town. I was raised in a beach front house some 45 minutes away from San Miguel. As a child, I knew Sigismund, his wife Charlotte Agnes and their son Alfred. Afternoons spent visiting him, while my grandmother had tea with his wife, ignited my interest in royalty. Hence the seeds of this royal tale were initially planted in the 1970s in a wooden farmhouse surrounded by a tropical forest faraway from Europe.

Prince Sigismund of Prussia.

Other than their tomb and memories kept alive by those who knew them, nothing remains of Sigismund and Charlotte Agnes' life in Costa Rica. The rain forest long ago took Finca San Miguel back. Prince Sigismund died in 1978. He is buried in Esparza, Costa Rica. His wife joined Sigismund eleven years later. Alfred survived until June 2013. To this day, nearly every time I visit my native Costa Rica, a respectful visit to their grave is on the agenda. A lifetime seems to have passed and as I approach the end of this journey, nostalgia for those halcyon days overcomes me. Sigismund, Charlotte Agnes, Alfred and my grandmother are now gone. Their memories live with me.

Prince Sigismund planted the first seeds of royal knowledge in me. He ignited my imagination with stories from his childhood; anecdotes that included personal reminiscences of Tsar, Kaiser and King-Emperor, all related to one another through shared ancestry and genealogy. *"They were all related,"* Sigismund used to remind me, *"and my great-grandmother Queen Victoria called them the 'royal mob' – they were very afraid of her, yet, they all flocked to her side when possible, and invited."*

Once Prince Sigismund pased away, San Miguel and his books were no longer available to me. In Costa Rica, obtaining books about Queen Victoria and royal genealogy was nearly an insurmountable task. As we were raised in a multilingual family and had relatives abroad, from early on I was able to get copies of some of the books Prince Sigismund had in his library. My grandfather once surprised me with a copy of David Duff's opus, *Hessian Tapestry*. I was also able to obtain books from Spain since one of the largest bookstores in Costa Rica could order them from Madrid. They were hugely expensive and would take months to arrive, but once I received the call from the bookstore, I dropped whatever I was doing and went to fetch it whether on foot, bus, taxi or in my mother's car. Once, a cousin brought me copies of several books written by Theo Aronson, a South African author. Later, Theo would not only become a good friend, but also a contributor to *Eurohistory*, a royalty journal I founded in 1997. Whenever we traveled to the United States, which we did every summer, most of my weekly allowance went toward the purchase of books about European royalty. I remember once spending my week's allowance of $35.00 on a book authored by Jeffrey Finestone and Robert Massie, *The Last Courts of Europe*. My father thought I was mad. My mother encouraged my spending money on books and replenished my allowance that time. *"It is best that he spends it on something that will teach him, rather then silly toys and candies,"* she told my infuriated father. That book, no doubt, played a large part in developing my interest in royal photos. Today, I own more than 200,000 images of royalty from the late 1840s to present day. As the years passed, my small collection of royalty books grew. By the time I completed law school in the mid-1980s, I owned several hundred books, not just on Queen Victoria and her descendants, but also on other royal families. To me it all seemed like an amazing puzzle that I could put together. Royalty replaced my fascination with Legos.

Prince Sigismund in his library, where this story began.

After returning home from a gap year spent traveling abroad, my parents expressed to me their hope that I would study law. I liked politics and the intricacies of the law, but lacked a passion for it. Still, off to law school I went. *"As much as you like politics, that ought to be enough to make you a good lawyer,"* President Mario Echandi, a childhood friend of my grandfather's, told me. At the time I was dating his niece, but that is another story. However, I lacked for legal studies the passion that I possess for history and genealogy. Much to everyone's utter shock and dismay, before legally becoming a lawyer, I left Costa Rica to pursue a degree in history in an American university. My father cautioned against such a move. *"Are you sure of what you are doing?"* my mother brokenheartedly inquired. *"You have no idea of what it is to be on your own and I fear that you will be back in six months flat,"* she told me at the airport before I boarded a Pan Am flight to the United States.

Luckily, I managed to survive on my own. From navigating school, finding a job and learning how to live on a budget (a foreign concept to me then), I made it through the first year. By then, my parents realized how serious I was about becoming an historian and their initial apprehension was overcome. With this change in circumstances, much to my delight, came an increase of funds – most of which went toward purchasing new royalty books. I would spend entire weekends going through every single used bookstore in Southern California. The book collection kept growing and my small apartment had to be let go for I ran out of space. This problem has continued and recently I was forced to add two new rooms to our home so I can house the book and photo collection. I am about to run out of space, again!

A summer visit to Europe changed the path my life was supposed to follow ... again!

As the Spring semester neared its end, I finalized travel plans to visit Europe. I flew to Costa Rica for a quick visit, *"to replenish his bank account,"* my father always said. From there, I returned to California and two days later I boarded a Pan Am flight to Frankfurt and then on to Athens. While in Greece, besides visiting the usual touristy spots, I tried to visit Tatoi, the former estate of the Greek royal family. I got in through a broken fence since the police kept the property off limits. I nearly made it to the main house before several rather ominous officers caught up with me and escorted the foreign intruder out. I always wondered if Queen Frederica had been more welcoming ... surely she would have, particularly once she knew my connection to her Prussian cousins ... thinking about that always gave me comfort – even though she probably would have thought me part of a different sort of 'royal mob.'

After a month in Greece, London beckoned. There, I joined a tour that took me to Eastern Europe. I visited Potsdam and Dresden, Prague and Konopiste, Bratislav and Budapest, before arriving in Vienna, where a cousin awaited me. Together, we toured the Coburg Palais, remnants of its past glories still present behind decades of grim abandon. I saw the Kaisergruft and toured the Hofburg and Schönbrunn. I went to Mayerling seeking the traces of Prince Philipp of Saxe-Coburg, a witness to the ghastly suicide of Crown Prince Rudolf of Austria. On the return to Vienna, Heiligenkreuz and the tomb of Baroness Vetsera called. By then, my tour had departed Vienna, but I stayed behind nonetheless. We managed to make it out to Ebenthal and Walterskirchen, and every day upon returning to my hotel, I would spend hours writing about the day's events in great detail.

Since I was now on my own, from Vienna I traveled to Salzburg and then on to Innsbrück, where I made contact with a Coburg, Prince Johannes Heinrich. I was kindly invited to coffee ... he found it interesting that an American knew so much about the "Catholic" Coburgs. I also met his wife Mathilde, who was delightful, if a little suspicous of this Gotha enthusiast sitting across from her. It was not the last time that I would see them, although in future both came across as shell-shocked and broken since their only son had died tragically.

Next on my itinerary was Munich, where I tried to make contact with several Coburgs, but was unsuccessful. I would simply open the phone book in my hotel room and see if any Coburgs lived where I was visiting. They all got a call from me. Then, I proceeded to Coburg, where unfortunately I lacked the time to get to all the sites on my list. That first visit to Coburg lasted one day, but I knew as I rode a night train to Florence, where summer school awaited, that one day I would return ... and I did, nearly a decade later!

Finca San Miguel, Esparza, Costa Rica.

A decade passed. While working for Goldman Sachs, I took two weeks off work and headed to London, Brussels and Coburg. I wanted to buy some rare royalty books, visit friends in Brussels and finally return to Coburg. The London visit went off well and I found some rare items to add to the growing archive at home. Brussels, always fun, provided me with several shops where more items were acquired. The photo and postcard antiquarians around the Grand Place always had "things" for me to look at ... they still do. Then, off to Coburg I went.

I rented a car in Brussels and drove to Frankfurt, where I stayed at Schloß Friedrichshof for a night. It was one of lifelong dreams to stay there. Then, the following day, I drove four hours to Coburg, where I spent the following five days. I visited all the Coburg-related sites: Schloß Callenberg, the Veste Coburg, Schloß Rosenau, the Edinburgh Palais and Schloß Burglaßschlößen. I found Schloß Ketschendorff. I went to several antiquarian shops and found amazing items. The owner of one of these shops phoned the hotel where I was staying and told me that she had talked with Prince Andreas, who was intrigued about a Costa Rican, who studied and worked in the United States and was an expert on the Coburgs. The following day, I met him for the first time and during the hour or so that we spent in his office the seeds for a great friendship were first planted.

By now, I have lost count of the number of times that I have visited Coburg. There was a time when I was visiting the city so often, that Prince Andreas suggested that it would be financially sound for me to just go ahead and either buy a flat or rent one permanently. It was during one of these visits that we first opened traveling trunks he had found in the attic of the ducal offices. Inside were long-forgotten photos and albums of Duke Carl Eduard and Duchess Victoria Adelheid. The images catalogued the couple's life from honeymoon to his death and beyond. They included the arrival of children, the Great War, the rise of National Socialism, the Duke's contacts with its leadership, his duties with the German Red Cross, journeys, family gatherings, weddings, baptisms and funerals. The find was a treasure trove and all these images are now in the Callenberg archive.

In 2001, Prince Andreas organized an exhibition at Schloß Callenberg. His goal, which he not only reached, but also surpassed, was to commemorate the centennial of Queen Victoria's death. I donated some pieces from my collection to the Callenberg Collection, while also loaning some others so they could be exhibited. Prince Andreas invited me to the opening ceremonies and I headed, yet again, to Coburg. It was a wonderful event. On opening day, several dozen Coburg descendants joined Prince Andreas for the festivities. I was put in charge of keeping Landgraf Moritz of Hesse company. Since he arrived early, we spent a long time talking about history and genealogy. I also met again Prince Johannes Heinrich and his now ex-wife Mathilde. Although divorced after the death of their son, they rekindled their friendship and were very civil together. By then, I had already met his daughter Felicitas and her mother, having spent time with them in Munich, Schladming and Grobming, where we had visited several Coburg sites. Present on opening was also Fürst Kraft of Hohenlohe-Langenburg, with whom I had a nice chat. Prince Michael of Kent and Prince Georg Friedrich of Prussia also attended and I was able to establish contacts with them. Duchess Sophie of Württemberg, a granddaughter of King Ferdinand of Bulgaria, and her brothers, all very helpful, were also there.

Prince Michael of Kent and Prince Andreas.

Later that year, I visited Coburg again to retrieve the items loaned to the exhibition. My parents came along, as did my dear friend Mary Houck. Prince Andreas walked us through the exhibition after it closed and we had several nice private dinners. From Coburg, where I also took my companions to visit the Kohary Gruft and the Glockenberg, we went to Gotha and toured Schloß Friedenstein and the ruins of Schloß Reinhardsbrunn. Then, we continued to Vienna, where I had arranged to meet Prince Philipp August, from the branch I have called "the Coburg of Vienna." He joined us for coffee at the hotel and we spent hours talking about the plight suffered by his branch: the destruction of the Kohary fortune, the dire consequences of World War II, the loss of the Coburg Palais and the countless tragedies that had befallen his branch of the dynasty. Our contacts continued, even though we have been unable to meet again.

A year later, Archduke Otto of Austria honored me with an invitation to attend the various celebrations around his 90th birthday. For that, I traveled to Vienna and while there I reconnected with several Coburgs, as well as countless Coburg descendants who were present. Chief among them was King Simeon of Bulgaria, who all along has been certainly gracious, and definitely patient, answering the many questions and inquiries I emailed him over the years. It was then that several of the Coburgs asked for the first time if my research was scheduled for publication any time soon.

In 2004, while on vacation in Boston, I received a call from Count Hans-Veit zu Toerring-Jettenbach. *"Arturo,"* he said, *"Kraft has died. Are you coming to the funeral?"* How could I not? We returned to San Francisco and quickly prepared my departure to Europe. The Fürst of Hohenlohe-Oehringen kindly arranged my lodging at one of his castles and I spent several days in Langenburg. The 'royal mob' attended Kraft's funeral in force. There were several hundred members of the Gotha at the funeral service, chief among them the Duke of Edinburgh, who later in the day would describe as "peculiar" a Costa Rican, who lived in San Francisco and was an expert on the Gotha. He was right of course, even though I did not need him reminding me of it. I had emailed Prince Andreas prior to departing for Germany and asked if he was coming to Langenburg. He confirmed that he was planning to be there. *"How is the book coming along?"* Prince Andreas inquired when we met in Langenburg. I explained to him that I was about to embark on helping Fürst Philipp, Kraft's son, cataloguing his family's vast photo archive, which would certainly cause delays to some of my projects. *"Don't trade Coburg for Langenburg,"* Prince Andreas jokingly cautioned. Unfortunately, I digressed and focused resources and energy on other projects, just as Prince Andreas had warned me not to do.

Prince Andreas at Schloß Langenburg.

Over the next few years, life became a bit more complicated. I married in September 2004. Six months later we bought a house. The day we were informed that our offer was accepted, I was packing a suitcase and readying to depart to Brussels. Grand Duchess Joséphine-Charlotte of Luxembourg had died and her funeral was in a few days. The Grand Ducal court granted me press passes and several of my royal correspondents told me that they hoped to see me there. Prince Andreas, unfortunately, could not make it to Luxembourg and was thus unable to partake in one of the largest gatherings of the 'royal mob' that I have witnessed. During the reception following the funeral, the Duke of York asked one of my friends, *"Now, I know I'm related to many here, but how so?"* *"Ah, through the Coburgs, of course,"* replied a princess whose husband is related to Prince Andrew's father. *"Are you still working on your Coburg project?"* she asked me a few days later at her home in Paris and while we shared our impressions about the Luxembourg funeral.

Everyone always asked me about the Coburgs, it seemed. By then nearly two decades had passed since my first visit to Coburg. I had collected several thousand photos and postcards of the dynasty's various branches, while adding hundreds of books about the Coburgs to my library. As if this was not enough, I had obtained subscriptions to several newspaper archives and had started downloading thousands of pages about the Coburgs. As the pool of information filled, I began to run away from it, fearful that I could never process everything I had gathered.

Meanwhile, *Eurohistory* began publishing books. *"Have you forgotten about the Coburgs?"* Prince Andreas always asked. I had not, I was just afraid that I could never write the book. *"I hope I live long enough to read the Coburg book,"* Princess Gabrielle said when we met in Rome at the beatification of Emperor Karl of Austria. Sadly, she died a few years later without seeing the book completed. Prince Johannes Heinrich also departed, as did Princess Viktoria-Luise, Prince Andreas's mother. Fortunately, she left behind her unpublished memoirs.

I had been unable to travel to Coburg in May 2009 when Hereditary Prince Hubertus married Kelly Rondesvedt, an American lady. They had met while he was working for a bank in New York City. The previous month, while visiting Prince Alexander and Princess Barbara of Yugoslavia in Paris, I became dreadfully ill. After spending several days in intensive care, the doctors released me with orders to fly to California immediately for further examination and emergency surgery.

It was not until Spring 2010 that I felt better. At times, I thought *Eurohistory* would not survive. I feared that the company was irretrievably lost. Nearly a third of my life gone to waste, I thought. Several longtime collaborators told me to fold the magazine and focus on publishing books. However, I could not let go of *Eurohistory*.

Two books we published gave me much hope. *The Gotha (Volume I)* and *The Grand Dukes*. They sold out and a second print followed, only to sell out soon afterward, requiring a third print run. *Majesty Magazine* began selling our books; Galignani in Paris and Hoogstraten in the Netherlands expressed to me their full support. Overnight it seemed that we were back in business. Plans to return to academia were put on hold, while I focused on rebuilding *Eurohistory*. We also redesigned the website and published several other books. *"So, when is the Coburgs coming out, now that you seem to have revived?"* one of my royal correspondents asked in the meantime. The Coburgs, always the Coburgs – they haunted me!

In March 2013 Prince Andreas turned seventy years-old. I sent him an email wishing him a happy birthday and he replied soon after. He reminded me that I had not been to Coburg for some time and wished to see me again. A month later, I traveled to London. From there, after a few days spent with friends and subscribers, I flew to Frankfurt, where I rented a car and drove to Coburg. That afternoon, after checking into a hotel, I headed to Prince Andreas' home. The next four days were spent in his company, every visit ending late at night. I never returned to the hotel before midnight. We sat in his study and talked. We had a lot of catching up to do. So much had changed since our last meeting. The prince had survived several health scares and he was slowly recovering. He showed me his mother's memoirs and gave me a copy. I promised that I would publish them. Prince Andreas also gave me hundreds of photos, private family images, to use with his mother's memoirs. Years before, I had told him, while he was visiting his mother in Louisiana, that his mother ought to write her memoirs. Luckily she did before dying in 2003. Now I had them in my hands. These memoirs were the catalyst needed to get the Coburg book finished and I knew then that the puzzle was finally complete. There were no longer any obstacles, other than my own fears.

Prince Andreas with Hereditary Prince Hubertus and Hereditary Princess Kelly, June 2013.

The first night of my stay in Coburg, I said to Prince Andreas, *"the Coburg book will be out this year … it is my promise to you, a gift for your birthday … I promise that you will get to see it in 2013."* Looking at me, somewhat incredulously, he replied, *"Well I hope I do, you have worked on it for a long time, and it would be nice to see it finished."* When I returned to the hotel, I opened the laptop and began putting together all the Coburg files. Every night I slept perhaps three to four hours, for once I returned to the hotel I continued working. I now had a purpose!

From Coburg, I headed to Munich, as I had arranged to visit the Toerring-Jettenbachs, who had been so immensely supportive of my book on Grand Duchess Helen Vladimirovna, Count Hans-Veit's grandmother. *"What are you working on now?"* Hans-Veit asked while he and I, accompanied by his son Ignaz, had lunch in his office. *"The Coburgs,"* I replied. *"Ah, I'm not one of them, nor are my children,"* he said. *"Yes, I know … but there is hope, I guess,"* was my reply. We all laughed! Later that evening, Ignaz showed me a beautiful painting of King Miguel of Portugal, his ancestor. *"It was a gift from my father,"* he said. *"His niece married a Coburg,"* I told Ignaz. We spent part of my visit to his home discussing how Queen Maria II had married into the Coburg dynasty, while her uncle Miguel lost everything. He ended living in Germany where he married a Löwenstein-Wertheim-Rosenberg princess, who managed to get their offspring sublimely married. One of Miguel's daughters, Maria José, in fact, was the great-grandmother of Count Hans-Veit, through his grandmother Sophie in Bavaria. One of Sophie's sisters, Elisabeth, was destined to become Queen of Belgium as consort of King Albert I. *"You may not be Coburgs,"* I told Ignaz that night, *"but you have plenty of Coburg cousins."*

Next on the itinerary was Schloß Langenburg, where I stayed a few days with Fürst Philipp and his family. I spent hours inside the archive as I always do. *"When is the Langenburg book coming out?"* Philipp asked me. *"Once the Coburgs is published, so perhaps next year I can focus on your family,"* I assured him. *"You know,"* Philipp surprisingly told me, *"that I have never been to Coburg. Never – and to think my family has such deep roots there."* We agreed that perhaps a visit could be arranged since indeed his family is so connected to Coburg. Philipp has five lines of descent from Duke Franz Friedrich Anton and Duchess Augusta of Saxe-Coburg-Saalfeld. Furthermore, if his eldest sister Cécile, who was once married to Count Cyril de Commarque, a descendant of King Léopold I of the Belgians, had any offspring, the children would have had six lines of Coburg ancestors. I love these genealogical puzzles.

I realized many years ago that when I think of the Coburgs, I think of the entire dynasty. Sometimes I sit at my desk and doodle on a notebook. My doodling is all genealogy, not funny Google-like imagery. I map out the ancestry of current royalty and aristocracy that descends from the Coburgs. Peculiar, no doubt, yet these exercises have turned into my own form of mental exercise. I can map out the line of Coburg ancestry of an overwhelming number of people. I suppose the Duke of Edinburgh was right … I am most peculiar!

Allow me, just before I leave you, a few thoughts. Somehow, my name became synonymous with the study of the Coburgs, at least among royalty and the ever-growing number of people who read *Eurohistory* and purchase our books. Perhaps as a joke, Fürst Philipp usually had me stay in the "Coburg Zimmer" at Schloß Langenburg. This last visit, for the first time, I was given a different suite. Indeed, the Coburgs are coming, but they are also leaving. They will never be far away though, for I will always continue gathering information, articles, archives and photos about them.

Prince Andreas and his sister Princess Beatrice, Coburg, June 2013.

A lot has transpired since those warm, sunny tropical afternoons spent on the verandah of the large wooden farmhouse at Finca San Miguel. I would have never thought that keeping my grandmother company on those lazy afternoons to visit the Prussians would have had such a deep impact on me. But it did and I don't have a single regret. The Prussians brought me to the Coburgs, who in turn brought the Gotha alive for me. However, in spite of my fears, I hope that I have done service to this amazing dynasty without which Europe's history, nay the world's, would be oh quite so different …

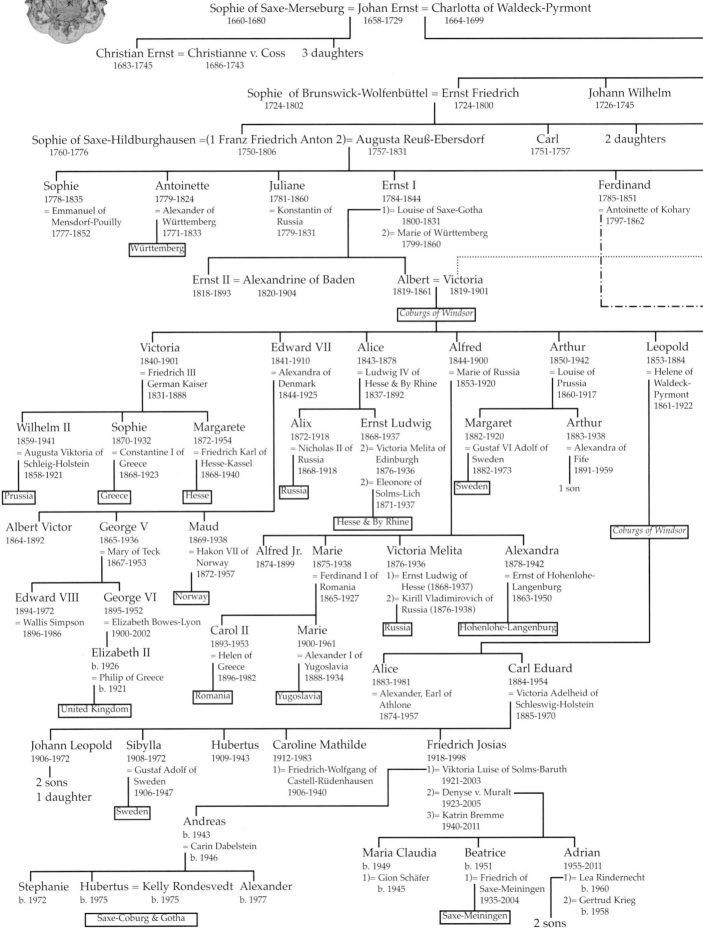

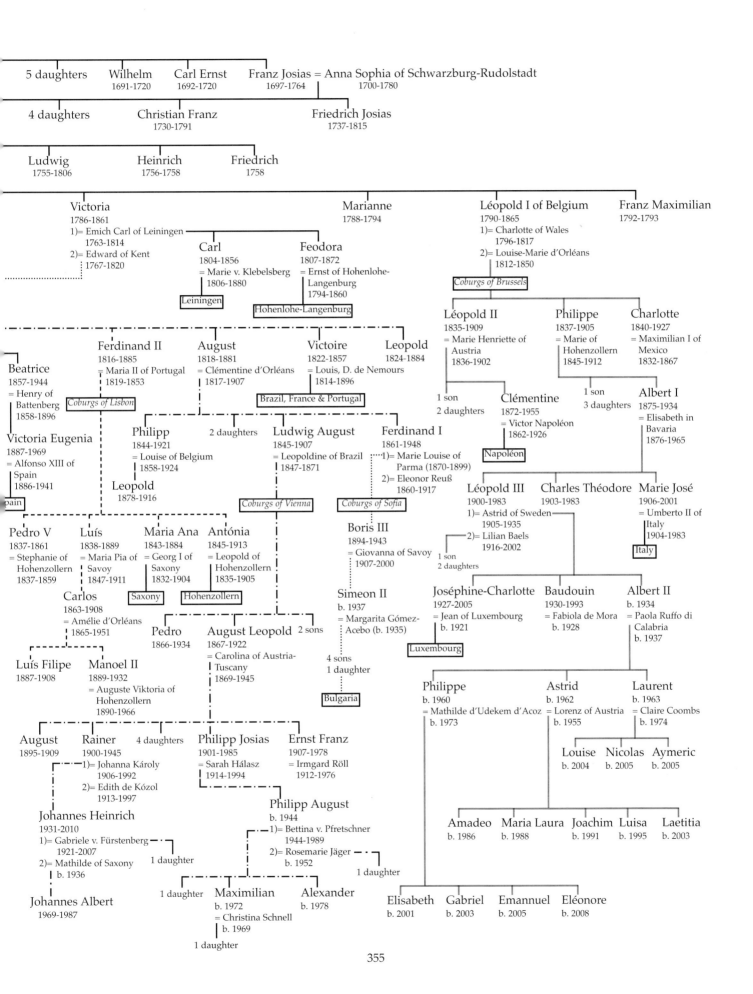

Coburg Ancestries

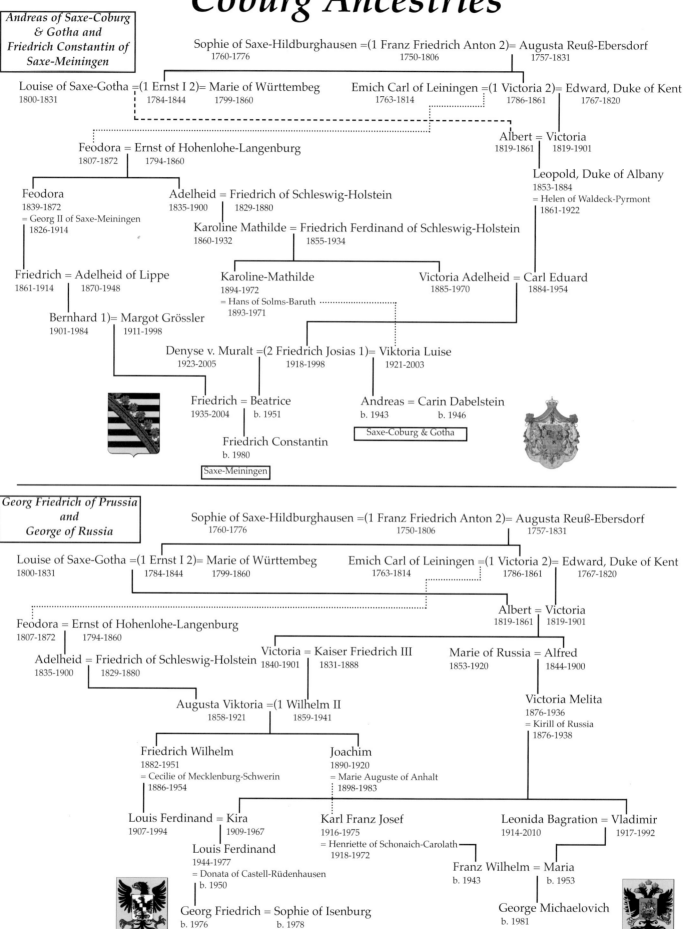

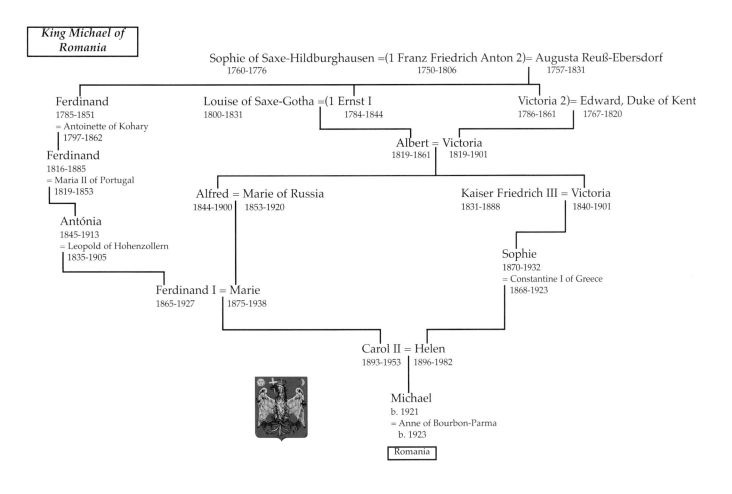

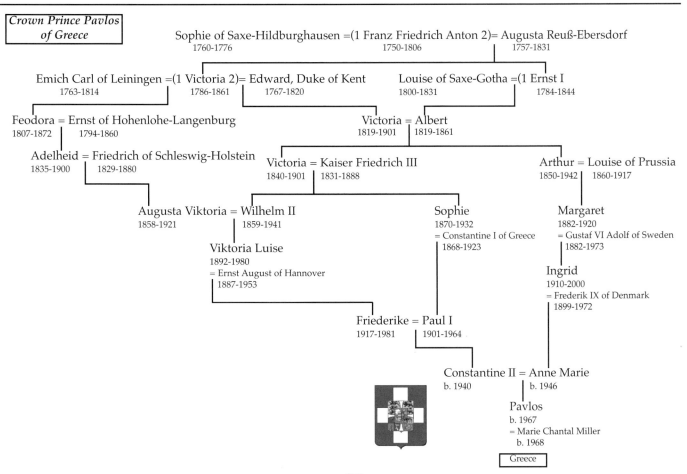

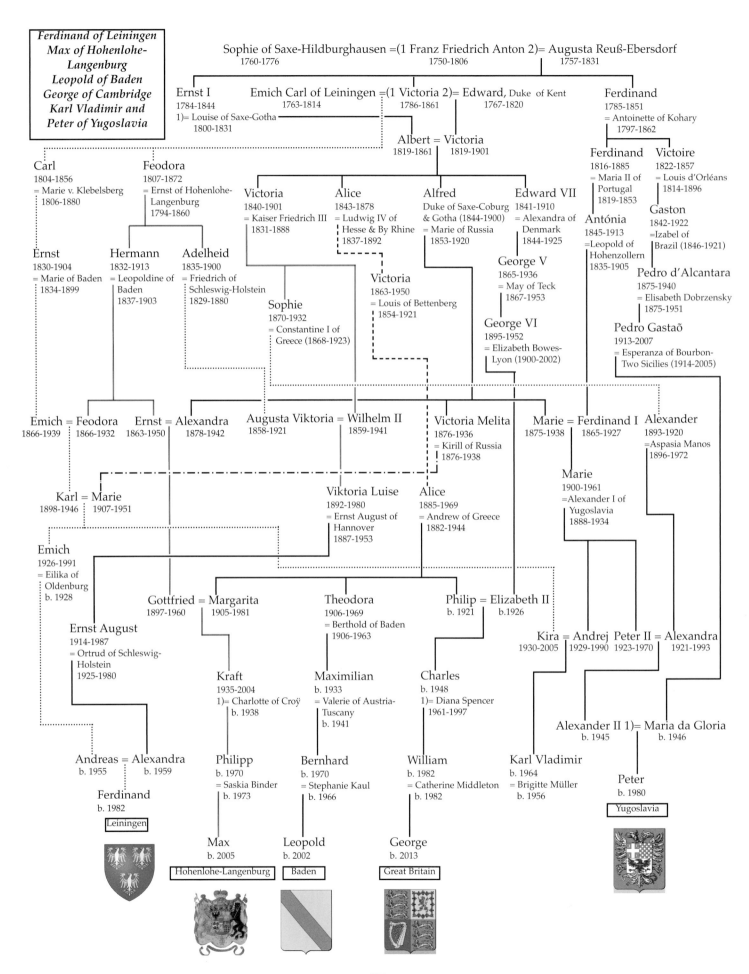

BIBLIOGRAPHY

Albert, Harold A. *Queen Victoria's Sister*. London: Robert Hale, 1967.
Argyll, Duke of. *V.R .I: Queen Victoria – Her Life and Empire*. London: Harper & Brothers, 1901.
Aronson, Theo. *Crowns in Conflict: The Triumph and Tragedy of European Monarchy 1910-1918*. London: John Murray, 1986.
Aronson, Theo. *Grandmama of Europe: The Crowned Descendants of Queen Victoria*. Indianapolis, IN: Bobbs-Merrill, 1973.
Aronson, Theo. *Princess Alice, Countess of Athlone*. London: Cassell, 1981.
Aronson, Theo. *The Coburgs of Belgium*. London: Cassell & Co., 1968.
Aronson, Theo. *Victoria & Disraeli: The making of a romantic partnership*. London: Cassell, 1977.
Ashdown, Dulcie M. *Queen Victoria's Mother*. London: Robert Hale & Co., 1974.
Ashdown, Dulcie M. *Victoria and the Coburgs*. London: Robert Hale & Co., 1981.
Aspinall, Arthur. (Editor) *The Letters of the Princess Charlotte, 1811-1817*. London: Home and Van Thel, 1949.
Athlone, Princess Alice, Countess of. *For My Grandchildren*. London: Evans Brothers, 1966.
Bachmann, Gertraude. *Herzogin Marie von Sachsen-Coburg und Gotha, geborene Herzogin von Württemberg, 1799-1860*. Coburg: Historischen Gesellschaft Coburg, 1999.
Balansó, Juan. *La familia rival*. 2nd ed. Barcelona: Editorial Planeta, 1994.
Balansó, Juan. *Los Reales Primos de Europa : Quién es quién en el mundo de los tronos, ocupados o vacíos*. Barcelona: Editorial Planeta, 1992.
Battenberg, Marie Princess of. *Reminiscences*. London: George Allen, 1925.
Battiscombe, Georgina. *Queen Alexandra*. Boston, MA: Houghton Mifflin Co., 1969.
Beéche, Arturo E. (Editor) *The Gotha: Still a Continental Royal Family, Volume 1*. East Richmond Heights, CA: Eurohistory.com, 2009.
Beéche, Arturo E. (Editor) *The Grand Duchesses: Daughters and Granddaughters of Russia's Tsars*. Oakland, CA: Eurohistory.com, 2004.
Beéche, Arturo E. (Editor) *The Grand Dukes: Sons and Grandsons of Russia's Tsars since Paul I*. East Richmond Heights, CA: Eurohistory.com, 2010.
Beéche, Arturo E. (Editor) *The Other Grand Dukes: Sons and Grandsons of Russia's Grand Dukes*. East Richmond Heights, CA: Eurohistory.com, 2012.
Beéche, Arturo E. *Dear Ellen – Royal Europe Through the Photo Albums of H.I.H. Grand Duchess Helen Vladimirovna of Russia*. East Richmond Heights, CA: Eurohistory.com, 2011.
Beéche, Arturo E., and Ilana D. Miller. *Royal Gatherings: Who is in the Picture? – Volume I: 1859-1914*. East Richmond Heights, CA: Eurohistory.com, 2012.
Beéche, Arturo E., and Prince Michael of Greece and Mrs. Helen Helmis-Markesinis. *The Royal Hellenic Dynasty*. East Richmond Heights, CA: Kensington House Books (a division of Eurohistory.com), 2007.
Belgium, Princess Louise of. *My Own Affairs*. London: Cassell & Co., 1921.
Belgium, Princess Stephanie of. *I Was To Be Empress*. London: Ivor Nicholson & Watson, 1937.
Benson, Arthur Christopher, and Viscount Esher (Editors). *Letters of Queen Victoria 1837-1861. Vols. I-III*. London: John Murray, 1908.
Blackett-Ord, Carol, and Richard Ormond. *Franz Xaver Winterhalter and the Courts of Europe 1830-70*. London: National Portrait Gallery, 1987.
Brockhoff, Evamaria, et al. *Ein Herzogtum und viele Kronen: Coburg in Bayern und Europa*. Coburg: Haus der Bayerischen Geschichte, 1997.
Brook-Shepherd, Gordon. *Royal Sunset: The Dynasties of Europe and the Great War*. London: Weidenfeld & Nicolson, 1987.
Brook-Shepherd, Gordon. *The Last Empress: The Life and Times of Zita of Austria-Hungary, 1892-1989*. London: HarperCollins, 1991.
Brook-Shepherd, Gordon. *Uncle of Europe: The Social & Diplomatic Life of Edward VII*. New York, NY: Harcourt Brace Jovanovich, 1975.
Brook-Shepherd, Gordon. *Victims at Sarajevo: The Romance and Tragedy of Franz Ferdinand and Sophie*. London: Harvill Press, 1984.
Brunswick and Lüneburg, Viktoria Luise Duchess of. *The Kaiser's Daughter: Memoirs of H.R.H. Viktoria Luise, Princess of Prussia*. Englewood Cliffs, NJ: Prentice-Hall, 1977.
Buchanan, Meriel. *Queen Victoria's Relations*. London: Cassell & Co., 1954.
Buchanan, Meriel. *Victorian Gallery*. London: Cassell & Co., 1956.
Calmes, Christian, and Raymond Reuter. *Jean, Grand-Duc de Luxembourg: un souverain et son pays*. Luxembourg: Éditions Luxnews, 1986.
Cannuyer, Christian. *Les maisons royales et souveraines d'Europe*. Paris: Brepols, 1989.
Cassels, Lavender. *Clash of Generations: A Habsburg Family Drama of the 19th Century*. Newton Abbot, Devon: Victorian Book Club, 1974.
Cecil, Lamar. *Wilhelm II: Emperor and Exile, 1900-1941*. Vol. II. Chapel Hill, NC: The University of North Carolina Press, 1996.
Cecil, Lamar. *Wilhelm II: Prince and Emperor, 1859-1900*. Chapel Hill, NC: The University of North Carolina Press, 1989.
Chaffanjon, Arnaud. *Histoires de Familles Royales: Victoria d'Angleterre – Christian IX de Danemark et leurs descendances de 1840 à nos jours*. Paris: Ramsay, 1980.
Chambers, James. *Charlotte & Leopold: The True Story of the Original People's Princess*. London: Old Street Publishing, 2007.
Cheboksarova, Tatiana, and Galina Korneva. *Russia & Europe: Dynastic Ties*. Edited by Arturo E. Beéche. East Richmond Heights, CA: Eurohistory.com, 2013.
Constant, Stephen. *Foxy Ferdinand, Tsar of Bulgaria*. New York, NY: Franklin Watts, 1980.
Corpechot, Lucien. *Memories of Queen Amélie of Portugal*. Reprint. Ticehurst, East Sussex: Royalty Digest, 1996.
Correia Guedes, Carmina, and Isabel Silveira Godinho. *Growing Up a Prince at Ajuda Palace (1863-1884)*. Lisbon: Ministry of Culture, 2004.
Corremans, Luc. *Philippe et Mathilde*. Braine-l'Alleud: Éditions J.M. Collet, 2000.
D'Auvergne, Edmund B. *The Coburgs: The Story of the Rise of a Great Royal House*. London: Stanley Paul & Co., 1911.
da Silveira Godinho, Isabel. *D. Luís – duque do Porto e rei de Portugal*. Lisboa: Palácio Nacional da Ajuda, 1990.
Danneels, Mario. *Paola – de la dolce vita à la couronne*. Bruxelles: Éditions Luc Pire, 2000.
De Fossa, Christophe, and Henri van Daele. *Six Reines*. Bruxelles: Éditions Racine, 1996.
de Launay, Jacques. *Léopold 1er*. Bruxelles: Éditions J.M. Collet, 1982.
de Sagrera, Ana. *Ena y Bee: En defensa de una amistad*. Madrid: Velecío Editores, 2006.
de Sousa, Manuel. *Reis e Rainhas de Portugal*. Mem-Martins: SporPress, 2002.
Defrance, Olivier, and Joseph van Loon. *La fortune de Dora: Une petite-fille de Léopold II chez les nazis*. Bruxelles: Éditions Racine, 2013.
Defrance, Olivier. *La Médicis des Cobourg: Clémentine d'Orléans*. Bruxelles: Éditions Racine, 2007.
Defrance, Olivier. *Léopold 1er et le clan Cobourg*. Bruxelles: Éditions Racine, 2004.
Del Priore, Mary. *O príncipe maldito: traição e loucura na família imperial*. Rio de Janeiro: Editora Objetiva, 2006.
Dimitroff, Pashanko. *Clémentine d'Orleans, Princess Augustus of Saxe Coburg: King-Maker Inveterate*. Sofia: Ascent 96, 1997.
Downer, Martyn. *The Queen's Knight: The extraordinary life of Queen Victoria's most trusted confidant*. London: Bantam Press, 2007.
Duff, David. *Alexandra, Princess and Queen*. London: Collins, 1980.
Duff, David. *Edward of Kent: Father of Queen Victoria*. London: Stanley Paul, 1938.
Dufoux, Georges. *Une dynastie mythique: Les Saxe-Cobourg-Gotha*. Fontainebleau: self-published, 2000.
Dujardin, Vincent, and Michel Dumoulin and Mark Van den Wijngaert. *Léopold III*. Bruxelles: Éditions Complexe, 2001.
Dumont, Georges-Henri. *La Dynastie Belge*. Braine-l'Alleud: Éditions J.M. Collet, 1994.
Ed. by the Chancellery of H.M. the King of the Bulgarians. *Libro Blanco – Al servicio de su patria*. Madrid: Imprenta «El Economista», 1969.
Eilers, Marlene A. *Queen Victoria's Descendants*. 1st ed. New York, NY: Atlantic International Publications, 1987.
Eilers, Marlene A. *Queen Victoria's Descendants*. 2nd ed. Falköping: Rosvall Royal Books, 1997.
Emerson, Barbara. *Leopold II of the Belgians: King of Colonialism*. New York, NY: St. Martin's Press, 1979.
Enache, Nicolas. *La Descendance de Marie-Thérèse de Habsburg, Reine de Hongrie et de Bohême*. Paris: L'Intermédiaire des Chercheurs et Curieux, 1996.
Enache, Nicolas. *La Descendance de Pierre le Grand, Tsar de Russie*. Paris: Sedopols, 1983.

Fenyvesi, Charles. *Splendor In Exile: The Ex-Majesties of Europe*. Washington, D.C.: New Republic Books, 1979.
Finestone, Jeffrey and Robert Massie. *The Last Courts of Europe: A Royal Family Album, 1860-1914*. New York, NY: Vendome Press, 1981.
Frankland, Noble. *Witness of a Century: the life and times of Prince Arthur, Duke of Connaught, 1850-1942*. London: Shepheard-Walwyn, 1993.
Friedrich, Otto. *Ketschendorf: Die Geschichte zweier Schlösser und ihrer Bewohner*. Coburg: Druck- und Verlaghaus A. Rossteutscher, 1973.
Fulford, Roger. (Editor) *Beloved Mama: Private Correspondence of Queen Victoria and the German Crown Princess 1878-1885*. London: Evans Brothers, 1981.
Fulford, Roger. (Editor) *Darling Child: Private Correspondence of Queen Victoria and the German Crown Princess 1871-1878*. London: Evans Brothers, 1981.
Fulford, Roger. (Editor) *Your Dear Letter: Private Correspondence of Queen Victoria and the Crown Princess of Prussia 1865-1871*. New York, NY: Charles Scribner's Sons, 1971.
Gelardi, Julia P. From *Splendor to Revolution: The Romanov Women, 1847-1928*. New York, NY: St. Martin's Press, 2011.
Genealogisches Handbuch des Adels: Fürstliche Häuser Band XIX. Limburg: C.A. Starke Verlag, 2011.
Gentile, Aniello. *Da Gaeta ad Arco: Diario di Francesco II di Borbone*. Napoli: Arte Tipografica, 1988.
Germany, Crown Prince Wilhelm of. *Memoirs of the Crown Prince of Germany*. Uckfield, East Sussex: The Naval & Military Press, 2005.
Glassheim, Eagle. *Noble Nationalists: The Transformation of the Bohemian Aristocracy*. Cambridge, MA: Harvard University Press, 2005.
Greece, Prince Nicholas of. *My Fifty Years: The Memoirs of Prince Nicholas of Greece*. Annotated and expanded by Arturo E. Beéche. East Richmond Heights, CA: Eurohistory.com, 2006.
Grey, C. *Queen Victoria's Memoirs of The Prince Consort: His Early Years*. New York, NY: Harper & Bros., 1868.
Groueff, Stephane. *Crown of Thorns: The Reign of King Boris III of Bulgaria, 1918-1943*. Lanham, MD: Madison Books, 1987.
Grützner, Günter, and Manfred Ohlsen. *Schloss Cecilienhof und das Kronprinzenpaar*. Berlin: Museums- und Galerie-Verlag, 1991.
Hamann, Brigitte. *Die Habsburger – Ein biographisches Lexikon*. München: Piper, 1988.
Hochschild, Adam. *King Leopold's Ghost: A Story of Greed, Terror, and Heroism in Colonial Africa*. New York, NY: Houghton Mifflin, 1998.
Hoffmeister, Hans; Wahl, Volker; et al. *Die Wettiner in Thüringen*. Arnstadt: Rhino Verlag, 1999.
Högel, Klaus-Peter, and Richard Kurdiovsky. *Das Palais Coburg*. Wien: Verlag Christian Brandstätter, 2003.
Hohenlohe-Langenburg, Feodora, Princess of. *Letters from 1828 to 1872*. London: Spottiswoode & Co., 1874.
Hohenlohe-Schillingsfürst, Franz Josef Fürst zu. *Monarchen – Edelleute – Bürger: die Nachkommen des Fürsten Carl Ludwig zu Hohenlohe-Langenburg, 1762-1825*. Neustadt a. d. Aisch: Verlag Degener, 1963.
Hough, Richard. *Advice to My Grand-daughter: Letters from Queen Victoria to Princess Victoria of Hesse*. New York, NY: Simon & Schuster, 1975.
Hough, Richard. *Victoria & Albert*. London: Richard Cohen Books, 1996.
Italy, Marie José, Queen of. *Albert et Élisabeth de Belgique: mes parents*. Bruxelles: Le Cri édition, 2000.
Jagow, Kurt. (Editor) *Letters of the Prince Consort, 1831-1861*. New York, NY: E.P. Dutton & Co., 1938.
Jonas, Klaus. *The Life of Crown Prince William*. Pittsburgh, PA: University of Pittsburgh Press, 1961.
Judtmann, Fritz. *Mayerling: The Facts Behind the Legend*. London: George C. Harrap & Co., 1971.
Katz, Robert. *The Fall of the House of Savoy*. London: George Allen & Unwin, 1972.
Kerckvoorde, Mia. *Charlotte: La passion et la fatalité*. Bruxelles: Éditions Racine, 2001
Kerckvoorde, Mia. *Louise-Marie d'Orléans: La reine oubliée*. Bruxelles: Éditions Racine, 2001.
Kerckvoorde, Mia. *Marie-Henriette: Une amazone face à un géant*. Bruxelles: Éditions Racine, 1998.
King, Greg, and Penny Wilson. *Gilded Prism: The Konstantinovichi Grand Dukes & the Last Years of the Romanov Dynasty*. East Richmond Heights, CA: Eurohistory.com, 2006.
King, Greg. *Twilight of Splendor: The Court of Queen Victoria during Her Diamond Jubilee Year*. Hoboken, NJ: John Wiley & Sons, 2007.
Kirschen, Gilbert. *L'Education d'un Prince: Entretiens avec le Roi Léopold III*. London: Didier Hatier, 1984.
Koninckx, Christian. *Astrid 1905-1935*. Bruxelles: Éditions Racine, 2005.
Lage Cardoso, Eurico C. E. D. *Manuel II: o rei patriota*. Lisboa: self-published, 2003.
Lage Cardoso, Eurico C. E. D. *Pedro V – O Esperançoso: Vida e Obra de um Rei Inesquecível*. Lisboa: self-published, 2006.
Lamont-Brown, Raymond. *Edward VII's last loves: Alice Keppel & Agnes Keyser*. Stroud, Gloucestershire: Sutton, 1998.
Lee, Sir Sidney. *King Edward VII: A Biography, from birth to accession*. New York, NY: Macmillan Co., 1925.
Lee, Sir Sidney. *King Edward VII: A Biography*. New York, NY: Macmillan Co., 1927.
Leitão, Ruben Andresen. *Cartas de D. Pedro V ao Conde de Lavradio*. Pôrto: Portucalense Editora, 1945.
Lincoln, W. Bruce. *The Romanovs: Autocrats of All the Russias*. New York, NY: The Dial Press, 1981.
Listowel, Judith. *A Habsburg Tragedy – Crown Prince Rudolf*. London: Ascent Books, 1978.
Longford, Elizabeth. *Queen Victoria: Born to Succeed*. New York, NY: Harper & Row, 1964.
Lorenz, Sönke, and Dieter Mertens and Volker Press. *Das Haus Württemberg: Ein biographisches Lexikon*. Stuttgart: Kohlhammer, 1997.
Madol, Hans Roger. *Ferdinand of Bulgaria: The Dream of Byzantium*. London: Hurst & Blackett, 1933.
Magalhães Ramalho, Margarida. *Fotobiografias século XX: Rei D. Carlos*. Lisboa: Círculo de Leitores, 2001.
Magnus, Philip. *King Edward the Seventh*. New York, NY: E.P. Dutton & Co., 1964.
Mandache, Diana. *Dearest Missy: The Letters of Marie Alexandrovna and of her daughter, Marie, Crown Princess of Romania 1879-1900*. Falköping: Rosvall Royal Books, 2011.
Marie Louise, Princess. *My Memories of Six Reigns*. London: Evans Brothers, 1956.
Martin-Fugier, Anne. *La vie quotidienne de Louis-Philippe et de sa famille: 1830-1848*. Paris: Éditions Hachette, 1992.
Masuy, Christine. *Princesses de Belgique: Laeken, les femmes de l'ombre*. Bruxelles: Éditions Luc Pire, 2001.
Mateos Sáinz de Medrano, Ricardo. *Estoril: Los años dorados*. Madrid: La Esfera de los Libros, 2012.
Mattachich, Comte Geza. *Folle Par Raison D'État: La Princesse Louise de Belgique*. Bruxelles: Le Cri édition, 1998.
Mead Lalor, William. *Royalty between the wars*. Falköping: Rosvall Royal Books, 1999.
Montgomery-Massingberd, Hugh. *Burke's Guide to the Royal Family*. London: Burke's Peerage, 1973.
Nikolaev, N.P. ; et al. *La destinée tragique d'un roi ; la vie et la règne de Boris III, roi des Bulgares (1894-1918-1943)*. Uppsala: Almqvist & Wiksells, 1952.
Nobre, Eduardo. *Amélia, Rainha de Portugal*. Lisboa: Quimera Editores, 2006.
Nobre, Eduardo. *Família Real: Álbum de fotografias*. Lisboa: Quimera Editores, 2002.
Nobre, Eduardo. *Paixões Reais*. Lisboa: Quimera Editores, 2002.
Noel, Gerard. *Ena: Spain's English Queen*. London: Constable & Co., 1984.
Oliva, Gianni. *Duchi d'Aosta*. Milano: Mondadori, 2003.
Oliva, Gianni. *Umberto II: L'ultimo re*. Milano: Mondadori, 2000.
Oporto, Duke of. *Memories*. Reprint. Ticehurst, East Sussex: Royalty Digest, 2004.
Packard, Jerrold M. *Victoria's Daughters*. New York, NY: St. Martin's Press, 1998.
Palmer, Alan. *Crowned Cousins: The Anglo-German Royal Connection*. London: Weidenfeld & Nicolson, 1985.
Paoli, Dominique. *Clémentine, Princesse Napoléon*. Bruxelles: Éditions Racine, 1998.
Paoli, Dominique. *Fortunes & Infortunes des princes d'Orléans : 1848 - 1918*. Paris: Éditions Artena, 2006.
Paoli, Dominique. *La duchesse d'Alençon: Sophie-Charlotte, sœur de Sissi*. Bruxelles: Éditions Racine, 1999.
Paris, Isabelle, comtesse de. *Tout m'est bonheur*. Paris: Éditions Robert Laffont, 1978.
Paris, Isabelle, comtesse de. *Tout m'est bonheur: Les chemins creux*. Paris: Éditions Robert Laffont, 1981.
Pellender, Heinz. *Chronik der Stadt und der Veste Coburg, der Herren und Herrscher über Coburg und das Coburger Land*. Coburg: Fiedler-Verlag, 1997.
Petropoulos, Jonathan. *Royals and the Reich: The Princes von Hessen in Nazi Germany*. New York, NY: Oxford University Press, 2006.
Plumtree, George. *Edward VII*. London: Pavilion Books, 1995.
Pollock, Kassandra. *Maria Pia of Portugal*. Unpublished.
Ponsonby, Sir Frederick. *Recollections of Three Reigns*. London: Eyre & Spottiswoode, 1951.
Pope-Hennessy, James. *Queen Mary*. London: George Allen & Unwin, 1959.

BIBLIOGRAPHY

Portugal, Carlos I, King of. *Cartas d'el-Rei D. Carlos I a João Franco Castello-Branco seu ultimo presidente do conselho*. Lisboa: Livrarias Aillaud e Bertrand, 1924.
Portugal, King Manuel II of, and Queen Augusta Victoria of Portugal. *Cartas do Rei D. Manuel II e da Rainha D. Augusta Victória para a sua secretária Miss Margrey Withers*. Lisboa: Fundação Casa de Bragança, 1997.
Priesner, Rudolf. *Herzog Carl Eduard zwischen Deutschland und England: Eine tragische Auseinandersetzung*. Gerabronn: Hohenloher Druck- und Verlaghaus, 1977.
Ramm, Agatha. (Editor) *Beloved and darling Child: Last Letters between Queen Victoria and Her Eldest Daughter, 1886-1901*. London: Alan Sutton, 1990.
Rappaport, Helen. *A Magnificent Obsession: Victoria, Albert, and the Death That Changed the British Monarchy*. New York, NY: St. Martin's Press, 2011.
Raskin, Evrard. *Princesse Lilian: La femme qui fit tomber Léopold III*. Bruxelles: Éditions Luc Pire, 1999.
Rebelo, Teresa. *Condessa d'Edla: a cantora de ópera quasi rainha de Portugal e de Espanha (1836-1929)*. Lisboa: Alètheia Editores, 2006.
Richardson, Joanna. *George IV: A Portrait*. London: Sidgwick & Jackson, 1966.
Richardson, Joanna. *My dearest Uncle: Leopold I of the Belgians*. London: Jonathan Cape, 1961.
Richardson, Joanna. *Victoria & Albert: a study of a marriage*. London: Dent and Sons, 1977.
Röhl, John C. G. *The Kaiser and His Court: Wilhelm II and the Government of Germany*. New York, NY: Cambridge University Press, 1996.
Romania, Marie Queen of. *The Story of My Life*. New York, NY: Charles Scribner's Sons, 1934.
Rose, Kenneth. *King George V*. New York, NY: Alfred A. Knopf, 1984.
Royalty Digest. Vol. 10. Ticehurst, East Sussex: Paul Minet, Jul 2000 – Jun 2001.
Royalty Digest. Vol. 5. Ticehurst, East Sussex: Paul Minet, Jul 1995 – Jun 1996.
Royalty Digest. Vol. 8. Ticehurst, East Sussex: Paul Minet, Jul 1998 – Jun 1999.
Rusk, John. *The Beautiful Life and Illustrious Reign of Queen Victoria*. Minneapolis, MN: Creore & Nickerson, 1901.
Ryan, Nellie. *My Years at the Austrian Court*. Reprint. Ticehurst, East Sussex: Royalty Digest, 2004.
Sachsen, Albert Prinz von. *Die Albertinischen Wettiner: Geschichte des Sächsischen Königshauses 1763-1932*. Gräfelfing: E. Albrecht Verlags-KG., 1995.
Sachsen, Albert Prinz von. *Die Wettiner in Lebensbildern*. Graz: Verlag Styria, 1995.
Salway, Lance. *Queen Victoria's Grandchildren*. London: Collins & Brown, 1991.
Sandner, Harald. *Das Haus Sachsen-Coburg und Gotha – 1826 bis 2001*. Coburg: Neue Presse, 2001.
Sandner, Harald. *Ein Herzogtum in aller Welt: Wie das "Haus Coburg" die Throne Europas eroberte*. Coburg: Tourismus & Congress Service, 2001.
Saxe-Coburg-Gotha and Other European Houses. Amsterdam: Sotheby's, 2004.
Saxe-Coburg-Gotha, Ernest Duke of. *Memoirs of Ernest II Duke of Saxe-Coburg-Gotha*. Vols. I and II. London: Remington & Co., 1888.
Saxe-Coburg-Saalfeld, Augusta Duchess of. *In Napoleonic Days – Extracts from the Private Diary of Queen Victoria's Maternal Grandmother*. London: John Murray, 1941.
Schiel, Irmgard. *Stéphanie, princesse héritière – Dans l'ombre de Mayerling*. Paris-Gembloux: Éditions Duculot, 1989.
Shoberl, Frederic. *House of Saxony*. London: R. Ackermann, 1816.
Solms-Baruth, Viktoria Luise Gräfin zu. *Memoir of My Life for My Children, Grandchildren and Great Grandchildren*. Unpublished.
St Aubyn, Giles. *Edward VII: Prince & King*. New York, NY: Atheneum, 1979.
Stéphany, Pierre, and Henri van Daele. *Six Rois*. Bruxelles: Éditions Racine, 1995.
Teixeira, José. *D. Fernando II: rei-artista, artista-rei*. Lisboa: Fundação Casa de Bragança, 1986.
Tourtchine, Jean-Fred. *Le Royaume d'Italie*. Vol. III. Clamecy : C.E.D.R.E., 1994.
Tuchman, Barbara W. *The Guns of August*. New York, NY: Macmillan Co., 1962.
Tuscany, Luisa of. *My Own Story*. London: Eveleigh Nash, 1911.
Valynseele, Joseph. *Les prétendants aux trones d'Europe*. Paris: self-published, 1967.
van der Kiste, John. *Edward VII's Children*. Gloucester: Sutton, 1989.
van der Kiste, John. *Queen Victoria's Children*. Gloucester: Sutton, 1986.
Veríssimo Serrão, Joaquim. *D. Manuel II (1889-1932): O Rei e o Homem à Luz da História*. Lisboa: Fundação Casa de Bragança, 1990.
Vicente, Ana, and António Pedro Vicente. *O Príncipe Real: Luiz Filipe de Bragança, 1887-1908*. Lisboa: Edições Inapa, 1998.
von Bothmer, Countess A. *The Sovereign Ladies of Europe*. London: Hutchinson & Co., 1899.
von Schwering, Count Axel. *The Berlin Court under William II*. London: Cassell & Co., 1915.
von Stockmar, Baron E. *Memoirs of Baron Stockmar*. Vols. I-II. London: Longmans & Co., 1872.
von Wangenheim, Rita. *Baron Stockmar: Eine coburgisch-englische Geschichte*. Coburg: Hirsch-Verlag, 1996.
Weber, Patrick. *Amours royales et princières: Mariages, liaisons, passions et trahisons de la cour de Belgique*. Bruxelles: Éditions Racine, 2006.
Weber, Patrick. *Elisabeth de Belgique: L'autre Sissi*. Paris: Éditions Payot, 1998.
Wiedau, Kristin. *Eine adlige Kindheit in Coburg: Fürstenerziehung und Kunstunterweisung der Prinzen Ernest und Albert von Sachsen-Coburg und Gotha*. Coburg: Kunstsammlungen der Veste Coburg, 2001.
Wilpert, August. *Short history of the Catholic, so called "Kohary" line of the Ducal House of Saxe-Coburg and Gotha*. By order of H.H. Princess Edith of Saxe-Coburg and Gotha. Munich: unpublished, 1990.
Wrangel, Comte F.U. *Les Maisons Souveraines de l'Europe*. Vols. I and II. Stockholm: Collection Hasse-W. Tullberg, 1907.
Zeepvat, Charlotte. *Prince Leopold: The Untold Story of Queen Victoria's Youngest Son*. Stroud, Gloucestershire: Sutton Publishing, 1998.
Zeepvat, Charlotte. *Queen Victoria's Family: A Century of Photographs*. Stroud, Gloucestershire: Sutton Publishing, 2001.
"The Wedding of Hereditary Prince Hubertus of Saxe-Coburg & Gotha and Ms. Kelly Rondestvedt – Coburg, May 23, 2009." Programme.

Newspapers, Magazines

The Illustrated London News (Various years)
The Graphic (Various years)
Eurohistory 1997-2013
Royalty Digest 1992-2005
Time Magazine (Various years)
Newsweek (Various Years)
Black and White (Various years)
The Sketch (Various years)
The Strand Magazine (Various Years)
Die Gartenlaube (1853)

Online Sources:

Austrian National Archive: www.obn.ac.at
Bulgarian Royal Family: www.kingsimeon.com
The Online Gotha: www.angelfire.com/realm/gotha/gotha/gotha.htm
La Nación, Costa Rica: www.nacion.com
The New York Times 1851-1997: www.nyt.com

INDEX

A
Acker, Achille van (Belgian Prime Minister) 267
Albania
  Zog, King of 288
Anhalt
  Aribert, Prince of 66, 121
  Leopold, Hereditary Prince of 114
Anhalt-Schaumburg
  Amalie, Fürstin of (née Nassau-Weilburg) 18
  Hermine, Princess of 18
  Viktor, Fürst of 18
Anhalt-Zerbst
  Sophie, Princess (see Russia)
Antonescu, Ion, Romanian dictator 283
Argyll, Duke of 66
Aubert, Louisa-Hilda d' 15
Austria
  Adelheid, Archduchess (see Savoy)
  Adelheid, Archcuchess (daughter of Karl I) 260
  Albrecht, Archduke 200, 231
  Carl Christian, Archduke 330
  Charles VI, Holy Roman Emperor iv
  Elisabeth, Empress (née Bavaria) 182, 239, 316
  Elisabeth, Archduchess (see Liechtenstein)
  Elisabeth, Archducess 207
  Elisabeth Christine, Holy Roman Empress (née Brunswick-Wolfenbüttel) iv
  Ferdinand Maximilian, Archduke (Emperor of Mexico) 47, 51, 59, 173, 224
  Franz II (I) Emperor 1, 25, 26, 54, 172, 213
  Franz Ferdinand, Archduke 38, 62, 71, 110, 126, 168, 206, 249, 278, 317
  Franz Joseph, Emperor 38, 47, 68, 71, 92, 93, 97, 105, 110, 168, 173, 200, 201, 202, 203, 204, 212, 230, 231, 239, 314
  Friedrich, Archduke 207
  Hermine, Archduchess 18
  Isabella, Archduchess 185
  Joseph II, Emperor 1
  Joseph, Archduke, Palatine of Hunhary 18, 172
  Joseph, Archduke (1833-1905) 96, 175, 220, 239
  Karl Ludwig, Archcuke 173
  Karl I, Emperor 315, 351
  Leopold II, Emperor 1
  Lorenz, Archduke of 272, 273, 298
  Ludwig Viktor, Archduke 201, 202
  Margareta, Archduchess (see Thurn und Taxis)
  Margarete Sophie, Archduchess (see Württemberg)
  Margherita, Archduchess of (née Savoy) 272
  Maria Carolina, Archduchess (see Two Sicilies)
  Maria Josepha, Archduchess (née Saxony) 239, 297, 298
  Maria Theresa, Empress iv, 172
  Maria Theresa, Archduchess 231
  Marie Antoinette, Archduchess of (see France)
  Marie Dorothea, Archduchess (née Württemberg) 172
  Maria Dorothea, Archduchess (see Orléans)
  Marie-Henriette, Archduchess (see Belgium)
  Marie Leopoldine, Archduchess (see Brazil)
  Marie Valerie, Archduchess 200, 239
  Mathilde, Duchess in (see Two Sicilies) 316
  Otto, Archduke (1865-1907) 314
  Otto, Archduke (1912-2011) 186, 297, 329, 350
  Rainer, Archduke 172
  Regina, Archduchess (née Saxe-Meiningen) 297, 329
  Robert, Archduke 272
  Rudolf, Crown Prince of 92, 101, 178, 184, 198, 199, 200, 201, 203
  Stephan, Archduke 18
  Stéphanie, Crown Princess (née Belgium) 92, 101, 174, 178, 179, 184, 198, 199, 200, 202, 203, 204, 317, 318
  Wilhelm, Archduke 200
  Zita, Empress of (née Bourbon-Parma) 105, 184, 186, 256, 259, 260, 267, 273

B
Baden
  Alexandrine, Princess of (see Saxe-Coburg)
  Friedrich II, Grand Duke of 251
  Hilda, Grand Duchess of (née Nassau) 251
  Josephine, Princess of (see Hohenzollern)
  Louise, Princess of (see Russia)
  Luise, Grad Duchess of 312
  Ludwig, Prince of 290
  Max, Prince of (Imperial Chancellor) 126, 303, 310, 311
  Max, Margrave of 329
  Victoria, Princess of (see Sweden)
  Valerie, Margravine of (née Austria-Tuscany) 329
  Wilhelm, Prince of 175
Baels, Henri 260, 263
Baels, Lilian (see Réthy)
Balkany, Robert de 324
Baratta-Dragono, Baroness Maria-Carolina von 212
Baratta-Dragono, Baron Richard von 212
Baratta-Dragono, Baron Richard-Pedro von 212
Battenberg
  Alexander, Prince of (see Bulgaria)
  Alice, Princess of (see Greece)
  Beatrice, Princess of (née Great Britain) 62, 66, 67, 148, 298
  George, Prince of 302
  Julie, Princess of (née von Hauke) 100
  Louis, Prince of 66, 68, 76, 79, 117, 302
  Louise, Princess of (later Mountbatten, Queen of Sweden) 249, 302, 313
  Victoria, Princess of (née Hesse & By Rhine) 66, 68, 117, 119, 298, 302, 308, 311
  Victoria Eugenie(a), Princess of (see Spain)
Bauer, Caoline 22, 38
Bavaria
  Adelgunde, Princess of (see Hohenzollern)
  Albrecht, Duke of 184
  Amalie, Duchess in 184, 186
  Augusta, Princess of (see Leuchtenberg)
  Elisabeth, Duchess in (see Austria)
  Elisabeth, Duchess in (see Belgium)
  Ferdinand, Prince of 186
  Franz, Prince of 186
  Franz, Duke of 329
  Franz Joseph, Duke in 184, 186
  Georg, Prince of 185
  Hildegard, Princess of 231
  Karl Theodor, Duke in 184, 316
  Ludwig I, King of 231
  Ludwig II, King of 58
  Ludwig III, King of 186, 211, 316
  Ludwig Wilhelm, Duke in 184
  Luitpold, Prince Regent of 186
  Maria Josepha (José), Duchess in (née Portugal) 184, 330, 353
  Marie Gabriele, Duchess in 184, 186
  Mathilde, Princess of 211
  Max Emanuel, Duke in 290, 329
  Maximilian I, King of 44
  Rudolf, Prince of 186
  Rupprecht, Crown Prince of 184, 189
  Sophie, Duchess in (see Orléans)
  Sophie, Duchess in (married Toerring-Jettenbach) 184, 353
  Therese, Queen of (née Saxe-Hildburghausen) 231
Belgium
  Albert I, King of the Belgians 160, 180, 182, 183, 184, 185, 186, 187, 188, 189, 190, 191, 220, 249, 255, 256, 316, 318, 319, 320, 353
  Albert II, King of the Belgians 258, 263, 266, 268, 270, 271, 272, 275
  Alexandre, Prince of 263, 267
  Astrid, Queen of (née Sweden) 255, 256, 257, 258, 259, 264, 326
  Astrid, Princess of 271, 272, 273, 298
  Aymeric, Prince of 275
  Baudouin, Prince of 29, 181, 182, 183, 258, 259, 263, 265, 266, 267, 268, 269, 270, 271, 272, 273, 275, 317
  Charles Théodore, Count of Flanders 185, 189, 190, 265, 298, 326
  Charlotte, Princess of (Empress of Mexico) 46, 47, 51, 170, 172, 173, 181, 224, 226, 318
  Claire, Princess of (née Coombs) 275
  Clémentine, Princess of (see Napoléon)
  Elisabeth, Queen of (née Bavaria) 184, 185, 186, 188, 189, 190, 191, 255, 256, 259, 260, 263, 265, 266, 269, 272, 319, 320, 327, 353
  Elisabeth, Duchess of Brabant 274
  Eléonore, Princess of 274
  Emmanuel, Prince of 274
  Fabiola, Queen of (née Mora y Aragón) 267, 268, 269, 270, 274
  Gabriel, Prince of 274
  Henriette, Princess of 181, 182, 183
  Joséphine, Princess of 181
  Joséphine, Princess of (see Hohenzollern)
  Joséphine Charlotte, Princess of (see Luxembourg)
  Laurent, Prince of 271, 272
  Léopold I, King of the Belgians iv, 29, 44, 46, 47, 48, 49, 50, 51, 53, 57, 61, 62, 88, 117, 143, 147, 170, 172, 173, 174, 175, 178, 181, 224, 228, 229, 230, 353
  Léopold II, King of the Belgians 29, 46, 47, 71, 113, 155, 170, 172, 173, 174, 175, 176, 177, 178, 179, 180, 182, 183, 184, 185, 190, 196, 203, 204, 205, 208, 318
  Léopold III, King of the Belgians 184, 189, 190, 255, 256, 257, 258, 259, 260, 261, 262, 263, 264, 265, 266, 267, 269, 279, 324, 326, 327
  Léopold, Duke of Brabant 29, 174, 176, 317
  Louis-Philippe, Crown Prince 29, 46
  Louise, Princess of (see Saxe-Coburg)
  Louise, Princess of 275
  Louise-Marie, Queen of (née Orléans) 44, 46, 47, 48, 49, 61, 88, 90, 91, 170, 173, 182, 196
  Marie, Countess of Flanders (née Hohenzollern) 47, 176, 182, 183, 186, 203, 231
  Marie-Christine, Princess of 266, 267
  Marie-Esmeralda, Princess of 266, 267
  Marie-Henriette, Queen of (née Austria) 46-47, 172, 173, 174, 175, 176, 178, 179, 180, 181, 190, 196, 203
  Marie-José, Princess of (see Savoy)
  Mathilde, Queen of (née d'Udekem d'Acoz) 273, 274, 275
  Nicolas, Prince of 275
  Paola, Queen of (née Ruffo di Calabria) 268, 270, 271, 272, 275
  Philippe, Count of Flanders 29, 46, 47, 170, 176, 180, 181, 182, 183, 231
  Philippe I, King of (duke of Brabant) 271, 273, 274, 275
  Stéphanie, Princess of (see Austria)
Belmont, Ernst-August (Knight of Hallenberg) 16, 23
Bentheim und Steinfurt
  Alexis, Fürst of 116, 117
  Pauline, Fürstin of (née Waldeck-Pyrmont) 116, 117
Bern
  Friedrich, Count of ii
Bernhardt, Sarah 150
Bismarck, Prince Otto von (Imperial Chancellor) 9, 51, 65, 73, 99, 100, 101, 104, 148, 152, 175, 201

Boël, Delphine 272, 275
Boelke, Bishop 336
Braun, Margaretha 23
Brazil
  Amélie, Empress of (née Leuchtenberg) 55, 56, 58
  Francisca, Princess of 54
  Isabelle, Princess d'Orléans-Bragança (see Orléans)
  Izabel, Princess Imperial of 46, 96, 202, 209, 210, 211
  Januária, Princess of 54
  Leopoldine, Princess of (see Saxe-Coburg & Gotha)
  Maria Francisca, Princess d'Orléans-Bragança (see Portugal)
  Marie Amélia, Princess of 56
  Marie Leopoldine, Empress (née Austria) 54, 213
  Paula, Princess of 54
  Pedro I (see Portugal, Pedro IV, King of)
  Pedro II, Emperor of 53, 54, 202, 210, 244, 252
  Pedro d'Alcantara, Prince of 211, 297
  Teresa Cristina, Empress of (née Bourbon-Two Sicilies) 244
Broglie, Yolande, Princess de 324
Brown, John 65, 67, 77
Bruneck, Baron Ernst von 23
Bruneck, Baron Robert von 23
Brunswick-Blankenburg
  Antonia Amalia, Princess of (see Brunswick-Wolfenbüttel)
Brunswick-Wolfenbüttel
  Anton Ulrik, Duke of ii, 11
  Antonia Amalia, Duchess of (née Brunswick-Blankenburg) ii
  Caroline, Princess of (see Great Britain)
  Elisabeth, Duchess of iv
  Elisabeth Christine, Princess of (see Austria)
  Elisabeth Christine, Princess of (see Prussia)
  Ferdinand Albert II, Duke of ii
  Juliane Maria, Princess of (see Denmark)
  Karl I, Duke of ii
  Louisa Amalia, Princess of (see Prussia)
  Sophia Antonia, Princess of (see Saxe-Coburg)
Buchanan, James (US President) 144
Buíça, Manuel reis 247
Bulgaria
  Alexander, Prince of 79, 96, 100, 101, 103, 300
  Beltrán, Prince of 292
  Boris III, King of 29, 106, 109, 111, 113, 276, 278, 279, 280, 281, 282, 283, 284, 285, 286, 287, 294, 321
  Boris, Prince of 292
  Carla, Princess of Panagjuriste (née Royo-Villanova) 292
  Eleonore, Queen of (née Reußzu Köstritz) 107, 108, 109, 110, 111
  Eudoxia, Princess of 107, 207, 260, 279, 281, 286, 288, 291, 321
  Ferdinand I, King of (né Saxe-Coburg) 29, 46, 71, 95, 96, 97, 99, 100, 101, 102, 103, 104, 105, 106, 107, 108, 109, 110, 111, 112, 113, 128, 207, 208, 209, 249, 276, 280, 282, 288, 294, 350
  Giovanna, Queen of (née Savoy) 113, 255, 280, 281, 282, 286, 287, 288
  Kalina, Princess of 292, 293
  Kardam, Prince of Tirnovo 291, 292, 294, 297
  Konstantin-Assen, Prince of Vidin 291
  Kubrat, Prince of Panagjuriste 291, 292
  Kyril, Prince of 107, 113, 216, 217, 279, 280, 281, 286, 287, 321
  Kyril, Prince of Preslav 291, 329
  Lucas, Prince of 292
  Mafalda, Princess of 292
  Margarita, Queen of (née Gómez-Acebo y Cejuela) 290, 291, 292, 293, 294
  María, Princess of Vidin (née García de la Rasilla) 293
  Marie Louise, Princess of (née Bourbon-Parma) 105, 106, 107
  Marie Louise, Princess of 281, 288, 289
  Mirko, Prince of 292
  Miriam, Princess of Tirnovo (née de Ungría) 292, 294
  Nadejda, Princess of (see Württemberg)
  Olimpia, Princess of 292
  Rosario, Princess of Preslav (née Nadal) 292, 329

  Simeon II, King of 282, 287, 288, 289, 290, 291, 292, 293, 294, 295, 297, 350
  Sofía, Princess of
  Tassilo, Prince of 292
  Tirso, Prince of 292
  Umberto, Prince of 293
Bush, Prescott 138

C

Calvi di Bergolo, Count Giorgio 255
Calvi di bergolo, Countess Matilda 255
Cambridge, Lady Mary 128
Caprivi, Leo von
Carroll, Lewis 114
Casa Riera, Marquess of 267
Cassel, Sir Ernest 151
Castell-Rüdenhausen
  Bertram, Count of 129, 139
  Friedrich-Wolfgang, Count of 129
Channon, Sir Henry "Chips" 169
Chrobok, Bronislaw 289
Churchill, Randolph 164
Churchill, Sir Winston 150, 262
Ciano, Count Galeazzo 322
Clifden, Nellie 147, 148
Commarque, Count Cyril de 298, 353
Conroy, Captain John 42, 43
Constantine, Eastern Roman emperor 13
Cornellian, Count 20
Cortina, Marqués de 290
Costa Alfredo, 247
Croÿ, Princess Isabella of 186

D

Daneels, Mario 272
David, Norman H. 138
Denmark
  Aage, Prince of 255
  Alexander, Prince of (see Norway)
  Alexandra, Princess of (see Great Britain)
  Alexandrine, Queen of (née Mecklenburg-Schwerin) 257
  Anne Marie, Princess of (see Greece)
  Axel, Prince of 255, 256
  Carl, Prince of (see Norway, Haakon VII)
  Christian VIII 145
  Christian IX, King of 59, 73, 145, 147, 148, 150, 329
  Christian X, King of 160, 257
  Dagmar, Princess of (see Russia)
  Feodora-Louise, Princess of 260
  Frederik V, King of iv
  Frederik VII 145
  Frederik VIII 145, 156, 159, 249, 255, 303
  Frederik IX, King of 259, 313
  Frederik, Crown Prince of 297
  Ingeborg, Princess of (see Sweden)
  Ingrid, Princess of (née Sweden) 259, 313
  Juliane Maria, Queen of (née Brunswick-Wolfenbüttel) iv, 12
  Louise, Queen of (née Hesse-Kassel) 73, 145, 146, 147, 148, 150
  Louise, Queen of (née Sweden) 159, 255
  Margrethe II, Queen of 313
  Margrethe, Princess of (see Parma)
  Marie, Princess of (née Orléans) 145
  Mary, Crown Princess of (née Donaldson) 297
  Thyra, Princess of 145
  Valdemar, Prince of 100, 145
  William, Prince of (see Greece, George I King of the Hellenes)
Deslys, Gaby 249, 251
Dietrichstein, Countess Alexandrine von 38
Disraeli, Benjamin 143
Dolgorukova, Catherine, Princess 11
Douglas, Count Robert 253
Dulles, Allen 138

E

Echandi, Mario (President of Costa Rica) 348
Egypt
  Farouk, King of 288
Eppinghoven, Baron Arthur von 49
Eppinghoven, Baron George von 49
Erbach-Schönberg
  Carolina-Ernestine, Countess of (see Reuß)
Eulenburg, Fürst Philipp zu 121

F

Fermepin, Sophie 18, 19
Fife, Duke of (Alexander Duff) 154, 159, 303
Filov, Bogdan (Bulgarian Prime Minister) 286
Fitzgerald, Mabel 82
Fitzjames-Stuart
  Alba y Berwick, Duke of 319
  Galisteo y Tamames, Duchess of 319
  Peñaranda, Duke of 319
Flahaut, Count de 90
France
  Charles X, King of 88
  Henri, Count de Chambord 105, 240
  Louis XIV, King of 1
  Louis XVI, King of 1, 240
  Marie Antoinette, Queen of (née Austria)
Franco, João 246, 247
Fruchaud, Dr. John 329

G

Galliera, Duchess de 241, 301
Gaulle, Charles de 319
Gersdorff, Johann Rudolf Ritter von 210
Gheorgieff, General 279
Goffinet, August 318
Golovina, Countess 15
Gregowicz, Lotte (aka Mila Rybicza) 205, 206, 207
Groitzsch
  Friedrich, Count of ii
Great Britain
  Adelaide, Queen of (née Saxe-Meiningen) 147
  Albert, Prince Consort (né Saxe-Coburg & Gotha) 4, 19, 21, 22, 23, 43, 47, 50, 62, 64, 65, 67, 73, 74, 75, 88, 114, 143, 144, 145, 146, 147, 149, 162, 224, 226, 228, 229, 231, 237, 245, 248, 297, 298, 299, 301, 308, 310, 347
  Albert Victor, Duke of Clarence 29, 149, 152, 153, 161, 162, 163, 174
  Alexander, Prince of 152
  Alexandra, Queen of (Princess of Wales) (née Denmark) 67, 69, 76, 78, 145, 146, 147, 148, 149, 150, 151, 152, 157, 158, 159, 160, 161, 163, 164, 166, 257, 303
  Alexandra, Duchess of Fife 249
  Alice, Princess of (see Hesse and By Rhine)
  Alice, Princess of (Countess of Athlone) 68, 82, 117, 118, 119, 120, 126, 128, 140, 189
  Andrew, Duke of York 351
  Arthur, Duke of Connaught 29, 62, 66, 86, 87, 119, 123, 128, 175, 249, 312
  Arthur (Jr.), Prince of 29, 66, 86, 87, 119
  Augustus, Duke of Sussex 34
  Beatrice, Princess of (see Battenberg) 62
  Caroline, Queen of (also Princess of Wales (née Brunswick-Wolfenbüttel) 30
  Charles, Prince of Wales 293
  Charlotte, Queen of (née Mecklenburg-Strelitz) 41
  Charlotte, Princess of Wales 18, 30, 32, 33, 34, 35, 39, 41, 44, 50
  Diana, Princess of Wales (née Spencer)
  Edward III, King of 143
  Edward VII, King of (Prince of Wales) 29, 38, 62, 64, 65, 66, 67, 68, 69, 71, 76, 110, 114, 116, 118, 122, 143, 144, 145, 146, 147, 148, 149, 150, 151, 152, 153, 154, 155, 156, 157, 158, 161, 162, 165, 166, 167, 175, 196, 245, 246, 248, 249, 303, 312
  Edward VIII, King of (Prince of Wales, Duke of Windsor) 136, 137, 164, 166, 169, 251, 282
  Edward, Duke of Kent 34, 41, 42, 143
  Edward, Duke of Kent (b. 1935) 290

Edward, The Black Prince 143
Elizabeth II, Queen of 169, 270
Ernest August, Duke of Cumberland (King of Hannover) 43
George III, King of 30, 35, 41, 43
George IV (also Prince of Wales, Prince Regent), King of 30, 32, 34, 35, 41, 42, 43, 62
George V, King (Duke of York, Prince of Wales) 66, 71, 81, 85, 117, 126, 134, 136, 137, 153, 157, 158, 159, 160, 161, 162, 163, 164, 165, 166, 167, 168, 169, 172, 184, 187, 248, 251, 281, 282, 297, 305, 311
George VI 164, 190, 266, 282, 283, 321
George, Duke of Cambridge 175
George, Prince of (Duke of Kent) 136, 164, 184
Helena, Princess of (see Schleswig-Holstein)
Helene, Duchess of Albany (née Waldeck-Pyrmont) 68, 116, 117, 118, , 119, 120, 128
Henry, Duke of Gloucester 164, 257
Leopold (Duke of Albany) 62, 68, 71, 86, 114, 116, 117, 118, 150
Louise, Princess of 21, 62, 66, 68
Louise, Princess Royal (Duchess of Fife) 149, 154, 303
Louise, Duchess of Connaught (née Prussia) 249, 312
Margaret, Princess of (see Sweden)
Maud, Princess of (see Norway)
Maud, Princess of Fife 249
Mary ("May"), Queen of (Duchess of York, Princess of Wales) (née Teck) 66, 67, 68, 153, 158, 160, 163, 164, 165, 166, 167, 169, 172, 303, 311
Mary, Princess Royal 164
Mary Adelaide, Princess of (see Teck)
Michael, Prince of Kent 350
Patricia, Princess of 249, 312
Philip, Duke of Edinburgh (né Greece) 302, 350, 353
Sophia, Princess of 43
Victoria, Queen of (Alexandrina Victoria of Kent) 7, 9, 22, 37, 38, 41, 43, 44, 47, 49, 50, 51, 53, 59, 62, 64, 65, 66, 67, 68, 69, 70, 71, 74, 75, 76, 77, 78, 79, 84, 85, 86, 87, 88, 90, 91, 94, 96, 97, 104, 105, 106, 114, 116, 117, 118, 119, 120, 134, 143, 144, 145, 146, 147, 148, 149, 150, 153, 154, 157, 161, 162, 163, 164, 165, 166, 168, 169, 172, 173, 174, 175, 181, 224, 226, 228, 230, 231, 232, 234, 239, 243, 245, 248, 289, 297, 298, 299, 301, 302, 308, 311, 312, 345, 347, 348
Victoria, Princess Royal (see Prussia)
Victoria, Princess of 66, 149, 154, 303
William IV, King of (Duke of Clarence) 32, 41, 42, 43, 147, 154
Greece
Alexander I, King of the Hellenes 276, 300
Alexia, Princess of 273
Alice, Princess of (née Battenberg) 302, 303
Andrew, Prince of 303
Anne Marie, Queen of (née Denmark) 313
Christopher, Prince of 113, 280
Constantine I, King of the Hellenes 62, 300, 301
Constantine II, King of the Hellenes 290, 297
Elisabeth, Princess of 184
Elisabeth, Queen of (née Romania) 281, 305, 306
Françoise, Princess of (née Orléans) 113, 280
Frederica, Queen of (née Hannover) 289, 348
George I, King of the Hellenes (Prince William of Denmark) 71, 73, 76, 145, 147, 148, 149, 156, 157, 159, 249
George II, King of the Hellenes 306
George, Prince of 329
Margarita, Princess of (see Hohenlohe-Langenburg)
Marina, Princess of 184
Nicholas, Prince of 307
Olga, Queen of 149
Olga, Princess of (see Yugoslavia)
Otto, King of (né Bavaria) 44, 59, 73, 75
Philip, Prince of (see Great Britain)
Sophie, Queen of (née Prussia) 62, 156, 297, 300, 301
Sophie (Sofía), Princess of (see Spain)
Greville, Francis (Earl of Warwick) 114
Grévy, Jules 242

H
Hanneken, General Hermann von 337
Hannover
Alexandra, Princess of (see Leiningen)
Ernst August, Crown Prince of (Duke of Cumberland) 126, 145, 169
Ernst August, Duke of Brunswick 167
Frederica, Princess of (see Greece)
Friederike, Princess of 77, 114, 117
Georg V, King of 114, 145
Georg wilhelm, Prince of Hannover 159
Thyra, Duchess of Cumberland (née Denmark) 145
Viktoria Luise, Duchess of Brunswick 130, 131, 167, 209
Hanstein, Alexander von 20, 21
Harden, Maximilian 121, 122
Hearst, William Randolplh 137
Heller, Athlone von 218
Heller, Eduard von 218
Heller, helene von 218
Heller, Marie-Amelie von 218
Henriques de carvalho, Cardinal-patriarch Guillherme 227
Hensler, Elise (Countess of Edla) 61, 236
Herzl, Theodor 204
Hesse-Darmstadt (also & By Rhine)
Alexander, Prince of 100
Alice, Grand Duchess of (née Great Britain) 62, 67, 76, 114, 231, 298, 301, 302
Alix, Princess of (see Russia)
Cecile, Hereditary Grand Duchess of (see Greece) 303
Eleonore, Grand Duchess of (née Solms-Hohensolms-Lich) 303
Elisabeth, Princess of (see Russia)
Elisabeth, Princess of (1895-1903) 307, 308
Ernst Ludwig, Grand Duke of 71, 79, 84, 119, 121, 156, 302, 303, 307, 308, 311
Friedrich, Prince of 302
Georg Donatus, Hereditary Grand Duke of 303
Irene, Princess of (see Prussia)
Johanna, Princess of 303
Ludwig IV, Grand Duke of 76, 114, 116, 175, 231, 301
Ludwig, Prince of 303
Margaret, Princess of (née Geddes) 303
Marie, Princess of (see Russia)
Marie, Princess of 302
Wilhelmina Louise, Princess of (see Russia)
Hesse-Kassel
Anna, Landgravine of (née Prussia) 114
Elisabeth, Princess of 114
Friedrich, Landgrave 114
Friedrich-Karl, Landgrave of 62, 300, 301
Karl, Prince of 290
Karoline Amalie , Princess of (see Saxe-Gotha)
Louise, Princess of (see Denmark)
Mafalda, Princess of (née Savoy) 287, 323
Margarete, Landgravine of (née Prussia) 62, 300, 301
Moritz, Landgrave of 290, 350
Heuss, Theodor 133
Himmler, Heinrich 134
Hindenburg, Paul von 133, 134
Hirsch, Baron Moritz von 151
Hitler, Adolf 131, 132, 133, 134, 135, 136, 137, 138, 139, 140, 141, 169, 191, 208, 212, 283, 284, 285, 287, 312, 336
Hochberg, Count Conrad von 338
Hohenberg, Sophie, Duchess of 168
Hohenlohe-Langenburg
Adelheid, Princess of (see Schleswig-Holstein-Sonderburg-Augustenburg)
Alexandra, Fürstin of (née Saxe-Coburg & Gotha and Edinburgh) 79, 84, 120, 298, 309, 310, 311, 312
Alexandra, Princess of 311
Alfred, Prince of 311
Cércile, Princess of 298, 353
Ernst I, Fürst of 40, 50, 55
Ernst II, Fürst of 79, 120, 310, 311, 312
Feodora, Fürstin of (née Leiningen) 40, 88, 114, 202, 289, 298
Gottfried, Fürst of 311

Hermann, Fürst of 310
Irma, Princess of 311
Kaft, Fürst of 290, 350, 351
Margarita, Fürstin of (née Greece) 298, 311
Marie Agnes, Princess of (see Löwensteti-Wertheim-Rosenberg)
Marie Melita, Pirncess of (see Schleswig-Holstein-Sonderburg-Glücksburg)
Philipp, Fürst of 351, 353
Saskia, Fürstin of (née Binder) 353
Hohenlohe-Oehringen
Kraft, Fürst of 350
Hohenzollern
Adelgunde, Fürstin of (née Bavaria) 316
Antónia, Fürstin of (née Portugal) 58, 181, 230, 239, 251, 298, 313, 315, 316
Auguste Viktoria, Princess of (see Portugal)
Josephine, Fürstin of (née Baden) 180
Joséphine, Princess of (née Belgium) 182, 316
Karl, Prince of (see Romania)
Karl Anton, Fürst of 180, 226, 316
Ferdinand, Prince of (see Romania)
Franz Joseph, Prince of 316
Friedrich, Fürst of 316
Leopold, Fürst of 59, 175, 181, 229, 230, 236, 237, 251, 315
Margarete, Fürstin of (née Saxony) 316
Maria Alix, Princess of (née Saxony) 316
Maria Teresa, Fürstin of (née Bourbon-Two Sicilies) 316
Marie, Princess of (see Belgium)
Stephanie, Princess of (see Portugal)
Wilhelm, Fürst of 251, 316
Holstein-Gottorp
Karl Peter Ulrik, Duke of 12
Horst, Baroness Feodora von der 129
Hoyos, Count Joseph 199, 200, 201

I
Izvolsky, Alexander 157

J
Jerome, Jennie (Lady Randolph Churchill) 150

K
Kennedy, John Fitzgerald (US President) 138
Kennedy, Joseph (US Ambassador) 137-138
Keppel, Alice 150
Keppel, George 150
Kohary
Kohary, Count Andreas of 195
Kohary, Countess Antonia (Antoinette) of (see Saxe-Coburg)
Kohary, Prince Franz Joseph of 25, 195
Konrad II, Holy Roman Emperor ii, 320
Krieg, Gerturd 340

L
La Harpe, Frédéric-César 13, 14
Lacroix, Caroline (Baroness de Vaughan) 178, 180179
Langtry, Lillie 150
Lavradio, Count of 224, 226
Leiningen
Alexandra, Fürstin of (née Hannover) 298
Andreas, Fürst of 298
Carl Emich, Prince of 40, 289
Carl Friedrich, Prince of 40
Christiane Wilhelmine, Princess of (née Solms-Rödelheim und Assenheim) 40
Emich Carl, Prince of 34, 40
Feodora, Princess of (see Hohenlohe-Langenburg)
Friedrich Karl, Hereditary Prince of 40
Karl, Fürst of 289, 308
Karl Wladimir, Prince of 289
Lindbergh, Charles 138
Liszt, Franz 22

Leuchtenberg
  Augusta, Duchess of (née Bavaria) 56
  Auguste, Duke of (King of Portugal) 56
  Eugène of (né Beauharnais) 44, 55
  Eugène, Duke of 44, 56
  Maria Amélia, Princess of (see Brazil)
Liapchev, Andrey (Bulgarian Prime Minister) 280
Liddell, Alice 114
Liechtenstein
  Barbara, Princess of (see Yugoslavia)
  Elisabeth, Princess of (née Austria) 184
  Franz Joseph, Prince of 184, 330
  Nikolaus, Prince of 330
  Tatiana, Princess of 273
Liverpool, Lord 32
Livingstone, David 177
lloyd george, david 262
Loscheck, Johann 200, 201
Loulé, Duke of 53, 233
Löwenstein-Wertheim-Rosenberg
  Adelheid, Princess of (see Portugal)
  Aloys-Konstantin, Fürst of 329
  Anastasia, Fürstin of (née Prussia) 329
  Constantin, Hereditary Prince of 55
  Marie Agnes, Hereditary Princess of (née Hohenlohe-Langenburg) 55
  Marie Therese, Princess of 252
Lower Lusatia
  Dietrich, Margrave of ii
Lundeen, Ernest (US Senator) 138, 139
Luxembourg
  Adolf, Grand Duke of (né Nassau) 145
  Charlotte, Grand Duchess of 184, 257, 326, 327, 328, , 330
  Dianne, Princess of (née de Guerre) 330
  Felix, Prince of (né Bourbon-Parma) 105, 328
  Guillaume IV, Grand Duke of 186
  Guillaume, Prince of 298, 328, 330
  Henri, Grand Duke of 328, 330
  Jean, Grand Duke of 266, 327, 328, 329, 330, 331
  Jean, Prince of 328, 330
  Joséphine Charlotte, Grand Duchess of (née Belgium) 258, 263, 266, 298, 299, 326, 327, 328, 329, 330, 331, 351
  Margaretha, Princess of 328, 330
  Maria Ana, Grand Duchess of (née Portugal) 330
  María Teesa, Grand Duchess of (née Mestre) 330
  Marie Astrid, Princess of 328, 330
  Sibilla, Princess of (née Weiller) 298, 330

M
Mafra, Count of 238
Mallet, Marie 119
Malmesbury, Lord 30
Manso de Lelaso, José Antonio 293
Marlborough, Sarah, Duchess of 147
Mattachich, Count Geza 202, 203, 204
Maynard, Daisy (Countess of Warwick) 114, 150
Mayrhofer, Luise 212
Mecklenburg-Schwerin
  Alexandrine, Duchess of (see Denmark)
  Elisabeth, Duchess of (see Brunswick-Wolfenbüttel)
  Hélène, Duchess of (see Orléans)
  Karl Leopold, Duke of 11
  Louise, Duchess of (see Saxe-Gotha)
  Maria, Duchess of (see Russia)
Mecklenburg-Strelitz
  Augusta, Grand Duchess of 146, 158
  Charlotte, Duchess of (see Great Britain)
Meißen
  Konrad, Margrave of ii
  Otto, Margrave of Meißen ii
Melbourne, Lord 38, 73
Mellon, Andrew 138
Mensdorff-Pouilly, Count Albert Viktor 38
Mensdorff-Pouilly, Count Alexander 37, 38
Mensdorff-Pouilly, Count Alfons 37
Mensdorff-Pouilly, Count Alfred 37
Mensdorff-Pouilly, Count Arthur 37
Mensdorff-Pouilly, Count Emmanuel 37, 38

Mensdorff-Pouilly, Count Hugo 37
Mensdorff-Pouilly, Count Leo Emanuel 37
Menshikoc, Alexander Danilovich 11
Metternich, Prince Clemens von 56
Metternich, Princess Pauline von 102
Meyer, Arcadia (née Claret) 49, 50
Monaco
  Albert, Prince of 246
Moncada, Salvador 267
Montenegro
  Elena, Princess of (see Italy)
Montezuma II, Azted Emperor 292
Morocco,
  Hassan II, King of 291
Mountbatten of Burma, Louis, Earl (né Battenberg) 76
Muñoz, Antonio (Kitín) 293
Muñoz y de Bulgaria, Simeon Hassan 293
Mussolini, Benito 130, 135, 153, 281, 282, 284, 321, 323

N
Napoléon
  Alix, Princess (née de Foresta) 319, 329
  Eugenie, Empress 68, 117, 318, 319
  Clémentine, Princess (née Belgium) 156, 176, 178, 179, 182, 298, 317, 318, 319, 320
  Clotilde, Princess (née Savoy) 319
  Hortense, Princess (née Beauharnais) 33, 44
  Jean-Christophe, Prince 319
  Joséphine, Empress 33
  Louis, Prince (Napoléon I's brother) 33
  Louis, Prince (1914-1996) 319
  Marie Clotilde, Princess 298, 319
  Napoléon, (Plon-Plon), Prince 226, 242, 317
  Napoléon I 7, 16, 18, 30, 33, 34, 37, 39, 40, 44, 53, 55, 57, 61, 319, 320
  Napoléon III 175, 226, 230, 235, 236, 240, 317, 318
  Napoléon, Prince Imperial 317
  Victor, Prince 178, 317, 318, 319
Nassau-Weilburg
  Amalie, Princess of (see Anhalt-Schaumburg)
  Hilda, Princess of (see Baden)
  Marie, Princess of (see Wied)
  Nicholas, Prince of 175
  Sophie, Princess of (see Sweden)
Netherlands
  Emma, Queen of the 116
  Wilhelmina, Queen of the 116, 262
  Willem I, King of the 30, 32, 44
  Willem II, King of the 30, 32, 33, 34, 39
  Willem III, King of the 116, 230
Nicolis de Robilant, Carlo Felice 218
Nightingale, Florence 301
Norway
  Astrid, Princess of 304
  Haakon VII. King of (né Denmark) 154, 155, 156, 160, 166, 249, 303, 304
  Harald V, King of 154. 290, 304
  Märtha, Crown Princess of (née Sweden) 255, 304
  Maud, Queen of (née Great Britain) 149, 154, 166, 297, 298, 303
  Olav V, King of (né alexander of Denmark) 155, 257, 303, 304
  Ranghild, Princess of 304

O
O'Brien, Sister Veronica 268
O'Farrell, James 77
Oettingen-Spielberg, Albrecht, Fürst of 329
Orléans
  Adelaïde, Princess 90
  Amélie, Princess (see Portugal)
  Antoine, Duke de Montpensier 237, 240, 244
  Charles, Prince 240
  Clémentine, Princess (see Saxe-Coburg)
  Emmanuel, Duke de Vendôme 182, 184, 251
  Ferdinand, Duke d'Alençon 182, 183
  Ferdinand, Duke d'Orléans 90, 239
  Ferdinand, Duke de Montpensier 240

Francisca, Princess de Joinville 209
François, Prince de Joinville 54
Françoise, Duchess de Chartres 145
Françoise, Princess (see Greece)
Gaston, Count d'Eu 209, 252, 297
Hélène, Duches d'Orléans (née Mecklenburg-Schwerin) 239
Hélène, Princess (later Duchess of Aosta) 152, 153, 240, 251
Henri, Duke d'Aumâle 88, 104, 196, 240, 242
Henri, Count of Paris (1908-1999) 267, 288, 289
Henri, Count of Paris (b. 1933
Isabel, Countess of Paris (née Spain) 183, 240, 243
Isabelle, Princess (Duchess de Guise) 183, 184, 240
Isabelle, Countess of Paris (née Orléans-Braganza) 218, 288
Isabelle, Princess (daughter of Henri, Count of Paris) 267, 289
Jacques, Prince 240
Jean, Duke de Guise 113, 240, 280
Louis, Duke de Nemours 27, 44, 46, 88, 96, 182
Louis-Gaston, Count d'Eu 46
Louis-Philippe, King of the French 27, 39, 44, 55, 88, 90, 196, 239, 240, 318
Louis-Philippe, Count of Paris 152, 153, 183, 239, 240, 241, 242, 243, 244, 317
Louise, Princess (see Spain)
Luisa fernanda, Duchess de Montpensier (née Spain) 240
Maria Dorothea, Duchess d'Orléans (née Austria) 239, 240
Marie, Princess (see Württemberg)
Marie, Princess (see Denmark)
Marie-Amélie, Queen of the French (née Two Sicilies) 44, 49, 90
Micaela, Countess of Paris (née Cousiño) 329
Philippe, Duke d'Orléans 183, 240
Robert, Duke de Charteres 145
Sophie, Duchess d'Alençon 182, 183, 184
Oldenburg
  Sophie Charlotte, Duchess of (see Prussia)
Oliveira, Maria 230, 231
Orlov, Gregory 12
Otto III, Holy Roman Emperor ii

P
Palmerston, Lord 51
Panam, Pauline 7, 9, 16, 23
Patch, General 327
Patton, General George 140
Pawel-Rammingen, Baron Alfons 114
Papacy
  Gregory XVI, Pope 55
  John XXIII, Pope 267, 270, 285
Parma
  Carlos Hugo, Duke of 329
  Cecile, Princess of Bourbon- 267
  Felix, Prince of Bourbon- (see Luxembourg)
  Margrethe, Princess of Bourbon- (née Denmark) 255
  Maria Antónia, Duchess of (née Braganza) 330
  Maria Pia, Duchess of (née Bourbon-Two Sicilies) 105
  Marie Louise, Princess of Bourbon- (see Bulgaria)
  Michel, Prince of Bourbon 324
  René, Prince of Bourbon- 255, 257
  Robert, Duke of 105, 106
  Sixtus, Prince of Bourbon- 257
  Xavier, Duke of 105
  Zita, Princess of Bourbon- (see Austria)
Petre, Mr. (Brisith Minister in Lisbon) 244
Pierlot, Hubert (Belgian Prime Minister) 261, 262, 266
Ponsonby, Sir Henry 77
Portugal
  Afonso, Duke of Oporto 234, 238, 247, 251
  Amélie, Queen of (née Orléans) 61, 239, 240, 241, 242, 243, 244, 246, 247, 248, 249, 251, 252, 253
  Ana de Jesús, Infanta of 53
  Antónia, Infanta of (see Hohenzollern)
  Auguste Viktoria, Queen of (née Hohenzollern) 251, 253, 316

Augusto, Infante of 58, 228, 237
Carlos I, King of 68, 71, 154, 234, 235, 237, 238, 239, 240, 241, 242, 243, 244, 245, 246, 247,
Carlota Joaquina, Queen of (née Spain) 53, 54
Duarte Nunõ, Duke of Braganza 252
Duarte Pio, Duke of Braganza 184, 252, 297, 329
Ferdinand, King Consort (né Saxe-Coburg) 26, 29, 53, 56, 57, 58, 59, 61, 122, 220, 224, 230, 233, 234, 236, 245, 252, 297, 298, 313, 314
Fernando, Infante of 50, 58, 64, 228
Francisco, Infante of 53
Francisco José, infante of
Isabel, Infanta of 53, 233
Isabel, Duchess of Braganza (née Heredia) 297, 329
João VI, King of 53, 54, 55
João, Infante of (son of Maria II) 50, 58, 229
João, Infante of (son of Pedro IV)
Leopoldo, Infante of 58
Luís I, King of 58, 59, 154, 175, 229, 230, 231, 232, 233, 234, 235, 236, 237, 238, 239, 301, 315
Luís Filipe, Duke of Braganza 243, 247
Manoel II, King of 61, 110, 224, 243, 247, 248, 249, 250, 251, 252, 253, 316, 321
Maria I, Queen of 53
Maria II, Queen of 26, 53, 54, 55, 56, 57, 58, 59, 88, 91, 122, 220, 224, 230, 233, 245, 252, 313, 352
Maria, Infanta of 58
Maria, Infanta of (b/d 1840) 313
Maria Ana, Infanta (see Saxony)
Maria Ana, Infanta of 243
Maria Antonia, Infante of (see Parma)
Maria da Assunção, Infanta of 53
Maria da Glória, Infanta of 58
Maria da Glória, Infanta of (b./d. 1845) 313
Maria Francisca, Duchess of Braganza (née Orléans-Braganza [Brazil]) 252
Maria Isabel, Infanta of 53
Maria Josepha, Infanta of (see Belgium)
Maria Francisca, Infanta of 53
Maria Pia, Queen of (née Savoy) 61, 231, 232, 233, 234, 236, 237, 238, 239, 242, 249
Maria Teresa, Infanta of 53
Miguel I, King of 53, 54, 55, 105, 184, 231, 251, 315, 328, 330, 352, 353
Miguel, Infante of 54
Miguel, Infante of, Duke of Braganza 252
Miguel, Infante of 252, 315
Pedro IV, King of (Emperor Pedro I of Brazil) 53, 54, 55, 56, 233, 352
Pedro V, King of 29, 50, 58, 59, 65, 181, 224, 226, 227, 228, 229, 230, 231, 245
Stephanie, Queen of (née Hohenzollern) 50, 181, 226, 227, 228, 315
Pouilly, Aubertin IV de 37
Poully, Baron Emmanuel de 37
Princip, Gavrilo 168
Prussia
Alexander Ferdinand, Prince of 130, 132
Alfred, Prince of 347
Anna, Princess of (see Hesse-Kassel)
August, Prince of 33
August Wilhelm, Prince of iv
August Wilhelm, Prince of 120, 130, 131, 132, 251
Augusta, Empress (née Saxe-Weimar-Eisenach) 172
Augusta Viktoria, German Empress (née Schleswig-Holstein-Sonderburg-Augustenburg) 68, 120, 122, 202, 300, 311
Charlotte, Princess of (see Saxe-Meiningen)
Charlotte Agnes, Princess of (née Saxe-Altenburg) 302, 347
Eitel Friedrich, Prince of 120, 123, 130
Elisabeth Christine, Queen of (née Brunswick-Wolfenbüttel) iv
Friedrich II, the Great, King of iv
Friedrich III (Kaiser) 62, 149, 152, 175, 299, 300, 301, 312
Friedrich Wilhelm I, King of 172
Friedrich Wilhelm IV, King of
Friedrich Wilhelm, Crown Prince of 120, 131, 139, 164
Georg Friedrich, Prince of 297, 350
Heinrich, Prince of 300, 302, 347
Irene, Princess of (née Hesse and By Rhine) 300, 302
Kira Kirillovna, Princess of 280, 298, 308
Louis Ferdinand, Prince of 33, 139, 298, 308
Louisa Amalia, Princess of (née Brunswick-Wolfenbüttel) iv
Luise, Princess of (see Baden)
Luise, Princess of 172
Margarete, Princess of (see Hesse-Kassel)
Oskar, Prince of 130
Sigismund, Prince of 300
Sigismund, Prince of (1896-1978) 302, 347
Sophie, Princess of (see Greece)
Sophie Charlotte, Princess of (née Oldenburg) 123
Victoria (Empress Friedrich, Princess Royal) (née Great Britain) 62, 64, 75, 84, 87, 118, 119, 146, 149, 152, 181, 224, 298, 299, 300, 301
Victoria, Princess of 100, 300
Victoria Luise, Princess of (see Hannover)
Waldemar, Prince of 300
Wilhelm I (Kaiser) 73, 148, 152, 172, 229, 312
Wilhelm II (Kaiser) 38, 62, 66, 67, 68, 70, 71, 80, 85, 86, 87, 104, 105, 109, 110, 114, 119, 120, 123, 126, 151, 152, 155, 156, 167, 168, 186, 187, 188, 189, 202, 249, 251, 297, 299, 311, 316, 347

R
Radziwill, Tatiana, Princess 329
Ravenstein, Philippe, Count of 179
Razumovsky, Alexei 11, 12
Reid, Sir James 85
Reindl, Maria Theresia 129
Réthy, Lilian, Princes de 260, 263, 264, 265, 266, 267, 269, 327
Reuß
Augusta, Countess of Reuß-Ebersdorf (see Saxe-Coburg)
Carolina-Ernestine, Countess of Reuß-Ebersdorf (née Erbach-Schönberg)
Eleonore, Princess (see Bulgaria)
Heinrich IV 107
Heinrich XXIV, Count of Reuß-Ebersdorf 4
Luise, Princess 107
Sophie Henrietta, Countess of 40
Reyna y Corvalán, Luis 324, 325
Reyna y Saboya, Azaea, 324
Reyna y Saboya, Raffaelo 324
Rockefeller, John 138
Reynaud, Paul (French Prime Minister) 262
Rindernecht, Lea 340
Roey, Cardinal van 264, 267
Romania
Carol I, King of 99, 101, 108, 180, 305
Carol II, King of 282, 283, 305, 306, 307
Elisabeth, Queen of (née Wied) 109
Elisabeth, Princess of (see Greece)
Ferdinand I, King of (né Hohenzollern) 79, 85, 110, 280, 304, 305, 306, 311, 316
Ileana, Princess of 280, 305, 306, 308
Margarita, Crown Princess of 329
Marie, Queen of (née Saxe-Coburg & Gotha and Edinburgh) 74, 78, 84, 85, 109, 128, 156, 163, 297, 298, 304, 305, 306, 307, 309, 311, 316
Marie, Princess of (see Yugoslavia)
Michael, King of 297, 306
Mircea, Prince of 305
Nicholas, prince of 305, 306
Radu, Prince of (né Duda) 329
Rommel, Field Marshal Erwin 336
Roosevelt, Franklin Delano (US President) 138
Roosevelt, Theodore (US President) 179
Ruffo di Calabria, Fulco, Prince 270
Ruffo di Calabria, Luisa, Princess (née Gazelli di Rossna e di Sebastiano) 270
Russia
Alexander I, Tsar of 13, 14, 15, 16, 32, 33, 34, 39
Alexander II, Tsar of 77, 78, 99, 100, 101
Alexander III, Tsar of 96, 100, 101, 104, 145, 163
Alexandra Feodorovna, Empress (née Hesse & By Rhine) 156, 167, 297, 307, 308
Alexandra Pavlovna, Grand Duchess 18
Alexei Petrovich, Tsarevich of iv, 11
Alexei Nikolaievich, Tsarevich 309
Anna I, Empress 11
Anna Leopoldovna, Grand Duchess 11, 12
Anna Pavlovna, Grand Duchess 16, 39
Anna Petrovna, Grand Duchess 11, 12
Boris Vladimirovich, Grand Duke 305
Catherine I, Empress (Martha Skavronskaya) 11
Catherine II, the Great, Empress (née Anhalt-Zerbst) 4, 12, 13, 14
Catherine Ivanovna, Grand Duchess 11
Catherine Pavlovna, Grand Duchess 30, 32, 33
Charlotte, Tsarevna (née Brunswick-Wolfenbüttel) iv, 11
Elisabeth I, Empress 11, 12, 13
Elisabeth Alexeievna, Empress (née Baden) 14, 15, 39
Elisabeth Feodorovna, Grand Duchess (née Hesse and By Rhine) 302
Ivan V, tsar of 11
Ivan VI, Tsar of iv, 11, 12
Kira Kirillovna, Grand Duchess (see Prussia)
Kirill Vladimirovich, Grand Duke 79, 132, 280, 289, 308, 309
Konstantin Pavlovich, Grand Duke 13, 14, 15, 16, 37
Maria Alexandrovna, Empress of (née Hesse & By Rhine) 77
Marie Alexandrovna, Grand Duchess of (see Saxe-Coburg)
Maria Feodorovna, Empress (née Württemberg) 12, 13, 37, 38
Marie Kirillovna, Grand Duchess (Fürstin of Leiningen) 289, 298, 308, 309
Maria Pavlovna, Grand Duchess (née Mecklenburg-Schwerin, Grand Duchess Vladimir) 107
Marie Feodorovna, Empress (née Denmark) 145, 158, 159, 163
Michael Alexandrovich, Grand Duke 71, 309
Natalia Alexeievna, Grand Duchess 11
Natalia Alexeievna, Tsarevna (née Hesse-Darmstadt) 12
Nicholas II, Tsar of 71, 85, 156, 159, 163, 167, 168, 302, 308, 309
Nicholas Alexandrovich, Tsarevich 145, 163
Olga Konstantinovna, Grand Duchess (see Greece)
Paul I, Tsar of 4, 12, 13, 38
Paul Alexandrovich, Grand Duke 311
Peter I, the Great, Tsar of 11, 12
Peter II, Tsar of 11
Peter III, Tsar of 12
Vera Konstantinovna, Grand Duchess 83
Vladimir Alexandrovich, Grand Duke 107, 308
Wladimir Kirillovich, Grand Duke 309

S
Salazar, António Oliveira de 252
Salisbury, Lord 244
Saltykov, Count Nicholas 13
Saltykov, Count Sergei 12
Santos, Manuel Inocêncio Liberato dos 233
Sapieha, Princess Zofia 273
Savoy
Adelaide, Countess of Aosta (née Torino)
Adelheid, Queen of Sardinia (née Austria) 232
Aimone, Duke of Spoleto and Aosta 322
Amedeo, Duke of Aosta (Duke of Aosta) 236, 237, 244
Amedeo, Duke pf Aosta 322
Carlo, Prince of 234
Carlo Emanuele I, Duke of 320
Clotilde, Princess of (see Napoléon)
Clotilde, Princess of Venice (née Courau) 324
Elena, Queen of Italy (née Montenegro) 13, 280, 288, 321
Emanuele Filiberto, Duke of Aosta 71, 153, 240, 251, 319
Emanuele Filiberto, Prince of Venice 324
Giovanna, Princess of (see Bulgaria)
Jolanda, Princess of 255, 280

Mafalda, Princess of (see Hesse-Kassel)
Margherita, Princess of (see Austria)
Maria, Princess of 260
Maria Beatrice, Princess of 322, 324, 325
Maria Gabriella, Princess of 267, 322, 323, 324
Maria Pia, Princess of (see Portugal)
Maria Pia, Princess of 322, 324
Marie José, Queen of Italy (née Belgium) 320, 321, 322, 323, 324, 325, 326
Maria Vittoria, Duchess of Aosta (del Pozzo, Princess della Cisterna) 236
Marie-José, Queen of Italy (née Belgium) 185, 186, 189, 259, 297, 299
Marina, Princess of Naples (née Doria) 324, 329
Oddone, Count of Aosta 320
Tommaso, Duke of Genoa 251
Umberto "Biancamano", Count of Aosta 320
Umberto II, King of Italy 288, 291, 320, 321, 322, 323, 324, 325
Vittorio Emanuele II, King of Italy 230, 232, 236, 239
Vittorio Emanuele III, King of Italy 71, 113, 255, 260, 280, 288, 320, 321, 323
Vittorio Emanuele, Prince of Naples 297, 322, 324, 329

Saxe-Altenburg
Charlotte Agnes, Princess of (see Prussia0

Saxe-Coburg(-Saalfeld) (& Gotha)
Adrian, Prince of 339, 340
Albert, Prince of (see Great Britain)
Alexander, Prince of 222, 223
Alexander, Prince of (son of Andreas) 342
Alfred, Duke of 29, 62, 74, 75, 76, 77, 78, 79, 80, 81, 82, 83, 84, 85, 86, 87, 117, 119, 120, 124, 132, 163, 237, 282
Alfred (Jr.), Hereditary Prince of 29, 78, 82, 83, 84, 86, 119
Albert, Prince of (see Great Britain)
Alexandra, Princess of (see Hohenlohe-Langenburg)
Alexandrine, Duchess of (née baden) 73, 74
Amalie, Princess of (Duchess Max Emanuel in Bavaria) 94
Andreas, Prince of, Head of House 223, 294, 297, 298, 336, 337, 338, 339, 340, 341, 342, 343, 344, 345, 346, 349, 350, 351, 352
Anna, Princess of (née Trauttmansdorff-Weinsberg) 211, 212
Antoinette, Princess of (Duchess Alexander of Württemberg) 4, 38, 39, 278
Antonia (Antoinette), Princess of (née Kohary) 18, 25, 26, 27, 50, 53, 88, 182, 193, 195, 231
Antonius, Prince of 211, 212
August, Prince of 26, 27, 46, 88, 90, 91, 92, 93, 94, 96, 122, 175, 193, 209, 220
August Clemens, Prince of 29, 213, 215
August Leopold, Prince of 29, 210, 211, 212, 213, 215, 216, 218, 220
Augusta, Duchess of (née Reuß-Ebersdorf) 4, 7, 9, 14, 15, 16, 19, 20, 21, 25, 33, 37, 38, 41, 143, 196
Beatrice, Princess of (see Spain)
Beatrice, Princess of 339, 340
Bettina, Princess of (née von Pretschner) 222
Carin, Princess of (née Dabelstein) 342
Carl Eduard, Duke of (Charles Edward, Duke of Albany) 29, 68, 86, 87, 113, 118, 119, 120, 121, 122, 123, 124, 126, 127, 128, 129, 130, 131, 132, 133, 134, 135, 136, 137, 138, 139, 140, 141, 156, 169, 208, 218, 251, 298, 311, 332, 336, 337, 338, 339, 341, 344, 346, 349
Carolina, Princess of (née Tuscany) 213, 215, 218, 218
Caroline Mathilde, Princess of 123, 129
Caroline Mathilde Prinzessin von 129
Christian Ernst ii
Christina, Princess of (b. 1995) 222, 223
Christina, Princess of (née Schnell) 223
Clémentine, Princess of (née Orléans) 27, 46, 55, 59, 88, 90, 91, 92, 93, 94, 95, 96, 97, 102, 104, 105, 106, 107, 193, 196, 202, 204, 207, 209, 213, 215, 220, 278
Clotilde, Princess of (Archduchess Joseph) 94, 220, 239
Daniel, Princz von 340
Denyse Henriette, Princess of (née von (de) Muralt) 339, 340
Dorothea, Princess of (see Schleswig-Holstein-Sonderburg-Augustenburg)
Edith, Princess of (née de Kózol) 216, 217
Ernst I, Duke of 4, 7, 15, 16, 18, 19, 20, 21, 22, 23, 33, 37, 38, 39, 47, 49, 122
Ernst II, Duke of 19, 23, 49, 73, 74, 75, 79, 88, 101, 163, 172
Ernst, Prince of 215, 221
Ernst Friedrich, Duke of ii, iv, 4, 14
Ernst Leopold Prinz von 129
Ferdinand, Prince of 7, 18, 25, 26, 27, 29, 37, 53, 88, 91, 122, 182, 193, 1965
Ferdinand, Prince of (see Portugal)
Felicitas, Princess of 220, 221
Franz Friedrich Anton, Duke of 4, 7, 16, 25, 33, 37, 38, 143, 196, 297, 298
Franz Josias, Duke of ii
Franziska, Princess of 223
Friedrich Josias, Prince of (Field Marshal) iv, 1, 112
Friedrich Josias, Prince of, Head of House 123, 127, 139, 298, 332, 334, 335, 336, 337, 338, 339, 340, 342
Hubertus, Hereditary Prince of (1909-1943) 29, 123, 139, 141, 294, 336, 338, 351
Hubertus, Hereditary Prince of (b. 1975) 342, 346
Irmgard, Princess of (née Röll) 221
Isabella, Princess of 222, 223
Johann Ernst, Duke of ii
Johann Leopold, Hereditary Prince of 123, 129, 338
Johanna, Princess of (née Károly de Károly-Patty) 216
Johannes Albert, Prince of 29, 221
Johannes Heinrich, Prince of 29, 216, 220, 221, 349, 350, 351
Joseph Ferdinand, Prince of 210, 211
Josephine, Princess of 211, 212
Juliane, Princess of (Grand Duchess Anna Feodorovna) 4, 14, 15, 16, 18, 23, 37, 50
Katrin, Princess of (née Bemme) 339, 340
Kelly, Hereditary Princess of (née Rondesvedt) 346
Klementine, Princess of 213, 218
Leopold, Prince of (King Léopold I) 4, 7, 14, 16, 18, 21, 33, 34, 35, 40, 41, 42, 44
Leopold, Prince of (Jr.) 27
Leopold, Prince of (son of Philipp) 29, 197, 198, 204, 205, 206, 207, 215
Leopoldine, Princess of (née Brazil) 209
Leopoldine, Princess of 215, 219
Louise, Duchess of (née Saxe-Gotha) 14, 19, 20, 21, 25
Louise, Princess of (née Belgium) 64, 91, 93, 174, 176, 178, 179, 196, 197, 198, 199, 202, 203, 204 , 311, 317
Ludwig August, Prince of 29, 94, 95, 96, 97, 209, 210, 211
Ludwig Gaston, Prince of 210, 211, 212
Maria Claudia, Princess of 339, 340
Maria Immaculata, Princess of 211, 212
Marie Karoline, Princess of 213, 215, 220
Marianne, Princess of 7
Marie, Duchess of (née Württemberg) 22, 23, 38, 39
Marie, Princess of (see Romania)
Marie Alexandrovna, Duchess of (and Edinburgh) (née Russia) 68, 77, 78, 79, 80, 82, 83, 84, 85, 86, 87, 117, 119, 132, 163, 169, 204, 308, 310
Marie-Gabrielle, Princess of (née Fürstenberg) 220
Maximilian, Prince of 7
Maximliain, Prince of 222, 223
Pedro (Peter) August, Prince of 29, 210, 211
Peter Albert Prinz von 129
Philipp, Prince of 29, 94, 96, 97, 101, 112, 178, 193, 196, 197, 198, 199, 200, 201, 202, 203, 204, 205, 206, 207, 208, 209, 215, 216, 217, 223, 311, 348
Philipp August 219, 220, 221, 222, 223, 350
Philipp-Josias, Prince of 215, 216, 217, 218, 219, 220, 221, 223
Rainer, Prince of 213, 216, 217, 218, 220
Sarah, Princess of (né Hálasz) 219, 220, 223
Sibylla, Princess of (see Sweden)
Simon, Prinz von 340
Sophia Antonia, Duchess of (née Brunswick-Wolfenbüttel) ii, iv
Sophie, Hereditary Princess of (née Saxe-Hildburghausen) 4
Sophie, Princess of (Countess of Mensdorff-Pouilly) 4, 37, 38
Stephanie, Princess of 342
Theresia, Princess of 215, 218
Victoire, Princess of (Duchess de Namours) 27, 46, 50, 88, 182, 252, 297
Victoria (Victoire), Princess of (Princess of Leiningen, Duchess of Kent) 7, 34, 39, 40, 41, 42, 43, 50, 122, 298
Victoria Adelheid, Duchess of (née Schleswig-Holstein-Sonderburg-Glücksburg) 122, 123, 127, 128, 131, 139, 140, 141, 218, 251, 298, 332, 336, 337, 349
Victoria Melita, Princess of (Grand Duchess of Hesse & By Rhine, Grand Duchess of Russia) 79, 84, 113, 128, 132, 280, 289, 298, 302, 307, 308, 309, 311

Saxe-Gotha
August, Duke of 19
Ernst I, Duke of ii
Friedrich IV, Duke of 19, 21
Karoline Amalie, Duchess of (née Hesse-Kassel) 19
Louise, Duchess of (née Mecklenburg-Schwerin) 19
Louise, Princess of (see Saxe-Coburg)

Saxe-Hildburghausen
Sophie, Princess of 4
Therese, Princess of (see Bavaria)

Saxe-Meiningen
Adelaide, Princess of (see Great Britain)
Bernhard III, Duke of 62, 300
Charlotte, Duchess of (née Prussia) 62, 299, 300
Friedrich, Prince of 340
Friedrich Constantin, Prince of 340
Konrad, Prince of 340
Regina, Princess of (see Austria)

Saxe-Weimar-Eisenach
Augusta, Princess (see Prusia)

Saxony
Albert, King of 314
Albert, Prince of 315
Alexander, Margrave of Meißen 220
Amalie, Queen of (née Bavaria) 314
Carola, Queen of (née Vasa) 314
Elisabeth Helene, Margravine of Meißen (née Thurn und Taxis) 220
Friedrich August III, King of 220, 314, 315, 316, 317
Friedrich-Christian, Margrave of Meißen 220
Georg, King of 174, 237, 314, 315
Johann, King of 314
Johann Georg, Prince of 251, 315
Louise, Crown Princess of (née Austria-Tuscany) 93, 99, 103
Margarete, Princess of (see Hohenzollern)
Maria Alix, Princess of (see Hohenzollern)
Maria Ana, Princess of (née Portugal) 58, 220, 230, 237, 239, 298, 313, 314, 315, 316
Maria Johanna, Princess of 314
Maria Josepha, Princess (see Austria)
Mathilde, Princess of 220, 221, 239, 314, 349, 350
Maximilian, Prince of 315
Sayn-Wittgenstein-Berleburg, Eleonore, Princess of 184
Sayn-Wittgenstein-Sayn, Alexander, Fürst of 329
Schauenstein, Berta von 15, 19, 23
Schaumburg-Lippe
Adolf, Prince of 300
Schiferli, Rodolphe Abraham 15
Schleswig-Holstein-Sonderburg-Augustenburg
Adelheid, Duchess of (née Hohenlohe-Langenburg) 298
Albert, Prince of 208
Augusta Viktoria, Princess of (see Prussia)
Dorothea, Duchess of (née Saxe-Coburg & Gotha) 184, 197, 198, 202, 203, 207, 208, 209, 212, 216, 217
Christian, Prince of 208
Ernst Günther, Duke of 202, 206, 207, 208, 217
Helena, Princess of (née Great Britain) 62,
Helena Victoria, Princess of 66, 169, 208, 310
Karoline-Mathilde, Princess of 114, 298
Marie Louise, Princess of 66, 169
Schleswig-Holstein-Sonderburg-Glücksburg
Alexandra Victoria, Princess of 131
Caroline Mathilde, Princess of (see Solms-Baruth)
Victoria Adelheid, Princess of (see Saxe-Coburg & Gotha)

    Friedrich Ferdinand, Duke of 114
    Wilhelm Friedrich, Duke of 311
Schmidt von Löwenfels, Edgar 15
Schmidt von Löwenfels, Eduard 15, 23
Scmidt-Schauenstein, Carl 18, 19
Schnirring, Captain Max 129
Seigneux, Jules-Gabriel de 15
Selys Longhamps, Baroness Sybille de 272
Simpson, Walles Warfield (Duchess of Windsor) 137, 282
Solms-Baruth
    Hans-Friedrich, Count of 340
    Hans Georg, Count of 139, 332, 335, 337
    Hubertus, Count of 338
    Caroline-Mathilde, Countess of (née Schleswig-Holstein-Sonderburg-Glücksburg) 332, 338
    Viktoria-Luise, Countess of 140, 141, 298, 332, 334, 335, 336, 337, 338, 339, 340, 351
Soveral, Marquis de 245, 248
Spaak, Paul-Henri (Belgian Prime Minister) 263
Spain
    Alfonso, Infante of (Orléans) 79
    Alfonso XII, King of 239
    Alfonso XIII, King of 166, 240, 246, 249, 267, 330
    Beatrice, Infanta of 79, 309
    Beatriz, Infanta of (Princess Civitella-Cesi) 298, 331
    Carlos IV, King of 53
    Carlos, Infante of 53
    Carlos, Infante of (né Bourbon-Two Sicilies) 240, 246, 251
    Carlota Joaquina, Infanta of (see Portugal)
    Cristina, Infanta of 273
    Elena, Infanta of 273
    Fernando VI, King of 293
    Fernando VII, King of 53
    Fernando, Infante of (né Bavaria) 321
    Francisco de Asís, King Consort of 88
    Isabel II, Queen of 176, 224, 236
    Isabel, Infanta of (see Orléans)
    Iabel, Infanta of, Princess of Asturias 224
    Juan, Count of Barcelona 267, 288
    Juan Carlos, King of 246, 273, 291, 292, 293, 324
    Louise, Infanta of (née Orléans) 240, 246, 251
    Luisa Fernanda, Infanta of (see Orléans)
    María de las Mercdes, Princess of Asturias 246
    María del Pilar, Infanta of 267, 288
    María Teresa, Infanta of 186
    Sofía, Queen of (née Greece) 292
    Victoria Eugenia, Queen of (née Battenberg) 156, 160, 166, 297
Stamboliyski, Alexander (Bulgarian Prime minister 276, 278
Stambolov, Stefan 100, 101, 102, 103, 104, 105, 106
Stanley, Henry Morton 176
Stanley, Lady 77
Stauffenberg, Claus von 139
Stewart, Anita 252
Stirbey, Prince barbo 305
Stockmar, Baron Christian Friedrich von 33, 41, 47, 143, 172
Strauss, Richard 124
Sullivan, Sir Arthur 81
Sweden
    Astrid, Princess of (see Belgium)
    Bertil, Prince of 313
    Birgitta, Princess of 267
    Carl, Prince of 255, 326
    Carl XVI Gustaf, King of 267
    Carl Johan, Prince of 313
    Carola, Princess Vasa (see Saxony)
    Gustaf V, King of 114, 312, 313
    Gustaf VI Adolf, King of 129, 289, 312, 313
    Gustaf Adolf, Prince of 113, 128, 313
    Ingeborg, Princes of (née Sweden) 255, 326
    Ingird, Princess of (see Denmark)
    Lilian, Princess of (née Davies) 313
    Louise, Princess of (see Denmark)
    Margaret, Crown Princess of (née Great Britain) 66, 129, 156, 297, 298, 312, 313
    Märtha, Princess of (see Norway)

    Oskar II, King of 232, 255
    Sibylla, Princess of (née Saxe-Coburg & Gotha) 113, 123, 128, 129, 136, 290, 313, 336, 338
    Sigvard, Prince of 313
    Sophie, Queen of (née Nassau) 255
    Victoria, Queen of (née Baden) 114, 312

T
Tasso de Saxe-Coburgo e Braganza, Carlos Eduardo 218
Taxis von Bordogna und Valnigra, Baron Lamoral von 218
Teck
    Alexander, Prince of (Earl of Athlone) 117, 218
    Francis, Prince of 303
    Franz, Duke of 153
    Mary ("May"), Princess of (see Great Britain)
    Mary Adelaide, Duchess of (née Great Britain) 153
Terceira, Duchess of 227, 228
Tervuren, Lucien, Duke of 179
Thurn und Taxis
    Albrecht, Fürst of 184, 209, 220, 239
    Elisabeth Helen, Princess of (see Saxony)
    Margareta, Fürstin of (née Austria) 209, 220, 239
Toerring-Jettenbach
    Carl Theodor, Count of 353
    Hans-Veit, Count of 184, 353
    Hans-Veit, Count of (b. 1935) 290, 350, 352, 353
    Ignaz, Hereditary Count of 352, 353
    Karl Theodor, Count of 184
Torby, Nadejda, Countess de 302
Torlonia, Allesandro, Prince of Civitella-Cesi 331
Torlonia, Olimpia 331
Trauttmansdorff-Weinsberg
    Anna, Princess of (see Saxe-Coburg & Gotha)
    Joephine, Fürstin of (née Pallavicini)
    Karl, Fürst of 211
Trotzky, Sergei 220
Tuscany
    Anton, Archcuke 280, 306
    Antonietta, Grand Duchess of (née Two Sicilies) 213
    Carolina, Archduchess 213
    Franz Salvator, Archduke 200, 213
    Immaculata, Archduchess (née Bourbon-Two Sicilies) 213
    Karl Salvator, Archduke 213
    Leopoldo II, Grand Duke of 213
    Louise, Archduchess of Austria (see Saxony)
    Teesa Cristina, Princess of Bourbon- (see Brazil)
    Valerie, Archduchess (see Baden)
    Walburga, Archduchess 218
Two Sicilies
    Antonietta, Princess of Bourbon- (see Tuscany)
    Carlo, Duke of Calabria 329
    Ferdinand I, King of 213
    Francesco I, King of 213
    Immaculata, Princess of Bourbon- (see Tuscany)
    Lodovico, Count of Trani 316
    Luigi, Prince of Bourbon- 54
    Maria Carolina, Queen of (née Austria)
    María de las Mercedes,Princess of Bourbon- 246
    Maria Pia, Princess of Bourbon- (see Parma)
    Marie-Amélie, Princess of (see Orléans)
    Mathilde, Countess of Trani (né Bavaria) 316
    Teresa, Princess of Bourbon- 213

U
Udekem d'Acoz, Countess Anna Maria d' 273
Udekem d'Acoz, Jonkvrouw Marie-Alix 273
Udekem d'Acoz, Count Patrick d' 273
Urach, Duke of 184

V
Vanderbilt, Gloria Morgan 311
Vestur, Hélène 330
Vetsera, Baroness Marie 199, 200

W
Waldeck-Pyrmont
    Emma, Princess of (see Netherlands)
    Georg Viktor, Fürst of 116
    Helen, Fürstin of (née Nassau)116
    Helene, Princess of (see Great Britain)
    Marie, Princess of (see Württemberg)
    Pauline, Princess of (see Bentheim-Steinfurt)
Waldstein-Waldenburg, Countess Maria Antonia von 25
Wells, H.G. 168
Weiller, Paul-Annik 330
Weiller, Sibilla (see Luxembourg)
Wettin
    Dedo, Count of ii
    Dedo II, Count of ii
    Dietrich, Count of ii
    Heinrich, Count of ii
Whitten, Captain Richard 340
Whitten, Victoria 340
Wied
    Elisabeth, Princess of (later Queen of Romania) 77, 145, 146
    Hermann, Fürst of 145
    Marie, Fürstin of 145
Witt, Count Serge de 319
Wolman, Léa (Princess Alexandre of Belgium) 267
Wren, Christopher 147
Württemberg
    Albrecht, Duke of 278
    Albrecht Eugen, Duke of 278, 281, 291
    Alexander, Duke of 38, 39
    Alexander, Duke of (1804-1885) 153, 278
    Alexander (Jr.), Duke of 39
    Ernst, Duke of 39, 88
    Friedrich, Duke of 39
    Margarete Sophie, Duchess of (née Austria) 278
    Marie, Princess of (see Saxe-Coburg)
    Marie, Princess of (née Waldeck-Pyrmont) 116, 117
    Marie, Duchess of (née Orléans) 39, 278
    Marie Dorothea, Duchess of (see Austria)
    Mathilde, Duchess of Württemberg 273
    Nadejda, Duchess of (née Bulgaria) 107, 113, 278, 279, 291
    Paul, Duke of 39
    Philipp, Duke of 231
    Sophia Dorothea, Duchess of (see Russia)
    Sophie, Duchess of 350
    Wilhelm II, King of 116, 117, 119

Y
Yugoslavia (Serbia)
    Alexander I, King of 276, 282, 306
    Alexander II, Crown Prince of 297
    Alexander, Prince of 324, 351
    Barbara, Princess of (née Liechtenstein) 324, 351
    Dimitri, Prince of 325
    Marie, Queen of (née Romania) 282, 306
    Olga, Princess of (née Greece) 321
    Paul, Prince Regent of 283, 284, 321
    Peter I, King of 282
    Peter II, King of 284

Z
Zedlitz-Trutzschler, Count Robert 120
Zoubkov, Alexander 300

Acknowledgments

The end of a wonderful journey is always bittersweet. For now, I have reached the end of my journey with the Coburgs of Europe. Over the last quarter century since I began gathering the information, photos, objects and vignettes that have allowed me to write this book, many are the ones who helped me reach the end.

First and foremost, I wish to thank Prince Andreas of Saxe-Coburg & Gotha for nearly two decades of friendship and support. It is to him that I humbly dedicate this book. He has shown that perseverance, upstanding character and respect for the past are the mantra of modern-day Coburgs. It is to him that his family owes its resurgence, for had he chosen to ignore the legacy he carries since birth, the Coburgs of today would be forgotten and unknown. He is an inspiration and example, and in his own way, the re-builder of his family's realm. I am deeply honored to be his friend and only wish that this book brought him the joy that our friendship brings me.

Of course, I couldn't have completed this journey without the support of my amazing life-partner, best friend and husband, Dave Higdon. Without his constant encouragement, his undivided attention and assistance, completing this project would have taken even longer.

I would like to thank everyone else who helped me with this project, specially those who are no longer with us, but who were instrumental in encouraging this book: Prince Johannes Heinrich of Saxe-Coburg & Gotha, Princess Gabrielle of Saxe-Coburg & Gotha, Prince and Princess Sigismund of Prussia, and their son Prince Alfred, Archduke Otto of Austria, Landgrave Moritz of Hesse, Prince Albert of Saxony, the Countess of Paris, and Fürst Kraft of Hohenlohe-Langenburg. I would also like to thank: King Michael and Queen Anne of Romania, Queen doña Sofía of Spain, King Simeon II of Bulgaria and his sister Princess Marie Louise, King Philippe and Queen Mathilde of Belgium, the Count of Paris and his son the Duke de Vendôme, the Duke and Duchess of Braganza, Princess Alix Napoléon, Crown Prince Alexander of Yugoslavia, Crown Princess Margarita and Prince Radu of Romania, Prince Alexander and Princess Barbara of Yugoslavia, Prince Dimitri of Yugoslavia, the Duke of Kent, Prince and Princess Michael of Kent, Duchess Sophie of Würtemberg, the Margrave and Margravine of Baden, Prince Ludwig and Princess Marianne of Baden, the Dowager Duchess of Croÿ, Prince Michael of Greece, the Margrave and Margravine of Meißen, the Prince of Tirnovo, the Prince of Panagjuriste, the Prince of Vidin, Hereditary Prince Hubertus of Saxe-Coburg & Gotha and his sister Princess Stephanie, Prince Philipp August of Saxe-Coburg & Gotha and his son Prince Maximilian (along with Princess Christina, Maximilian's wife), Princess Felicitas of Saxe-Coburg & Gotha and her son Nikolaus Trotzky, Duke Borwin of Mecklenburg, the Prince of Naples, the Prince of Venice, Archduchess Helen of Austria, Archduke Maximilian of Austria, Archduke Christian and Archduchess Marie Astrid of Austria, Princess Victoria of Bourbon-Two Sicilies (Mrs. Nomikos), Archduke Michael Salvator of Austria-Tuscany, Archduke Markus of Austria-Tuscany, Duke Rudolf and Duchess Alexandra of Croÿ, Fürst Philipp and Fürstin Saskia of Hohenlohe-Langenburg, Dowager Fürstin Irma of Hohenlohe-Langenburg, Princess Cecile and Princess Xenia of Hohenlohe-Langenburg, Count Hans-Veit of Toerring-Jettenbach and his son Hereditary Count Ignaz, Fürst Hugo and Fürstin Sophie of Windisch-Grätz, Princess Elisabeth of Oettingen-Wallerstein, and Princess Tatiana Radziwill and Dr. John Fruchaud.

I would also be remiss if I forget to thank Greg King, Seth Leonard and Katrina Warne, whose help with editing, fact finding and revisions was invaluable. They are greatly responsible for the completion of this project, as well as providing sincere guidance and suggestions, even when I did not want to hear any more about it.

Other friends whose encouragement and support must be acknowledged, include: Ilana Miller, Charles B. Stewart, Penny Wilson, Russell Clarke, Larry Russell, Geoff Teeter, Wayne Hodge, Katie Tice, Mary Ann Fogarty, Brian Fogarty-Wall, Phil Perry, Leslie Sieren, Rick Hutto, Kassandra and Sabrina Pollock, Lynda Levin, Mark Andersen, Netty Leistra, Hilde Vieveen, Annet Bakker, Coryne Hall and Henry Wong. I am indebted to Marianne van Dam, Stefan Sohn, Netty Leistra, Albert Nieboer, Stig Nielsen and Lilian van Reijen for supplying photographs to *Eurohistory*. Their artistry and persistence to obtain unique shots have over the years enriched the pages of all my publications.

Last, and by no means least I would like to thank my parents (who finally realized it was not whim), our sons (for not getting too upset with their father having to work through countless weekends), and my dear friend Mary Houck, whose support, encouragement and constant pestering to get the book done in her lifetime gave me the last push I needed.

6300 Kensington Avenue, East Richmond Heights, CA 94805 USA
Phone (510) 236-1730 – Email: books@eurohistory.com

The Coburgs of Europe
The Rise and Fall of Queen Victoria and Prince Albert's European Family
ISBN: 978-0-9854603-3-4
By Arturo E. Beéche

Copyright © Arturo E. Beéche, 2013
Copyright © David W. Higdon and Arturo E. Beéche (artistic design), 2013

All rights reserved. No part of this book covered by the copyrights hereon may be reproduced or used in any form or by any means without prior consent of the publisher, except for brief passages covered by reviewers or fair use by other authors. Reproducing passages from this book by any means, including mimeographic, photocopying, scanning, recording, or by any information retrieval system is an infringement of copyright law.

THE AUTHOR AND PUBLISHERS ALSO EXPRESS THEIR GRATITUDE TO THE FOLLOWING INDIVIDUALS, FOR SUPPLYING ILLUSTRATIONS FOR THIS PUBLICATION:

The Prince of Tirnovo
Princess Elizabeth of Yugoslavia
Prince Andreas of Saxe-Coburg & Gotha
Princess Felicitas of Saxe-Coburg & Gotha
Count Hans-Veit of Toerring-Jettenbach
Stig Nielsen
Marianne van Dam
Albert Nieboer
Lilian van Reijen
Katrina Warne
Netty Leistra
Stefan Sohn
The Eurohistory Royal Photo Archive